Practice Management in Optometry

Second Edition

Neil Gailmard, OD, MBA, FAAO

ISBN: 978-0-9991336-6-8 Hardcover
ISBN: 978-0-9991336-7-5 Paperback

Library of Congress Control Number: 2017910416
Walnut Ridge Publishing
Munster, Indiana

For Susan,
my partner in business and in life,
with love and gratitude for your
inspiration and support.

Contents

Foreword

I've had the privilege of being involved with Dr. Neil Gailmard since he introduced the *Optometric Management Tip of the Week* in 2002, when he was chief optometric editor of *Optometric Management* magazine. At the time, the e-media group that supported *OM* and its sister publications was in its early stages: Internet connections were still primarily dial up and our e-mail activity had only begun ramping up the year before, and the profession was still adapting to getting information by e-mail. Acquiring e-mail addresses from readers was an ongoing effort; people weren't accustomed to providing them, and were often changing Internet providers along with their addresses.

We were publishing only one other editorial newsletter then, *Contact Lenses Today*, the first of its kind in vision care. When the *OM Tip of the Week* launched, it quickly surpassed *Contact Lenses Today* in the number of times recipients opened and clicked on links in the e-mail. Readership quickly got to the point, as I often said to sponsors, where it had a "cult following." And the cult continued to grow, as did sponsorship interest in being associated with the newsletter. We hear anecdotally that eye care practices print paper copies of the newsletter – which our tracking data confirms – and share it with staff in their weekly meetings. We routinely receive requests from associations and doctor groups around the world for permission to reprint editions of the *OM Tip of the Week* in the print and electronic newsletters they send to their members. Just recently, the president of an eye care company told us that every past issue is required reading for all new employees, as it provides the most complete catalog of information optometrists need to successfully manage their practices.

In short, the *OM Tip of the Week* established a new standard for practice management information delivered regularly in capsular form, and spawned a virtual industry of focused newsletters that our company PentaVision now publishes, covering everything from glaucoma to color contact lenses.

In 2005, Neil made the decision to resign from his role as chief optometric editor of *Optometric Management* so he could spend more time working with his practice and practice management consulting business. That decision, he said, included discontinuing the *OM Tip of the Week.* We were dumbstruck, intimately aware of what Neil had single-handedly accomplished in a now vibrant medium: an invaluable source of information our readers depended on that could be easily read, absorbed and implemented – and make a real, immediate difference in their practice success. We were also intimately aware that no one could replace Neil, whose down to earth, friendly style – not to mention his vast experience and knowledge – resonated with optometrists everywhere. I immediately shared these concerns with Neil, and suggested that the *OM Tip of the Week* would be a valuable means for him to reinforce his bona fides as a practice management consultant to existing and potential clients. In his always thoughtful and humble manner, Neil recognized the unique value of what he built and, thankfully for all of us, continued.

At the time of this writing, Neil was just approaching his 800th weekly tip. As a former magazine editor, I always felt the unrelenting pressure of producing a monthly editorial. But that responsibility pales in comparison to Neil's prolific output *every week* for more than 15 years...and counting. What Neil has accomplished is nothing short of amazing. Indeed, he is the Energizer Bunny of optometric information.

I could go on about my admiration for Neil's work on the *Optometric Management Tip of the Week*. What matters most about Neil is his commitment and service to a profession in which he has enjoyed enviable success – and his unhesitating willingness to share the wisdom he has gained in the process to help other optometrists do the same.

Thank you, Neil. And whatever you do, keep those tips coming.

Roger Zimmer
Publisher
Optometric Management
June 2017

Preface

The purpose of this book is two-fold: to provide a guide to eye care professionals who want to take their practices to the next level of success and for optometry school faculty members and students as a textbook in their practice management courses. My hope is that the book can be easily read from cover-to-cover or it can be used as a reference for help on a specific topic.

I have always attempted to bring a real-world practicality to my articles and lectures and the same is true for this book. While I taught required practice management courses at three schools of optometry over a period of 30 years, I also owned and operated a successful practice at the same time, which afforded me the practical know-how that makes this book so useful to students and practitioners.

The text in the following chapters is adapted from my long-running series of articles published as the *Optometric Management Tip of the Week*. I spent many hours reviewing, selecting, revising, expanding and organizing the tip articles into sections for this book. I believe simply having the sections grouped under chapter topics will make them much more useful and easy to reference, but I have also brought much of the content up to date.

I launched the *Optometric Management Tip of the Week* series in 2002 because I strongly believed there was tremendous value in a good idea and there were many good ideas in existence that most ODs did not know about. And there were millions more ideas that we had not yet thought of. I love the experience of finding a new idea (on my own or shared with me by a colleague) and implementing it in my practice. On many occasions, I witnessed a new idea turn into increased profitability or efficiency and I found that extremely exciting. I saw the *OM Tip of the Week* series as a way to share those new and potentially big ideas with other optometrists.

I must admit that I really did not know if the tip of the week venture would be successful or how long it would last. I didn't know I would write an article per week for over 15 years (and still counting). I started numbering the tip articles with the very first one and I'm now approaching Tip #800. As I reviewed and organized the articles for this book, I discovered that I have written well over one million words in this tip series.

What I did know was that I had a passion for practice management and I loved to teach. I liked to write in a casual, conversational style and I enjoyed making topics simple and practical. It turned out that ODs liked it also. The tip series caught on and became one of the most successful publications in optometry. Within a year, we had over 15,000 opt-in subscribers for the *OM Tip of the Week* and currently over 25,000 eye care professionals subscribe to this ongoing series. I was told by the publisher that the click-open rate has always been extremely high. It's easy to deploy mass emails, but it is quite another story to get people to open them and read them.

I also have direct evidence of the success of the tip e-newsletter by the very large number of emails I receive from readers. The response depends on the topic, but it is usually dozens per week and has reached 100 or more on occasion. I quickly discovered that my audience was not just optometrists in the United States; I am pleased to receive emails from eye care professionals from the United Kingdom, Australia, the Philippines, South Africa and literally all over the world. I am gratified by the optometrists who frequently come up to me at conferences to tell me how much they enjoy the tip articles.

About the *OM Tip of the Week* Format

I selected slightly less than half of the total number of published tip articles for this book, eliminating many of the older ones and those that were duplications. Some articles that were written more than ten years ago, however, are still surprisingly valid and are included. This is especially true when the topic is based on principles. You may see references to current events or pop culture from early time periods. I also tried to use real numbers when I wrote about practice finance and metrics, but the reader should realize that some numerical norms change over time. The numbers still serve as good examples and should be easy to adapt to present day benchmarks.

I elected to leave intact some of the language that informed the reader about my plans from one week to the next and other comments that colored an article. I feel this original context retains the informal writing style that I prefer.

Even though many articles were eliminated because they were repetitive, I retained two or more articles on the same topic if each one presented some important concepts that were significantly different. I generally grouped these articles together so the reader can choose to skip some or read them for the nuances.

Best wishes for continued success,

Neil Gailmard, OD, MBA, FAAO

Introduction

I hope that by sharing some background information about the two phases of my career, the reader will glean an understanding of the sources for many of the principles and strategies in this book.

Gailmard Eye Center

I have loved practice management ever since I graduated from Illinois College of Optometry in 1976. I opened my own practice cold, right out of school and working to make it grow fueled my passion for business. My practice was very meager in the beginning. I had difficulty finding a bank to give me a loan to buy a single lane of basic equipment. When I finally secured that, I rented an office in a medical building in my hometown of Munster, Indiana (in the Chicago metropolitan area). It was very professional but had almost no visibility to the public. That office was only 540 square feet and I could barely afford to pay the rent! The furniture in my reception area consisted of lawn chairs. But I was too proud of my office to be embarrassed. Instead, I visualized how my office would look someday and I was driven to achieve my dream practice. I was naïve and idealistic, which turned out to be good traits to get me through some lean times. To me, it was exciting!

I could not afford to hire a highly skilled staff, so I hired a part-time receptionist and I did most things myself. That worked out fine because I had very few patients at first. Necessity really is the mother of invention; I learned every aspect of my practice, from answering the phone to fitting glasses to financial reports. I found that business administration is much easier to learn when you're dealing with your own money and your own employees! That background still serves me well to this day in practice management.

I knew I would not be able to derive any income from my practice in the early years, so I was thrilled to receive an offer of employment from Illinois College of Optometry as a full-time faculty member upon my graduation. It was an odd experience to transition from student to professor overnight, but I found out that I loved to teach, I had a steady paycheck, and I still had enough time to work in my practice.

Fortunately, I met my future wife when she was in her fourth year at ICO in 1980. After her graduation, Susan joined me in practice, and we were married a year later. I had recently moved into a larger and nicer office (a respectable 1,700 square feet) a few blocks from the first location. The practice was far from ready for a second doctor, in fact we still had some financial struggles, but we liked working together and I was spread a bit thin with my growing patient volume and teaching schedule.

Patients took to Susan extremely well, although female doctors were still rare in the early eighties and she recalls situations where patients said they preferred to see the other Dr. Gailmard – the man doctor. But that disappeared fairly quickly and Susan's schedule became full. Her clinical skills, excellent financial production and ability to manage all aspects of the practice allowed me to pursue the management consulting side of my career and I'm very grateful for that.

Together, we built Gailmard Eye Center into one of the largest and most successful independent optometric practices in the country. In 1985, we bought commercial land in town and designed and built a 7,000 square foot eye clinic. Five years later we bought more land and built an addition to the facility, bringing the total to more than 10,000 square feet with an expanded optical department.

The practice is still going strong with 35 employees and three full time associate optometrists. We have 14 exam/procedure rooms and we utilize state-of-the-art clinical instrumentation. We provide medical eye care and advanced contact lens services. The eye center includes a huge optical dispensary with an onsite surfacing and finishing lab. We have ample office space for administrative use. GEC is a very busy practice with a large patient base and strong profitability. A reader survey by our local newspaper named us as "Best Vision Center" for the fourth year in a row! It is a far cry from that first office of mine.

Susan and I sold Gailmard Eye Center to Keplr Vision, a private equity firm, in 2018 and we retired from clinical practice. That transaction was an excellent experience and I have a great relationship with Keplr.

In many ways, Gailmard Eye Center served as a laboratory for practice management strategies. It gave me the opportunity to test new concepts in the real-world, many of which do not always work as intended. But mostly, it showed me what is important in building a successful optometric practice and to that end, I will share what I learned in this book.

Practice Management Consulting

The practice management side of my career started in the early 1980s when I was asked to teach the lecture course in practice management to the third year class at ICO. Being the sole instructor of a required lecture course was a big step for a young faculty member and I loved it. I brought in some expert guest speakers, but I taught most of the course myself for about 15 years. I immersed myself in trying to learn all I could in the field of practice management, eventually earning an MBA degree in 1998 by attending graduate school at night and on weekends.

I have been actively writing journal articles, lecturing at state and national conferences, and consulting within the optical industry over the past 30 years. Some of the bigger projects included serving as Chairman of Practice Management University for the American Optometric Association from 1998 to 2003. I was also a founding faculty member for the Management and Business Academy (MBA), a ground-breaking educational program sponsored by Alcon and Essilor, from 2005 to 2013. I served as Chief Optometric Editor at *Optometric Management* magazine. I taught parts of the practice management course at University of Houston, serving as the Benedict Professor in 1999-2000. In 2011 to 2016, I presented guest lectures in the Eye Care Business Management courses at University of California, Berkeley.

I started Gailmard Consulting in 1996 so I could provide one-on-one management consulting services to independent optometrists in the United States. Since then, I have worked with well over 1,000 OD clients to help them increase profitability and productivity in their practices. In 2011, following several discussions about the concept of buying groups and alliances in optometry, my good friend Jerry Hayes, OD approached me with the idea of partnering with him to form Prima Eye Group. Jerry had a history of success as an entrepreneur in the optical industry and owned two traditional buying groups: HMI and Red Tray. Our idea was to develop Prima into a new type of alliance that would combine group buying power and one-on-one consulting for independent optometrists with a low monthly dues structure.

I was president of the company and served as the primary consultant in the early days. Prima grew very quickly in membership and we added specialty consultants in the fields of finance, human resources, and marketing, as well as another OD/MBA. We held national conferences with leading speakers on practice management. We championed the concept of full-day roundtable meetings with small groups of ODs and we offered separate training programs for staff members.

Long before Prima was launched, I became friends with the founder and owner of a much larger alliance group: Mark Feder, OD of IDOC (Independent Doctors of Optometric Care). I provided some lectures and webinars for IDOC and I always respected the work they did for independent optometrists. Mark contacted me in the spring of 2015 and proposed meeting with me and Jerry Hayes at Vision Expo in New York City to explore the possibility of merging our companies. We took the meeting and after months of soul-searching, due diligence, and extreme vetting of Prima by IDOC's private equity partner, IDOC bought Prima Eye Group by the end of that year.

I stayed on at IDOC as Chief Optometric Officer for three years and assisted with the transition of the combined companies. The company is led by Dave Brown, CEO and Oliver Spandow, CFO; both are industry veterans who are doing a great job and have my utmost respect.

Chapter 1. Starting and Organizing a Practice

1.1 Opening Cold and Practical

I presented a lecture to optometry students at Vision Expo West recently and it seemed to generate a good response. I recommended a different business model for opening cold than the one I usually see outlined by consultants and practice management instructors. My approach is much more practical and costs much less than the typical practice start-up plan. It's enough to make new graduates actually believe they can do it! Of course, that's the point and they absolutely can do it.

Optometry school graduates are not the only folks interested in owning a practice. Many ODs in various employed modes of practice or in retail leases are contemplating it as well. I'll share my practical approach in this article and in a few more to come. I opened my practice cold using this method and I've helped other ODs do it as well. It works.

The road to ownership

There are many excellent paths to owning your own practice. You could buy a practice from a retiring doctor. You could buy into an established practice and become a partner. There is nothing wrong with these scenarios and they may be the best option in many cases, but the method I like best, and advise doctors to look strongly into, is opening cold. Starting your own practice is:

- The least expensive way to own a practice.
- The one sure way that you will not pay too much.
- The one sure way that you won't buy things you don't need.
- The best way to follow your own vision.
- The way that allows you to build your own reputation.

When to do it

Many new optometry grads today want to work for a year or two before opening their own practice. I understand the reasoning. New ODs have high student loan debt and they would also like to gain some real-world experience. There is no right or wrong answer here, and it is a personal decision, but it is often based on a concept that owning a practice is extremely expensive. That is not necessarily true and if the cost of start-up is low enough, the decision may change.

I think the best time to open a practice of optometry is directly out of school. Generally speaking, life only gets more complex as time goes on. It becomes harder to do it. A new graduate has the highest level of drive, energy and idealism and those are factors that are extremely important in starting a business. In the first few years out of school, many people begin to have families, buy cars and other consumer items, and they buy a house. The cost of the lifestyle increases dramatically and it becomes difficult to take a step down in income. As life gets more complex, it takes more time to manage it. Many optometrists intend to open a practice someday, but never feel they are at the right time to proceed.

I realize that even with my low-cost approach to opening cold, it may still be impossible for many people right out of school. If that's the case, go ahead and accept a job, but stay determined to save money and reach your goal as soon as possible.

The start-up cost

I think of the cost of a start-up practice as having two parts: the initial start-up costs and the ongoing monthly expenses. As we develop a mini-business plan over the next few tips, we will keep these separate and we will consider both.

The initial start-up cost can vary greatly based on many factors. Here is one simplified example that is fairly typical:

- Exam equipment $60,000
- Optical displays $25,000
- Frame inventory (500 frames X $60) $30,000
- Computers/office equip $15,000
- Office furniture $10,000
- Build out/Decorating $75,000
- Other stuff $20,000
- First three months expenses $50,000
- TOTAL $285,000

A price of nearly $300,000 is enough to make anyone think twice and probably choose another route. Fortunately, with some creativity, you can own your practice for much less.

$62,000!

Tune in next week and I'll show you how to open a new practice for $62,000. That's the price of a new car. A very nice car, but a car! That is a price tag that many ODs can arrange to have financed, or borrow from a relative, or work hard and save up. Here are some additional benefits of working with a low start-up cost: the monthly loan payment is quite affordable and the total risk of the business venture is reduced.

I know critics will say that one of the leading causes of new business failure is underfunding and that it would be foolish to start a practice without far more resources than I'm advocating. I say another leading cause of new business failure is spending far more money than necessary and not being able to pay the bills! Stay open-minded and wait until you see more next week.

As my friend Irving Bennett, O.D. says: don't open cold – open hot!

1.2 Opening Practical, Part 2

I can tell I piqued your interest last week with my encouragement to open a new practice from scratch and to do it on a modest budget as low as $62,000. So, let's dive into how I came up with that number.

Your personal income

We must be clear that my model for a low cost practice start-up does not have any room to pay the doctor a salary during the first year or more. You must be willing to work in another practice as an employee as your sole source of personal income. That should not be difficult – optometric jobs are plentiful and they pay very well. You may want to find a position in a practice that is located far enough away from your office so it is not in the same market. You could work in corporate optometry or in a private OD or MD office.

Depending on your willingness to work long hours, you may be able to work nearly full time in the outside employment position for a while. Your practice will not require that many doctor hours in the early stages, and I advocate trying to schedule patients together as much as possible. The appointment times that are in greatest demand are evenings and Saturdays, so try to reserve those for your practice.

Gradually, your new practice will begin to pay all its monthly expenses and have some amount left over as owner profit. As that occurs you can reduce the number of hours worked per week at the other practice and increase the patient care hours in your practice.

Start-up costs

Remember that we are going to separate initial start-up cost and ongoing monthly expenses. Our first goal is to keep both of these as low as possible while still providing excellent eye care services and products. Our second goal is to move as many costs as possible into the monthly category and not pay for them up front.

Here is the sample budget for initial start-up costs totaling $62,000.

- Exam equipment — Lease – No upfront cost
- Optical displays (DIY) — $10,000
- 200 frames X $60 — $12,000
- 300 frames — On consignment
- Contact lenses — Free trials only
- Computers/office equip — $3,000
- Office furniture — $5,000
- Decorating — $2,000
- Other stuff — $10,000
- First two months expenses — $20,000
- TOTAL — $62,000

As you can see, this is a rather bare-bones office. I see many business plans for start-up practices that are much grander and that is another way to go. This plan allows you to grow into greatness over time, but given that you are going to see very few patients in the early months, I'm opting for a modest, affordable practice. Equipment is just the basics. No retinal camera to start and maybe not even an autorefractor. Frame displays are also basic for now and maybe you have a friend who can help you with a do-it-yourself project.

There are really no funds for an office build out, so you may need to find an older office building that had a previous tenant in which you can make the rooms work. This is a temporary office. You will move to a better one when you can afford it and when patient flow increases. Or maybe the landlord will cover your build out costs; it is a renter's market out there right now.

Obtaining part of your frame inventory on consignment holds down one large start-up expense.

You should start with an office management software program and electronic medical records, but that does not need to be expensive for a small office and you already own a computer or two.

Reserve fund

I realize there is not much room for unexpected costs in this budget (and there often are some unexpected costs with any new venture), but I have $30,000 labeled as "other" and "first two months". With such a low reserve fund, however, this model depends on the practice being able to pay its monthly expenses in month three. I will make a good case for being able to do just that when we analyze monthly expense (more next week), but we really can't be certain of that. Therefore, it would be best if you had a bit more of a cushion. Maybe you can increase the budget to $90,000 and have more in reserve (just don't spend it). Or maybe you can have a line of credit at your bank in case of emergency. Perhaps a relative will help you out if you need some additional operating costs. Or, you might be prepared to supplement your practice income from your wages earned from your other job.

That last strategy is quite realistic if you are really dedicated to making your practice a success. I don't know your personal financial needs, but let's assume you are a recent optometry school grad. You may be able to earn $80,000 per year in your outside job and you may only need $50,000 to live on (OK, not for long, but bear with me). That provides you with $2,500 per month that you could invest in your practice during the early going.

Monthly expenses

I'll tackle this next week and it is really the key to the whole business model. What will those monthly expenses be and will you bring in enough income to handle them? You may be realizing that we are actually constructing a business plan as we go along, but it is much more fun this way. I'll itemize realistic monthly expenses and project patient income in a practical way, so you'll see when you can expect to reach a breakeven point.

What about your dream practice?

Don't be disappointed at the prospect of opening with a very basic practice like the one I'm describing in this series. I hope you know me well enough to know that I want you to have a large, beautiful office, the most advanced clinical instrumentation, a highly delegated staff, and a fantastic optical dispensary. Keep that image in mind as you start modestly with a practice you can afford. As soon as you are in the black with positive cash flow, go right ahead and buy the next great thing for your office. Continue to invest in your practice. Move to a nicer office in a few years.

I started my practice in a rented office of 540 square feet. I was turned down by several banks before I found one willing to give me a loan for my basic equipment. My reception room furniture consisted of lawn chairs when I first opened! You may be able to have real chairs right from the start.

1.3 Opening Practical: Monthly Expenses

In this third segment of our four-part series on opening a start-up practice, I want to concentrate on projecting revenue and monthly expenses. This can be the most difficult part of a business plan, but also the most crucial: how much business will the new practice generate and can we pay our bills?
This part involves some guestimates and assumptions, but a good business plan always backs up every projection with facts.

If you recall, we are building a model to open a very modest practice, while earning all personal income by working in another practice as an employee. We have limited our initial start-up expense and we hope to pay our ongoing monthly expenses fairly soon; such as by the fourth month.

Monthly expense overview
My friend, Jerry Hayes, OD, is often credited for developing the seven major expense categories that many ODs use to track expenses and compare norms with other practices. Let's look at those and how they relate to our new practice.

1. Cost of goods. This is an expense that I don't mind at all, because it is only incurred when we sell something! This is a variable expense and it is usually about 30% of gross revenue. We will cover this expense when we analyze the practice income below by deducting it from revenue.
2. Staff payroll. This will be a big expense, but for a new, small practice it is not too bad. I don't recommend much of a staff to start and the optometrist will have to do many tasks that eventually I would never want him or her to do. I strongly believe in delegation, but not in the beginning. The doctor may do most of the eyeglass dispensing and may even have to answer the phone at times. We want positive cash flow first, and then hire more staff. Maybe a spouse or family member can help out as a receptionist. At any rate, we will budget for one staff member as a receptionist at $2,000 per month.
3. Occupancy cost. This is the biggest expense for the new practice. You must have an office and even if it is small and not the fanciest, you can spend a lot. You may have some build out expense rolled into the rent. Let's plan on $3,000 to $5,000 per month.
4. General overhead. Office supplies and miscellaneous items go into this category, but you can keep it low to start.
5. Equipment. We have an expense here, but since we resisted buying a retinal camera and only chose a basic exam room set-up which is leased, I would estimate the monthly cost to be around $600.

6. Marketing. We need to get the word out to the community about the new practice, but we can also do a lot of marketing by participating in the Chamber of Commerce, and other local groups. There will be some expenses, such as a big grand opening celebration, a couple of large direct mail pieces to local zip codes and some newspaper announcements. I would have a great website and a business Facebook page that is active. Do more marketing as cash flow permits, but be careful because many forms of advertising just break even or lose money.
7. Net income to owner. This is zero to start. You earn a personal income from your other job.

If we add these up and throw in some wiggle room, I'd estimate the cost for our new practice at about $10,000 per month. Let's look at how we might be able to pay for this.

Income projection

This part is a bit more of a guess, but let's assume we can attract just two patients per day on a five day week. That is ten patients per week but you will more likely see them on one evening and Saturday. Or on a couple of half days per week. By the way, I want the office open five days per week with your receptionist, but the doctor is by appointment only and is not in the office every day.

Given that we see 40 patients per month, follow my math based on typical clinical experience and realistic fees:

- Multiply 40 times a weighted average of exam fees, including medical eye care: 40 patients X $100 = $4,000. This could be higher but I'm being conservative.
- Project that 70% of the patients buy glasses. Some buy none, some buy two pair. 28 patients X $350 (gross for now) = $9,800.
- Project 30% obtain contact lenses. 12 patients X $370 (service and product) = $4,440.
- Total income = $18,240 per month ($218,880 annually).

That is pretty impressive for a new practice seeing only two patients per day!

Cash flow

Breaking down the income and expense looks like this:

- Monthly gross revenue = $18,240.
- Deduct cost of goods sold at 30% of gross = ($5,472).
- Subtotal or gross margin = $12,768.

- Less monthly expenses from above = ($10,000).
- Subtotal or net income = $2,768.
- This is simplified; we did not consider debt service, taxes, unforeseen events, etc. But we did have a generous monthly expense that will cover some of that.

Based on this scenario, we actually are making a net profit of $2,768 per month! We are not relying on the practice for personal income so that would accrue in the practice checking account to be used as needed. These calculations are based on an average month, but income and expenses will vary widely.

You may not see two patients per day in the first week or month, but it is quite possible to do so by the fourth month. We had three months of office expense built into our start-up costs.

1.4 Opening Practical: An Overview of Practice Growth

This is the final part of our four part series on opening cold with a modest budget. I've really enjoyed the personal stories many readers have shared with me about their experiences in opening a practice. I'm pleased that many of you have told me that this series inspired you to consider opening your own private practice.

Since we started our hypothetical practice on an initial budget of only $62,000 and we have very low monthly expenses, we obviously have a very modest practice. The great thing about new practices is that they can grow very fast. It is not unusual to grow 100% or more in revenue from year one to year two. After two years, you are beginning to see more patients returning for eye care while you're still attracting a high number of new patients. You are seeing positive cash flow and you are reinvesting available funds into the practice in more equipment, more staff, and nicer office décor. Let's review some of the details we glossed over in our start-up practice and then let's look ahead to the future.

Projected revenues

Since this tip series is really a mini-business plan, let's look closer at the projected gross income from last week. When I refer to practice gross revenue, I always mean collected gross income for the practice after insurance adjustments. It is a total of all fees paid to the practice and deposited in the bank. Our hypothetical practice income for the first year

$218,880. Is that possible and reasonable? The closest data I have on that is from the Management and Business Academy (MBA program), which gathered data from newly formed practices that were open up to three years. The mean annual revenue was $286,000. If we look at data for all established optometric practices in the United States, we find median annual gross income (one full time equivalent OD) is about $550,000 according to AOA surveys and about $688,000 from Management and Business Academy surveys. I've known many single ODs who generate gross revenue of $1.2 million and much more in a busy practice.

Where do patients come from?

There are all kinds of innovative practice marketing ideas available. As CEO of your practice it will be up to you to read about them, think about them and try them.

If you ask any successful optometrist where most patients come from, you will hear word-of-mouth referrals. It is the best way to build a thriving practice. The key to generating lots of word-of-mouth is outstanding customer service. Of course, you also need to provide excellent eye care services and products, but that is generally expected. Customer service (showing patients that you care about their wants and needs) is extremely important. Word-of-mouth referrals occur much faster than most people think.

One other major source of patients is vision plans. Established optometrists may complain about the discounted fees, but vision plans are a huge resource for new practices that need patients very badly. Medical plans are equally important, of course, and I recommend that new ODs practice full scope medical eye care, but vision plans drive more patients to the office because they cover routine exams, contact lenses and glasses.

Some final points

Here are a few practice building tips to get you thinking:

- Visualize what you want your practice to eventually become and stretch to make it look like that.
- Don't always wait for the perfect sign to make a change, like "As soon as we get busier, I'll move to a nicer office." Moving to a nicer office could make you become busier. You have to take some risks in business.
- You may not be able to have your office open long hours at first due to working elsewhere and a limited staff, but ideal office hours are weekdays from 9am to 5pm plus two or more evenings until 7pm

plus Saturdays 9am to 1pm. Longer hours than that are even better. Early morning hours are great too. Even in the beginning keep the office open with a receptionist most days. People want to call and speak to a real staff member – not an answering service that knows nothing and not voice mail. People do not want to find your office door locked in the middle of a weekday.

- Develop your priority list and reinvest money in your practice. Only you can decide how best to do that. You are the CEO. Borrow or lease as needed, but do so safely so you're not overextended.
- Hire more staff and train them to be the best. Make legendary customer service the core of your office culture. Let the patient win.
- Eventually, own your office building, hire associate ODs and open branch offices. Eventually, plan to work on your practice; not in your practice.

1.5 Write a Winning Business Plan

Your practice will become your career and likely one of the largest financial assets you will ever own. It deserves to be planned properly.

My final course in graduate business school was dedicated solely to writing a start-up business plan. I submitted my finished B-plan, as we called it, to the faculty committee who decided whether or not I would receive my MBA. Fortunately, I passed.

In this article, I share some of the basic steps of writing a business plan, as well as some of the lessons I learned while starting my own practice.

Go to Guide
Some excellent sources to consult as you begin your quest for business facts include:

- Practice management lecture notes
- Optometry practice management textbooks
- Articles in optometric journals
- Original surveys or market research (just ask people)
- Practice management consultants. Although these experts charge professional fees, they may provide easy answers to questions at no charge for the goodwill value.
- Established practitioners

- Printed materials and Web sites from vision care plans, medical insurance and Medicare
- Optical suppliers, labs and equipment vendors
- The AOA and other professional optometry organizations

Why a Business Plan?

Many optometry practices probably started without a formal business plan, but that doesn't mean you should try to do the same.

Typically, business plans are presented to potential lenders, from banks to venture capital firms, to obtain financial support for a new enterprise. Most O.D.s starting a new practice or buying an existing one will need financial assistance, but even if you don't, a business plan is an essential exercise for checking the feasibility of the venture. It is the due diligence for a huge investment of your money and time.

Lenders and some landlords may require a business plan, but you also may want to share a copy with your accountant, future partners and associates. However, the most important person who can benefit from your business plan is you, because it makes you consider and research every aspect of your practice. A good business plan becomes the blueprint for your future operations.

When I opened my practice cold, I needed a bank loan to finance the equipment, inventory and start-up costs. I didn't know how to write a business plan back then, but the bankers requested some of the same elements, such as financial statements, projected costs and projected revenue. I learned the impression I made on the loan officer had a huge impact on his approving my application. When you think about it, all you have to offer a lender is yourself and your plan, since your business does not exist yet and you have no track record.

If I had approached the bankers with an impressive business plan meeting all their requirements and more, I have no doubt I would have obtained more financing at a better interest rate.

Elements of a Successful Business Plan

You don't need to follow absolute rules for writing a business plan, but it should be as comprehensive as possible. In addition to the cover page, table of contents and executive summary, you should include:

- Information about ownership and management
- Plans for staffing the practice

- Financial data
- Marketing strategies
- Analysis of local competition
- Plans for selling your services and products
- Details about the customers and suppliers with whom you plan to work
- Daily production and operations procedures
- Plans for meeting government regulations (compliance, licensure, etc.)
- Summary of information presented in the business plan (strategic planning)
- Appendices listing the references and documents used to create your business plan

Build a Good Case

As you begin to develop your business plan, keep in mind the one tenet my business school instructors drilled into me: Every assumption you put in your plan should be based on facts, not conjecture. At first, that may seem impossible when you have to predict how many patients you'll see per day or how much each patient will spend, but you can consult resources to back up your projections. (See "Go-to Guide" above for a list of resources.)

An effective business plan uses information from these sources to back up every statement. Remember to cite sources in the text and list them in the appendix.

Here's an example: If you project you'll see four patients per day for comprehensive eye exams and two for contact lens check-ups, follow up with a statement that your estimates are based on interviews with other ODs who started cold and on survey data obtained from the American Optometric Association.

Business Plan Basics

The required components of a successful business are too numerous to list here, so I'll limit my discussion to a few of the most important. (See "Elements of a Successful Business Plan" for a complete list of topics.)

A typical business plan is 30 to 40 pages long plus an appendix of supporting data. This document should start with a cover page and a table of contents showing the name of the business, the names of the owners and a list of topics covered in the plan. Next, include a one- to three-page executive summary that:

- Describes the services and products you plan to offer
- Lists consumer benefits
- Summarizes your accomplishments
- Discusses how much capital you will need
- States facts about the eyecare market size and growth rate
- Identifies any market niche of the practice.

In addition to describing your business and why it will be successful, the executive summary also should grab the reader and encourage him to keep reading.

Don’t Forget the Details

Consider developing a checklist to keep track of your progress as you prepare your business plan.

Many different elements go into developing a successful business plan and it's sometimes easy to overlook the small details. Make sure you include:

- A curriculum vita for each owner
- Job titles and descriptions of proposed staff members
- A copy of your fee schedule and mark-up formulas
- Professionally designed copies of your practice name and logo
- A description of your proposed practice recall system
- The name of the office management software system you plan to use.

Vital Financial Data

Many businesses fail because they are undercapitalized. Be sure to ask for enough money, but be conservative by limiting your equipment and inventory to just basic requirements at first. Keep the budget lean, and stick to it. You always can reinvest once you're in the black. Important financial information to have at hand includes:

- A personal financial statement. This is also called a net worth report, and it lists all assets and all debts (liabilities). The difference between your assets and liabilities is your net worth. Many recent college graduates have a negative net worth, which can make financing more difficult, but not impossible. As small businesses go, optometry practices are very low-risk. Banks provide blank forms for borrowers to fill out, which can serve as a helpful guide if you're not familiar with financial statements, but don't actually use the form. Provide the same data in your own format.
- Practice financial statements. Incorporate a detailed statement of income (profit and loss [P&L] statement), balance sheets and projected cash flow.

- Pro forma (projected) practice P&L statement. This can be difficult, because you have to gather information to make an educated guess, but this step is extremely important, not just for the lender but also because you'll get an advance look at your potential financial situation.
- Income and expense information for a stated period of time. (See "Projected Budget" for a list of typical expenses.) Provide projected monthly and annual P&Ls for 3 years into the future, showing growth in units, revenue and profit. Remember that you will start to see established patients in addition to new patients after year one. Calculate your break-even point (when your income passes your expenses), making sure to factor loan payments back into the expenses. Some banks may let you pay interest only, or they may not require any payment for the first several months. Of course, interest keeps accruing, but it can help you through a period of weak cash flow.
- A list of all clinical equipment. Don't forget to account for optical display and office furniture, as well as clinical equipment. Provide a price for every item on your list.

Projected Budget

Use these figures with care when you're estimating income and expense information because a new practice does not have enough gross revenue to ensure accuracy. Cost of goods sold should remain correct, since it varies with volume, but the other expenses should reflect your actual marketplace.

- Cost of goods sold: 30%
- Equipment: 3%
- Rent: 7%
- General overhead: 7%
- Staff payroll: 18%
- Net: 32%
- Marketing: 3%

The practice net income (profit) is the amount left over after all expenses.

Get the Word Out

Lenders will be interested in how you plan to attract patients. Begin with a summary of local demographics, and research growth trends, age groups, household income levels and average education. Use national census data and information from the local Chamber of Commerce. Next:

- Tour target market areas and document growth spots.
- Provide national statistics about the eyecare and optical industry.

- Discuss how you will attract new patients, such as local newspaper advertising (announcements), press releases, office open house or a direct mail campaign.
- Describe insurance plans (vision and medical) for which you will be a provider and how patients select doctors on these plans.
- Cultivate referral sources, such as other doctors and school nurses.
- Discuss your community involvement in civic groups and participation in vision screenings and health fairs.
- Provide speeches and seminars on eye care topics.

Scout the Territory

If you want to establish a strong practice, you need to know your competition. Include this information in your business plan by:

- Providing a list of all other eyecare providers within the market area. This should include private O.D.s, ophthalmologists, optical shops, optical chains and mega-mart optical stores. A map with colored dots is a helpful visual aid.
- Discussing how you will differentiate your practice from the competition. Will you offer superior customer service or specialty niches?

Restate Your Argument

The second to last section of your business plan should bring together and coordinate all the previous sections. Restate the major goals and the overall vision of your practice and make a strong case for why you will be successful. Discuss your practice in the context of SWOT: Strengths, weaknesses, opportunities and threats.

Follow the strategic planning section with appendices that list all the supporting documents you used to prepare your business plan. Include items like invoices, sales quotes, correspondence, copies of articles and Web sites, market research, office policies, fee schedules, examples of advertisements, licenses, awards and achievements.

Reap the Rewards

Writing a winning business plan is hard work, but it should also be a labor of love. Get off to a good start by recognizing your role not only as a doctor, but also as the CEO of your company. This philosophy will serve you well throughout your professional career. Develop your vision of a truly great practice and devote the time and energy required to make it happen.

1.6 Advice for new optometry grads

I received an email from a fourth year optometry student asking the following questions: "I was wondering if you have any recommendations on finding private practice opportunities in this tough economy. Also, from your perspective, what does a new graduate have that may seem attractive to an established doctor?"

Here are some thoughts that may help students and recent grads as they enter their professional careers, but I hope my comments are also of interest to independent practice owners who should be assessing how new doctors can help them reach their practice goals.

Not everyone wants to own a practice!

It is important for optometry school graduates to consider their goals for practice ownership. Many excellent young ODs today want to practice clinical eye care in a professional environment but they do not want to manage and operate a practice. These doctors would like to work a 40 hour week and go home to their families. They would rather not have the time burden of building a patient base, the stress of managing a staff and the business risk of borrowing money. Those of us who own practices can certainly understand that and fortunately for all, there are now practice modalities that facilitate this career goal.

Many ODs mistakenly believe that you must either own your private practice or work in a retail store or optical chain. Many senior ODs mistakenly believe that to recruit and retain a good OD into their practice, they must offer some form of future ownership. Actually, a growing trend is for independent private practice owners to employ ODs and pay them an excellent salary and benefits.

How can a practice benefit from another OD?

As the new graduate approaches practitioners about the possibility of becoming an associate, it is good to have an awareness of how the practice owner might benefit.

How any associate can help a practice:

- Can dramatically increase revenue production (if there is some unmet patient demand).
- Could help build the practice by assisting with projects (see more below).

- May allow the senior doctor to reduce clinical hours and use time for practice management or personal life.
- May play a role in the senior doctor's exit strategy by buying into the practice or buying all of it at retirement.

Why a new grad may be better:

- New grads may be hired for a lower salary than an experienced OD.
- New grads may be more amenable to practice procedures and policies than a doctor who is set in her ways.
- New grads bring the latest optometric training.
- New grads extend youth to the practice demographics which often ages with the practice owner.
- Enthusiasm! Idealism!

What to promise

Here is some advice for new grads seeking a job position. If you bring up these ideas in a job interview situation, I guarantee the senior doctor will be impressed. Of course, you must be willing to follow through with them if you are hired.

- Be friendly and personable. Smile.
- Lose any arrogance and don't have a fragile ego. Mention that you will be respectful and considerate toward practice staff members; you are not better than them.
- Pledge that you will pitch in wherever needed. At first, you will not be very busy with patient care. You will actually be costing the practice money – possibly a lot of money! Be willing to do the extra things like dispense eye glasses, do your own pretesting, join a civic organization.
- Indicate that you would make an effort to meet the patients. Hang out in optical when you are not busy and introduce yourself to whoever drops in. Offer to see all emergency visits.
- Offer to assist with office projects that are not direct patient care: research new office computer systems, implement electronic medical records, train staff to expand their testing ability or scribe, work on practice marketing projects, be the point person for a new practice website, overhaul the practice fee schedules, analyze practice data.
- Ask if you can observe the senior doctor doing eye exams if you are hired. Ask if you can sit in. You may know the technical aspects of refraction and ocular disease very well, but you will learn valuable skills in patient communication and efficiency by watching and listening to someone who has been doing it in the real world for 10 or 20 years.

- Bring a new specialty to the practice... vision therapy? Low vision? Dry eye therapy? Treatment of glaucoma and eye care for senior citizens? Nursing home visits?
- Can you give in-office presentations (seminars) to the public? Can you visit local physicians to introduce yourself and discuss referrals both ways?

Chapter 2. Office Design

2.1 Your Office Space

I think many eye care practitioners don't give enough thought to their office space. It just sort of happens and once it does, doctors often stay put longer than they should. The selection of an office often goes like this: the doctor 1) decides where he or she wants to practice, 2) looks around for office space to rent, 3) makes the best choice of what's available and 4) makes the most out of what the facility has to offer. For something as important to your success as your office, it probably deserves more.

Potential advantages
If we take a broad overview of the most important things an office can do for you and your practice, I can boil it down to two major benefits:

- The investment value of the real estate.
- Office space as a competitive advantage in the marketplace.

These two factors convert to two action points:

- Own – don't rent.
- Make the office impressive.

If you don't currently enjoy both of these factors, it may be time to project ahead and develop a plan for the future.

Own – don't rent
A recent study revealed that over 50% of optometrists with above average sized practices rent their office space. I'm shocked. I'm sure these doctors don't rent their homes, and office space is really no different. Here are a few of the many good reasons to own your office building:

- Build equity in the real estate as you pay "rent". Your mortgage payment could be about the same as the rent you'd pay for similar space. And even if it's higher, the payment is going from one pocket to the other – you're the landlord!
- Appreciation. You not only build equity as you pay the mortgage, real estate almost always grows in value over time.
- Tax benefits from interest payments.
- The real estate asset will pay off in retirement. You could sell the practice some day, and continue to own the building and receive rent; then eventually sell the building.
- Freedom to modify the facility as you see fit.

How to begin

Start by studying the area where you want to practice. Drive around and look at commercial districts and growth regions. Read the local paper and talk to people in the know about business development. Look at commercial real estate want-ads in the paper. Talk with a commercial realtor, your CPA and your banker. Consider the following real estate categories as you assess your local opportunities:

- Existing buildings that could be remodeled.
- Vacant land in areas zoned commercial.
- Buildings with teardown potential. This could include old houses in areas that are being transitioned from residential to commercial.

Make it impressive

The second way to make your office work for you is to make it a competitive advantage. Ask yourself why a patient should choose your practice over all the others in the community. The answer to that key question is a competitive advantage and you need as many as possible to build success. Your big competitive advantage could be you (your dynamic personality and charm), or it could be your staff, or it could be your office. Having all three things going for you is the best of all.

There are many ways to make an office impressive, but let's not kid ourselves; large is good. People like space, and that includes patients and staff members. Reception rooms that are not crammed, optical dispensaries that offer lots of inventory, wide hallways, exam rooms and pretest rooms that don't feel like closets; these are all features that make an impressive office.

Sure, one must consider the cost of a larger building, and cavernous wasted space is not good either, but in general, it's best to stretch as much as you can as you enter a real estate investment. What seems expensive today, and what seems large, won't feel that way in five years. Space allows growth and you are planning to grow.

Other ways to make your office impressive

- Exterior and interior design.
- Signage.
- Landscaping.
- Equipment and furnishings.
- Flow and internal efficiency.
- Good visibility.

- An eye care identity and destination. While owning a building and renting some of the space to other professionals may be a very smart move in the early stages (possibly a financial necessity), your practice ends up appearing as just another tenant. There is quite a bit of marketing power in using the whole building and positioning it as a dedicated eye center.

Can you afford it?
Of course you can. Don't let the price of real estate scare you. Like a house, you don't have to actually pay for the office building; you only have to make the monthly payments. You may very well end up paying off the mortgage, but it's irrelevant as you enter the investment. Real estate is not a consumer purchase that declines in value. If you ever want to retire, or move or get out, just sell the building and pay off the mortgage. You will need a down payment, and there are taxes, insurance and building maintenance, but even with all that, ownership is almost always a smart move.

Worried about moving?
Don't be. Sure, it's a lot of work to move – but I wouldn't worry about losing patients as long as you stay within a few miles of your present office. Moving is actually a huge practice builder. Moving will get you noticed by your patients and the community at large, and as long as the move appears to be to better and larger facilities, it's a very positive thing. It signals that you are big player in the eye care market and that you are growing. It offers benefits to your patients and your staff members become more enthusiastic. You'll see a jump in your practice volume.

2.2 Office Design Concepts

I have the opportunity to assist many eye care practitioners with the design of their office floor plans and I've designed six offices for my own use over the years, so I've seen lots of innovative concepts as well as plenty of design mistakes. Office space is always limited to some extent, so it is necessary for the practice owner to prioritize the various options. It can be challenging to decide what to leave out due to lack of space, but that's much preferable than omitting a design element or room function because it wasn't thought of.

Frequent omissions
Consider these rooms and functions that are often omitted due to space limitations or because the designer didn't think of it. Some of these are big

mistakes while others are merely luxury features that one can live without. Which is which is often in the eye of the beholder.

- Multiple pretest areas. I see many offices designed with one pretest room, but when you consider the goal of maximum delegation along with the new advancements in clinical instrumentation, it won't take long until the limited pretest office space stifles practice growth. In addition to the usual pretest instruments (like autorefractor/keratometer, visual field screener, non-contact tonometer and lensometer) plan ahead for the threshold field unit, retinal camera, corneal topographer and nerve fiber analyzer. Larger practices need at least two of the basic pretest instruments to avoid a bottleneck. One should also consider the dilemma of choosing to put multiple instruments in one larger room or using several smaller rooms with each one having only one instrument. The latter has the advantages of faster room turnover while offering complete privacy for only one patient at a time, but it has the disadvantage of moving the patient among more rooms. I use both and I've found that a room size as small as 6 X 10 feet works well for one procedure.
- Multiple exam rooms. Plan to have at least two exam rooms per working doctor. I think the ideal size for the exam room is 10 X 14 feet but 9 X 12 is still comfortable. Smaller rooms will certainly work but I would try to avoid it if possible.
- Technician workstations. Where do we expect technicians to work when they aren't with patients? Ideally, they will have many other duties, such as placing orders, talking to patients on the phone, verifying contact lenses, updating office records on paper and computer. This area can also serve to store diagnostic contact lenses, lens care kits and pharmaceutical samples.
- Staff lounge. This serves as a lunchroom, conference room for staff meetings and special project room. Plan for a sink, microwave, refrigerator and TV. It is a very important room to staff.
- Private executive office for the doctor. This would be high on my priority list even if it is a small space. Successful doctors do much more than examine eyes, they also run a business.
- Private administrative office. In addition to the front business office that is seen by patients, this is a workspace for an office manager, insurance coordinator, and others who work on projects behind the scenes, such as monthly mailings, bulk photocopying, bank deposits, accounts payable and more. Even paperless offices have a need for some space for filing cabinets.

- Large optical. The optical dispensaries in so many optometric offices today seem to be planned as minor entities right from the start. Some serious square footage is needed to make it impressive.

Other innovative ideas

- A private washroom for the doctors. The benefit is self-explanatory. A shower is a handy luxury. Try to place the patient washroom near the reception area. A restroom just for staff is a much appreciated perk.
- A vestibule or lobby to buffer the reception room from extreme cold or heat.
- A coffee bar with a small sink in the reception area.
- Granite countertops at the coffee bar and front desk.
- A flat panel TV, wall-mounted in the reception area.
- All rooms wired for computer data jacks.
- Some rooms can serve double duty. Contact lens patient training, for example, can be conducted in a variety of spaces and a dedicated room for this is often underutilized.
- Plan for some empty space. Don't place patient waiting chairs too close to the front desk. Maintain plenty of room around each dispensing table in optical. People like space and some degree of privacy.
- Lockers built into a hallway wall so each employee has a place for a coat, purse and personal items.

Only you can decide what the priorities are for your office facility, but it helps to enter the process with lots of ideas.

2.3 Owning Your Office Building

If you own your own practice, unless you're nearing retirement, ownership of the office building that you work in is one of the best investments you can make.

First of all, real estate in general is a very good investment, because it usually appreciates in value over time, and there are some excellent tax benefits. The problems of being a landlord and finding good tenants may be the biggest obstacles in commercial real estate, but that is completely alleviated in the specific instance of owning your office building, because you'll always have an excellent tenant – yourself! This tenant, an optometrist, is willing to sign a long-term lease, always pays the rent on time, takes good care of the facility, does not complain much, and you'll probably find him or her to be a very nice person!

The optometrist, in turn, generally finds the landlord (still you) to also be a great person to do business with. While the rent may seem a little on the high side, the landlord generally agrees with any ides the optometrist/tenant has, such as signage, landscaping, hours of operation, parking, remodeling, etc. And, if something changes in the practice or in the optometrist's personal life, the landlord can be very flexible and understanding with the terms of the lease.

You probably always knew you would own your own home after you got out of college, and not rent an apartment. All renters realize that their monthly rent checks could just as easily be mortgage payments, and if they were, the renter would be earning more equity in the real estate with each passing month. When it comes time to move, the house is sold and some net profit is usually earned. There are also some nice tax benefits available to home owners. It's really the same philosophy with your office building.

If this idea appeals to you, you should discuss it with your CPA first. The usual scenario for professionals who own their own building is to own the property personally, and lease it to their professional optometric corporation. You actually will sign a lease with yourself, and the rent will be based on the going rent for commercial property in your geographic area. It's common to make this a triple net lease – which means the tenant is responsible for real estate taxes, insurance on the building and all building maintenance – in addition to the rent. These become business expenses for the optometric corporation. As long as the rent payment is more than the mortgage payment, you the landlord will earn positive cash flow every month.

It's best to think of the ownership of an optometric office building as a separate asset and financial transaction from the practice. You could buy (or sell) them both together, but you certainly don't have to. The appraised value for the building would be done by a real estate appraiser, while the appraised value of the practice would be done by a practice consultant or CPA. A retiring OD who owns his or her building could sell the practice to a new doctor, but retain ownership of the building and continue to collect rent well into retirement. The new doctor also becomes a logical future buyer for the building, eventually.

There are many ways to acquire and use the real estate. You may want to buy a vacant lot in the commercial district of town, seek an architect, and design and build your own building. You may find a better deal by buying an existing building and remodeling for your needs. There are condominium medical complexes, strip malls and free standing buildings. Even homes can be converted to office space if the zoning will allow it (but make sure you can have adequate parking for future growth). You may want to make the entire office building into a clinic for your practice only and enjoy the entire identity, or only use part of the building yourself and rent the rest out to other professionals.

2.4 Office Design Tips

Last week's tip focused on the advantages of owning your own building and making the office impressive. I'll continue that theme with some ideas to consider when designing an office. Having seen many optometric offices in my career and designing several for my own use, here are a few design tips that I think make an ideal office.

The big picture

- A large optical area is important. This idea is not real popular because most ODs really like clinical work much better, and they want to emphasize the exam areas. There are so many wonderful diagnostic instruments available today, and the efficiency of multiple exam rooms is undisputed, so the tendency to devote space to clinic is understandable. But resist it and make the optical bigger, if revenue is of interest to you. The competition for the eyeglass sale is growing increasingly fierce, and private doctors must offer an obvious reason for patients to stay put with their Rx. Optical dispensing is important to the most important person in the office: the patient. And optical produces about 50% of gross revenue in the average optometric practice. That revenue is achieved without the doctor, so don't pass it up.
- If you really want a lot space for exam rooms, try to make the whole office facility larger than the usual 1500 to 3000 square feet. I would like to see the optical area at least 1000 square feet.
- I prefer to see a real waiting area when you walk in the front door – not an optical shop. But I think it's ideal if the patient can see the optical from the reception area.
- Two entrances (one for the clinic and one for the optical) have some real advantages, but they both must be staffed at all times.

- A parking lot that is larger than you need is a must.
- A large illuminated sign with your practice name and logo is a sound investment.

Details to consider

- Have at least four exam rooms. I find 10 by 12 or 9 by 14 feet to be good sizes.
- Include several pretest and special testing rooms. How these rooms are used may change over time. Very small rooms for a single instrument, like threshold visual fields, make sense. Placing a retinal camera and corneal topographer together works well.
- The doctors and the office manager need private offices. You aren't just seeing patients; you're running a business. It will be much more successful if you take that part seriously. Solid core doors prevent conversations from being overheard.
- Include a technician station near the clinical area, but with some privacy for placing orders, calling patients, and doing the administrative work of patient care. It could be coupled with the contact lens and pharmaceutical sample inventory.
- A dedicated room for contact lens dispensing seems outdated to me. Most offices could better use the space for other purposes.
- File rooms are less important because the future is with electronic medical records. Still some file space is needed for business records.
- Inner waiting or dilation rooms can be a fine idea – but a larger general reception area may be more comfortable and more impressive. Many patients are taken to the optical while dilating anyway. A widened hallway or alcove with chairs is smart so patients can be held for a few minutes while waiting for a busy room to open up.
- Include an on-site optical lab. Plan enough space for surfacing and finishing.
- More storage space is always needed. I'd design a basement or second story for storage if suitable in your area.
- A staff lounge is not a luxury. They are great for lunches, breaks, staff meetings and conferences. Including one helps staff morale and retention.
- Some separation between the waiting area and the frame displays is nice, but the areas are still connected. If space is really tight, you could have very few chairs for waiting and just have a larger frame display area with chairs here and there.

- A refreshment center in the waiting area. I think Keurig coffeemakers are great and patients help themselves with minimal mess. They take very little space. Plan for a small sink if you can.
- A private back entrance for staff and doctors. This is extremely handy if anyone is arriving late, leaving early and at lunchtime.

Keep in mind that these tips are aimed at designing the ultimate office, which may not be financially possible in the early stages of practice. But visualizing the ultimate goal is one of the keys to making it a reality.

2.5 More Office Design Tips

Some of the best optometric office design ideas come not from architects and designers, but from veteran ODs who have lived through various designs (good and bad) in the real world. I'll put myself in that group. I've progressed through various office settings from my first startup office of 750 square feet in a medical complex to a second story professional building in a shopping area, to my current 10,000 square foot freestanding building. I've also had the opportunity to tour many of the top practices in the country, which always results in many good ideas.

So here is a non-exhaustive list of random design tips to consider as you remodel, expand or build new.

1. Reception room. Also known as the waiting room, make this area large enough for families and drivers who come along, patients waiting for pupil dilation (unless you have an inner holding area) and future growth. Ideally, a patient washroom should be located immediately adjacent, but with some buffer or divider to provide privacy. Consider your practice philosophy as you decide how to position the frame display area. I prefer a reception room that affords a view of the optical, but is completely separate from it. The first impression is often the reception area and I like the feel of a completely professional, medical office. Consider a coffee counter with sink, a water cooler, and cable TV in this room.

2. Business office. This area should interface with the reception room, and I prefer an open design without barriers like sliding glass windows. One good design provides a counter at the reception room for check-in and a second, more private, inner counter off the clinical area for check-out and payment. Typically, the business office houses file cabinets for patient records, although usually there is

only room for very current files. A storage room in a remote are of the office is usually needed for more files. This is where the value of electronic medical record software is obvious. I also like to see a private administrative area next to the business office. This area could have a private office for the office manager and additional desks for an insurance clerk and general administration. A photocopier and a mailing center can also be located here.

3. Pre-test and special procedure rooms. Plan for more of these than you think. Most patients will go through this room, even if you have multiple exam rooms, and it's not a good idea to keep a patient in the pre-test room too long or else it becomes a bottleneck. I like to limit the number of tests that can be performed in the pre-test room to about 3 or 4. A 10 by 12 foot room works well, and a sink should be included for contact lens handling. In addition to the basic pre-testing (such as IOP screening, field screening, auto-refraction, lensometry) additional small, single-use rooms may be considered for visual fields and nerve fiber analysis, since these tests take a little longer and are best done without the distraction of other people.

4. Exam rooms. Gone are the days of 20-foot long rooms. I used to have them and I actually think shorter rooms look and feel better, while saving valuable office space. I think an ideal size is about 10 feet wide (you can get by with as narrow as 8 feet) by 12 to 14 feet long. Refraction mirrors are easy to set up and they work great. I originally made my exam rooms 10 X 20 feet, and several years ago I shortened four of them by 7 feet by having a new dry wall partition installed. This made the exam rooms 10 X 13, and created four new 7 X 10 special testing rooms, which we use for fields, nerve fiber analysis, retinal photography and corneal topography. We spend a lot of time in these rooms, so I'd make them comfortable and big enough for a couple of side chairs for family members. I like a refraction desk or counter which can handle a computer monitor and allow additional room for a scribing technician. Plan for at least 2 exam rooms per working doctor and then allow for some more rooms for growth. Doctors who work out of 2, 3 or 4 exam rooms are very efficient, with technicians getting patients ready in one room while the doc is in the other. Don't forget that several pre-tests, such as acuity, blood pressure, color vision and even the case history, can be performed by a tech in an exam room – freeing up a pre-test room.

5. Technician workstation. This is a valuable behind-the-scenes area for technicians to work. Located in a central spot in the clinical area, this multi-purpose room is for staff only. It may contain a large counter and wall cabinets for central drug storage and hand instruments. A lensometer and radiuscope is handy here, and an ordering desk with a computer for ordering contact lenses and other supplies. A contact lens lab and inventory storage may also be kept in this area.

6. Optical dispensing. Consider giving this area a separate entrance and parking area, if possible. I like having the optical separate – but not too separate. We operate our optical under our practice name and within the same business organization, because patients like knowing we are responsible for all aspects of their care, and they like writing one check. Internally, we can walk from the clinic to the optical with no feeling of separation. But the separate entrance and a second reception desk allows us to serve a large number of patients who drop in for eyeglass pick-up or repair without appointments – and it has helped us build our walk-in optical sales, filling Rxs from other doctors and selling non-Rx sunglasses. If you have room, consider building special dispensing stations, with built in countertop desks to work across and mirrored partitions to separate patients who are having adjustments. This frees up dispensing tables for frame selection. The dispensing tools and sink can be positioned nearby, saving steps for the opticians.

7. Optical lab. My main tip here is to have one. I'm still a believer in doing in-office lab work because it gives us control over our products, and reduces cost of goods. A finishing lab makes sense for practices of any size, and in-office surfacing or lens molding is within reach of many larger offices. More on optical labs next week.

2.6 Silent Signal Lights

Did you ever miss an important phone call because you were in the exam room with a patient? Has your staff ever tried to let you know that you have a call, only to create an awkward moment as you excuse yourself from the patient you're examining? Here's a simple answer that has worked for me for years.

In every exam room, I have a small red glow light mounted on the wall behind the patient's chair, which is turned on and off by a light switch located in the business office. This easy-to-install and inexpensive device has served me well for years, because the patient does not know that I've been signaled. Here's how it works.

If I'm needed for any reason – an important phone call or something happening in the office – the receptionist or office manager just flips the switch that controls the light in the appropriate room. The light stays lit, and I can't help but see it when I look at the patient. Now that I know I'm needed for some good reason, I can excuse myself from the patient for any reason I come up with. I may be nearly done anyway, and I'll just let the receptionist wait a minute (she knows I'll be out soon). Or, it may be time to dilate and I'll tell the patient that my assistant will instill the drops and I'll see him later. I may tell the patient I need to re-verify the Rx in his old glasses, or I need another instrument, or whatever – anything is better than being called out for something more important.

If you're working toward building a practice that's based on excellent patient service and higher fees, the patient wants to feel like he or she is most important. When an assistant knocks on the exam room door and asks you to step out, or calls you on a phone or intercom, or buzzes you in some way, the patient knows he is secondary. It may be minor, but it reduces the experience a little bit.

If you're even a little handy with mechanical things, you can install these lights yourself with a trip to a hardware store. Just tell the salesperson what you have in mind and he will fix you up. You'll need low voltage wire, the glow light fixture, colored lens and light bulb assembly, and possibly a cover plate to allow you to install the light onto drywall. You'll also need a small plug-in transformer. You will run the low voltage wire from the transformer to the switches in the business office to the lights in each exam room. If you have a suspended ceiling, this should be easy enough, and then you will drop the wire down inside the walls in between the wood studs. Another option is to just hire an electrician.

It's a good idea to meet with your staff and set up advance ground rules about when you want to be called out of an exam. There may be specific people who are always put through, and various rules about patients and other doctors calling. Also, I like to let my staff know day by day whenever I'm expecting a specific call and want to take it to avoid playing phone tag.

You may find a commercially available office light signal system (even wireless ones) that will do this for you also, but those are often geared toward calling a technician, or doctor to a room more than calling someone out of a room, and they may have a chime or beep to get the signal noticed, which I don't want in this case. And, in my personal situation, I don't have a need for a total office light system because I use scribes in the exam room and never have to call one to the room.

2.7 Office Design with Staff in Mind

Attracting good employees, maintaining high staff morale and reducing turnover are important goals for owners and managers of eye care practices. You simply can't build a great practice without a great staff. Human resource issues are often described as the most challenging of all practice management duties. The office culture that leads to a high level of job satisfaction for employees is made up of many diverse and complex factors, but many of them begin with office design.

The design of an eye care office is generally determined when the space is initially built out. The practice owner, a designer or architect and a contractor collaborate and draw up a floor plan. Since office space is limited, rooms and features are selected and prioritized based on function and importance. Even with the best design effort, most offices evolve and change after the tenant moves in.

Whether you are considering a minor office update, a major remodel, a new addition or a completely new location, be sure to consider the spaces that are devoted to staff. Here are some ideas to consider, some of which require very little square footage, but go a long way toward making the office a pleasant and efficient environment for employees.

- Technician workstation. Ideally located in the center of the examination area, this is a desk or counter with a computer and phone. Technicians can be available to assist the doctor, manage contact lens orders for patients, schedule appointments, make follow-up phone calls, arrange referrals, work with pharmacists and a host of other duties. Sometimes a wide section of a hallway is sufficient, or this area could be built into a contact lens laboratory and inventory room.
- Business office. This generally serves as the receptionist's area. The room may have a counter that interfaces with the waiting area and an inner counter for patient checkout and appointment scheduling. Consider the number of people who may work in this area at once and have enough phones and computers for all.

- Administrative area. This behind the scenes area may include a desk for the insurance coordinator and also serve as a space to take care of printing and mailing projects. A private office for an office manager can be located here if space permits. More and more offices are using an out-of-sight dedicated phone desk that handles all incoming calls, schedules appointments, and makes many outgoing calls, so the receptionist does not have to be distracted from patient service.
- Optical lab. I believe in having room for lens finishing equipment, but if you dispense you need a space to adjust eyewear, make repairs, place orders and check on job status. I like having a window so staff can see the frame area and patients can see the workings of the lab (as long as it is kept clean). This room often doubles for other purposes mentioned in this article.
- Staff lounge. It may seem like a luxury in smaller offices, but having a place to eat lunch or take care of personal issues before and after work is an amenity that employees love. Consider having a television, refrigerator, microwave, sink and even vending machines. This room can double as a conference room and a large table works great for staff meetings.
- Staff restroom. A washroom dedicated just for staff, with cabinets for storing some personal items, will be much appreciated and it takes minimal space.
- Lockers. I had actual metal lockers installed in a wide hallway off the entrance door used by employees. These are like the type you would see in a locker room of a workout facility and they are lockable with a key. These basically fit into an extra thick wall. Staff members love to have a safe, private space to put coats, purses, umbrellas, shoes and personal items – and they can decorate the inside with photos or knick-knacks.
- Entrance and parking. This is not just a staff need, but having plenty of nearby parking for a growing staff and a growing patient base is an important perk. If employees have a separate entrance, parking may be close to that door without taking away prime spots from patients. A separate entrance allows doctors and staff to come and go without being seen by patients in the reception area.

I strongly discourage staff members from hanging out in the business office when they have down time. While this may be a natural place to go when there are no patients to care for, it creates a bad impression when someone walks into the office. Generally, the employees are chatting away about personal issues and they stop abruptly and everyone stares at the new person who interrupted the party. In addition to requesting that staff avoid this habit, it's best to tell them where they should go and what work assignments should be attended to.

2.8 The Exam Room as a Pretest Room

Pretesting is widely utilized in eye care and its popularity is understandable because office efficiency is greatly increased. Delegating most of the data collection during a comprehensive eye exam allows the doctor to focus on higher-level tasks like ocular health assessment and patient consultation. While pretesting is performed to some degree in most practices, there is a huge range of techniques and procedures. In the interest of pursuing more of a good thing, if your pretesting process is limited to one area, let's consider expanding it to the exam room.

The floor plan

The approach I like best uses one or more pretest rooms, a separate retinal imaging room and at least two exam rooms per doctor. In this arrangement, the pretest room is used to take autorefraction and auto-keratometry readings, measure intraocular pressure with a non-contact tonometer and screen the visual fields with a small autoperimeter. If the patient has eyeglasses not made by our office, lensometry is performed in this room during the field screening.

Since most patients will go through the pretest room, we make an effort to avoid a bottleneck by minimizing the activities performed there and moving into any available exam room as soon as possible. Multiple exam rooms allow a tech to work in one room while the doctor works in another. Ideally, there will always be a patient waiting for the doctor (but not too long of a wait!) and the doc simply moves between two (or three or four) exam rooms.

The tech in the exam room

Here are some pretesting activities to conduct in the exam room.

- Case history. The doctor will review and expand on the history, but having it recorded by a tech in advance greatly speeds up the exam. Case histories can become time consuming, so I prefer the tech to do it in the exam room. If some personal chit chat develops between tech and patient, all the better. We like the personal touch and we want to have time for that.
- Reinsert contact lenses. Contacts are removed for the automated pretest instruments, but I usually like to have them back on the eye

when I see the patient. We have patients remove contact lenses in pretest and hand carry them into the exam room to reinsert there.

- Visual acuities at far and near. I prefer to have the acuity measured on the same eye chart that I will refract with because it avoids variations that exist with different display systems, room lighting and chart distances. I like to have very accurate acuity before and after the refraction and that is best achieved by using the same chart. I believe preliminary acuity should not be measured by the doctor; it's a huge drain on time.
- Color vision. I feel this test is part of a thorough eye exam and I like to have it tested at each full exam. Color vision books are inexpensive enough that they can be duplicated in all exam rooms. Doing this test in the exam room instead of the pretest area helps improve patient flow.
- Stereopsis. This is an excellent pretest because it's easy to perform by a technician at any skill level and it provides me with a good gauge of binocularity. Stereo books and polarized glasses are in every exam room.
- Blood pressure. I like to have blood pressure performed at every eye exam because it's an important screening for general health and it's often a major factor in eye health. We've used several automated cuffs, but we always go back to the standard sphygmomanometer and stethoscope. It's easy to measure with the patient seated in the exam chair and the technician on a stool to the side.
- The technician wipes the exam instruments with alcohol in front of the patient.
- We have the tech dial the starting lens Rx into the phoroptor to speed up the refraction process. We tried delegating refraction to techs, but we migrated back to having it performed by a doctor in most cases.
- The doctor is paged by the tech on a simple numeric pager in vibrate mode. Wait time for the doctor is minimized by placing the page a few minutes before the end of pretesting.
- Patient education video clips may be displayed on the exam room computer while the patient waits for the doctor. We make this optional in most cases.

Refining and increasing your pretesting routine pays big dividends in patient flow and efficiency.

2.9 Exam Room Size and Function

A great way to increase productivity and patient flow in your practice is to add an exam room. Multiple exam rooms per doctor are a necessity for efficient delegation of clinical testing to your technician staff. Whether you are converting some existing office space into a new exam room or designing a floor plan for a completely new office, the size of the exam room is an important consideration.

I'm seeing a trend in office design that leads to smaller and smaller exam rooms. With the cost of office space at a premium, you naturally want to get as much functionality as you can from your space, but it's possible to go too small. Here are my thoughts on optimum room sizes.

The exam room

I'm defining this room as one that houses a traditional exam chair and stand with a phoroptor, acuity chart and slit lamp. Here are some considerations:

- Realize that you will spend a large portion of your life in these exam rooms. Make them comfortable and pleasant to work in.
- Patient perception matters and a room that's too tiny and cramped does not create the wow factor.
- The patient often has a guest that needs to be in the room also, so allow space for at least one side chair. This guest may be a parent, caregiver, interpreter or friend.
- Plan for space for a technician to sit and function as a scribe. Even if you don't currently use scribes, I would not build a new exam room without considering it for the future. The technician needs a small area out of the way of the patient's visual path and near the refraction desk or counter. She will need a small desk area to write on paper forms and access the computer keyboard, mouse and monitor for electronic records and images. There are many possibilities for computers, from laptops to tablet PCs to standard desktops with wireless keyboards and mice, but they all need some workspace. A corner of the room works well for the tech because I'd like her to stay in the background while the doctor is with the patient.
- Consider the location of the sink so it's near the exam chair but not in the way of the scribe or patient guest. The corner behind the exam chair and to the left (as you face the chair) often works well.
- The exam room door location can cause problems if the room is very small and it opens onto the technician or guest space.

- I like the refraction desk/counter to be about 30 to 32 inches high rather than the usual counter height of 36 inches. This allows more comfortable use of the desk while seated on a stool.
- I like to use a mirror system for the acuity chart and I strongly recommend digital visual acuity monitors over any projector. Long refracting lanes, to come close to the 20 foot distance for optical infinity, are simply a waste of space and the room proportion is not very pleasing.
- One could simply place the acuity monitor on the wall opposite the patient for direct viewing and reduce the size of the letters for proper calibration at that distance. I'm sure refractions done that way in a short room can still be quite accurate and the practitioner could add -.25 diopter if necessary to compensate for accommodation, but I prefer to use a mirror and obtain the long viewing distance. Only one mirror is needed with this setup. The acuity chart (monitor) is placed on the wall behind the patient, usually high and to the left. A refraction mirror is placed on the wall directly in front of the patient (when they look through the phoroptor). This mirror has angling screws that cause the chart to be seen as perfectly centered in the mirror.

I have found an exam room that is 10 feet wide and 14 feet long to be luxuriously large while not wasteful. The smallest exam room I recommend is 8 X 12 feet. Any dimensions between those will work fine and it's certainly possible to go smaller with some limitations on the points made above.

The pretest room

Pretest and special test rooms are as important as exam rooms in the design of your clinical area. With new advanced instrumentation, we need more of these data collection spaces than ever before.

- Pretest rooms can work with many different room sizes, but they are usually not larger than 10 feet by 12 feet. 8 X 10 works well for three instruments on a power table.
- A side stool for a caregiver is nice to have, but not a requirement.
- Wall hooks for coats and purses are handy.
- Even though pretest equipment is expensive, if you're fortunate enough to have strong patient flow and more than four exam rooms, you will want two pretest rooms plus additional special testing rooms.
- Very small rooms, such as 6 feet by 10 feet, can work well for single purpose testing like visual fields or nerve fiber analysis. It is

sometimes an advantage to have only one instrument in a room because it opens up quicker for the next patient.

- In large areas, it's possible to have two different patients being tested by two technicians on different instruments. It is distracting when the other people are speaking, however, and it can be awkward when it is time to switch instruments. I prefer to design pretest rooms for one patient at a time.
- Don't forget that the technician can perform some pretesting in an unused exam room, vacating the pretest room so the next patient has access.

2.10 You Need Two Exam Rooms and One More Technician

Much of my work involves helping optometrists to be more efficient. If the practice happens to have enough patient demand so it is booked ahead even for a few days, the steps we take will instantly generate more gross and net income. If the practice is not booked ahead, greater efficiency still pays off because it allows the doctor to see the same number of patients in fewer days, leaving more time for other projects inside or outside of the practice.

Many optometrists find it very difficult to change their office procedures and one of the big challenges is what to do first. How can you see patients more efficiently (faster) without causing stress and reducing quality? It is a great question and the answer can vary depending on many factors, but a good place to start lies in the title of this article.

Invest in infrastructure first

When implementing change, it is best to start with the things you need in place to allow the change to occur. This may be a bit painful, because it requires some money up front, but you have to make a commitment to this change or it won't happen. The risk is usually quite small and you are simply making a business investment. It is actually more painful to try to change your operational process without making the investment first. That causes stress on staff members and service quality often suffers, which hurts your reputation.

In most cases, you will start to see a rapid return on your business investment and the increased profit can be quite large.

Multiple exam rooms

Having at least two fully-equipped exam rooms per working doctor is certainly not a new principle in practice management, but many offices don't have it. Consider these situations:

- There is simply not enough space in the office for a second exam room. This can certainly be true, but I have been able to create the second room in some extremely small spaces. In some cases, you have to get rid of some junk and move it off site. In other cases, a room may serve multiple purposes at different times. Maybe offices, labs and administrative areas can be moved to an upper or lower floor, which creates space for exam rooms and pretest rooms.
- An ideal exam room size might be 10 X 14 feet, but you can make it much smaller. 8 X 10 feet is about the smallest I'd go without feeling too uncomfortable.
- If available, try to acquire some additional office space next to your office from the landlord or from another tenant. · If there is really no more space to be had in your office, consider looking for a new, larger location close to your current one.
- There may be a second exam room, but it only has a slit lamp and it is used for follow-ups and dilations. It's better than nothing, but nowhere near the efficiency you need.
- The office has three exam rooms, but there are often two doctors working at the same time. The goal is to have each doctor working out of two rooms and this does not achieve that. The efficiency is gained when a technician prepares a patient in the second room while the doctor is working with a patient in the first room. The doctor should ideally just go from room one to room two and back again.
- There is a second exam room in the office, but it is not equipped because the doctor is not that busy yet. This is a judgment call, but even a slight increase in efficiency will easily pay for the equipment.
- Three or four exam rooms per doctor are even better than just two, but the big jump in efficiency comes when you move from one to two.
- Multiple exam rooms per doctor should be a goal all practice owners work toward because a huge increase in efficiency occurs.

Adding another technician

If you want to see patients at a faster pace, hire and train another staff member first. After all, you will have to delegate more procedures and you will need more help. You will need someone to perform some additional tests for you. You may want someone else to insert contact lenses, instill eye drops or walk the patient out to optical. You may have your new technician educate patients on eye care, write up fees, make a referral or discuss insurance billing. Finally, there will be more patients looking at frames at the same time than there used to be and you will need staff members to assist them. We have just scratched the surface on the tasks you could delegate, but first you need someone to delegate to!

Don't worry about the increased cost of the additional employee. You will generate a lot more revenue when you see more patients per day.

2.11 Is it Time to Move Your Office?

As I look back on my own experience and that of many other optometrists and ask myself what single tactic has resulted in the most practice growth, I have to place moving to a new location in the top three. Most optometrists don't think about moving as a marketing strategy, but it can be a powerful way to get your practice noticed. In this article, I'll cover some important considerations about moving to a new office location.

Benefits of moving

One of the most common reasons for moving is to gain more office space and that factor alone can account for an amazing increase in practice profitability. The limited physical space of your office can definitely restrict your production. If you have good patient demand, more square footage would allow you to add employees and give them space to work. You could add more exam rooms and special testing rooms, which can increase patient volume per day and pave the way to adding another doctor. You can make your optical dispensary larger, which is greatly needed in most optometric offices, will increase optical sales and allow you to handle the increased patient flow.

In addition to more space, here are some other advantages:

- You may be able to improve parking for patients and staff. People want convenience.
- You can give your practice a better image. You can make the décor nicer and a larger facility is a sign of success that will be noticed by your patients and the general public.
- Moving can improve staff attitudes and office culture. You may be able to give your staff some perks there are no room for currently.

Employees respond well to having their own work space and a pleasant work environment.

- Better visibility and signage. Many optometric practices are successful without much exposure, but there is no question that you are better off with it. Times are changing; let the public see your office.

Where to locate?

If you intend to keep your current patient base, you should limit your move to a very small area near your present office. The actual radius varies with population and geography, but think in the three mile range. Your present patient base is very valuable and you will retain all of them if you don't move too far. This may limit the opportunities to the point of making a move impossible, but be sure to look. In some cases, additional space may be available in the same complex you are in. You may be lucky enough to acquire adjacent space and add on without moving. Or consider swapping your space for a larger unit.

If there is a new part of town that looks to have great growth potential, but is further away, I would think about opening a second office at least 10 miles away and leave the current office where it is.

What type of building?

This a matter of personal taste for the practice owner, but I encourage you to think out of your comfort zone. I think a free-standing building with the entire space being used for an eye center is a great way to go, but short of that, I think an upscale strip mall presents a great practice image. I'm talking about a very nice mixed use center with beautiful architecture, landscaping and lighting. An optometric practice that has a medical image with a medical practice name, but located in a retail setting which offers convenience and feels more approachable, is a great combination. We see more professional and medical offices of all kinds in this setting. Doctors don't have to be buried in a multistory office building and that is especially true if you have a great optical.

How much space?

The key is to get considerably more space than you have now. If the average practice is about 1,800 square feet, I would think at least 2,500. It is smart to plan for growth, stretch the budget a bit and obtain more space than you need at the present time. You may decide to not equip or even finish all the space at first if you go really big. In many ways, the size of the office could dictate how much your practice can grow. Even though ODs are far more interested in medical eye care, I would make the optical very large, possibly up to one third of the total space.

When should you consider owning the real estate?
Buying commercial land and constructing a new building or buying an existing building should always be on your radar. There are many financial advantages to this arrangement and the only reason not to own your building is if the initial cost is too great or if you don't need a large space yet and you plan to move in a few years. As soon as you approach 3,000 square feet or larger, the monthly rent you will incur becomes so large that is close to the same as a mortgage payment. In that case, you should try to buy the property. All you need is a down payment. Talk to a commercial loan officer at your bank and find out if you can meet the requirements.

Floor plan design
Since you already have an office, you should use the good and the bad of your present location to design the new one. You should work with a consultant or designer who is familiar with ophthalmic offices. Our needs are unique and most architects and contractors will need lots of input.

Build outs are expensive
Be prepared to invest a lot of money in the build out of a new office location. This cost varies greatly by amount of square footage and also by the finishing materials chosen, but it can easily exceed $100,000. The marketing power and practice growth of a new location generally provide a very good return on that investment, but try to get the landlord to cover more of the build out cost, since he gains some value in his property. Also, consider office space that had a previous tenant where you may be able to use some of the rooms and reduce your cost.

2.12 When Should You Move to a New Office?

My answer to the question in the title is that the right time for an optometrist to move to a nicer or larger office is either when the practice is very busy or when it is not busy enough. I don't mean for that answer to be contrary, even though it sounds that way. My point is that it's obvious that a very busy practice can benefit from a larger space, but I've also seen many practices that are not that busy do much better when they move to a new location. Moving to a new office helps the practice get noticed by the community and it signals strength and progress to the existing patient base and the staff. Moving is one of the best marketing strategies I've ever seen in optometric practice. Any time can be the right time.

One of the most important lessons in business that I've learned is to take action before it is obvious. Act as you mean to go. Make your practice look like the way you want it to be. If you wait for a clear signal that some action is the right decision, it may never happen. You have to take some risks in business. Of course, you should also do some cost and income projections and make smart investments. In some cases, you may have to wait until you can afford a major investment and have some cash reserves. Having said that, I think many optometrists stay in the same location too long.

Here are a few things to consider as you contemplate moving your office.

Don't move very far from your current location if you expect to retain most of your current patients. I'd keep it to less than a few miles.

- Ask the new landlord for help with the buildout costs. Get some buildout quotes from contractors before signing your lease. Speak to your banker about a loan or line of credit.
- Look at office space that already had a previous tenant. You may be able to make that buildout work for you with minor modifications.
- Play hard to get. Have another office space in mind that will work and let the landlord know his rent is higher than you want to go and it may not work. Negotiate.
- Try to stretch a little and make the office slightly larger so you can grow into it.
- Make the optical large. Most ODs design offices with lots of exam areas, but the optical is not very impressive.
- Look at signage options. You want a large illuminated sign with your practice name and logo.
- Look at parking during peak hours.
- Ask if you can have an exclusive right as the only eye care provider in the complex.
- If the square footage is over 2500 square feet, consider buying commercial property instead of renting. The monthly rent amount plus common area maintenance costs could easily be the same or greater than a mortgage payment.

Be sure to market your new location heavily to your patient base and to the community. Play up the benefits for patients, such as larger optical showroom, more exam rooms, and state-of-the-art technology. Have signs in your office showing pictures of the new place well in advance. Plan for an open house, patient seminars and a frame fashion show.

2.13 How Can You Redesign Your Office to Better Utilize Space?

There are many factors in our profession that we can't control, so I tend to focus on the things I can change that will provide a good return on investment. One of the best ways to increase profitability in your practice is to see more patients per day. In many cases, an additional exam room or pretest area can help you do that. Seeing patients more efficiently reduces wait times and improves the patient experience. We also know that the less time patients spend on the clinic side, the more time they will spend on our optical side.

Use this article as a guide to help you look at your office space and see if some minor construction changes could help you to be more efficient. In most cases, your office space is fixed and limited, so if you find some space to devote to a new purpose, you must take it away from something else. There will usually be some aspect of the change you don't like, but the point is to decide if the new functionality will be more valuable than the old.

What do you need?

Begin your analysis by considering what additional rooms your practice needs most. Another exam room would be at the top of my list if you only have one. Ideally, each working doctor should have at least two exam rooms. I think 9 feet wide by 12 feet long is a good size for a full refracting lane, although I converted a 6 X 10 space into a nice exam room with room for a tech and a visitor chair.

Think about where the bottlenecks to patient flow are usually located in your daily operations. It may be at the pretest room and that is often because there are too many instruments in there. It can take a long time to do all those tests and that ties up the room. If you can create a new special purpose room, for the retinal camera, OCT or corneal topographer, another technician could access that device and not have to wait.

Repurpose

Walk through your office and ask yourself these questions about each room or section: Is this space helping to improve productivity or is it just nice to have? How often is this space utilized?

Review this list of rooms that often can be repurposed or divided into multiple sections.

- Contact lens training rooms. I think these rooms are outdated, but they are still extremely common in optometric floor plans. Insertion and removal training can occur in many different places and does not need a dedicated room any more. However, these rooms often serve as the place to store a huge inventory of diagnostic lenses as well and I admit those must go someplace. The room may also be used as a work space for technicians, which is also important. But if the lenses can be moved to another space near the exam rooms, maybe an open wide hallway, then the CL dispensing room could become an exam room.
- Storage rooms or large closets. We all need storage, but it does not produce revenue. Consider throwing out a lot of old junk or moving it to a nearby rental storage unit.
- Any room that is larger than it needs to be. This could be a waiting area, private office, lab or any other space. A carpenter can build a new partition wall and make it butt up against the existing ceiling and now you have two rooms.
- Vacant space adjacent to your office. If you have unused or unfinished space in your office or even in a rental unit next door, you could remodel it for your use. You can usually break through from one rental unit to another and create a new hallway so they are connected. It may be smart to snap up the additional office space while it is available. At least you would not have to move.
- Basement or second floor space. Spaces that are not on the ground floor are not ideal for patient care, but they could allow you to move administrative offices, optical lab, a call center, and insurance coordinator's space and many other functions. If this creates more space on the ground level, you can convert that to a new purpose.
- Space for files. With electronic medical records, you may be able to free up some space that holds paper records. Consider scanning in the old charts or move them to your off-site storage unit.
- I do not recommend taking space away from optical in most cases. Most optometric offices need a larger optical.

Construction basics

Here are a few things to remember as you plan your new space. The decisions are up to you, but talk to your contractor about the items you need.

- Will you need a new heating and air conditioning vent in this space? Probably yes, unless the new area is open most of the time. A small fan can help you get by.
- Will you need a sink? Some offices just use hand sanitizer pumps.
- Is the lighting adequate and where is the light switch? If the room needs to be dim for testing, a desk lamp could be enough.
- Will you need a door for privacy or to control sound and stray light? I like it completely dark for retinal photos.
- What will the floor look like when you are done? Do you have any spare carpet remnants or extra floor tiles?

2.14 Improving Flow in Your Existing Office Space

Patient flow is often the key to practice efficiency, which in turn allows increased productivity. A smooth-running practice not only allows you to see more patients per day, but it also creates a more pleasant experience for doctors, staff and patients. Perhaps you feel like you would love to improve flow and increase delegation in your office, but you just don't have the space. Here is an idea I've used to improve flow in my office and others.

Form and function

Patient flow refers to how well patients move through the office and how many can be seen in a given timeframe without bottlenecks. One of the fastest ways to increase flow is to increase the number of pretest rooms and exam rooms. Matching an increase in exam rooms with increased instrumentation and delegation dramatically increases flow and ultimately, revenue. If you are able to find a way to remodel your office space, use the opportunity to change how you and your staff work to delegate more testing and see more patients per day.

Bottlenecks

Most offices have a single pretest room with all the automated instruments in it. The problem with this arrangement is that the room is tied up for a long time because there are so many things to do in there. This creates a facility bottleneck. You may have another technician waiting to start the next patient, but no room is available. Once a backup occurs in the schedule, it's hard to correct it.

Whenever multiple instruments share a room, problems can occur with patient flow. One of the most common examples of this inefficiency is when threshold visual field testing ties up the pretest or retinal camera room. Perhaps you try to sneak a patient into a room for a test while another patient is already there. This is not a good arrangement because it distracts both patients from their procedure at hand and it lacks privacy.

Clearly, you can't have one room for each instrument; it would take too much space and it would be inefficient in a different way. But there is a happy medium.

The exam niche

I've found that creating a very small room dedicated to just one instrument can alleviate huge flow problems because it lets multiple tasks happen at once. If the test is long, the niche avoids bottlenecks, and if the test is quick, the room turns over fast. I call it an exam niche and you can often take the space from another area that is larger than it needs to be. An exam niche works well if it is 5 or 6 feet wide and 9 or 10 feet long. This is perfect for an instrument table, a patient chair and a technician's stool. I set it up so the instrument is against one wall, allowing the technician to walk around the table to operate it. The patient sits facing the instrument with his back to the doorway. A table or counter can be placed in the rear of the niche for technician supplies. A visual field instrument is operated from the side, so it can be placed up against the rear wall.

Exam niches are perfect for special tests that:

- Take a long time, like fields.
- Need special lighting, like retinal photos.
- Are not done on every patient, like an OCT.
- Are done on many patients but there is only one instrument, like corneal topography.

Construction details

A carpenter can easily construct a partition wall from lumber and simply set in place so it just butts up to the suspended ceiling without even changing the ceiling grid. The carpenter can also break through an existing wall and create a new doorway, effectively making two rooms out of one. Give some thought as to whether an actual door is needed; some tests need true darkness and isolation from sounds, but it's nice to have no door on a small room. If there is no door, you may not need a heating/air vent. If the testing runs a long time (like fields) you can have a furnace contractor add a duct and vent above the ceiling.

An exam niche may not need any lighting or wall switch, since the instrument often provides enough light and many tests are done in semi-darkness. A floor lamp or night-light may be used if needed. You obviously need electrical outlets, but rooms generally have these on all walls, so there is probably one that will remain in the new niche.

Creative design

To find potential office design changes, I find it helpful to look at an office floor plan on paper first, and then walk through the space when there is no one in the office. Think beyond the existing walls and look for wasted space. Think "What if?" and be creative.

Chapter 3. Instrumentation

3.1 Instruments That Pay; Directly or Indirectly

Some advanced clinical instruments can be added to existing practices at virtually no cost. I consider these investments as no-brainers because they improve the level of care that is offered, they provide a wow factor for practice building and they increase net income.

Projections

The basic premise to determine the break-even point of an instrument is to project how many times you will likely use it in a month and multiply that by the typical additional fee you will receive. That dollar amount represents your gross revenue from that instrument. The next step is to determine the monthly cost of the instrument, assuming you finance it. You can find out by asking the instrument sales rep for leasing terms or by asking your local banker to determine the monthly loan payment for you. If your gross fees exceed the monthly cost, you have a no-brainer decision and you should buy the device.

If you are close to a break-even situation it is still a smart move to buy the instrument in most cases because you will still have all the benefits of the new device, and when you pay off the cost in a few years you will generate a profit at that time. Besides, the chances are good that your practice will grow and your utilization will increase, which would result in a profit even sooner.

Be sure to review the tax benefits of buying or leasing instruments with your tax advisor. Section 179 deductions are still available which basically create an effective discount of about 33% off the cost of instrument within the first year of use.

What instruments

There are several great devices that I consider to be in the direct profit category, if you have sufficient patient demand, and there are other good ones that provide an indirect return on investment. I'll cover the direct paybacks in this article and the indirect ones next week. I consider the following to be the top candidates:

- OCT. The new generation of instruments that perform optical coherence tomography are very quick and easy for both technicians and patients. They provide a wealth of valuable data that will help the practitioner manage and monitor macular and retinal diseases and glaucoma.

- Digital retinal camera. These are fantastic devices that assist in the examination of the fundus in routine cases and are also helpful in documenting abnormalities. The only reason this idea may not be much help is that you probably already have one. A recent survey of large optometric practices showed that 82% have a retinal camera. If you don't, I think you should strongly consider acquiring one.
- New macular technologies. There are a few new instruments that show promise in evaluating risk factors and in quantifying macular degeneration. These include devices for highly specialized central visual field tests to devices that measure macular pigmentation. Of course, the aging population trend places these devices in a strong position.
- Visual field instruments pay for themselves, but they are generally a requirement for practice so a new instrument would not provide a new service or result in more procedures. Visual field screeners are excellent tools but I would not charge an additional fee for this test.

How will you charge?

There are several good ways to charge a fee for your new service, often depending on the instrument and on your practice. Here are some considerations:

- Procedure code. While you don't have to have a procedure code associated with the test to make it generate a profit, it is helpful. Once the code is known you can find out the approved fee by Medicare and private medical plans in your area. Since the procedure is covered by Medicare and by private insurance, you will generally concern yourself with how many patients you see who have corresponding diagnoses and how often you will run the test.
- Screening vs. full test. Will you use the instrument as a screening device or will you only use it only when medically necessary – or both? Screenings are often run on large groups of patients; in many cases it's offered to every patient presenting for a routine exam. Typically, a fairly nominal fee is charged on a private pay basis, not covered by insurance. Digital retinal photos offered as an optional screening generally result in a 60 to 80% patient acceptance rate. Most coding experts feel that using a device as a screening tool is a different test than when it is used as a medical procedure (including interpretation and report) and it can be used both ways.
- Include in exam fee vs. offer at additional cost. Instruments can be used as a screening, but rather than offering it as an option, you could simply include the test on every routine exam and raise the exam fee. The advantage to this method is that every patient

benefits from the service and experiences the wow factor. The doctor also gets the advantage of the data and efficiency in every case.

- Vision plans. Vision plans generally permit providers to offer a special technology to patients at an additional fee as long as the service is not considered part of the routine exam requirements. The special test must be offered and the fee explained in advance and it must be optional. Document the record by using an educational handout initialed by the patient to indicate his preference. Practices with a high concentration of vision plans might do well to offer the special test as an option for an additional fee. Practices with low participation with vision plans may do better to just include the advanced test in the exam routine and raise the fee.

How many will you do?

If there is a procedure code associated with the test you can research the diagnosis codes that are approved by your medical plans. Most state carriers for Medicare will have a section on its website that will list the diagnosis codes. (This is usually referred to as local coverage determination or LCD). Once you know the diagnosis codes, consider if you would really need and use the test for those types of patients. I would never recommend doing a test just because it will be paid by third party. Run a data search of your office computer system to determine how many patients you saw last year with the diagnoses on your list.

You may be able to correlate your future usage of a test based on other test procedures you currently use. For example, some experts feel the average practitioner will perform an OCT twice as often as threshold visual fields. If that is true, you can simply look up how many visual fields you performed last year and you can get an estimate of OCT usage. If you have a device that you currently use for glaucoma only, consider that adding macular degeneration and diabetic retinopathy patients which may easily double the number of patients who need the test.

If you will use the instrument as a screening test, estimate your usage based on 60% of your average number of exams per month. Multiply the fee you will charge.

Can you offer too many patient options?

I think it's important to not go overboard with screening tests. I'm all for using technology in innovative ways, but I think one optional upgrade is enough. Patients can be confused with too many options and may have a difficult time making a decision.

Things to ask

If shopping for high tech instrumentation:

- Be sure to investigate the networking capabilities of the device and any additional costs if you intend to view the test results in exam rooms after the test is done by a technician in a pretest room. This is strongly preferred for imaging procedures.
- What changes in the instrument are expected in the near future? Will software upgrades be included in the purchase price?
- What is the warranty and what are the costs of future maintenance agreements?
- Will your technicians be able to operate the instrument; is training included?

Combo instruments

There are some exciting instruments on the market that can perform multiple functions, such as:

- Autorefractor/keratometers that can also do non-contact tonometry (NCT) and even pachymetry.
- Autorefractors that are also wavefront aberrometers and corneal topographers.
- NCTs that do pachymetry.
- Retinal OCTs that have an anterior segment OCT feature.
- OCTs that also have a non-mydriatic fundus camera.

Consider these pros and cons of combination instruments:

- Smaller footprint. Many offices struggle with bringing in new technology because they simply do not have enough space for more instruments.
- Having the technician seat the patient, adjust the chin rest, explain the fixation target, and focus the device takes time, so it is very efficient to collect more data at one sitting.
- There is often a cost savings over buying separate instruments to perform all the functions.
- If the device breaks down, you may lose the ability to perform several tests.

3.2 Instruments That Pay, Part 2

Last week I discussed instrument purchases that have a direct return on investment and how to calculate projections for usage and revenue. Today, let's focus on specific instruments that offer a great bang for the buck even though the return on investment is indirect.

Here are some instruments that pique my interest:

Computerized refraction systems

These automated phoroptors have made great advancements in the past few years and they now truly offer the best technology available for subjective refraction. This is not a question of is it as good as a traditional phoroptor because it works exactly the same way, with real lenses, prisms and a Jackson Cross Cylinder. Of course the lenses are changed and turned electronically instead of mechanically, so lens choices are precise and fast. The lenses and the eye chart are manipulated by using an electronic control panel.

There are many advanced features with these systems that make them better than phoroptors. One example is the simultaneous display of a target during the cylinder test for axis and power, which allows the patient to see both choices at the same time. This eliminates having to remember the sharpness from one flip to the other and you don't have to repeat the choices. Another feature is the ability to compare the old eyeglass prescription with the new one by just touching one button. The integrated electronic acuity display offers many more types of eye charts and it can be programmed to your preferred sequence. It is fast and impressive!

Many of these systems are bought with the intention that the optometrist will use them, but I think we should also evaluate the potential for these instruments to be used by technicians under a doctor's supervision. I know the concept of technician refraction has been controversial in the past, but we must continue to seek ways to increase efficiency in clinical practice. As technology improves, old ideas must be constantly challenged. The subjective refraction is one of the most time-consuming tests we perform, so any savings there could be significant. Keep in mind that to delegate refraction is not the same as delegating prescribing. The former is data collection and the latter is a professional skill that takes years of experience and knowledge.

I'm studying the concept of technician refraction carefully and I'll bring you more in the future. Always follow the laws of the state or jurisdiction where you practice.

Corneal topography

Many practices still do not have a corneal topographer, but I think it is an extremely useful instrument that I would hate be without. Much more than a device that is used in managing keratoconus and pre- and post-op refractive surgery, I use it on every contact lens patient every year.

The topographer provides valuable data for monitoring corneal health and integrity. It is part of the annual contact lens evaluation that I perform in addition to the routine annual eye exam. We charge an additional fee for the contact lens evaluation and this is typically not covered by insurance (or part of the insurance allowance is applied to this fee). Providing advanced technology like this justifies a higher contact lens evaluation fee.

I strongly recommend using a topographer that is fully networkable, so a technician can perform the procedure in pretesting and the images are displayed in the exam room for the doctor to review. This creates a perfect opportunity for patient education about the shape of the cornea.

Automated lensometry

I often say that if an OD performed lensometry as often as his or her staff, he would own the best autolensmeter on the market. Lensometry is a tedious test that is done every day on every pair of glasses that is received from your lab, plus the glasses of every new patient seen. It can be challenging for newly- trained technicians to perform perfectly. With all the automation we see in other pretests, lensometry is the biggest obstacle to training new employees.

My experience with most autolensmeters has not been that great if you move beyond single vision lenses. I found that even in my hands, trying to neutralize a pair of progressive lenses was difficult. If I would measure the same pair of glasses twice in a row, I would get two different values. I need to know a patient's habitual Rx exactly in order to judge subtle acuity variances and to prescribe properly.

Fortunately, there is a new generation of automated lensmeters that are very easy, but accurate and repeatable. Some models work by just setting the glasses in a tray and pushing a button. Ask your instrument dealer about the new entries to this market.

3.3 A How-to Guide to Instruments That Pay for Themselves

I've written articles about the clinical, financial and marketing benefits of adding instruments to your practice in the past, but here I'll present a how-to guide to determine if an instrument will pay for itself. If you perform this analysis and find that an instrument will pay for itself, you should definitely buy it.

What instruments?

A variety of instruments can pay for themselves. Some may be used in medical billing and some may function as screening tests for an additional fee that is not covered by insurance or vision plans. Some instruments can be used with both methods of payment. Here are some to consider:

- Digital retinal camera. Most eye care practitioners (ECPs) already have this instrument but if you don't, it may be the best example of an instrument that pays for itself. It can be used as a screening device offered to all patients for an extra fee and it can be used for medical documentation and billed to Medicare or medical insurance with an appropriate diagnosis code.
- OCT (Optical Coherence Tomography). With the large number of glaucoma suspects, macular degeneration patients and diabetics seen in many practices, this instrument makes excellent sense, even though it is fairly expensive.
- Macular pigment optical density test. This is relatively new technology that is used to screen for a risk factor for macular degeneration. It is not billed to medical insurance but a small additional fee could be charged to patients who opt-in for the test.
- Visual field. Most ECPs would agree that an auto-perimeter is a requirement to practice, not optional like many others on this list. But there is a CPT code and it would pay for itself in most practices with use.
- Pachymeter. The usual fee paid by Medicare is low for this test, but the overall cost of the device is relatively low as well.
- Anterior segment camera. CPT code 92285 can be used with many diagnoses of the external eye and anterior segment.
- Corneal topography. I don't bill medical insurance for this procedure very often but an annual topography test is required in my practice for contact lens exams and a separate fee is charged to the patient.
- Specular microscope camera for endothelial cell check. Many specialty contact lens practices use this device on a regular basis to investigate the physiological impact of contact lenses on the cornea. It could be billed to medical insurance or it could be charged to the patient as a screening test.

Projecting gross fees

The first step to determine if a device will pay for itself is to determine how much gross revenue it will produce in your practice. We must analyze how many tests will you do and how much will you be paid for each one. Consider these factors:

- Patient demand in your practice. You can generate data from your office management system to tell you how many people you saw last year with specific diagnosis codes, in certain age groups or with Medicare. If the new device will be a screener that is paid directly by the patient, determine how many comprehensive eye exams you did last year and use a factor for the percentage of patients you believe will opt-in. It will vary by the test but 60% would be realistic.
- Will having the device produce more cases than you have seen in the past? Many practices see more of a certain type of case than they did before the instrument because the device helps them to more accurately diagnose cases. Also, you may receive referrals of more patients because you have the instrument. To be conservative, you could simply ignore this potential and work from what you actually have seen in the past.
- Pent-up demand. You may generate a larger number of tests in the first year of owning an instrument because you have many patients on file with a specific history or risk factor who you could contact and urge them to come in for the procedure.
- Diagnosis codes. If the procedure will be billed to Medicare or medical insurance, you can often obtain a list of diagnosis codes that will be paid by checking the local coverage determination (LCD) for the plan. The LCD may be on the plan's website. If a list of diagnosis codes is not available, ask the instrument rep for the information. Be sure you are aware of all the potential for an instrument. OCTs have a large number of applicable diagnosis codes for retina and optic nerve issues, but some can also scan the anterior chamber and cornea, which opens up the device for many additional patients.
- How often will you do the test? You can check the LCD again or just use your judgment while considering the accepted standard of care in the profession. You can often use one test per year for this analysis, even though you may be able to do more than that based on the case.
- What is the fee? If there is a CPT procedure code for the test you can determine the current approved Medicare fee by checking the website at the Center for Medicare Services (cms.gov). If you factor in potential payments from private medical insurance be sure to

consider if some percentage of those claims will be uncollectible due to high patient deductibles or other reasons. If you will use the device as a screening test, just decide on a fee that will be high enough to generate a profit but low enough that most patients will opt-in for the service.

Projecting expenses
The next step is to project how much the instrument will cost on a monthly basis. Consider these points:

- Cost of the instrument. Get the best deal you can by attending eye care conventions and comparing features and costs.
- Monthly expense. If you choose to lease or finance the purchase, just find the best terms and determine the monthly payment. Even if you pay cash for the instrument, use a hypothetical monthly payment with interest because you are tying up the use of your money that could have been invested elsewhere.
- Additional expenses if any. Consider lab supplies, maintenance agreements or any other extra cost that will be incurred by using the instrument. I would not typically include staff expense or the use of office space because most practices will use existing staff and space that are already paid for, but you could make a case to factor it in.
- Express the monthly expense for one year. Multiply the total monthly cost by twelve.

Resultant cash flow
Simply deduct the projected annual expense of the instrument from the projected annual gross income determined above and you have the profit you will generate in the first year. Any profit at all is a good thing when you consider that you'll also benefit from the additional clinical data and the public relations value of the wow factor. I'd buy the instrument even if it were a break even scenario in the first year because usage will often increase in subsequent years because having the advanced technology often leads to diagnosing more cases. And don't forget that the monthly payment is typically for three to five years and after the instrument is paid for, the entire gross income becomes profit.

Tax incentives
In the United States, the IRS continues to provide strong income tax benefits for business owners who invest in capital equipment such as diagnostic instruments. Section 179 of the tax code allows a business to deduct the full amount paid for the device in the year it is purchased. Rather than having to depreciate the cost of the machine over seven years, you may take it as an

expense all at once. This deduction converts to a discount of an amount equal to your tax bracket. If you are in the 35% tax bracket, a $60,000 instrument would actually cost $39,000. I don't actually work this tax savings into the projection calculations, but I view it as a very nice bonus.

3.4 Corneal Topography: How Can It Increase Profitability

I think corneal topography is a very valuable clinical instrument that is underutilized by optometrists. If you have a topographer, read on for possible new ideas on how to get maximum utilization; if you don't have access to a corneal topographer, this article will show you how you can buy one and have it pay for itself immediately.

The usual uses

Most optometrists who have a corneal topographer use it on a variety of cases, including monitoring keratoconus, screening for LASIK candidates, diagnosing irregular astigmatism and corneal distortion and prescribing contact lenses in orthokeratology. These are all excellent uses for the instrument, but the problem is that those cases are relatively rare in most optometric practices. In most practices, this amazing instrument ends up being relegated to sitting in a room with a dust cover on it. The instrument has much more potential than that and it can produce significant practice revenue.

Don't look just to a CPT code

While most of us look to CPT codes when it comes to generating revenue with clinical instruments, corneal topography can also be used very nicely even when there is not a medical necessity and the procedure is not billed to medical insurance. CPT code 92025 can still be used when there is a medical diagnosis to go with it, but the test can also be billed to the patient as part of routine contact lens fitting or evaluation with no code at all. In my experience, Medicare and private medical insurance can be a little finicky when it comes to this code; it is not a universally covered procedure and you may meet with more rejections than other medical procedure codes.

When you require corneal topography for all contact lens evaluations every year, you will use the instrument on a very high number of patients, rather than for the relatively small group of patients with corneal abnormalities. A bonus for this higher utilization is the wow factor that your contact lens patients will experience. In my practice, every contact lens wearer has corneal topography performed every year by a technician as a pretest. The corneal map images are displayed on the computer monitor in the exam room before the doctor sees the patient. The doctor briefly reviews and discusses the maps with the patient. This elevates what would have been a routine visit with no noticeable difference from a basic eye exam, into a high-tech digital corneal examination.

Contact lens evaluation fees

There are two ways to charge for corneal topography as part of routine contact lens care. You can either bundle the procedure into your contact lens evaluation and fitting fees or you can itemize it as a separate procedure. In either case, you may want to require the test on all patients on an annual basis, not make it optional as you might for routine retinal photos or Optomap. If you elect to include the test in your contact lens evaluation fee, you should raise the fee significantly from what it is now. If you itemize the procedure, consider setting the fee at the same amount as what you would charge if it were billed medically; that way you do not have any problems with charging different fees for the same procedure. A time of service discount could be applied and remember that many vision plans require a discount on contact lens fitting services.

Your decision to itemize or bundle could depend on how most of your vision plans handle the contact lens benefit. If the plans usually provide an allowance, bundling everything into one fee may be easier and the patient pays any balance that is not covered anyway. If most vision plans have a set benefit for the contact lens fitting, you may be better off making topography a separate non-covered service. Always follow the terms of your contract with any insurance plan.

Tips on instruments

I strongly advise that you choose a corneal topographer that will be easy and fast for technicians to use. The operational differences can be significant so be sure to test the instrument yourself and consider if your average staff member could learn the technique easily. Handheld instruments tend to require more skill to operate. If topography is to be widely used in your practice, it can't be a doctor-only device. Corneal topography can be as simple as an auto-refractor, in fact there are combination instruments that do both of those tests at once.

Ask the equipment vendor about networking and if there is additional software needed for multiple viewing stations. Find out if there is an additional cost for each workstation. You want to take the measurement in a pretest room and view and manipulate the images in any exam room. Finally, find out if the instrument integrates with your EHR software.

3.5 Your Equipment Wish List

I love technology and instrumentation in my practice. There are three good reasons why investing in clinical instrumentation provides a very good financial return:

- It allows you to provide new services that are billable to insurance plans or patients or both.
- It increases your efficiency and speed, often through delegation to technicians.
- It creates a wow factor for patients, elevating your exam services and causing more word of mouth referrals.

Consider the tax benefits of buying equipment and speak to your accountant about the timing.

My list of must-haves and wish-I-hads

Here is a list of clinical instruments that I think you should already own or have in mind for the future. I'll start with the basics and move up to the advanced. It should be understood that new startup practices should not overextend the budget and can rightfully get by with less. Instrument decisions are relative to the size of the practice, but it is smart to push forward and reinvest as cash flow permits.

- Autorefractor. Most optometrists have one, but surprisingly, quite a few do not. They are quite accurate and they make the subjective refraction much quicker. I know I'll hear from the purists, but for most patients we can just drop retinoscopy and let the technician do autorefraction. There are many wonderful combo instruments out there with autorefraction plus keratometry, topography, wave-front analysis and even non-contact tonometry! I love all that in one footprint!
- Visual fields. Some form of perimeter is needed to practice. I like to have traditional fields for managing glaucoma plus a fast electronic field screener that is used in pretesting.
- Autolensmeter. If you are willing to spend more money, you can find some that are extremely accurate and repeatable, even for progressive lenses. For the medium to large practice, autolensmeters are very helpful for clinical technicians.

- Digital refracting systems. These have many applications for doctors or technicians and lots of wow factor for the patients. You can test for cylinder while presenting the choices side by side instead of flipping. You can also compare the habitual Rx to the new one with one click. And you can remain at your desk or console the whole time.
- Non-contact tonometer. I love these instruments and the widely believed fear and hatred by patients is greatly exaggerated by colleagues who don't own one. A good alternative is the iCare tonometer. But the NCTs are simple for any technician to use and the measurements are very accurate when compared to Goldmann. It pays for itself by saving the doctor up to an hour per day (do the math)!
- Retinal imaging/photography. This instrument is the best non-essential instrument in eye care. The decision may be about non-mydriatic retinal cameras or Optomap. Both are great and I have both in my practice. The former is more affordable but the latter allows an amazing view of the periphery. Choose based on your budget and your goals. I recommend using the device as both a screening tool for an additional fee not covered by insurance plans and also for management of eye disease.
- Corneal topography. This instrument elevates your contact lens services and I believe you should require it as part of the yearly eye exam for all contact lens patients. Raise your evaluation fees accordingly.
- OCT. Truly a break through instrument that allows us to provide a better level of eye care. Depending on your practice size and demographics, this instrument may be a no-brainer because you may be able to bill enough procedures to Medicare and private insurance to pay for the significant cost. Fees dropped a few years ago, but we can now bill for retina, optic nerve or anterior segment, plus the office visits in many cases.
- Many other technologies are out there that could make your list, such as visual evoked potential, endothelial cell cameras, macular pigment optical density tests, and even digital devices for optical dispensing.

What's on your wish list?

3.6 Your Plan for New Equipment

As we come to the end of the calendar year, it is a good time to consider your equipment wish list for your practice. The IRS section 179 income tax deduction is limited to $25,000 at the present time, although there is hope that it may be increased in the coming year. Regardless of that regulation, there are many great reasons to invest in instrumentation for your practice.

While not an exhaustive list by any means, I'll share a few of my thoughts about equipment that can help your practice, clinically and financially.

- **Second exam lane.** This could easily be overlooked when we compare it to high tech diagnostic tools, but if you don't have two fully equipped exam rooms per working doctor in your office, it may be the most bang for your buck. For relatively low cost, a chair, stand, slit lamp, phoroptor and digital acuity chart can allow you to be much more efficient than working out of one room. A second or third lane will greatly impact your profitability. The life of this equipment is quite long, which makes used equipment a good value also.

- **Retinal camera or Optomap.** These devices are now in most optometric offices, but they deserve to remain high on our list because of the clinical value, the wow factor and the profitability. Prices have come down for these and Optos now sells their imaging instruments outright, eliminating the leased only model that many doctors did not like. You can use cameras and Optomaps as a screening tool for an out-of-pocket fee and also bill it medically.

- **OCT.** This instrument has quickly become the most coveted advanced instrument in optometry and for good reason: it helps doctors to diagnose conditions at an earlier stage and manage them better. Even with the drastic cut in Medicare fees for this procedure, most optometric practices have enough patients who need the test to make this instrument pay for itself.

- **Topography.** No longer new, but I think this test should be run at every annual eye exam for contact lens wearers and you can increase the evaluation fee accordingly. Also, orthokeratology is growing in popularity and represents an exciting new service for many practices.

- **Tonometer for technicians.** Various non-contact tonometers and the iCare tonometer are the leading candidates for accurate intra-ocular pressure measurement in pretesting. These are huge time savers for the doctor. They do not require an anesthetic and are easy for techs to master. I have both in my practice and we love them both.

- **Macular pigment density test.** If you are not prescribing fairly large numbers of nutritional supplements for patients, this device can help your practice. Patients love the fact that you are doing something to help prevent age-related macular degeneration (AMD) and they opt in for this screening test at a nominal fee not covered by insurance. The test helps determine one important risk factor for developing AMD by giving you a score for pigment density.

- **Finishing lab (edger).** Edging systems today allow your staff to finish all kinds of lenses in your office very easily with minimal training. You can greatly reduce your cost of goods by having an inventory of stock lenses and by cutting lenses that are surfaced at your wholesale optical lab. With VSP and EyeMed now paying independent offices to do the finishing work, you can increase your payments and profit from these plans.

- **The basics: autoperimeter, autolensmeter and autorefractor/keratometer.** In case you somehow skipped ahead and never acquired these three instruments, you should go back and get them. They are so common in practice and have been around so long that we can't really call them advanced, but there is a reason they have become standard. You really can't be a good clinician without a good visual field device. Some autolensmeters are now extremely accurate (spend more to get an accurate one) and they are huge time savers for staff. Autorefractors help make the subjective refraction go much faster, which is reason enough to get one. Stop doing retinoscopy unless you are doing it on kids for accommodative dysfunction. Yes, I've heard from ODs who love their retinoscopes, but there are better ways to gather the information and I'd rather save the time by letting a technician run an autorefraction in pretesting.

3.7 Is It Time to Add In-office Finishing to Your Practice?

I realize that most optometrists in private practice have a long list of items they would like to buy. Investing in your practice is a very smart business strategy that produces a great return, but you can only handle so much spending at one time and you must prioritize. In this article, I'll make the case for you to purchase or lease an edging system.

I'm often asked to provide a specific metric on when it makes economic sense for an OD to install in-office finishing. My answer is that it makes sense for any optometric practice of average size or greater. There is not a precise metric, but for most practices, an edging system will pay for itself fairly quickly.

Ways to make money

There are three main ways to save money by doing in-house lab work:

- Use stock lenses instead of surfaced. There is a huge difference in cost between stock uncut lenses and custom-made lenses, but for common prescriptions, the quality is the same. Your wholesale optical lab could use stock uncuts in suppling a complete job for you, but many will surface the lenses specifically for any given job and charge you more. When you edge the lenses yourself, you decide and you know for sure when stock uncuts are used. Stock uncuts are only available in single vision (and some spherical multifocals), but you can easily save $20 or more per pair when you use a stock lens instead of a surfaced lens.
- Save the cost of edging on private jobs. Wholesale labs generally charge about $8 to $12 to edge a pair of lenses for you. If you did that task on your optical orders that are not sent to a vision plan laboratory, you would save that amount on each one.
- Get paid by vision plans to do the edging. VSP and EyeMed both have a program that pays optometric practices to do the edging on single vision jobs. The payment varies depending on the type of lens material, but it can range from $7 to $30 per pair of lenses.

When you add up all three of these methods, you get an idea of how profitable it can be to have your own in-office edging equipment.

Gain more control of your product

In addition to the direct cost savings an edger brings you, there are some very important service advantages as well.

- Many of your eyeglass orders can be made completely in-house. You take the frame off your display and you pull a pair of lenses in the correct Rx and they are done. When you don't have to rely on others and you don't have a shipping factor, the chances of error are greatly reduced.
- Fast delivery. If you have the lenses in stock on your shelf, the entire job will take your staff about 20 minutes. Patients love it when you are fast.
- You can stock lenses in CR-39 or poly, with and without a premium antireflective coating already applied. A rough power range would be a pair of lenses from +2 to -4 and up to 2 cylinder. You don't have to carry a large inventory of lenses and you can build it gradually. You can order stock uncuts a pair at time if you don't mind waiting a day or two. But these lenses are not very expensive and it makes sense to have some stock on hand.
- The quality of the work when you edge a pair of stock uncuts is extremely high.
- Having an edger gives you more ways to "save the day". When a patient is in extreme need due to lost eyewear or when a custom Rx job has to be rejected, your office can make a pair of temporary glasses very quickly to help get the patient through a tough spot. That type of service builds your practice reputation very fast.

Drawbacks

Some ODs tell me they don't want to hire more staff to do edging. To each his own, but I disagree with that. In the early going, your current staff can be easily trained to edge lenses in addition to their other duties. It is incredibly easy with the technology available today and most staff have some down time at various times of the day. If your staff does not have much downtime, then this may be a good time to bring on a new employee who can do some edging and also help in other areas of the practice.

It is true that edging systems are a bit expensive, but this is a device that will pay for itself as you use it. Just do some projections on how much you can save per month based on the dollar amounts given above. If you can save more than your monthly lease payment on the machine, you should do it.

Go to Vision Expo East or the AOA annual meeting for a good overview of edgers and other lab equipment or just call one the edging companies for an in-office demo.

3.8 A Guide to Lensometry for Techs

Last week's tip offered ideas for increasing delegation of clinical procedures to staff. In my experience, one of the trickiest instruments for a technician in training to master is the lensmeter. Here, I will provide a simple, step-by-step guide that can be printed and kept near the lensmeter as an aid.

A lensmeter measurement of the habitual eyeglasses is a basic element of the eye exam that should always be delegated to staff. The procedure takes a bit of practice but any good employee can master it, saving a significant amount of doctor time.

Autolensmeters
Of course, the guide in this tip is for manual lensmeters, but I should acknowledge that automated lensmeters are wonderful instruments that take much of the skill out of the process. I think every practice should have an autolensmeter, but the reality is that it may be one of the instruments on that future purchase priority list. Autolensmeter technology is improving rapidly, but many models have their own nuances, so a manual lensmeter is still a very valuable tool.

I'm still amused by a hiring experience I had years ago, soon after opening my practice. During a job interview, I asked an applicant if she could perform lensometry. She answered yes, and assured me that she did it all the time in her previous job. I hired her and on the first day of work I showed her our manual lensmeter. After looking at it for a moment, she said "Oh – I only know how to use the kind where you press a button."

A challenging technique
Lensometry is second nature to those of us who have mastered it, but when you think about the steps involved, one can see why it can be tough for a newbie. To find a cylinder axis requires both the power wheel and the axis wheel to be turned at the same time. The number line concept and some basic algebra can be a little beyond those who haven't used it much. And if you skip a step or focus the wrong mire pattern first, the result will be wrong. These are some of the areas where I've found the guide useful.

Disclaimer
This guide is written as a very practical and quick guide that will actually be used on the job. It assumes that the technician has been given some training and practice on a lensmeter by an experienced user. The guide is merely a

refresher – a cheat-sheet, if you will. It is not textbook complete and it does not delve into PD or prism. I think those aspects are best trained in person. A technician who is not skilled in those areas can be taught to ask for help when a mire pattern will not move to the center of the reticule.

Print the section below
Lensometry Guide

This guide is to assist you in accurately measuring the lens prescription in a pair of glasses. It assumes you will record the Rx in minus cylinder format using a manual lensmeter with an American style target. The target that you focus on is called a mire pattern and it looks like a cross pattern of illuminated bars. They may be green, white or some other color. If the Rx has cylinder, the bars running one direction will focus at a different power reading than those running in the opposite direction. Every step below is important and you must follow this guide exactly.

1. Release the lens holding mechanism, place the eyeglasses on the stage platform so both lenses rest squarely, center the mire pattern for the right lens, and carefully secure the lens holder.
2. Always start with the power wheel in very high plus.
3. Turn the power wheel to reduce plus power, while turning the axis wheel, until a set of mire stripes come into focus and the bars appear straight and unbroken. Refine the axis and power wheels until the set of stripes is very sharply focused and unbroken.
4. The single line mire (3 stripes close together) **must** come into focus first when coming down from high plus in the previous step. If the triple line mire (3 stripes far apart) came into focus first, turn the axis wheel 90 degrees and the single line mire will be in focus.
5. Write down the sphere power reading and the axis wheel reading.
6. Continue to turn the power wheel reducing plus (or adding minus, which is the same thing) until the triple line mire comes into focus. You should not have to turn the axis wheel during this step. The amount you turned the power wheel is the cylinder power. It is the **difference** between the reading at the single mire and the reading at the triple mire. You may wish to write down the reading of the triple line mire and subtract it from the single line mire reading.
7. Bifocal add power is determined by turning the power wheel to focus the single line mire through the bifocal portion of the lens. Move the stage up so the lensmeter aperture is placed in the bifocal seg area. Do not move axis wheel from the location found previously. You will always need to add plus power. If the single line mire is not visible or will not focus, move the glasses until the

problem is corrected. Progressive lenses may show distorted mires if the seg area is not positioned properly on the aperture. Subtract the distance sphere power from the near sphere power to get the add power.

8. Repeat sequence for left lens.

Chapter 4. Strategic Planning

4.1 What is the Secret to Success in Eye Care?

There are many factors that contribute to building a successful practice, but I'm occasionally asked to name one overriding thing. I actually have an answer and if you ever attended a lecture seminar of mine, you may already know it. What would your answer be? Let's define success as a practice with very high gross and net incomes, strong patient demand, high productivity, a large, excellent staff, high tech instrumentation and a great optical. We may all define success differently and that may not be your definition, but let's assume it is.

Drum roll, please...

I want to build up a little drama before I name the single biggest factor in building a successful practice. Are you ready? It's customer service. Whenever I reveal that answer, I always wish it were something more dramatic that no one ever heard of before. But it is what it is. I believe legendary customer service is at the core of every great company and it's no different for eye care practices. But sadly, customer service in health care is at an all-time low. While we might like to think our offices are the exception, I find many that are not as great as the owners think. I work on service continuously in my practice and ours could be better.

By the way, I prefer to use the term customer service in this context rather than patient service because the latter implies something clinical, and I'm not referring to clinical care at all. I always use the term "patient" in the real world, but this publication is about business, so I occasionally use business terms.

Whose wants and needs?

I like to look at customer service by looking at the usual policies and procedures that occur in an eye care office. It all comes down to whose wants and needs are being served by the policies. The definition of marketing is identifying and satisfying the customer's wants and needs, but I find many office policies are based on the owner's wants and needs or sometimes the staff's.

Of course, the policies are up to the owner and he or she can have them anyway he wants, but I have to think that these doctors don't get it. Sure, we tend to set policies that are easy for the practice and there may be some short-term advantages in getting what you want, but if your goal is a practice similar to the one I described in the first paragraph, the tough-love approach is not going to do it.

Many eye care practitioners have a difficult time with an approach that lets patients win. After all, the public can be so unreasonable. The mantra is often that the practice is better off without this type of patient. And if you give in to these folks too much, the practice will gain a reputation that it's an easy mark and then everyone will want special care! Frankly, I can't think of anything better than a reputation like that. It's not as easy to build as one might think, but if you really become known far and wide for having a practice that patients love, you've got it made. You will let patients win all the way to the bank.

How far do you have to take customer service?

My short answer is how much money do you want to make? How fast do you want to make it? If income is important to you, I'd go ahead and take customer service all the way. Make it an obsession. Don't worry too much about when to draw the line. Try to say yes first; try to satisfy the patient's needs another way if possible, but when you have to say no, do so diplomatically and explain why your stance is necessary and fair.

Since many of the times when you must stand firm involves the billing and collecting of fees, you can go a long way toward avoiding problems if you adopt a policy that no one will ever be asked to pay anything unless they were told in advance. Telling patients the tough news in advance is an amazing equalizer that makes everything OK. Don't tell them and you risk unhappy patients and angry confrontations. It's really not that difficult. Start by telling every patient over the phone if your office will accept their insurance plan and if not, tell them what the exam fee will be - even if they don't ask! Think you can't do that because (insert your favorite excuse here)? I think you aren't really trying.

Specifics

We all know what customer service is, but consider how well you do with these basic examples.

Convenience

- Office is on time for appointments (at least 90%)
- Very little internal wait for the doctor
- Very little wait for drop in visits (eyeglass adjustment, pick up contact lenses, etc.)

- Office hours of 9 to 5 every weekday plus some evenings until 7pm and Saturday mornings
- Office not closed at lunch or other special times during the week
- Phones answered promptly by knowledgeable employees and no voice mail during office hours
- Ample, easy, free parking near the office entrance
- Eye exam moves along quickly and is not boring
- A large selection of great frames
- Fast service on glasses (same day or one day)
- Fast service on contacts (some brands in stock for immediate sale)

Comfort and happiness

- Reception room and exam rooms that are tasteful and attractive
- A friendly receptionist who makes eye contact right away is always at the front desk
- Optical displays that are beautiful
- Quiet and peaceful
- Spacious
- Impeccably clean
- A friendly and attentive staff
- A friendly and attentive doctor who explains conditions well
- Fresh coffee, tea and water is available in the reception area
- A clean rest room that is easy to find without asking
- An accurate diagnosis and correct prescription (kind of goes without saying)

Service recovery

- Entire staff is empowered to do whatever is needed to satisfy the customer (patient)
- Doctor is easy to see for a recheck at no charge and he/she doesn't have an attitude
- No excuses given when something goes wrong - sincere apologies are stated when mistakes are made
- Refunds cheerfully given when satisfaction is not met
- Follow up calls to ensure all is well

4.2 Your Practice Positioning

Have you ever thought about your market philosophy for your practice? Many ECPs start their practice with a very general positioning statement, such as: "We provide excellent service and high quality products at reasonable fees." The goal of this philosophy is to attract as many people as possible, but in my experience, this approach usually falls short of greatness. These practices often end up in the vast middle of the practice spectrum. They do OK, but there is no true competitive advantage.

Three positioning levels

This may be an oversimplification, but for the purposes of this article, we can really divide eye care practices into three types. Which one best describes your practice?

- Low price. Must see a lot of people and generally must advertise heavily, but some of these providers are extremely busy and profitable.
- High end. Beautiful décor, excellent customer service, the best equipment including advanced medical diagnostic capability, expensive frame lines, high fees.
- Middle-of-the-road. Good services but nothing very unique or special. The patient's experience is similar to previous eye exams. Fees are competitive with most other providers in the area.

The first two business models give the consumer some strong reasons to choose them, but the middle-of-the-road model is nothing special at all. This makes that model the worst of the bunch in my opinion, yet it is by far the largest group. No one sets out to make their practice middle-of-the road, but that is simply where many practices end up because they don't have a plan; they have no vision.

Pick two and call me back

There is an old joke where the shopkeeper is on the phone to a customer and he says "You say you want great service, high quality and low price? Pick two and call me back." It illustrates that in business, you can't be all things to all people. Businesses try all the time to be great and still offer a low price, but something has to give. Think about this as you consider what market philosophy you want for your practice. If you are not currently positioned the way you want, change it, but let's start by determining what is best for you. Think about the service / quality / price ratio in retail business in general (non-optical) as examples of other successful business models.

- The truly successful low price outlets give up something. Some mega-discount retail stores like Costco do this by making the stores similar to a warehouse. They do not have a large staff and personal service is not their strong point.

- Internet shopping can offer very low prices, but there is no human service at all and no products for the consumer to see or touch.
- Could a Nordstrom's or Nieman-Marcus store offer extremely low prices? Not really. They have a higher cost of doing business because they have excellent employees to serve the customer, beautiful display furnishings and high quality, exclusive products.
- Fast food restaurants usually have a low price but the restaurants are not upscale, the customer must serve himself and the food quality is not at gourmet standards.
- Could a fine restaurant set the price for a hamburger the same as McDonald's? No, because it uses ground steak, fresh bakery rolls, a staff of waiters and a gourmet chef.
- Compare the experience of a Days Inn with a Ritz-Carlton hotel.

We can go on and on with examples, but the point is that successful businesses choose a model that lets them focus on doing one or two things really well. If your profit margins are small, you will not be able to say yes to patients and let them win. You will be forced to be tougher with your policies and your initial plan to be great goes out the window.

So decide on the type of practice you would rather work in and the type of patient you would rather see. Also, decide on the business model that you can successfully compete within. For most independent private practices, the best model provides excellent service and high quality, not low price.

What about vision plans?
Some ECPs may feel that they can't choose the high-end practice model because discount vision plans are too strong in their market area. I don't think that should stop you at all. Many vision plan patients want an eye care practice that is way above average; they want premium optical products, expensive frames, and advanced eye care beyond the routine vision exam. While it is true that the patient with a vision plan may obtain the basic services and products at a very favorable price, there are many non-covered items that could move into higher profit margins.

4.3 Reinvent Your Organization

Independent eye care practices, like any other business, can easily grow stale over time. At key intervals throughout the life of your practice, I think it's smart to reinvent the organization. Practice owners should perform an objective introspection, formulate fresh goals and develop a plan to implement change. This task can seem a bit overwhelming, but let's break it down and simplify it.

Strategic practice positioning

The biggest and most common problem eye care practitioners (ECPs) have with strategic planning isn't that they choose the wrong philosophy; it's that they don't choose any philosophy at all! Most docs I know have never really thought about how to position their practice. They just want to do the best job possible for as many people as possible. The pricing model is typically "to be competitive". This approach is so general that the practice ends up being lumped together with most other eye care practices in a sea of sameness.

The good news is that it's easier than one might think to change your practice positioning. Just start acting like your practice is how you want it to be in every way possible and patients will get the idea very quickly. Patients adapt very nicely to change when they like what they see and they don't remember your old philosophy all that well anyway. Evaluate your current practice philosophy and consider what would best serve your business needs, such as profitability, professional satisfaction, rapid growth or whatever your priorities are.

If we are very basic, you may want to start by thinking of just three practice philosophies:

- Low price and high volume. This model can be very profitable, although it is obviously difficult for an independent practice owner to compete with national discount mega stores. Continuous advertising is the norm in this type of practice in order to maintain volume. This practice tries to produce a high gross income through volume but will have a lower profit margin than other forms of practice. Even a low net percentage, however, can produce big net dollars if the gross is large enough. Patient loyalty is not very high in this strategy because the loyalty is really to the low price, so if other practices ever undercut your pricing, you could be hurt.
- Average service with high dependence on vision plans. The vast majority of optometric practices are in this model, especially if the owner did not proactively select a position and simply let the practice gravitate on its own. This practice type is middle of the road on everything. Since the practice cannot freely set fees, gross and net incomes are both usually low. It may seem impossible to break free of this model once it takes hold, but if investments are made in the practice and staff, fees can be increased and some of the poorest

vision plans can be dropped. The change can be implemented gradually so income does not decrease.
- High fee structure with advanced service. This is a great model for independent practitioners. If you can build fairly high volume in this model of practice, which is really quite possible because patient loyalty is high, you will have it made. There is always a market for the best, even in middle class local economies.

Budget
The vast majority of ECPs do not have any practice budget at all, which is surprising because most business executives would never operate a company without one. Setting an annual budget can help you control expenses and increase your net income. Here is an easy way to do it.

Take your practice profit and loss statement (income statement) for the year 2007. If you don't have this at your fingertips, you need to set up a meeting with a CPA immediately! I like to reallocate the dozens of expense categories usually shown into just seven major ones, as made popular by Jerry Hayes, O.D.

Once you have those seven expenses, express each of them as a percentage of your gross income. Compare your percentages with the norms given in Tip #266 and decide if you can make any improvements in them and what you could realistically expect your percentages to be in 2008. Next, set your goal for gross income. You could just add 10% to the 2007 gross, or you could be more aggressive here and set an even higher number.

Once you have the projection for your gross, multiply it by the percentage for each of the seven expenses and express that category in dollars. You now have your budget for 2008 - both the income side and the expense side. I would divide those figures by 12 to arrive at a monthly budgetary goal. The hard part is holding to the budget, but you'll have to be creative and work to find a way to do it each month.

While we all love to keep expenses low, here is a word of caution. You can't cut your way to prosperity. Be careful of a strategy that tries to cut expenses to the bone to the point that services drop. You can create a downward business cycle where patient demand drops due to the reduced service, then income drops, then you make more cuts, and so on.

Your investment plan

I believe that ECPs should reinvest in their practice every year, even if you have to borrow to do it. Some years may warrant a large purchase (or two) and sometimes a small financial outlay will suffice. Develop your priority list including instrumentation, technology, physical office space, a branch office, staffing, marketing, in-office optical lab services and any other concept that will help your growth.

4.4 Act as You Mean to Go

If you want to make your practice more successful, start by emulating other successful practices.

For many optometric practice owners, the biggest challenge is that there is not enough patient demand. These doctors would make some outstanding changes in their practices if they just had the patient volume which would provide the necessary cash flow. My advice is begin to make those changes even if you don't have the patient volume. Make your practice look like it is busy and successful, even before it actually is.

This is not really such an unusual approach; it is followed by successful businesses all the time. It requires an ongoing investment in your company and the acceptance of some business risk.

What would you do?
If you had lots of patient demand, plenty of cash flow, and you were able to design your dream practice what would it look like? Your list may be different but here are a few of the possibilities:

- A larger, nicer office
- New office design, nice finishes, attractive furniture
- A larger staff with excellent training
- More delegation to staff
- A focus on excellent customer service
- An office culture that is respectful, happy and low stress
- High fee structure
- Multiple exam rooms
- Clinical instruments with advanced technology
- See patients efficiently; compress them into fewer days
- A marketing plan which includes community outreach
- An office manager to assist with the management

- A fantastic optical department with beautiful decor and amazing frame lines
- An in-office lab for fast optical service
- Associate optometrists so the owner can work on practice management
- Evening and weekend hours which are covered by the associate optometrists

How much at once?
All of the above sounds great, but you may be thinking that a small or average practice can't possibly achieve all that. True enough, at least not all at once. But if you review that list, you'll notice that many of the items do not require a financial investment at all. They may require effort and time.

Many things on the list require a very large investment and for those, you must be careful to not overextend your budget. But many ODs stop investing completely. They try to cut expenses to maximize their net income, which is not a good strategy for the long term. As the leader of your practice, it is up to you to decide on your priority list. What will give you the most bang for the buck? You may change this list over time, but keep the top items in mind and try to find a way to make them happen.

Make your practice look like the way you want it to become. Fake it 'til you make it.

4.5 How Can You Think Big?

Many optometrists wish their practices would grow faster. Many are stuck in a mode that has average production and average profit, but they are not sure what to do about it. After trying a few marketing ideas that don't work very well, most ODs just assume there is nothing they can do. They hope for business to improve, but unless there is a change in strategy, the chances of significant growth are highly unlikely.

If the approach you have taken to date has produced results that you feel are less than stellar, why not try something different? Why not try something big? Your career is flying by. Life is short. If we look at the areas of your practice that you can control, there are only a few that produce very strong results. Read on and decide which ones you want to implement.

Raise your fees

Raising fees is one the easiest big things you can do and it can provide the instant resources to do other big things. Many strategies that are really productive require a financial investment first and a fee increase can provide that. Yes, even in this era of managed care, fee increases still work. Here are some important points on why fee increases work and how to implement them.

- It is extremely important to realize that the vast majority of patients are very loyal to your practice and they won't leave you over a fee increase. Most patients have insurance anyway and they don't even pay the basic fees.
- Your staff may resist fee increases. They mean well, but staff members are not experts in this area. They react with emotion and they sympathize with the patient. This is an area where the OD/owner needs to be the leader and run the practice. Don't ask for input about fee increases, just announce them.
- As you evaluate the effect of a fee increase, do so with a scientific approach. Anecdotal reports from your staff are not good enough. Measure your Rx retention rate.
- Many doctors tell me they don't bother raising fees because most of their patients are on vision plans and it will not make any difference. That is not true at all. Many vision plan patients buy products or services that are not covered by vision plans or only covered in part. If you increased your frame mark-up formula, more patients would pay a higher overage. If you raised your contact lens evaluation fee, many patients would pay more after their allowance was applied. These are just examples; there are many areas where optometric fees are vastly too low.
- Do you offer retinal photo screenings as an optional test for an additional fee? Do you perform macular pigment testing and prescribe nutraceuticals? Do you prescribe a high percentage of digital progressives with premium antireflective lenses? There are untapped opportunities galore in optometric practice.

Hire another employee

Many ODs will not hire more staff members because a) they view staff as more headaches to manage and b) they are concerned that their payroll costs are already higher than the national norms. This is small thinking and we are now thinking big! You can't do great things in your practice if the doctor has to do everything. Delegation is the key to growth and it can be dramatic. Make one of the new staff appointments an office manager and she/he can take over most of the headaches of managing the others. Don't worry about the metrics such as staff expense as a percentage of gross or gross production per full time equivalent (FTE) staff member. Those metrics often improve with additional employees because revenue goes up much more than their salaries!

Many good things happen when you hire more staff:

- Customer service improves because there are more staff members to answer phones and take care of people. That is the key to growth and word of mouth referrals.
- Production increases because staff and doctors have time to recommend treatment options.
- Doctors delegate more because there are staff members to delegate to.
- Existing staff often improve their performance because they see other staff capable of doing their jobs.
- Stress levels decrease because staff members are not rushing all the time.

See patients faster

It may be time for a major change in your clinical routine. Push out of your comfort zone and try seeing patients at a faster pace. With more delegation and data collection, clinical quality does not need to drop at all. Many doctors take great pride in how much time they spend on patient education but most patients really wish they could get through the eye care visit faster. Even if they tell you how much they appreciate all the time you spend, most are really not having that much fun in your exam room. Delegate more and shorten your appointment slots.

Move to a larger office

Most doctors don't even consider moving unless the practice is bursting at the seams with patients, but a large nicer office can be a great marketing strategy that will get you noticed in the community and will drive more patients. The more impressive your office, instruments and optical... the faster your practice will grow!

Join more vision plans

I realize it is in vogue to talk about dropping vision plans, but many of those doing the talking don't actually own a practice or if they do, they have a small one that does not produce big profits.

- Vision plans are very strong and they provide routine eye care benefits for huge numbers of patients in the U.S.
- It is quite possible to make a nice profit with any vision plan.
- Many people with vision plans also need medical eye care.

- It is very difficult to grow a large, successful optometric practice while not accepting vision plans.
- Joining a new vision plan can quickly increase the number of patients a practice serves.

Remodel and expand the optical

The optical dispensary in your office is responsible for a huge amount of revenue in your practice, yet most offices have a fairly small, modest optical. Many appear outdated. Optical consumers today are willing to spend big money for the right products and service. And they have many vendors who are vying for their business. The patient is yours to lose and you can retain at least 90% of them if you have a great optical. It needs to be larger in space and in frames on display. It has to be fantastic! Invest in your optical.

4.6 The Circular Logic of Service, Profit and Demand

Here is an interesting observation about the interrelationship of three extremely important factors that contribute to practice success. I have found that these three factors depend on each other a great deal and if you start with excellent customer service, you can increase patient demand and create a strong profit margin. These three factors continue to work in a circular manner: as one factor increases, the others increase as well.

The cycle of success

Here is the three-prong cycle that will lead your practice to growth and profitability. I am going to use the word "customer" to refer to our patients because customer is the universal term in business and customer service is well understood by all. I will refer to "letting the customer win" as an action phrase meaning great customer service. Notice that the final step in this cycle leads back to the first step. Continuing to improve in all three factors creates business growth.

- You can let the customer win if you have a strong profit margin.
- You can create strong profit margins if you have enough customer demand.
- You can have enough customer demand if you let the customer win.

Analyzing each step

In my experience, a business that has a weak profit margin can't continue to deliver great service for very long. With weak profits, the business owner must begin to cut corners and that causes customer service to suffer. The business must seek employees who will accept lower pay. Suppliers are selected based on lowest price, rather than best quality. Many optometrists intend to offer great customer service, but they price themselves so low in the market that they can't sustain it.

A big factor in creating strong profit in a company is related to customer demand. If there are enough customers wanting goods and services, the business can charge more. And even if it can't charge more, it can increase the volume of customers handled per day through technology and efficiency and that increases revenue and profit.

The best way to achieve high levels of customer demand and volume is by providing outstanding customer service. I'm talking about legendary service that gets people talking about the business. Customer service leads to word-of-mouth referrals and customer loyalty. In any business that is not a pure commodity, people want great service.

Putting this to practical use
Of customer service, strong profit and high customer demand, the factor you have the most control over when starting a practice is customer service. It is true (as I stated above) that you will need some profit eventually to keep the great service going, but that is the phase of a business where you inject working capital and wait for the profit to occur. As you continue to work hard to provide fantastic customer service, even when the customer seems unreasonable, you will see demand increasing. You will gain more customers as the public learns how great you are! As the numbers of customers increase, your profit will also increase and you can even begin to raise prices. You then take that extra profit and re-invest in equipment, staff, inventory and décor, which improves customer service.

4.7 Perform a SWOT Analysis on your practice

Like any well-run business, your practice needs a marketing plan. That does not mean you need to advertise, but rather that it is important to know your market - your patients and your community. Are you providing what the potential pool of patients wants?

A good way to start that plan is to conduct a SWOT analysis - which is an acronym for: Strengths -- Weaknesses -- Opportunities - Threats. Write each of these words on a blank sheet of paper and ask yourself how your practice rates in each of these categories. Obviously, you must be brutally honest and objective, and it is important to get the input of others. Ask your staff for their opinions, as well as a spouse or friends. The good things are easy to list, but you may have to get a tough skin to hear the weak areas.

Once you have your list, consider how well it matches your philosophy of practice. Is it the kind of practice you set out to build? Are you on track to meet your goals? A threat to one model of practice may have little impact on another.

The strengths will form the core attributes about your practice that you should promote - make sure the public knows about these. The weaknesses are the factors that need your attention and a plan to change. Opportunities are goals that you can pursue and invest in. Threats require strategies to insulate your practice and to turn negatives into positives.

This kind of reflection is valuable to your practice; it's part of your ever changing business plan. After the SWOT analysis, ask yourself what are your competitive advantages? Or, why would a new patient select your practice over all the others in the community? If you have trouble coming up with a few solid reasons, you may need to develop a stronger competitive advantage.

4.8 Quick – Can you name your top three competitive advantages?

To build a highly successful practice, you need competitive advantages, but when ECPs are asked about this, I often see a blank stare. I can almost hear that cricket-chirping sound. The basic question you should ask yourself to evoke your competitive advantages is "Why should a patient choose your practice over all the others in the area?" The more answers you have, the more successful your practice will be. If you are struggling to come up with good, solid reasons, then you need to acquire some new competitive advantages.

As you analyze your competitive advantages, I urge you to be objective and brutally honest. Avoid weak, general statements like "We provide excellent service and high quality products at reasonable fees" because every ECP can say that and to the consumer you have not really offered anything unique.

Competitive advantages are now on sale

When you think about it, you can actually buy competitive advantages and that could be a very smart business investment. Here are a few things that money can buy:

- A larger, nicer office.
- A computerized refraction system.
- A truly great staff.
- A large, beautiful optical.

On the other hand, realize that many competitive advantages are free and it certainly makes sense to adopt as many free ones as possible. The following competitive advantages do not cost anything:

- An office that sees patients within five minutes of the appointment time, 95% of the time.
- Excellent customer service; a staff that is friendly and caring.
- Convenient office hours that include evenings and Saturdays.
- A large scope of service; a practice that offers medical eye care, optical products, low vision and pediatric vision care.
- In some cases there is an indirect cost to achieving these factors, such as more employees or staff training programs.

Customer service and convenience

Competitive advantages that are based on customer service are extremely important because they create patient loyalty and that generates word-of-mouth referrals.

Facility

I have always been amazed at the huge practice building effect of a new, larger office. The office itself can be a big competitive advantage, including:

- Décor
- Cleanliness
- Lack of clutter (papers, files, stacks of stuff, old instruments, electrical cords, etc)
- Extra features, like beverages
- Space, so people do not feel too close to each other
- Frame displays in optical
- Lighting
- Pleasant music

Equipment

Clinical instrumentation defines your exam. While it may be true that an excellent clinician can diagnose and treat eye problems quite well with just basic tools, the public understands and is impressed by advanced technology. It may be partly wow factor, but there is usually additional or more accurate data supplied by high-tech equipment. You can treat glaucoma without an OCT, but many would say you can do a better job with one.

Products

Optometrists are increasingly focused on growing the medical eye care aspect of their practices, but a large percentage of our patients still see us primarily for eyeglasses and contact lenses. The quality of those products that we prescribe and dispense is a long lasting reminder of our services. We must work hard to not allow the product aspect of our practice drop because we are concentrating on other specialties.

- Stay up to date on the benefits of new contact lens designs and materials and recommend them to your patients even if they have no complaints. Upgrade them.
- Offer a large, diverse frame selection so you can satisfy the wants and needs of your population. This includes a wide range of price points from economy to high-end. Keep the frame styles continually current.
- Concentrate on staff training so the service aspect of dispensing is high quality. Work to reduce remakes and errors in seg heights and frame fitting.
- Speed of delivery still matters. Work with your labs to speed things up. Do in-office edging. Maintain a sellable inventory of your contact lens brand of choice.

Price

Low price is a strong competitive advantage. As discussed in last week's tip, I do not think low price is the best market philosophy for independent private practices, but there are many optical vendors who do quite well in this arena. And there is a strong market that wants low price. So decide if low price is really the market that you can do well in. Consider these points:

- Large chain retailers have tremendous buying power and can usually buy at much lower cost than independents.
- Consumers who are mostly interested in price are less loyal and are more likely to go wherever the lowest price is next time.
- Product quality is lower with low prices, so there may be more dissatisfaction issues.
- Low priced services require higher numbers of patients per day to make the same profit.

Independent private practices still compete in the price-conscious market by accepting vision plans. Vision plans allow the patient to obtain routine services and basic optical products at little or no cost. Private practices may also successfully implement an occasional aggressive price strategy, as long as it does not become the norm. For example, my practice does not pursue a low price structure, but we always offer 50% off on second pairs of glasses (purchased at the same time). This approach appeals to the price awareness that exists in most consumers and results in higher multiple pair sales.

4.9 Your Strategy for Greater Profit: Answer One Question

I'll start with the assumption that you would like to see greater profitability for your practice in the year ahead. To help you formulate the strategy that will achieve that goal, I need you to answer one critical question:

Which of the following statements most closely describes your typical backlog of patients?

- Strong (Appointment schedule is fully booked two weeks ahead or more.)
- Moderate (Appointment schedule is almost fully booked one to two weeks ahead.)
- Weak (Appointment schedule is almost fully booked three to seven days ahead.)
- None (Appointment schedule is not fully booked even three days ahead.)

The strategy

Every week I speak with ECPs in all of the four categories above and even those with moderate to strong patient demand often are not earning anywhere near their true potential. Doctors with weak demand obviously have even more trouble generating high income levels. Read on for a super-simplified strategy to increase profits based on your current level of patient volume.

Stronger demand

If you answered a or b above, you have fairly strong patient demand. That is a wonderful situation in this economy and you are indeed fortunate. I view those patient appointments that are in the future as a very strong asset and I strongly urge you to convert some of it into cash flow.

- Delegate more.
- Hire more technicians and opticians.
- Use scribes.
- Consider allowing technicians to assist with refraction and contact lens fitting.
- Always follow your state law about delegation, but if your state law is holding you back, maybe it should be changed.
- Change your appointment schedule to allow you to see more patients per day.
- Hire an associate optometrist if you still have excess patient demand after implementing the above. This doctor does not need to be a partner. Pay straight salary with excellent benefits.
- Look for larger office space to allow each doctor to have at least two exam rooms.

It can be difficult to change the way things are done in your practice, but everything around us is changing very quickly and practices that don't adapt will decline. You can make changes in a step-by-step fashion over time. This type of practice is fairly easy to change because the revenue will increase right away. Just get started and make things happen.

Weaker demand

If you answered c or d above, you are like most eye care practices and you have weak demand. Our focus is different for this practice. Increasing profitability is harder and will take longer, but it can be done!

- Be sure you and your staff are passionate about customer service. Look at everything you do from the patient's point of view. Let the patient win. You are working to increase word of mouth referrals.
- Be sure your practice has a fantastic website and a Facebook page.
- Add one or more vision plans. Of course you would rather see private pay or medical patients, but you need more demand. You can still be profitable with vision plans.
- Buy or lease a new instrument that can generate more income. A new instrument like a retinal camera or a macular pigment density test allows you to offer a new service and generate fees.
- Use your available time wisely. Ask every patient to try on a pair of contact lenses. Don't worry about finding the perfect candidate right away. Just let them have a cool experience.
- Improve your optical. Work with sales reps to bring in the best styles. Increase the size of your inventory. Get someone with decorating skills to help you give the optical a makeover.

- Drop in at the offices of primary care physicians, meet the nurse and/or doctor and drop off some business cards. Tell them the kind of patients you want to see and ask if you can refer patients needing their specialty.

4.10 Quality vs. Price in Your Practice

I attended a workshop on marketing last weekend and the speaker drove home a classic point about the value proposition. A consumer defines value as the right combination of quality and price. Which factor do you think is more important to your patients? Let's assign a percentage to price and quality as an indicator of the relative importance of each factor. Suppose we have the following choices. Remember, this is from the patients' point of view:

- Price 80%, Quality 20%
- Price 50%, Quality 50%
- Price 20%, Quality 80%

The interesting point of this is to realize that you have much more control over what patients think than you realize.

Price

If price is the dominant factor for your patients, it simply means that you have not yet differentiated your practice sufficiently to make them see the value. When price is the main thing that customers look at, it means the product (or service) is a commodity. It means that the product is virtually the same from all the sellers. Two classic examples of commodity products are electricity and sugar. Buyers of those items are mostly concerned with finding the lowest price because the items are all the same. Yet, if you think about it, even the sellers of electricity and sugar have been able to build the value proposition for their product by educating the buyer about the differences. By doing so, they are able to charge a higher price and people will pay it.

I realize that you may not actually shop for electricity, but municipalities do and so do large factories. If a power utility company can demonstrate that they are more reliable, have fewer power outages, fewer power surges and are able to respond quickly to emergencies, they will win contracts and they can charge more. When you shop for a bag of sugar at the supermarket, will you pay a few cents more to get a national brand name? Many people do and it's because they believe the major brand may be a little more pure or somehow a little better.

If electricity and sugar can be differentiated to cause customers to spend more – just think what you can do with eye care! Eye care services and products are complex and highly variable and they are not commodities.

Your marketing plan

If you want your patients to not focus so much on price, you must first give them the reasons. You must make your practice not appear to be like every other practice. You must differentiate your product and services. This will teach your current patients that there are other factors in eye care that are more important than price. It will also attract new patients who are less price sensitive than your current patient base. Through word of mouth referral and other forms of marketing, your reputation as a leader in eye care and a provider of high quality products will become widespread.

Quality

The greater the emphasis on quality, the higher the fee can be. But what do we mean by quality? Quality can refer to many aspects of eye care and we should pay attention to all of them, but it is smart to consider how your customers define value. Determining this is why many companies hold focus groups; to bring their customers together to ask them what is important and how quality can be improved. Eye care practices can certainly hold focus groups as well; but you may get similar results if you just ask some patients in your office and if you conduct patient surveys.

It is common for a business owner to focus primarily on the quality of the products he sells but customers often prioritize quality factors differently. For example, an optometrist might rank the accuracy of a contact lens or eyeglass prescription as a top indicator of quality. But the patient may place that far down on his list with things like friendly staff, short wait times and a large frame selection garnering higher rankings. A person who is looking for a fine restaurant may think about ambiance and waiter service before food quality.

Consider these factors in eye care and try to project how your patients would rank them as critical to quality.

- Ease of getting an appointment.
- A practice website that gives a great overview of the practice.
- Courtesy of staff on the phone and in person.
- Ease of handling insurance plans.

- Length of time in the waiting area.
- Easy parking.
- Office cleanliness.
- Friendliness of the doctor.
- A doctor who is not boring and does not drone on and on about eye care just to make himself feel important.
- Examination equipment that is up to date.
- A thorough eye health exam.
- Contact lens fittings that are fast and easy.
- An optical department that is high fashion and offers lots of choices of style and price.
- Clear vision through new glasses or contacts.

4.11 Increasing Practice Net Income: There Are Only Five Ways

The overriding goal of any business, including a professional practice, is to increase income to its shareholders. As optometrists, we do that by providing excellent eye care services and products, but let's look past what we do and concentrate on the revenue. It is extremely helpful to step way back and see the big picture in its simplest form.
It turns out there are only five ways to increase practice net income:

- See more patients per day.
- "Sell" more to each patient.
- Raise fees (or reduce discounts).
- Avoid costly errors.
- Reduce expenses.

When we break down the profitability goal in that way, it seems quite achievable! Each of those five factors will make an excellent topic for the next five tip articles. Rather than choosing one or two of these profit generating methods — let's develop a plan for you to improve in all five of them.

The challenge of seeing more patients
Lack of patient demand is a huge problem for most eye care providers (ECPs), but let's acknowledge that there is a practical limit to how many patients per day a doctor can see and some practices have achieved that. There will be some variation of opinions on what that per day number should be, which is understandable, but I think most ODs place the number way too low. Based on advancements in exam technology and the economics of managed care, I

put the goal at roughly 25 exams per eight hour day per doctor. This would be a mixture of comprehensive exams and follow-ups, with about 75% the former.

If you are already consistently performing at that level, congratulations. The only way I see for your practice to increase patient volume is to hire more ODs and open additional locations. If you do not see around 25 patients per day, read on and try to determine which of the following situations best describes your practice. There are actually three different reasons why most practices don't see more patients. Once we determine the obstacle to you seeing more patients per day, we can go about fixing the problem.

Some ECPs think they don't want more patients
The reasons for this feeling may vary, but many ECPs are not that interested in net income. That's perfectly fine, of course; it is a personal decision. But some doctors come to this conclusion based on misconceptions, such as seeing more patients will require harder work, or create more stress, or will result in poor quality care. I disagree with those thoughts. Seeing 25 patients per day is no more work for the doctor than seeing 10, if you have enough good staff. And the quality of care can be excellent, if you have a good staff. You might think it is nearly impossible to build a good staff, but it isn't that hard if you are willing to spend some money. Where do you think the money will come from? How much additional cash flow is created if you see 25 patients per day?

Some ECPs don't have enough patients
This is completely true and a perfectly valid reason to see a lower number of patients, but let's consider it temporary! A practice like this needs marketing! What can you do to work on the challenge of creating more patient demand? You may have to invest in the practice to make this happen, but the return on that investment is historically excellent. Don't forget that the most important form of marketing is based on excellent customer service which creates more word of mouth referrals.

Some ECPs have plenty of patients, but can't see them
This situation is what I consider the low hanging fruit. If you have plenty of patient demand (you are booked with appointments well in advance), but you only see 10 to 15 patients per day, you can quickly generate much more net income. Begin with a plan to shorten your exam routine by delegating more of the data collection to qualified technicians. Analyze how much time is spent on other aspects of the patient visit and change it. If personal chit chat with the patient takes a lot of your time, try to delegate that as well.

Think of your assistants as eye care professionals your patients can also bond with. Don't assume that patients love to hear long explanations about their eye problems or that they are super-impressed with all those tests in the phoroptor. Most are very polite to their doctor, but they would really like to get on with their busy lives.

Part of your new plan to increase efficiency and take advantage of your patient demand may include more exam rooms, more pretest rooms and a larger optical. You may need more automated instrumentation. That may also mean a larger office. Go for it. Your patient backlog is worth a lot of money.

4.12 Increasing Practice Net Income: Step #2

Last week's tip started with the premise that there are only five ways to increase your practice net income. As a review, here they are:

- See more patients per day.
- "Sell" more to each patient.
- Raise fees (or reduce discounts).
- Avoid costly errors.
- Reduce expenses.

I'm covering each of these five steps in a series of tip articles and today we'll focus on "selling" more to each patient. I hesitate to use the word "selling" to optometrists because I know many of my colleagues find the word offensive, but I really don't know what else to call it. Yes, we actually prescribe our treatments and we recommend optical products, but from a broad business perspective we are still selling ourselves and our services.

Regardless of what we call it, this strategy deals with the patients you already have rather than trying to attract more of them. This method of increasing net income does not require you to see more patients per day. Let's analyze the ways your current patients might purchase more eye care services and products. If your practice is underperforming in any of the following categories, you have an excellent opportunity to increase your per patient revenue and your practice net. Embrace and invest in the missing categories.

Multiple pairs of glasses

This is the classic factor we think of when it comes to selling more to each patient and there is a huge range of success among practices. Some offices sell multiple pairs very well and some are terrible. My practice used to be terrible until we implemented an aggressive policy of offering a 50% discount on the second complete pair (and the third, fourth, etc.). Yes, we also offer the same discount to patients with vision plans. Overnight we started to sell lots of multiple pairs. We still make an excellent profit on the second pair and smaller profit is better than no profit.

I have heard the concern that patients will immediately presume there must be way too much markup in the glasses if I can offer 50% off, but they really don't think that way. They already know there is a lot of markup in optical and all they really focus on is how the policy affects them. I've never had to justify how we can give 50% off, but my response would be that our lab gives us a discount when we order two or more pairs for a patient at the same time and we save time in processing and dispensing both pairs at once.

There are plenty of other ways to sell multiple pairs of glasses without a big discount. One of the major ones involves the doctor recommending and prescribing special purpose eyewear in the exam room. This includes Rx sunglasses, computer glasses, TV glasses, golf glasses or whatever is appropriate. The other major factor is the concept of lifestyle dispensing. The optician must begin the patient encounter by asking questions. Don't begin by showing patients what you have; begin by asking them what they need. Begin by asking them about their life: work, hobbies, sports, driving, and computer use.

Sunglasses

It takes an investment in great inventory, but optometric practices can become the go to place for quality plano sunglasses in the community. And many people want quality and will pay for it. You need a great selection of great brands like Wiley-X, Rudy Project, Maui Jim, Oakley, RayBan, and Nike, to name a few, plus many high fashion designer brands. Carry that and they will sell. My practice is in the Chicago area, not exactly the sunbelt, but we sell lots of sunglasses all year round.

Contact lenses

Most ODs do not bring up the idea of contact lenses unless the patient asks for them. Be honest – are you in that group? Imagine how many contact lens fittings you could do if you suggested a free try-on in your office to most of your patients? You could just delegate the matter to a technician and only become involved if the patient agreed to a fitting. Many of these patients would order contact lenses, buy a pair of plano sunglasses to wear over them and also purchase new Rx glasses as well! Now we're talking about selling more to each patient.

Medical eye care
Additional diagnostic testing and follow-up office visits also qualify as selling more to each patient. Take courses in medical eye care and in billing and coding. Invest in an OCT this year.

Optional screening tests
Many patients with vision plans will opt in for a special screening test and pay out of pocket because they know it offers advanced technology and a higher level of eye care. Screening retinal photos and macular pigment density testing are excellent examples and you could bundle those together. Many eye care practices are beginning to use an OCT in a screening mode.

Nutritional supplements
Patients really like it when their eye care professional advises them about nutrition and vitamin use. They are happy to buy a better product from their eye doctor's office or via the practice website.

Low vision
The population is aging and there is a growing need for help with magnification. You probably have a large number of patients already in your practice who need basic low vision care. Why not have some good hand held magnifiers and a demo unit for an electronic magnification device?

Average sale per exam
This metric goes by many other names, such as average gross revenue per patient among others, but it is extremely useful and easy to track. Simply take your collected gross revenue for the month and divide by the number of comprehensive exams performed. The national average for independent optometric practice is $307 according to the MBA program, but I know many OD practices where the number is over $500. All of the eye care services listed above contribute to a higher revenue per patient figure.

4.13 The Third Way to Increase Practice Net

Continuing in our series covering the five methods to increase your practice net income, let's focus on the practice fee structure. As a review, raising prices or reducing discounts is the third way to increase profitability. Here is the list we are working on:

1. See more patients per day.
2. "Sell" more to each patient.
3. Raise fees (or reduce discounts).

4. Avoid costly errors.
5. Reduce expenses.

Raising fees increases the net

When most of us think about raising fees, we realize that it will increase gross revenue, but we should also know that it has a huge effect on the practice net as well. Most of the expenses in your practice are considered fixed costs; in fact, the only variable cost is cost of goods. Because you are already paying the fixed costs, the vast majority of any collected fee increase will fall directly to your bottom line net. That is a big jump in profitability.

One of the fastest ways to increase your net income is to increase your gross income.

What are you worth?

As I consult with ODs and analyze practices throughout the US, I find that we routinely undervalue our services. This is especially true for routine eye exams, which we have somehow convinced ourselves must have a much lower fee than medical eye exams. I think we should charge the same fee regardless of the medical diagnosis and regardless of the insurance plan.
When you consider the importance of good vision to the public, the level of training of the OD, and the investment in equipment, inventory and staff, it becomes obvious that the average routine eye exam fee is too low. So are many other fees like contact lens fittings, frame mark-ups and ophthalmic lenses. I often compare optometric fees to those charged by other occupations, such as lawyers, plumbers, and ophthalmologists. When you think of the fees those professionals charge I believe you see my point. Are optometric services worth less? I have one more service I like to compare to: a "cut and color" at a hair salon. If we charged for eye exams what hair stylists charge for a cut and color, we would be doing very well.

Fee increases don't matter with vision plans

The usual mantra from optometrists about raising fees is that it won't make any difference anyway because they see so many patients with vision plans. My response to that is: In that case, why not raise them? Most of the concern over fee increases is that the practice might lose some patients (which is actually not true in my experience). But you certainly won't lose any of the vision plan patients because they don't pay the full fee anyway. So why not raise them?
Even with vision plans, two good things happen when you raise fees:

1. The patient's perception of the quality of your service improves. People equate the value of the service with the fee, especially when they can't really evaluate the technical aspects themselves.
2. Vision plan patients still buy some goods and services that are not covered by the vision plan and when they do, you need to make a strong profit. Patients may need an eye exam or may want to buy a pair of glasses before they are eligible for benefits. They may buy a pair of sunglasses or they may get an eye infection. These services and products are not covered by the vision plan and they are paid for out-of-pocket or billed to medical insurance.

What if you lose patients?

The fear of losing patients is the main factor that prevents ODs from raising fees and makes staff members worry about it. Yet, if you ask doctors what happened the last time they raised fees the usual response is that nothing happened. Most likely no one noticed or complained. Even if some patients do notice, they really understand that prices sometimes must go up. Professional fees and optical prices in a doctor's office setting is just not that price sensitive. People will not leave a trusted doctor over a fee increase. Did you ever notice that the eye care practices with high fees usually have plenty of patients? Price is not the only factor when a patient chooses an eye doctor.

What about discounts?

Getting rid of a discount is basically the same as raising fees and both can help your bottom line.

When considering offering a discount to patients, here is the test question I ask: Will the discount result in many more purchases that would not have happened anyway? Many discounts I see do not really increase sales – at least not enough to cover the reduced profit. One example is the use of lens packages or bundles. Typically, some of the most popular lens features are grouped together and sold as a package at a lower price than the items would have cost individually. I would argue that the vast majority of patients would have bought all those features at the regular price. A time of service discount is another example; most of those patients would have paid the full fee.

Discounts to family members, employees or professional courtesies are not part of this. Those discounts are given as a benefit or as a gift and profitability is not the main goal.

Vision plans require huge discounts and the decision to accept them or not can be complicated. That topic is beyond the scope of this article, but it is smart to analyze all vision plans regularly and decide if you may be better off dropping some of them. I have seen many examples of practices that dropped a vision plan and the owner reports that they saw fewer patients but had the same net income. That sounds like a good move to me.

4.14 Office Errors Can Reduce Your Net

Continuing in our series covering the five methods to increase your practice net income, let's focus on the fourth item on our list: reducing administrative errors. Here is the complete list we are working on:

1. See more patients per day.
2. "Sell" more to each patient.
3. Raise fees (or reduce discounts).
4. Avoid costly errors.
5. Reduce expenses.

Errors in the broad sense

I refer to administrative errors as a catch-all category for anything that doctors and staff may do that costs the practice money. I'll provide some examples and some tips for preventing these oversights and omissions, but in the broad sense this category could include any office inefficiency.

Fees that are not posted or collected

One would think that forgetting to charge and collect fees would be a rare occurrence in any business, but it is actually fairly common in optometric practice. Part of the problem stems from office management software programs that are slow and burdensome on the staff. In an effort to check patients out quickly, many offices do not post charges to the patient account while the patient is in the office. Many staff members are just too busy to handle that task at the moment the patient appears at the front desk after spending well over an hour in the office. The patient wants to go and the staff member writes up a paper receipt of some kind, accepts some form of payment from the patient and places the record to the side to come back to and finish later.

With the charges placed on hold and the patient gone, any number of problems can occur that will prevent the charges from ever being entered into the management system. One example might be that another employee cleans up the front desk and files the record away. The danger is that when eyeglasses or contact lenses are dispensed, most office staff members simply look at a patient's record to see if there is a balance. If a balance exists, the staff member collects it. If the balance is zero, the staff member sends the patient on his way and says "Have a nice day!" Of course, if charges are never entered, the balance will be zero!

There are many other scenarios for not entering charges. Contact lens orders placed over the phone is a common one. If an order form is generated, but no charges are entered, the contacts can easily be dispensed and never charged.

We should also mention that optometrists often provide services and procedures at no charge. This might be a free OCT test or retinal photos or a refraction fee that is waived. I do not understand this. I do not believe this gesture results in much patient goodwill. The patient just assumes those tests had little or no value. If the doctor had charged for the tests, the patient or the insurance plan would pay it.

Monthly procedures not followed

Many offices do not get around to sending billing statements in a timely manner to patients. Likewise, these offices may not review payments and claim rejections from insurance plans on a regular basis. No one is really monitoring the accounts receivable aging report. It is imperative that a staff member be assigned with sufficient time dedicated to manage billings and collections for insurance and for patients. Rejected claims can be corrected and re-filed. Balances can be transferred from insurance plans to patients (in some cases). Patients who are past due on payments can be called. Time is of the essence. If these issues are not handled quickly, the chance of successful collection drops dramatically.

Another monthly procedure is patient recall. No matter what system you use, if you omit recall efforts or have an inefficient recall system, you will pay a big price. There is a cost to that.

Theft and embezzlement

While not technically an error, I place employee theft in this category because it is a management oversight if it is allowed to happen on a large scale. I've heard far too many stories told to me by colleagues about employees who steal cash, write fraudulent checks, and take frames, sunglasses or contact lenses for their own use or for friends. I'm sure this has happened in many offices, mine included. We may never be able to completely prevent theft, but using strict accounting procedures and maintaining a close watch on inventory can greatly reduce the problem.

Be sure you have a system in place that requires financial accuracy. The daily production report must always balance exactly with the cash drawer at the end of the day. Have two working cash trays with a predetermined amount of cash to start the day so the other cash drawer always stays with that day's production report until it is balanced. Any over or under cash amounts must be explained. Bank deposits should always match the day's receipts exactly in the form of cash, checks and credit card payments. Bank deposit receipts are returned to the owner and monitored.

Inefficiencies

There are many ways that a practice can be inefficient and to some extent, those are management errors. One common example is insufficient delegation. Another would be a practice that does not encourage patients to buy annual supplies of contact lenses. Selling annual supplies reduces the transaction cost of having your staff place multiple orders throughout the year. Shipping lenses directly to the patient also reduces transaction cost.

None of us are perfect, but if you review your office procedures and design them to reduce errors and omissions, your practice net income will increase.

4.15 Reduce Your Expenses to Increase Practice Net

Today we reach the final article in a five part series covering ways to increase practice net income. I encourage you to develop an action plan that will improve your performance in all five of the factors.

It's certainly logical that if you cut your operating cost, you will increase your net, at least in the short term! But I urge you to consider the big picture of your practice and be very careful where and how you reduce expenses; I often say you can't cut your way to prosperity! Cutting expenses often means cutting service and quality, and that can lead to a loss of patient loyalty and reduced referrals. This can create a downward business cycle with reduced patient demand leading to reduced cash flow requiring more cuts to services. I think it's great to buy smart and shop for good values, but in some areas of your practice spending more will lead to higher profits in the long run.

Shop around

Most optometrists and their staffs already do an excellent job of finding good deals on all the supplies, products and services needed to operate a practice. We all have a natural tendency to shop for good values, change vendors when service or quality suffers and buy in bulk when it makes sense.

Some practices provide an incentive bonus to staff members based on net income or expense percentages, and I'm sure that can be effective, but if there is a good system of management and supervision in place, I don't think it is a necessity. My staff can only order from specific suppliers that are pre-approved.

How to negotiate with suppliers

While most ODs do a good job of comparing prices, most do not try to negotiate better deals. If they tried, they could save money. The best way to negotiate a better price is to have some form of leverage. You can't go to a supplier and just say you would like a better price. A better approach is to go to a competitive vendor and say you are considering moving some business to them and you would like the best price quote they can offer. Compare this pricing with what you are paying for similar products now. If it is much better, go to your current supplier and tell them XYZ company has offered you better pricing and you wanted to give them a chance to keep your business and see if they can do better.

It is very important, however, to realize that changing suppliers can easily result in unhappiness. The cheaper company may not provide as good service or quality or speed of delivery. Your staff may be very unhappy dealing with the new company. Patients may be disappointed in the product. All of this may not be worth the lower price! Be careful not to burn bridges. I would send only a small percentage of orders to the new company first and even if you switch to a large degree, keep a good relationship with the first vendor because you may want to go back.

I think we have a responsibility to negotiate in an ethical way with suppliers. It will work in your best interest in the long run because business relationships are important. One way to do this is to not share price lists or invoices from one competitor to the other. In my example above, you obtained the pricing information and made the decision yourself without giving copies of invoices and saying can you beat this pricing? Each vendor quotes the best price they can offer and they compete in the marketplace.

Return products

Be sure your staff keeps up to date with returning products that are covered under warranty or can be returned or exchanged. Sales reps may assist with this in many cases, but there are plenty of returned products that must be packaged and addressed and shipped back. If an office is understaffed, there may not be time to get around to this and the products pile up in a drawer or a box and eventually no one knows what to do with them.

Every staff member should have a side job that he or she is responsible to manage as time permits. Be sure products are retuned for credit in a timely manner and the credits are received on your account.

Buying groups and doctor alliances

One way for independent ODs to get optimum pricing is to belong to a group purchasing organization. By way of disclosure, I am currently employed as Chief Optometric Officer at IDOC, a leading alliance group that offers vendor savings, education, networking and consulting services to independent optometrists. There are many different ways that these groups work, but the new generation of alliances is different than traditional buying groups because they additionally bring practice management services and educational programs to doctors and staff members. Alliances also differ because they do not typically bill and collect payments from members for purchases. The member doctors maintain direct accounts with vendors and they are afforded excellent discounts and rebates that are typically not available to individual practices or small chains. The basis for the increased discount is that the alliance group will work to build loyalty and increase purchasing volume for these preferred vendors. There is often some exclusivity of vendors within business categories with alliances, while buying groups typically represent nearly all vendors. Alliance groups typically charge a membership fee in the form of monthly dues; buying groups often keep a percentage of the discount the account earns as an administrative fee.

4.16 Office Hours: It's Not Personal!

In my consulting work with optometrists, I frequently find office hours that are ideal for the OD and the staff members, but not very convenient for patients. Changing this is usually very difficult because the staff does not want to work evenings or Saturdays. In many cases, the OD does not want to either. Of course, this only matters if the practice wants to grow and generate more income. If the practice is already busy enough and already profitable enough, then it's fine to leave well enough alone. But if you want to grow, convenience factors are a big part of marketing.

There is a tendency to view the hours the office is open as quite personal, but let's view the practice as separate from the doctor and the current staff. Let's consider what is best for the practice and we can worry about staff later.

Convenient hours aid growth

In addition to normal business hours, which are generally regarded as Monday through Friday, 9am to 5pm, practices that are open some evenings and Saturdays generally grow faster and produce more income. Part of that is simply the fact that the practice is open more and therefore can see more patients in an average week. Some of those patient visits are by appointment for exams and some are just drop-in visits for optical dispensing or contact lenses. The other factor is the convenience aspect of evenings, Saturdays and early morning. These convenient hours are preferred by many patients who work or go to school and when your practice meets patient's wants and needs, you earn higher points for patient satisfaction and loyalty. You become easier to do business with.

The other big void in office hours for many optometric practices is the lunch hour. Many offices simply close during lunch because it is easier for staffing. It is not so easy for patients, however.

Of course, Monday through Friday, 9am to 5pm is a 40 hour week, so any additional hours must be managed with additional staff members and more complex scheduling.

Practice growth in phases

It is helpful to view the practice in growth stages and understand that there is a transition from one phase to the next. A new start-up practice can't afford a large staff so office hours must be limited. Even in the small to medium phase of practice size, we find many offices close on a weekday or on a half day. This allows the staff to work some additional convenience hours and not exceed 40 hours per week.

As a practice moves into the medium production phase (median practice gross revenue with one OD in the U.S. is about $680,000), the owner should make a decision: he or she can transition into a large practice or can hold back and stay small. A practice of this size has great potential to grow, especially if there is some degree of patient backlog (appointments scheduled in advance).

Additional staff

To take the practice to the next level, the owner should hire more employees and move to expanding office hours. A goal is set to not be closed any weekdays and to not close for lunch. There should be at least two evenings per week until 7pm and every Saturday (at least morning hours on Saturday). Many offices find that early morning appointments before 9am quite popular. These hours easily add up to over 50 per week.

As you expand office hours, you'll naturally need more staff, and this is a perfect opportunity to hire new people who will work the evenings and Saturdays. You may also find some of your existing staff would like a day off during the week and will work those hours. Each employee is different and if you speak with each one individually, you may find some way to reward those who want to help the practice move forward.

This is also the perfect time to hire an associate OD if you have some patient demand. Again, I'd only accept ODs willing to work two evenings per week and every Saturday. I find ODs and staff members easily accept these hours during the hiring process. After hiring a new OD, the senior doctor may want to cut back on his or her patient care hours and spend more time on practice management.

4.17 Evenings and Saturdays

I consult with many private practice optometrists who do not have evening or Saturday hours. Since office hours impact one's personal life, I certainly understand why doctors and staff would prefer to not work those hours. Evenings and Saturdays are often reserved for family or personal time. But the question I have to ask is... are we looking at the owner's personal life or are we looking at the business?

In many cases, the owner and the practice are tied very closely together. So much so that they feel like the same entity. But they are not the same and I urge you to separate them. As your practice grows, it is very smart to try to develop a system that does not depend too much on the doctor/owner. Build a business model where the doctor is also the CEO of a company. I would never try to make the case that the business is more important than one's personal life, but the office hours do not have to be covered by the owner or the existing staff. Let's look objectively at office hours as a business strategy and forget the personal aspect.

Practice growth and patient demand
Successful optometric practices are mostly built by word of mouth referrals by happy patients. The key to marketing a professional practice is a high level of patient satisfaction and loyalty and that is directly dependent on customer service and convenience. Many optometric practices can deliver high quality eye care, so success comes down to how easy are you to do business with?

Do you have many competitive advantages compared to other eye care providers in your area?

Convenient office hours are a huge part of customer service. There are many providers open many evenings per week and Saturdays and even Sundays. Marketing is identifying and satisfying the customer's wants and needs.

Ideal office hours

I believe ideal office hours for a private optometric practice would be every weekday from 9am to 5pm plus a couple of evenings per week until at least 7pm and every Saturday from 9am to 1pm. That is at a minimum. If you can be open more late evenings and weekend hours, all the better. The office does not close during the lunch hour and is also not closed any half days or full days during the week.

I realize that small practices and start-ups can't be open all those hours. My basic plan above has the office open 48 hours per week and since you should open the doors about a half hour before the first appointment and you may not finish until a half hour after closing, you could easily be staffing for 54 hours per week. It is OK if you can't achieve those ideal hours in the early stages of a practice, but if you are trying to grow the practice, I would be working hard to reach that goal. So I would elect to be open some evenings and Saturdays and be closed on a weekday.

Misconceptions about office hours

Here are some important tips as you consider your office hours:

- Being open until 6pm means that your last appointment is around 5pm. That is not an evening. That is when people get off work and they can't make it to your office in time for that appointment. You need to be open until 7pm to really have an evening.
- Early morning hours (before 9am) are great and they have some big fans, but they are not a substitute for evenings and Saturdays. I know they may be preferred by the doctor, but we aren't talking about the doctor's wants and needs right now. There is a large segment of the population for which early mornings will not work. Evenings and Saturdays are the times with the greatest demand. If you can offer all those options, that would be great.
- I often hear about the number of no shows on Saturday as a major reason for being closed. It is a myth. I have to think this is mostly a rationalization by people who do not want to work Saturdays. I'd rather they just say we don't like to work Saturdays and that would be perfectly understandable. There may be a higher percentage of

no shows on Saturday but it can be easily managed and it does not make up for the thousands of dollars that can be generated in four hours. Saturdays are always booked further ahead than any other day in optometric offices. They are often booked weeks ahead. Even a brand new associate can be booked solid on Saturdays. If staff members report to the owner that Saturdays are not very important to patients, I think that staff member does not want to work them.

- I realize that changing the hours of operation can be difficult and staff may resist the change. It is understandable and the owners and manager should be sensitive to each individual. The current workings of an office become the norm and staff may not want to give up what they feel are good things about their job. Some employees have important family demands and a change in hours won't work. If you want to expand your office hours, I'd speak to each employee individually and find out what his or her thoughts are. Some may like having a day off during the week and an evening and Saturday may be OK. Some may work those new hours if they got a raise. Some could be "grandfather-claused" in with the present hours, while new employees are hired only with the new hours. I have noticed that those evening and Saturday hours are no problem for people who are applying for a job.
- Evenings or Saturdays by request does not really happen very often. It becomes a special exception and staff members usually don't offer those times. It would mean the doctor and some staff would have to make special arrangements. It is too complicated.
- It is not necessary for the office to have a doctor on duty all the times it is open. Doctor's hours are by appointment and people can't walk in and always expect to be examined immediately. But the more convenient doctor's hours you have the better.

By the way, patients who want evening and Saturday appointments are highly desirable for your practice... they are the ones who have jobs!

4.18 What if you raised your fees and nobody cared?

I'm always perplexed at the prevalence of low fees in optometric practice. I'm not referring to the discounted fees paid by vision plans; I'm focusing on the fees set by practice owners for exams, spectacle lenses, frames, and contact lens fittings. In my opinion, if you look at the actual value of eye care compared to other products and services in our society, optometrists charge too little.

It's actually hard to say what the average eye exam fee is in the United States. A recent large survey resulted in an average figure of $110, but if we examine the question, which I always want to do in surveys, we see that it asked for the "undiscounted, full pay" fee. You can see how that muddies the water with many eye care practitioners charging a reduced fee for private pay through time of service discounts, s-codes and other discounts. I would be interested in the average fee for a comprehensive exam including refraction that is actually charged in most cases. I think it would be under $100 and I see many practices in the $80 to $90 range. Consider the cost of dinner (with tip) at a nice restaurant for a family of four... and how much is a "cut and color" at a hair salon?

Let's project what would happen if you raised your fees.

On private pay transactions

This is where you will realize an increase in practice net income. Most of the fee increase will fall directly to the net income line because your fixed expenses are already being met. Yes, there will be some cost of goods sold, but even that was being met with the old fee structure and those costs did not go up.

It is important to realize that even vision plan members make some private pay transactions. Not everything is covered by the plan. If a vision plan patient needs another pair of glasses six months after his exam or if he has problems with his contact lenses or if he buys a pair of plano sunglasses, it is a private pay transaction. And based on the revenue typically collected for covered vision plan services, we must maximize revenue on the non-covered ones.

Based on my experience and that of many others (possibly your experience too?), there is generally very little reaction from patients to a fee increase. Typically, no one even notices. But look at the example practice below to see the true effect of patient loss on net revenue.

On vision plan transactions

I often hear the logic that there is no point in raising fees because it has no impact on what vision plans pay. While that is true, I would counter that there is no reason not to raise fees within this group. Vision plans certainly don't care if you increase fees because most of them place a maximum on covered goods and services and providers may not charge the patient any more than that.

Patients also don't care what the fee is for the goods and services covered by their plan. But there is a side benefit to the practice when fees are increased for covered items: patients will perceive a higher value for the service, even though they are not paying for it. Many consumers use price as a barometer for the value of things, especially for items that are difficult to evaluate. When I look at audio speakers for a home theater system, all I know is that the more expensive ones are better. Even size of the speaker is not a good indicator of quality.

On medical plan transactions

This is a mixed bag because medical insurance often pays pretty well, but not always. And they typically do not cover refraction, eyeglasses and contact lenses, so those items move to the private pay category. But in any case, I would not expect much of a negative reaction to a fee increase in most practices.

Example practice

I assume the main reason most ECPs do not raise their fees is fear of losing patients. While I believe there is much less price sensitivity among patients of independent professional ECPs than one might think, this example shows that you could withstand a large percentage of patients leaving and still net the same amount.

Let's make some assumptions for a hypothetical practice:

- Solo optometrist.
- Annual gross collections of $600,000.
- Sees 2000 patients per year (for comprehensive exams; we will ignore all other office visits for simplicity).
- Average revenue per exam is $300.
- Practice net income is 30% of gross or $180,000.

Now let's suppose that you raised fees by 20%. Of course, the prevalence of discount vision plans in the practice has a huge effect on whether a fee increase will be realized or if it is simply written off. But most practices are a mix of private pay, medical plans and vision plans. Let's assume that all fees (exam, optical and contact lens) were raised by some large amount so there was a net increase in fees paid to the practice by 20%. This may not be realistic for some practices, but it will help me make a point and many practices are so grossly undercharging that they truly could increase fees dramatically.

A 20% average increase in fees would take our practice to a gross of $720,000 and the average revenue per exam would jump to $360. Under this scenario, you could lose 333 patients or 16.6% of the entire patient base and still net the same as you did with the old fees. With 1667 patients each averaging $360 in fees, the practice would gross about $600,000 again. Assuming practice expenses remained the same, the net would be the same with far fewer patients. It is highly unlikely that you would lose 16% of patients, but even if you did you would work less and earn the same.

How to justify a fee increase
Many ECPs and staffs worry about how to justify a fee increase. If you have that concern, set out to improve your service. Treat patients better, run on time for appointments, be caring and friendly, and find a way to say yes to patients. Let the patient win in a dispute. I like the exam to be thorough, but don't make it take longer in an attempt to justify a fee increase. Patients will actually pay more if the eye exam doesn't take so long.

4.19 What if you raise your fees and patients leave you?

Fear of losing patients is one of the main reasons optometrists don't raise their fees. But will they really leave you? Or will an unfounded fear cause you to undervalue your services and earn less than optimum profit?

As you evaluate your fees, there are many factors to consider, including your local economy, local demographics, participation with insurance, and cost of doing business, but based on my experience with many practices, ODs frequently set fees extremely low. I don't call for ODs to overcharge, but just charge fairly based on the true value of the service and the costs of business operations.

There are other reasons ODs are afraid to raise fees, so let's look at those first.

Insurance plans make fees irrelevant
When optometrists tell me they don't bother to raise fees because vision plans are so dominant in their practice that it would make no difference, I always give the same response: then why <u>not</u> raise them? These doctors have less reason than most to keep fees too low. After all, if patients have services or products covered by a vision plan, they really won't care what the fee is.

There are some good reasons to raise fees even with a high percentage of patients on insurance plans.

- Many items are purchased without vision plans. These may be non-covered services, multiple products or services and products that are not timed to qualify for coverage. We must grant large discounts to vision plans that we participate with, so it is very important to make a strong profit when non-covered items are purchased.
- Some of the items purchased with vision plans have a co-payment or overage that is based on the usual fee. Some vision plans have the patient pay a percentage of the usual price for some items. Contact lens fitting often pays an allowance and the patient covers the balance. Frame overages are often calculated based on the usual retail price. Shouldn't you maximize these co-payments by setting your fees higher?
- Consumers often judge the quality of services and products based on price. This is especially true with highly technical services that people can't easily judge. Higher fees create a perception of a better practice, even if the patient does not pay that fee out of pocket.

If I raise fees, it will just hurt private pay

If your fees are currently undervalued for the services and products you deliver, then raising them is perfectly fair. Set your market philosophy to be the best practice in terms of your exams, your products and your customer service; then set your fees appropriately. Patents who do not have insurance realize they must pay high fees for health care. Many people who do not have a vision plan have some form of medical insurance and the eye exam may be covered. If the patient has no insurance at all, they may be eligible for Medicaid or they may soon qualify for insurance under the Affordable Care Act.

Ability to test the market

One of the big advantages of running a small business is that you can try new strategies and change policies quickly. You can test your market by raising fees and if there is a huge adverse reaction by patients, you can simply change the fees back. How much damage can you do in two weeks?

The reality is that when optometrists typically raise fees, no one notices. Patients don't remember what it was last year. Most of it is covered by a third party anyway. Patients love you and your staff and they are not going anywhere. And patients realize that you provide a very high level service and product.

What if patients leave you over higher fees?

I've taken a long time to get to the theme of this article as reflected in the title, so let's get to it. Consider these points if you raise fees and your staff comes to you and tells you they are noticing patients asking for their spectacle Rx and not ordering glasses.

- How many are really leaving? Two patients in a row does not make a trend. You need to really dig into this issue and be very scientific about your analysis. You should be tracking your spectacle Rx retention rate (the inverse of the walkout rate) and ideally, you should know that rate before you raise fees so you can monitor the change.
- Is it a random bounce? The fee schedule is very important, so bear with me if I belabor this point. Analyze any reported patient loss very thoroughly.
- Which type of patient is leaving and why? Are you losing only private pay patients? Do you offer them a time of service prompt pay discount? Do they know that is available?
- Are you making more money anyway? It is quite possible that you could lose a small percentage of patients and still increase net income. That is still a great outcome: see fewer patients and make more income.
- Do you have less expensive options for patients that are still very desirable? I had an OD client who raised his frame price mark-up formula, but he had not yet ordered new lower priced frames. He found there was a void in his inventory at the low price point of $90 to $180. There are some excellent value lines at low wholesale prices that work great in this price point and offer excellent profit margins. He beefed up his selection in that range and everything was fine.
- Are staff members on board with a fee increase? This can be a big problem because if staff don't support a concept, it may not go over well. Staff members often have a good heart and they feel like patients are family. They may sincerely feel that a fee increase will hurt the patients they care for. With all due respect, the staff may not get it. They may not see the whole picture, including the big discounts mandated by vision plans, the rising practice expenses, and the relatively small profit at the end of the month. They may need more loyalty to the practice and less to the public.
- In fairness to staff, it is up to the practice owner to communicate the business side. You must lead them to participating in the business aspects of the practice and make generating a profit part of their job description.

Be sure to train your staff to start by offering every patient the best eye care services and products, but be able to gracefully move to the second best option if price becomes a factor.

4.20 Pretend Your Services and Products Are Free

I was speaking to my friend, Walter Choate, OD, of Nashville, TN, by phone today and he shared a novel idea that he said I could use in a tip article. It's a great way for doctors and staff members to overcome price bias and prejudging patients. So here it is: recommend eye care services and products as if they were free. What would you prescribe or recommend to your patient if everything was free? How does that treatment plan differ from the one you usually would design?

Let's take a look at this approach in various areas of your practice.

Contact lenses
If contact lenses were free, and if the fitting services necessary were also free, what would you prescribe? What disposal period? What lens material? If you examined a patient wearing an older lens design, would you simply replace that lens with no change? Under our fantasy conditions, many optometrists would prescribe a high percentage of daily disposables. Many would recommend silicone hydrogels. In the real world, patients are left to wear older technology every day, without the optometrist even bringing up the idea of trying something new.

Of course, lenses and fitting services are not free and I don't think we should be insensitive to the financial impact of eye care on patients, but I think we it's a disservice to patients when we prejudge their ability to pay or what is important to them. I believe doctors and staff should recommend the best eye care, not the cheapest. The "what if it was free" exercise lets us see past our bias. It may be easy to just let patients stay with their old contact lens technology; it is certainly less risky, but it's not the best eye care.

Optical dispensing
If optical products were free, would optometrists be so shy about telling their patients about eyeglass features in the exam room? Would you simply write the spectacle Rx and let the optician handle it? Probably not. If glasses were free, ODs would want to help their patients with their lens options and they would very likely recommend free-form lenses, high index materials, a

specific brand of premium antireflective coating and additional options like Transitions.

What about frames? If frames were free optometrists might actually advise patients to get a new one! Why not enjoy a new look and the latest fashion? Why not get a frame that fits better and looks better? No one would ask the question "Do you want to use your old frame again?"

How about multiple pairs of glasses? Patients would select a few colors and styles of frames to change their appearance and match various outfits. Doctors would write prescriptions for a special pair of glasses for office use and additional Rxs for hobbies and TV viewing. Of course, prescription sunglasses would be selected for every patient.

Opticians would no longer lead patients to the budget frame display first. Instead of spending a lot of time discussing various levels of progressive lenses, they would simply recommend the best.

Exam services

Exam services and diagnostic procedures may be a little more immune to the "what if it was free?" test, but there are still some lessons to be learned. I think eye care professionals don't hold back on necessary testing when vision and eye health is at stake. We order the tests that are needed—no more, no less. But look at the following services and consider if there are times you might recommend them if they were free:

- A panoramic laser image of the retina
- A screening OCT
- A thorough low vision evaluation
- A comprehensive binocular vision evaluation for a child
- A multifocal contact lens workup
- More frequent follow-up visits to monitor a problem
- A wave front analysis coupled with corneal topography and a computer program to modify the subjective refraction to produce a spectacle prescription that optimizes vision in a patient with higher order aberrations.

Of course, eye care is not free and we should have options for patients who indicate cost is an issue. And I'm not recommending that we order diagnostic tests that aren't needed or bill insurance plans for things outside the standard of care. But it would be just as bad to pre-judge the patient's budget based on his clothing or the kind of car she drives. The people you least expect can be millionaires and people with average income may place a very high value on eye care and optical products. Let's let them decide what they want by offering the best first. It is good for the reputation of your practice.

4.21 Most Important Goal Other Than More Profit? More Free Time.

When I work with optometrists who own their practices, I ask them about their goals. The most common goal I hear revolves around some aspect of creating a larger financial profit, but a very close second is how to create more free time. Of course, everyone has their own priorities in life. The younger OD might want more time with family, including more participation in kids' activities. The mid-career doctor may want time for hobbies, sports or travel. The optometrist closer to retirement might want any of these options, but generally does not want to work so many hours.

Whatever your reason for wanting more free time, let's look at some big picture ideas for how to create it, without reducing your gross or net income.

Free time must come from somewhere

The best way to create more free time is to become more efficient in certain parts of your life. We can analyze this by dividing your life into three buckets: personal time, patient care time and business management time.

We want to create more personal time, so I won't try to reduce that. I find most ODs do not spend enough time on practice management, so I'd rather not cut that. I think many ODs (not all, but most) are inefficient when it comes to delivering clinical care, so I'll provide some ideas on how to see the same number of patients per week in less time and without stress.

The amount of time you can save varies, but it could easily be 10% to 50%. If you are currently seeing patients 30 hours per week, you may be able to do the same work in 20 hours. Could you use 10 free hours per week?

Delegation

The first step to being more efficient in your clinic without stress is to delegate more. Only you know what items you could delegate that you are not now. Make a list on paper of all the steps you perform in a typical eye exam. Check the items that you could delegate if you had the staff support. It might be having staff take more of the case history. It might be more pretesting or scribing. Some ODs still do tonometry on all their routine patients. Make this exercise idealistic, even if you don't have the staff for it yet.

Hire more staff

The fastest way to push yourself to delegate more is to just go ahead and hire another employee. Most ODs are very guarded about doing this because of the payroll cost, but sometimes you just have to take a chance in business. Nothing will make you delegate more than having staff members standing around doing nothing and that would be a good step! In most cases, the additional salary cost is more than made up for with increased exams per day and increased sales in optical.

Hiring another employee also reduces the push-back you might get from your current staff if you go to them with the idea of delegating more. They really can't complain if the extra work is not falling on them!

EHR

One might consider electronic health records as an administrative duty and not patient care, but since it happens at the same time as patient care and because it is so time consuming, let's cover it here. The first easy answer to reducing doctor time spent on records is to use scribes, but let's also consider immediate ways to speed it up. Consider if you might be too much of a perfectionist when it comes to your records. You can use some shortcuts and abbreviations as long as they are standardized and you have a log detailing what they mean. And if there is some aspect of your EHR system that is terribly inefficient, you could devise a work-around that involves paper and abandon the method that is hurting your speed. All EHRs have a method of scanning a paper document, so have your staff do that if it is much faster.

Change your exam routine

Are you still doing some test procedures out of habit, and they are not usually adding anything useful in your diagnosis or treatment? Do you perform some tests because you think it might impress the patient? Be honest. If so, I would rethink that and save the time.

Time spent talking

Take a cold hard look at how much time you spend on patient education and explanations about what you are doing. We can all agree that that those are very valuable activities to some extent, but it is easy to provide more than the patient needs or wants. Don't kid yourself into thinking patients love those detailed mini-lectures on the eye or refraction. It may be more interesting to us than it is to them. They might smile and nod because they are being polite.

Reappoint
Most of us tend to try to get everything done in one visit, so we don't inconvenience the patient. But realize that health care is changing and the reimbursement for a routine exam is quite low and it should be matched with a short visit. If medical issues are present, we can and should reappoint to take care of them.

Change your appointment template
Finally, as you make the changes above, you will need to make your appointment slots shorter in order to take advantage of the increased efficiency. This step can be a little scary to doctors and staff, so try them on a limited basis at first and make some tweaks in your routine. But eventually, you must change the 30 minute slots to 20 minute slots (or 15 minute). When you do that, you will find ways to be more efficient because you have to.

4.22 Your New Patient Appointment Template

I have written many times about the need for optometrists and their staffs to be more efficient with eye exams. I know that concept can spark a negative response because it may seem like quality of care will be sacrificed or the doctor and staff will be stressed. That is simply a misconception, however. Neither of those factors has to be true. If you want to increase practice profit in this era of managed care and vision plans, let's find a way to work faster, not harder.

Start by changing the appointment template
There are dozens of good ways to design your appointment schedule and if you have a system that works for you, lets you see about 25 patients per day, and you stay on schedule the vast majority of the time, then stick with it. But many doctors waste a tremendous amount of time because they have appointment systems that are outdated.

It is likely that you will need to change some aspects of your exam process to be more efficient, but the quickest way to do that is to start with the end in mind. If you change the schedule and you have shorter time slots for each patient, you will figure out what needs to be done. It usually involves more delegation, it may mean hiring more staff and you may need to eliminate or shorten some of the testing and talking. Don't worry, we can do that and still deliver great care and still make patients love your practice.

15 minutes

My practice has four optometrists and we work with an appointment system that is amazingly simple, which is the main reason I like it. Every slot is 15 minutes long and we don't care what kind of exam it is. That is about it! But there are some details that may help you implement this system:

- While the appointment slots are only 15 minutes long, we insert block outs at several points throughout the day that allow us to stay on schedule and even handle emergency squeeze-ins.
- With the block outs considered, we actually have about 20 minutes per patient. We could just have 20 minute slots with no block outs, but I prefer the shorter slots. It makes me think in shorter terms with each patient.
- I like the psychological aspect of more appointment slots with some blocked out. These empty slots give my staff some place to enter additional patients if needed.
- We only schedule doctor time, not technician time. The patient may be in the clinical area of our office for 45 minutes or more even though they only have a 15 minute slot with the doctor. We have plenty of clinical technicians who do pretesting and also scribe. I hire the right number of staff to keep their part moving.
- I find that with ample delegation to a great staff, a comprehensive eye exam does not take any more doctor time than a follow-up visit or a contact lens check. Fifteen minutes is plenty of time, even with a dilated fundus exam (DFE). Of course, some patients are more complex and may run over the 15 minute time slot, but some are very easy and take less than 15 minutes. The block out slots allow you to catch up when some patients run longer.
- The doctors in my practice dilate about 90% of their exams, even though we have an Optos. In most cases, a technician just works the patient back into any available exam room after dilation and the doctor completes the exam fairly quickly. This DFE is not actually scheduled.
- Having all the slots the same helps my staff to fill last minute cancellations because they don't have to find just the right patient type. See the section below on specialty exams.
- You can't control all aspects of the appointment schedule, so just fine tune it with block outs placed at strategic points during the day and let it work itself out. Some patients arrive early and some are late, some are easy and some are difficult. Work on perfecting the

average for your practice. Doctors can stay on schedule if they are flexible with their routine and what order they do various procedures. It is critical for the doctor to be aware when the next patient is ready to be seen. We use silent pagers for this, but light systems would work as would an online popup message.

What if you can't fill the new schedule?
I would set up the fast template anyway, even if it has empty slots. It is better to actually see the full capacity of what your schedule should be and not get lulled into a slow-paced routine. I would also close off some full days or half days in order to group patients together on days when you can see patients efficiently. This also frees up those other days and helps you manage your time better. Here are some thoughts:

- Use those days for practice management. Since you need more patient demand, marketing would be a good topic to focus on, but there are many more projects that need the owner's leadership. What could be improved in your practice?
- Work in another practice or see patients in nursing homes.
- Become involved in the community or with civic groups.
- Enjoy some of that time for your personal life.

In this new appointment model, your practice appears to be quite successful and busy on the days you see patients! Patient notice this and the perception of your practice improves.

Specialty exams
There can be some exceptions to the 15 minute appointment slot, namely specialty work like low vision, orthokeratology, binocular vision and developmental vision. You can train your staff on the proper appointment time needed for this work, what days to offer this care and how many of these appointments you can see per day.

4.23 How to Sell from the Chair

I know many optometrists are quite uncomfortable with the topic of selling optical products. Mention the word "sell" to a group of ODs and you may see them squirm a bit. Some will talk a good game and say how they always recommend products from the chair, but I think many of us cave quite a bit when we are actually in the moment. I think it is time we got over our aversion to selling and realize that our patients are coming to us for our recommendations for the best eye care possible. Let's not deprive them of that as we try to prove our ultra-professionalism.

Opticians often marvel at how easy it is to sell premium optical products and multiple pairs of glasses if the optometrist recommends it first. Here are a few tips you can use to improve your skills in that area.

- Use the word "prescribe". For example: "In addition to updating your general lens prescription, I'm also prescribing computer eyewear for you with lenses that are specially designed for that task."
- Don't give the patient a list of options to choose from; make a firm recommendation. Tie your recommendation into one of the complaints you gathered during the case history or into the visual demands of the patient's job or hobby.
- If the prescription change is significant, just say "I'm prescribing new glasses for you because I'm seeing a noticeable change in your astigmatism (or whatever refractive state is involved)." Don't make an option out of it; he needs the new Rx.
- If the prescription change is small, tell the patient there is a slight change but it can make a big difference in visual comfort and efficiency. Demonstrate the change with your automated refraction system or by holding trial lenses over the patient's old glasses. Ask the patient if he sees the improvement and go from there.
- Know what vision plan benefits are available for each patient before you start the exam. Develop a method so you can easily see that information on every patient. Patients generally want to use their benefits as soon as possible, so if a new frame or lens is covered, include that fact as you discuss your recommendation.
- Be sure to include a very basic question in your case history about getting new glasses. It is best for a technician to ask the question verbally before the doctor sees the patient. Keep it short and simple: "Are you planning to get new glasses today?" The tech records the answer and the doctor sees it before starting the exam.
- Don't think that refractive changes are the only reason a person needs new glasses. Think about advances in lens technology as well. You might say: "Mr. Jones, we have seen major improvements in the technology of progressive lenses since we made your current pair of glasses. I recommend we update your glasses with the newest lens design that offers edge to edge clarity and they are thinner and

lighter than ever." After all, if you were working with a contact lens patient who was wearing an older design, you would feel a duty to discuss the latest advancements. It should be no different with eyeglasses.

- If the exam shows little or no change in lens prescription, tell the patient he is fortunate and that this is the perfect time to update his prescription sunglasses.
- A great way to begin any sales opportunity is to ask questions. As a doctor, you may be able to pull this from the case history or simply ask: "Tell me how you use your eyes at work" or "Are you involved in any outdoor activities?" The answers sell products.

Once you start talking about optical products at chairside, it will quickly become completely natural for you. When that happens, patients perceive it as the normal routine of eye care. The biggest difference will be in your practice's financial bottom line.

4.24 Diagnose Your Management Problem Before Treating It

Just as in providing good clinical eye care, you must diagnose your practice management disorders before you can treat them! Busy optometrists often just take a shotgun approach to practice management; when business seems down, they hold a trunk show or do some extra telephone recall. A better approach is to analyze the business and develop an action plan that goes beyond one or two events. Develop a complete strategy rather than some new tactics. After all, you wouldn't treat a red eye without knowing the etiology.

Got data?
Many practice management problems can be identified with business data, so that is a good place to start. Be sure you are familiar with the reports you can generate through your office management software system and from your accounting software (like QuickBooks). If you are not sure how to run reports, consult your user manual, or call customer service if needed, and go in and start producing reports. Once you get it, make notes about how to run and save these reports every month or every quarter. You could assign some of the reports to staff members and ask them to send them to you on a specific time schedule.
Here are a few basic metrics you should have:

- Collected gross revenue per day and per month. Compare to the same time period of the previous year. Practice revenue should always grow.
- Average total fees (revenue) per comprehensive exam.
- Eyeglass Rx retention rate.
- Multiple pairs of glasses sell rate.
- Appointment fill rate (number of exams performed divided by number of appointment slots available).
- Revenue per staff full time equivalent (FTE).
- Revenue per OD FTE.
- Cost of goods sold and other key expense categories.

It is helpful to also know the national norms for some of this data, which is available from various professional organizations and management consulting firms.

In addition to data, be sure to spend some time observing practice operations. Many things can't be determined by data, such as customer service, staff morale, office culture, efficiency, traffic flow, marketing projects and more.

Patient demand

Not being busy enough is a frequent problem for optometrists. You generally know it if you have it, but be sure you have your appointment schedule template set for enough slots. The treatments for low patient demand are not usually easy or fast, but focus on customer service and the patient experience, vision plans, medical insurance plans and practice marketing.

Office size

The size of your office can limit your growth. If you have enough patients, but can't see more per day because you don't have enough exam rooms, not enough workstations at the front desk and not enough room in the optical to handle more people at once, you may need to expand your office space. Increasing your number of employees may not be possible if they don't have space to work. You may not be able to do much about it until your lease ends, but recognize the problem and develop a plan for more space. You may be able to reallocate your existing usage of space. Perhaps there is an empty office in your existing complex you could move into or add on.

Efficiency and flow

You may have fairly good patient demand, but you feel like you are always running behind schedule and there is no way you can see more patients per day. Then it is time to look within and diagnose why you are taking too long with patients. In many cases, the first step in treating this problem is to hire another full time employee. You may actually need to delegate more, but the best way to learn to do that is to hire an extra staff member. When you actually have that person on the payroll, you will quickly figure out what you can have her do. You will delegate more if you have someone to delegate to.

As an OD, consider the things that you do fairly often that could and should be delegated. Do you do your own routine tonometry? Do you ever take your own entrance VAs? Do you ever do autorefraction or retinal photos or fields? Do you insert trial contact lenses on the patient yourself very often? Do you ever do lensometry on the patient's habitual Rx? If so, you need another technician.

Service and product mix

An excellent metric to look at is average collected gross revenue per comprehensive exam. Just take the total collected revenue for the month and divide by the number of comprehensive eye exams performed that month. This data point removes patient demand from the equation because it is revenue per patient. The national average for optometrist is about $307, but I know many ODs who do more than $500.

If this metric is low for you, consider adding more services and carrying a larger mix of high-end frame lines. That does not mean you won't still carry affordable frames, but the mix could skew higher. You also may need to raise your fees. Yes, fees still matter even if you have a lot of vision plans because many services and products are not covered by insurance, or the exams are billed to medical insurance which pays better.

On the service side, invest in specialty instrumentation and offer more services, such as medical eye care, orthokeratology, low vision, nutrition counseling, vision therapy, sports vision and more. Be sure to offer a retinal screening and other optional testing to your vision plan patients.

Staff morale

How do you treat a problem such as staff members who can't get along with each other and are basically unhappy? Read up on organizational culture and staff management. Think about the job from the employee's point of view. What factors create good or poor levels of job satisfaction in your office environment? Studies show that employees want to be appreciated by their bosses and coworkers. They want respect and a feeling of self-worth. Can you give that to them? Do you have weekly staff meetings and many positive interactions every day? The culture comes from the leaders in an organization. Just show staff that you care and treat them as equals.

4.25 Why Do ODs Resist Hiring More Staff?

When I consult with ODs one of the key factors I look at is the level of staffing in the practice. I find many optometric practices are understaffed and if the OD would simply hire an additional employee, the practice would grow.

Why the resistance to hiring?
Generally, ODs resist increasing the staff because they are concerned that the increased payroll cost will take away from the practice net income. They may be looking at a metric such as the percentage of payroll cost to gross revenue. This reasoning is often faulty and hiring more staff would actually increase productivity much more than the payroll cost. More on this below.

One other factor that causes ODs to pause when it comes to hiring more staff is they perceive staff management issues to be so unpleasant and difficult that they want to contain it. This really comes down to each individual's goals. If you want your practice to grow, a larger staff is part of that process. If you are content with your current gross and net revenue, then keeping the staff small may be the right move.

Good things happen
Several good things happen to a practice when more staff members are added. Consider these factors:

- Customer service improves. It's easy to see why; more people to take care of patients' needs.
- Productivity increases. If doctors and staff are not rushed, they have more time to educate patients and discuss additional products and services.
- Delegation increases. You would delegate more if you had someone to delegate to.
- May be able to expand office hours. Evening and Saturday hours are highly desirable for patients. Some existing staff members may resist these hours but new employees can easily be hired with those hours as a requirement.
- Stress decreases and attitudes improve when employees are not over worked
- Easier to handle call-offs and vacations
- Existing staff may perform better

Staff metrics

Many doctors avoid increasing staff because their payroll expense percentage is already at what they feel is higher than it should be. We must realize that the data that is reported as norm in our profession is not necessarily the right figure for your practice. Furthermore, increasing the number of staff does not necessarily increase your payroll percentage. It is very likely that gross revenue will increase more that the new salary and benefits. It is quite possible that hiring another employee may cause the payroll percentage to drop! I believe 21% is too low for a large thriving practice that has advanced services, higher fees and drives growth through excellent customer service. That practice could have a 25% payroll figure or higher and it would be fine with me.

One useful metric is annual gross revenue per employee. I like this number to be about one full time employee per $135,000 of annual gross revenue. Calculate your full time equivalent (FTE) number of employees by adding part-timers together. While not absolute, your gross revenue per FTE employee should not be too high or too low. There is a tendency to think that we would like the figure to be as high as possible. If we can achieve gross revenue of $200,000 per FTE, isn't that better than $135,000? It really is not better because it is likely that it can't be sustained. It is likely that the doctor is not delegating efficiently and could increase revenue and production if more staff were involved. It is likely that customer service is suffering and stress may be high.

The best way to determine the proper staff size for your practice is to observe the operations over a period of about two weeks. Over time, we see the unusual random events even out, such as a big rush of patients, or an unusual span of no shows, or staff call-offs and vacations. We want a good balance between staff being crazy busy sometimes and having time for side jobs and conversations with co-workers at other times.

4.26 Who Really Controls Your Staff Schedule?

If the practice owner does not pay close attention, some staff members will exert gradual influence over their work hours and have a big impact on their total compensation. With the recent expansion of federal overtime rules under the Fair Labor Standards Act (FLSA), optometrists should be more vigilant about work hours than ever, but even without that, it makes good business sense to control your staff schedules. In this article, I'll describe a common way that staff work hours can become out of balance and what you can do about it.

Staff work habits can begin innocently enough, but they often have a way of becoming embedded into the norm and then are harder to change. Practice owners and office managers should be aware that what seems to be a great work ethic by a well-meaning employee can actually hurt the practice. Sometimes you have to just say no when staff members want to change their hours.

The work situation

Here is how the problem starts: an employee alerts you to a problem with getting the work done. It could be lab orders not getting out, insurance claims not filed or any other task. He or she also proceeds to offer a possible solution, such as coming in early, staying late or working through lunch. A busy doctor or manager could easily jump at the welcome answer to the problem, but there may be better solutions. At best, allowing extra work hours should be temporary, but it may be best to say no upfront.

What is really happening during the day?

The initial proposal from the employee could be innocent or even noble, but if the staff member likes the extra hours because it results in a bigger paycheck, he could easily start to slow down on work during the normal work hours in order to justify the additional hours as necessary.

What is the employee's real motivation?

The big benefit to staff is the increased pay they receive for the extra work hours. A secondary factor might be that the additional time works out well with their personal life. I have had employees want to start work early because they need to get a ride with their spouse and that person's commute is quite early. Some employees don't like to eat lunch and they would love to work through it and snack at their desk. Some staff members do not want to go home at 5pm because the house is empty.

I'm not saying you can't accommodate these special needs, but understand the true reasons and only agree if it is also good for the practice.

Not necessarily overtime

The additional hours may not cause an overtime problem, but if it does push an employee into more than 40 hours per week, the situation is more serious. Employers must pay time and a half in that situation (with some exceptions) and you should not agree to pay straight time, even if the employee offers it.

New overtime rules will take effect on December 1, 2016 which will increase employee eligibility for overtime based on salary and exemption requirements.

I would rather hire an additional employee than authorize overtime on an ongoing basis.

What to do if you already allow it?
If you already allow an employee to work certain hours that you do not feel are beneficial for the practice, here are some ways to return the schedule to normal and re-establish control of it.

- If the hours are not creating overtime, you might agree to special hours as a grandfather clause, but don't allow it in the future.
- Explain to the employee why you can't continue with the special hours. Perhaps you need an additional employee anyway or the overtime pay is not in the budget. Maybe the situation is not fair to other employees.
- Consider letting the employee move back to the correct schedule gradually, so it is not too big a shock to their personal budget.
- Require that employees take a lunch break and define how long it is. It is a good policy for employees to take a break and they can also take care of personal things like phone calls and texts. Many practices have staff work through lunch when they are small, but as the staff grows, it is best to take lunch in two shifts with no patients scheduled.
- Hire another employee so the staff member who was working extra can't complain that he is stressed out and overworked.

4.27 A Story about a Second Office

Let me present a hypothetical situation. We have an optometrist who has been in practice more than five years but less than thirty years. It is a traditional private practice that grosses about $500,000 per year and nets about 30% of that gross. The OD works 40 hours per week and she has a staff of three full time and one part time employees. All is well enough, but the doctor feels like she works very hard and does not have a lot to show for it. There is a fair amount of stress. The practice has grown very slowly over the past few years, in spite of the doctor trying many marketing strategies and participating with most vision plans and medical insurance. This is a bright, personable doctor who provides great service and truly gets the importance of patient satisfaction. What can she do to break out of mediocrity?

That description above actually covers a huge number of optometric practices in the United States today – maybe close to 50%. While the ideas that could create growth in this practice are many, I like to think big so let's focus on a strategy that can lead to big results: opening a second office.

Why a second office?

In some cases, the population and demographics of a market area are simply not sufficient to sustain a large practice. There may be a huge population, but there are also a huge number of eye care professionals (ECPs) as well. Or, there may be relatively few ECPs, but the market area is slightly rural and there are just not enough people to keep everyone as busy as they need to be.

If we look at this doctor's $500,000 practice, she may only see about 1,400 patients per year, which is about 28 patients per week, which is only about five or six per day. In today's eye care economy, that is not a full time practice. With moderate staff support, the OD could see that number of patients in three half days per week. When looked at that way, it seems like a waste of valuable skill for this doctor to put 40 hours per week into this practice.

If the practice is growing rapidly, as often happens with a new cold start practice, the situation is different, and having the doctor present full time may provide the leadership that is needed to keep it growing. But in this example, the practice is not growing much in spite of considerable effort.

The satellite office

A very reasonable strategy for growth in this situation is to open another office. The new office location would be selected in a different market from the first office, but close enough where the doctor (and maybe some staff) can drive between them. The new location might be in an upcoming area with lots of growth and good median household incomes.

The doctor would divide her time between both offices. She would incur many new expenses in rent, staff, equipment and overhead cost, but the plan is for the increased patient demand in this new market to quickly offset those costs and provide a profit. The vision is that the doctor can generate the same profit as before in office #1 and at some future point do the same in office #2.

She is still working 40 hours per week, but her income will double; or could possibly more than double.

Business plan

A venture such as opening a second office requires careful planning, which I won't go into here, but you would need a business plan. It is basically like opening a practice cold, except there is one major advantage: the doctor already has a successful practice. The business process is already in place. All one has to do is repeat what exists in the first office. Maybe some things can even be done better, but all that experience will be very valuable.

There is a starvation period in a new start-up. It should be projected in the business plan and there should be enough capital to cover operating expenses until the break-even point is reached. The break-even point is when the revenue from patient care equals the monthly office expense, but there is no salary yet for the doctor. Some new offices reach that in the first year; some may take two or three. Everything beyond the break-even point is income for the doctor.

Cost and Risk

Many ODs do not follow the path of opening a second office because it seems too expensive and too risky. They may view the first office as not as successful as they had hoped and not want the extra work of another office. That really depends on your entrepreneurial spirit, but I don't see it that way. I see the first office as an extremely successful two day per week practice. And with the marketing power of a second office (and maybe a third one eventually), all the offices could grow significantly.

A new office can be opened in a grand fashion with the hope of attracting tons of upscale business, or it can be more modest: nice decor, but not overly expensive. That decision depends on market factors, but I favor the latter. I favor seeing the business move past the break-even point very quickly and keeping start-up costs in check fosters that.

I like to view the start-up costs in two categories: Up-front cost (like the office build out and some equipment and furnishings) and ongoing monthly expense (like rent and staff salaries). The up-front cost could easily be under $100,000, especially if equipment is leased. The monthly expense could be quite reasonable and could be covered by patient revenues by the six month point. It does not seem very risky to me.

Marketing punch

The public perception of this two-location practice is far different than the initial scenario I presented. The organization just expanded! It must be highly successful! There is an opportunity for a big marketing splash for the new location, and any ads or announcements will always feature both locations.

The doctor will be busier immediately, because the existing patients will have to be seen in fewer days, but that creates an even bigger image of success. The doctor and staff even feel differently about the practice. They think of themselves as successful and that makes all the difference.

4.28 How to Get Your Patients to Love You and Your Practice

The title of this article is meant to attract your interest, along with the corollary I could have used as a subhead: "How to get your staff to love working for you." After all, if I could show you a way to achieve both of those characteristics, you would have the essence of a very successful practice! What if there was a thing you could do that would achieve that? You could keep growing those two factors by continuing to do the "thing". It would be brilliant. It might be the best business strategy in the history of business!

I actually think I know the thing that achieves these amazing results. I learned it over many years of operating my own practice and studying ways to increase patient loyalty and improve our organizational culture for employees. I studied it further in business school but still did not quite get it at first. I made a lot of mistakes along the way. I will share it with you here and hopefully save you a lot of time and effort.

You have to love them first.

That is really it. That really is all there is to it. You have to love your patients first and they will love you back. And you have to love your staff first and they will love you back. For the most part, anyway. There are always outliers in any experiment.

Patients

Many optometrists never take the chance and allow themselves to be vulnerable enough to really feel that way toward their patients. In a way, I'm talking about customer service taken to a much higher level than we normally see in optometric practice. I'm referring to the practice that says yes even when the patient is being unreasonable. I'm referring to the practice that lets the patient win almost all the time. Many practice owners and managers can't stand the feeling of being taken advantage of, so they hold firm and say no. They think they are doing the right thing. They don't realize that extreme customer service is strategic. It is in the best interest of the practice in the long run.

Staff

Many optometrists never ask themselves: "What is so great about working in my office?" They never think about job satisfaction and why should employees be happy and smile all day. Most ODs don't really see the job from the employee's point of view. The paycheck is certainly the main reason why people work, but truly loving a job goes way beyond the pay. It goes to the culture of the organization which is largely based on respect and appreciation. It turns out that to build a great staff, the leaders of the organization must act as if they like the employees! It is even better if you really do like them! You need to show them in various ways. Who knew?

You may wonder why you need to show the love first. Why can't patients love you and your practice and behave the way you prefer and then you'll give them excellent eye care and treat them well? Why can't your staff behave the way you have trained them and then you'll give them their due rewards? It took me a long time figure out that it just does not work that way. I think it is because, as the doctor and the employer, you are the leader in both of these relationships and the culture is always created by the leader.

4.29 Fighting the Gloom and Doom

Things are never quite as bad – or as good – as they first seem.

Lately, I have heard a great number of what I call "gloom and doom" statements about optometry. These statements are often made by vision plan companies, industry publications, optical vendors, eye care consultants or optometrists in online forums. There is usually a certain amount of sensationalism associated with the statement. In some cases there may be a hidden agenda or profit motive behind the revelation. Usually there is a basic statement that is true followed by some assumptions or conclusions, which sound plausible, but are not always based on fact.

I think optometrists have enough challenges facing them every day and we would do better if we fought the battles that are here and now. Don't be distracted and waste energy on things that may or may not happen or are simply beyond our control.

It seems to me that optometrists are masters at worrying about what might happen, even though a high percentage of the assumptions are incorrect or never actually come true. I have seen many threats and scares to the optical industry in my 30+ year career. Some of these turned out to be no big deal and in other cases, optometrists found a way to manage the issue. The profession of optometry is still doing very well and I believe there will be even more demand for our services in the future.

As examples, here are a few gloom and doom statements I've heard recently that have some ODs in private practice very worried. I'll place the statement in italics and my comments in regular print.

- *VSP recently started requiring providers to accept the Choice plan, which is regarded as a low cost plan. This will lead to lower reimbursements.* My practice decided to accept all the VSP plans long ago and the Choice plan pays less on some items but allows us to collect more on others. The Choice plan is calculated differently than the Signature plan, but our practice profitability is about the same with both. I don't see this move as a sinister plot to hurt optometry.
- *EyeMed is vertically integrated with retail optical stores and they are steering patients away from private practice optometry.* I'll admit that I don't know their inner corporate strategies, but I've been an EyeMed provider for many years and have never experienced this. If they have done some marketing to benefit their retail outlets, it has not made any difference to my practice. It seems to me that for EyeMed to be successful as a vision plan, it needs providers in all categories. EyeMed knows that many patients prefer private practice ODs and there is often strong loyalty to one's eye doctor. I think EyeMed is best served by a very broad provider base. I don't think EyeMed is out to hurt private practice optometry.
- *Online optical sales are growing by leaps and bounds and private practice ODs will soon lose that segment of business.* I think we all understand that e-commerce is changing buying habits of products in all industries and categories, but I don't think ODs realize that it is happening relatively slowly for prescription glasses. The Vision Council conducts the only large-scale study I know of for online optical sales each year. Here is the percentage of prescription eyeglasses sold online to U.S. consumers for the past several years: 1.9% in 2008, 2.9% in 2009, 2.8% in 2010, 2.4% in 2011. I have not

seen 2012 data yet and I would not be surprised if we see a noticeable jump at some point, but if we look at the facts, the segment is small and growing slowly if at all. We will have time to adapt and find new profit centers in our practices. There will likely be a leveling off of online sales at some point in the future. Patients like to try on glasses in person and they value the help of a trained optical professional.

- *Specsavers is an extremely successful chain of discount optical stores in the United Kingdom and Australia and they may be coming to the U.S. They are capable of putting independent optometry out of business.* A new concept in eye care that is extremely well-managed and well-financed could certainly start here, but I would not underestimate the power of independent ODs. We have competed with many optical discount stores for over 100 years and the trust between doctor and patient has remained quite strong.
- *Obamacare will cause a huge decrease in fees being paid by health insurance plans and Medicare.* We are just starting to see some of the effects of healthcare reform but we won't really know the true impact for a few years. Medicare fees have been maintained for 2013. We may see some reimbursements decrease in the future, but optometry may benefit from the increase in numbers of patients. Unlike many medical specialties, optometrists generally need more patient demand. ODs may also find they are allowed access to health insurance panels they were previously excluded from.
- *Wellpoint (Blue Cross/Blue Shield) recently bought 1-800 Contacts and they will market online contact lenses to their members, cutting out the OD. And now Wal-Mart is launching its own brand of contacts.* I'm sure 1-800 will market contact lens products to the best target groups it can, but we have competed with 1-800 and Wal-Mart quite well for many years and I don't see that changing. Private practice optometrists have a very loyal base of patients who really prefer to do business with them.

I recently watched a movie titled "The Best Exotic Marigold Hotel" and I loved the optimistic quote by the main character, Sonny, which seems quite appropriate for this gloom and doom topic. He said, "Everything will be all right in the end... and if it is not all right, then it is not yet the end."

Chapter 5. Organizational Behavior

5.1 Fairness and Teamwork

We know that a great practice depends upon a great staff, but exactly how does a doctor/owner achieve a great staff? Some offices have staff members who have a true spirit of helping each other and trying, while other offices have employees who try to do less and leave more work to their co-workers. The latter frequently presents with an attitude like "that's not my job". The latter may be plagued with staff members who often call off work or show up late.

The easy answer might be to hire the right people and I certainly agree with that, but if you have experience in owning and operating a practice, you know that is easier said than done. And even if you could identify the "right people" from an interview/hiring process, I have found that even good people can be pulled into poor behavior if the office culture leads them that way. Also, most practices have staff turnover at some point, so the mix of employee personalities changes over time.

Read on for advice on how to inspire the teamwork you want to see in your staff.

Not easy to build the culture

Let's acknowledge that building a positive organizational culture and a staff team that is cohesive and supportive is no easy task. It starts with the practice owner caring and trying. Some owners may wonder if they should even bother, but I think they should because a great staff is the key to practice success.

Office culture refers to the unwritten rules of the organization. The leaders of the organization create the culture, but don't assume that the leaders are always the doctor or the manager. Strong staff members can also be leaders and in the absence of a doctor and manager who act as leaders, other staff members could fill that void in a negative way. The doctor and office manager should work to become good leaders and to foster the values and processes that provide a great work environment.

Steps to follow to become a better leader

- Foster open and frequent communication. This starts with weekly staff meetings that encourage employees to participate. It also means creating time for the owner or manager to meet with individual employees to listen to their concerns and to ask questions of them. But communication is not always positive. Owners or managers must also take the time to tell employees when they make errors or could improve in other ways. This news can be delivered in a sensitive manner, but it must be done.
- Fairness. When employees perceive that they are not treated fairly, they describe it as favoritism. They can easily think that the practice owner or manager is giving special advantages to some employees for personal reasons. The reality is that the employee may not have all the information or may misunderstand, but smart leaders will care a great deal about the fairness issue. One way to greatly increase fairness is to have policies in writing. Have the basic rules of employment in an office manual and add to it as new policies are decided.
- Exceptions. Even though you have rules, the day to day challenges of people's lives require some exceptions to be made. Employees value that and it makes your practice a good place to work, but you must provide the exceptions fairly. Ask yourself if you would say yes to any employee in a similar situation. Do not have favorites among your staff. This is especially difficult if family members of the owner are employees.
- Never take anything away. When you need to make a change that the whole staff (or an individual) will perceive as negative, either don't do it or give them a benefit that is just as good as what you are taking. Compromises and make-up gestures can work wonders.
- Explain why. Take the time to explain your thinking when you want to make a change or when you must say no. It is easy for practice leaders to think it is none of the employee's business, but silence is interpreted as not caring.
- Gratitude and praise. Congratulate and thank employees for a job well done. Give plenty of praise.
- How should you handle the employee who is lazy and waits for others to do a job? Your office culture can help create better teamwork, but ultimately, your practice needs an active supervisor. Staff members need a boss. Ideally, that is an office manager and not the doctor, but this person is empowered to supervise and direct staff members. Employees will not always have the right priority on the job, but a manager can give them a friendly reminder to get back to work or take the next work-up.

- All of this can be summed up by the owner caring and trying on an ongoing basis. Even if the outcome is not perfect, employees can tell if you care about fairness in the workplace and that makes a huge difference.

5.2 Developing a Happy, Loyal Staff

A staff with a cheerful, friendly and caring attitude is extremely valuable. Those characteristics alone can build a practice. That positive attitude can mean the difference between a practice that grows quickly and one that is struggling. The demeanor of the staff can create loyal patients who return for future care, while they also refer their friends and relatives. Read on to see how you can have this valuable resource in your practice.

How can you control staff attitude?
It's a trick question. You can't really control staff attitude. You can develop it, foster it or encourage it, but you can't dictate it. Stop and think about what makes employees happy in any job. A high salary might do it, but studies show that pay is not the most important factor. More important would be things like:

- Respect from supervisors and co-workers.
- Acknowledgment of a job well done by the boss.
- Having some perks and some occasional fun in the office.
- Having others ask your opinion and preference.
- Making a suggestion that the boss considers and implements.
- Co-workers who care about you personally and ask about your life.
- Attractive office décor.
- Happy patients.

Organizational culture
The factors listed above describe features of the office culture. Some offices have scenarios like those every day, while others may never have them. Individual personalities have some effect, but a caring culture can be developed with a wide range of people. Caring and respect is contagious. If others show you respect, you will typically show it in return.

The culture in your office is created by the leaders. Typically, that would be the doctors and the office manager. Those individuals have leadership by default because of their job position, but if they don't exercise their authority and set a strong example, anyone can become a leader. It may be staff member who likes to be a trouble-maker. It may be an older employee who is burned out.

The doctor or manager can rebuild a negative culture by leading the staff to think differently. The way to achieve that is to actually care about your employees. Lead by example. Give positive feedback. Don't think you are better than they are. Do something nice for the staff as a group. Praise the staff at a staff meeting. Begin a new focus on excellent customer service. Lead that focus by not complaining about patients and by letting patients win, even when they are unreasonable.

Your competitive advantage in staffing

As you analyze your office policies and culture, ask yourself what is so good about working in your practice. See the day-to-day activities as an employee would see them. While we must have rules and policies and we must set limits, a good employer cares about the working conditions and how people feel. It is OK for staff to have some personal conversations on the job within limits and when appropriate. A staff member with a complaint may just need to vent to a manager who is sympathetic. A doctor who intends to instruct a staff member might do well to give some praise first, because employees are very sensitive to criticism.

Developing a staff with a great attitude takes some effort and some attention to detail, but the rewards are significant.

5.3 Go the Extra Inch

I had the pleasure of attending an educational conference at Disney World two weeks ago. It was a fantastic meeting with a great sense of sharing of ideas among the doctors and staff who attended. We enjoyed an excellent keynote speaker from the Disney Institute, Chris Caracci, who specializes in applying the Disney principles to health care. Chris shared a concept that I absolutely loved and I introduced it to the staff in my practice when I returned. The concept is that many companies and staff members say they go the extra mile for the customer, but it is far more effective to go the extra inch.

We have all been saying that phrase in my practice frequently ever since I heard it. Go the extra inch. The beauty of this concept is that we can all do some small thing for a patient that will be meaningful. We can actually make the small things happen. If we think of providing very big things, like an extra mile, we probably won't do them at all. We can go the extra inch many times throughout the day and we can do it many times in various ways for many people. And the small details make a huge difference in the patient's experience.

Here are a few examples of how our practice goes the extra inch:

- A patient walked into our optical dispensary without an appointment. Our optician greeted her with a big smile and a warm handshake and said "Hello, Mrs. Smith! It is so nice to see you again! How can we help today?" He was truly delighted to see her. The optician knew the power of using a person's name and making her feel important, but he was completely sincere about it. Most staff members never use the patient's name, even though they know it.
- We had a cold, windy, snowy day recently in the Chicago area. I saw (through my window) one of our technicians walking an elderly patient out to her car, holding her arm firmly. Our tech did not even have a coat on!
- Our receptionist went into the waiting area and informed a patient that the doctor was running a few minutes late. She apologized for the delay and asked if she could get the patient a cup of coffee or tea.
- A female patient was trying on frames, assisted by one of our opticians. Another staff member, who was not busy, walked past and stopped to tell the patient how cute she looked in that new frame style. A third staff member saw this and joined the group and soon they were all enjoying the excitement of choosing new glasses.
- Every pair of glasses we dispense is delivered on a velvet tray with a chocolate truffle candy. There are no job tickets or plastic bags involved.
- A patient arrived at our front desk with two young spirited children. The young mom commented that she knew she was late for her appointment (about 30 minutes late actually). Our receptionist smiled warmly and gave her an understanding nod and said "Don't worry about a thing. We're glad you're here now and we'll get you in for your exam as soon as possible. Hi kids! Here are two coloring books about visiting the eye doctor. Would you like to sit at that table and color? We also have a cool train set over there you can play with."
- A staff member calls every patient about one week after they pick up their new glasses and says something like this: "Hello, Mr. Jones, this is Sandy at Gailmard Eye Center. The doctor wanted me to call and check to see how you are enjoying your new eyewear?"

After introducing this concept to your staff, ask them to take note of the various ways your practice goes the extra inch and to bring them to the next staff meeting. When you see a staff member doing a nice thing for a patient or co-worker, tell her "Way to go the extra inch!" Encourage all your staff to say that phrase to their co-workers when appropriate. Make "Go the extra inch" your new mantra in the office.

5.4 Can Your Staff Do the Right Thing?

I enjoyed an amazing family vacation in Hawaii last week. We stayed at a beautiful resort that is known for great service and it generally lived up to that for us. But, as is often the case, there were some lapses. I always find that I can learn some valuable lessons in practice management by observing other businesses outside of the optical industry.

How customers react to lapses in service varies widely. Some will just let an incident go with the understanding that nobody's perfect all the time. Others will complain about any deficiency. I'm mostly in the former group, but if service is extremely poor, I think most people will speak up to management. A lapse like that occurred one day at lunch at our resort, and I informed the waitress a few times that we had been waiting a long time for our food. The response was always the same: an apology along with a statement that the food should be right up. But it wasn't. It was like the staff did not really listen to me and really could not do anything outside of their usual process.

A two-part review

The point of this story is to inspire you to reconsider two aspects of the process your staff follows when they are faced with a complaint from a patient: (1) How is your attitude when a patient complains? Do you (the doctor or manager) generally view these people as troublemakers? Are they usually being unreasonable? (2) Are your staff empowered to take corrective action on their own or do they have to check with the doctor or manager? Is the process to fix a problem rather complicated? These two factors will have a huge impact on your customer service. Let's look at them closer.

The leader's attitude

The culture of a practice is an extension of the philosophy of the leaders. How staff members feel about patients who have a complaint, legitimate or otherwise, is a function of what they observe in the practice owner and the office manager. If you vent behind the scenes that patients are irresponsible, or not very bright, or in some way unfair, your staff will feel that way too. Invariably, they will not cover those feelings very well when they are on the front lines of the public. They will send signals of annoyance and they will be protective of the practice, often to the point of digging in their heels about office policy when the better move would be to let the patient win.

The first response on the front lines carries great importance when we consider the patient's perception of the practice. You may be able to undo some damage, but you shouldn't have to. Also, the practice leaders will be faced with the uncomfortable position of needing to support the staff member vs. doing the right thing for customer service. Ideally, these two positions should not be at odds.

Staff empowerment

The second phase of service recovery is for staff to quickly fix the problem. Train the front line staff to be able to make decisions about how the practice can resolve an issue. Teach them to own the problem for the patient and to take the necessary steps to see that it is resolved. Practice how to handle sticky situations, such as:

- Refund requests
- Calling to cancel glasses
- Requests for frame information
- Requests for PDs
- Calling to be late for an appointment
- Complaints about vision with new glasses or contacts
- Complaints that glasses or contacts are taking too long

As you work through how to handle these challenges, consider adopting office policies that are not based on the practice owner's wants and needs. Consider having policies that are ridiculously patent-friendly. Do that for three years and the results will amaze you.

5.5 Inspiring Staff to Support Change in Your Practice

There are many exciting practice management strategies out there, but most of them involve changing some aspect of how the practice operates. Change can be good, in fact, it is a necessity in any business, but if staff resist change, the great idea can become a failure or it may simply never happen. Read on for tips on how to get your staff to be open-minded to change.

Don't give an edict; explain why

I know doctors are very busy people, but if you want to implement a new idea in your practice, it is best to not rush it. Plan to devote some time to explain the reasons why you want to try the concept and convince your staff that it will be good for the practice and ultimately good for them. The best place for this may be at your weekly staff meeting because you can address everyone all at once and get feedback. This tends to squelch the rumor mill and prevents having only part of the story told to others.

People tend to support what they help to invent, so begin by talking about the problem that you hope will be addressed by your new concept. This could be a need to increase practice profitability or office efficiency or patient demand. Go on to describe your new idea and how it will produce the desired outcome and ask for input and opinions. Be sure to listen; staff members often see things you might have missed.

It should be implied that things that are good for the practice are also good for the staff, but you may need to help them see that. They may perceive the change as benefitting the doctor and not them and that is a recipe for failure. We all want to know "what's in it for me" and there is nothing wrong with that. Remind your staff that part of their job duties is to help the practice as a business and when they do that, it helps them grow in their career. I think we all agree that employees who support the vision of management and help the practice reach its goals will receive rewards in many forms. It could be a raise, promotion, bonus, or job perks or it might be personal gratitude and respect. You don't have to be specific, but make sure your staff understands that rewards will follow good performance.

See their fears and overcome them

Before discussing the change you have in mind, see it from the employee's point of view and think about what might worry them. This is important because employees may not be willing to share some of their concerns, but if you can predict what they might be, you can reassure them in advance and gain their trust and confidence.

Here are a few possible staff worries:

- This will make me work harder. Now I'll have to do my work and the doctor's work.
- This new work will fall on me more than my co-workers. It is already not fair.
- I won't know how to do this new task. I might be embarrassed in front of patients if I don't do it right.
- This will take more time and I get stressed if we run late with patients.
- I don't like to sell things and this will involve selling.

Next, think about how you can overcome these concerns and work that into your talk at the staff meeting. For example, you could say:

- We don't want you to feel stress on the job so if this concept works for us, I'll hire additional staff members.
- I'd like to test this concept on a small basis first with a pilot program. We'll invest more resources if it looks like it will be successful.
- We will provide you with all the training you need before we implement this idea and we are also designing new forms and installing new software that will make it easy.

Inspire through leadership

If you follow the examples above, you will automatically be thinking like a leader. You will inspire the staff to work with you and you'll convey a feeling that we are all in this together, rather than it is me against you. Caring about others and treating them with respect creates the kind of culture you want in your practice.

Don't be shocked at the domino effect

I discovered long ago in my practice that when we change one thing, there are about 10 other things that are influenced by that. The problem is that I can't always predict what those other things will be and if I tried, I might become so paralyzed that I would never try anything new. I just remind my staff that there will be some unintended consequences and we will deal with those as they occur. We control the impact of change by testing it on a small scale and proceeding slowly. But I'm never shocked when someone tells me about some negative aspect of the change; I'm expecting it and I'll manage it.

5.6 Want to Implement Change? Hire a New Employee First.

Do you ever feel paralyzed about making changes in your practice? Perhaps you have an idea for a new service or a new marketing strategy. Maybe you want to delegate more tasks to your staff so you can see a few more patients per day. Whatever the new thing is, you may feel frozen because you just can't ask any more from your staff. Or you're concerned that if you do bring up the idea, it will meet with a resounding rejection from the staff.

When any of us make a change in our practice operations, there are many moving parts. This is important to consider because a good idea may fail if it is not introduced properly. Even if you know some of the major items that need to happen, it can be difficult to decide what to do first. Here is a guide to implementing change.

Gaining support for change

There is a natural resistance to change among most employees. It springs from fear over what the change may bring. It is simply easier to just continue to do things the way we have been doing them. The only problem is that if businesses don't change, they will eventually die. It may take many years, but businesses must keep pace with changes in society and must grow financially or they will stagnate and then decline. Even better than just keeping pace is to lead change in a positive way. Highly successful businesses offer new services and products to customers, delivered in unique ways. These changes create great customer experiences.

The first step to introduce a change in procedure is to discuss the reason for the change and ask for input. This may be in a staff meeting or you could talk to staff members one-on-one. Start by reviewing the very simple reasons why you are proposing the change. This most likely revolves around the need to increase revenue or profit, or patient demand. Your staff should have an interest in the business aspects of the company, but you may need to remind them about that side.

Many ODs and staff members are so focused on patient care that profitability takes a back seat. But a short presentation about how important it is for the practice to make a profit quickly reminds employees that if their career is going to grow, the practice must grow.

We want staff input because people support what they help to create. Staff members often have excellent ideas that can help the project and they may see legitimate obstacles that should be considered in advance. Start with a statement about a business problem (i.e. "We need to create more revenue and profit.") and ask for ideas on how to achieve that goal. Eventually, work in your new idea and get help in developing it.

Anticipate and head off fear

The next step is to think in advance about what some staff members could be concerned about if the changes are implemented and then reassure them about how you will prevent or remedy those problems.

Here are the main fears staff members have about changes and what you might do about them:

- They may have to work harder. Reassure this worry by saying you will hire more employees if the new concept proves successful. Remind employees that you do not want anyone to feel stress and that customer service is extremely important to your vision of the practice. On the other hand, you expect everyone to work hard and if that creates increased profit, some of that can be paid out in salary increases.
- They may be asked to perform tasks they don't know how to do. Pledge that you will provide plenty of training and that you realize the new skills will take time. Encourage staff that new responsibilities are a way to create advancement in their career. As the practice does better, life in the office can be better.
- They may not like the new tasks. This is not likely, but you should consider it. Most changes do not involve a different type of work. If I'm asking an employee to take on a much different job than she is used to, I usually have a one-on-one chat with her first. I explain the new job, why I think she would be good at it, and then ask if she is willing to take it on.

It is often reassuring to test a new idea and call it a pilot program. Tell staff in advance that you can't predict every aspect of the new program, but you will all adapt and learn as you go along. If the pilot is successful, more resources and funds can be allocated to make the changes permanent.

Hire first

If your staff already seems very busy with patient care and administrative duties, consider hiring a new employee before a change is started. This relieves a great deal of pressure on staff and it counteracts any negative staff response that is more fear-based than real. In many cases, a new employee motivates existing staff members to perform better and try harder, because they realize that someone else could replace them.

Don't worry about the increased cost of the additional employee. You are making an investment in growing your practice and the new idea should increase productivity far more than the additional wages. The first step of adding to the staff demonstrates your confidence in the new program. The new staff member will provide some breathing room for all employees to learn new techniques.

Who is in charge?

In the end, the optometrist/owner should lead the practice. Inspire your employees to support your vision. Make decisions for the good of the practice and proceed. It is possible to make the office culture overly collaborative, where all employees have an equal vote in every decision and if you do not have unanimous approval, nothing happens. If that describes your practice, take steps to change that practice. Listen to staff input and then make the decision as you see fit and announce the change.

If some staff members resist all change, in spite of your best efforts to be inclusive, then you really learned something important about them. Those employees are not as great as you might have previously thought. They are really not team players. That is an important part of your ongoing employment review process. In the worst case, you could be better off in the future replacing that employee with someone with a positive attitude.

5.7 The Above and Beyond Award

I recently attended a conference that had numerous breakout groups for the doctors and staff members. Groups of 10 to 12 people of similar size practices were provided a conference room in the hotel and they had all day to discuss practice management issues. The goal is for each member to ask for help on some topics and provide help on others. These study groups provide extremely powerful ideas because they tap into the experiences of many people. This conference included a wrap-up session on the final day and the moderator of each study group presented the best four or five ideas to the larger combined audience of all attendees.

There were dozens of great ideas, but I'll share one that I have implemented in my practice: the Above and Beyond Award.

Staff recognition

The idea is really quite simple, but it has a powerful effect on your staff morale and office culture. We invite all employees in the practice to nominate a co-worker for the Above and Beyond Award. The award is given to a staff member who does something special or makes an extra effort for a patient or co-worker. Our practice purchases gift cards from a popular retail destination (Amazon, Target, Starbucks or any other you wish) and the manager or doctor presents the gift and the honor to the winning employee at our weekly staff meeting. We have notes about the good deed and the details are provided before the winner is announced. There is a round of applause, there are lots of congratulations, and the winners are listed on plaque on our staff bulletin board.

Our gift cards are in the amount of $25, but the recognition is more important than the dollar value. We only present one award per week, but if we have multiple nominations we can save some for a following week. The Above and Beyond Award always makes our staff meetings end on a positive note, even if some of the topics we discussed that day were not so positive.

Good deeds are contagious

Since you can't nominate yourself, the award causes staff members to pay attention to the good work of others. Staff members who frequently nominate others find that they get nominated as well as a thank you. Some employees who are naturally considerate and often go the extra mile for patients end up getting numerous awards. This makes those who have not received an award try a bit harder so they will be recognized. The focus is on providing exceptional service and the award makes all of us think about it and talk about it.

In smaller practices, you can recognize and reward staff members for good deeds without having them nominate each other. Just pay attention to jobs that are done well and thank the person with a gift card at your meetings. I highly recommend weekly staff meetings for all practices.

5.8 A Plan to Reduce Stress in the Office

Many optometrists and staff members feel stress on the job. It's an uncomfortable feeling that leads to bad attitudes, negative office culture and more frequent errors. If you feel stress fairly often in your workplace, review these tips and take some action to reduce it.

Weekly staff meetings

Stressful situations can be due to many causes, but if you communicate about them with your team, things will improve. Enhance the communication by scheduling staff meetings at least once per week and allowing at least a half-hour per meeting. You can hold daily meetings as well, but you need more time to flush out issues and set policies for the future. Simply pick a day and time of the week that will be your regular staff meeting and block it off from appointments. Block it way ahead in your schedule, like six months or one year. You are always going to need the meetings.

Review the problems of the past week and discuss how to improve and prevent these situations. Don't blame anyone and keep the meeting positive. Ask staff members to tell you about one thing that makes patients unhappy.

Work on office policies
Review all your office policies with an eye on customer service. Let most policies be patient-friendly. The goal is to identify and satisfy patients' wants and needs. Convert your office culture to one that is based on excellent service and letting the patient win. It will create a happier office.

Lunch breaks are required
Work toward requiring all staff members to take a lunch break. Try to change habits if some staff have decided to work through lunch in order to finish their work, but be careful in the process because staff often use this tactic to increase their paid work hours and taking lunch could mean reducing their pay. Never the less, taking a legitimate break and not thinking about work is a good way to decrease stress. Talking to co-workers about one's personal life or going out to lunch helps people relax. My staff get a 45 minute lunch period and they must take it.

Reserve some openings in the schedule
I'm a big believer in efficiency in the clinic and seeing a high number of patients per day, but if you are constantly running behind schedule, you will feel stress. Begin by finding ways to save time in the exam process by delegating more to staff and possibly talking less. But also consider inserting a couple of blocked appointment times every day to allow everyone to catch up or to create some space to add an emergency.

Have enough staff
This may be the best way to reduce stress: be sure you have enough help. More employees reduces stress for the doctors and staff. I know we must keep an eye on the payroll cost, but most of the time, an additional employee increases production and gross revenue more than the additional salary. Having enough staff means the phone can be answered and not go to voice mail. It means there will be someone at the front desk and patients will be served well. It means someone can check on insurance benefits before the day of the appointment. And it means if someone calls off sick, you will still have enough staff to not go crazy.

Hire a true manager
Optometrists feel stress when they try to handle too much at once. A busy week of patients along with managing the staff and handling administrative duties is too much. Delegate some of the staff issues and administrative duties to a manager. A manager can be trained to handle most of the problems that arise with staff and also resolve patient complaints. That feels

like less stress already! But don't expect a manager to know how to do it all; the practice owner will still have to lead and will have to coach the manager on how to do a good job. That takes time, but not as much time as doing it yourself.

It is important that all staff know that the manager is now their boss. That can ruffle some feathers, but a manager can't be effective as a supervisor unless she/he has the authority that only the practice owner can give.

Hire an associate OD

Most optometrists hire a manager to run the business side of the practice so they can continue to see patients. I think that is the wrong way to look at it. I would rather you hire an associate optometrist to see patients so you can have time to run the business! Obviously, a manager is still needed, but he or she can't replace the OD/owner. The practice needs the leadership and vision of the owner. It needs a CEO mentality and no one can do that better than the owner. The transfer of patients can occur gradually, but as the practice grows larger, it needs more management time.

5.9 Overmanage; Don't Micromanage

I recently attended a practice management conference at Disney World in Orlando, Florida and one of the special events was the "Business Behind the Magic" tour. This was the third time I've taken this tour which is produced by the Disney Institute and I was still inspired with new ideas that I could apply to my practice. One of the tour guides told our group that Disney leaders do not micromanage, but they do overmanage. I thought about that concept quite a lot and it correlates extremely well to achieving a great patient experience in an optometric practice.

What is Disney Overmanagement?

The tour guide told us that overmanaging is different from micromanaging because: a) it is intentional and b) the intent is extremely positive.

Here is what Disney means by the overmanage concept:

- Think about your challenge or goal differently and to a greater degree.
- Pay extraordinary attention to the details.
- View what is "typical" or "corporate best practices" as a baseline as opposed to an acceptable standard.

Apply the concept to your practice

When you overmanage your practice, you can create consistently pleasant experiences for your patients, which results in greater patient loyalty and word-of-mouth referrals. And as anyone who has visited Disney theme parks knows, you can charge high fees and still have your guests (patients) feel they received a good value.

Begin by listing each interaction that occurs between your office and the patient during a typical visit and then discuss each of those points with your staff. Disney calls those interactions "moments of truth". Brainstorm ways to make each event more pleasant and memorable for the patient.

Here is a quick list of moments of truth to consider and improve upon:

- The phone call to ask about services and fees.
- Scheduling an appointment.
- Planning for insurance benefits to be used.
- Confirming the appointment.
- Greeting the patient upon arrival.
- The waiting experience.
- Asking for information and approval for screening tests.
- Calling the patient in for pretesting.
- The case history.
- Introduction to the doctor.
- Recording data in the EHR system.
- The examination including dilation.
- Contact lens trial and fitting.
- Patient education and treatment plan.
- Eyewear selection and the ordering process.
- Additional medical testing.
- Notification and delivery of eyewear.
- Ongoing communication and satisfaction survey.
- Recall system.

If you refine these points and invest in them with money and through staff training, you will build a more successful practice. Exceed the Patient's expectations the way Disney does with their Guests.

Have a magical day!

5.10 Free Food Helps Office Culture

I occasionally read about the world's best companies to work for in business magazines like Fortune and Forbes. I agree with the concept: making your business a great place to work results in happy employees and that is good for business. But many of the job perks I read about are just not practical for my practice. Companies like Google can have nap rooms, massage services, or on-site day care centers, but I don't have Google's budget or physical space. I have implemented a new perk that is going over extremely well, however: free food and drink for all staff.

My goal is to make my practice a great work environment, and I should stress that I don't think I can buy a positive organizational culture with free snacks. The doctors and managers of the practice really care about employees and we work hard to set an example of respect and friendliness. The culture of an organization is created by leadership.

Taking a step up

Many businesses offer some degree of free refreshments, even if it is just coffee and the occasional bagels or catering lunch at times. We did this as well, but more and more companies are providing unusual perks on the job with the result of higher job satisfaction ratings, which leads to better staff attitudes and more happiness, which leads to better customer service. More perks also improve our ability to recruit and retain better employees.

We had some vending machines in our staff lounge with snacks and soft drinks for several years. We also have a staff refrigerator, microwaves and a coffee machine. I was not sure what free food and drink would cost for our staff of 30 people, but we decided to test the concept. We got rid of the vending machines and we remodeled the staff lounge. We appointed a food committee which was charged with the task of deciding what kind of food and beverages we should stock. The committee orders many food items online but they also make regular trips to our local supermarket to buy fresh food. Now that this program has been in effect for a few months, I can tell you that we seem to be settling in on a food and drink budget of about $500 per month.

Food and drink choices

We now have something for everyone in our staff lounge and we find that food indeed makes work more fun. We have healthy foods like yogurt, granola, vegetables, cheese, humus and fresh fruit. We have comfort food like cookies, chips, ice cream and muffins. We offer hot drinks in our Keurig machine and we keep cans of soda, juice and iced tea in the refrigerator. We have large open shelves with baskets of food. We are getting a popcorn machine soon. Everyone just helps themselves!

Comradery

We have seen a great response from staff members to our free food initiative. Employees enjoy each other's company over snacks before and after work, during breaks and lunch time, but we have not seen any problem with too many breaks or abuse of time. I am happy with the return on investment.

5.11 Casual Fridays and Saturdays

I've always tried to develop a good office culture in my practice with my staff. I truly believe that if staff members like their job and feel respected by their bosses and co-workers, the result will be better attitudes and a stronger desire to achieve the goals of the organization. If all goes to plan, in addition to creating a more pleasant work environment, the practice receives a big benefit in the end because customer service is better and the patient experience is enhanced. That results in more word-of-mouth referrals of new patients and better patient reviews on social media. A strong organizational culture can be a big factor in building your practice.

That is all well and good, but how does one build a positive office culture? It is both simple and complex at the same time, but read on.

Starts with the leaders

The culture of an organization is really a reflection of the leaders. That is typically the owners, doctors and office managers, and if you're one of those, it starts with you. At the simplest form, you need to really care about employees as people and you need to show that you care with actions. Treating staff with respect, kindness and fairness is a good start. Treating patients the same way and demonstrating the customer service culture yourself as you work with difficult patients are additional ways to set the tone of the practice. You are a role model for staff and you set the prime example of how to act.

Holding frequent staff meetings and communicating well are important factors in building your culture. Be interested in your staff. Ask them about their lives, without getting overly personal. Ask for their input and opinions on practice decisions and projects. Give employees verbal praise when deserved and be patient when they make errors.

Having some fun
We are also trying to find ways to make our office a more fun place to work. There are many great ideas for this and I'll share a few in upcoming articles. The one we are working on right now is casual Fridays, which is spilling onto Saturdays as well because it might make working Saturdays a bit more bearable.

We have always provided staff uniforms in my practice as an employment benefit. We have cycled through many variations of health care uniforms, pants, tops and jackets in various colors or prints. We like a professional look and we replace the items twice per year so they look good. There are always challenges in getting all the sizes we need and choosing materials that wash well with few wrinkles. We don't make every staff member perfectly happy in every case, but we have become veterans in the uniform process and we do very well.

Once per year, we have a special event for the Susan G. Komen Breast Cancer Foundation where staff members get to wear blue jeans to work and they make a donation to the cause for the privilege, which is matched by the practice. Everyone enjoys this day so much, and since society is changing, we decided to begin having casual Fridays (and Saturdays) every week. To keep the staff looking like a team and to enhance the identity of the practice, we printed t-shirts for all employees with the practice name and logo and they can pair this with jeans and any shoes they want (within reason).

We bought the custom t-shirts online from one of the many places that sell logo sportswear. We chose a bright color shirt which is thicker and higher quality than most t-shirts. It comes in a big range of sizes and there are cuts for men or women in round or V-neck. The shirt has the practice logo on the front left chest and a very large version on the back. This year happens to be the 40th anniversary of our practice and we had a special logo designed for this year only that has the number 40 worked into it. We are using the tag line: "Providing 20/20 to Northwest Indiana for 40 years."

The t-shirts can be worn with a long sleeve shirt under it if the employee wishes. We are also supplying a zip up fleece jacket with the practice logo.

You may wonder if I can be sure that all this trouble and expense will pay off. I don't know that I can be sure, but it is just my instinct.

Chapter 6. Human Resource Management

6.1 Your Staff: Cross-Train or Departmentalize?

As you analyze and refine your practice operations, consider the job descriptions of your staff. Is it better to cross-train your staff or to assign staff to more specific job duties? How you decide on this can make a huge difference in your practice efficiency and on patient satisfaction.

Your practice in phases

The answer to my question is not as easy as you might think at first. I look at the optometric practice in phases and I believe the best staffing strategy varies depending on the phase. I've been through all these phases in my practice and here is the model I followed at different times:

- Early growth phase. This practice has a small staff and they are generally all cross-trained. Everyone does everything and that serves the practice well at this stage. Even the doctor handles tasks that will eventually be too basic, but at this early stage, the staff is not trained at a very high level. The role of the staff member may best be described as an optometric assistant. The assistant answers the phone, greets patients, and performs basic pretesting and simple optical dispensing. Anything more complex is handled by the doctor.
- Need for accuracy. As the practice grows, there is a need for staff to function at a higher level and it becomes difficult for each assistant to learn everything well. If a larger staff tries to do everything, more errors are made and it is hard to track down who is accountable. A logical strategy is to make the staff more specialized. Some employees are opticians, some are receptionists and some assist the doctor with clinical care. Having some employees specially trained to do specific tasks helps them to do a better job.
- Expansion and delegation. With more delegation and new technology, there is a need for even more specialization. The practice may add an in-office finishing lab. There is a need for a dedicated insurance coordinator. The practice may begin to use scribes. Technicians could be trained to refract.
- Full circle. In larger practices that are highly delegated, there may be very busy times that are highly productive and other times that are relatively slow. This change in demand may be random or due to other factors like one or more doctors taking time off. The larger patient volume can cause the optical dispensary to get very busy at certain times when people drop in without an appointment. This phase of practice has many employees who are well-trained in

specific duties, but they can also be cross-trained to perform other jobs fairly easily. In my practice, for example, all the clinical technicians are also scribes and opticians. This gives us great flexibility to put staff where they are needed. They can handle a heavy load in the clinic or a busy rush to pick up glasses or select frames in optical. We also train our lab technicians (whose main job is making glasses) to dispense eyewear to patients. Our insurance coordinator and a couple of specially trained clinical technicians can help out at the front desk when needed.

Departments

Here are some typical departments to consider as your practice moves through the growth phases.

- Business Office
- Clinic
- Optical Dispensary
- Optical Laboratory

In addition to these departments, other special areas include: contact lens department, insurance department, office manager, frame buyer, and marketing specialist.

The formation of departments can happen gradually, with staff learning advanced techniques in specific areas over time. As new employees are hired, the department of need is identified and candidates with appropriate skills and experiences are recruited.

When these departments grow to include more staff, it may make sense to appoint a department manager. Typically, there is already a general office manager in place at this point, and the practice can benefit from a group of assistant managers who can fill in when the general manager is off work or busy with other matters. The practice may have extended office hours and need supervision at times and the department manager can become an assistant manager. This approach also recognizes strong contributions from staff members who have performed well by promoting them.

One of the disadvantages of departments is there can be some competition and lack of cooperation between staff members in different areas. Usually this is not a problem if the practice has developed a culture of teamwork and fosters mutual respect among coworkers.

6.2 Tips for Hiring Staff

Finding the best candidates for employment can be very tricky. You can do the best interview in the world, but you never really know an employee until he or she has worked a few weeks. Here are some innovative ideas to help you through the process.

How to advertise the opening

I use both the traditional newspaper and the electronic media for placing a simple help wanted ad. The ad describes the job, the hours, our excellent benefit package and it specifies any experience or training that is required. For technicians and opticians, we try to find excellent people with optical experience, but it is more important to find the right personality and we will train to develop the skills as needed.

One thing that I do that is slightly unusual is that I put the name of my practice in the ad and it states: apply in person. No phone or fax number is provided. I really don't mind if other eye care providers or the general public see that we are hiring, so I don't use a blind box number for replies. I actually prefer for job seekers to see the name of my practice because it may increase responses.

Other sources

Keep your eyes open for great people when you are in other public environments. If you are in a retail store or restaurant and you are receiving great service, consider giving the person your business card and saying you are looking for someone with the kind of skills she demonstrates and, if she has any interest, to please give you a call.

Patients can be good sources of future employees. You already have some insight into intelligence, personality and current job. The patient knows something about eye care and your office and obviously likes your office. If you or your staff know someone you all love to see, you could call her and ask if she is interested in applying for the job.

I do not believe in raiding the offices of other eye care practitioners (ECPs) for staff members out of respect and professional courtesy. If I run a want ad in the paper, however, and an employee of a local ECP responds, I feel that person is fair game. After all, she was obviously reading the employment ads.

Resumes and job application forms

We certainly receive preprinted resumes by mail and fax, but we just call those candidates and ask them to stop by during business hours and complete an employment application. Preprinted resumes are useful, but the handwritten application gives me much more information. After all, you never know who actually wrote a resume. Consider the information we get when the candidate completes a form in our office. I'll use feminine pronouns in this article since most of our staff are females.

- My office manager and I get to see the candidate in person. Someone on my staff speaks to her and we find out quite a bit about her demeanor, speech, communication and personality.
- How long does it take for the candidate to complete the application form? It is one sheet of paper on both sides. Take too long and we lose interest.
- We observe clothing, hair, accessories, piercings, etc. I relax our standards a bit because I realize the candidate is not expecting a job interview, but we still learn a lot.
- A quick review of the completed application form lets me see the neatness of the handwriting and basic spelling and grammar.
- Pertinent job and wage history is available at a glance on the form

The interview

Typically, my office manager conducts all job interviews and she will often do it on the spot unless the candidate proved unworthy during the quick look described above. If the manager is not available at this drop in visit, our receptionist will take the application, thank the candidate and tell her that we'll call if we wish to arrange an interview. But the manager will often do an interview and then let the candidate go. After we see several applicants, we will call the best ones back for a second interview with the doctor and the manager.

The starting wage

The application form asks for the desired salary and has blank space. This is a valuable bit of information. If it is left blank, the manager or I will press for an answer by saying how much it helps us to determine the correct wage; it's generally not difficult to get an answer. The form also has a place to list the last four jobs and includes spaces to indicate the salary, which would include the present salary if the person is currently working.

In general, once we are ready to offer someone the job, I like to pay the amount requested on the application. I compare the amount desired with other factors, such as the applicant's experience and how desirable I feel she is. I also consider what I'm currently paying my other employees with similar job descriptions and experience. If the wage requested is higher than I wish to pay, I might offer less, but I realize I may not have a completely happy employee and she may continue to look for another job even if she accepts my offer.

I find that most job candidates cite a figure near the lowest acceptable wage, quite often less than I might have offered, because they want to get an offer. While I believe in paying employees well and I know that very bright people will command higher wages, I'm always trying to keep business expenses down.

Probationary period?
When I discuss the hiring process with other eye care professionals, someone often brings up the concept of telling all new employees that there is a 30 day probationary period and employment may be terminated for any reason during that period. I don't really like that practice because I wish to preserve the right to dismiss an employee at any time. Most states have employment at will laws which allows an employer to end employment for no specific reason, as long as there is no discrimination of a protected class of individuals. To give a 30 day period during which employment may be ended seems to imply that after the 30 day period, dismissal is not as easy. Even if we don't consider the legal aspects, it may confuse the employee.

It is fine to have a 30 day waiting period before health insurance or other employment benefits begin.

6.3 Where to Find Good Staff Members

I often speak to optometrists who know they are understaffed but just can't find good employees. This issue varies among local job markets, but there are many geographical areas where staff members are hard to find. In some cases, the practice is looking for people with optical training and experience, but the candidates don't have the people skills. In some cases, the practice has hired several new employees over a period of a year and they simply don't last. They either quit rather quickly or they perform poorly and have to be dismissed. It's enough to make the doctor/owner just give up.

In this article, I'll describe a true story and provide some motivation for not giving up.

Recruiting staff

When a job market is very difficult, I'm occasionally asked about the idea of recruiting employees directly from other eye care offices in the area. We all know it happens, but I don't recommend it. I wouldn't actually cold-call or solicit any individual in the optical field because I think it is best to remain in good standing in the eye care community and I think the other eye care professionals would view such action as crossing a line. Of course, it is fine to advertise quite heavily that you have a job position available. You can make the position very attractive by indicating that you offer special training and excellent salary and benefit packages. If employees from other practices are looking for a new job and see the employment ad, they are fair game.

Craig's List is still the standard for job related ads in most communities, but I would also place a classified ad in the local newspaper in both the print and online editions. Many practices only use Craig's List or other similar websites, but I have found the newspaper is still a good resource. Newspaper help wanted ads are incredibly expensive, but this is a time to think big. I would run the ads every day until the position is filled and forget about the cost.

Read on for more innovative ways to find employees.

Hire for personality; train for skills

If the pool of good job candidates is small in your area, I'd give up any requirement to have optical experience. It is much more important to find someone with the right personality and attitude. You really can train the optical skills on the job in your practice and have the employee take additional courses, live or online. Of course, you should always follow the laws in your state or jurisdiction; this approach obviously does not work if you need a licensed professional. But once you remove the experience requirement, the pool of good people increases greatly. Some of them will respond to your employment ads and in other cases, you can just go out and find the person you are looking for.

I think direct solicitation of someone you meet in everyday life in a field outside of eye care is just fine. We have all heard of this technique, but I've used it several times and it has worked very well for me. Here is a recent example:

My wife and I were having dinner in a nice restaurant a couple months ago and the waitress was excellent. I'm sure you know what I mean; sometimes you interact with a person who just seems to get it. This waitress smiled all the time, she got our order perfect, she was attentive, smart, had a nice appearance, etc. As we were closing out the check, I gave her my business card and told her that we were looking for an optometric technician/optician in our clinic and that she is the kind of person we need. I said if she had any interest in exploring a new career to please call our office manager. I wrote the manager's name on the card. I told the waitress we would train her for all the skills she would need.

She called. Our manager asked how much money she wanted to earn and her response was in the normal range for my practice. We interviewed her and hired her. She completed basic training in about two weeks and she is now working for us. She is still that smart, happy person we liked and she is fitting in with our staff very well. Of course, this person could come from any vocation, including retail sales, industry sales rep, auto dealership, hair salon, housekeeper, and many more. You can even find these great people within your own patient base if you look.

A few more tips

Consider these additional points to make the hiring process better:

- Pre-employment testing. A test of job-specific skills and a personality test before making a decision to offer the job provides very valuable insight. There are a few sources in our industry of such tests. The tests are often taken online and graded electronically.
- Staff sabotage. If new employees frequently quit, consider the possibility that one or more of your current staff may not want anyone to join them. Some employees want to protect their turf. There are two sides to every story.
- May need to pay more. If you are in a market where it is extremely hard to find good employees, you may have to pay higher wages to attract them. A better staff can give you an advantage that results in more business and better profits.
- Hire two? I usually recommend assimilating one new employee at a time, but there are exceptions. If you are extremely understaffed, hiring two new people at once can make sense. Training both at once is not much more work than training one person. Your current staff will see that you are very serious about expanding your practice.
- Don't always use today's revenue metrics. Some doctors won't hire a new employee because of some metric, like their payroll cost is already 22% of the gross and they don't want to exceed that. But operational experience and judgment always trumps numbers. Practice gross revenue with that additional employee could jump up by much more than the additional salary.

6.4 Are You Having Trouble Finding Staff?

Not having enough staff is a huge problem facing optometrists. I see practices every day that are understaffed. Frequently, the practice owner or office manager has been searching for weeks or months, but can't find the right person. In many cases, the office has given up the search. In the short term, one might rationalize that the best decision is to simply not act, but there is a very large opportunity cost if you don't hire someone. It could be that doing nothing is costing your practice a great deal in lost profit and reduced service quality. These negative factors can be invisible because you don't miss what you never had, but they are quite real.

It is very hard to generalize about the reasons why a practice may have trouble finding a new employee. Much can depend on the local job market and on the philosophy of the owner or manager. I understand from decades of hiring in my own practice and in helping other doctors staff their offices properly, that it is not easy to find great employees. But as hard as it may be, I would never allow my practice be understaffed for very long. At some point, I would simply hire the best candidate I can find and go about training him or her.

Where can you look?

The usual resources for hiring include online job boards, such as Craig's List, Indeed.com, Monster.com, and many more. I would certainly post the position available in one or more of these standards and they usually work quite well. But not always. They can sometimes produce almost too many candidates with none of them very qualified. That is a problem, but you can screen them and be selective about whom to interview. You could also rewrite the ad to require more experience.

I also find the local newspaper is still a good source for find employees. It may be true that newspapers are declining in readership, but they all have an online version and many people who are looking for a job check those classified listings. Running an ad in a newspaper may have a cost, but hiring the right person is very important. Go ahead and pay for the ad!

There are many other more creative ways to find new staff members:

- Hire a patient. After all, you already know them. Peruse your files and call a few up and ask if they would be interested.

- Look for candidates in real life. You know a great personality when you see one, in retail stores, restaurants, hair salons, wherever you work with people. If you interact with someone you think might be good for your office, give her a business card and ask them to call you if they are interested in making a career change. Tell her that your office is looking for bright people like her. Obviously, this will not result in a candidate with optical experience and you will need to train the person.
- I do not believe in stealing employees from other eye care providers from an ethical standpoint, so I would not solicit anyone. If you run an ad in the media and an employee of another practice is looking and replies that is different and quite acceptable.
- There are web-based services in the optical industry that can help you search for job candidates.
- Local colleges have placement services for their graduates in medical fields, business management and even opticianry.

Experience or no experience

It is smart to hire a great personality with excellent training and optical experience if you can find such a candidate, but it is often not possible. Realize that the pool of people who have all those qualities can be quite small. In general, you are better off hiring someone who has the brains and personality you want, even if they don't have experience. You can train the skills, but you most likely can't change the personality or the IQ. After some reasonable time period, you have to move on and change the ad to read: "no experience needed; will train." That should open up a larger group of candidates for you to interview and choose from.

How will you train a new employee if you are already understaffed? Well, this may be one of the rare times that you need to authorize some overtime for one your existing employees to work with the new employee. The doctor may also need work some extra hours and teach some skills. There are some very good online videos and other training programs that the new employee can take while on duty in your office. Finally, don't underestimate the value of having the new employee shadow some current staff and the doctor. If the office is busy, the senior staff do not have to teach or communicate at all. The new one can just silently observe the veteran and she will still learn a lot.

Could it be you?

The old adage "hire slow; fire fast" sounds great and we can all agree with the principle, but there is a limit to how slow you should be. If you have searched and searched and found no one, you may have to lower your expectations. Also, be realistic about the pay scale you are offering and the type of person you are seeking. You may have to either raise the pay level or lower the minimum skill requirement.

Many optometric offices are using the following tools to look for the best employee possible:

- Background checks
- Credit checks
- Personal references
- Interviews with former supervisors
- Excellent results on pre-employment tests (I strongly believe in doing this one)
- Perfectly-written resume

These are all excellent tools in the right job market and with the right candidates, but you also need to know when to lower your standards and take a chance on an individual who shows promise in the interview. I would use these tools as support factors, but if you are too strict with the results they could cause you to reject someone who would be great. In the end, we really never know for sure how a new employee will perform until he works for you. There is always some degree of chance and some employees just won't work out and you will have to part ways.

If you are really unsure about a candidate, consider having her come in for a full day working interview and pay her a pre-agreed upon fee.

6.5 Making the Good Hire and the Part You're Overlooking

Most ODs are very cautious to not hire a job candidate who will not work out. We go to great lengths to screen out the wrong type of employees during the interview process. This is understandable, of course, but I think we should be just as concerned about missing out on a good hire. Most employers don't think about that aspect as they recruit job candidates. It is just as problematic if we pass on a person who would have been a good employee based on assumptions that are inaccurate. In spite of our best efforts, both of these situations occur: we occasionally hire the wrong person and we occasionally reject a good person. Being aware of both possibilities will help you improve your chances of finding good employees.

How we hire a bad person

Most of the current strategies we use in the recruiting and hiring process are geared to prevent an employer from making a bad hire. In spite of all this effort, experienced managers will agree that we never really know a new employee until he or she has worked the job for a few weeks. Eventually, the true work ethic, job skills and personality traits come out, but job applicants can become masters at not revealing their true selves during an interview. People always put their best foot forward and suppress their negative traits in order to get a job offer.

The interview is still the best tool we can use to select the best person for the job, but it is far from foolproof.

- I've hired employees who seemed extremely happy and pleasant in the interview, only to have them never smile at patients and actually be quite rude.
- I've hired staff members who said they are great team players, only to have them create hard feelings among their co-workers and hurt office morale.
- I've hired a person who had great experience in previous eye care jobs only to find out that she was really not that bright.
- I have called colleagues for references and received positive reports only to have the new hire be chronically late for work and frequently call off sick. I think the reference source was afraid to tell me the truth for fear of legal action.

When the new person is not quite what you hoped, it is best to have a talk about the issues right away. You must let the new employee know what your expectations are. I always give staff members plenty of chances to improve and train, but if you don't see improvement quickly it is best to part ways early and resume your search.

How we overlook a good person

In my consulting work, I often come across optometrists who know they are understaffed and have been searching for the right person for months. They may have hired someone during that period, but it did not work out and they are still looking for the right employee. In those cases, I have to look at the practice owner and ask some tough questions. Except for very unusual circumstances, it should not take that long! The goal in hiring is not to seek perfection, but rather to hire the best person available in the job market at the wage range the practice can afford. I think we have to do a reasonable search of that job market and make an offer to the best person, even if that person is far from perfect. Just pick the best person in your pool of candidates. If the new hire is lacking in some skills, it is up to the practice to train him or her.

Some of the applicants who were rejected by the owner or manager would probably have become excellent employees or at least average ones.

- The person you thought was not friendly was actually just very nervous in the interview because she wanted the job so badly. Once she gets past her nerves, she has a great smile and she uses it often.
- When you called another OD in town for a reference, he told you the applicant caused a lot of problems when she worked for him. The truth is, she was a good employee but he views your practice as a threat to him and he does not want to help you.
- You did a credit check on the applicant and found that she had a history of financial problems and a low credit score, so you did not hire her. There could be many reasons why a person had financial problems, but could still be an excellent employee. She may need another chance. She certainly needs a job.
- You noticed several spelling errors on an applicant's resume, so you passed on hiring her. Instead you hired someone with a perfect resume, but you did not realize that her brother-in-law created the document for her, much of it was not true and she can't spell well either.
- You did a phone interview and you got a bad vibe about a candidate. She seemed timid. But without seeing her body language, her excellent appearance and her eye contact, you misjudged her and she now works for another practice in town.

Trust your instinct but don't be shocked

The more I study human resource management, the more I rely on my instincts about people. I look at education, job history, professional experience and other factors on the resume. I think pre-employment testing for job skills and personality is a very useful tool. But the interview is how I get to know the person. In some cases, if we are not sure about a candidate, we will invite him or her to observe the practice and conduct a working interview for a day or two at an agreed upon pay rate.

If my instinct and that of my managers is good, we make a job offer and hope for the best. But I'm never shocked if it doesn't work out.

6.6 Extending the Job Offer

I received a nice email from an OD in Ohio who found some past tip articles on staff hiring to be helpful, but he suggested I write about "the offer" part of hiring. Great idea! I have not seen anything on that before.

After going through the process of advertising the position available, reviewing resumes and interviewing candidates, we all make the best selection we can. So how do you decide how much to offer?

The starting wage

There may be several factors a job candidate will consider before they say yes to a job offer, but the big one is the pay. If you get the wage right, the candidate will usually accept. Deciding on the starting wage is more art than science and experience in hiring certainly helps, but I'll tell you what makes it easier for me. I have all candidates complete a two page job application form while seated in my reception room. This allows me to control the information more than a prepared resume, which could have been written by the applicant's brother-in-law.

Two of the questions on my application are: "Date you can start", and "Wage desired (per hour)". The wage desired question is key to my hiring process. My office manager conducts the initial interviews and she always pays attention to that figure. If the question is left blank, our manager will ask the candidate to please name an amount. She will even push for it if necessary, in a respectful way, indicating that it will be very helpful to us. We almost always get the number and we do not reveal what wage we are willing to pay. I actually don't have a firm number in advance anyway.

The reason I like the candidate to state the wage number first is because I find that most people will give the lowest number they can accept, since they want to get the job offer. They know if they go too high, it may mean no job. I often find that the wage requested is lower than I would have been willing to pay.

So how much?

There are several factors to consider when you decide on how much money to initially offer.

- What are the applicant's job experience and skills, including non-optical skills like computer technology?
- Will the candidate need the normal training or much more than that?
- What was the candidate's wage history at previous jobs and is she asking for much more than her most recent job?

- What are the wages currently being paid to your other employees with similar job experience and skills? Even though you may have a policy that wage information should be kept confidential, realize that co-workers often share this with each other. While you should not have to defend what you pay any employee, it is a good test to ask yourself.
- Is the wage requested realistic for a good employee in a non-optical career? What is a typical annual salary for a teacher or a retail clerk? A quick way to convert hourly wages into a full time salary is to double the hourly wage and add three zeros. For example, $16 per hour is $32,000 per year. Is $32,000 per year considered a high salary in general terms? Consider that the U.S. Government placed the 2012 poverty threshold for a family of four at $23,000.
- Overall, how much do we like him or her? This considers personality, appearance, communication skills and other traits.
- Does he need health insurance? You may be able to offer a much higher hourly wage if no health insurance is needed.

The points above are important to consider, but I always go back to the desired wage as stated on the application and if possible, I try to offer that amount. If I go lower than that, I run the risk of the candidate accepting the job but continuing to look for employment elsewhere. I see little point in paying more than what was asked for, because I am trying to keep payroll costs as low as possible, but I have occasionally offered more when the amount requested was very low. If the amount requested is higher than I can comfortably manage, I generally pass on this applicant or I may have a very frank conversation about the wages and take it from there.

Do you offer benefits?

For many job candidates, the employment benefits can be more important than the wages. This is especially true with health insurance for people with lower wage jobs. To attract the best employees you need excellent benefits, so look closely at what you offer in health insurance. Even though it is incredibly expensive, I would try to provide an excellent program, such as 80% of premiums covered in a major PPO plan with a drug benefit. A high deductible is usually accepted well. Other benefits matter also, like a retirement plan, vacations, paid holidays, paid training programs and more. If you put a nice package together and if your office presents a nice impression, you'll get most of the people you want.

What are the deal breakers?

Some aspects of compensation are negotiable and you can give more if you have a great candidate, but decide in advance what items are not negotiable. Don't be swept away and give away the farm; keep in mind that most employees have faults and you will find them within the first couple weeks in almost everyone. One of the deal breakers for me is that every employee must work two evenings per week until 7pm and Saturdays from 9am to 1pm. When we make that a requirement of the job, nearly every applicant says it is no problem at all.

6.7 How to Fire an Employee

Not a very pleasant topic this week, but sometimes firing an employee is a necessity to keep your practice operating at the highest level. We don't see this topic tackled very often in our professional literature, but I'll share some practical thoughts on it here, based on my experience.

Training and Rehabilitation

Depending on the nature of the problem, I believe in giving an employee a chance to correct deficiencies and in assisting in that process with specific training. As employers, we have a duty to inform an employee of shortcomings, unless an offense is so grievous that there is simply no possibility of overcoming it. This due process before dismissal is also the smart thing to do as a manager. It is difficult to find employees and we can't simply fire everyone who makes a mistake. No one is perfect.

When an unwanted behavior is noticed, it's important for the doctor or manager to discuss it in private with the employee. This may not seem like an easy task for some people, but avoiding it is worse because it appears that you have accepted the behavior by not addressing it right away. Some judgment is needed here, of course, because if a boss intervenes in every minor oversight or staff disagreement, the office culture can be adversely affected.

As problems are discussed, notes should be made in the employee's file. Performance should be monitored and if improvement is not noted, additional meetings should be held. One need not make a big deal out of the meeting; just ask the person to step into your office or other private room and say what you need to. It may only take two minutes.

When I first bring up a deficiency to an employee, I start very gently and I usually begin by finding something that the person does well, to acknowledge the good with the bad. Some staff members have difficulty accepting any criticism and even a mild admonishment can hurt their morale. I like to see the employee acknowledge the criticism and adopt an attitude that he will work on improving. If the employee does not know what in the world I'm talking about, I usually find that there is little hope for positive change.

As meetings continue, I become less congenial and eventually I issue a warning that job termination will occur if the behavior can't be improved. I will give a date as a final deadline for improvement. These notes are documented in the file.

Employment at will

Most states adopt a legal doctrine called employment at will, which means the employer does not need a reason to fire someone – as long as the firing is not discriminatory against a protected class. This seems fair to me, since employees don't need a reason to quit. It's kind of interesting really, that employees often just tell the employer that they found a better job, with very little warning. That act is comparable to the employer telling a staff member they found a better receptionist. Yet it is not really viewed the same way, and that is understandable because companies are bigger than individuals. Much of employment law favors the employee, but employment at will gives some power to the employer.

Employment at will can be lost if a company gives an employee a contract or makes other rules about the dismissal process, so it's usually best to keep employment simple.

Discrimination

It is against federal and state law to fire someone because he or she belongs to a protected class. That doesn't mean you can't fire someone who is in a protected class, it only means the class can't be the reason you fire. Protected classes vary by state to some degree but usually include race, color, religion, national origin, age, gender, sexual orientation, marital status and disability. You may "discriminate" against factors that are not protected – but that's not really discrimination. Poor manners, tardiness, excessive absences, sloppy hygiene, poor grammar, bad attitudes and odors of cigarette smoke are all non-protected.

How to actually do it

When you decide that your practice would be better off without an employee, I recommend keeping the process short and simple.

- Resist the temptation to explain why you are firing. It's too late and trying to prove that you are justified in your action is futile because you are asking the dismissed person to agree that he is not worth employing. Pretty tough to agree to. Allow the person some dignity.
- The two sentences to say are: "Things are just not working out." and "I think it's best if we part ways." If pressed for a reason, just repeat those two sentences. As long as you aren't discriminating, you don't need a reason.
- You may wish to give the employee an opportunity to resign, before actually firing him. Some people may prefer to have a resignation on their resume and on your records. Resigning also benefits the employer because an employee who resigns will have difficulty filing a claim for unemployment benefits.
- I prefer to end employment immediately after the dismissal meeting. There is no benefit in having a fired employee finish the work day or any additional days while you look for a replacement. I ask for the key to the office right now.
- It is routine practice to change our office alarm code on the day an employee is discharged, so duplicate keys will be of no use.
- The end of a work day may be the best time to terminate employment.
- I often provide severance pay equal to two weeks salary because I am not giving the employee the two weeks notice I would ask for if he quit. You don't have to provide severance pay, but it's often the right thing to do.
- You may want to have the final paycheck and severance check ready to hand to the person, or hold these checks until company-owned materials (uniforms) can returned (check with your state law about when the final check must be delivered).

Unemployment benefits

Each state has a program to assist the unemployed. I do not let that system influence my decision to keep or fire and employee. As an employer, I pay into the fund which provides money for the state to award. Like insurance, if I have a claim, my premiums may go up temporarily. Having the state grant benefits to a former employee and charge your account does not mean that your dismissal was wrongful. It only means that the state is assessing more risk to you because of this experience. You may fire someone for very legitimate reasons and still find that the state awards benefits. That may be quite valid; the person is still unemployed.

Unemployment tax is a cost of doing business and retaining a poor employee is much more costly. If I'm contacted by the state employment office, I write a letter stating the facts of the employment and the discharge, because the office needs to receive both sides of the situation to make a correct determination.

6.8 How many staff members?

Last week's tip article prompted a strongly positive reaction from readers, so I'm going to use this article to dive into the most common question I received: How many technicians does a practice need to manage 24 patients per day per doctor? If you missed the last article you can click on the past tips button at the end of this message.

Practice variables
Since no two practices are alike in how they operate and in the duties that are assigned to staff members, it's impossible to give a blanket answer to the question of how many employees are needed. As you seek to compress your existing patients into fewer days with more delegation, it is likely that you'll need another technician. Don't worry about that increased cost, however, because typically more income is generated with the additional employee. It does not take much more gross revenue to make up for the additional payroll expense.

As we compare the staffing needs of one practice to another, we must try to compare apples to apples. We must analyze how the practices operate. One of the biggest variables to consider is if the practice uses scribes and if the scribes are cross-trained to perform pretesting and optical dispensing. The more traditional approach is to have separate pretesters and opticians and for the doctor to not use scribes.
My practice uses the scribe approach and we try to schedule three scribes per working doctor. On a three doctor day, we would have nine of these scribing technicians. Scribes in our practice are not assigned to a specific doctor, but they go wherever they are needed most. Three scribes per doctor sounds like a lot at first, but remember that these staff members are also called to optical to do adjustments, repairs, deliveries and walk-in frame selections.
If you do not use scribes, I would estimate you would need two full time technicians per working doctor to manage the fast paced flow of 24 patients per day.

Additional staff

Staff requirements will also vary based on other duties. We have a separate business office staff of six people plus an office manager. I like to have some specialized training for staff who greet patients, handle money, file insurance claims and book appointments.

We have two full time opticians who do not perform pretest or scribing duties, but always stay on the floor in optical. We find we need these experts in optical to give us the high quality service we need and they are very good at sales. Typically, the scribe stays with the patient they cared for in the clinic and just continues if frame selection is needed, but if the clinic is extremely busy and we need their technician skills, a hand-off is made to one of the opticians.

We also have two full time and one part time lab technicians. These individuals make glasses with our own surfacing and finishing equipment and place orders to outside labs. On rare occasion, a lab tech will be called out to work with a patient in optical.

Hiring can jump-start your practice

Most ECPs tend to avoid hiring an additional staff member, but I've always found that doing so actually stimulates practice growth and profitability. Four good things happen when you hire a new employee:

- Customer service improves because you have more staff to take care of people.
- You will delegate more because you have someone to delegate to.
- Staff performance improves because staff members are less stressed and the presence of a new employee often increases the effort of existing staff.
- Productivity increases because everyone has more time to educate patients and sell premium products.

Useful metrics

The best way to determine if you have enough staff is to observe practice operations over a period of weeks. There should be a good balance of general activity; some non-busy time for socialization in the office is OK, but not too much. Beyond that, here are two rules of thumb to consider:

- The AOA and the Management and Business Academy say that the median staff payroll cost in optometric practice is about 19%. That is actually too low for my model of a highly delegated practice with excellent customer service. I would try to hold at 22% to 24%. This expense category does not include any ODs or lab technicians. It includes all costs of employment including payroll taxes, uniforms, etc.

- The collected gross revenue per full time staff member should be about $135,000. If your practice grosses $600,000 per year, you should have about 4.5 employees. If you gross a larger number per staff person, it either means that you are very good at sales or you are understaffed.

6.9 Four Strong Reasons Why You Should Hire Another Employee

In my consulting work with optometrists, one of the most frequent ways I've been able to help is by identifying the need for an additional staff member. I actually find most optometric practices are understaffed. Most OD/practice owners resist hiring more employees because a) they are concerned about increasing their payroll cost and b) they dislike the management challenges that are brought on by a larger staff. I teach my clients that the first concern is usually without merit (see reason #1 below) and the second concern is holding back their practice growth.

Let's look at the four major benefits you could realize if you hire one more staff member.

1. Productivity will increase

Hiring another employee often increases production by any metric you care to use: gross revenue per day, number of exams per day, average sale per exam, collection of fees, etc. Having more staff allows everyone, including the doctor, to function at a higher level and to spend more time with patients. Not feeling rushed allows opticians to explain a lens feature better or to bring up the benefits of a second pair of glasses. Doctors who have enough staff support might recommend a new patient try on a pair of bifocal contact lenses. A receptionist who has time can check the exam history of a patient's family members and recommend scheduling appointments. There are many ways productivity increases with more staff.

The increased production is also the reason why a new employee will not reduce the practice net or drive up the payroll cost. Gross revenue typically increases more than the cost of the new employee. Usually much, much more.

2. Customer service will improve

This one is pretty obvious when you think about it. An extra staff member will allow everyone to spend a bit more time with patients, greet them a little quicker, explain things slightly better and stay on time for appointments more often. Do I need to mention how important customer service is for practice building? Do you want to get more five star reviews on Google? In this way, an extra staff member can actually increase patient demand because there will be more word of mouth referral. Word of mouth is the biggest source of new patients in private practices.

3. You will delegate more

Delegation is one of the best strategies there is for increasing practice revenue and profit, yet it is widely underutilized by ODs. You would delegate more if you had someone to delegate to! You could provide high quality clinical care with less doctor time. Start by challenging your clinical routine by asking what you could delegate. Eventually, you could increase the number of appointments you offer and the number of patients you see per day, without working any harder. You can see more patients per day with no added stress if you have enough good technicians to assist you.

4. Current staff members will perform better

Bringing in a new employee often improves the behavior and performance of existing staff members. This occurs because of one of two reasons (or both): the current staff member a) feels a bit of competition and tries harder or b) feels less stress on the job because there is someone to share the workload. Current employees often develop a better attitude, try harder, become more punctual and try to learn new skills.

If current employees do not perform better, having the larger staff will make it much easier to discipline, retrain and possibly even dismiss problem individuals.

Next week I'll present some ideas on how to evaluate your practice to see if you need more staff members and how to go about recruiting them.

6.10 How to Tell If You Need More Staff

Last week, I wrote about the practice-building power of adding staff members. This week, let's look at the issue of deciding when your practice is ready for an additional employee and how to find the right one.

Observe the practice for two weeks

We can talk about rules of thumb and practice metrics, but the best way to determine if you need another staff member is to observe your practice in action. All practices have random ups and downs in patient flow and it is important to analyze staffing over a long enough period for that to even out.

It's OK if staff members are extremely busy for a while, as long as the activity settles down to a normal pace so staff have time to complete the administrative aspects of the job. Mistakes happen too often when people are rushed and stressed. It's also OK for staff to have some time to socialize with co-workers on the job, as long as it is not excessive. Where that work demand line should fall is a judgment call that the practice owner and manager have to make. I would think about the overall vision of the practice as that judgment is made. If your practice is designed on the basis of excellent customer service, I would move the line to having more staff available even if you have to raise your fees. If the goal of the practice is basic eye care at low prices, I would favor fewer employees.

I often hear doctors and managers say they would not need an additional employee if the current staff would just not call off so much. But the fact is that staff members do call off and that is the norm that must be factored in. Not every day will be staffed perfectly, but most days should be.

Other changes that call for more staff

In addition to adding staff to keep up with growth, you might want to make a change to your usual practice model. Some of these changes may require another employee. There is some normal business risk when you make a proactive change, but the risk is extremely small and there is great upside potential. Change stimulates growth. Here are some examples of strategies that require more staff, but also produce much more revenue.

- You have a plan to delegate more. This is always a good move. Even if you don't have a lot of patient demand, I would try to compress the patients you have now into fewer days so you can use the other days to build the practice.
- You want to expand your marketing reach. The doctor and manager may intend to do more but never get around to it. You could hire a new front desk staff person and assign the side job of Director of Marketing. She owns this new role and spends dedicated time on community outreach, social media, email marketing and more.
- You are hiring a new doctor. This is a wonderful step that greatly increases patient volume and revenue. This additional technician will pay for herself immediately.

- You have a staff member who you want to dismiss. Never a pleasant task, but if you have tried to rehabilitate a problem staff member with no success and are ready to part ways, consider hiring a replacement employee first. Let the new person get onboard, fully trained and proven to be a keeper, and then you can let the other one go. You will have a larger payroll for a few weeks, but you will avoid a difficult period of being understaffed.

How to find candidates

Craig's List has become the standard for employment ads. It is an excellent resource, along with other online services that specialize in employment. There are also some optical industry employment websites. The cost is low and these services really work, so be sure to list your job opening there. If you don't get a good response with these web-based services, place an ad in your local newspaper. While this is more expensive, many people still look in the paper when they are seeking job opportunities and the newspaper will run your ad in an online and print version.

One other good way to find the right person is to be on the lookout when you are dining out or shopping in retail stores. If you work with someone who takes very good care of you and obviously "gets it", give him or her your business card and say you are always looking for employees who provide great service like this and ask the person to call if she wants to make a career change. Of course, you will have to train this person to have optical skills, but finding the right person is more important than the skills.

I like to give the name of my practice and address in the employment ad and ask people to apply in person during normal business hours. We can tell a lot by just looking at the candidate and having them complete our own employment application. My office manager calls the ones who look good to come in for an interview. After that process is completed, I meet with the manager to review the best candidates. I may do a second interview myself, or just formulate a wage and job offer. The manager calls the applicant back and makes the offer.

6.11 Staff Bonus Programs: Mixed Reviews

If you ask optometrists if staff incentive programs work, you'll get a mixed response. There is a large segment who are strong believers in some kind of bonus program and they typically point to their own success in their practice.

But you'll also find a large segment who say they have tried bonusing staff and it became an entitlement program and really did not change behavior.

Many ODs who know me think I don't believe in bonus programs, and that is not quite true. I have tried and continue to test many different programs in my practice, from straight commission to goals with a bonus pool to spiffs for selling products. I would love to offer bonus programs if I was sure there was a cause and effect relationship between the reward the goal. In reality, there are many variables in play that can cause a specific result. I think I see why we don't have universal agreement on the effectiveness of staff incentive programs. Sometimes they work and sometimes they don't.

In this article, I'll look deeper at staff bonus programs and help you decide what to do about them in your practice.

Test the effectiveness

If you are starting a new bonus program or already have one in place, I recommend that you analyze it to see if it is doing what you want. Based on the scientific training we all had, I'm surprised we don't seem to apply those principles to business topics. We should.

- If you start a bonus program in June and practice revenue increases, can you conclude the bonus was a success? No. It depends on what else is going on.
- An initial successful experience can lead us to believe that the bonus is working, but something else may have caused the good results.
- Business cycles. May is often a slow month for ODs due to school summer vacation beginning and family schedules are up in the air. Business may return in June and go way up in July and August.
- Compare to what? Most businesses compare sales figures to the same period (month or quarter) as last year. Assuming you have that data and assuming revenue increased this year over last, does that mean the bonus is working? No. Maybe you took a vacation last year and had fewer doctor days. Perhaps you signed up for a new vision plan in the past year and you now see more patients per day. What if you raised your fees in the past year? Maybe the economy is better. Maybe the local population is increasing. Maybe a local OD retired. Did you change the patient flow and volume per day? Did you start offering a new service or product line? Management decisions may drive business much more than staff.
- What about Pearson's Law: "That which is measured improves. That which is measured and reported improves exponentially." Starting

or changing a bonus program signals to staff that the doctor and manager are paying close attention to this task. There is some form of measurement of data and it will be reported. It seems logical that the attention alone will cause an improved outcome.

Good data

In order to control all the variables, you need a lot of high quality data about your practice. This will help you make many smart decisions about the business side of your practice. Work with your practice management software system and consider getting special software to help you collect and analyze the data. Here are some good data points:

- How many exams were performed?
- How many pairs of glasses and pairs of contact lenses were sold?
- What was the collected gross revenue?
- What is the Rx retention rate?
- What is the appointment schedule fill rate?
- What is the no show rate?
- What is the multiple pair sale rate?

Start by thinking about your practice

As you evaluate bonus programs for your practice, think about the following points:

- What motivates your staff? In my experience, some staff members are motivated by money, but the majority are not. Financial rewards may have a very minimal effect on employees who are not that interested in money. For them, just telling them that selling multiple pairs of glasses is important because it will enrich the patient's lifestyle could work just as well.
- What are the goals of a bonus program? Do you want to attract more patients? Do you want to sell more products to existing patients? Do you want to reduce costs? You could say all of the above, but if you are specific, the next point becomes clearer.
- Does your staff have direct control over factors that influence the goals of the program? If part of the bonus goes to saving cost, but the staff is not involved in selecting the suppliers or checking prices, then they have little control over that. If the goal is to see more patients, but staff does not make decisions about marketing projects or vision plan participation, they can't influence it.

- Bonuses work best when the employee has direct control, so if the whole office is rewarded when a revenue goal is met, each individual will feel less direct control. The reward depends on the others doing their part. These "group shares equally" programs are very popular, but I call them "feel good" bonuses because I think the staff and the doctor feel good about them, but they do very little. They don't do any harm either; these bonuses just become part of the general compensation.
- Is what you are bonusing really part of the basic job – something staff should do anyway? I hate to pay extra for what should happen anyway.

Bonus programs instead of management?
I think busy doctors who can't spend much time on staff management may jump quickly to a bonus program with the hope that it will solve their problems. They may have staff members who don't have the right priorities and don't follow procedures. Paying more money to incentivize them to focus on specific tasks may not work. The alternative is to have a manager supervise the staff and direct them to do the tasks properly and in the right priority.

6.12 Feel-Good Staff Bonus Programs: Do They Work?

I'm always interested in the topic of staff incentive programs. I'm highly skeptical about the effectiveness of these programs, but I'm always hopeful to discover just the right formula that will motivate staff without creating any ill will and dramatically increase sales and profits (or whatever I choose to measure and reward). I experiment with bonus programs in my practice and I study the theory behind employee motivation.

Staff bonus programs are extremely popular in optometric practice and the majority of them are what I call feel-good programs. These programs typically involve setting a goal, such as gross or net practice revenue, generally based on the same time period from the previous year plus some growth amount. If the goal is reached, a monetary reward is paid to all staff members. These programs are popular because they make logical sense at first glance and because optometrists would love to find a fast-track to managing and training employees.

This type of program reduces the risk of upsetting anyone because it uses a total revenue goal rather than individual sales results and because it rewards all employees rather than just those who do the selling. Those same factors, however, make these programs much less effective at achieving the desired performance. In many cases, these programs simply become an entitlement for staff members and they don't really change behavior at all.

Read on to find out why feel-good staff bonus programs don't really work very well.

Degree of correlation

For an incentive to work well there must be a high degree of correlation between the measured outcome and the reward. Using total optical sales or total practice revenue dilutes the incentive for an employee because those metrics correlate very weakly with an individual's sales effort. One person has relatively little control over whole practice revenue. On the other hand, if my pay is based on my own sales receipts, that is something I can control to a great degree. Of course, tracking individual sales may lead to some office conflicts, but if the goal is to increase sales, greater correlation works.

Optometrists often like to include the entire staff in one bonus system, with the argument that everyone is part of the team and the receptionist must schedule appointments in order for the optician to sell eyewear. I get the theory, but the reality is that the receptionist does not directly cause the sale; her involvement is very indirect. It is quite likely that if some staff members try very hard to increase sales and are very good at it, they may resent the weak contribution by some others who still receive the reward. It may be better to set up a different program for front desk staff centered on a different objective, such as recall success.

Group Dynamics

Ironically, setting up a group bonus program with the hope of keeping all staff members happy can do just the opposite. If the reward is based on a total revenue goal that means employee Mary's compensation is partially based on employee John's effort. Clearly, she has an incentive to watch what he is doing and vice versa. The result of that dynamic will depend on the personalities involved, but my experience is that one staff member telling another what to do causes hard feelings.

If Mary can't actually see and judge John's efforts, John has an incentive to "free ride" on Mary's efforts. Worse, Mary may sense that John is free riding, which will not create the sense of teamwork we are going for. If extra effort is costly to John (and it must be if this sort of incentive scheme makes any sense at all), then John would rather do less of it. If John's compensation is based on total optical sales or total practice revenue, he has a good chance of maintaining constant pay with little effort.

How much money is at stake?

The reason that most of these bonus programs don't usually cause morale problems is that the money at stake is too low to worry about. But that point is another reason why these plans are not that effective! A typical bonus amount is about $100 per employee per month. This may actually be measured and paid on a quarterly basis, which I believe is much better than monthly because it evens out noise the employee can't control and therefore it increases correlation.

If the amount of money at stake is $100 per month and a full time employee works about 160 hours that amounts to about 62 cents per hour. If this staff member is paid a wage of $16 per hour, the bonus is less than 4% of the compensation. If the effort-to-bonus correlation is low, the reward is too small to worry about, especially if the chances are good that the practice will make the goal anyway.

It is very likely that feel-good bonus programs do very little harm or good, but they perpetuate because the practice grows due to other variables that are not even measured.

Final thoughts

Employee motivation strategies are complex and it may be better to just hire good people, pay well, recognize good performance with praise and raises, and train them continuously to do a better job. Having an active manager in a supervisory role helps maintain excellent staff performance.

I've been trying a new bonus program in my practice that pays an individual spiff of $10 for each pair of digital free-form progressive lenses sold. The correlation of effort to reward is obviously extremely high! Sales in that category have tripled compared to the same period last year. I have not seen any problems with staff morale; they are excited about the opportunity!

Next week, I'll talk about how to get rid of a bonus program that is not working.

6.13 Getting Rid of Bonus Programs That Don't Work

The last article presented several reasons why bonus programs may not work as well as we might have hoped. In many cases, there is not much correlation between the work required and the reward. In other cases, the incentive is taken for granted and old behaviors creep back into place. Some bonus programs cause staff to be competitive or to resent the success of others. Whatever the reason, if the practice owner simply takes a bonus away, staff morale will likely suffer.

Don't reduce benefits

The most important thing about ending a bonus program that has been in place for a long time is to give back something of at least similar value. Once employees become accustomed to a benefit, whether it's financial, a preferred schedule or other perceived perks, they do not like to lose it. Fortunately, it is not that difficult or costly to find something you can offer instead.

Several years ago, I wanted to drop all bonuses and incentives and just return to paying good wages for a job well done. Before announcing that we were dropping the bonus program, I calculated the average bonus payment per month received by each employee over the past six months. I converted that dollar amount to a per hour figure for each employee. It was different for each staff member but it amounted to roughly 50 cents per hour. I told the staff that we were dropping the program because I did not believe it was working well, but that each person would receive an hourly wage increase determined by the average amount of their bonus history.

This change was well received and staff morale was fine. It seemed quite fair to my staff; maybe even generous because they would earn the same amount without the risk of not making the bonus. When you think about it, however, the change really did not increase my cost. I still paid on average the same payroll I was already paying.

If you want to change the bonus program, rather than drop it, you can simply try to make the new program have the same potential for rewards as the old one.

Keeping the program fresh

You may want to make your bonus programs have a preset expiration date so it is understood by all. I find quarters of the year to be a good time interval because it evens out random business cycles and it results in a larger check that monthly periods. This approach is actually better because it allows you to promote different metrics, services and products each quarter, which stimulates new behavior and interest.

Update on my spiff program
Many readers emailed me to ask if the $10 spiff program I implemented this quarter for selling a pair of digital progressive lenses is paid to the individual staff members or if it is accumulated and distributed to all. It is individual; those who sell more earn more. I'm trying to see if a high degree of correlation between the work and the reward pays off and in my experience it makes a big difference. We do not have a program going on right now for the front desk staff, although we have had some in the past. It has not caused any hard feelings. Sometimes you just can't tell until you try it.

6.14 Your Office Policy Manual

Don't you love it when an employee stops you in the hall and asks you if she can leave at 2pm to attend a personal event? Or how about the industrious staff member who mentions that he is going to come in extra early in the next few days to get caught up on some work? The experienced manager or owner knows that the response to these seemingly innocent questions can have far reaching effects. There is often a domino effect where one thing causes something else or there may be a delayed reaction where a secondary problem isn't noticed until much later.

Fairness
There is no easy answer for staff issues. A good manager will consider many factors and will think of the problems that may be created, possibly bringing them to the employee's attention. If you aren't sure of the consequences, a delayed answer may be the smartest way to go, such as "let me think about that and get back to you". When I consider an employee issue, I use a two step guide: I look to our office policy on the matter and I always ask myself if my response will be fair to the other employees.

Fairness is one of the most important characteristics employees look for in an employer and believe me, they're looking. Part of the challenge in managing a staff is simply knowing the policies that have been set up in the past. Having office policies in writing is a big advantage because there is no doubt about what the rules are and 90% of the fairness test is met if the employee knows a policy in advance.

Writing your manual

A few of my recent tip articles have focused on some items that are typically covered in an office manual, and I've been encouraging practice owners to begin to write a manual or revisit the existing one. It occurred to me, however, that we should step back and get an overview of the topics you might want to include in a policy manual. Listed below is a table of contents of topics that I think should be in the manual. Read the list and see if you have a policy or statement for all these items. I'll write more about many of these topics in tips to come, but email me if there is an area that you are struggling with and I'll try to address it.

I like to think there are two different kinds of employment manuals. There is a policy manual, which I'm addressing here and there is a procedure manual, which covers how to perform actual tasks in the office. Both are very important and beneficial. A policy manual would describe how an employee requests a vacation while the procedure manual would describe how an employee performs keratometry on a patient. We'll also cover writing procedure manuals in a future tip.

Can it have too much detail?

While it's important to give details about the rules of the office, too much detail can cause problems. You will generally have to follow the rules of the manual. That may seem fine, since that's the point in the first place, but remember that one set of rules does not always fit every situation. You may not think of something when you devise a policy and if it's very specific you may lose any flexibility. For example, if you list the steps that are supposed to occur if an employee is disciplined or discharged, you may be bound to follow those steps. If you give a job description that is very detailed, it may be difficult to ask and employee to do something not listed. An office manual could be treated as an employment contract by a court of law or by a state department of employment.

Topics to include

Here are some topics that should be covered in your office manual.

1. General Philosophy of the Office
2. Vision Statement
3. Our Practice Motto
4. History of the Practice
5. Practice Ownership
6. Employee Benefits
7. Health Insurance
8. Uniforms and Personal Appearance
9. Continuing Education and Travel

10. Eye Care Benefits
11. Financial incentives from suppliers
12. Work Schedule
13. Paychecks
14. Vacation Days
15. Personal Days (Sick Days)
16. Personal Time Off
17. Overtime
18. Complaints by Patients
19. Employee Parking
20. Confidential Patient Information
21. Confidential Proprietary information
22. Alcohol and Drug Use
23. Personal Telephone Calls and Internet use
24. Chewing Gum
25. Smoking
26. Maternity Leave
27. Jury Duty
28. Lunch Period
29. Probationary Period
30. Employment at will
31. Resignation or discharge

6.15 Employee Benefits

My reader email tells me that there is a need for more articles on staff management, so I'll keep them coming. I've had several requests for more information on employment benefits and I'll cover that in this tip article.

An excellent benefit package

I think it's extremely important to offer great employment benefits to full time staff in your practice. I realize that payroll costs are already very high for most practices and in this economy, everyone is looking to reduce expenses, but we have to look at the big picture. You can't build a great practice without an excellent staff and you can't recruit and retain an excellent staff without very good compensation.

We use the term total compensation or compensation package to refer to all expenses that go to an employee. It includes salary plus the value of all fringe benefits, such as health insurance, paid vacation, uniforms (if provided) and every other item paid for by the practice on behalf of employees.

Your practice is an employer and it must compete with all other employers for employees. If we look at the landscape of employers, the excellent ones provide good wages and good benefits. It is the norm. No one who is smart and ambitious wants to work for a company that doesn't provide good benefits. They won't think of that job as long term. People who want to make their job a career look for companies that provide benefits. Benefits are even more important for employees who earn less than $50,000 per year because they can ill afford to pay for extras.

New practices may have to wait to expand their benefit package to include the more expensive items like health insurance, but it's smart to set it as a goal. Established practitioners who want to grow their practice should find a way to budget for an excellent benefit package. So what is an excellent benefit package? It's subjective, but people tend to know it when they see it. I'll provide some food for thought.

Health insurance

When we speak of employment benefits, the biggest component is health insurance. To some, it's synonymous. This benefit is highly valued by the general public and all practices should strive to provide it. It's tempting to presume that your employees don't need health insurance because they have a spouse who provides it, but health insurance is rarely free for dependents. In fact it is usually very expensive.

Health insurance is a complex enough topic that I'll cover it in a separate article.

Typical benefits

Here is a list of some of the usual employment benefits that are provided by eye care practices. I'll cover most of these in more detail in the next tip, including citing some specific examples on how to structure each one. Of course, opinions on what benefits to offer will vary. This list is not exhaustive, nor is it necessary to provide all of them. Review the list and make a note of what your practice offers and which ones you would like to offer.

- Health insurance
- Paid time off (personal days / sick days)
- Paid vacation
- Paid holidays
- Eye care benefits
- Uniforms
- Continuing education

- Retirement fund
- Dental insurance
- Life insurance
- Disability insurance

A description of each benefit should be included in your office policy manual. Employment policies must be provided fairly and equally to all employees and we just can't rely on memory. It is certainly possible to offer different benefits to different groups of employees. This allows the employer to make changes without taking away benefits from existing employees.
Additional payments are made on behalf of employees for matching of social security withholdings and workers compensation insurance, but since those items are mandated by law they are not usually considered a benefit. But they are part of the total compensation package.

Annual compensation summary
I don't think employees truly know the dollar value of all their benefits, so I furnish each of them with a private summary sheet that details all amounts paid on their behalf each year. It includes all wages, but also itemizes all the other benefits and lists the dollar amounts paid. A grand total is provided, which is quite a bit more impressive than the IRS W-2 form or the annual salary figure alone. Employees generally don't react much to this statement of value, but I think it makes a subtle impression that their employer pays for many items besides wages.

6.16 Employee Benefits Part 2: Health Insurance

I made a case last week that the average eye care practice would do well to improve the employment benefits offered to staff. Of the typical benefits provided by most employers, health insurance is the biggest challenge because it is very expensive and the cost has generally increased dramatically over recent years. Even with the high cost, I'm convinced that eye care practices are better off providing a health insurance benefit because it greatly improves your ability to attract and retain excellent employees.

A complete overview of health insurance is not possible in a brief article like this, but I will provide some practical insights to get you started in your own analysis.

Hard to shop

Shopping for health insurance is very time consuming because there are many complex options and it is difficult to find the information you need. Find a good local insurance agent to work with, but even then it will prove frustrating. One of the basic factors we all need when we shop is the price – but that is elusive until you can provide an employee census with names and ages, and a price quote is not really accurate until the insurance underwriter obtains actual applications from the employees. You will want to obtain quotes from a few insurance companies.

In my experience, some health insurance plans will provide a reasonable bid for the first year but when it comes time for renewal, the premiums may jump significantly; often 25% or more. That may be part of the marketing strategy or it may be based on actual claims experience with your employees.

You may want to poll your employees about their interest in health insurance and at what cost, and also benefit features, including the importance of drug plans, deductibles, co-payments and choice of physician.

There are many choices to explore, including PPOs, HMOs and health savings accounts (HSAs). In addition to working with a trusted insurance agent, I also recommend discussing the options with a CPA. CPAs work with many small business owners, know the norms, and know how to assist with the payroll deductions that you will put in place. They are often small business owners themselves and have navigated the waters for their firm. They may even recommend a specific insurance plan.

What to offer

There are unlimited options for how much of the health insurance cost your practice should cover. Some practices offer a flat dollar amount and then let the employees shop for individual insurance on their own. Some provide 100% of the premium. Some practices pay for 50% of the premium and withhold the rest of the from the employee's paycheck. There is no right or wrong, but the employee will judge the value of the benefit when they see the actual personal cost and they make comparisons with what other employers do.

There really is no official standard for small business in regard to health benefits, and it is changing rapidly as health insurance costs skyrocket and as businesses struggle in the current recession. Keep in mind it is very difficult to ever cut employment benefits, so design your policy to protect your business.

It should be noted that payroll withholdings for health insurance are made before tax withholdings, so the benefit is not taxed.

I certainly made some mistakes over the years with the health plan for my employees, but here are a few points to consider.

- I only provide a benefit for the employee. Dependents like spouse and children may be included in our company health plan, but the employee is charged for 100% of that portion of the premium.
- It is very important that the employee pay some portion of his or her own premium. In the old days, an employer might pay 100% of the premium cost, but that makes it very difficult to ever shop for a new plan or to reduce benefits to cut costs. If the employee has some stake in the cost, they are happy to look at more economical alternatives. Having the employee pay a portion of the premium prevents those who can obtain insurance through a spouse from joining your plan needlessly.
- I believe the employer should pick up the majority of the cost, but the employee should have a significant stake. I prefer percentages to dollar amounts because dollars change too rapidly and can quickly become out of date. I settled on the practice paying for 80% of the premium for the employee.
- I offer a PPO plan because it includes the vast majority of doctors in my area and freedom of choice is extremely important to people.
- I moved to a high deductible ($2,000 per individual) to keep premiums lower.
- I include basic drug insurance coverage because the cost of prescription drugs is prohibitively expensive for many people without it.
- I don't offer dental insurance or vision plans in an effort to keep costs down.

6.17 Employee Benefits: Paid Time Off

This tip article will focus on employment benefits such as personal days, vacation and holidays. Of course, there are many creative ideas and there is no one right way to set employment policy. Some practices don't like the term sick days and just call them personal days. Some add vacation time into the mix. Some practice owners offer more paid time off based on seniority or number of hours worked and some offer bonuses if sick days are not used. Some practices allow personal days to accumulate, while others require that they be used each year and some simply pay for unused days at the end of the year.

It's all really a judgment call. Generous benefits can help foster a good relationship with employees, but they also increase costs. To some extent, it is important to consider what other employers do because your practice will be compared to them. There is really no exact standard, but it is smart to be within the typical range.

Perhaps more important than the specific rules of each benefit is that the rules are known by employees when they are first hired and the rules are applied uniformly and fairly. The descriptions of your benefits should become part of your office manual. Avoid changing the rules randomly as you go along.

Should you change?

Once you begin with a benefit or a policy, it can be difficult to change. I don't recommend taking away or reducing benefits unless you compensate by giving something new, such as additional benefits or pay. Another effective way to change your employment policies is to create a "grandfather clause" for existing employees, and make the new policy effective for all new employees. This allows the practice to adopt more efficient or cost effective rules for the future without changing senior staff who did not agree to the new terms when they were hired. This works well for employment benefits and for other points of contention, such as working evenings and Saturdays.

What is full time?

Generally, employment benefits are only provided for full time employees. I like to have an exact definition of what "full time" means. For example, our office manual reads: Full-time employment is defined as a minimum schedule of 32 hours per week (lunches excluded & Saturdays averaged). We use the scheduled hours as our guide, which is determined by management, not the actual hours worked.

Personal days and sick days

The typical small business will allow five or six personal and/or sick days per year for full time employees. Usually these days off are with pay, but they don't have to be. My practice allows five personal days off, but they are without pay. Vacation days may be used for days off with pay.

A big problem can occur if an employee calls in sick after his or her sick days are used for the year. Even though the time off is without pay, excessive call-offs place a large burden on the other staff members and morale suffers because it feels unfair. On the other hand, we want to be compassionate toward the employee who has a serious illness or has a string of legitimate health problems. We handle this by requiring a written doctor's excuse for every absence after the sick days and vacation days are used. Vacation days are not required to be used for illness but may be used if the employee wishes. Without the written medical excuse, employment is terminated.

My practice encourages trading days with other employees as a way to allow time off without impacting the practice.

Vacation policy

Here are the basic rules for vacation in my practice.

- Two weeks of paid vacation is provided after one year of full time employment and three weeks of vacation after five years. One week is defined as five work days.
- Vacations are compensated on the basis of 40 hours of pay per week. One day off shall equal eight hours of vacation pay, one Saturday off shall equal eight hours. Only four Saturdays per year can be requested as vacation pay.
- Only one person may be approved for vacation from a department at the same time. Our departments are business office, patient care, optical dispensing and optical lab.
- Employees are asked to submit requests for vacation between January 1st and 15th. During this time, vacation requests are granted on a seniority basis. If two employees request the same time off, it will be granted to the employee with the most seniority. After January 15th, vacation time will be granted on a first come first serve basis.
- Vacation days cannot accrue into the next year. If an employee does not use vacation days, they are compensated as extra pay.
- Part time employees may take vacation time without pay based on the prorated percentage of their normal work schedule.

Paid holidays

Six paid holidays are provided in my practice: New Year's Day, Memorial Day, 4th of July, Labor Day, Thanksgiving, and Christmas. The extra holiday pay is provided even if it falls on a Sunday or on an employee's day off.

Management makes decisions to close the office for additional days or half days surrounding these holidays based on the calendar. For example, if Christmas were to fall on a Friday in a given year, we would close the office on the day after Christmas (Saturday) to give everyone a long holiday weekend. If the office closes for additional days, that time off is without pay. Based on experience, I have found that our staff is generally happy to have the additional time off even without pay, but I am also sensitive to the need for continuing income and to our patients wanting the office to be open.

6.18 What to Do About Holiday Pay

The best time to think about your office policy for holidays is when there is not a holiday looming in the near future. That makes this a good time to review and improve your policy.

Do you ever wonder how to handle the pay of an employee who has a scheduled day off on a holiday? What if a holiday falls on a Sunday? Do you struggle with what to do for part time vs. full time? What about hourly vs. salaried? Like many employment policies, there is no one right way to manage holidays in your practice, but in this article, I'll share what I do in my practice and give you some help to decide what will work for yours.

At least have a policy

Many optometric practices don't have written office policies, but that just makes you have to reinvent what to do over and over. And it leads to hard feelings by some employees who may have envisioned things differently. Once you have a policy and get past any objections, all becomes easy and fair. So just write down what you decide and you will have the start of an employee manual, which can be revised over time.

The two main factors to consider are which holidays the office will always be closed and how employees will be paid for those days. You can still make special decisions for additional days off depending on the day of the week and other factors.

Which holidays?

Before deciding on which holidays, you may wonder if you should have any paid holidays as an employment benefit. It is very standard practice for full time employees, so I think it is a good idea. It is expected by the workforce and it helps you attract and retain good employees. The typical holidays most companies pay for in the United States are: New Year's Day, Memorial Day, Independence Day, Labor Day, Thanksgiving and Christmas Day. Of course, this is up to the business owner and you can choose whatever days you wish. Some progressive companies are trying to increase employment benefits and adding Christmas Eve and the day after Thanksgiving. Some may be closed for Jewish holidays.

How will you pay?

There are many ways to go, but I'll describe the method that works best in my practice. It is different for hourly employees vs. salaried. Most of our employees are paid hourly so let's talk about that first. By the way, you should decide on your definition of full time for hourly staff and put that in your office manual. What is the minimum number of hours per week a person must be scheduled to work to be considered full time? Many businesses use 32 hours of scheduled time, but some government programs are moving toward 30. Businesses can generally still decide when it comes to issues like holiday pay and other employment perks. Of course, you can still schedule most employees at 40 hours if you wish, but it is good to have your definition for special situations.

Hourly employees in my practice are simply paid extra for each holiday during the pay period it falls in. This eliminates any discussion about if the holiday is on an employee's usual day off or if it falls on a Sunday when the office is usually closed. It doesn't matter. The employee gets paid for the hours they clock in for plus the extra holiday pay. If the holiday falls on the day off and employees get paid more than their usual amount for a pay period that is fine with me.

Salaried employees get their usual salary every pay period, regardless of holidays. They get holidays off.

Special days off

As a small business owner, you can make special decisions about days to be closed on an ongoing basis. I recommend looking well ahead at the calendar and what days of the week holidays fall on. Then use your judgment if you (and your staff) want additional days off or not. For example, Christmas is on a Sunday this year. You might decide to be closed on Saturday (Christmas Eve) to give everyone a nice holiday weekend. You could even extend it into Monday.

Here are some important factors to consider:

- What is the policy for paying employees for these optional additional days off? No right or wrong here, but have a policy. In my practice, hourly employees are only paid for hours worked, so there is no additional pay for special days when we are closed. Salaried employees receive their usual salary.

- Based on the point above, I try to balance the general enjoyment of extra days off work with the need for employees to earn a full paycheck. If you don't close the office too many additional days and if you listen to employee feedback, you can strike the right balance.
- Keep patient convenience in mind. I realize that one's own personal and family life matters the most, but if you are trying to build a practice, patients' needs matter a lot as well. The ideal situation is to work toward having other optometrists in the practice so the owner can take personal time off without closing the office.
- Revenue and profit are reduced when the office is closed.
- Always use extra care when changing your office policies, even if they were not in writing. It is generally not a good idea to take anything away from employees without giving them something of equal or greater value at the same time. Setting a grandfather clause often works well to allow existing employees to continue with a policy, while changing it for the future.

6.19 Staff Lunch Policies

A recent tip article focused on office policies and I recommended that all practice owners write an office manual. Even doctors who already have a policy manual generally find that it is an evolving document that undergoes occasional revisions. In this tip and in more to come, I'll cover some of the topics that we all wrestle with as we try to decide on the details of employment policies. There is really not a right or wrong way to do these things, but I'll share what I do and give you some food for thought.

Patient service first

The motto in my practice is "We look at everything we do from the patient's point of view." That overriding philosophy is what builds success over time. I've seen many practices where the policies are primarily decided with the wants and needs of the doctor or staff in mind. As much as possible, I believe we should base the policies on the wants and needs of patients.

Because of this approach, I believe in keeping the office open during the lunch hour. While it is certainly nice for the staff and doctor to just close up shop, I don't like patients to find the office door locked or to have phone calls routed to voice mail. Remember that lunch time is the only opportunity many people have during the day to take care of personal errands, like scheduling appointments or picking up glasses or contact lenses.

Policies for small and large practices

How you manage to keep the office open depends on the size of practice. Many small practices simply do not schedule any appointments during the lunch period, but they require employee(s) to eat lunch in the office and take care of any drop-ins and phone calls. Many employees like this arrangement because they are paid for the lunch period and in smaller practices, there is not much lunch time activity anyway. I would probably make the lunch period one hour long in this case, to allow employees to have enough time for a nice break even with interruptions. Of course, food should be eaten in a break room, back office or lab, rather than the front desk.

Keep in mind that lunch breaks are not always started precisely on time if the morning patients take longer than expected. Since we need the afternoon appointments to start on time, we must allow for that by making the lunch period long enough or placing a block-out before lunch.

As the practice grows and there are more employees, I like to hold lunches in two shifts, with half the staff working the first shift and the other half working the second shift. Again, management would designate a period of time when no appointments are scheduled. I use one hour and thirty minutes in my office, so each lunch shift is 45 minutes long. This allows me plenty of time in the middle of the day to finish the morning patients, catch up on management issues, return phone calls and enjoy a relaxed lunch. Employees punch out on a computer time clock software program when they go to lunch and they punch back in when they return to work. In this scenario, staff members may go out to lunch or eat in the office. Our office manager supervises who is assigned to first or second lunch so we maintain good office coverage, but we try to honor requests when possible.

A few more points

- We start the lunch period at noon on days that we close the office at 5pm, but we start lunches at 1pm on days that we are open until 7pm.
- Our office manual states that employees must start work as soon as they punch in, so any personal tasks such as touchups of hair or make-up should be done prior to that.
- We do not have any scheduled breaks other than lunches.

- If an employee is due to start lunch but is busy with a patient, we may assign another employee to interrupt and take over in order to maintain our schedule.
- My office has a staff lounge with refrigerator, microwave, sink, and soft drink and snack machines for people who choose to bring their lunch. Cable television in this room has proven quite popular.

6.20 Employee Benefits: Eye Care Services and Products

Continuing with our series on employment benefits, let's look at eye care services for staff members. Obviously, since you provide eye care, you can provide a nice employment benefit to your staff at no direct cost. But it's best to define the policy clearly in writing so all staff understand and do not take advantage of the practice.

Most eye care practitioners provide professional services at no charge to the employee and possibly for immediate family members. Optical materials are often provided at the actual lab cost, although some practices provide a pair of glasses or supply of contact lenses completely free, and some may simply provide a discount off the usual price of materials rather than bother with tracking the actual lab cost.

The exact policy is up to you, of course, but I would design a benefit that employees feel is generous. Free eye care is a strong perk that comes with working for an eye doctor!

Fine tuning your policy

Here are some concerns to watch for:

- Is there a limit to how many pairs of glasses or contacts that an employee can purchase per year at cost? Personally, I see no reason to have a limit as long as they are truly for the employee.
- Can an employee purchase items at cost and give them away as gifts? Is there a limit on that?
- Are family members allowed to purchase products at cost or at a discount and if so, how do you define family? Does it include parents? Step-parents? Half-brothers? Live-in partners who are not married? Does it matter if the employee lives with her parents or lives on her own? Children? Stepchildren? Husband's children living elsewhere? How you define the benefit may hurt someone's

feelings, but not defining it in advance can take unfair advantage of the practice and having to reduce the benefit is more difficult.

- Can employees accept complimentary eyeglasses or contact lenses from a lab, even if the lab will not provide that for all employees? Should the practice track usage of complimentary products?
- Should employees report their usage of eye care services and products to management and if so, how?
- How is the product cost paid by the employee? What system is in place to ensure charges are entered? Can the staff be allowed credit? What if they are slow to pay the balance?

A sample policy

Upon completion of a 30 day waiting period, eye care services will be provided to employees and their immediate families at no cost. Optical materials will be provided at our office's wholesale cost or complimentary when available from the manufacturers. Family members who qualify for this benefit are spouses and children under the age of 23. An employee's mother, father, brothers, sisters, and children over the age of 23 shall receive a 25% discount off of normal professional and material fees (contact lenses are excluded from this program and are not discounted).

Whenever an employee or family member receives eye care benefits at no charge or at cost, or at a 25% discount, a cost authorization form must be requested from the office manager. This form should be completed and approved by the manager prior to examination purchase or start of a lab order. The cost authorization form shall then be returned to the office manager's desk the same day that services are rendered.

All materials must be paid in full at the time of dispensing.

If any materials are to be received complimentary (or at special discounts) from a supplier, they must be ordered specifically for the employee and not taken from stock. The supplier must be willing to extend the same courtesy to all employees, or the materials cannot be accepted.

An important side point

Labs and suppliers who are willing to give free products to our staff are much appreciated, but it prompts me to mention the potential problem of key employees accepting gifts and rebates from suppliers. I recommend that your practice have a clear policy prohibiting this practice and requiring all gifts and rewards to be sent to the practice owner. You may then distribute the gifts in an equitable manner if you wish or keep the reward as a perk of ownership.

Many eye care practitioners have had the experience where they did not even know that a supplier was giving gifts to an employee who makes buying decisions for the practice, because the gifts are sent to a personal residence. There are obvious conflicts of interest with this reward system. Talk with your staff to be sure this isn't happening and review your policy with your sales reps.

6.21 Staff Dress Code

Staff dress codes and uniform policies can be very difficult to manage. Sometimes it seems like you just can't make everyone happy, including the practice owner! I don't pretend to have all the answers, but the way your staff looks on the job is important to your practice success. I'll provide some tips in this article that will help you develop your office policy and make most people happy.

Staff apparel should reflect the personality of the practice. There are many different looks that work very well and I can't advise you on what to choose. Think about your practice marketing goals and the image that fits with that. It could be medical, upscale retail, corporate, family-friendly, professional, formal or casual. Look at other businesses in and out of health care for inspiration.

Make it an employment benefit

While I can't advise you on what style to choose, I will recommend that the practice provide uniforms or some part of the apparel as an employment benefit.

The image of your practice to patients is far better when everyone looks great. Providing uniforms lets the practice owner control the look.

- There is a big impact when most or all employees wear the same styles and colors. You can decide if the uniform is exactly the same for all or has coordinating mix and match pieces.
- The practice logo has a positive impact on the perception of quality. I recommend you have your practice name and logo embroidered or screened onto the garments for a customized, upscale look.
- Employees may not buy good quality or replace uniforms frequently enough if they are paying for them.
- Employees may not use good taste if they choose the uniform on their own.

- Staff members have a better attitude and more self-confidence when they like what they wear and when they look good.

Where to buy?
There are many good sources for uniforms. Local uniform shops may give you better service, including quick help with replacements, fill orders for new employees, exchanges, advice, and try-on service. There are also very good sources online. Land's End Business is a popular source for an upscale look. Logo sportswear shops online can supply something different for special needs.

How often and how many?
This depends on the practice budget to some extent and something is better than nothing. I think the practice should supply at least a minimum amount of tops and pants so a person does not have to buy them. You might provide uniforms twice per year, possibly two pairs of pants and two tops for each person. You may also supply a clinic jacket to wear over the top for warmth on a less frequent basis. Depending on your climate, you might choose different styles or colors for winter and summer. Of course, employees can buy additional items if they choose.

Special considerations
Here are a few tips based on experience:

- Unless your practice is unique, I would look for some amount of polyester in the fabric so it won't wrinkle too much when washed.
- You will most likely need a product that comes in a size range from extra small to XXX large. Look for that early in the shopping process.
- Consider buying a couple of sample pieces in different sizes to allow staff to try them on for size before ordering a large quantity.
- Wash the sample garments to see how they look and try them on again for the shrinkage factor.

Who should wear the uniform?
There are many opinions on this and I think it is ultimately up to the practice owner. You may want an office manager to wear business apparel and not a uniform. The doctors will most likely dress differently as well. There is a school of thought that says people who wear high fashion clothing can sell high end optical better. There is also something to be said about the impact of more people wearing the colors and styles of the uniform. That is impressive to patients and they can immediately tell who works for the practice. In my experience, it is easier to sell eyewear when it is prescribed

and has a medical perception. When it feels more like retail, the patient becomes more of a consumer. I suppose the best image for optical sales is borrowing a bit from both retail and health care.

It might be time to change your thinking

Be aware that times are changing and so are social values. We may not all like that, but if you want to keep your practice image up to date, you can't think the same way you did 30 years ago. Consider that the dress code can have a big impact on the moral and attitude of employees. It is OK to have some fun in the office! We are moving to casual Fridays with our practice supplying a colorful long sleeve T-shirt with our logo and the employee's first name screened on the front and a motto screened on the back. The staff members can wear blue jeans with this – which they love! We are also supplying fleece half zip pullovers. We all like this so much it may become the normal uniform and not just for Fridays!

6.22 Staff Use of Cell Phones

I received several reader emails describing frustration over the issue of employees who use their cell phones on the job for personal phone calls or texting, so I thought it would make a good topic.

Office policies

Every practice has employment policies, even if they are not written down. Policies are the rules you operate under; they are simply how you do things. Of course, it is far better to have them written down and it is really just as easy as typing the rules in a Word document. Save the document as a file titled "Office Manual" and you're all set. This document is always changing and evolving as you learn a better way to do things or as problems arise and you figure out a way to prevent them. Each new topic can become a heading in your office manual. Written policies are much better because the rules are clearly stated in advance and you avoid the confusion of relying on someone's memory.

Staff use of personal cell phones should be a topic and you need a policy for it. Enforcing the policy is another challenge, but having it clearly stated is a great start.

How tough should policies be?

This is not as easy as it might seem. Practice owners and managers who are too tough risk developing an office culture where staff are unhappy and have a bad attitude. If you are too lenient, employees can take advantage and become lazy and selfish. Smart employers care about the wants and needs of employees and they want the practice to be a good place to work. In a service profession like ours, we need staff to care about the patient experience and to be friendly and thoughtful. Good attitudes are developed by bosses who care and are respectful of employees.

I believe in looking at each policy individually. We should consider the policies from the employee's point of view, but balance that with the need to make the practice profitable. I try to be very supportive in some areas, but in others I find it is best to be strict. Use of cell phones while on the job is one of the latter for me. My reasoning is that it is too difficult for many employees to draw a line when it comes to personal gratification like talking or texting with friends and family. Clearly, the employee is supposed to be working, so prohibiting personal phone calls is hard to argue with. Enforcement is too difficult if we allow it to some degree because the office manager can't monitor everyone all the time.

My policy is to simply not allow use of cell phones or personal digital assistant devices by staff at all when on the job. They should be turned off and put away. They may be used at lunch and before and after work. We are sensitive to the need for employees to receive emergency phone calls and even for children to check in with their parent after school, but these calls must be made to our general office line and they must be kept very brief. Emergency calls should obviously be infrequent.

Office phones and computer use
A similar topic is the use of office phones and computers for personal use. Just as with cell phones, I take an approach that prohibits it. Using the Internet on office computers for personal use is a double problem in that it wastes staff time that you're paying for and it opens your computer system and data to damage from adware, spyware and viruses.

Hold the line on certain staff areas that are frequently abused. Just say no.

6.23 Extra Staff Hours: Who Should Control?

A staff member sees you in the hallway and says... "I'm so backed up on my lab work that I'm going to work through my lunch hour." Or, "I'm staying late tonight because I need to file insurance claims and we've been so busy I can't get to them." Sounds like a model employee with a great work ethic, doesn't it? This person clearly has the best interest of the practice at heart. Or does she?

The other possibility is that this staff member would like to increase her paycheck and since she is the only person who can perform certain tasks, she simply wastes time during the regular work week so she can work extra hours. Those extra hours may actually be very convenient for her if she does not want to take lunch or if her morning routine at home has her ready to arrive at work an hour early. Maybe her spouse has to work later anyway so she might as well stay late.

Who controls the hours?

The problem arises when the practice owner or office manager simply accepts an employee's word that she needs to work extra hours. It can be rather awkward in the beginning because the proposal to work overtime seems like it is good for the practice. The employee may say it as a statement (I'm going to stay late.) rather than a question (Is it OK if I stay late?). At first glance it feels like the owner should thank the tireless worker.

I think the practice owner should decide on staff hours and work schedules in conjunction with the office manager and the manager should supervise and enforce the schedule. I like to have a system that everyone follows. I like a policy that staff members may not decide on their own to start work early, work through lunch or work after closing without approval in advance from the manager or owner.

Staff payroll is a huge expense for a practice and it is important to supervise the details. Over a period of time, even an extra 15 minutes per day adds up to a significant cost. I recommend that all practices use a virtual time clock program on one of the office computers and every employee must click in and out for starting, quitting and lunch breaks. An employee may not begin work more than ten minutes before the scheduled start time or it won't be paid. When a staff member punches in, they must be ready to work, not go to the bathroom, work on hair, get coffee, etc. Employees should be told to go home as they are no longer needed at the end of the day, possibly in tiers if the staff is large.

Special circumstance or the new normal?

Once an employee is allowed to call the shots on the hours worked, it can easily become the normal office routine. After a long period of time, it becomes harder to change the policy because the employee feels like the flexible hours are part of her verbal employment agreement. When employees offer to work additional hours, owners and managers should carefully consider the situation. Don't be rushed into approval. You might say: "Let me think about that, but for now let's just stick to your usual schedule.

- Is the task really crucial or can it wait? Does practice revenue depend on it? Is there a deadline?
- Is there a good reason why the work could not be completed during the normal work schedule?
- Is this likely to be just temporary overtime or will it keep occurring?
- How will other employees feel about it? Is it fair to all? Will they want to skip lunch or start work early also?

Additional employees

I would rather hire an additional employee than continuously approve additional hours for existing staff. I view a larger staff as an asset that improves customer service, fosters more delegation and improves productivity, so more people are better.

Scheming for more hours often goes along with employees who are the only ones who can do something. Having office tasks that only one person can do often spells trouble because it gives too much power to one person. Granted, in smaller offices it may not be possible to avoid, but that is an advantage of growing into a larger staff. Having more than one staff member work on a task provides important back up if someone quits. It also provides a check and balance system so one person cannot waste time and just not work very hard.

Think about tasks in your practice where the owner and manager have little knowledge and go about changing that. Typical areas are insurance billing, lab work, and computer technology. You may find that the one employee who is knowledgeable in a task is not very willing to share the knowledge with co-workers, even after repeated requests. That is a red flag that says the person is controlling her turf.

Overtime regulations

One final reason for concern is the issue of overtime pay. If you do authorize an employee to work more than 40 hours per week, even on a temporary basis, you should always pay time and a half wages and follow the regulations of your state government. Generally, salaried individuals are not held to any standard for maximum hours, but there may be rules about who can be salaried. Be very wary and don't agree to a proposal by an employee who says he is willing to work extra hours for regular pay. That person can file a claim with the state labor agency much later and fines and penalties could be imposed on the practice, in addition to the back pay.

6.24 Staff Issues 101: Employees Taking Too Much Personal Time Off

I've received quite a few emails on this topic lately, so I'll share my thoughts in this article. Managing a staff is the most challenging aspect of owning an optometric practice and there are no shortcuts or quick answers that work every time. A great staff is crucial to practice success and I recommend that OD/practice owners work to develop their management skills rather than trying to avoid staff issues.

It is very easy for a practice to become too lax in the management and supervision of employees. After all, much of this falls to the optometrist and he or she is usually very busy with patient care and other matters. The OD typically expects the staff to follow their own good judgment by putting the best interest of the practice first, but that often does not work out very well. This is why I recommend that all practices have an office manager. But even with an office manager, which definitely helps, the OD/owner must be aware and involved even if at a higher level.

Back to the issue at hand, what should you do if an employee frequently requests days off, half days off or a few hours off for personal reasons such as child school activities or special errands. Further, what if an employee has used up all of his/her available time off and still needs more time, possibly for illness?

Your office policies

All employees need some time off sooner or later, for personal reasons, vacation or sickness. To address this in a fair manner, you need an office policy. There are many ways to structure your policy, but the point is to think about it, decide and write it down. The written policy becomes part of your office manual which is a reference for all employees. Time off could be with pay or without pay.

Consider what other companies usually offer their employees, since you compete with other firms to attract candidates in the job market. Fairly typical might be five personal days which are also for illness, two weeks paid vacation (that would be 10 work days). In many cases, some of this time off must be earned before it can be used by a new employee. Some employers prefer to lump it all together and call it personal time off (PTO). Paid holidays are an additional employee benefit, but I consider it differently because the employee does not get to choose when to use it.

- If you have a policy but have just not enforced it; you can start enforcing it. This is similar to changing the policy though because what has become commonly done in your office is the policy, even if it is different than what is written in the manual. I would give employees some advance notice that the policy needs to be enforced better.
- If you have learned that your previous policy is not practical, you can change it. More on this below.
- If you don't have a policy, announce to your staff that you need one and tell them what it is.

How to change the policies

It can be very difficult to change office policies for existing staff. If they perceive that you are taking something away, morale and attitudes may suffer. You may want to consider not changing some policies and just living with them. You may want to grandfather clause some existing staff, while requiring the new policy for new employees. You may want to give the current staff some other benefit to compensate for something you must take away. Or you may have to just do what you think is right and be ready for some fallout and even some resignations.

- Explain why the change in policy (or new policy) is needed. Possible reasons include: To be fair to all staff members..., For excellent customer service..., To make the practice more efficient...
- Be honest and up front. It is OK if there is a business and profit motive. That is why you are in business. One aspect of all employees' job duties includes helping the company generate a profit.
- Review what the policy has always been, even if it has not been enforced very well.
- Don't surprise staff with a change in policy. Give them some fair warning that the rules have changed. You don't want staff to come to you with an important request to go home early only to be told with no recourse.
- State what the new policy will be. Not everything in your practice is a democracy. In some cases, the owner must simply make a decision. If you ask for input and then don't go with the prevailing view, you make matters worse.

Hourly vs. salary?

I recommend that most employees be paid on an hourly basis and that the practice has a virtual time clock program installed on an office workstation. This reduces the temptation for employees to call off and if they do anyway, at least you save the payroll cost. Hourly employees are not allowed to work overtime unless approved in advance by the owner, and it rarely will be approved in my office.

It is fine if the office manager and associate doctors are on salary, but I still make a specific work schedule and expect them to start on time and stay until the end of the work day. If salaried employees work slightly more than their schedule, it is just part of the job and no pay adjustment is needed. If they work a lot more than scheduled or if they work a special day (like attending a conference on Sunday), I would give them a future day off to compensate for that additional work time.

Disciplining an employee

Sometimes you need to tell employees that they need to improve in some aspect of the job. It could be that they are asking for too much time off or it could be some other behavior. I always start this process in a calm, gentle and respectful manner. I ask the employee to meet with me in a private area so I don't embarrass him/her in front of co-workers. I know that staff can take any criticism very hard sometimes, so I try to start with acknowledgment of something they are doing well and I'm understanding about the things that are not going well. But I make my point very specifically about what I would like to change. I make some brief notes with the date in the employee's file after the meeting.

If the behavior does not improve, I speak with the employee again and gradually over several meetings, my tone becomes more serious. Goals and deadlines are set and I monitor the situation more closely. I always hope the employee acknowledges and agrees with the problem as I describe it, but if she denies there is a problem, I know we have very little chance of resolving the issue. Eventually, depending on the nature of the problem, the employee may have to be dismissed. When you get near that point, I think you owe it the employee to tell him that his job is at stake. You might say that if the matter does not show some improvement, you will have to part ways. Follow through, of course.

6.25 Staff Late for Work Again?

I've consulted with many ODs lately who have raised the issue of staff members chronically arriving late for work. It may be just a coincidence, but I also believe that society in general has become more tolerant of being late for appointments and events. Patients seem to arrive late for appointments more frequently and people in general seem to have less concern over running late. Of course we can't change societal trends, but we can adopt and enforce standards in our practices.

I don't think it is good for the practice culture for staff members to routinely arrive late for work. It fosters a sense of not caring about others. It creates ill-will among co-workers who have to cover for the late person. If your practice has been tolerant of some frequently late arrivers, I think it is time to change the rules and enforce them. I'll show you how.

A check list

Here are some points to consider as you adopt a new approach to staff punctuality in the office.

- Start fresh. If your policies about arriving to work on time have become lax, it is best to announce to all concerned that the rules are changing and explain why. This is actually fairly easy because everyone knows they are supposed to arrive on time. I would announce the new standard for punctuality at a staff meeting, admitting that the office has not enforced the rules very well in the past but that you will be in the future. Mention how arriving on time is important out of respect for co-workers and to provide excellent patient service. You may want to announce some rules about arriving a bit earlier than the schedule calls for, but not too early. Announce other changes based on some of the items discussed below.
- Doctors should have the same standard. It is a good idea if the doctors, manager and owners of the practice adopt the same standards required of staff. Staff may be scheduled earlier to get the office ready, but doctors should not show up late for their first appointment or meeting. Doctors and managers are leaders in the organization and a successful culture is built when the leaders demonstrate the desired behavior.
- Office manager. We need an office manager who has authority to direct and discipline other employees. In other words, we need a supervisor. This could be the doctor, but for punctuality issues, it works better if it is a manager. We need someone to track late arrivals and to continually correct and discipline employees who break the rules. If you do not have a manager, you need one. You

could appoint this job position from within or hire a new person for that job. Managers can serve dual roles in smaller practices, such as manager/receptionist or manager/optician. In larger practices, there is enough administrative work that the manager will rarely work with the public.

- Definite staff schedule. There should be a written staff schedule that is determined by the manager and doctor. Employees cannot change the schedule without approval from management. It shows each employee's name, the day of the week, start and stop times and days off. It could include lunch breaks, but if there is a preset constant lunch then it is not necessary. As you formalize the schedule, make sure you have enough staff starting early enough. If the first patient appointment is 9am, you need some staff to arrive at 8:30am to be sure the doors are open, lights are on, thermostats are correct, equipment uncovered, coffee is made, etc. Staff should understand that they must remain until all patients are completed and that can run past the scheduled closing time. I schedule most full time employees at about 37 hours per week so staying late does not drive them over 40 hours per week.
- Time clock. I strongly recommend using a virtual time clock on office computers for hourly employees. A sign-in sheet is notoriously inaccurate. Employees punch in in the morning, out and back in for lunch and out at the end of the day. The accuracy of this system will save a great deal of money over one year and it makes payroll accounting much easier. Many inexpensive time clock programs are available online.
- Policies. Consider adopting some policies about the work schedule. My practice does not allow staff members to start work more than 10 minutes early, lunch breaks may not be skipped and working extra hours must be approved in advance. Be careful about changing policies that have long been established, however. It is never smart to take away an employment benefit without giving something of equal value back.
- Catch the late arrivers. After announcing the new effort for punctuality, it is very helpful if the manager is present at the time clock workstation at the time employees are supposed to start. She may need to catch some offenders arriving late for them to learn that management is serious. I would start out very understanding about a late arrival, but if it continues, the manager must become stricter about it. Speak to offenders in private about each tardy incident. Let the employee know that a record is being maintained about each late arrival (just print the time clock data for the week). It

is OK to embarrass the staff person about it; ask why he was late and then indicate that the reason is not sufficient. If there is traffic, the employee should start sooner. As time goes on, become less tolerant of excuses. After numerous late starts, you may have to tell the employee that the habit is cause for dismissal and be ready to carry it out. It is necessary to set the right example for all employees.

I realize that many doctors and managers want to be a good boss and treat staff well, but letting some people arrive late is not treating the others well. Your good employees will appreciate your effort to make the workplace fair.

6.26 Having a "Talk" with a Staff Member

Do you ever get that uncomfortable feeling when you know you should have a talk with an employee about some problem, but you kind of dread the whole process? The confrontation can be stressful and in many cases, the situation goes from bad to worse. Many doctors prefer to just put the whole thing off and live with the problem! In this article, I'll share some tips that will make it easier, based on my experience.

How you approach a meeting with a staff member depends greatly on the nature of the problem or the new concept you are proposing. My advice has to be general in nature but you should always consider the individual, the personality and the history surrounding the event that led to this conference. It is also important to consider who should be at the meeting. Some items are best discussed at a full staff meeting; other things may best be handled in a small group and sensitive matters should be handled with one-on-one private meetings. Be considerate and don't embarrass employees in front of co-workers. Be respectful and allow them their dignity.

Don't try to fix everything

My first bit of advice is to realize that the practice owner, doctor or office manager should not try to solve all minor petty complaints or squabbles. Sometimes getting embroiled into a battle over who did what to whom just deteriorates into a bigger mess than it was to begin with. It often works to just let people cool off and they often can resolve their difference themselves. This is why it is best for doctors and managers to not become close personal friends with staff. Be friendly and caring, but not best pals.

I think an important role for an office manager is to allow employees to vent about something and to offer some sympathy and understanding, but to not necessarily take action. This requires judgment because some complaints by staff are justifiable and could lead to a change in office policy or additional staff training in order to preserve fairness to all. But pick your battles carefully and be willing to let some things go by the wayside.

Start softly

Let's assume that the purpose of the meeting surrounds some behavior or performance issue with a specific staff member. It could be frequent tardiness, repeated errors, lack of team work or just a poor attitude.

If a behavior is hurting the practice, you really must address it. Don't make it a big deal, just find the staff member when she is not too busy and say you would like to talk for a minute. Go into a private office and sit down. Depending on the circumstances, try to lighten the mood. Realize that this employee is most likely worried about this private meeting and could be defensive. Smile. Start by saying something positive about this employee's work, if possible. Realize that employees can be extremely sensitive to criticism, so start calmly and slowly. Don't become angry; if you display any emotion, disappointment may be more appropriate. If the staff member becomes angry, be understanding about the feelings but ask her to try to be calm. Reassure her that you want to hear her side.

Ask questions first

Begin by describing what you have observed or what the problem is, and ask the employee to tell you what she knows about the issue. Try to not talk too much in the very beginning but ask for the employee's input. Ask how the employee feels and if there are any problems. You may want to state the obvious, such as "you don't seem to be happy on the job."

Listening to this input will help you decide where to go next in the discussion. If you have relied upon others for a description of a problem, be prepared for a different set of facts that might even change your mind. There are always two sides to a story and the truth probably lies somewhere in between. This is one reason why it is best to start the discussion by asking questions; your initial impression may change.

If you want to change or add to this employee's job duties, ask if she would like to accept the new task and let her know how it would help the practice.

Present the issue clearly

After gathering the facts, just follow your instincts about what is best for the practice. Try to be fair to all parties. Propose a compromise or ask this staff member to make a better effort or to be the first to extend the olive branch to a co-worker.

Be prepared to clearly present the main issue you want to see changed or improved. It is best if you have some facts or data to draw upon, not hearsay and conjecture that is easily challenged. After explaining the problem, I like to see if the employee acknowledges her role in it and projects a desire to fix it. In many cases, staff members just deny the issue completely and act like they don't know what I'm talking about. That does not bode well for fixing it. In those cases I make my point and keep a close watch on the situation. Another meeting is very likely.

Protect confidentiality

Be considerate of your other employees when you share a problem that must have been told to you by a co-worker of the offending staff member. If I'm given a heads up about a problem by another employee, I make it my business to observe the issue myself so I can present it as something I saw or heard myself.

The domino effect

Be aware that changes you implement in your office procedure often have a domino effect. One change aimed at solving a problem can cause many other problems you may not have anticipated. Try to prevent that by thinking about all aspects of the practice and the patients. Also, consider staff input.

I like to think of managing my practice as similar to steering a cruise ship. You just can't turn it on a dime. Most changes are best made in small increments and adjustments.

6.27 Why Aren't the Rules Fair to Employers?

Do you ever feel like the balance of things favors the employee and the employer does not get a fair shake? That point of view may change depending on if you are an employee or an employer, but many readers of this column own a practice and they are employers. I know from my experience as a practice owner, I have felt that way in the past, but I got over it and I see it differently now. I'll share that perspective here with the hope it will help some of you to better manage your practice.

First, I'll give you some examples of ways that the employee/employer relationship can seem out of balance:

- Staff members can quit if they find a better job and we are supposed to be happy for them, but if an employer fires someone with the hope of finding a better employee, it is not well accepted.
- Unemployment benefits are often paid by the state even when the employee quits or was dismissed for valid reasons.
- Staff are not always appreciative of efforts to do something nice. This is not always the case, of course, but I have organized parties, dinners, outings, trips, picnics, bowling nights, etc. only to have some employees not show up (after accepting the invitation) or complain about some aspect.
- Sometimes staff members who you really trust will let you down by breaking the rules of the office. An example might be an office manager who is texting or posting on Facebook for personal reasons while on the job. This can feel like a disappointment to the boss. Or employees who are chronically late; being late with their paycheck would not be tolerated well.
- What I realized many years ago is that it does not have to be fair. Of course, poor behavior on the job should be corrected, I'm not saying we don't try to improve job performance, but I am saying try not to take it personally. Don't view it as an insult.
- The difference is that the employee views the practice as a corporate entity; not really as a person. In fact, the employee may view the corporate entity as quite wealthy and powerful and not see their attitude as disrespectful in any way. It is just how some employees think. To some extent, ODs contribute to their own disappointment by thinking of their practice as an extension of themselves personally. I prefer to think of the practice as separate from me. It is a business and it is not me, personally.
- In reality, the rules should not be the same for employees as employers. Employers decided to take on some business risk when they started; employees have not opted for that risk. In return for that risk, employers stand to make as much profit as they can, but employees do not share in most of that profit. The business is indeed more powerful than an individual employee; the business has greater financial resources and things that are paid for by the business are tax deductible. So, expectations are higher for the business and it can absorb a letdown easier than a person.
- As employers, we certainly place a high value on employees who have a positive attitude and who think more like an owner. But I no longer take it personally when an employee thinks like an employee.

6.28 Changing Staff Policies for the Worse

I learned a long time ago a basic principal of human resource management that has served me well: Don't take anything away from employees that is perceived as a benefit. At least, not if you care about employee morale and about preventing turnover. In spite of what seems like common sense to me, I talk with optometrists fairly often who are in the process of implementing a change that takes something away from staff.

The office policies that are in place now become the norm that employees understand and work from. It does not really matter if those policies were not originally intended or designed to be the way they are. Once they become common and accepted, even with the passage of time, they are the policies.

Here are three ways that I see ODs and managers make negative changes to employment policies. With a little creativity, the backlash from these changes could be avoided with little or no cost to the practice.

Drop a bonus program
If you have a staff bonus program that has been in operation for some time, but does not seem effective to you or it has become an entitlement, realize that employees see it as part of their normal compensation. You have two options, replace the current program with a different one that offers similar opportunities for rewards or buy the old program out and replace it with higher wages.

The first is best if you still believe in bonus programs. I recommend that you announce the new program rules and indicate that it will run for one quarter only and then it will change again. It works well if you pay the bonuses after the end of the quarter with a separate check from the normal paychecks. Changing the bonus programs frequently allows you to focus on different specific goals and it keeps the staff from taking it for granted. They have to change their behavior to earn the bonus.

The second method works much better than it sounds. Tell the staff that the bonus program is ending, but the practice will give each employee a raise in their hourly wage equal to the average bonus they earned in the past. Calculate that amount for each employee individually based on their actual bonuses paid over the past six months or more, and based on their usual hours per week. Some employees will have a bigger hourly wage adjustment than others, so keep this confidential. This raise does not cost the practice anything; you will still be paying the same amount you always have, but you got rid of a bad program once and for all. As new employees are hired, it is no longer a factor. As you give raises to existing employees, you can decide in each case if a raise is deserved and continue to normalize the wages.

Begin to charge employees for a benefit

A good example of this is in the situation where a practice provides health insurance to full time staff members as a full benefit, but due to ever increasing premiums, this becomes too big of an expense. This happened in my practice many years ago. When employees do not contribute at all to their health insurance, they will take the insurance benefit even if they don't really need it and they are resistant to changing the insurance plans or moving to higher deductibles in an effort to lower the premium.

I wanted to change the policy to requiring a 20% contribution from the employee toward their premium. The practice would cover 80% of the premium. We already charged the employee the additional premium cost if they wanted to add dependents. When I announced this change, which would have reduced take-home pay for the staff, I also implemented an off-setting raise in each employee's hourly wage. This raise did not cost the practice anything because I was basically compensating for the increase by getting some help with the health insurance premiums. The staff accepted the change quite well because they did not see a change in their pay.

Cut pay or charge a penalty

There can be many variations in this category, but they amount to cutting an employee's pay or cutting scheduled hours (in a punitive way) or charging staff a financial penalty for errors made or poor behavior (like punctuality problems). It should be noted that some of these actions could be against state department of labor regulations. I don't worry much about those state laws as I would not take these actions in any case, because I think they are a poor human resource strategy.

I think if we cut an employee's pay, and if the employee does not quit, we end up with an unhappy staff member who resents that action and will likely retaliate in some way, even if it is just with a poor attitude. The practice owner may think the move was quite fair and justified, based on the facts of the situation, but it is very unlikely that the employee would agree. If I have an employee who makes errors or does not follow procedure very well, I take the responsibility to retrain and rehabilitate the person. If that process does not work, I'd rather fire the employee than cut his or her pay.

I realize the playing field can seem uneven in favor or the employee in many cases, but realize they are individual people and your practice is a company. It is not the employee vs. you personally, it is the employee vs. your company. We need to develop a great staff to reach your practice goals. Start by never taking anything away.

6.29 One Employee with Special Knowledge

A potentially big problem exists in many optometric practices when one employee handles a specific task and no one else knows anything about it. That situation results in two negatives for the practice: 1) the employee could resign and take her (or his) special knowledge with her, making it difficult to operate the business and 2) the employee with special knowledge can, in effect, hold the practice owner hostage, demanding raises, overtime or special treatment and using an unspoken fear of quitting as leverage. Let's take a look at your practice, identify if this situation exists and explore remedies for it now, before a problem develops.

In any small business, it is important to have all operational procedures documented. How you do things becomes the essence of a practice procedure manual, but the vast majority of practices do not have such a document. In most cases, the office procedures just develop over time and key employees learn them and change them as needed. I believe it is a very smart goal to write a procedure manual for your practice, but this article will focus on the more immediate need of avoiding a situation where only one employee knows everything about a specific task.

Who should have backup knowledge?

The best way to protect your business operations is to have multiple people know the basics about each task. In a large practice, with many employees, it is possible to assign two or more people to each procedure through some degree of cross-training. There may be a primary staff member who does a task most of the time, but another employee who is also knowledgeable and serves a backup role. This makes your operation more efficient if work flow increases and allows work to continue even when the main staff member is on vacation or out sick.

In smaller practices, the best person to have the backup knowledge is the optometrist and practice owner. This is the only person we can be sure will remain employed in the practice and we are also certain that he or she has the best interest of the practice uppermost. Additional staff members can also serve as backup, such as an office manager, but I strongly recommend the OD learn the key elements of every aspect of the practice. If an employee quits, the OD has enough knowledge to train the replacement and provide more resources to stay up and running.

You might think you don't know anything about billing insurance, making glasses or many other topics, but you would be surprised at how easy it is to remove the mystery around these things once you dig into them. You have the core knowledge needed and if you spend just a little time with your staff members, you can protect your practice in a pinch.

Some optometrists open their practice with a leadership style that conflicts with the doctor doing everything. Thinking big, the OD may decide to hire others to manage various aspects of the practice. I understand the thinking behind everyone working at their highest level, but as a small business owner, you leave yourself vulnerable.

Tasks that need a backup

Here is a list of office procedures that may have only one employee who knows how to handle them. The backup person does not need to be an expert in these areas, but should know the basics about what is done and have the resources (people, phone numbers, websites, manuals, etc.) to learn more, if needed. Consider how well you could manage each of the following tasks if a key employee left your employment.

- Medical insurance claims and billing
- Insurance credentialing updates
- Compliance with regulatory issues: HIPAA, records, etc.
- Vision plan authorizations, claims, and payment reconciliation
- Balance the cash drawer and make bank deposit
- Bookkeeping
- Recall methods: confirmations, email and post card
- Facebook page and practice website: administrator and passwords
- A complete list of user names and passwords for every supplier and vendor
- Software updates
- Payroll
- Hiring process for new employees
- Training process for new employees
- Scheduling of employees
- Optical lab work (in office and outside labs)

How to approach the special employee
It is not unusual for an employee who has special knowledge to be somewhat reluctant to train others in the practice. We might call it protecting one's turf. It may seem innocent enough, but I find the practice owner must become very involved to overcome this tendency. Just telling Mary to show Jane how to do some task may not do anything. Also, if Jane does not actually perform the tasks on a regular basis, she may easily forget the key elements.

I find that honesty is the best policy and it works well if the practice owner simply reserves some time in his/her schedule and meets with the employee. I would not inform the employee in advance or make a big deal out of it because it can create stress. You can say something like this: "I'd like to learn more about our process for filing claims with Medicare and medical insurance plans (or any task). I want to see if we can improve our efficiency and I also would like Jane to learn some of this as well to serve as your backup. Please walk me through an example of what you do."

I think it is fine to expose the elephant in the room if the primary employee seems hesitant or offers excuses. You can say that for the good of the practice and in case the employee is ever out sick or on vacation, you want to understand the process.

Be sure to take notes as you learn the process. These notes become the beginning of your office procedure manual and you can share that project with the employees as well.

6.30 Does Each Person on Your Staff Have a Side Job?

If your office is like mine, there are times when the staff is really busy, and there are times when they aren't. I believe this is normal, and because our philosophy places high importance on patient service, we actually staff for the busier times. To keep production high and to maximize the use of staff time, our practice assigns every employee one or more specific side jobs. The side job is the employee's responsibility to manage, and the task should be worked on whenever there are no direct patient care duties. He or she owns that job. Our office manager maintains a list of employees and their side jobs and the performance of those jobs is reviewed.

If there is an undue amount of chit-chat going on (and I believe some personal conversation is normal and beneficial, if it is done in private areas), the manager can simply inquire about side jobs. There is always something to do.

Side jobs encompass a variety of duties, some rather menial in nature, but all are important in keeping the office looking good and running efficiently. If the job is small, one employee might have several. Some of the side jobs we use are:

- Check and restock all paper towel and soap dispensers
- Check and restock brochures and paper forms in all exam rooms, dispensing area and waiting area
- Return contact lenses that were defective or exchanged for credit
- Return frames and lenses that were returned under warranty for credit
- Check the "to-be-dispensed" cabinet drawers for glasses and contacts that need to be picked up, and call overdue patients to remind them
- Make follow-up phone calls to patients who picked up their glasses in the past 2 weeks to see how they are doing.
- Check the accounts receivable list and call patients and insurance companies about balances
- Confirm tomorrow's appointments
- Check every frame on our displays to see if it is in standard adjustment (so they feel better when they are tried on)
- Clean all clinical instruments (we prefer to have our staff do this rather than our janitorial service)
- Clean all mirrors and counter surfaces in dispensary
- Check office supply inventory - contact lens inventory - drug inventory - solution inventory - and order as needed
- Straighten waiting room, organize magazines and make fresh coffee
- Check and stock rest rooms
- There are many more

Slower times in the office are also excellent opportunities for staff training, which I believe is something that never ends. And sometimes a necessary part of training is simply practicing. Technicians can practice on each other to improve their skills in using pre-test instruments, or inserting and removing contact lenses on another person. Staff can also work individually on tasks they could be better at - like measuring parameters of RGP lenses, neutralizing glasses on a manual lensometer - especially with prism or progressive lenses, spotting and marking the segments on progressive lenses, restringing a rimless frame, etc. Having a staff member observe a co-worker in another department is also time well spent. It fosters better inter-department cooperation and can even lead to cross training of duties.

6.31 Annual Employment Reviews

Continuing with my expansion of the top ten misconceptions in practice management in the order of reader interest, this article will cover the idea of annual employment reviews. I realize that this is a very standard business tool and I believe that reviews are valuable in many organizations, but I'm not so sure they actually help the typical eye care practice.

The importance of staff management

I want to stress how important human resource management is to the success of any practice. Practice owners and managers must continually strive to improve their skills and knowledge in this area. To maximize job satisfaction among employees, we must create an office culture where doctors and staff members have mutual respect for each other. This fosters the pleasant attitude, strong work ethic and good morale that we value so much. This reminds me of the classic joke about a sign that hangs in the employee break room that reads:

The beatings will continue until morale improves. -- The Management

Taking an interest in staff members lives, being the first to extend a pleasant greeting, and praising a job well-done are gestures that go a long way to creating a positive work environment. Additionally, paying better wages, providing good benefits and having policies that stress fairness to all employees are important factors in attracting and maintaining the excellent staff we all want.

Rather than holding a formal annual review either at the beginning of each calendar year or at the annual anniversary of the start of employment, I prefer to provide feedback on a more frequent basis. This may be with just the employee and me in a private setting or it may be more general at our weekly staff meetings. The discussion might be positive feedback about things we are doing well or it might be the correction of a deficiency. I often ask for staff opinions and input about how to handle situations.

Formal reviews and raises

I used to perform an annual evaluation of each employee's performance. I found the exercise resulted in one of two things:

- The review would result in an automatic raise in wages, even though I was often not really wishing to give one. I realized that I was prompting raises that might not have occurred at that point in time.
- If I felt I did not want to grant a raise, I had to present a negative review to the employee to convince him or her that a raise was not deserved. This would hurt the morale of an employee that was doing average work and was really quite acceptable.

Because of this no win situation, I let the regular reviews drop away. Instead, I gave feedback informally and more often without any connection to the thought of a raise. I still give unexpected raises or bonuses when I see excellent work performance. But overall, I now rely on employees to ask to be reviewed for a raise when they feel it is appropriate. These requests are made to our office manager, who brings the request for a review to me (and my wife who is an OD/partner). Some employees request a review on an annual basis, but many will go several years before asking for a raise.

It often works out that employees who are in that middle range of performance, not bad but not stellar either, are the ones who sense that and remain content with their current salary. These are employees I do not want to dismiss, but I also do not feel a raise is warranted. I am quite content to let these people drift along without rocking the boat.

Additionally, the formal reviews took a great deal of time and seemed to always be looming ahead for someone. They just did not help foster the culture and teamwork I wanted.

Granting raises and how much?
When I receive a request for a review, it is considered informally with the office manager. Our practice is managed so closely that it only takes a few minutes for me to decide to grant a raise or not. Usually the answer is yes, but if there are factors such as poor attendance or punctuality, the answer could be no with that explanation given. If the negative factor can be improved and sustained, the raise may be granted at a later date.

A cost of living raise is really not a raise at all, it is simply staying even. For most of our employees, that would result in a 50 cent per hour raise. So even with mediocre performance, that amount of raise can be offered and morale is maintained. If performance has been good, then a $1 per hour raise is common.

Our office manager generally meets with the employee who requested the review and gives a short verbal summary of the person's work performance and indicates the amount of any raise.

While I want to maintain an excellent staff, I'm also interested in keeping operating costs at a minimum. That is the balance that is required in managing a business. I am willing to accept a payroll percentage of gross in the 22% range, but if allowed to go unchecked, it could quickly rise much higher than that.

6.32 Are You Giving Your Staff Enough Feedback?

Many optometrists and office managers don't get around to supervising staff members in action and giving them feedback on job performance. It's understandable: a) we're all busy and b) criticism can feel like a confrontation and it can cause a drop in staff morale in some cases. Nevertheless, the biggest management challenge I hear from ODs and managers has to do with staffing. And a major reason for low production can be traced back to staff who make errors or who have poor attitudes.

Many ODs who own practices believe they should simply communicate their vision of the practice to the staff and then let them go do it. In my experience, that will lead to disappointing results. Staff members do not innately know how to do their jobs very well. Some may do well and some won't. Staff members frequently change the procedures to meet their personal needs. They need ongoing supervision and training by someone who has the best interest of the practice at heart. If the OD is too busy seeing patients, which should be the case, then an office manager is needed. We need an active manager.

Staff reviews

One formal review per year or even per quarter is simply not enough feedback! In fact, I don't even like scheduled employee reviews. They often result in a raise that may not be deserved. We should be talking to our staff on nearly a daily basis. This separates the job feedback from the idea of a raise. Frequent communication, on both the good and bad aspects of job performance, helps employees improve and prevents them from becoming overly sensitive about receiving criticism.

Don't forget the good things

As employers, we need to be careful that we don't always focus on the deficiencies of job performance. We must balance that with praise and acknowledgement of good work. We all know this, but it can be very easy to overlook.

Make a point of reviewing your patient surveys during staff meetings and be sure to single out any good surveys that mention a staff member by name. Print these and display them on a bulletin board or pass it along to the person mentioned.

Simply telling employees that they did a great job with a certain task or with a specific patient does wonders for your office culture and staff morale.

To be sure we notice good performance in my practice, I implemented a program where we give away $10 Target gift cards to employees when they do a great job. We have three managers in the practice and each one gets one gift card each week and they have to give it away when they see good work. So that is twelve good deeds per month that we recognize. I like Target cards for this because Starbucks can feel a bit indulgent for some people. We used to make a presentation about this at a staff meeting, but that sometimes became too competitive so we now give the reward one-on-one without the peer pressure.

Staff training is like coaching

I believe the training never stops for staff. None of us will ever be perfect, so we will continue to try to improve. If we look at on-the-job criticism as a form of training and if we present it in a constructive manner, it does not have to be unpleasant. This management style requires that staff members have a boss who actually observes their day-to-day work. That is often not the case with optometric staff, but I believe it results in the best job performance. It means virtually all offices should have a manager, because the doctor can't do it unless the practice is brand new or very small.

I view the manager's role as similar to a coach. The manager is a teacher in many respects. When an error is made or when a situation is not handled well, it is the manager's job to use that opportunity to teach the employee to do better next time. Of course, it would also be a mistake to micro-manage every aspect of job performance. The manager must allow for some independent thinking and know when to step in and when to stay out. And there should be many levels of correction or discipline with an employee; at first starting out extremely understanding and caring and gradually becoming more serious if the same issue continues to be a problem.

The manager also has a boss, typically the practice owner. Ideally, the practice owner will train the manager on how to become a better at that job. Managers don't always do everything perfectly either.

6.33 Salary Creep and Pay Caps

In my consulting work, optometrists often share their concern with me that some employees have reached very high salary levels. The doctors want to know how to handle raise requests from these individuals, who are often excellent staff members they don't want to lose. Some doctors wonder if they should implement a salary cap for certain job positions that will establish the upper pay limit.

The term salary creep generally refers to an employee who has been with you for a long time and regular raises or bonuses have added up to a larger than normal compensation for a certain job position.

Don't overreact
When I evaluate the actual wages being paid to optometric staff members when salary creep is the issue, I usually find that the situation is not that bad. I rarely find that an employee is being paid a wage that is completely beyond what I consider reasonable. In most cases, the salary creep is more of a worry about what might happen in the future rather than remorse over the current wage.

It is important to recognize the true value of a staff member who has been with your practice a long time. If the employee does excellent work, has a great attitude, is liked by patients and co-workers, and knows every aspect of your practice procedure, he or she is worth fairly high compensation. It is very hard to find a person that has all those qualities. An employee like that will generate a great deal of revenue for the practice.

I would never announce a range of wages or a pay cap for a certain job position. It would hurt morale for employees to think they could go no further in their career and I see no benefit in telling a person that. I don't think it would even be that useful because you will want to manage each employee individually and circumstances do change. Don't lock yourself in with your own policies. Leave them flexible. Some policies should not be too specific.

Compare wage amounts to other fields

When you wonder if an employee is being paid too much or if a possible raise makes sense, compare the compensation with other occupations. After all, wages are based on the job market and that is based on what other employers are paying for people with a specific skill set. In this case, let's assume we are evaluating a very smart, likeable, dependable employee with considerable skills as an optician or manager. Determine this person's total compensation with wages and bonuses averaged and express it as an annual salary prorated for a 40 hour week. A quick rule of thumb is to take the hourly wage, double it and add three zeros. For example, a person earning $26 per hour is about equal to a $52,000 per year salary.

When you consider a career for a bright person earning a living for his family that pays a salary of $52,000, what do you think? It is a reasonable salary level, but I think most people in the U.S. would not think of it as extremely high. It depends on the job, of course, but on the scale of all jobs, it may be middle to low.

This analysis helps me realize that the salaries paid by many optometric practices may not be so out of line after all.

So what can you do?

As you do reviews for higher earning employees in your practice, you should not feel forced to give a raise. You can let the highly paid staff coast along a little bit. You may tell them they are doing great but a raise is not in the budget at this time. You may give them a small raise to show that the practice likes their work but it is only 25 cents per hour. It is just a token, but maybe better than no raise. We never know how staff will react to a raise; they could be insulted or upset, but you have to cross that bridge when you get to it.

Most reasonable people know that the economy is in trouble and jobs are scarce right now. Even a 50 cent raise, which would seem pretty good to most staff, may only equal a cost of living increase. You do not need to tell the employee that it is just cost of living. Let them feel good about it. But you should realize that a cost of living raise is really not a raise at all. Your practice must find a way to also keep up with cost of living. Your practice should be increasing in profitability more than the cost of living each year.

If you feel like your wages and payroll costs are getting too high, it may be because your practice is not profitable enough. You may need to raise fees or see more patients or bring in a new service. If you applied your current payroll expense to a higher gross revenue number, the payroll percentage would be lower. You effectively could afford to retain and pay the best staff.

You might also consider a bonus program for these highly paid employees instead of a conventional raise. If this employee found a way to achieve a very high level practice goal, you may be very happy to pay more.

Annual employment reviews
One final point... I don't do annual staff reviews that are forced by the calendar. I know many human resource management books say you should (I earned a concentration in human resources with my MBA degree). Many smart people disagree with me on this and that's fine. But our practices are not large corporations where we can't keep track of our employees and how they are doing. I know exactly who is doing well in my practice and who is just so-so.

Reviews that are forced by the calendar based on the anniversary of employment always result in the employee expecting a raise. Even if you say the reviews are not related to raises, they always are. So when you do the review, you must either give a raise you did not want to give or you must tell an employee why they are not good enough to deserve a raise – which will usually demoralize them and change their attitude at work. So, you may want to slowly migrate away from giving forced annual written reviews and give more frequent feedback, like daily or weekly comments. I believe in giving feedback to employees so frequently that a raise is not even on the radar. And proactively give raises or bonuses when you see good work and keep up with it. You must pay well to keep good people.

6.34 Employee Compensation Summary

Employers everywhere will agree, employee fringe benefits carry a very high cost. In addition to wages or base salary, there are many additional expenses incurred by employers. I'm well aware of this, because I see the bills and I see the total cost of staff compensation on my financial statement – but I realized years ago that my staff members were generally unaware of the real value of the perks we provide.

To gently educate our staff, I devised an employee compensation form, which we distribute at the end of the calendar year with the employee's W-2 wage and tax form. This form lists every employment expense incurred for the individual during the year. We either keep our own records of these items or our CPA provides them. Eye care benefits, for example, are tracked by each employee filling out an "employee usual and customary fee slip" whenever they receive free eye care or buy optical materials at cost.

I've provided my form below as a sample. Determine if you provide some additional benefits – and remove the line completely if you don't provide a listed benefit.

You'll notice that some of the items listed are not really benefits – but are government mandated payments – such as social security matching and unemployment insurance. I list them anyway because this is an educational piece and I consider those payments part of the employee's true compensation.

The TOTAL COMPENSATION value tells the staff that they are actually earning much more than they thought. For hourly employees, we recalculate their effective hourly pay rate based on this total compensation dollar amount.

Employee Compensation Summary

Employee Name, Date
Period covered on this summary
Wages paid
(Vacation and paid holidays included here)
Profit sharing / 401K contribution
Health insurance premiums
Eye care benefits
Uniforms
Continuing education fees
Social Security matching
Workers compensation
Unemployment insurance
Miscellaneous

Total compensation

Total number of hours worked
Effective hourly rate

Chapter 7. Office Managers

7.1 Why You Need a True Office Manager

I'm surprised that so many private practices do not have office managers. Or some practices have them (also known by other titles such as team leaders, department coordinators, and practice administrators), but the manager really has little or no authority to direct others. I think a true office manager is a vital factor for a fast-growing and efficient practice. In this tip, I'll describe why you need a manager with full authority to manage.

Is staff management a challenge?
Staff management ranks as the most difficult issue I hear about from ECPs who own practices. It ranges from employees not showing up for work on time to battles with co-workers to texting on the job to generally poor attitudes. Many employees are not really horrible, but they are not great either. They have no enthusiasm; the spark that elevates a practice from average to great is missing. Yet many of these ECPs don't have a real manager on duty. The doctor hopes that after telling the staff how to do the job, they will carry out the vision. The hope is that they will do the right thing. Usually, an incentive program is in place which pays a small bonus if certain goals are met.

Unfortunately, in the real world, most employees need more structure than this. They need supervision. But in many practices, the doctor is the only person with real authority and he or she is in the exam room. An office manager has many roles in most offices, but most important is making sure the rest of the staff is productive and projects the best image.

Not just a payroll expense
It might seem that promoting an employee to manager or hiring a new person for that role will cause an increase in payroll and a decrease in net income. That's why many ECPs continue to drift along with minimal management year after year. Trust me; it's not true. A good office manager will greatly increase practice profitability by accomplishing the following:

- Vastly improved customer service. A manager will be sure staff members go where they're needed. If employees don't respond to a patient in optical or if there is no one at the front desk, the situation is remedied.
- Continuous training. The manager is like a coach and when she sees or hears something that was not done perfectly, it can be a learning moment for the employee.

- Better performance. When staff members know that someone is watching and may indeed pull them aside and correct them, they try harder.
- Fewer squabbles. Managers play a key role by being a good listener and letting employees vent some frustration. Not every complaint needs to be acted upon; sometimes an understanding ear is enough.
- Greater productivity. A little social interaction among staff members can be a good thing, but they often take it too far. A supervisor is needed to communicate, often with a just look, to stop the chit-chat and get to work. Employees may all have side jobs and managers can make sure they get done.
- Handling administrative tasks so the doctor doesn't have to. From bookkeeping to staff scheduling to patient communications, there are many jobs the manager can handle which lets the doctor work at a higher level and develop the vision of the practice.

Those factors contribute to practice growth in many different ways, but there is no doubt that the manager's salary is covered many times over. Every eye care practice, large or small, should have a manager.

Manager's duties

Smaller practices can have a manager who has a dual role. She might be manager and optician or manager and receptionist. But the goal is for the manager to become a full time administrator and not work directly with patients. It is a great achievement when your practice is large enough to need a full time manager.

I like to leave the exact duties of the manager rather unstructured. I want it to evolve over time as I learn the person's strengths and as she gains respect from the staff. As my trust in the manager grows, so will the duties of the job. Don't try to describe it too fully at the outset.

Authority and responsibility

It can be difficult to tell your staff that they have a new boss, but it's necessary if the manager is to be effective. The doctor/owner must give the authority to the manager by communicating it directly to the other staff. The manager can't take the authority herself. Without the authority to deliver consequences, the manager will not be successful.

As the manager uses her authority, she can be given more responsibility. The practice owner should always maintain supervisory control over the practice finances.

7.2 More on Office Managers

In my last article, I wrote about how important it is for every practice to have an office manager. I received many questions and comments in response to that article, which I really appreciate. This week, I will address some of those concerns and issues.

Duties of a manager

Thanks for the tips on office managers, but I wish you would be a little more specific on their duties. Mine tends to sit in her office.

I don't want to define the duties too specifically because the needs of practices vary and so does the skill level of the manager and the comfort level of the owner. I think the duties should evolve over time and the doctor should seek to give the manager more and more responsibilities. I do not believe that a manager should spend all of his/her time in a private office. If the practice is very large and there is that much administration, then an assistant manager or another administrator may be needed. I would like to see the manager spend 25 to 50% of the time in the clinic, at the front desk and in the optical supervising and observing staff members. You may need to have a private chat with the manager to review her current duties and help her delegate more to others. Discuss the tasks that she is working on and realign her priorities to mesh with your goals.

The transition

Could you expand on the most effective way to promote an existing employee to manager and make a lasting and positive transition?

First, talk with the employee you have in mind and make sure she wants the job and understands the duties. Explain to the employee that the good of the practice must be her primary responsibility and that she will have to separate friendships with staff members while at work – and maybe even outside of work. Explain that the job may involve difficult challenges with patients or staff members who have complaints. Point out that she may work with patients very seldom and her duties will be administrative.

If all that goes well and you have a good candidate for the job, hold a staff meeting and explain to all employees that the office has grown to the point that you need a manager. Proudly announce your selection and note that this person is now the supervisor of everyone else in the office. Ask your staff to go to the manager with questions and concerns from now on and ask them to help make the transition easy for her. Observe the staff interactions and step in if needed to have a private discussion with any employees who have trouble with the new role. Understand that some staff may feel a little jealousy or insecurity for a while, but just reassure them.

Hire from within or out?

Do I want someone with managerial training?

I would look at your current staff first and decide if there are any good managerial candidates and if there is already a manager by default without the official title. If you have a natural leader who has the respect of the staff and who you like to work with, go with him or her. If not, advertise in the usual places for office manager position available, managerial experience or training required. It is nice to have optical experience, but it is not a necessity. Finding a smart person who will be patient and empathetic with staff, and who understands the importance of great customer service is more important. The manager can always go to an optician or the doctor with eye care questions.

I have read articles that state that having a manager is not the right way to go and everybody should be on a level playing field – what do you think?

I disagree with that philosophy. I prefer a direct management style more than one where everyone participates. I have a vision for how I want the practice to operate and while there is room for some individual personalities, I believe we will be more successful if I design a system and train the staff to follow it. In a participative management style, you will have employees deciding how the practice should operate, but they may care more about their own wants and needs than the patient's.

Pay level

I won't quote an actual dollar range in this forum, but managers are usually one of the higher paid employees in an eye care practice. I think the pay should be commensurate with what the employee has been earning if he or she is already employed in the practice. A slight raise might accompany a promotion, but more raises should come after some success on the job has been achieved. Like any job, wages are based on the value and experience the person brings.

7.3 A Practical Guide to Working with an Office Manager

Many optometrists are unsure about how to hire and train an office manager. Here is a very practical look at why your practice needs one and how to find a good one.

Yes, you need a manager
An office manager is a job title that can have vastly different duties depending on the size of the practice. In a smaller practice, the job is a dual-role, such as manager/receptionist or manager/optician. In a larger practice, the manager will hardly ever work with patients at all because there is so much administrative work to do. The management role typically changes slowly over time as the practice grows.

I believe it works best to design the practice from the start to operate like a large, successful practice, so why not appoint a staff member as manager early on? The optometrist will be heavily involved in management when the practice is smaller, but the operation of the office will be built around the presence of a manager and everyone becomes comfortable with that concept. The doctor increasingly delegates more tasks as the practice grows and as more staff members are hired. This optimum delegation includes optical dispensing, clinical data collection and office administrative duties. This builds a system where the practice is not solely dependent on the doctor/owner. Eventually, when associate ODs are hired, the practice can function just fine without the doctor/owner being present.

Qualities of a good manager
Many people think a good manager is a powerful personality who will demand great work from the staff, but that type is not what I'm looking for. I want a person who has compassion and empathy for staff members and who will be patient and understanding as we work toward our practice goals. Staff members often need someone who will listen and care as they vent some frustrations from the job. We are not operating a factory; we take care of patients who trust us with potentially serious eye problems. We need a leader who can inspire the staff to have happy attitudes and great morale. We need a positive office culture.

Additionally, I am looking for a manager who understands customer service and is as passionate about it as I am. Many managers are somewhat protective of the practice and they try to be sure that we are not taken advantage of by unreasonable people in the general public. I understand the philosophy, but it tells me that the person who feels that way does not get it. I want a manager who will let the patient win and one who can say the words "I'm sorry" when the situation calls for it. My manager and I understand that the unreasonable people are really no different than you and me when you look at things from their point of view. That is how large, successful practices are built.

Of course, I can list many other traits of a good manager, most of which are common sense, but the two traits above will get you off to a great start.

Manager duties

The actual duties assigned to the manager should gradually evolve to include increasingly more important tasks as the owner gains confidence and trust. There is no handbook for this, but here is a list of jobs that good managers perform:

- Supervise and direct the staff. This is a big one and it can't work unless all staff members know that the manager is their boss. It can be an awkward moment, but the doctor/owner must tell everyone that the manager has the authority to tell them what to do. Without that authority, which can only be given by the practice owner, the manager can't be effective. The more you hide that authority with vague terms like office coordinator, the less cooperative employees will be. Staff members need to be supervised. It would be great if we could simply share our vision of the practice with the entire staff and they would carry it out, but in reality, most employees look out for their own self-interest first. The manager must look out for the best interest of the practice.
- Staff management such as scheduling, training, remediating and refereeing disputes. Also, managing requests for vacation, days off, sick days, and to leave early.
- Supervise billing and serve as a back-up to the insurance coordinator. I never like to see an important task in a practice that only one person knows how to do. Staff members may try to protect their turf in some areas, but the manager should insist on learning it as well.
- Supervise the handling of payments to the practice including reconciliation of the cash drawer with the daily production report

and bank deposits. The practice owner should also receive a report and bank receipt every day that provides a paper trail.

- Assist with bookkeeping and accounts payable. Again, the practice owner should supervise and approve all payments to suppliers, but the manager can do much of the work.
- Marketing the practice. This can include recall and many other projects.
- General administration. There is so much here I can't list it. It becomes obvious if the owner simply thinks... what would happen to the office if I were not here?

7.4 The Perfect Office Manager

I wrote that title to get your attention, but I actually think it is nearly impossible to find a perfect manager. Of course, none of us are truly perfect in any endeavor, but even if we don't take the term literally, I think great managers are made, not found.

Many optometrists want to hire that special person who can take over the business aspects of the practice and the staff management issues so they can concentrate on seeing patients. Many ODs who own their practices want to delegate the business side to a well-paid and competent person so they do not have to think about it. Unfortunately, my experience in consulting tells me that is not usually the best philosophy. Oh, there are a few rare cases where a manager leads a practice to greatness by herself or himself, but far more often, practices that are extremely successful have a doctor/owner who is also involved with the business and with leadership.

We need someone to know a little bit about everything

I often talk to doctors who want to delegate or outsource most administrative aspects of the practice. They would love to buy their way out of operating the practice themselves. These are often smart, ambitious doctors who want to use their time and skills to treat eye problems and have a personal life. Many have grown their practices fairly quickly but they have reached a choke point where the business seems out of control.

The problem with delegating and outsourcing the management is that you put this important task in the hands of people you don't know and they may let you down. Employees, including managers and insurance coordinators, will eventually quit. Outsourcing firms may start out doing a good job, but they could have some staff turnover and the service suffers. These failings can occur slowly and by the time the practice owner realizes what happened, there can be a serious loss of profit and damage to the practice reputation. If the practice owner knows nothing about the tasks at hand, he or she can become desperate for help and that is not a good situation.

I prefer the doctor/owner, sometimes with a partner or spouse, to learn everything in the practice. These are the only people who are permanent! We need this core group to be able to train others, including the manager. I think it is ideal for the doctor to know something about areas that many doctors do not really like, such as optical dispensing, frame buying, lab ordering procedures, setting fees, insurance billing, daily bank deposits, staff management, accounts receivable and accounts payable.

It may seem like a very tall order for the owning OD to see all the patients and learn everything about the business operations, but it is really not so bad. I think we simply have to organize our time to be more efficient with clinical eye care. See the same number of patients in fewer days of the week and spend some days on management.

The phases of a practice

As the practice grows through phases, from start-up to medium size to high production, the need for the doctor/owner to know everything diminishes. The owner can increasingly depend on others because the staff is getting larger and there can be some redundancy built in when multiple staff members all know the same task. I don't like it when there is only one person in a practice who knows how to do something important and complex (and is not the owner).

I believe strongly in delegation as the practice grows, but it is still best if the doctor/owner knows the basics about everything. This serves the owner well as he or she monitors the practice and reviews employee performance. And in a tough pinch, which usually happens eventually, the doctor can train a new employee or at least know the resources for where to go for help.

Train your own manager

This same philosophy fits perfectly with my preferred method for finding a great manager. I'd like the practice owner to find someone who has all the skills and traits you would expect in a manager. She or he could be someone already working in the practice or could be hired from outside. I want someone who is compassionate, patient and caring about staff members and understands the importance of great customer service. Beyond that, I'd prefer someone with managerial experience, great computer skills and generally intelligent. A college degree is desirable as is optical training, although not a requirement in my book.

Once you make the selection, I think it is the responsibility of the practice owner to train the manager. This training occurs over years of working together and typically results in a gradual increase in responsibility. Managers don't start their job knowing everything.

7.5 Finding the Right Office Manager

A reader emailed me the following question and I thought it might be of interest to others.

"On the subject of delegation, we really would like to hire an office manager to help take some of the daily burden off our plates. Our problem is how do you suggest finding and hiring a qualified candidate for the job? Maybe you can consider this as a topic for one of your upcoming tips?"

There are many good things that a strong manager brings to a practice, but from a big-picture perspective, none are bigger than these two factors:

- A manager can supervise, direct and improve the performance of all the other staff members. The optometrist simply can't watch what's going on throughout the office and I believe supervision is key to a great staff and a great practice.
- A manager is instrumental in developing a practice system that does not depend solely on the doctor/owner. That is an excellent goal for one's career and life.

Finding the right person for the position of office manager can be challenging, but a good place to start the search is by looking at the status of the current staff.

Promoting from within
In many cases, it's best to reward solid, loyal performance on the job with one of the few promotions available in an eye care practice. It just depends on the people.

Quite often, even in a practice that does not have an official manager, there is an employee who is the acting manager. Perhaps this person has more experience and the other staff members seek her out with questions. Perhaps she already coordinates days off, vacations and lunch breaks. If this de facto manager without the title is good at the job, she may be the natural best choice. Consider how well you communicate with her and if she is loyal to the practice. Problems can occur, however, if this person is too close of friends with her co-workers and will have difficulty disciplining and correcting others.

Sometimes the current staff members in a practice are just not management material. In filling this position, I'm looking for someone who will be compassionate and understanding when faced with a staff member who has problems or complaints. I also insist on a manager who shares my passion for customer service. Finally, we need strong loyalty to the owners and the best interests of the practice. You really can't teach those qualities, so don't promote a staff member and hope to change her.

Bringing in outside talent

Most office managers have experience in eye care and that can obviously be very valuable. But it is not a necessity. In some cases, it is better to find someone who has experience and training in business management even if they come from another field.

I have taken this approach in my practice with success and I've seen it work in many others. My feeling was that to find a great manager within the small pool of optical people in my area would be too constricting. And after all, I already had many employees who knew optical. If the new manager needed knowledge in technical areas, we had plenty of people who could provide it. In reality though, the new manager learned the technical aspects of eye care very quickly. How could she work in our office every day and not learn it?

In some ways, bringing in an expert from another field sets the new manager apart from all the other co-workers our employees have worked with. A fresh perspective can be very helpful.

Multiple bosses and team leaders

I just don't care for the strategy of using team leaders and profit center coordinators where no one is actually a boss. I get the concept of a team approach to achieving goals, but in my experience many optometric employees don't respond well to that management style. Many staff members are just not self-disciplined and self-motivated, although they can still be outstanding employees when given some direction and guidance. I find that the tried and true organizational chart where one person is in charge and everyone knows it, works best.

This is an area where many eye care practitioners make a mistake because they want to delegate some of the practice administration and staff management, but they don't want to upset any staff members by announcing a new boss. But a manager without any authority is unable to be effective. The effort to keep the peace often backfires because the manager and staff often work against each other in a battle for authority.

Upsetting morale

There is no question that appointing someone as manager has the potential to cause a problem with staff morale. We can all understand the fears that will exist in this situation; perhaps there is worry that the new boss will not be fair or that the workplace will become stressful. There is also the potential for someone to feel she was passed over for the job and feel some jealousy.

I certainly think we should work hard to maintain positive staff morale, but this is one situation where the end result is so important and so beneficial that it's best to push through with the task. Appoint someone to the job and explain to all staff that the new manager has the authority to tell them what to do. The side effects will blow over and the practice will have a true manager.

Diplomacy and the role of staff

One excellent way to head off some morale issues is to talk to your current employees in advance. Don't surprise them, but rather keep them informed even if it feels a bit awkward. In some cases this may be with a private one-on-one talk. Alternatively, general announcements can be made at a staff meeting. If you're seeking a manager from the outside, tell your staff you're doing so. They'll learn of it anyway and it really should come from you. You may say that you're seeking someone with managerial experience (as a way to hedge why you're not considering current employees).

If you have an individual who may be an excellent optician or receptionist, but who you don't feel would be a good manager, consider this approach. Describe how the role of the new manager will eventually become almost 100% administrative and will have virtually no contact with patients. You can go on to tell the optician that she is simply too valuable in her technical role to lose to a behind-the-scenes role. The office manager job is not necessarily the most important job in the practice and may not even be the highest paid job. Let the valuable employee know this and let her know that the skill she has shown in patient care is too important to lose.

7.6 List of Duties for Office Managers

I frequently help optometrists who are promoting or hiring a new office manager and a question often comes up about what should be included in the job description. I think it is important that the duties of the job evolve over time with the practice owner actively providing training and guidance. I think the list of specific duties will be obvious as the OD/owner gradually delegates more tasks, but I am asked about this often enough that I'll provide a list of job responsibilities in this article.

Dual role

I think all practices should have an office manager (or other similar terms for this job position). The optometrist can certainly fill that role in smaller practices, but I think it is best to begin to develop a business model that encourages delegation of some of the administrative tasks.

In smaller to medium sized practices, the manager usually has a dual role such as optician and manager, or front desk and manager. This works out well and allows for a gradual increase in administrative duties as the practice grows. It allows the manager to have a full time position and still provide some patient services.

As a valuable staff member is identified for the manager role, it is wise to keep in mind that as the practice grows, the role will usually become completely administrative and managerial. That staff member may not work much with patients anymore. The practice owner should decide if that is the best use for that employee.

New manager will not know everything.

I sometimes find that an optometrist would like to be completely rid of most or all of the administrative burden of owning a business. The OD hopes to outsource the management, but that rarely works out very well. A new employee will not know how to automatically be a good manager for that practice. It is up to the owner (with some staff support) to share his or her vision of the practice and train the manager on how the practice operates. I look at this as a long process that could take years to become completely effective. It is best for the OD to always be involved to some degree in the operation of the business. I would rather the OD/owner hire another OD to see some patients if needed in order to create enough time to effectively lead the practice.

Important trait

A manager is a leader in the practice and is therefore partly responsible for the organizational culture. That becomes the personality of the practice; it shapes the morale and attitudes of the staff members. To build a positive culture, it's important that the manager be compassionate and caring. Rules must be enforced when managing employees, but I don't look for someone tough who can rule with an iron fist. Staff often need to vent about frustrations on the job and the manager should fill that need by being understanding and fair.

List of duties

Here is a list of typical tasks that are often assigned to managers. Depending on the size of the practice, the manager may delegate many of these items to others, but he or she should supervise and be responsible for them. The manager may act as a backup person. I recommend that the practice try to avoid ever being in a position where only one person knows how to complete an important task. In fact, the OD should have some knowledge about most items as a backup to the manager.

- Supervise daily reconciliation of payments.
- Supervise bank deposits and receipt verification.
- Manage all aspects of staff: scheduling, punctuality, time off with or without pay, complaints.
- Supervise and direct staff in day-to-day operations.
- Supervise all aspects of optical dispensing, contact lenses, product orders and delivery. This area may be delegated to a co-manager or department manager.
- Ongoing staff training and remediation.
- Recruit, hire and fire staff.
- Plan and conduct staff meetings (weekly).
- Manage patient complaints.
- Supervise all office supplies.
- Supervise all aspects of customer service.
- Manage recall tactics (monthly and daily).
- Print and mail statements to patients (monthly).
- Track data; produce reports (monthly and as needed).
- Supervise and assist insurance billing and claim filing.
- Review and manage accounts receivable aging reports for patients and insurance plans.
- Open mail and distribute unopened mail to practice owner.
- Manage bookkeeping; enter data into QuickBooks or other.
- Manage the practice marketing plan and calendar; logistics of marketing.
- Order and supervise maintenance on the facility and equipment.

- Assist with information technology.
- Test new procedures and policies.
- Maintain an office policy manual (employment issues) and a practice procedure manual (how-to guide).

7.7 Delegating Sensitive Information to a Manager

I have long advocated that OD/practice owners appoint an office manager. It represents a major step forward in building a practice that does not depend on the doctor for everything. It can free the practice owner to focus on other tasks, be it patient care or higher level management. Many ODs have an employee with the manager job title, but struggle with how much financial information should be shared.

This article will give you some direction on how to delegate more to your manager, but preserve the privacy of some data.

Management philosophies
There are many degrees of information-sharing in a business, with traditional management at one end of the spectrum and open-book management at the other. How much you share depends on your business philosophy; it is really up to you. But even advocates of an open-book system may want to keep some data private, such as wages of certain employees or personal income of the owner.

Here is a list of some of the items you might like to delegate to a manager, but you may not be sure how much to reveal.

- Employee wages
- Associate doctor salaries
- Owner's personal salary or draw amounts
- Bonus amounts
- Bank deposits
- Practice check register
- Manager's ability to sign checks or use credit cards

Employee wages
Letting the manager be aware of the wages of most employees offers a big benefit to the practice owner. Once you get past that hurdle, the manager can truly take over most of the hiring process and employment review process, with your guidance. Managing the staff is a huge drain on time for

the OD/owner and it is one of the most important tasks a manager can do. You can still hold back some salary information and I'll show you how below, but consider meeting with your manager and delegating the wage and review process.

When you first break through with this procedure, it is possible that you will upset some people, so develop a plan first, but realize that once you get past the initial change, your practice will be much more efficient. First consider what salaries you don't want to share. Maybe you will not share the doctors' salary information. Second, consider if the manager will likely be unhappy if he or she learns that another employee is earning more. In general though, it may be best to try to share as much information as you are comfortable with. After all, there are no rules that say a valuable optician should not earn more than a manager.

A nice side benefit of getting your manager involved in staff wages is that the other employees begin to truly see the manager as their boss, which will make the manager more effective. After all, the person who makes your initial job offer, and the person who does your review and tells you the amount of your raise is a person you consider to be your boss.

To be clear, we consider wages a private and personal matter and while the manager may learn the wages of others, you must make it clear that this is highly confidential and may not be shared with anyone.

Payroll service

I highly recommend that you use a payroll service, which could be a national company or some local CPA firms also offer this. By using a service, the payroll reports can be separated by employee category and can be delivered only to the owner, if desired. Or some categories are delivered to the owner and some to the manager. Also, payroll services can deliver paychecks (for those who do not use direct deposit) in sealed envelopes. The manager can simply receive the envelopes and distribute them.

Your office manager can still track the hours of all employees, preferably with virtual time clock software, and submit the hours worked, sick days, vacation days and any other payroll information to the payroll service.

The actual record of employee wages and dates of raises can be kept on a spreadsheet or in a ledger book that only the manager and owner have access to. The owner may leave key employees out of this record and handle them personally.

Separate bank accounts

Another factor in keeping wage information private is the practice bank account the payments are drawn from. Ideally, the manager will also have access to the checking account register in order to assist with accounts payable. A payroll service can print and issue checks on this account and provide a grand total for the entire pay period, without showing the actual names on the checks and the individual amounts. A large total is deducted from the bank balance and just labeled as payroll, so the manager can't tell who received what.

Additionally, it is helpful for the practice to have a checking account and a separate money market (savings) account, and the manager may only have access to the former. The practice owner can move funds from one account to the other. These accounts are both still corporate and moving money does not change the income tax situation as it does when money is taken by the owner personally. If cash flow is strong and profits are good, the owner can move some money from checking into savings. Also, if money is tight, the owner may need to move some money from the savings account into the checking account in order to pay bills. Be sure to code this type of deposit as a fund transfer and not as practice income. A payment of profit distribution to the owner personally can occur from the money market account and need not be visible to the manager.

7.8 More Sensitive Information for Managers

Last week, I wrote about how to delegate sensitive information, like employee wages, to managers. I'll continue with that theme here in an effort to help you prepare your practice to be fully operational without the doctor/owner having to be present. With proper training, a manager can handle more and more of the day-to-day responsibilities of the office. Ideally, the OD owner can work on other aspects of the practice or even be away from the office for extended periods of time.

Daily bank deposits

Your manager can be trained to handle most of the financial aspects of the practice, with some owner supervision, which I will expand on below. Starting with the basics, the manager can be in charge of making a daily bank deposit. I recommend a daily process to reconcile the cash drawer with the daily production report, which basically proves that cash, checks and credit card receipts from the previous day are accounted for. I use a process where the bank deposit always matches the previous day's receipts exactly and multiple days are not combined so we have a reliable record. The staff member who actually takes the deposit to the bank must always receive a receipt showing the amount of the deposit and that is given to the practice owner.

Check register and accounts payable

An office manager may serve as an in-house bookkeeper. Most ODs use QuickBooks or a similar financial software program and I think these work very well. A manager many have password access to the practice checking account, but no access to other accounts the owner may have. Develop a system and train your manager to receive and open invoices and statements received via U.S. mail or email and post the payments in the check register. Auto-payments are posted for our records and payments that need a physical check are posted but must be approved by the owner before the check may be issued. With remote login or cloud-based programs, the owner and manager can both view the check register and make entries or check marks.

The owner should generally have a good idea of the appropriate amounts due to various suppliers and if an amount seems out of line, it can be researched further before paying. After payments are approved, the manager can print and sign checks or a check signature stamp can be used.

Credit card and petty cash

In addition to the practice checking account, which the manager may not be authorized to initiate payments on without direct approval, it is useful to have an additional checking account called petty cash. This would be a joint account with the manager and practice owner, but it will mostly be used by the manager to pay for smaller expenses that arise unexpectedly such as a service call or purchasing an item for the office. Risk is small with this approach because the balance in this account may be kept fairly low, maybe $1,000 maximum, and it is replenished as needed. Receipts can be kept as a record of the expenses on this account. A check can also be written for cash from time to time if cash is needed.

A business credit card with the manager as an authorized signature is also very helpful and can have a moderate credit limit for safety. This card can be used to order items online and it is paid by the business checking account on a monthly basis.

Handling contractors and repairs

Generally, all assorted repairs and maintenance issues fall on the practice owner, but the owner can delegate these tasks to a manager. Begin by having the manager be part of a few meetings and cost estimates with contractors or service people and then turn the job over. The owner can advise the manager about the scope of a job, which service firm to call, and approve the estimate, but let the manager handle the details.

Ongoing supervision
I think it is good practice for the owner to always remain involved and aware of practice finances. We may assume that our employees are honest and will do the right thing, but embezzlement and theft do occur. Additionally, we must always be aware that employees can resign at some point and if the owner does not know how to jump in and perform a task until a replacement is found, big problems can occur. It is smart to delegate, but don't give up control.

7.9 Five Success Factors for Office Managers

I work with office managers (or practice administrators) quite often in my consulting work and this article will be directed at that group and to optometrists who want to train and lead managers to greater success. I think the office manager position is very important in any optometric practice and if your practice does not currently have that job position, you should set a goal to develop it and fill it.

In many practices, the manager has a dual role and is coupled with other duties that are directed at patient care, such as optical dispensing or front desk work. As the practice grows larger, the manager will generally become so busy with administrative tasks that he or she drops the other tasks. I think the best formula for success is an optometrist/owner who has some dedicated time for practice management working with an office manager.

Here are my five key points for successful managers:

1. Make money. I'm often amazed at how many optometric staff members do not think generating revenue is part of their job. It is, and especially so for managers! Some managers are so focused on the delivery of good eye care and optical products they forget they are operating a business and, unless it is a charitable endeavor, the primary goal is to make a profit! And revenue must increase every year to keep up with rising costs and hopefully create more profit. Once a manager starts thinking about generating revenue, he or she

can have a huge impact and I'm positive the practice owner will love it! Rewards follow employees who help the company achieve its goals.

If you are unsure about how to help your practice generate more income, remember that there are only three ways for a practice to do that. Lead and inspire your staff to embrace these factors:

- See more patients per day. You may need more staff to do that, but the revenue potential is much greater than the extra wages. You can see more patients per day without stress.
- Sell more things to each patient. When I use the word "sell" it can mean many things. We sell the reputation of the practice, we sell by making appointments (sooner, not later), we sell by delivering medical eye care, we sell by getting compliance with recall messages, and we sell multiple pairs of glasses and contact lenses.
- Raise fees or reduce discounts. Your fees may be out of date. Raising fees helps profitability even if you have a lot of vision plans.

2. Cut expenses. We never want wasted operating costs or overpayment for supplies in any business, but be careful because cutting some costs could reduce service or quality and that is a bad move. Basically, be sure you save the practice money whenever you can and not hurt services. That might include returning products under warranty, watching the spoilage rate if your lab makes lenses, letting some hourly staff go home early if they are not needed (assuming they agree), and shopping for supplies to get the best price.

3. Make patients happy. Word of mouth referral is still the biggest source of new patients to a practice and most practices need far more patients. You have to make customer service truly amazing in order to garner the maximum word-of-mouth impact. You may have to go against your sense of fairness and let the patient win and smile about it. Does that sound difficult? Read up on the greatest companies in the world or think about the stores and businesses that you love and see how they do it.

4. Make staff happy. You want your office to be a great place to work. You want it to be a pleasant and happy work environment. You want the staff to smile and be friendly to each other and to patients. It is the culture of the organization that causes that and the culture is created by the leaders. A great manager is compassionate and caring. Even if you can't say yes to every request from staff members, you can listen and be understanding and be sure the office policies are applied with fairness. In fact, it is the fairness factor

that is often the reason you can't say yes. But try to say yes as much as possible or try to find a compromise that everyone can live with. Always treat co-workers with respect. I don't think there is ever a need for anger in the office. Maybe disappointment, but not anger.

5. Increase efficiency. This is a counterpart to factor #1, but it is very important. Wasting time is just like wasting money. We don't want to rush to the point that it causes mistakes or creates stress, but some people need to work faster. Work with the practice owner to delegate more tasks to staff members. Help the doctor work at his or her highest level. A manager should supervise staff members and when their priorities are off, the manager directs them to the right action. Managers are like coaches in sports; they are continuously training the team.

Chapter 8. Staff Training and Meetings

8.1 Staff Training: Your Secret Weapon

I've always had great pride in my staff; since opening my practice cold with one receptionist to the present day with a very large staff of opticians, technicians, front desk specialists and managers. I'm a teacher at heart and I've always worked to continuously train my staff in clinical eye care, optical dispensing and customer service. I've held staff meetings every week for over 30 years. I send staff to major conferences like Vision Expo or SECO as well as local meetings. I recently learned it is not enough. I need to do much more with staff training and if I do, I'm quite sure it will help my practice.

What I learned about scribes

We have had our clinical technicians working as scribes with our doctors for a very long time and I have studied the various benefits we derive from that approach. I just came across a new one: having the technicians listen to the doctors as they perform tests, diagnose, treat and educate patients has made the techs very knowledgeable in clinical eye care. They now have the confidence to intelligently talk to patients all by themselves and explain eye conditions and treatments. This is a benefit for our practice. Patients often don't think of everything they want to ask when they are with the doctor and talking to an assistant can be quite comforting.

We still need staff to continue learning about clinical eye care and billing and coding, but observing an expert every day provides a great knowledge base.

More optical training

The area that I think my staff needs much more training in is optical dispensing. Staff members don't typically get a chance to observe others in optical. Of course, we hire opticians with excellent training and experience whenever we can, but the reality is that their backgrounds are widely diverse. Many were trained on the job at a previous employer. There are a wide range of skill levels among opticians and optometric technicians. We may have a new employee learning from someone who is not performing at the highest level.

This becomes more difficult because optometrists themselves are not always well-trained in optical dispensing. And most ODs know nothing about sales techniques. It is very hard to design an in-office training program if you are not an expert in that field.

Because of these issues, I think most optometric staff members need much more training in optical products, proper eyeglass fitting and measurements, and sales.

Customer service

The third topic area we need to train staff in is customer service. This is vitally important in order to increase patient demand and it must be continuous. We need specific training programs in patient satisfaction, but it also should become part of the office culture. When great service and convenience is woven into the day-to-day policies and procedures, no one has to think about what to do; it is just the normal way we do things.

DIY

I think the core training program in a practice should be designed and provided by the owner, doctor and manager. Staff members can also participate in training their co-workers by sharing areas of expertise. All it takes is knowledge of the subject matter and organization.

Training may be as simple as just talking about real world situations. You could begin by sharing with staff exactly how you would perform a frame selection and lens design. What would you say if you were the optician? How would you explain each optical product? How would you respond if the patient asks tough questions about price? Let your staff share their experiences and challenges.

At a higher level, you could choose a topic and give a mini-presentation. Pick a clinical topic or an optical product or a customer service issue and talk about it. Prepare a handout with bullet points.

Training can occur at weekly staff meetings, but I'm beginning to think we need more than one hour per week. That staff meeting is often used up with administrative issues and we don't have time to do real training. I'm certain the investment in training is more valuable than the patients we could have seen in that time period.

Training resources

In addition to your own core training sessions, there are many benefits to providing your staff with professional training. Some of these resources have a cost, but I believe that is money well spent.

- Major eye conferences. Send one or two staff members and they will return very excited about their job.
- Lab, frame, contact lens, and equipment reps can make presentations to your staff during regular staff meetings.
- Professional speakers or consultants can come to your office and present a workshop for a fee. Close the office for a half day.

- State optometric meetings. There are special programs for staff and the cost is low with minimal travel.
- The AOA is now accepting optometric staff as AOA associate members and they have a strong training program. Visit http://www.aoa.org/paraoptometrics for more information.
- Essilor has a wonderful staff training program that includes online videos for in-office education. It is called ECP University.
- Join a doctor's alliance group that has staff training programs and meetings.
- Many companies in the industry offer webinars on a variety of topics of interest to staff.

8.2 An Idea to Make Training New Staff Easier

All practices have staff turnover at some point. Larger practices have more employees and therefore more turnover. The whole process of interviewing and hiring new employees is very time consuming. So here is an idea that will immediately make the task easier: as you train the next new employee in your office, use your smart phone to make a series of video recordings about each procedure. You or a staff member are going over each job function anyway; it takes no more time to tap record and make a video.

Don't worry about making it perfect; these videos are for your internal use only and they don't need to be perfect. The recording will be just like real life, and it is not perfect. The next time you hire an employee, you will have a library of short training videos that are customized for your practice.

Staff training
Most practices assign the training of new employees to senior staff members. This works well, but some staff do not enjoy the process of training others. Making videos will reduce the need for current staff to train newcomers, so the idea should be well received.

Start with a list of job duties the new employee needs to be trained on. This depends on your practice, but it could include:

- Front desk duties like scheduling an appointment on office software
- Confirming appointments
- Preparing files and paperwork
- Clinical technician duties like taking retinal photos
- Measuring visual acuity

- Doing autorefraction
- Lensometry
- Performing visual fields and OCT
- How to use electronic health record software
- Optical dispensing duties like frame selection
- Measuring PDs and seg heights
- Writing up an eyeglass order
- Pricing with vision plans and billing

Making the video

The important thing about the video recording process is to break the files up into separate topics. It is better to have more videos and make them shorter. It is also important to name the file accurately by using the name of the job duty or instrument that is being trained.

Ideally, you will have a senior employee showing the newbie how to do something and a third employee may be present in some cases to act as a practice patient. In this case, the third employee can record the video and act as the patient at the same time. In some cases, the new employee can handle the smart phone camera and pay attention to being taught at the same time.

Another idea is to move the camera (phone) far enough away that it can record the whole area and prop it up using a device on a table. Inexpensive phone and iPad holders are available online and in retail stores. Then just hit record and leave it alone. This method does not allow for a close view of a screen or other target and it does not allow for panning, but it still gets the job done.

Store the videos on a hard drive in your office computer or server and keep a backup. You can make the videos available to any staff member and they can watch them as many times as need.

8.3 Hosting Your Own Lunch and Learn Series

Optometrists occasionally ask me what to do about staff members who make errors. In some cases, it seems like a great many errors. The OD sometimes seems rather surprised and wonders how these mistakes can happen. I have to remind these colleagues that when we hire an optician, receptionist or office manager, we can't expect perfection. They don't know everything. It is the practice owner's responsibility to provide training for staff members and that should continue for more than the first two weeks of employment. We will never completely eliminate mistakes because we are all human, but an ongoing training program can greatly reduce them.

In this article I will describe a new program I implemented in my practice and you may want to do something similar.

Staff meetings vs training programs
We have always had weekly staff meetings (in addition to our daily morning huddles with key staff) and I strongly recommend that doctors plan these frequent and regular meetings. My intention is always to use some of that staff meeting time for training, and we discuss many topics that we need to improve upon, but we often don't have time to do a real educational presentation.

I decided to continue with my weekly staff meetings, but add a new monthly training meeting called Lunch and Learn.

Lunch and Learn logistics
The Lunch and Learn educational series is different from staff meetings because it offers a couple of small perks to the attendees: 1) it occurs over the lunch break and the practice will pay employees their normal wages (my staff are usually not paid for lunch breaks) and 2) the practice brings in a nice lunch for the group. Staff members have a good feeling about this meeting.

A benefit to the practice of having the meeting over lunch is that we do not have to block any of the patient schedule. You will have to plan how this will work for your practice. In my office, we need some staff to manage walk-ins and phone calls, so we limit the number of employees who can attend a Lunch and Learn. We will repeat the same topic again on a different day for other staff members if needed. We currently schedule one Lunch and Learn per month, but we may increase that in the future.

We have a variety of people present the educational program. Most often, it will be one of our senior employees, but it could be a doctor or a representative from an industry supplier. I would not force an employee to speak to the group if they are not comfortable, although a small group of co-workers is not difficult for most people to talk with. I do expect the presenter to put in some preparation time in advance.

Possible topics

I think you will find no shortage of topic ideas once you get started with your Lunch and Learn series, but here are a few to consider. Some topics are targeted for opticians, some for clinical staff and some are for front desk assistants.

- Proper frame fitting
- Digital lenses: why are they better?
- Vision plan review: how to price products
- The medical model: how to bill medical insurance when the patient has a vision plan
- Lens materials: when to use what
- Visual fields: what are we really testing?
- Asking for additional appointments
- Digital dispensing measurements with our device
- Patient communication
- These glasses have prism (I think)
- Online optical: what to say when asked for a PD
- Presenting the option for routine retinal photos
- What to say when you dispense new glasses
- HIPAA review: what you can and can't do
- Suggesting second and third pairs of glasses
- Ocular nutrition and preventing AMD

Support materials

I encourage the presenter to use PowerPoint slides to help them to be organized and to let the audience have a visual aid. One of your staff can help those who are not familiar with PowerPoint; if you can type you can create a presentation in minutes. You may want to install a large flat screen TV on a wall in the room where this meeting will be held. You can just plug a laptop or tablet into the TV or many devices offer mirroring technology.

In many cases, the presentation could include a demonstration with an actual instrument or with real frames or lenses. This works great with the small groups we will have. The staff may be able to practice on each other in some cases.

I would always require a handout. It may be only one page, but the attendees should leave with something to remind them of the key points and keep all the handouts in a notebook.

Always encourage and leave time for questions and answers.

8.4 Policy for Staff Education and Travel

A few weeks ago I wrote about the importance of staff training and I've had several colleagues ask how to handle the issue of wages and travel expense if employees are sent to major conferences that are out of town. I think sending one or two staff members to a major conference provides a level of training that can't be matched in your office, plus the staff receive a huge morale boost for their career. The AOA, SECO, Vision Expo, AAO, and national alliance groups all put on outstanding meetings with world class speakers and a vendor exhibit area that is also educational.

There is a significant cost to sending an employee on an educational trip, but it is a pre-tax business expense investment and the return on investment is very strong. A well-trained staff elevates your practice. You can decide how many staff members you can send and how frequently. It can be viewed as a bonus for high level performers and it may stimulate other employees who would like to be considered for the opportunity next year.

Office policy
To keep the expenses under control, you need an office policy for staff training and education. When I wrote the policy for my practice, I wrestled with how much to pay and how to do it. I had to realize that even though a trip to a conference is more fun than a day at the office, it is still work for the employee and they should be compensated for their time, plus the travel expense.

Here is the policy I came up with for my practice:

Education and Travel Policy

- Education is not mandatory; employees do not have to attend meetings outside the office except under special circumstances that will be announced.
- Educational programs and specific courses must be approved by the doctor. Several factors will be evaluated and not all requests can be honored.
- The practice pays the employee's usual wage for full days or half days spent at educational programs and in travel. It makes no difference if the days are usually scheduled for work or not.
- The doctor will determine how many full or half days are spent in education and travel.

- The practice pays for the registration and educational course expense.
- The practice pays for travel expense but hotel and air fare arrangements must be approved by the doctor in advance of booking. Driving is reimbursed at the current IRS mileage rate.
- The practice will reimburse the employee for reasonable meal expense, taxi, parking etc. upon submission of receipts. The allowance for meals shall be $50 for a full day unless special arrangements are approved.
- Employees who register for courses but cancel or do not show will be charged for any fees or travel expenses that are not refundable.
- If the practice is closed for education courses, no hourly wages are paid to employees who choose to not attend the education.
- A spouse or guest may accompany the employee to an out-of-town conference provided it is clearly understood that the purpose of the trip is for work and the employee must spend the entire full day or half day at the conference. Also, any additional travel or meal expense will be paid by the employee.

8.5 Staff Meetings 101: The When, Why and How

After Vision Expo West and then another practice management conference in Toronto, I'm realizing that many eye care professionals don't have regular weekly staff meetings. I think most practice owners and managers know they should have them, but they just don't get around to making the time. Many doctors used to hold regular meetings but stopped. Now is the time to put weekly meetings back on the books and begin to reap the rewards. I think you need to meet once per week with the whole staff, but daily five minute meetings with key people is also a good idea.

There is no one right or wrong way to hold staff meetings; the important thing is that you meet. I'll offer some guidelines here in an effort to pave the way for you.

When

I would schedule the meetings for every Monday from 9 to 10am. Just block the appointment schedule in advance so no patients are booked. Go ahead right now and find the first Monday that is empty in that time slot and block it off along with every Monday after that. Once you have it on the books, you are committed and the odds are good you'll actually meet.

Don't worry about the lost revenue from that one hour per week. The improvement in your staff and in your office operation is far more important and well worth the cost. Besides, you really should be able to delegate a little more and still see those patients so production need not be lost.

I don't like to hold staff meetings before work or after hours because employees have families they need to care for. We want to be a good place to work and we're considerate of employees' wants and needs. I also don't like to close the office for routine meetings. It's not good customer service for the patient to find the door locked or voice mail on during normal business hours (Monday through Friday, 9 to 5).

You may be able to meet with your whole staff at once if the office is not very busy during this non-appointed hour and just designate someone to take care of the rare walk-in or phone call. Just work around it. If there is just one doctor and one employee, I would still hold a regular meeting each week. If the practice is larger, you could meet in two shifts like I do. The first session is with the business office staff while the technicians and opticians take care of phones and walk-ins. Then the groups switch places. Some of the items on our agenda may have to be repeated for each group, but many issues are specific to just one department anyway.

I prefer everyone to attend the meetings: practice owners, associate doctors, office managers, lab technicians and staff members. If you have multiple offices, that can be a challenge. Each office can meet with its staff only and the owner may not be able to attend all of the meetings so an office manager may chair the meeting.

Why

You need to meet with your staff on a regular basis to improve communications and to provide leadership on many issues. This is how you improve the culture of your practice and build a better staff. You can inspire and motivate staff to provide better customer service and to have better attitudes.

Here are some examples of how the improved communication can help you manage your practice:

- Work with staff on how to handle customer service issues. Use real examples that occurred in your office.
- Discuss office procedures and review how you do things.
- Announce new events and marketing programs.

- Review administrative procedures such as billing or ordering supplies.
- Provide staff training on clinical or optical procedures. Occasionally, a sales rep may be invited to participate. Or the doctor can explain a technical procedure. An educated staff is a better staff.
- Present new products such as new contact lens designs or new frames that are available.
- Get feedback from staff about patient phone calls, complaints about fees, use and interest in new vision plans, obstacles to making an appointment, walk-in Rxs from other doctors, requests to take spectacle Rxs out, and patient interest in online sales of contact lenses and eyeglasses. There are many things you need to know!
- Brainstorm new ways to grow the practice and improve word of mouth referrals from patients.

How

Begin by noticing the good and the bad in your office for one week. Carry some note cards with you and jot down things you see and hear that are examples of excellent service and issues that need work.

Take your list to the meeting and ask other key people in your office to bring any times they wish to discuss each week.

- Be sure to focus on some positive actions. Don't overlook all the things your staff does right. If you had a compliment from a patient, share it.
- Don't single anyone out as an example of bad performance. Criticize individuals in private only. You may bring up and work on problems that affect the office as a whole, but keep emotion out of it. Anger is counter-productive.
- Be sure to let others talk. Encourage questions. Ask questions of the group to encourage interaction. Role-playing works well. Invite someone to discuss how they handle certain situations. It may take a few meetings for some staff members to feel confident enough to participate.
- Invite other key staff to bring anything new to the meeting form their departments and also to bring up problems. The doctor or manager can serve as a moderator to prevent the tone of the meeting from becoming too negative. Keep it constructive and positive.
- If you aren't sure how to handle a tough situation, which easily happens, don't be pressured into making a bad decision on the spot. Say you'll think about it and get back to the staff.

If you need ideas for staff meeting content, consider these:

- Ask employees to describe for you one thing they noticed that makes patients unhappy. Overcoming the problem is a great topic.
- Ask staff for help doing a SWOT analysis on the practice: list the strengths, weaknesses, opportunities and threats of the practice and discuss how to make the most of the good and prevent the bad.
- Review or develop the practice mission statement. What business are you really in? What are your priorities? How well are you living up to the mission?

8.6 Ideas for Staff Meetings

I received an email from a colleague who said he was one of those optometrists I mentioned at the end of last week's Tip on time management who has abandoned staff meetings. He went on to ask what should go into a good staff meeting. He said he discusses practice metrics with his staff, but sometimes it feels there is nothing else to cover.

I think many ODs are in that situation. Read on for ideas on how to make your staff meetings more productive.

Just meet and talk
Many optometrists and managers do a masterful job of preparing for staff meetings and for those who want to go to great lengths, I think it is great. But the important thing is that staff members and doctors meet and talk about the practice on a frequent basis. Don't let preparing an agenda and coming up with topics stop you. Just meet every week at the same time. Block out the appointment schedule. Pay the staff. The communication will result in a much stronger practice and I have no doubt you will increase your gross and net revenues.

I rarely present practice metrics at my staff meetings. There is nothing wrong with doing it and many ODs and business leaders get great results by using data-driven goals. Some like to use charts and graphs. Some feel staff members are motivated by friendly competitions. It is just not me and not my style. Being true to yourself and believing in your message is the most important thing.

Ideas for meetings
Here are some topics you can use to inspire your staff meetings:

- Who should speak? Before we discuss what to say, let's consider who should say it. I think meetings are better when several people contribute. I would tell some key staff members that you'd like them to talk about a few things at the weekly meeting. Let them prepare in advance, but make sure they know it is very informal. They can make some notes during the week about anything in their area that could be improved. Or just ask some questions about a problem.
- Of course, I also think it is good for one or more doctors to speak at every meeting. Doctors are natural leaders in the practice and they have great knowledge of eye care. Practice owners also generally have a feel for the business aspects of the practice and they should be prepared to talk about that in general terms.
- Do you have an office manager? If not, I think you should appoint one and then she/he can assist with the staff meetings.
- What is new? I observe my practice all week long and I make notes on what I see. I always see things we could do better. I can't imagine not having something to talk about. I'm always working on something new. If you are not, try to think about how you can improve things. In many cases, it is more efficient to instruct the whole staff at once rather than just one person at a time. But the big rule is to not embarrass any individual in front of their peers. If an issue is really with just one person and everyone knows it, speak to that person in private, not at a staff meeting.
- What else is new? Any new frame lines? Office forms? Medications? Instruments? Insurance plans? Bring it to the meeting.
- What is good in the practice? I try to make staff meetings mostly positive. Tell staff what they do well. I often bring some of our patient surveys to the meeting and read them - especially if a patient mentions a staff member by name in a good way.
- What could be better? It is necessary to talk about problems in order to improve upon them. You may even be able to get some help with solving a problem by asking for staff input. Employees have some great ideas and they may be closer to a situation than the doctor. But be careful about asking for input if you already know what you want to do. It can hurt morale if you ask but don't give the input a serious chance of working. There is an art to bringing up bad news without making people feel terrible. Try to avoid blame. Definitely avoid anger. Try to state the facts and work toward improving the situation in the future.
- Eye care education. Staff meetings are a perfect time to teach staff about eye care. It could be medical eye care, the reason we do certain tests, what is a true ocular emergency, contact lenses and

there are plenty of things about optical dispensing. ODs can discuss their thoughts about dispensing glasses. A senior optician could present on some aspect of measuring and fitting glasses. A lab technician can demonstrate how to do a difficult repair.

- Invite sales reps on occasion. I like to screen the content somewhat, unless I know the rep really well, but sales reps can bring high quality education to your meetings. They might be from an optical lab, a contact lens company, an equipment dealer, a drug company or a software firm. Consider providing them a flat screen TV to connect their laptop for PowerPoint.
- What does the practice need? Seriously, what do you need most? More patients? More multiple pair sales? Higher frame price points? Faster pretesting? More sales of full year supplies of contact lenses? More sales of premium digital progressives? A higher opt-in rate for screening retinal photos? Better results with recall? A decrease of no shows? Just tell your staff what you need and see if they can help. Employees support what they help to invent!
- How can we speed up patient flow so we could see more patients per day without stress?
- What is affecting the business in general terms? How do we compete with online optical vendors or big chain stores? How can we embrace medical insurance as part of health care reform? Are vision plan discounts taking a big bite out of profits? Let staff know what is happening in the profession and industry.
- Teach staff not to prejudge the patient's ability to pay. Let's focus on providing the best eye care first; not the cheapest. It is very unfair for staff to assume they know best about what a patient wants or can afford. Judging based on appearance, clothing, occupation or town of residence is a big mistake and it is discriminatory. Let the patient tell us when they want a more economical option and we will help them with that, but start with the best.
- Review the patient experience. Have your staff list every point of contact your office has with a patient, starting with the first phone call. Walk through a typical visit. What does the patient see and hear? Consider the eyeglass sale and delivery. How could the experience be improved? How is the customer service at each step?
- Do a SWOT analysis. Make a list with your staff of the strengths, weaknesses, opportunities and threats to your practice. Discuss how to maximize the good things and overcome the bad.
- What marketing projects could the practice undertake? How is your community outreach? Practice Facebook page? Website? Recall system? Can staff members help with the projects?

Ask questions

A great way to start staff meetings, possibly after some general announcements, is to ask questions of the staff. This is a great way to make the meeting not always one-sided with the doctor and manager doing all the talking. There are many aspects of the practice that staff know more about than anyone else. You don't need to have the answers to your own questions; you can often figure out solutions as you get staff input.

I recommend that someone take notes at meetings. This will help with following up on issues and the notes can be read by anyone who misses the meeting. In some cases, if you are brainstorming, you can take notes on a large paper easel or white board. Someone can take photos of the boards with their smart phone for a record before erasing them.

Here are some possible questions to get you started:

- How could we improve the profitability of the practice?
  - It's OK to let staff know that the practice is a business and like any business, you need to continuously increase profit.
  - There are only four big ways to make more money: see more patients per day, sell more things to each patient, raise fees and reduce expenses. See if your employees come up with these.
- How could we sell multiple pairs of glasses at the same time?
  - Do staff bring up the idea now?
  - Are opticians too busy to bring up a second pair?
  - What discount do you offer?
- How could we improve efficiency?
  - What are the bottlenecks that often slow down the process?
- What are some examples of waste in the office, in time or money?
- What are some of the most common errors we all make?
  - In billing?
  - In optical measurements?
- What are some of the hardest questions patients ask you?
- What questions do we get that we don't have a good answer for or the answer is not what the patient hopes to hear?
- What are a few things that we do that make patients unhappy, uncomfortable or embarrassed?
- If we get a complaint, what is it likely to be about?
  - What can you do to prevent and resolve the unpleasant experiences?

- What data should we measure? How can we measure these things?
    - Metrics like these are good: Rx retention rate, multiple pair sales as a percentage, and percentage of contact lens patients who buy a full year supply.

Staff members are more likely to support what they help to invent. Try not to deliver edicts, but enlist staff to find solutions with you.

One other good exercise for staff meetings is to have a virtual walk-through for a typical patient visit to the office. Start with the first phone call for an appointment, then review every step, every communication through the exam, everything the patient sees and any dispensing of products. As you discuss every step, consider how well you are doing it and if it can be improved.

Chapter 9. Customer Service

9.1 The Practice Building Power of Customer Service

I'm sure all optometrists know that customer service is important for practice growth, but in my consulting experience, there are obvious lapses in putting that into effect. And many ODs and their staffs may not fully understand just how powerful customer service is as a tool for increasing patient volume. In my opinion, customer service is the most effective tool there is.

The biggest problem facing optometry today

Let's put the importance of customer service in perspective by realizing that lack of patient demand is the biggest problem facing optometry today. As you consider all the challenges facing our profession (and there are many), understand that they all go away if you have enough people calling your office for eye care. Although rare, some practices have the wonderful problem of "too many patients". That is a problem that is fairly easy to manage and capitalize on. Let's look at how those practices got that way.

Word-of-mouth

Optometrists who own independent private practices generally agree that word-of-mouth referral is the largest source of new patients. Even though marketing trends are changing rapidly, ODs still do not do a lot of traditional advertising. Happy, loyal patients telling their friends, family members and co-workers about how much they love your practice has always been extremely powerful. This still happens in live conversations, but it also occurs on social media. It is all considered word-of-mouth. Even patients who say they found you on an insurance provider website may have been aided by word-of-mouth. They may look up doctors in their zip code area, but when they see the list of names, they remember a friend who said she went to your office.

All practices obtain some word-of-mouth referrals from happy patients, but some practices receive a huge amount. Why is that? Of course, the size of the patient base is a factor, but the beauty of word-of-mouth is that it grows exponentially. A core of happy patients recommends you to others and then they recommend you to others, and so on.

Word-of-mouth referral occurs when patients are beyond satisfied with your services. We must set a higher goal than merely satisfied. We must reach for enthusiastic. We achieve that through the patient experience.

What is great customer service?

We may all think we know great customer service when we see it, but let's break it down to the real world of optometric practice. The doctor and staff must be really great in all of the following areas:

- The facility. Much of the patient experience is based on factors that have nothing to do with eye care. The appearance of the physical office affects the perception of everything else. This includes the décor, the interior design factors, colors, flooring, furniture, countertops and more. Unnecessary, but thoughtful touches aimed at patient comfort are a factor. Smells and noises are a factor. The exterior of the building, parking and landscaping are factors. The appearance of the clinical equipment and the optical dispensary play a big role. Even the clothing or uniforms worn by staff influence the perception. At the very least, the entire office must be impeccably clean, even the bathrooms.
- The interpersonal factors. This is really just being nice to people. It includes good manners and being attentive and thoughtful. Smiling has a huge effect. Using a patient's name (even though you don't have to) builds relationships.
- Convenience. You might not think of convenience when it comes to customer service issues, but you should. Making wait times minimal, reducing the paperwork for patients, easy parking and accepting most insurance plans are examples. Being open some evenings and Saturdays and telling people with an urgent need to come right over are also factors.
- Easy to do business with. This is related to convenience, but I'd use examples like quick check-in and check-out and fast delivery times on glasses and contact lenses. Explaining policies and quoting fees in advance are other ways to earn points in the patient experience.
- The professional services and products. This may seem obvious, but the patient must think the eye exam was performed well and any optical products purchased must meet or exceed expectations for visual function, comfort and cosmetic appearance.
- Service recovery. How well does your office handle matters when something goes wrong? It's easy to provide great service when the patient loves you and cooperates, but how do you handle the unreasonable person? This takes a deeper understanding about the big picture of customer service as a business development tool, but ODs who get this and inspire their staff to get it are usually the recipients of lots of word-of-mouth. Big picture, long term profitability is worth far more than the minor cost of letting the

patient win. Don't let your ego get in the way of your business goals. In my practice, we have office policies that work 95% of the time but we make exceptions to those policies whenever someone is unhappy.

9.2 Is the customer always right? Where do we draw the line?

My last few articles focused on patient satisfaction and customer service. It's one of my favorite topics because it's the main factor at the core of every highly successful eye care practice. Whenever I write about extreme examples of letting the patient win, even when not truly necessary, it sparks an emotional response from eye care practitioners (ECPs).

The emails I received following this series is no exception. Most ECPs agreed with the concept of practice building based on legendary service, but many shared specific examples of incidents in their offices which proved challenging. I love real case examples like those because it goes beyond generalities like "we'll do whatever it takes." We can all learn from examples of service challenges and it turns out there are some very creative ways to manage them.

Is the customer literally always right?

No, I don't mean it literally. There are always extreme situations where you just can't say yes. I'm the first to say we must run our practices like a business. That means we need to be paid for our services! We need to make a profit. But how we say no is critically important. If you listen to patients on a case by case basis, and if you really try to help them within the limits of good business policies, you can make 99% of the people happy. You can be sincerely empathetic and still stick to your policies.

One of the best responses when you can't give a patient what he wants is to say "in order to be fair to everyone..." Another important guideline is to simply be honest and upfront. When confronted with a complaint like: "You used to give me a discount if I paid cash, why didn't I get that today?" a good response is honest: "I'm sorry we had to drop that program due to our own cost increases, but we try hard to keep our fees in line with the high quality we provide." People may be disappointed a little, but they really just want to know what happened. Did you forget the discount he was entitled to?

We can reduce the occasions where we have to say no if we tell people what to expect in advance. Smart business owners work on this. Anything that can be a source of problems, such as fees, payment requirements, vision plans, warranties, appointment times, return policies and more, is best disclosed in advance. This may be done verbally or in writing. It doesn't solve all the problems, but advising in advance prevents most of them and it helps to be able to point out the advance notice when a problem arises. Since fees and payments are a big source of misunderstanding, just think how much easier life would be if your staff told every patient what the fees would be in advance and when payment was expected.

It's all about making money!

Some of the reader emails I get on this topic seem a little antagonistic; like the ECP who was annoyed with me for advocating that we be nice to patients even if they are wrong. These ECPs think it's wimpy to give in to patients or to go above and beyond the call of duty. Let me be very clear, this whole approach of catering to patient's needs is anything but wimpy! It is clearly designed with the goal of making the practice owner wealthy! It's a business strategy and it works.

We have to draw the line somewhere on how much we can give in to a patient's wants and needs, but in my analysis most ECPs and their staffs draw the line much too soon. More damage is done by drawing it too soon than too late.

What if vision plans are involved?

Many of the examples of frustration sent in by readers revolved around patients with vision plans. The essence is that under normal circumstances with decent profit margins, one could afford to let the patient win. But with the steep discounts required by vision plans and with some of them forcing the ECP to use a sub-par lab, it can be hard to practice good customer service. I understand that having a third party involved between the buyer and seller can create difficult and unusual circumstances, but I hate to give excuses to my patients and I won't sacrifice my principles of excellent service. We must look at the big picture in these cases. If a vision plan does not allow you to practice the way you want, you may not be able to participate. But if you do choose to participate, there must be enough business advantages to overcome the disadvantages.

Should the squeaky wheel get the grease?

I think some ECPs are troubled by the thought that it's simply not fair for the complainers to get special breaks. Why should we give in just because someone complains loud enough? This does not bother me and here is how I justify giving in. First, it's good for business and that is of overriding importance to me. Second, I really do treat all patients the same. I'll give anyone who is unhappy with my services the same consideration. My policy is to guarantee satisfaction and I admit that achieving satisfaction occurs in various degrees among people. Most are easy to satisfy; a few are not so easy. One final benefit: life in the office is much less stressful. Employee attitudes improve as a result.

An example of high standards
A colleague emailed me with a great story from his practice. He was trying a new optical lab and it became evident that they provided very poor work, took too long and did not communicate well. One patient's eyeglass order had several problems in a row and was rejected multiple times. Mistakes were made and promises were broken. The job took much longer than it should have and the patient was obviously upset. When the glasses were finally ready, the ECP had prepared a check for the amount paid toward the glasses and the optician presented it to the patient with an apology and then dispensed the eyewear. The doctor said he may have still lost the patient, but he felt he did the right thing and at least he avoided bad word of mouth. I agree and I also think the staff learned a valuable lesson about how important excellent service is in their practice culture. I also think the chances are very good that he'll keep the patient for life. It was not a waste of money; it was a smart investment in the practice.

9.3 When the Patient Is Not Always Right

I often receive emails from colleagues who present a specific situation that occurred in their office and they're not sure how to handle it. These cases involve a patient who is dissatisfied with a product or service but is also being unreasonable in some way. I love these challenging situations because it helps me check my own standards for customer service. Read on for some tips that will help you and your staff manage these unpleasant confrontational situations.

An example
Many of the cases that are really annoying involve a time element on the patient's part that goes beyond reasonable behavior. For example, a contact lens patient who returns eight months after the fitting of new lenses to report that the contacts are not working as well as they should. The optometrist is willing to see the patient and prescribe new lenses, but

practice policy calls for a new office visit fee to be charged. The patient objects to the professional fee and says he will find a new optometrist if the fee is not waived.

The usual thinking is to not allow this patient to take advantage of the practice. Doctors will reason that it's the principle of the matter that is important; not the office visit fee. After all, doctors must charge for their time and expertise. In fact, the practice may be better off without this type of patient.

The problem with the thinking above is that it's all from the point of view of the doctor or the practice. It does not consider the patient's point of view. The patient's point of view is not really of interest because if it differs from the doctor's – well, then it's simply wrong.

Let the patient win

This type of situation is one that a staff member will typically refer to the doctor and quite often the doctor ends up speaking to the patient directly about it. A disagreement ensues and quite possibly some anger exists on both sides. This kind of confrontation upsets the doctor and the staff. It creates stress. The doctor will think about it for hours. The patient will stew over it and tell his version of the incident to family, friends and co-workers.

I would like to know more details about the patient, the fee system, the history, etc., but in general it is best to let the patient win. Yes, I know there will be large percentage of readers who will be upset by my approach, but hear me out and rest assured that my conclusion is a smart business strategy that is aimed at making more money. I'm not just taking the easy way out.

Your practice reputation

It's a clever strategy to let patients win because doing so quickly creates a reputation that your practice is great to work with! From the patient's point of view, you are the best! You operate a gem of a practice. Optometrists are often concerned that their reputation will become that of a practice the public can take advantage of, but I disagree. In fact I'm happy to let the public take advantage of me all the way to the bank! Happy patients send more patients. Happy patients return more often and buy more goods and services.

The second major reason to follow "the customer is always right" approach is that it creates the office culture you want. Your office is less stressful and staff members are happier on the job. Standing up to patients might stroke your ego, but it teaches staff members to say no and act tough to patients.

How to back down gracefully

When a patient objects to your usual office policies or fees and you can tell they are sincerely unhappy, here is a good way to let him win. Just say: "John, you are an important patient to my practice and we value your business very much, so I'm going to make an exception in your case and waive the office visit fee." Then simply move on and don't make a big deal about it. The patient may not show it, but he will be very happy and impressed. You have just removed a great deal of stress for him as well. Was it really that hard?

Don't sweat the small stuff

I assume these objections are rare. If they are not rare, then there may be bigger issues in your practice that should be worked on. But typically, the complaints in an optometric practice are a very small percentage of cases. The cost of giving in is insignificant. It is usually the doctor's ego that stands in the way, but if you can view this as small stuff and not worthy of upsetting the patient relationship over, you can come off as the hero.

Let's look at the big picture. The patient is unhappy about something. From his point of view, accurate or not, something you or your office did was not right. He is not satisfied. When you think of it this way, the right thing to do is make the patient happy. And don't worry that it is not fair to all the other patients who do not complain; the point is that you will handle anyone who is not satisfied in the same manner. Some people are just easier to satisfy than others.

Examine your vision

Many companies say they believe in great customer service, but that vision falls apart as soon as the going gets tough. How you handle the unreasonable patient provides true evidence of your level of commitment.

Truly great companies, like Disney, Zappos, Ritz-Carlton Hotels, Nordstrom, Lexus, and many more understand the customer service philosophy. Great service is at the core of how these businesses were built. These companies get it.

Part of your management vision relates to your fees. If you have a low fee structure, you really can't be the hero and let the patient win. What I want to do to reduce to small stuff (and it really should be in the big scheme of your practice) will feel like big stuff if your profit margins are slim. All of the great companies mentioned above have a higher pricing philosophy, except maybe Zappos and they are in a different price-value category because they only do business online.

What took you so long?

In discussions like this with a time element, I find it helpful to ask the patient (with no sarcasm or attitude on your part; just sincerity): "John, what took you so long to let me know about this problem?" This does three things: 1) It implies to the patient that he has some responsibility as a consumer to let you know about dissatisfaction in a timely manner. There could be warranties from your lab or other time sensitive issues. 2) The answer might provide you with some useful insight into one aspect of the situation that could make you be more understanding (wife has cancer or the patient was out of the country, for example). 3) It could help the patient see things from your point of view and be more open to a fee or a compromise. Play this by ear; you will know how to handle it based on the situation.

9.4 Back to Basics: Prevention of Common Service Problems

Let's face it, eye care practitioners (ECPs) are busy seeing patients and don't always have the time to observe the day to day activities of the office. Office managers are also likely to become consumed with an increasing work load to the point of not noticing the little details. But the little details are exactly what differentiate the average practice from the multi-million dollar one. You could be delivering the best clinical care in the world but if basic customer service factors are not met, your practice will wallow in mediocrity.

It's important to make time to watch and listen to what happens in areas of the office that are not typically in the doctor's domain. Do this covertly at first, so you can really take an accurate pulse of your practice. Pay attention to your staff on the telephone, at the front desk, in pretest areas, in the dispensary and in behind-the-scenes areas, like the optical lab.

Managing problem employees

Unfortunately, overcoming problems can be challenging because it usually means you need to have a frank discussion with an employee about attitude and behavior. That confrontation can be so unpleasant that it drives some

ECPs and managers to simply avoid the issue. Some doctors would rather turn a blind eye to the problems and rationalize that all is well or that it really doesn't matter. The little details actually have a significant impact on patient satisfaction and loyalty. Don't let a stubborn employee ruin your potential to build a great practice.

Start by holding a staff meeting to analyze and discuss the following frequent customer service problems. Focus on how important excellent service is to the growth of the practice. Recognize that some of the issues listed below are larger than simple employee behavior and may require changes only the ECP can make.

If there are one or two specific employees in your practice who have bad attitudes, meet with them privately and let them know that it's time for a behavior change. Start with a positive approach but continue to monitor behavior and let offenders know that lack of cooperation with the new customer service culture will result in dismissal. Follow through with that after several attempts at remediation and warnings.

Frequent Service Problems

Here are some commonly seen service breaks in eye care practices. How can they be prevented in your practice?

- Rushed and rude behavior by staff over the phone. This is a big one and there are many degrees of poor phone manners, so it can be hard to define. We want friendliness and a caring attitude, just as you would expect a person to speak to a family member.
- Poor initial greeting at the front desk. It should be warm and welcoming and use the patient's name before he says it, if at all possible.
- No one at the front desk. There are valid reasons why staff members must leave the front desk, but I like to watch this factor because it's objective and measurable. Find ways to be sure there is always someone at the front desk to greet people walking in. Discuss multitasking such as making eye contact and gesturing to a person approaching the desk while on the phone.
- The long wait in the reception area or the inner office. Doctors and staff must work together to keep wait times to less than 10 minutes.
- The out-of-date office. Is it time to remodel?
- The dirty office. Do you have a professional cleaning service and are they doing a good job in the corners of rooms?
- Embarrassment over fees or insurance. Ask front desk employees about how patients react to your procedures about billing vision

plans or medical insurance. Billing is not just between you and the third party. Patients will leave your practice over this issue if they are unhappy.

- The broken promise; order not ready. Review the delivery times that staff members tell patients for contact lenses and eyeglasses. Develop a system that helps employees keep track of the status of all orders.
- Not calling patients promptly. It's crucial to call the patient right away if a problem occurs with an order that could prevent you from making the promise date. Watch closely for products that are backordered. Patients are very understanding when you make the call – not so much if they make the call. Also, be sure to call promptly when orders are ready to pick up.
- Using poor terminology in front of patients. Discuss the right way to say things in the office
- The rude staff member. Some employees will take out their personal frustrations on patients by being crabby.
- Odors, chronic coughing, worn clothing. Issues like this require tact and sensitivity, but they must be corrected.
- Problem attempted but not solved. Review the lens remake changes that opticians make when trouble shooting Rx problems. Avoid shooting from the hip when staff is not really sure what the cause of the problem is. It's better to get the doctor or a senior optician involved.
- The arrogant doctor. I find most doctors aren't really arrogant, but they can be perceived that way if they have a serious demeanor. Work on your own interpersonal skills. Smiling makes a world of difference.

9.5 Favorite Phrases for Patient Service

I don't usually give my staff full scripts to use in various office situations, because I like them to use their own words. We do, however, work on the right response and I try to teach principles more than policies. I have found that a specific leading sentence can get my staff (and me) started on the right foot when responding to patient complaints. Here are a few phrases that I've found helpful. Discussing patient service and reviewing these phrases makes for an excellent agenda at a staff meeting.

- **"Oh, that's horrible."** This is a great response phrase after hearing a complaint from a patient. It puts you in the right frame of mind; it clearly says you care about the problem and it should never have happened. It tells the patient that he won't have to go any further to convince you to take action. Now what can we do to fix the problem? Credit a great business book for this phrase: *Customer Satisfaction is Worthless* by Jeffrey Gitomer.

- **"What took you so long to tell me about this?"** This is very effective when a patient brings up a complaint about something that occurred a long time ago – like months or even years. This question allows you to get that time factor out in the open and to imply that there is a fair responsibility on the consumer to voice complaints within a reasonable time period. It's an issue because warranties expire and lab polices for return are limited. Listen to the answer – it will often be enlightening and it can guide your response, which may be nothing at all, or propose a partial credit of some amount.
- **"What do you think would be fair?"** We often want to let patients win and go with the customer-is-always-right philosophy, if we could just figure out what they wanted! In those situations, I like to just ask them – but if you try this approach then be prepared to give them what they ask for. Usually the patient is easier on you than you would have been.
- **"Hello, Mr. XX, I see you're about 15 minutes early (or late)"** There is an art to checking patients in for appointments. It's best to acknowledge (without a negative attitude at all) if a patient is early or late at the moment you greet him or her. If you don't, the early patient who is called in for his visit 10 minutes after the appointed time feels like he was made to wait 25 minutes. And the late arriver will not understand that you had to take the next patient ahead of him and now it will take a while until you can work him in. By acknowledging the situation up front, you can indicate that you'll do all you can to accommodate the scheduling mishap.
- **"I want to make an exception in your case..."** finish this sentence with an ending of your choice, such as "because we must not have informed you about our policy" or "because you have been such a good patient and we value your business". You are letting the patient win, but there is sometimes value in letting him know that you are treating him special, while educating him that your office won't be able to honor such a request again in the future.
- **"Thanks for your patience as we work on this. We want your glasses to be perfect and sometimes problems like this can't be foreseen in advance."**
- **"In order to be fair to everyone..."** While I'm a big advocate of always trying to say yes to patients and not worrying too much about drawing the line, there are times when you have to say no.

This phrase is a great way to do that. Alternatives are: "In order to provide the excellent service we stand for..." or "In order to protect your eye health...".

- **"I'm sorry."** Sadly, you don't hear those two words used much by optometric staff or doctors, yet a sincere apology is sometimes exactly what is needed. Consider your own feelings about when it's appropriate to say I'm sorry and how often you say it, and then talk about it with your staff. Too often staff members are worried about taking the blame for something if they say I'm sorry, but a practice culture that does not focus on blame fosters an environment of honesty and mutual support by co-workers. And doctors sometimes worry about the implied admission of making a mistake, but we're not talking about potential malpractice issues – just eyeglass issues. Admitting you made a mistake, and not passing the buck, is a humbling gesture that disarms what could become an angry confrontation. Even the disgruntled patient knows everyone makes mistakes – usually all he wants is acknowledgment of it.

9.6 Four Common Breaks in Customer Service

I believe customer service is the single most important element in practice building. Great customer service is responsible for everything you want to achieve in your practice: high patient demand, high fees, and higher sales per patient visit. In view of that, let's take a look at how your practice is performing with four key convenience factors.

My goal in this exercise is to identify specific examples where many eye care practices fall short. I do that with the full understanding that there are good reasons why practices struggle with these factors. I'm not saying the remedy is easy. But the really great eye care practices work toward excellence in areas like these.

You may reason that these four items are not that important, but they are if you want to grow your practice. They are just four signs of how much emphasis you place on customer service. If you have some lapses in these areas, chances are good there are additional service breaks occurring in your practice. The culture in your organization turns to what is best for the staff instead of what is best for the patient.

Voice mail

Do you ever notice how often incoming phone calls go to your office voice mail? It is easy for the practice owner and manager to not be very aware of this factor since they don't answer the phones very often. Pay attention to it and check it yourself from time to time.

Patients who call your office but fail to reach a human on the first try are being inconvenienced. When your staff finally gets around to calling back, the patient may no longer be available. The appointment does not get made and lots of things can happen; including finding an ECP who is more convenient.

If your front desk staff allows many calls to go to voice mail, you should investigate the cause and fix it.

- You don't have enough phone lines. This one is not your staff's fault – the phone doesn't even ring when someone calls and the lines are tied up. It goes straight to voice mail. Remember that your lines are used for outgoing calls also. Easy to fix.
- Not enough staff. If you think you are saving money by not hiring that extra employee you really need, you may actually be losing more in patient good will. In some cases, there may be enough staff, but too few who answer phones.
- Staff members who don't care. Many employees don't know that letting calls go to voice mail can be damaging. Other times, employees are lazy or they are trying to send a message to management that they are overworked. This is a deeper problem, but once it is identified you can go about the training and culture building to change the bad attitudes.

Evenings and Saturdays

I know that evening and Saturday office hours are not desirable work times for staff and for doctors. I get it. But customer service is not about what is good for you – it's about what is good for the customer. Your competition is open on evenings and Saturdays and these times are very attractive to a patient group which is very important to you: those with jobs!

Practice owners who don't want to work evenings and Saturdays should look for an associate doctor who can work them. Work with existing staff to identify those who would not mind evenings and Saturdays in exchange for a full day off in the week. Hire all new employees with the understanding that evenings and Saturdays are a requirement.

Squeeze-ins

How accommodating is your staff when patients call with an urgent need? Of course, some judgment is needed and you can only accept so many people per day before you begin to adversely affect the quality of care, but have you checked this lately?

Let's face it; there is a very real incentive for staff members to accept fewer patients. Their day becomes easier. Of course, some employees keep the good of the practice uppermost at all times, but if one can follow the rules and still say no to a caller, many will do just that. If your office procedures were more streamlined and if you delegated more, would you be able to say yes to a few of those urgent needs? If your appointment schedule were not so rigid, would you be able to see a few more exams each day?

If you were to make a change in this area, your annual practice revenue would jump up significantly. And many patients who really need you would become extremely loyal to your practice. Perhaps your staff is not sure which calls are really urgent and which are not. If the patient thinks it's urgent and if you are able to see them, I'm not sure it really matters. True medical emergencies should always be seen the same day. Talk about it with your staff.

Delays to call the patient in

Many doctors work pretty hard to stay on schedule only to have inefficiency and apathy at the front desk cause delays in getting the visit started. Patients wait and become bored as they begin to think about the other things they need to do in their lives; the experience at your office quickly slipping into dissatisfaction. You may be able to recover with the good things you do during the exam, but why start out in the hole? Observe and review the steps your front desk and technicians are taking before calling the patient in. Can you change some of it to get them in quicker?

- History questionnaire. Can you shorten it? Can you just use it for new patients only? Can your staff tell callers to go to your website, download the form and complete it before they arrive?
- Insurance verification. This really can be done before the patient arrives.
- Organizing forms and papers. Do it the day before the appointment.
- Enter patient demographic data into the system. This can be done in advance and more data added after the patient is called in.
- Technicians need to review the previous exam record before beginning the pretesting. A quick review is good, but I see some techs who feel they must memorize every detail. Just get started.

Let me know how your practice performs in these four areas, whether it is good or bad.

9.7 How Does Your Staff Handle These Challenging Situations?

I thought I would present some examples of real world issues that face many eye care practices every day. Some of these cases present ethical dilemmas or other sticky situations. Consider using these vignettes at a staff meeting to get feedback on how your staff handles them. Provide some guidance on ways to improve patient communication and prevent unpleasant confrontations. I'll share my thoughts briefly on each issue, but just use that as a starting point for your preferred management.

You answer the phone and the caller asks "How much is an eye exam?"
The key is to train your staff to ask a question back to the caller. We want to have a conversation so the caller sees how friendly and caring you are. Ask about insurance plans first, which speaks to the real issue of the cost of an exam. It may be free or just a co-pay! I recommend that you actually quote the fee eventually because we don't want to dodge a direct question, but also comment on how thorough the exam is and what kind of tests are performed. Next, ask if the caller is having any problems with his vision. Listen, show concern and comment about how good the doctor is. It is important to have enough staff so these calls are not rushed.

A patient is checking out at the front desk and questions the contact lens evaluation fee; he does not want to pay for it.
I believe in being proactive and telling patients about these services and fees over the phone when they schedule the appointment – even if they don't ask! I find that patients don't really mind the contact lens evaluation fee, but they hate to be surprised by it. Train staff to look up the established patient's record while talking to them and see if he wears contacts without asking. You will have to ask new patients. Explain that contact lens patients require additional testing that other patients do not need. Most staff members don't mind this procedure once they get used to it because it prevents complaints at the front desk. For general questions about contact lens fees just say that a new fitting and lenses start at $XXX, but the fee varies based on the type of lens and complexity of the fitting.

A patient has both a vision plan and medical insurance and your office accepts both. The doctor found a medical problem and bills the medical plan, but the patient wants to bill the vision plan.
Don't lose the patient and family over billing aggressively to medical. The patient does have a financial stake in this decision. Most doctors see patients for the first exam under the vision plan and bill medical for subsequent visits and tests. Don't schedule subsequent visits if they are not really needed. One new strategy I've heard is to bill the medical insurance if you have a medical diagnosis but waive any co-pay or deductible and waive the refraction fee unless it is covered. In other words, remove any cost to the patient so they don't care which plan you bill. Of course, you only do this if the medical insurance payment is higher than the vision plan and it may not always be! Also, be aware that your contract may not allow you to waive patient fees, this is especially true with Medicare.

A patient calls to check on a contact lens order from two weeks ago and you look it up and find it was never ordered. What should you tell the patient?
We never lie to a patient, but we don't have to tell them everything. The first thing to do is apologize for the delay and then give a firm statement about when the lenses will be in. For example: "I'm so sorry but your contacts are not in yet. I spoke to the lab and they said they will be shipped tomorrow and I'm having them sent overnight express at no charge to you."

The office manager notices a staff member made an error earlier in the day on the fee calculation for a vision plan patient or realizes the patient was not eligible for a particular benefit, i.e. frames, exam.
The technician who made the error calls the patient right away and sincerely apologizes, but explains that an error was made in the calculation and the correct amount is _____ and the balance will be____. Apologize again and thank the patient for understanding. Turn the call over to the office manager if the patient does not agree. At that point, is a judgment call on how to handle it, but if materials have not been made yet, you should be able to collect the correct fees. Mistakes happen. The patient can check with the vision plan support line if necessary.

A patient wants to buy more contact lenses but the Rx has recently expired.
Be helpful and give a grace period. Optometrists can sometimes be extremely tough on these situations without good reason. An important factor is that the patient must actually schedule the needed re-exam on the spot. If he does that, we will sell him one box for each eye or give him a trial pair to hold over.

A patient supposedly does not know a basic office policy, like he is picking up new glasses and he says he did not know he had to pay the balance due. I like for my office to take the blame in a situation like this, even though we know we communicated the policy very well. It saves embarrassment for the patient. I would actually want our optician to apologize for our office not making the policy clearer. Then we would say that we will be happy to hold the glasses until the patient can return with the payment. We will not release the glasses, but we are very nice about it! I've seen many patients in this situation produce a credit card and pay the balance.

Notice that some of these tough situations are made easier by the staff member saying I'm sorry. Yet, in my experience, it is extremely rare for eye care staff or doctors to ever speak those words. When something goes wrong, an apology is really what we all want to hear and when we get that response, everything is much better.

9.8 Getting Rid of the Complainers

How does your office handle the patient who is not easy to get along with? What do you do with the person who has a complaint that is truly unreasonable? In many practices today, the doctor or a staff member will explain the facts to the patient and if he persists with an unreasonable demand, the doctor or staff person will suggest or imply that he go elsewhere for future eye care. The reasoning is that the practice is better off without these unreasonable patients. If we let this type of patient take advantage of us, they will keep doing so and they will send more people like them.

If this sounds a bit like your practice, please hear me out and consider a different approach. If you are interested in generating maximum revenue and profitability, I think the let's-get-rid-of-them approach is misguided.

What is unreasonable?
Before we dig deeper into the management strategy behind patient management, realize that my premise above is based on the patient being *unreasonable*. That is critical to our discussion because by definition we might justify strong actions if a person is unreasonable. But the question becomes who judges what is unreasonable? Typically you would base that on your opinion and judgment, but what if you based it on the patient's opinion? I'm fairly certain that the complaining patient does not think he is being unreasonable at all! To him, something was not handled well by your office.

This is the key to understanding the customer service mentality; look at everything you do from the patient's point of view.

As you try to try to reassess these challenging issues in your practice, ask yourself whose opinion matters more: yours or the patient's? The answer may lie in how busy your practice is. If your practice is booked solid for weeks in advance, customer service may not be all that important (at least not at the moment). If you need more patient demand, and most practices do, then the patient's opinion is far more important.

Why would you want that type?

Getting rid of the complaining type of patient is a bad idea because there are too many of them! We work with the public and at some point in time anyone could be that type! You have probably even been that type when you had a run-in with a retailer, a restaurant or a service business over some misunderstanding. There are some very good, normal people who can become that type. It is a huge mistake to think we can do away with people who ask too much of us or become unhappy with something we do. The smarter approach is to become better at dealing with those issues and to let the patient (customer) win. I believe this is the better business approach if you want to generate maximum profit.

An argument could be made that the actual number of people who are dismissed from your practice is fairly small, but the bigger concern is that your office culture will become negative when the doctor or key staff members feel this way. It becomes harder and harder to know where to draw the line. When a patient makes a special request, the protect-the-practice mode takes over and the answer is "no, we don't work that way." When a complaint is lodged, a staff member explains why the problem is not our fault. Most patients don't take it any further and therefore are not actually dismissed, but they sense the attitude. They realize they do not have any recourse. What should concern all of us is what these patients do next. Some will just quietly go to another eye care provider next time. They certainly will not refer their friends and co-workers to your practice.

When this negative culture (protecting the practice against so-called abuse) is spread over all your patients over a long period of time, the result is a practice that does not grow as fast as others. Word of mouth referrals are less frequent and more patients migrate elsewhere than practices which really get the customer service concept.

We are pushovers

My practice is known as one of the nicest places around to do business with; we are total pushovers! We let the patient win and I'm happy about that all the way to the bank. To the local population that is hard to get along with, I say come see us; take advantage of us; welcome!

9.9 How Do You Manage the Upset Patient?

I'm sure it will come as no surprise to readers of this column that I'm going to say we should let the patient win in a confrontation or complaint. Most eye care professionals (ECPs) who I talk with agree with that approach – at least in principle! But I also receive many emails from ECPs who struggle with the real-world application of this concept. I read many posts in various optometric chat rooms and forums that convey stories of patients who are unreasonable and how it is best to show them the door.

In this article, I share my thoughts about how to handle unpleasant confrontations and how to not let them ruin your day. As a bonus, if you apply these principles, you will actually build patient demand in your practice and greatly increase your profitability.

There are many variations of the upset patient and I'll try to write this to apply to all of them. In some cases, patients come into your office upset about something. In other cases, they come in just fine, and something you do upsets them.

Why let them win?
Please understand that my policy of letting the patient win in virtually every case is not because I'm a wimp and afraid to stand up to people. It's because my policy makes an unbelievable amount of money! Letting the patient win is an extremely smart business strategy. The practice growth that occurs when you are extremely easy to do business with is phenomenal. Your reputation as a great doctor increases many times over, just because you make people happy. The word-of mouth referral rate is huge when you take good care of people, especially when it is was not very easy to do so. The cost that is incurred when you give in is nothing compared to the preservation of your image.

Most ECPs go along with this until the patient becomes unreasonable, and then they don't want to be taken advantage of. I let patients take advantage of me all the way to the bank! Actually, most of these patients are not really being unreasonable if you look at the situation from their point of view. You and I could easily be those unreasonable people if we were the customers in a different setting. Just let the patient have it his way if at all possible. Your decisions get easier and your stress level drops enormously.

Agree with the patient

Train your staff to empathize and agree with the patient when they come in with a complaint. Share the patient's unhappiness by saying "Oh, that's horrible!" as author Jeffry Gitomer writes. Then convey to the patient that you will take care of the problem. Take the patient to a more private area and listen without interrupting, even if you've heard this dozens of times before. The patient needs to vent.

Accept the blame – apologize

The greatest tendency for ECPs is to shift the blame to someone else. Resist this urge to say it was the lab's fault or a nameless co-worker's fault. On behalf of the practice, accept the blame. Say that never should have happened. It is not acceptable and it is not our usual standard of quality or service.

It is extremely important to say the following two words: "I'm sorry". Those words are so seldom spoken in an optometric office that it may be a good idea to practice saying them. Staff members need to know that it is a good thing to say. Doctors should also say those words to patients sometimes. Your office does make mistakes; no one is perfect. And when consumers feel like a mistake was made, they want an apology. It is the polite thing to do.

In some cases, you can apologize for not having explained the policy in advance well enough. It doesn't matter if you actually did explain it; in this case the patient did not get it. Let the patient save face by you taking the blame for an awkward moment. It works wonders! The patient who was about to be backed into a corner is allowed to avoid embarrassment and he will love you for it.

Go to the manager — not the doctor

A patient may come in with a problem with his eyes or glasses or contact lenses and he wants you to do something you can't do. He might want to buy a new supply of contact lenses but his prescription is expired. He might want to cancel his recent order for glasses with digital progressive lenses, but the job is already finished at the lab. He might be a non-adapt to new progressive lenses and you proceed to remake them into a flat top, but he now wants a refund of the difference in the price of the two types of lenses. The staff member will generally state the office policy and nicely explain why you can't do what the patient wants. In most cases, the patient will understand and will accept the policy. That is a good reason for having the policy; most people will accept it.

When the patient is not happy with the policy is when special action is needed. If the staff member is trained and authorized to handle the upset patient properly, fine. If not, the staff member should ask the patient to wait while she speaks to the office manager. I do not recommend that staff members take complaints and issues like that to the doctor. Let's keep the doctor out of it.

If your practice does not have an office manager, you need one.

Make an exception

An excellent way to let the patient win is to make an exception to the policy. This allows you to support the first staff member who was involved and who first explained why some course of action could not be done. The policy does exist and was stated correctly, but the manager is deciding to make an exception to the policy in this case. This also conveys that the policy will be followed in the future, but perhaps it was not well understood this time. It is very effective to say: "Mr. Jones, you are a very important patient in our practice and I'm going to make an exception to our usual policy and..." Let the patient feel good about it.

Extra gesture when indicated

In some cases, especially when our office makes a mistake, we give the patient a gift or a credit as a make-up gesture. Have items on hand for this purpose. We keep a supply of plastic gift cards from my practice in $50 denominations. It is good like cash in my office, but the patient has to return to us to use it. We also have a supply of $10 gift cards from Starbucks and some other logo gift items like coffee mugs, t-shirts, and nice pens.

Letting the patient win has many benefits, and one final consideration is that you will gather many positive online reviews and very few negative ones. Let the new age of online reviews work in your favor.

9.10 Manners 101

I study customer service and marketing in use by all kinds of companies, within the eye care industry and in my personal life. I learn a lot and it gives me ideas that can help my practice. One of my favorite fast food restaurants is Chic-fil-A. I was placing an order there recently and I said "Thank you" for something. The clerk used a phrase that I've heard many times by the staff at Chic-fil-A restaurants all over the country: "It is my pleasure." This phrase is not unique to Chic-fil-A, of course. The Ritz Carlton organization made it famous and many other business use it as well, but I was impressed at how universally well-trained the servers at Chic-fil-A are. After all, most of the servers that I work with appear to be under age 20. And yet, they do not seem to forget and revert back to the more frequent response today when a customer says thank you, which is "no problem" or the popular alternative: "no worries". And they sound natural when saying "my pleasure"; not forced or scripted, even though it obviously is.

Well, this made me think about my own staff and how they sound to patients and how well we use our manners. In my opinion, society today has gotten away from using what I was taught as good manners. It has become somewhat out of date or certainly not regarded as all that important. But when people hear kind words that convey respect and consideration, they notice and it makes them feel good.

Many optometrists and office managers never take the time to train their staff on the intricate details of good manners, yet that is precisely what some of the best companies do. If it has been a while since you talked about using the right words with your employees, why not make it the topic of your next staff meeting?

I'll provide a list of items to cover in your manners check, but we all probably know these preferred phrases. The important thing is to take the training seriously and practice it enough so it becomes internalized by your staff... like they must do at Chic-fil-A.

- When someone says "thank you", I like the sound of "my pleasure" as a response, whether over the phone or in person. Of course, "you're welcome" always works too, but that really won't be noticed as anything special. I would avoid responses like "sure" or "no problem".
- I think it is a nice touch to use people's names even when you don't have to. I teach my staff to use Mr., Mrs., and Miss and the last name if the person is older than you. We use first names if the person is about our age or younger. But the important thing is to use the name. It builds relationships and people love to hear their own name. We make an effort to pronounce names correctly and to make a record of it for others.

- I think the use of the words "I'm sorry" are conspicuously absent from common speech today and especially in health care offices. I prefer my staff to own our mistakes. When a patient or consumer thinks something was not handled well, an apology turns the tone around almost instantly.
- There are many other phrases that will enhance the patient's experience in your office. Having staff members introduce themselves by name and shaking hands when appropriate. I like the use of "may I place you on a brief hold?" instead of just "hold please". It's perfectly fine to use words like "yes sir" or "yes ma'am".

It is up to the leaders of your practice to initiate a training program on good manners and make it part of your office culture. It will help grow your practice.

9.11 Revisiting Customer Service

I realized that I have not written about customer service in a long time and that is unusual for me, so stick with me and read this tip because it is the most important topic there is for building a successful practice. It is important for all of us to revisit our own beliefs about customer service and then lead our staff teams to embrace it as well. If you don't continue to make customer service the dominant factor in your office culture, service will decline. Complacency will set in. It takes an ongoing, renewed effort.

Do you understand the strategy?
Legendary customer service truly has the power to lift your practice to very high levels of production and profit, but I think many doctors don't really get it. I've talked with and read social media posts by some ODs who actually scoff at the concept. I think they get some kind of ego boost by letting patients know they are the boss. If a patient asks for something unusual or difficult, they become quite annoyed.

I think these optometrists often mean well and they simply don't want to be taken advantage of. They don't think they should have to kowtow to people who are unreasonable. The problem with that thinking is two-fold: first, the patient never thinks he is being unreasonable. There is a difference of opinion on that point. I wonder whose opinion counts more if the ultimate goal is to increase business. Second, it doesn't even matter if the patient is trying to take advantage! If you let them win (within reason, but liberally) you will make far more money. They will buy more services and products, return more often and send many other people to see you. I let them take advantage of me all the way to the bank.

These doctors may actually be nicer to people than they let on with their bravado, but complaining about patients even behind the scenes can cause more harm to their practice than they realize. The culture of an organization is determined by the leaders and if staff members realize the doctor has little compassion for the public, they will emulate that and take it even further.

Are you complacent about customer service?

Another group of doctors truly understand that customer service is an important factor in practice building, but they are not passionate about it. This group of owners may be so busy with clinical eye care that they delegate customer service to the staff and assume it is being handled well. In my experience, customer service often erodes over time in the absence of firm leadership because staff begin to focus on their own wants and needs more than the patient's.

Nearly all the extremely successful practices I have consulted with provide excellent customer service in a consistent manner. The owners get it. They live it and breathe it. As expected, the practices that are owned by doctors who are indifferent to customer service are generally mediocre. It stands to reason because professional practices are driven by word-of-mouth and strong recommendations. Of course, the value of customer service is well documented in virtually all business categories.

How to improve your customer service

Here are some ideas for leading your staff to provide great service:

- Say yes to patients, even when it is not easy. There are some times when you can't say yes, but those situations are really quite easy to manage. Just explain to the patient, honestly and patiently, why you can't say yes in this instance and don't embarrass the patient in the process.
- Review your office policies and try to change them to reflect the wants and needs of the patient. Stop thinking about what is convenient for the doctor and staff.
- Talk about customer service frequently at staff meetings and as daily decisions are made.
- Explain to the staff about the importance of word-of-mouth referrals and the total patient experience.

It is actually fun to practice in an environment with outstanding customer service. There is far less stress and staff members are happier. There is a feeling of pride for doing wonderful things for others. And patients act better and are more grateful when they realize they are being treated well.

You can have everything you want in life if you just help enough other people get what they want (Zig Ziglar).

9.12 A Patient-Friendly Policy for Late Patients

Many things go into building a large and profitable practice, but if I had to pick one factor that has led to success in my practice, it would be delivering excellent customer service, even when it is difficult. One of those times that it is difficult is when patients arrive late for an appointment or when they call our office to let us know they will be arriving late.

My staff and my associate doctors have wanted me to take a hard stand with these patients from time to time. They would like me to set some number of minutes, after which, we would refuse to see the patient that day and we would reschedule them. Rescheduling may be the best answer, but I insist that we decide that on a case by case basis with the late patient. It is not a mandate based on policy.

The last time we discussed this issue at a staff meeting, I asked my staff members to consider how they would feel if they arrived late for a doctor's appointment, due to some factor that was beyond their control. Maybe they had trouble with child care at the last minute or perhaps traffic was very heavy due to an accident. Let's assume they really needed to be seen and delaying the visit a week or more would have caused a real hardship. How would you like to be treated by the person at the front desk? How would you feel if she was very understanding and wanted to find a way let you see the doctor?

A memo to my staff

As part of staff training in my practice, I often put my thoughts in writing and pass them out to all for discussion at a staff meeting. It keeps me organized and it helps staff members to remember the key points. Here is a handout I wrote for my staff on the topic of late patients:

1. Our primary goal is to provide great service for the patient, not to do what is most convenient for us. Look at the situation from the patient's point of view first.
2. We don't usually have to stay much past quitting time, but we will have to sometimes. That is the nature of our work. We stay until we are done with patients.
3. Setting an exact number of minutes for which we will turn a patient away is not advisable. We will handle each case as it arises after looking at various factors such as:
    a. The nature of the patient's needs. How urgent and serious is the eye problem? How important does it seem to the patient that he/she be seen today?
    b. How much past the original appointment time will the new time be?
    c. How close will the new time be to quitting time?
    d. How busy are the doctors expected to be at that time based on the schedule?
    e. It is fine to ask for input from the doctors or the office manager about the situation, but I expect them to follow these principles and guidelines as well.
4. If the new start time seems difficult for our office to manage, offer to reschedule or ask if the patient would rather reschedule given the circumstances. Do not dictate that we must reschedule. Work with the patient.
5. We will not inconvenience other patients who are on time for appointments. They will be given priority and if the late patient will truly impact others, we just explain to the late patient that there will be a wait until we can see them due to other appointments. This may make the late patient choose to reschedule for their own convenience.
6. If a different doctor has an opening or has faster patients, the late patient may be asked to see the other doctor.
7. Many late situations are pretty easy to decide if we should see the patient today or not. But if the decision is borderline or hard to decide, then go ahead and see the patient. That is always the right decision and we can often improve the situation if we spend less time thinking, talking and worrying about it and just get started. If the patient wants to be seen, we will usually do so unless circumstances are extreme. We can see a patient in 15 minutes or less. Don't make it a big deal.
8. When we see a late patient, receptionists, technicians and doctors should consider changing our usual office routine to be more

efficient. Possible examples: Skip the history form for now (we can do it later and take it verbally). Start the pretesting faster (don't stand there and read the previous exam data, just call the patient in). Let the doctor see the patient without pretesting (especially if no tech is available and if it's an established patient). Do frame selection before the exam if the clinic side is busy. Just see the patient and figure it out as we move forward. Once we begin working with the patient, you will find the situation will get easier. The patient will know he is late and will be accommodating to us. Some services can be reappointed as needed if there is a time issue. This includes frame selection, which can always be done with no appointment needed. A practical solution can be found once we talk to the patient.

I realize that my patient-friendly approach will not be well-liked by some optometrists. It is, however, very well-liked by patients. Some ODs feel that letting patients win in cases like these just enables them to take advantage of us. I have not found that to be true, but even if it were, I wouldn't care. The practice-building power is simply too great to pass up.

9.13 A Five Point Quiz on Customer Service

When I ask optometrists how their practice performs in the area of customer service, the answer I always get is: great! Every OD I speak with knows that customer service is very important in growing a practice. If you talk to patients, however, and if you really observe practices in operation, you see that the service is not nearly as good as the owners think. Some of that difference may be because customer service is intangible. It is hard to describe and the standards vary widely. It's easy to be nice to people when things are going well. A bigger test occurs when you think the other party is being unreasonable. When should you give in and when do you draw the line?

There are some judgment calls needed as you navigate how generous to be, but my experience is that letting the patient win is a very smart business strategy.

In an attempt to assess your customer service more accurately, and just to have some fun, take this quiz. Read the following five statements and decide if each one is true or false. Be objective and follow the spirit of the statement.

1. At any given moment, there is a good chance there is no one at your front desk. Patients want to be greeted by a friendly, caring person as soon as they walk in. If you are reading this during office hours, stop and walk up to your front desk and take a look.
2. Your office hours (with a doctor) do not include two or more evenings until 7pm and some hours every Saturday. Part of good customer service is convenience. I realize that many doctors and staff do not like to work these hours, but we're evaluating what is good for the patients and the practice, not you personally.
3. If a patient no shows or cancels at the last minute, your staff will give them a stern warning or charge a fee or take some other punitive action. This is a tough one because the patient is clearly in the wrong, but really great practices are understanding and see things from the patient's point of view, not from their own. A Medicaid practice or other situation that has a high no show rate gets a partial pass, but I think better appointment confirmations and booking closer together based on experience are better ways to handle it.
4. When you call your own office, you sometimes get voice mail or you are put on immediate hold. This one depends on how often it happens, but voice mail should be extremely rare during office hours. If you have a menu tree that makes callers choose options, score this statement as true.
5. It is not uncommon for a patient to wait in the reception room more than 15 minutes after their appointment time or for the patient to have an internal wait of more than 15 minutes for the doctor.

If you scored zero true statements, you have outstanding customer service and not due to coincidence, I predict you also have a very successful practice. If you had one to three true statements, you have an average optometric practice, but who wants that? If you have four or five true statements, you should work on improving customer service. Start by taking the quiz again with your staff and talking about each point.

9.14 Project SMILE

The more I wander around my office and observe our day-to-day activities, the more things I find that we need to work on. My practice will never reach perfection, but I am going to continuously work on pursuing it. The latest thing is that the staff who work at the front desk don't smile enough. So my office managers and I have embraced this as our latest mission in staff training and motivation.

I want to be clear that I have long insisted on hiring and developing a pleasant, friendly staff. I look for happy people in our hiring process; we administer personality tests; we talk about smiling and being friendly before and after we hire someone. My managers and I work hard to create a positive organizational culture where we care about our staff members and treat them with respect. We offer a good pay and benefit package plus other perks. Excellent customer service is at the core of our business model and we talk about it at every staff meeting. In spite of a great deal of effort, I notice the front desk staff rarely smiles.

To be fair, it is not that easy to smile all the time. Most of my staff are perfectly happy on the job and they will smile if something amusing occurs, but most of the time, they are busy and they are working and there is nothing to smile about. I realize that it won't work to simply command my employees to smile. I can't just say "Smile, darn it!" I must show my staff why they need to smile and what it will do for them and for the practice.

It was actually a personal experience that motivated me to pursue Project Smile in my practice. I went to a new restaurant in town a few times and I noticed that the hostess and the wait staff were extremely friendly and it had a profound effect on me. I really enjoyed going there. Keep in mind that I study business models and marketing strategies, so I see behind the strategic curtain pretty easily, but this restaurant even had me thinking that the staff really liked me. It was mostly the hostess; she smiled at me and made eye contact with me. It was not always the same person, but the hostess always seemed very pleased that I was there. She seated me and told me the specials or whatever, but that was secondary to how she made me feel. I almost thought for a moment that she might have been flirting with me, but I quickly came to my senses on that point. Even when I realized that her interest in me was the result of corporate training, I didn't really care. I liked it.

I would really like all my staff and our associate doctors to smile more. I realize that it is a powerful relationship builder. It creates a great patient experience. I'm working on helping everyone in my practice to understand this, but the front desk staff is most critical.

Here are some of the points my managers and I are making with our staff on Project Smile.

- Understand that a smile is an extremely powerful tool to build relationships and improve the patient experience.

- The patient experience is a key factor in practice building: it drives patient referrals, repeat business and higher sales.
- The growth of our practice as a business directly benefits the employees. It lets us provide raises and better employment benefits. It helps us make our office a better working environment. Employees who embrace new projects and help the practice achieve its goals will be rewarded.
- The managers will remind the staff to smile. One great way to do that is for the manager to give the staff member a smile of her own. Smiles are contagious.
- Target and Starbucks gift cards will be given to individual staff members by managers whenever they see a strong pattern of smiles.
- Two important side points in this project are to make eye contact with patients and to remember patient names and use those names in the greeting and in conversation.

9.15 Customer Service: How to Say No

Readers who follow my philosophy on practice building know that I place an extremely high value on customer service. I think patient satisfaction (loyalty) is the most important factor in creating a successful and highly profitable practice. I've written many times on letting the patient win, patient-friendly office policies, and saying yes most of the time is a very smart business strategy.

But, what about when you or your staff can't say yes? When do you draw the line and tell a patient no? And how do you say no without alienating the patient? I really do have a good way and I'll share it below, but first let's look at saying yes.

The unreasonable patient

Eye care professionals who really understand the power of the customer service concept are able to provide it even when the patient is unreasonable. It's easy to give great service when the patient is cooperating with everything you want to do. But once you make the transition to being kind and understanding even when patients are difficult, you will find a self-confidence that will lead your practice to more patient referrals and more revenue production. Think about how you handle these patients:

- The two family members who booked appointments together and no show.

- The patient who says they have no insurance, but two weeks after getting their glasses, they tell you they have a vision plan and they want everything rebilled.
- The patient who wants to cancel their eyeglass order and they would also like their PD.
- The patient who is 30 minutes late for their appointment.

You could tell these people no. You could try to penalize them in some way, such as an extra fee or advising them that they can't have an appointment in the future. You could decide to dismiss them from the practice. I would not do any of those things; I would be very understanding about these issues in my practice. I don't think these people are being unreasonable. I think all of us can appear to be unreasonable sometimes to the staff at various businesses we patronize.

Preventing problems

In my practice, we try to let the patient win this time, but we learn from the event and we may educate the patient (in a nice way) for the future. We prevent problems by always telling patients in advance about what to expect with out-of-pocket expenses. We tell people some things over the phone before the appointment. We tell patients other things before we do special tests or before we fit them with contact lenses. We go the extra mile to check for insurance plans before the patient's visit.

We talk about problems we have encountered at our staff meetings to give everyone a heads up about what can happen and we discuss how to prevent it in the future.

How to say no

OK, here is my big secret on how to say no to a patient! Are you ready? You apologize when you do it. It really is brilliant, I think. Look at everything you do from the patient's point of view and if you must say no, say "I'm sorry" first. Take the blame for having to say no. Take the blame for not explaining the policy better and in advance. Save the patient from any embarrassment. Make it your fault. Express that you feel badly for having to say no.

Now I realize that this means you and your staff must be able to utter the words "I'm sorry" and I know many people have extreme difficulty saying that. I think some people can't admit they made a mistake or can't take the blame for others in the practice. You should get over it and say the words. You are not perfect and your practice is not perfect. When a patient does not get his way, he feels disappointed and those words make a huge difference.

It does not matter if the patient is correct or not. It does not matter if you think he was right or not. What he feels matters more.

Here is an example where the staff in my practice would say no: A patient picks up his new glasses and has them adjusted and dispensed. As he is leaving, the following exchange occurs:

- Optician: "Mr. Smith, I see you have a balance of $480 on your glasses, I'll take you to the front desk so you can pay that."
- Patient: "Oh, I forgot my wallet and checkbook. I'll just send you a check when I get home."
- Optician: "Oh, I am so sorry! I must apologize if we did not explain our payment policy when you ordered your glasses, but we must have payment in full when glasses are picked up. I'll be happy to hold the glasses for you until you can return with your payment. I feel so badly about this Mr. Smith, I hope you understand."

You can apply this method to just about any situation where you must decline a patient request. Start with the words "Oh, I'm so sorry..."

9.16 Customer Service: How to Say Yes (Even If Your Office Policy Says No)

My tip article last week was all about how to say no to patients (even though we try not to). It is certainly much easier to say yes, but what if your staff member already told this patient no? Or what if you have a written office policy that states something is not allowed? Should you go against that?

Customer service and the patient experience are so important to the success of your practice that I favor letting the patient win, even if we already said no. But that can be awkward if you are going against a staff member who was just following the office policy.

How to say yes
I like to find a specific phrase that we can use in special circumstances to get my managers and staff started in the right direction. Here is one that works wonders in our office when we want to let the patient win, but we also want to acknowledge our policy. We simply say we are going to make an exception in this case. We say this quite often in our practice.

- It lets the patient know he is important to us.

- It lets our staff member save face for having said no to the patient, but is now being overruled.
- It informs the patient that we can't do it this way again in the future.

Why have a policy if you are going to say yes?
I don't like to flood the patient with policies that seem negative, but having some handouts, discreet signage or some policies printed on the back of your walkout receipt is a good practice. Having some rules about refunds, insurance billing, appointment cancellation or Rx rechecks helps to gain cooperation from the vast majority of patients. It also helps give our staff some guidelines on how to handle difficult situations. Printed policies serve as a resource.

I don't feel badly about making an exception for the small number of patients who do not feel our policies are fair or who feel they warrant special consideration. I'd rather make the patient happy and loyal to our practice then stand on policy.

9.17 What's in a Name?

Those of you who read this newsletter every week know that the content is not rocket science [well, maybe a few of them come close :)]. My management tips are often just common sense observations and solutions that I see in my practice or in consultation with other doctors. I have the luxury of time to make those observations and to test new concepts. I see patients in my practice only one day per week, and I only do that to keep in touch with the "customer" and to keep up with clinical optometry. I spend the other days studying practice management and working as CEO of my group practice.

This week's tip is one of those observations that will not come as a huge surprise to you, but if it makes you focus on something that is important and perhaps forgotten, I've done my job. The tip is the power of using a person's name. It turns out that remembering a patient's name when it's not expected, and using that name in conversation, can have a big effect on building your practice.

I'm fortunate to have an optician employed in my practice who is a master at interpersonal skills. People love John. Patients actually write me letters praising him, and he is frequently mentioned by name in our ongoing patient survey postcards. He is a fantastic salesperson, by the way, selling multiple pairs, high-end frames and premium lens options.

John does many things to instill confidence and win trust, but one of the most important things he does is remember people's names and use them. The nature of our optical department (like most) is people drop in without an appointment. They need an adjustment or repair, or they want to buy something, or they're picking up a pair of glasses. John greets the patient in a friendly and respectful way, and he uses the person's name! Seems pretty simple, doesn't it? When he does that, the patient feels important and highly valued, and that is the beginning of building a strong, loyal relationship.

I have a group of receptionists that also frequently call people by name, although that occurred more by training than by nature. I once asked my staff if they often know a patient's name upon sight. The answer was an unequivocal "yes". Several of my receptionists happen to just be good with names and after seeing a patient and preparing their paper and computer files, they know the name whenever they see the person, even a year later. I then asked my staff if they often used a person's name in a greeting. Here I got blank stares. I already knew the answer anyway. My staff, like lots of people today, did not often say a person's name – even when they knew it!

This lead to an excellent discussion about the value of saying people's names, and the obstacles that prevented my staff from doing it. The reasons were not very logical and they were easily overcome – but we had to talk about the issue before it could be changed. Some staff refrained from using names because they were afraid of being too personal, or making a social error. Some said they did not know if they should use Mr., Miss, Mrs. or Ms. – or just use the first name. Some said they weren't sure how to pronounce some names. Some said they just never thought about it.

Once we acknowledged these potential stumbling points, we simply adopted office rules to get past them. For example: always use the Mr. or Mrs. title if the patient is older than you, unless the patient requests otherwise, or unless the relationship has become friendly. The correct title was asked for in our new patient questionnaire, so that's where we look for it. We decided where to write name preferences and nicknames in the chart. We all know how to write a name phonetically so we can pronounce it correctly in the future. We are not too shy to ask a new patient how to pronounce his name – once. And we all try to remember names, and use them in our greeting. The exact rules you adopt for your office is not nearly as important as getting the issue out in the open and adopting something.

Doctors have the luxury of usually having the chart in front of them when they greet a patient, and they also have the day's appointment list handy, so it should be pretty easy to greet patients by name in your office (not so in the supermarket - right?). But do you use your patient's names very often? If not, why not? This name initiative is not just for staff. Be aware, of course, that you can overdo it and sound phony, but you can't build a relationship without using a person's name.

9.18 Managing Patients Who Want It for Free

I received an interesting email from a reader who asks about a very real situation that I'm sure we all run into in our practices. Here is the email:

"In the age of no responsibility or accountability that we live in, how do you handle those situations where patients don't feel they have to pay for services rendered? Particularly those contact lens patients whose prescriptions have been finalized and return one, two, or three months later with issues they want resolved. Is there a charge for these appointments? How do you handle this? This has been a recurrent theme and has the staff continually on edge and in a defensive posture. Do you bill their medical insurance if there is a relevant issue on a medical level? I know you espouse a heightened level of customer service, but there is a point to let a patient take their issues elsewhere where they get services for 'free?' How do you handle this whole arena? I would appreciate your insights to aid us in handling these situations which are very recurrent."

From the patient's point of view
Before I give any advice on how to manage these sticky situations, let's first try to understand them better. The reader has presented us with a good understanding from the doctor's point of view but it is always helpful to see these things from the patient's point of view as well. Why would these patients expect the visit to be free? We know these patients have "issues they want resolved" but another way to phrase that is they have a complaint about a product they purchased. I'm not saying an error was made in the prescription of the lens and I'm not assigning blame, but from the patient's point of view, the contact lens he recently bought is not working right.

In my practice, we would describe this type of visit as "CL Trouble." This office visit goes by many other names in our profession, such as Rx trouble (if it were about eyeglasses), Rx problem, grief case, Rx complaint, trouble-shoot,

Rx remake visit, Rx re-do, Rx recheck, etc. It doesn't really matter what we call it as long as we are talking about the same thing. Of course, the reader may be referring to some variation of this and I may be oversimplifying, but let's begin here.

To me, it makes no difference if a complaint is about contact lenses or eyeglasses. In either case, the patient is dissatisfied with a product I prescribed. I also don't know the reason for the dissatisfaction yet or whose fault it was. I'll determine that when I examine the patient.

Was the problem there from day one?

I think the answer to the question above is primary as we try to assess if it's fair to charge the patient for additional professional care.

If the patient alleges that the problem (discomfort, blurred vision, redness of the eye, etc.) was always present with a new product, I would generally see them for an office visit at no charge. Yes, the patient could be dishonest with his answer in order to gain sympathy, but I will probably discover clues to that as I go along and it is really a separate issue anyway.

Of course, the time period from the date of dispensing is also important. Our reader's email gives an example of one, two or three months later. More on this in the next section.

I know there is a school of thought that all care by the eye care practitioner (ECP) should have a fee associated with it, even if it is a follow-up to a complaint, but that approach is a bad idea if you are trying to build a practice. Our society and marketplace simply won't accept that because the ECP is also profiting from the sale of the product. That is one key difference between an ECP prescribing glasses or contacts and a general physician prescribing a drug.

What took you so long to tell me?

When I'm seeing a patient with CL trouble or (Rx trouble) and the time period from the date of dispensing is beyond reasonable, I find that asking the question above makes a huge difference. Try it and you'll see what I mean. I can't tell you exactly what to do in every circumstance, but when you hear the patient's answer, you'll know. If the patient gives you a surprising answer, like "I've been out of the country and just got back" or "My wife was told she has cancer and everything else had to wait," you will be more understanding. If there is not a great answer, the patient usually says "Yeah, I know I should have called you sooner but I thought it might go away." In the latter case, however, at least you communicated to the patient that he has some responsibility to let you know of a problem in a timely fashion. If you decide to help the patient at no charge, at least you get some good will credit for being very understanding.

If the patient's answer is "Well, it didn't start bothering me until last week" and the contacts were dispensed four months ago, you may be justified in charging an office visit fee. Continue to examine the patient and find the cause of the trouble and you'll know what to do. You might even consider asking the patient what he thinks would be fair regarding the fee.

Tell patients in advance

This point is vital in so many aspects of patient satisfaction issues. Consider how the following could help prevent a sticky situation.

- The doctor or a clinical technician could have told the patient at the time of the fitting that follow-up visits are not included in this service (to keep costs low) so if you have any problems with these new contacts be sure to call us right away.
- The receptionist could tell patients over the phone that there may be an office visit fee. Train your staff to look at the date of dispensing while taking the call to schedule an appointment. If your policy is to see complaint visits within 30 days and it is beyond that, the receptionist should say so. You may still make an exception based on the circumstances, but the time to bring up the possibility of a fee is over the phone. Doing this prevents confrontations at the front desk after the visit.

Charge higher fees and include follow-up care

Since the need for follow-up care is recurring frequently for our reader, I would raise the contact lens professional fee so follow-up visits can be included if needed. I presume the ECP is trying to be a nice guy and keep the initial patient fee low when he believes the contact lens fit is final, but since that is often not the case, I would raise the fee and require a follow-up visit. Or raise the fee and make follow-up care optional.

I made the point just two weeks ago in tip # 431, but I'll repeat it here. Great customer service is very hard to deliver when the fee schedule is value oriented. Raise your fees in general and you'll find it is much easier to let patients win these scenarios. If vision plans are very dominant in your practice, raise the fees anyway.

Medical insurance

To answer the reader's question about medical insurance, I would make such billing secondary. I would decide about a fee first, as if the patient was going to pay. I like to presume that the patient has a $2,500 deductible (and many do). I will bill medical insurance if there is a fee for the visit and there is a medical diagnosis. A good test for billing medical insurance is if the patient wants you to or not.

9.19 Service Recovery

The last two tips have been about patient satisfaction and practice culture and I stressed how important it is to believe in the philosophy that the patient is always right (at least 99% of the time). In this tip, let's take a close look at how your office handles situations when things go wrong. And let's face it, things will go wrong. I do wonder though, why it seems that multiple things have to go wrong with the same person on the same job! Does that happen in your practice, too?

The initial response is key
The perception of quality and integrity of your practice is largely determined by the first few words out of an employee's mouth (and the supporting body language) when initially confronted with a complaint. It's so important that you should have a staff meeting to work on that issue alone. Well-meaning employees may try to mitigate the "damage" by trying to explain why the problem occurred or worse, trying to make a case that there is no problem.

The correct response to a patient complaint is one of complete understanding and agreement that the situation is intolerable and that a sincere effort will be made to correct the problem or at least learn from it.

A good response from a staff member to a serious complaint would be "Oh, that's terrible."

As customers, we all know that things will sometimes go wrong; what we judge closely is what will happen next.

Unresolved problems represent a huge hidden cost
It's short-sighted to look at the immediate lab costs that may be incurred by fixing a problem with glasses or contact lenses or at the lost sale that occurs with a refund. And fixing a problem begrudgingly, while letting the patient know that you are not happy with the situation, is a double loss: you incur the

immediate cost and still lose the patient goodwill. Realize that the public relations damage done by a patient who feels they were not treated fairly can be severe and long-lasting. Picture the patient who spent hundreds of dollars on glasses at your office but can't wear them for some reason. They sit in a drawer. That person will retell his story over and over every time eye care comes up in conversation. The damage to your practice reputation will be fairly invisible to you, but none the less real.

Listen

An important step in the service recovery process is to listen to the patient. Provide reassurance up front that you will resolve the problem, take him to a private area of the office and ask him to tell you about the problem. Don't cut the patient off. Make eye contact and nod in an understanding way. Take notes for the record if appropriate. You will be surprised at how easy it is to disarm a person's anger once you show support.

Empower staff

Make it easy for staff to fix problems. Be sure to train staff on how to troubleshoot a problem and to do whatever it takes to make the patient happy.

Don't make the doctor inaccessible

Remember that it's important to get the problem corrected on the first try. If your staff member attempts to solve a problem but does not have the knowledge to diagnose it properly in the first place, a wasted effort will be the result. When you have to get involved after two or more unsuccessful attempts, the patient will have lost confidence by then and will be losing patience as well. Be willing to get involved early with a no charge office visit, or with a behind the scenes review of the issue at hand.

Don't worry about blame

Resist saying the problem was the lab's fault. It's your lab and the patient is dealing with you! They don't want to hear about the problems you encounter in running your practice. Train your staff to not display anger or frustration at co-workers when faced with having to correct a mistake. Just admit the error and accept the blame on behalf of the office. Even doctors may have to check your ego at the door. Patients don't want to hear long-winded excuses about why the Rx didn't work.

Use the words: I'm sorry

It is extremely rare for eye care staff or doctors to say I'm sorry - but that is exactly what is needed in most cases to reach a successful resolution. You may never reach complete patient satisfaction without it. When things go wrong, most of us just want to hear a company representative admit that a problem occurred and express an apology. Once we get that, attitudes change instantly! Even the toughest meanest person will soften. What's the big deal about saying I'm sorry? Are we afraid it is an admission of fault? It may be helpful to actually rehearse saying it out loud.

The late complaint

How do you handle the patient in your chair who says her glasses have never been right and it's eight months after dispensing? Most of us are happy to resolve issues, but we expect the patient to be reasonable. When I'm faced with this I say: "I'm sorry to hear you're having problems with the glasses; why did it take you so long to let me know about this?" The response to this key question will lead you to the right resolution and just asking it lets the patient know, in a nice way, that she had some responsibility in the matter. The patient will typically soften up. Consider a few example responses and how it will change your point of view:

- I did let you know four times but your staff refused to correct the problem.
- My husband has cancer and I was just too distracted to take care of it.
- I really should have come in sooner but I wasn't sure if there was a problem or not.
- I just noticed the problem last week.

In some cases, a compromise may be reached that will be fair to all. You might say: "Of course, your prescription may have changed in eight months time, but I'll recheck it today at no charge and if we have to make a change in your lenses I will reduce the cost by 50%."

Ask the patient what to do

Sometimes I find I would be happy to fix a problem if I only knew what the problem was! In cases where nothing more can be done it's best to explain that to the patient. Often, that may be all that's needed. If you can't resolve a problem and the patient is still unhappy, it may help to ask him what he would like you to do. Listen and comply.

Refunds are allowed

Refunds are a sensitive topic among eye care practitioners, with some vehemently refusing. My philosophy is of course to try all other remedies first, but if a refund is requested, I grant it right away. I may even proactively offer a refund if I know I can't make a situation right. But refunds are extremely rare. I believe refunds should be limited to products and not professional fees since the service was provided, but if a patient did not agree with that, I would refund professional fees as well. Life is too short to worry about it and I stopped letting these matters upset me or my staff long ago. We simply move on and feel good about it. Don't sweat the small stuff.

Chapter 10. Practice Marketing

10.1 A Primer on Eye Care Marketing

In my opinion, the biggest problem facing optometric practices in the United States is the lack of patient demand. There are exceptions, but the vast majority of practices are not busy enough. Some ODs rationalize that they don't want to see more than 10 to 15 patients per day, but actually in many cases, there are no more to be seen even if they wanted to.

Many of the management challenges we face would go away if we just had more patient demand. The first benefit would be an increase in profit and cash flow, which could then fund many great changes and advancements. Most ODs would love to manage the problems of a practice that has too many patients!

Given this state of the profession, one would think optometrists and managers in private practices would do more marketing, but actually, most do very little. The marketing budget is typically 2 to 3% of gross revenues and much of that is actually for postage on recall notices. Marketing and advertising is the key method that businesses use to find customers, so let's look at your marketing effort and see what you can do.

Customer service
I always like to begin any discussion on marketing with a review of the vital role of customer service. Doctors in general are getting worse in this area, which may not matter if you are in a specialty that has tons of patients. But if you need more patients, realize that word of mouth referral is the biggest source there is for doctors. You'll get some word of mouth referrals if you simply get most of the eyeglass prescriptions right, but if you treat people really well and if you're super-easy to do business with, you can attract a huge number.

Talk with your staff about the importance of customer service and letting the patient win. Look at everything you do from the patient's point of view.

Director of marketing
As you embark on a new world of marketing campaigns for your practice, decide on who is going to do the work. You would do well to appoint someone on your staff to take on the additional role of Director of Marketing. If your current staff is already overworked and you can't give anyone more assignments, then go ahead and hire a new employee. It will be part-time

duty in most practices, but it takes time. The marketing projects will produce a financial return that more than covers the increased payroll cost. Choose a person who understands the business side of the practice and has a creative flair. Appoint someone who has excellent computer skills and uses social media.

Practice logo

Evaluate your practice image and consider the name of the practice and the logo. If it is time to freshen that image, get help from a local advertising professional. Consider your logo colors and a tagline you can use with various media and advertisements.

Website

Your practice website is the cornerstone of your marketing plan. Virtually every patient you see, new or established, will visit your site. It must be impressive. It must be beautiful. Have a custom designed website built for your practice by a company that knows eye care. Be prepared that a great website requires more than just writing a check to the designer; it requires a great deal of your Director of Marketing's time to take photos, write and edit copy and shoot videos. You will want to work with third party plug-in software. You will want to make the site interactive. And you will want to be able to make most changes yourself with user-friendly administrative access.

Social media

The major thrust here is Facebook, so even if social media is not your thing, at least have your Director of Marketing administer a business page there. Think of it as free marketing. Most of your patients check Facebook several times per day. Once you get these patients to "Like" your page (easy to do), then all your posts appear on their newsfeed. Unlike your website, which people must actively go to in order to see it, Facebook lets you push your posts out to your followers.

I also recommend paid advertising in social media, like Facebook ads and Google AdWords.

Recall related

Most of us do some form of patient recall, but it can be so much more than just sending a post card once per year. Reminder messages about the need for eye care may be the most powerful marketing tool we have. Whether you choose to use preappointing, email, regular mail, telephone or a combination of all of the above, be sure to continually work to perfect your procedures.

The recall success rate is important, but so is the perception you create about your practice, so look at it from the patient's point of view.

In addition to reminder notices, re-activation letters with special promotions and special telephone calls for patients who have not responded to traditional recall are very effective. If you create an accurate list of patients who are well past-due for eye care, your assistant could call twelve people and schedule two for eye exams. Consider a bonus program for these appointments.

Electronic communication

I highly recommend that you sign up with one of the companies that provides email and texting service through integration with your patient database. Companies like Websystem3, Demandforce, Solutionreach and 4PatientCare offer much more than appointment confirmations! They are your vehicle for newsletters; they get you more Facebook likes and they promote more online reviews.

Community outreach

Being active in your community and supporting worthy causes will earn your practice a great reputation. That converts to more patient demand in an indirect way, but still very effective. If the doctor wants to be involved in Rotary Club or other service groups, that is fine, but if not, your Director of Marketing can participate and represent the practice. Chamber of commerce, parks and recreation programs, local school and sports events are all good things to be involved in.

Vision plans

While the marketing projects mentioned here are effective, none of them will result in a huge increase in your patient volume all at once. If you want a larger and faster change, consider something bigger like adding another vision plan or accepting Medicaid. I realize that these programs require a large discount and adding them is a major decision. They are not right for everyone, but they can deliver a large number of patients. This is especially helpful if you have an associate OD. I view the discount provided under these plans as a marketing expense. Many of these patients actually need medical eye care, which improves revenue considerably. Many vision plans allow the provider to balance bill the patient for contact lens fees after a small discount, so we can do well there.

There are many other great marketing ideas available for your practice, including: direct mail, trunk shows, in-office seminars, open houses, telephone reactivation and much more. Embrace marketing for your practice and increase your patient demand.

10.2 Making Your Practice Busier

The biggest problem facing optometrists today is insufficient patient demand. Most practices are simply not busy enough. If you can solve that problem, nearly all of your other problems would go away.

I'd like to present a series on marketing ideas for the independent private practice designed to fill your appointment schedule. These projects will require time, energy and some expense, but if you own a practice, remember that your job description is more than just examining eyes. You also must actively manage your business. That aspect is not always easy, but embrace it and you will be rewarded.

The first step
The most important marketing strategy is to stimulate more word-of-mouth referrals and the basis for that is outstanding customer service. I will concentrate on specific marketing tactics in this series, with an emphasis on the practical details, but don't overlook the importance of an office culture that is built on customer service. Work on that first. It does little good to attract new people to your practice if you leave many of them dissatisfied and spreading negative word-of-mouth comments.

About this tip miniseries
Each week, I will present an idea for a specific marketing project that you can put into effect to increase patient demand in your practice. Of course, each idea won't appeal to everyone, but try to stretch out of your comfort zone and adapt the concept into ways that will work for your practice and with your resources. Choose the projects that appeal most to you and develop a plan to do the others in the future. I'll make some basic decisions and present very specific instructions for each topic to make it easy to get started. But many alternative methods will also work so modify as you see fit. Questions and comments via email are welcome.

Host an in-office seminar
The marketing tactic this week is to host an in-office seminar on an eye care topic of your choice. I'll choose contact lenses for presbyopia, but there are dozens of eye care specialties that will work. Present a different topic later in the year.

You do not need to be an eloquent speaker to present a seminar. The simple approach that you already use when you speak to a patient who is interested in bifocal contact lenses will work just fine. You'll just do the same thing for a small group instead of one person. In fact, it is best to limit the lecture to only about 20 minutes and to use simple layman's terms.

An in-office seminar is a great marketing concept because:

- It brings people who are interested in a service or product into your office.
- It makes use of your resources like office space and staff when you are not busy enough.
- You and your practice are positioned as expert in the eye care topic.
- The advertising you do for the event is great publicity for your practice.
- Even people who do not attend the seminar will think of your practice when they are in need of that service in the future.
- It makes an event happen that creates a buzz among your staff and patients.

Plan and promote the project

Here is a list of things to do to:

- What is the event? I suggest you make it a seminar and free screening. The doctor will give a presentation on new advancements in multifocal contact lenses and a free trial contact lens screening will be offered for anyone interested. Refreshments will be served. You must make the event enticing to people and this fills the bill. People can learn about contact lens options, talk to a doctor and see if they qualify to wear specialty contacts, all at no cost. That is compelling.
- Select a date. The optimum time will be when people can attend and not have to miss work, so late afternoon or evening is best. In this case, you will need as many staff members as possible to assist with the screening. You could pay overtime or, if you are not very busy, just chose a date when you typically have evening hours and close it off to appointments. Choose a date well into the future so you have time to make the arrangements.
- Consider a time like 4pm so people can stop on their way home from work before dinner or 6pm so people can come out after dinner. There is no perfect time that will appeal to everyone.
- Prepare the seminar. Use PowerPoint to make slides and buy or borrow an LCD projector. The slides actually guide you through the

talk so you don't need notes. Have about 10 slides with bullet points of what you want to say, but don't put everything on the slide. Explain presbyopia (very simply), the disadvantages of eyeglasses, the benefits of contacts, how bifocal contacts work for near and far and discuss modified monovision as an additional option.

- Be sure to encourage questions after the talk. Have a staff member ask something if no one else does to break the ice.
- Be prepared to answer questions about price. Consider offering a 10% discount if a fitting appointment is scheduled at the seminar.
- Offer appointments. Ask attendees to schedule a fitting appointment after the presentation and have staff ready.
- Have handouts. This can be a simple outline of what you will talk about (a copy of the PowerPoint works well) and you can include brochures from the AOA and your contact lens manufacturer of choice. You can also include your office brochure and business cards.
- Plan for the screening aspect. Ask people in attendance to sign a list if they want to try contacts in the office after the seminar. Have your staff determine their approximate Rx by autorefraction or lensometry of present eyeglasses. Insert trial lenses and let the patients walk around the office to adapt while the doctor speaks to each one individually. The doctor should ask all good candidates to schedule a fitting exam.
- Decide on refreshments. I would not serve alcohol. Cookies, coffee and cold bottled water should be sufficient.
- Ask your contact lens sales rep for assistance and ideas. Co-op financial support may be available for some projects. Can you get some slides with diagrams or photos of bifocal contacts?
- Promote the event on your website and on your business Facebook page. Tip: if you can't easily do these tasks, make the needed investments so you can use electronic media more effectively in the future.
- Advertise the seminar and screening in your local newspaper. This part can be expensive, but you are getting the word out and it will pay off. Newspaper ads reach your current patient base as well as everyone else in the community.
- You could send a special invitation to a select group of patients (search your records for the right age group) if you wish. Your staff could also call a select group and personally invite them for a better response.
- You could send invitations by mail or email to the local community or to certain zip codes. Speak to a local printer about this; use post cards and bulk mail pricing.

- Put signs up in the office for the event and ask candidates in person if they can come back for the seminar.
- Require people to reserve a spot by phone in advance. Space is limited.
- If you find that you have a bigger response than you can handle, add another date.
- If you find that you get a very low response you can increase the promotion effort. Postpone the date if necessary. A small group is OK.
- Confirm attendance by phone the day before and be prepared for some no shows. Accept 20% more than ideal to plan for no shows.

Measure your results
It is not always possible to know how much new business is generated from a marketing project, but keep good records and do the best you can. Make notes about:

- Cost of advertising and cost of other invitations.
- Cost of food and drink served.
- Additional staff wages outside of normal business hours (if any).
- Day, date and time of the seminar.
- Number of people confirmed/ number actually attended.
- Number of appointments scheduled in the next week.
- Number of actual cases fitted with the product as a result of the project.
- Gross revenue generated.
- What you would do differently next time.

10.3 A Busier Practice, Part 2: Community Outreach

I tried to get you started last week by jumping right into a marketing project and I'll present more in the weeks ahead. Building a practice with plenty of patient demand is a process that requires time and effort, but you will be rewarded with greatly increased profitability and the potential to enjoy both your personal and professional life more. There are many facets to practice building, so let's continue to tackle one per week. Make time in your schedule to work on these projects. Visualize the great things you could do if you had plenty of patients wanting your services!

Is your community aware of your practice?

Many practices are nearly invisible to the public. I'm not really talking about how many people see your office location (although that certainly helps), but rather how many people know you, think of you and talk about you. While there are many ways to promote your practice, this article will focus on community service. Spend a little time out of your office doing good things for others and key people in your local area will notice. Some of these people will become your patients and others will just talk about you in a positive way, but this kind of exposure is very good. Pay it forward. Give away your time and skill and the public will pay you back.

The biggest impact will be found if the doctor and/or practice owner performs the community service, but really any representative of the practice can make a difference, including opticians and office managers.

Community research

Start by making a list of community organizations and projects that exist and then select the ones that you would like to pursue. You can ask key leaders in your community, check your local library, visit your town website or just ask your friends and staff members for ideas. Here are some possibilities to look for:

- Service clubs. Examples include Rotary, Kiwanis, Lions, Jaycees and many more. These often meet once per week at breakfast or lunch. Ask a current member if you can come as a guest. Learn about the goals, rules and local projects. If you join and become active, you'll gain many other business leaders as patients and that word of mouth becomes very valuable.
- Church. If you do more than just attend services but also volunteer for committees, projects or choir, you'll gain the trust and admiration of many people.
- Business clubs like the Chamber of Commerce offer many opportunities for networking with other professionals and business people. Join the group, pay the dues and attend the functions.
- Charities from Salvation Army to Red Cross to United Way and others need volunteers. How can you help?
- Hobby-based clubs. Pursue your interest by joining a local club for gardening, books, photography, or whatever it may be.
- Take a class – or give a class. Does your city parks department or community college offer adult education classes?
- If you are good in sports there are many opportunities to volunteer as a coach or umpire for little league baseball, Pop Warner football, soccer, and school sports programs. Even if you can't play sports, how about joining the high school booster club?

Time is more important than money
Community outreach events do not usually require much expense. There may be a sponsorship donation or a registration fee, but usually the contribution is mostly in the form of time and effort. Participating in community organizations requires time by the doctor or staff or both. Consider how much time each person can devote to these events per week. It is great for the doctor to have some involvement as described below, but I believe it is also a good investment to pay staff their usual wages to have them participate. Some employees may participate in the community on their own, and that is great, but if they are doing it for the practice, you should treat it as work for them.

If an event or meeting requires staff to participate in the evening or on weekends, consider giving them some compensatory time off in exchange. Always observe rules for paying overtime if required. You may need to hire another employee to give your office the proper coverage for patient care, but I would embrace that and try it. I want the staff to grow larger because your practice will grow larger as well. Make something happen.

Chamber of Commerce
The local chamber is a good place to start because this group focuses on all kinds of events in town. You'll meet other business leaders and share ideas on what they have done to build their businesses. The chamber often sponsors events for the public that will showcase your practice. Pay the dues, become a chamber member, attend the meetings and volunteer to participate.

Parks and Recreation
Keep up with your city or neighborhood to learn about events that will be hosted, often through the parks department. There may be fairs, festivals, or educational programs. Your practice may be able to have a booth and have your staff present to talk to people about eye care, give away practice brochures, free gifts and do vision screenings.

Sponsorships
Say yes to some of the community events that ask for help to get your practice logo on signs, T-shirts and in programs as a sponsor. Sponsor a little league team or the high school speech and debate club.

Fund raising support

Many organizations have fund raising events like silent auctions and raffles. While you will have to say no sometimes, consider donating a pair of sunglasses. If you do this, be sure to play up the marketing value by placing the sunglasses and case in a basket with lots of extras, like tissue paper, a bow, a practice brochure and business cards, and some give-away gifts like a lens cleaner and cloth.

Civic groups
Active membership in organizations like Rotary Club, Lions Club or many others is a good idea because it builds your network of local leaders. These are excellent patients and referral sources. If you join, however, make a commitment to attend meetings and be active in club events. And approach the club primarily with an attitude of how you can help others, not how to attract business. The business will follow.

Charities and church
Get involved in charities especially one that means a lot to you and is vision related. If you have a special promotion in your office, like a frame trunk show, you could donate a portion of the profit to a charity.

The right motivation
If you pursue these organizations and projects, do it with the attitude of providing a service without personal financial gain. Don't think about your own business development and it will actually just follow naturally. Placing your own needs first is a sure way to make the effort backfire.

10.4 A Busier Practice, Part 3: Why Your Practice Should be on Facebook

I continue to monitor optometrists' use of Facebook as a practice marketing tool by asking for a show of hands during my lecture presentations. While admittedly a very rough, non-scientific poll, I'm now estimating the percentage of ODs who use FB for business to be about 50%.

If you are in the group that does not have a Facebook business page or has one but rarely posts anything, here is why you should change your ways: it's free marketing that can easily reach thousands of people!

Social media overview
If you are new to social media you may find it overwhelming as you hear about the growing number of social sites. How do you decide whether to use

Twitter, LinkedIn, Google+, Pinterest, Instagram and so on? I'll make it easy for you; select the one that more of your patients are using on a daily basis and that would be Facebook. There are over a billion users! Many of your patients check their Facebook news feed several times per day, on their computers, iPads and smartphones. This is not just a fad; it is a change in social communication and it is not going away. You can look into the others later, but start with Facebook.

Facebook can actually be very good for your practice because it gives you an up to date image and it allows you to connect with your patient base and the general public on your terms. Most practices need more patients very much and FB is a great way to market your services and products.

Different than a website

I believe you need both an excellent practice website and an active practice FB page. They are different and both are extremely important to your marketing plan. Here is one major difference: your website requires people to actually seek it out. A viewer must do a Google search and find you or otherwise know your web address and type it into a web browser. The person must click on your web address and want to visit the site. With Facebook, you get to push your content out to the viewers and it appears on their Facebook newsfeed. That is a huge advantage!

Your FB posts are seen by people who have "liked" your page, which is FB terminology for clicking on a button. Think of these people as subscribers to your page and your practice. Your practice reaches many more people, however, when any of your fans likes one of your posts or comments on a post. In those cases, all of their friends will also see the post. So you may have a few hundred fans who like your page, but you can reach thousands more!

Your website is still important because it can offer so much more than a Facebook page. It is the primary source of information about your practice and it provides a much more robust platform with many more features than Facebook. Use your website for people who want to find out more about your practice and use FB to push out updates, news and greetings to your followers so they keep thinking about you.

How to get more "likes"

It turns out that it is extremely easy to get people to like your page. All you have to do is ask them. Most people who are active users of Facebook like many pages and they are happy to comply with a click. When a person likes your page, all of his friends instantly see that "like" as a post on their newsfeed, so you get some immediate publicity. Facebook is so powerful because it builds upon other people's networks of friends.

Once you have established your practice FB page, simply train your staff to ask each patient who visits your office if they are on Facebook. This could be at the same time they are confirming the patient's email address, which is fast becoming the preferred method for communications and appointment reminders. If the patient replies that he is on Facebook, the charming receptionist simply says "Great! Our practice is also and we are trying to get more likes; would you please visit our page and like us?"

Many practices have signs made up asking patients to log onto the FB page and "like us". You can also run a contest for a free pair of designer sunglasses. Just monitor new likes for two weeks and enter those names into a drawing. Of course, you can take a photo of the winner and post it on Facebook!

What to post

Facebook posts are short by nature. It should be a quick headline or sound bite that will be of interest to your patients. The best FB posts have a photo, a video or a link to go along with your text. You can certainly share facts about eye care from educational websites like allaboutvision.com or the AOA or consumer publications, but I think the most interesting posts are ones that are unique to your practice. Just share what is going on and take a photo with your cell phone to go with it. Maybe it is a new frame or sunglass line, maybe you have a new instrument, perhaps you went to a conference, or put a photo of a new staff member. Try to mix it up and just use your judgment about what people will find interesting and make your practice look good.

Consider these ideas for posts:

- What's new in your practice? Take a photo or short video of it, upload it and write a few sentences about it.
- Do you have a new frame line coming in?
- Did you acquire a new instrument?
- Are you participating in a community event?
- Are you hosting an in-office seminar or screening (see last week's tip).
- Have a running "meet the staff" feature, with a photo and short personal bio.
- Optical illusions are always a hit. Find a website and post the link.
- Look online to any resource about eye care or news organization that has an eye story and post the link. Allaboutvision.com is a great source along with the AOA.

- I've seen posts when offices have an opening in the patient schedule due to a cancellation — asking if anyone wants it.
- Facebook is a very inclusive network. Follow other practice pages and see what they post. Most ECPs would not mind in the least if you repost their posts; after all they are seen by a different circle of patients.

I recommend that you appoint a staff member to manage your practice Facebook page. Select someone who understands social media and work with him or her on developing the right content on a frequent basis.

10.5 Time to Get Serious with Patient Email and Texting

I think most ECPs already use email for patient communications to some extent, but now is the time to really move this effort into high gear. If you are not using patient email yet, you really should develop a plan to begin now. The benefits are huge and this is a trend that will only grow larger.

I find email to be the primary form of electronic communication, but many people use their cell phones extensively as organizers and calendars and they may prefer text messages. It is smart to offer both options to patients.

What to communicate
Just about everything you need to communicate with patients can be done by email. And email is so easy and efficient that you'll even undertake some extra communications that are not required but just kind of nice. When done well, these communications will build your practice.

- Recall notices
- Appointment reminders
- Glasses or contacts are ready
- Welcome to our office
- Please take our satisfaction survey or write a review
- Thank you for the referral
- Appointment waiting list
- Happy birthday greetings
- Practice newsletter
- General announcements and promotions

Better than the postal service or telephone

There are several good reasons to begin to use email for patient communications, but here are my top three: saving money, office efficiency (which is still saving money) and patient satisfaction (which is making money).

Some communications are quite large, like recall notices. Email saves money on this monthly project by avoiding the cost of postage, printing, and staff time. Add up your typical cost to mail 1,000 post cards per month and you'll see what I mean. Don't resist the email process because you think you will still have to some mailing, so why bother? You could cut your mail recall in half very quickly and over the next few years, virtually eliminate it. But you have to start.

Other communications are more individual, like confirming appointments for tomorrow or letting patients know their glasses are ready. Currently, you use the telephone for much of this, but ask your staff how often they place a call and do not reach the person intended. They get voice mail more often than people. Your staff leaves a voice message but who knows if the correct person ever retrieves it? How inefficient. Email is always there and the service I use indicates if the message was delivered and even if it was read.
Still other practice communications are simply not happening because they are too much trouble for your staff. Welcome letters after an exam is completed or birthday greetings, for example. I only recently started sending birthday greetings by email in my practice and I was surprised to see a few of those messages were used to request an appointment for an eye exam! I assumed the birthday effort would generate some patient goodwill, but I did not expect appointments. The online communication company I use searches my records for birthdays and sends the email greetings automatically and there are virtual buttons along the bottom that encourage the patient to schedule an appointment or refer a friend.

How to get email addresses

I've long been disappointed in the small percentage of patients who gave us email addresses for our records. Obviously, we must overcome this issue if we are to reap the potential benefits of email communication. I'm happy to report that we went from collecting email addresses on about 10% of patients to 80% almost overnight. All I did was meet with my front desk staff and office manager and we discussed how important email is and how we would like to use it. I told them that getting an email address from each patient is just as important as getting the phone number.
Of course, many people do not want to share email information with businesses, possibly for fear of spam, but we developed a strategy about how to respond to that resistance. By assuring the patient that we will never

share the email address with anyone and by explaining that we would like to use it for appointment reminders and other forms of communication, most people are quite willing to cooperate. We have pads of paper at the front desk to help us get the email address correctly.

We have even made a dent in the large number of patient records from the past that do not have email data. Our communication company offers a service that searches internet email directories for names that match our patient names and residential addresses. The company then sends an automated email message asking the person to confirm the email address and if we may have permission to communicate with them via email. I pay a small fee for each email address that is found, if the person opts in.

Online communication companies

There are several excellent companies that can assist you with the email process. Some of these companies started out in the field of dentistry and have now moved into eye care and other fields. Just ask your colleagues or visit a major eye care conference or email me for a list of names. These companies work with your office management software program and upload all the information so the process is automatic.

There are many other services these online companies offer, such as assistance with "reputational marketing" in order to increase and improve reviews of your practice by patients which show up on Google, Yelp, Yahoo and many other review sites. The firms also provide an interface for your staff, a dashboard, to show the appointments for the day and the status of confirmations. The companies can even help your practice on Facebook. This is the future of marketing and appointment management and it looks bright.

10.6 Practice Websites, Part 1

A recent survey of large optometric practices (greater than $1 million gross revenue) revealed that 29% do not have a website. I was surprised that the percentage was that high and it prompted me to appeal to all eye care providers who do not have a website and those who have one that's only very basic. I'll also offer some food for thought for practices that already host a site.

Why have a website?

All eye care practices should have a website because without one, the practice appears to be out of date. A website offers many strong business benefits, but the mere absence of a site sends a very negative signal. Today, strong businesses, large and small have a site because the Internet is such a widely used business tool and websites are so easy and inexpensive.

Many eye care providers think that the Internet is so big that it won't be effective in attracting new patients to their practice in the local environment. That assumption is incorrect for a few reasons:

- Consumers frequently perform a search via Google or other search engines for terms like "eye care" followed by the name of the city and state they are located in. Without a web site, your practice will not likely pop up as an option in the results. With a website, your practice name will appear with a link allowing the consumer to move directly to your site with one click of the mouse.
- A practice website facilitates word of mouth referrals from existing patients. Consider the patient who loves your services and wants to tell a co-worker about it. Let's say he does not have your business card, but he knows that you are called The Eyes Have It Eye Center. He types that name into a Google search window, but doesn't find a hit for your practice because you have no website. This is not a good impression for the co-worker and the referral may be delayed or lost. On the other hand, an instant hit on Google and a jump to your website reveals a list of your services and specialties, photos of the office and plenty of assistance with how to make an appointment. The co-worker easily remembers your practice web address (called a URL) and he can revisit your site on his own anytime.

Beyond the marketing power of attracting new patients, your website is a valuable tool for established patients who need more information. Often more convenient than the phone book, many people use the Internet to look up phone numbers or addresses. In fact, most local communities have yellow pages online and will list your practice there and allow you to include a link to your website URL. See below for features you may want to include on your website.

What should be in a website?

In its most basic form a practice website is like an electronic brochure, but it can also be much more than that. It should tell a visitor the key features and benefits of your practice. It's a marketing piece that allows you a great opportunity to showcase your office. Spend some time writing short and interesting statements about each aspect of your practice. Consider these elements for your website design.

- Practice name, location and contact information. Be sure to include an email address in addition to a phone number and fax number. You are communicating with people who use the Internet. But be sure someone checks that email mailbox every day and responds immediately. Email is meant to be fast.
- A map of the area showing how to get to the office.
- Information about your services.
- About the doctor and staff.
- Photos are very important, of doctors, staff members, instruments and the optical area.
- Insurance plans accepted and methods of payment.
- Promotions and events in the practice.
- Links to other websites of interest about eye care.
- Articles about eye care topics.
- Animated educational videos about eye care topics
- Office forms (such as patient history and registration) that can be completed and submitted online or printed by the patient and completed before the visit.
- Online appointment scheduling.
- Online ordering of replacement contact lenses.
- Virtual frame inventory with a virtual try-on feature.

Domain names

Tune in next week for some tips on how to get help designing and publishing your practice website, but in the meantime, here is some homework for you. Select and reserve your domain name. A domain name is a unique name that includes the.com or the.net part of an email address or website URL address. It should be related to the name you use for your practice, which could be the doctor's last name or other practice name.

I strongly believe that you should have your own domain name and not add on to another entity that might host your website. Your practice needs its own identity, not that of another company. For example, if your practice name is Migilicutty Eye Care, you might like to own the rights to Migilicutty.com, or MigilicuttyEyeCare.com. That would mean your website could use www.migilicutty.com and your email address could be DrM@migilicutty.com.

It's very easy to own a domain name, or actually you rent it on an ongoing basis for about $10 per year. The difficult part is finding the domain name that you want, now that millions of names are already taken. If you have an unusual name, the one you want may be available. If you have a more common name, you may want to consider alternative domain name suffixes. While.com may be the most popular and most desirable for many people, you may have to go to.net or.org or.biz or others to get the name you want. These suffixes may be slightly more difficult for people to recall. There are also country codes that can make a suffix unique.

To check if a domain name is available, use the Internet to visit the website of a company that registers and hosts domain names. You can perform a Google search for "domain name" and you'll see many options, such as networksolutions.com or godaddy.com. These websites will do an instant check on any names you wish and offer alternatives if yours are not available. Be creative. If MigilicuttyEyeCare.com is taken, MigilicuttyEye.com may not be.

Once you find a domain name you like, get out your Visa card and reserve it. Later, you can use that name to host your website.

Next week, I will list a few website design firms to help our readers make an informed selection. Please send me an email if you know of a company that should be included.

10.7 Practice Websites, Part 2

Chances are good that you already have a practice website, but if you don't or if you would like to change some aspects of your current site, here are some ideas to consider.

Designing your website
While it's certainly possible to design and program your own website, the computer code language that is used may be a little difficult to master for the uninitiated. Besides that, a great website should have design elements that may be best left to professionals. The primary language used in websites is called HTML (hypertext markup language). Some commercially available software programs (such as Microsoft Frontpage, Expression Web or SharePoint Designer) are available to guide you through the web authoring process.

A far easier way to obtain your own website is to use a company that specializes in web design. The services available from a website development firm range from personalized work with an individual designer to complete self-service where you just type your text into a template and upload your files for photos and printed forms. You'll get more creative personalization and a more unique website with the former, but you'll find a lower cost and possibly more control with the latter.

There are many website design firms available to you. The list below contains some companies that have experience creating websites for eye care professionals but it is by no means exhaustive nor does inclusion constitute an endorsement or recommendation. You should evaluate and select a company that matches the needs of your practice.

What to look for in a web development company

Whether you use a local boutique web designer, a national firm specializing in eye care web design, an Internet do-it-yourself company, a web template service offered through a vision plan, or your brother-in-law who dabbles in computers, be sure to insist that you have direct access to your website so you can make changes easily by yourself. I think it's important to be able to log on to your website file with a password and delete, change or add text and files. If the web designer wants to assist you with every change or update, you'll find that you avoid making changes because it's inconvenient and may trigger an additional fee. You should own the website and have direct access to it yourself anytime you wish.

Here are some additional features to consider:

- Can you use your own domain name independently from the web hosting name?
- Can the web design firm host your site for you on its computer server and what is the cost for this service?
- Can you get hit statistics about your website?
- Does the firm offer features such as online contact lens ordering, appointment scheduling and office form completion?
- Is technical support available?
- Will the firm assist you if you wish to send emails to your patients?

10.8 Take Patient Surveys up a Notch

Optometrists, along with many other small businesses, are surveying their patients and customers more than ever before and that is a wonderful trend. Asking patients about their experience in your practice shows you care and the information you collect can help you to improve your services and your marketing. Email and the internet have made it much easier to conduct surveys and having the responses in electronic format allows you to analyze the data.

Read on for a simple tip that will help you to ensure higher levels of patient satisfaction and will improve patient reviews that you receive on social media.

Surveys in general

The electronic communication firms that specialize in eye care do a fantastic job of asking your patients to complete a brief survey and reporting the results to you. If you aren't currently using one of these services, I highly recommend that you select one and subscribe to it. To be clear, these firms offer many marketing services in addition to surveys.

The survey process begins with an email, which is sent from your practice to each patient who was seen for an eye exam today. The email content is written by you in advance and the communication service pulls the patients names and email addresses from your office management software. The entire process is automated and does not involve your staff at all. The email message thanks the patient for selecting your office for eye care. It also says how we value your feedback, we are always looking for ways to improve, and please click here to complete a brief survey. If the patient completes the survey, the results are sent to the practice owner or manager. In some cases, the communication service may also invite the patient to post a review on Google, Yelp, Yahoo or other review sites.

The companies I'm aware of that offer patient surveys are:

- Solutionreach
- Websystem3
- Demandforce
- 4PatientCare

Ask for feedback at checkout

Here is a great idea to enhance your efforts to obtain patient feedback: ask them. Train all staff members in your office who work with patients at the end of the visit to smile and say the following: "Hi, Mr. Smith. How was your visit with us today? Is there anything we could do better?" It seems simple enough, but I'm quite certain there are very few optometric offices that do this.

Asking patients for verbal feedback right there, in person, provides some strong benefits:

- If there were any shortcomings, it is best to know right now before the patient leaves the office. In many cases, an adjustment or correction can be made.
- If the issue can't be fixed, at least an apology can be delivered.
- Addressing the issue at the office will usually prevent the patient from posting a negative review on a website or writing about it on Facebook.
- Patients can become angrier about an issue when they stew over it after leaving your office and after they speak to others.
- You may want to have some gift cards on hand ($10 Starbucks and $50 gift cards from your practice) and empower staff to give them out as needed on the spot – with an apology.
- Thank patients for sharing a negative experience with you and assure them that your office cares very much about patient service and that the office will review this and learn from it.
- If everything went well, the patient still appreciates that you cared enough to ask.

10.9 The New World of Online Reviews

I've been asking every patient seen in my practice to complete a satisfaction survey for over 25 years. We used a simple prepaid post card for many years but we now send a thank you email after each exam and we invite the patient to take the survey by clicking on a button. I wrote Tip #17 about surveying patients in May 2002. I still read every patient survey we get and I learn from them.

Patient surveys have always been important but the concept has been elevated to a higher level with the popularity of online reviews. Whether it's on Google, Yelp, Angie's List, Yahoo or a host of other sites, patients no longer just tell you when they are not satisfied with their eye care; now they tell everyone. If your practice has not received a negative review yet, it's just a matter of time.

Do reviews really matter?

Um, yes, they do. The vast majority of patients who contact your office look you up on the internet. They may do a Google search for your last name or they may type the word optometrist plus your city name. They may only be looking for your phone number. But when the list of practices pops up, if yours has a reference to a review or some number of stars, do you think the patient will read it? Of course they will. People who are shopping love to read reviews and they can be quite informative. I'm sure you've read them for some products or services.

The best strategy for reviews

Here is the best strategy for success in the new world of online reviews: get a lot of them! There are two reasons why you are better off if you have dozens of reviews. First, your practice is probably quite good in the area of patient satisfaction. Most reviews will be very positive and if you have a very small percentage of bad reviews along with many great ones, you still look great. The rare negative ones actually add credibility. Second, if you receive many reviews, a bad one will quickly be pushed downward in the list and will not be as visible.

The best way to get a lot of online reviews is to ask patients for them! Train your staff to ask happy patients to write a review for you. Post a sign telling patients you appreciate their reviews. And the most effective way I've found for getting more online reviews is to work with an online communication and marketing company (like Websystem3, Solutionreach, Demandforce, etc.).

Preventing bad reviews

There are many ways to prevent bad reviews, including placing customer service at a very high level, but here is a specific technique that will stop most of them. Adopt a technique used in many restaurants: ask each patient as they check out "Was everything satisfactory with your visit today?" Every time I've had a complaint in my practice, I wondered why we didn't know the patient was unhappy. I'm always pretty sure that if I knew, I could have corrected the problem. Of course, the question must be sincere and with real interest.

If the staff member can determine that something is bothering the patient, she must take decisive control. She should apologize and advise the patient that we will fix the problem. She must show she cares and the office will not leave the matter alone. In most cases, the office manager should be alerted or a promise made that someone will be in touch.

What to do if you get a bad review

I recommend you have a protocol and a staff member in charge of how to respond to a complaint, a bad survey or a negative review. In my office, a high level staff member calls the patient as soon as possible. She apologizes and takes any steps she can to correct the problem. We also tell the patient that we are sending a $50 gift card as a token of our appreciation for his business and as a gesture of our concern. Plastic gift cards with the practice name and logo serve many purposes for us.

This approach prevents bad reviews, but if the review is already posted and the patient can't remove it, we post a short, polite response so readers can see we care. The important thing in responding is to not be defensive. I like to see an apology for the problem and thank the patient for bring this to your attention. We pledge that we truly care about customer service and we will work to improve in this area. It's not about revenge for the original poster, it's about making others see that you care.

10.10 What Should You Do about a Bad Review?

I think it is great that so many optometrists are now asking patients to complete a short survey about their eye care experience. Credit the success of electronic communication companies that now make it so easy for ODs to send emails and text messages to patients automatically. Understanding the customer (patient) is extremely important to the success of any business (practice).

While most of these surveys (and the online reviews they often lead to) are positive, we are increasingly seeing the big impact a complaint can have on the reputation of a practice. Not too long ago, if a patient had a complaint, they called your office and let you know. In most cases, you worked things out and everyone was happy. Now, instead of contacting the doctor's office, many people just write their comments on the survey that came to their inbox, or they go to Google, Yelp, Angie's List, Yahoo, Facebook or other social media. Whether the facts presented by the patient are right or not, many other people will read the comments.

This seems a bit unfair to business owners, but fear not; it is really not that bad. Here is my short list on what to do if you get a bad survey or review.

- Make sure you get a lot of reviews. A bad review is only a problem when you have only three reviews. The bad one gets way too much attention in that case and it never goes away. If you have 50 reviews, no one notices if there are a few negative ones and even if someone notices, it makes your practice look credible. Also, since new reviews are frequently being posted, the bad one gets pushed out of sight fairly quickly and it becomes irrelevant.

- We have to presume that the vast majority of people who come to your office leave happy, so if you had lots of reviews, most will be great. If most people are not happy, solve that problem first.
- The best way to get a lot of reviews is to work with one of the electronic communication companies like Solutionreach, Websystem3, Demandforce, 4PatientCare and I'm sure there are others. Use this service to email every patient after each eye exam, thank them for selecting your practice and ask them to complete a survey or to write a review. Also, train your staff to encourage happy patients to give you a review.
- I don't like to incentivize patients in advance to post a good review, but if someone does so on their own you can certainly thank them and give them a small gift like a $5 Starbucks card.
- If you get a bad survey or review, investigate what happened by talking to the staff involved based on the patient's comments. You want the truth, so be understanding with your employees about the situation. Show your staff the comments and get their side of the story.
- Resist the feelings of anger or hurt that you feel when you read a bad review. You will probably feel the person is not being fair, but that reaction is not the best for your business. Accept that your office made a mistake, even if it is only in the perception that the patient had. Force yourself to see this from the patient's point of view.
- If you can figure out who the patient is (some reviews are anonymous), call the patient right away. Don't give excuses or try to change the patient's mind. Instead, thank the person for bringing the problem to your attention. Assure the person that you take the issue seriously and that you will implement better staff training and that your office will improve. Apologize for the problem. That last one is especially hard, but it is what the patient wants and needs and it works wonders.
- If appropriate, offer to solve the problem or give a refund.
- Be sure to call the patient fairly quickly after getting a survey and you may be able to prevent a bad review online.
- If your phone call goes very well, you might consider asking the patient to remove or edit the bad review. Only the person who posted the review can do that. But don't worry about that; it is not a big deal.

- Always post a comment under a negative online review. Be careful with this because many people will judge your response. Follow what I advised you to do on the phone above: thank the person, talk about training and improving, apologize... and if anonymous, ask the person to contact your office so you can correct the problem.

With this approach, negative online reviews do not have to be such a big problem... and a large number of good reviews is great for your marketing plan!

10.11 Whose Wants and Needs?

The single biggest factor in driving more patients to your office is customer service. Great customer service stimulates word of mouth referrals and that is how independent practices are built. Yet, customer service in most small businesses and in most health care offices is mediocre at best. I think eye care practitioners in general fail to realize the direct connection between outstanding customer service and profit. Most ECPs think they are pretty good at customer service, but they spend 90% of their time in the exam room so they really don't know.

Review your office policies

The definition of marketing is *identifying and satisfying customers' wants and needs.* Yet many policies in eye care practices are designed to satisfy the *doctor's* wants and needs. Or the staff's wants and needs. Let's take a look at a few hypothetical situations and ask yourself if the policy is based on the patient's wants and needs – or the ECP's? See if any of these situations exist in your practice.

- The office closes at noon on Friday and reopens on Monday morning. This works great for the doctor and staff. Not so great for patients who love Saturday hours. Oh well, there are plenty of other eye care offices that are open during the convenient hours. I've heard the argument from offices that are closed on Saturdays that they just had too many no shows, but I see the thousands of dollars that are generated from 9am to 1pm on a single Saturday and I see that these appointments are booked weeks in advance.
- The office closes at lunchtime. Great for the staff isn't it?
- Patients who drop in to pick up glasses or have an adjustment may have to wait more than 15 minutes before they are served. This way the office only needs one optician.

- Patients must fill out long history forms at every visit. This helps the staff not have to ask as many questions and it helps the billing department in case the visit may be billed at a higher CPT code (even though that hardly ever occurs).
- The waiting area and the optical are very small. This helps keep the rent low. Is a small office a customer service issue?
- Many phone calls go to voice mail. This allows the office to reduce costs with fewer phone lines and it prevents interruptions when the staff is busy.
- Tell patients who miss an appointment that they will be charged a no-show fee if it happens again or that they will be double-booked. This makes people realize they are lucky to get an appointment. The practice is better of without this type of customer so if they go elsewhere, so be it.
- Patients often walk in and find no one at the front desk. The staff is busy; they have to be in many places in the office.

So what's wrong with having it your way?
Nothing, as long as you have all the patients you could ever want. And truly, that is why some businesses have such horrible customer service. Primary care physicians are often so busy that they can set their policies to be anyway that suits the doctor and staff and they will never have a shortage of patients. Unfortunately, optometry is not like that. We need more patients and our approach must be very consumer friendly.

My local cable television company is another example of a business that has plenty of customers, so they do things their way. With very few local options for television service, the cable company is thriving in spite of poor service. The cable boxes work poorly and there is a line out the door at the local office to exchange them. After you wait about an hour, the employees are very rude. But businesses like this are vulnerable because the marketplace is always changing. With satellite, fiber optic and internet-based television options on the way, those cable customers are ripe for the picking.

Some policies are hard to change
I realize that it is not easy to overcome some of the examples listed above. Many of them will create additional expense, such as more staff, and that can seem impossible. That's fine as long as the practice owner and manager know it is a shortcoming and there is a desire to improve. I opened my practice cold and I know very well that you can't do everything at once. But think of the practice as a business – not as an extension of you. Realize that the business must be convenient and a pleasure to work with for the

customer. Try to build a system that does not depend totally on the practice owner. Visualize a time when you can hire an associate OD and more staff, and try to make that happen. Look at new, larger office space before your lease is up for renewal. Don't wait for things to happen to your practice; make things happen.

10.12 A New Twist on Attracting Referrals from Primary Care MDs

I was at a conference last weekend and I was in a breakout group with some very smart and successful optometrists. My friend, Jay Binkowitz, an astute consultant and business owner, made a comment that stuck with me. It is a rather simple idea, but it was a new perspective on an old marketing concept. That is the value of meeting with colleagues to share practice management strategies: invariably a new point of view is discovered that can make a huge difference in how you do things. Then all you have to do is implement the idea and reap the benefits!

Calling on physicians
We've all heard of the concept of dropping in on the offices of physicians in the community to introduce yourself and just say hello. This strategy is a very effective way to gain referrals of new patients but I think relatively few optometrists actually do it. We tend to attract most of our new patients by referral from other patients. Those word of mouth referrals are extremely valuable, of course, but if you can establish a referral pattern from a local MD, you can greatly increase your patient demand.

Optometrists may have felt some insecurity about approaching MDs at some point in the past, but there is no reason for it anymore. We have been diagnosing and treating eye disease for many years and most primary care MDs are more interested in clinical skills and local relationships than political battles between professions. In my experience, physicians are quite happy to refer patients to ODs once they get to know them. We all have many MDs who are patients, which proves the point. We also have had drop-in visits from retinal specialists and general ophthalmologists, and we know that it goes very well and often results in more referrals from us.

Professional courtesy
The twist I heard at the conference was not rocket science and I'm sure many readers have done it, but it was an eye-opener for me. The idea is to drop in

at a physician's office and introduce yourself, handling the visit in the usual way (more on this below)... but also offer a special professional courtesy to the entire staff and physicians of 50% off your usual fees for any service or product, including exams, services, contact lenses, glasses or sunglasses. Encourage the staff and the doctor to stop in at their convenience to browse your optical and to schedule an appointment if they need an exam.

Here is why this courtesy discount is a good idea:

- It makes your drop-in visit easier because you have a purpose that is not self-serving. There is a big benefit for the medical staff.
- Many of the medical staff will take advantage of the generous offer.
- Once the staff experiences the quality of your eye health care and begins to enjoy the attractive new eyewear, they will become loyal to your practice.
- The receptionists and nurses talk to many people every day. They may refer patients who need eye care and they will also simply talk to people about your office as they respond to compliments about their new glasses.

Points to consider

I don't think there is a right or wrong way to call on physicians. Just do what comes naturally. But here are few additional thoughts.

- An office manager of other staff member could accompany the OD. Gives the visit more importance and may make the conversation easier.
- Ask to meet the physicians in the office if they have a brief moment, but also make a point to spend time and have interest in all the staff. The nurses and receptionists may prove more valuable than the doctor for generating referrals.
- Give a brief overview of the kinds of eye cases you would like to see – indicate that you would appreciate their referrals. Pledge that their emergency referrals will be seen the same day.
- Ask what kind of report letter the practice would like to receive from you.
- Ask if the practice is open to your referrals and ask what types cases they specialize in.
- Drop off a supply of your business cards and ask for some of theirs.
- In addition to family practice docs, call on any medical specialty that has some relationship to eye care, such as dermatologists, pediatricians, allergists, plastic surgeons, and more.
- Consider sending a follow-up gift if you hit it off well, such as a nice breakfast treat or fruit basket.

10.13 Trunk Shows: Excellent Marketing and a Profit Booster

When I talk to ODs about their experiences in hosting a trunk show, I usually get one of two responses: either they do great and produce a tremendous amount of revenue or they are a complete bust and not worth the effort. My practice held a trunk show a few weeks ago and I'm happy to report we were with the former group! I can't guarantee that all trunk shows will be successful, but in this article, I will outline what we did.

The Benefits

There is no question that planning and hosting a trunk show is a lot of work, but I found three major benefits for the practice that made it a good investment:

- Profit. We did extremely well with revenue production. We have a large practice base to draw upon, but we sold well over 100 complete pairs of glasses plus many pairs of non-Rx sunglasses in one day. Even after subtracting all the marketing expenses and discounts provided, gross profit was more than three times greater than an average day.
- Publicity. Our practice made a strong connection with many people in the area because of the trunk show. Many people came to our office and had a wonderful experience and many more did not attend but learned that our practice offers fantastic eyewear. We marketed to our patient base and to the public at large. Once you decide to hold an event, there are many great ways to talk about it! More on the marketing effort below.
- Team building. My staff had a lot of fun at the trunk show and it was definitely good for morale! I sensed a certain amount of pride that we held a big event and it was a success. We had very good attendance by the public and it was quite different from the usual routine. Many staff members went to the restaurant next door for a drink after the event.

The Promotion

There are many excellent ways to promote a trunk show, but the key is to invite a lot of people. I think most trunk shows that do not turn out very well may be due to inadequate promotion.

- I hired a graphic artist to design an eye-catching flyer for our trunk show. We used versions of this flyer in several different media; it became our eblasts, invitations, ads, Facebook posts and signs. Freelance designers are not very expensive and it gets away from that home-made look.
- Invitations are the main method used to promote a trunk show; you can send them via postal mail or email and you can send them to your patient base or to the community at large. There is no right or wrong to that as long as you send thousands. We have over 6,000 active email addresses so we used only that method and no direct mail. That provided a huge saving in printing and postage cost. We sent two email blasts to our patients at one month and at one week prior to the show.
- We advertised on local pop radio for a couple of weeks before the event, including sponsoring a "Women's Working Wednesday" event held at a local bar by the radio station. We provided designer sunglasses for a raffle at this live broadcast.
- Three full color ads ran in our local newspaper the week of the event. Newspaper is not the leading media anymore, but it was a cost-effective way to reach the general public.
- Signs were made up for the reception room and optical.
- We posted about the show many times on our practice Facebook page and we had a special pop-up ad about the event on our website.
- We had strong support from our local Chamber of Commerce. Several officers attended our event and local businesses helped us promote it. We had several cross promotional items with some hair salons, restaurants and a local chiropractor.
- We had several raffle prizes, including a large Coach purse, a Kindle, several pairs of Varilux-S lenses, a Polo shirt and more. Our lab and the frame reps donated some of these items and we bought the rest. The prizes draw people and make for a fun event.
- The main attractions of the trunk show were to see the complete line of frames from four major brands and to receive a 50% discount on frames when purchased with Rx lenses. We also offered 30% off plano sunglasses. These discounts could not be combined with other discounts or vision plans.

The Event

- We held our trunk show on a Friday from 1pm to 7pm and continued it the next day from 9am to 1pm. These hours offered something for everyone, but looking back on it, I think one day would work just as well as long as it runs until at least 6pm to catch the after work crowd. We were surprised to see traffic starting to slow down around 6pm.

- Four frame reps were at our show, which worked out fine and they all had plenty of sales, but I think two or three reps would be plenty in the future. To reduce the competitive feel, all the reps worked for the same parent company, but each had a major brand to present. We assigned one of our opticians to work with each rep and be the "right-hand man." The rep did most of the styling presentations but our staff member wrote up the sales and handled the details.
- We asked any staff who were not scheduled on the show days to work the event and offered time and a half pay.
- We had large folding tables with tablecloths for the reps to display on.
- Wine, cheese and fruit were served during the evening hours and coffee, tea, bagels and Danish the next morning.
- We had nice gift bags printed with our logo and filled them with give-away items and brochures from our practice and discount offers from our supporting local businesses.
- A very good patient of ours plays the dulcimer in a three piece band. We hired the group to play live background music and that added a nice touch.
- We performed eye exams as usual during the trunk show, but we decided to avoid our busiest days which have three doctors all working at once. We would have not had enough staff available for the walk-in shoppers.

If your practice can use the publicity and the profit, speak to your frame reps about hosting a trunk show. I recommend that you place a very competent staff member in charge of the event because there are many details to manage, but our experience was very positive!

10.14 Increasing Patient Volume

I often say the biggest problem facing optometrists today is lack of patient demand. Just think about what your practice would be like if you had tons of patients calling your office for eye care! I love to help optometrists manage the problems they face because they have too many patients! Once you have the cash flow that a higher volume of patients produce, you can hire more staff, install advanced instrumentation, move to a larger office, expand your optical and then just continue to set goals and grow! The irony is that once your practice reaches that high level, you attract even more patients because you offer such great service in an awesome facility. You have more competitive advantages and an upward business spiral occurs.

As important as patient demand is, most optometrists seem to think it is something outside of their own control. They seem to just take what comes their way. Most ODs do very little marketing. I think one reason for that is often because they simply do not have the time or make the time. Let's take a look at some simple steps you can take to market your practice and grow your patient volume.

Marketing

Marketing and advertising are actually very complex. Many promotional efforts do not work very well. Many can result in a financial loss. But marketing is extremely important to practice success and should be part of your daily activity.

Most optometrists have not been trained in marketing, but you can learn.

- Learn by trying things and keeping records of costs and revenue produced.
- Learn by talking with colleagues about what has worked for them.
- Learn by attending courses and reading books.
- Learn by hiring a consultant or a local advertising firm to help develop your marketing plan and guide you.

How to design your marketing plan

- For most optometrists: start by appointing someone from your staff as your marketing coordinator. If you are already short-staffed, hire a new employee with a plan for someone to work with you on marketing. There are many details with marketing projects and you will not have time to do it all yourself. Your marketing specialist should be enthusiastic about the goals of bringing in more patients and increasing practice revenue. The marketing duties may total 10 to 20 hours per week in an average practice. This is an investment that should produce a good return. Work closely with your marketing director.
- Make a list on paper of projects you do now and list new ideas that you could take on.
- Prioritize your ideas and develop a timeline. Put your projects on a calendar for the next 12 months.
- Decide on an annual marketing budget and indicate the amount you will spend on each project on your list. The typical optometric

practice spends about 3% of gross revenue on marketing, but you may decide to invest more than that.

What works

A truly effective marketing plan involves a comprehensive review of the practice and many aspects of your practice. It is far more than just the direct promotional ideas. It includes fee schedules, product mix, office hours, practice image, customer service issues and much more. Marketing is defined as identifying and satisfying patients' wants and needs.

To get you started, here are a few projects that usually work well to increase patient demand:

- Use your computer software system to search for patients who have not responded to recall notices and are past due for eye care. Have a very friendly staff member call these patients and ask how they are doing.
- If you are new to practice and don't have that patient history, drop in on various primary care MDs and other health professionals to introduce yourself. Discuss referral possibilities both ways. Invite the physicians and staff members to obtain eyewear at your office at a 50% discount. You want them to wear glasses from your practice.
- Community outreach can be an effective way to improve your reputation. Participate in community events through the chamber of commerce, the parks and recreation department, local civic organizations, sponsorship of school events and sports team, and other local activities. Have a booth for your practice, give away free stuff, do vision screenings and talk to people. Get your staff involved in these events.
- Host events in your practice, such as in-office seminars, screenings, open houses, and trunk shows. Once you plan events, you can promote those events on your practice Facebook page, website, to your patients via email and to the community at large via newspaper or local radio.
- Cross market with other local businesses. Help promote them and they will help promote you.

10.15 Summer Is Sunglass Season

Most optometrists I know are very sensitive about selling anything at chairside. Understandably so, we have our patients' best interest at heart and our job is not to sell them optical products. Our job is to diagnose and treat conditions in order to improve vision and ocular health. We are ethical and professional and that approach actually serves us very well from a business standpoint because it garners trust from the patient. And that turns out to be a very important factor as the patient goes on to buy optical products.

Even though I understand that very well, I think most ODs go too far with the professionalism and they develop an aversion to proactively talking about optical products. There is a balance between overtly selling and not educating patients at all.

Excuses for not talking about sunglasses

Sunglasses are a perfect example of an optical product that optometrists don't talk about enough to patients. It might be due to the professional paranoia mentioned above. Or, if we are busy and running behind schedule, we may not bring up any new topics that are not in the patient history. And we may feel that a discussion about sunglasses is the optician's responsibility. In this article, I'll provide you with a very simple way to talk about sunglasses to all your patients that will be very professional and only take a few seconds. I hope your optician does talk about sunglasses, but we also know that if the doctor recommends a product, it carries an extreme amount of importance and makes the optician's job much easier.

Push yourself to say this to every patient

Here is one way to bring up the topic of sunglasses to your patients. Memorize this and say it at the end of each patient visit: "With summer upon us, your eyes need protection from UV light just like the rest of your body. UV exposure from the sun can increase the progression of cataracts, macular degeneration and other eye problems. Do you have a good pair of sunglasses?" If the patient has a full time spectacle Rx, refer to them as "prescription sunglasses". If the patient wears contact lenses or does not have an Rx, you are obviously talking about plano sunwear.

Patients understand all about ultra-violet protection, but they often do not associate it with their eyes. They apply sun lotion on their skin; women wear makeup with UV protection, they wear hats to keep UV off their face and they buy clothing that has extra UV protection built-in. Remind patients that their eyes need protection, too.

Notice that I ended the sunglass comment with a question. Listen to the patient's answer and go from there. You might conclude that the patient's sunglasses are fine. You might simply recommend that the patient speak further about this with the optician. You may find that the patient does not understand much about UV light, polarized lenses, Transition lenses or cheap gas station type sunglasses and you can offer some advice. If your office carries some of the leading sunglass brands in your optical, you might even mention those by name (I know I'm really pushing it now).

The power of bringing it up

If you simply ask each patient about his or her sunglasses, your office will greatly increase the number of sunglasses you sell. You could easily double the number of sales of Rx and non-Rx sunwear. You will increase your practice profitability and you will help to protect patients against damaging UV exposure without ever having to sell anything!

We all know that sunglasses are important in all four seasons, but summer makes it very easy to bring up the topic. Once you're comfortable with it, I can hear you saying: "Even in winter, your eyes need protection from UV..."

10.16 Two Quick Ways to Fill your Appointment Schedule with Zero Cost

Seeing more patients is the most effective way for most practices to increase profitability, but that is often easier said than done. Many strategies that increase patient demand take a long time to reap the benefits. In this article, I'll describe two methods that will keep your schedule busy and productive right away.

Vision plan family members

I'll admit that many of you have heard of this tactic before, but I think the odds are good that it is no longer being done on a regular basis by your staff. Even if you've heard of it before, it is so good that it is worth revisiting.

Here is the concept: Patients with vision plans call your office every day to schedule an appointment for themselves. As your staff member speaks to the patient, he or she brings up the patient's name in the authorization section of the vision plan website. This is helpful because the staff person can see the patient authorization while still on the phone. Most vision plan authorization systems show all family members on the opening page along with their dates of eligibility for eye exams and materials.

Your front desk staffer looks to see who else is eligible and says something like this: "OK, Mrs. Smith, I have your appointment set up with Dr. Gailmard on Monday, August 15 at 2pm. By the way, I see your husband Bob is also eligible for an eye exam and so is your daughter, Brittany. Would you like me to schedule their appointments now as well? These visits will be covered by your insurance."

As good as this method is, I must note that I have had an ongoing battle with my staff to keep doing it. I have implemented the procedure only to ask them six months later how it's going and I discover we are no longer doing it. Many ODs have shared the same experience with me. When I ask why, my staff replies that they don't always have time. Clearly, we have our priorities wrong, because I think there is nothing more important than scheduling additional appointments. I have had some success if I place a notebook at the front desk and ask the staff to keep a daily log of the names of people who are offered a vision plan family member appointment and how many say yes.

Walk-ins in optical

The second quick method of adding patients to the schedule involves the people who walk into your optical every day for an eyeglass repair, adjustment or warranty replacement. The number of people who do this may surprise you. In many offices, the staff just provides the service and does not even bother to pull the patient's record because we think it may provide some good will and the vast majority are patients who bought their glasses from the practice.

Here is a better way: begin asking for the patient's name every time someone wants optical service. An easy way to do this is to have pads of paper (4 X 5.5 inch) that are preprinted with blanks to write on. When patients approach the desk, the staff asks them to write their name on the form and indicate the type of service needed. The receptionist asks the patient to be seated and pages an optician. In the meantime, she looks up the patient record and writes the date of the last exam on the paper form along with the recall date and any other information such as vision plans or diagnosis. The form is given to the optician, who takes care of the optical needs as usual. Before the patient leaves, the optician says something like this: "Mr. Jones, I see that your last eye exam was in June of 2014. The doctor wanted to see you back in one year to check your eye pressure. We really should set up an appointment for that now; is that OK with you?" Further discussion about insurance coverage can follow.

We all have many patients who are non-compliant with recommended recall dates, but when we have them in the office, in-person, we have a great opportunity to ask them about it. The success rate of scheduling these folks is very high when the staff is already working with them.

A side benefit of this technique is that you can collect data about walk-in services and you may want to only provide service on glasses that were purchased from your office. The optical form can be scanned into the EHR system and provides a record of the visit.

10.17 Three Long Term Ways to Fill Your Schedule

My last Tip article focused on two quick tactics to add patients to your schedule, so this article will look at the bigger strategic picture of keeping your practice busy. I often say that the biggest problem facing optometrists today is lack of patient demand. If you had enough patients wanting your services, you could overcome almost any challenge. It is interesting to note that some optometric practices are extremely busy, maybe even too busy, while others are very slow and struggle to make a profit. If we analyze the busy practices, we can learn some valuable lessons about what made them that way.

Location, population, and competition are factors that can have a big impact on patient volume, but those should be considered before opening a practice. Once the practice is up and running, these aspects are difficult to control, so I will not cover them in this article. For our purposes, there are three main factors that bring patients to your office. Read on and ask yourself how well your practice performs in each area.

Word-of-mouth referral
This has historically been the biggest and most important factor in practice growth: one satisfied patient telling his family, friends and co-workers. It occurs slowly at first, but grows exponentially and can become extremely powerful. Even in this age of marketing through social media and websites, word-of-mouth is still at the core of how it works. Even as we give credit to medical insurance and vision plans for bringing patients to us, word-of-mouth is underlying it because that leads to which provider patients choose.

All practices receive some benefit from word-of-mouth referral, but certain ones generate far more than others. The practices that get the most leverage from word-of-mouth referral are truly great in all aspects of customer service. They excel with intangibles like these:

- Easy to do business with

- Fast and convenient
- Friendly
- The wow factor
- The patient experience
- The physical facility and decor
- High quality services and products

Vision Plans

Vision plans are so prevalent in the U.S. that they belong in a category all by themselves. Many ODs feel they are better off without vision plans, and that could be the case in some instances, but I also see many doctors make bad decisions about vision plans because they make them on emotion and not fact. I have analyzed the profitability of all the major vision plans and there are some widespread misconceptions about them. I have found that all vision plans generate some profit and it is often greater than the practice owner thinks. More importantly, vision plans bring large numbers of patients to your office and many of them need medical eye care or other non-covered services. Doctors who are not providers for a major vision plan see very few patients who are members of that plan.

A very important factor to consider in deciding if you should become a provider is how full is your appointment schedule? How many exams do you see per day on average? If you have appointment slots that are not filled or if you set up your schedule with relatively few slots per day, then even a low profit patient is better than no profit.

Marketing

Aside from the two factors listed above, everything else can be put under the umbrella of marketing. Marketing offers huge potential to bring in more patient volume, yet most ODs take very little action in this area.

Marketing can be expensive and you should establish a reasonable budget (2% of collected gross revenue is a good start), but many projects are little or no cost. They do require time and commitment, however. They require someone to handle the details and logistics. Someone must do the planning. An ideal situation is when a doctor/owner works with and delegates the marketing details to a staff member who has some creative talent.

To get started in marketing, consider two broad areas that have worked well:

- Community outreach. This is a big category that involves the doctor or some staff members donating time to community events. This could be vision screenings, career day at schools, providing an eye care booth at fund raising events, participating in chamber of commerce projects, civic organizations, charities, sponsoring youth clubs and sport teams, or parks and recreation events.

- Host and promote events in your office. Frame fashion trunk shows can be big, but you could also host seminars on eye care topics or have sales and celebrations in your optical. Once you have planned the event, promote it on social media, with in-office signage and email blasts.

Do you feel like you don't have enough staff to make these projects happen? Hire another full time employee and rearrange the job duties. You have to make growth happen.

10.18 Your Marketing Team

Marketing is vastly underutilized in most independent optometric practices, which is ironic because most of them desperately need more patients. In this article, I'll look at why most ODs do not do any serious marketing and how you can easily overcome that tendency. Next week, I'll review some of my favorite marketing projects that will put more patients in your exam chair.

Reasons why ODs don't use marketing

I think there are two main reasons why optometrists don't often use marketing techniques to grow their practices:

- It takes too much time. It is true that marketing projects can take a large amount of time in the planning stages and time is something most ODs and don't have enough of. Even if you have a dedicated administrative day, there are so many other tasks that need the OD / owner's attention, there is no time for new projects. This is a cycle that you must change. The best solution I have found when I'm facing a time management problem is to delegate more of the tasks to others. As the practice owner, you must break away from the mindset of doing everything yourself. More on this below.
- Uncertain results. As I look back on all the marketing projects I have tried in my practice, I must admit that some seemed to work, but many did not. I define a successful marketing effort as one that generates a profit after the marketing expenses and any promotional discounts are applied. Of course, there is value in improving your brand perception in the community, and that is not

measured in profit dollars. It can be difficult to accurately measure the financial result of a specific marketing project because some of the good will created will result in a sale well into the future. I would not let the uncertainty of direct profitability stop you from trying various marketing projects. Just get in there and take your best shot and measure the results the best you can. Learn from these results and keep repeating the ones that work best.

Your marketing team

I recommend that you begin to think of marketing in your practice as a team effort. Here are the players you should have:

- The doctor. I recommend that the doctor / owner delegate a great deal of marketing, but I still think he or she needs to be involved in the decision making. The doctor, as CEO of the business, has valuable knowledge of the needs of the patient base. The doctor knows the philosophy and ideal image of the practice. There are budgetary decisions to be made and those will include unexpected options and changes along the way. I see the doctor's role as meeting with the marketing director to give direction and to approve concepts. This role does not need to be very time consuming.
- An employee as marketing director. I recommend that the practice appoint or hire an employee to serve as part time marketing director. This job assignment may take 5 or 10 hours per week (it will vary) and it can be handled as a side job for an optician or front desk associate. The role involves taking care of all the logistics and pricing of various marketing projects and working with local organizations to implement them. It is best if this person has a creative flair and I also look for someone who wants the job. It is also important that this person have some experience with technology and social media, since much of marketing today is in that area. If you want to give the marketing job to an existing employee, but you feel he or she will not be able to give it the time needed, then hire a new employee to cover this person's previous job. Think big and trust that the marketing campaigns will bring in enough new profit to more than cover expenses like this. It is possible that the marketing director could work from home, but I prefer him or her to be in the office to allow closer collaboration and better monitoring of the work.
- An advertising agency or marketing consultant. To give your practice the professional image it deserves, you should work with a real marketing professional. This could be a local agency or some optometric alliance groups and consulting companies provide a

marketing expert for its members. A graphic artist is another professional you should have a connection with. These specialists will present you with new ideas and valuable guidance as you plan and implement your program. You should control the budget for this service. Ad agencies can be expensive so I would start small and build as you see results. Understand any contracts you are presented with: always ask how it can be ended.

- Electronic communications firms. This may include companies like Solutionreach, Websystem3, Demandforce, 4PatientCare and others. It would also include a website design company and possibly other internet services.

Start by holding an initial planning meeting with these stakeholders. Review your past marketing efforts and plan for the future. You may want to create a marketing calendar for the next 12 months so projects can be spread out properly and to avoid the pressure of having to rush the details. This also helps your determine an annual budget. After that, meet with your marketing director as needed to provide the decisions and support needed to implement the plan.

I'll present some marketing ideas in the next issue.

10.19 What to Do If Your Practice is Not Busy Enough?

The biggest problem facing optometrists today is that they are not busy enough. There are certainly exceptions to that statement and those doctors who have more patients than they can handle may not always agree with this, but from my point of view they are blessed. Sadly, many optometrists who are not that busy have come to accept the meager patient demand and rationalize that it is enough.

Of course, there are only so many patients to go around and not every optometrist can be super-busy. But there are always some optometrists in every market who have achieved excellent practice growth and very high production. Why not you? We can hope the Affordable Care Act will be our savior and bring us lots more patients, but I have plenty of concern that the fee levels of these insurance plans will be at the Medicaid level.

Review your current production and growth rate

Let's start this growth project by looking hard at your practice production numbers and deciding if your current strategies are working. The average full time optometrist in the U.S. produces collected gross revenue of about $650,000. If that is average, you want to set your production goal higher than that; I think at least $800,000 per full time equivalent (FTE) OD is a good goal and many practices well exceed that. If you are already at that level, congratulations and your next decision may be to add another optometrist and try to double that gross revenue.

If you are not at the $800,000 level, that could still be fine if you are showing strong growth from year to year. In the early years of a practice, growth rate can be very strong, often 30 to 50%, but as revenue increases, the growth rate typically slows. If your annual practice revenue is below $800,000 and you are not seeing at least 10% growth each year, read on for my four point plan for increasing your patient demand and ultimately, your profitability.

Review your market strategy

Many optometrists have never really thought about their market strategy very much, but it is a good idea to consider it in relation to the community you practice in, the demographics, median household income, local eye care competition, office environment, practice image and other factors. If your current strategy has not worked as well as you would like, begin to work on changing it. If you started with a boutique optical image and it has not done well, you could convert to a medical eye care model. If you tried to be upscale but the community has not responded, you may need to appear more approachable and affordable. If you have a practice name that is aimed at pediatrics, you may need to become known for caring for all age groups.

An adjustment in your market strategy can be easier than you think. Consider modifying your practice name while retaining some elements of the old brand. Freshen up your logo, invest in new signage, and focus on the new image in your marketing efforts.

Be certain customer service and convenience are excellent

A practice that does not have enough patient demand could have a problem with customer service and patient satisfaction. The patient experience in your office is a huge factor that relates to word-of-mouth referrals and repeat business. Evaluate your staff and the culture of your office. Culture starts with the leaders of the organization, so re-examine how you feel about working with the public and the message you send to staff behind the scenes when you talk about patients and the business challenges you face.

Review your office policies and try to change them to be more patient friendly. Set your policies as much as possible to satisfy the patients' wants and needs; not yours or your staff's. Part of customer service is convenience:

do you have some evening and Saturday hours? Are you open during the lunch hour? Are you almost always on time for appointments?

Work on marketing

If you need more patient demand, I would review your marketing plan. This should include your practice website, use of social media, email communication, recall methods, reactivation phone calls, special events (like trunk shows and patient seminars), professional referrals, and community outreach.

Consider accepting more vision plans

While not very popular in many circles, if you have worked on all the factors above and still have moderate to low patient demand, it may be time to rethink your strategy with vision plans. Many optometrists have felt it was best to not become a provider for certain plans, but in some cases (ironically) that decision is hurting them.

- Is your decision to not participate based on what is good for our profession or what is good for your practice? Vision plans have such a huge network of willing providers, it is very unlikely that abstaining will hurt them in any way. Work with the AOA and other organizations to fight for a level playing field.
- There are many misconceptions about vision plans. Most optometrists react emotionally and don't really know the facts.
- No matter how good your practice is, if you are not a network provider for their insurance, most people will not choose you for their eye care, unless you have a very low-priced business model.
- When people call your office, what vision plan do they ask about that you do not accept? Ask your staff.
- Accepting vision plans can give you access to a large number of patients, many of whom will need medical eye care and will have their services billed to medical insurance plans.
- It is definitely possible to make a profit with all vision plans and with the right strategies, that profit can be increased. I accept most plans in my practice and I've analyzed the profitability of each one.
- I don't advocate all vision plans for all practices, but most practices need more patients.

Chapter 11. Recall and Reactivation

11.1 A Recall Review

A colleague recently asked me about the patient recall system I use in my practice and he mentioned that he did not remember seeing a tip article on the subject. He's correct that I don't write much about recall methods, even though it is a very important procedure in practice management. To me, the type of recall system utilized is an individual practice decision and I'm not out to change your mind on which method is best. Recall procedures should fit the personality of the practice. Having said that, I'll review the options available and discuss the nuances of each system. No matter what recall method you use, it's very important to do it well.

Recall starts in the office

Successful recall begins with the patient in the exam chair, regardless of the method used. It's too late to begin a recall effort one year later when the patient is due for reexamination. One of the most important ingredients for improving success is for the doctor to tell the patient the reason the next exam is needed. That will vary on a case by case basis, of course, but it should be part of the case summary and recommendations for every patient.

Staff members play an important role in recall management, but the doctor is the one who decides when and why the patient should be seen again and the message has maximum punch when the doctor discusses it. There is often more than one reason for the next exam, but it's effective to single out the main factor for the patient. Ocular health concerns are far more effective than refractive issues if you have multiple diagnoses. The doctor may say, "Jim, I want to see you for another exam in one year so I can monitor your risk factors for glaucoma. My office will send a reminder card when you are due for your next appointment." Following the statement, look for agreement from the patient.

It's very helpful for technicians to reinforce the recall message by mentioning that key tests should be performed yearly or more frequently, as the case indicates. Receptionists should review the recall date and how the patient will be notified or reminded.

For patients who have completely normal visual systems, you should decide on your philosophy for regular eye exams and share that with the patient. Some doctors feel the intervals should vary by age group, but I generally recommend a yearly eye exam.

Preappointing

Setting up the next appointment before the patient leaves the office is a popular recall system and doctors who use it are often strong proponents. Here are a few thoughts:

- Preappointing is generally regarded as having the highest recall success rate.
- There is an art to presenting the concept to the patient, especially if the case does not have a serious medical diagnosis. Some patients will embrace the idea of setting up an appointment a year from now, but many will feel like it's pushy. Patients often don't reveal their true feelings at the time; they may go along with the office routine just to be congenial. If preappointing is perceived as a way for the office to generate business more than serve the patient's need for eye care, the image of the practice will suffer.
- Is it a real appointment or not? Many offices obtain good acceptance of preappointing by making it seem less specific. "We'll reserve some time for you in our schedule for next year and we'll confirm the date and time when it gets closer" is a typical statement used by receptionists. Patients may not think they actually have a firm appointment.
- The appointment schedule should have some way to indicate which appointments were preappointed a long time ago and which ones were actively made by a patient who called on the phone
- Preappoints must be confirmed and reconfirmed. Some practices send a written notice of the appointment date and time and ask the patient to call to reschedule if needed. Patients who don't respond are called by the office staff to confirm. These calls must be made far enough in advance to allow vacated appointment slots to have a good chance of being filled by others. A final confirmation call may be done the day before the appointment.
- Even with all the confirmation effort, preappointing usually results in a higher no show rate than a conventional appointment system where people call to schedule themselves. Some patients are not really ready to spend the money for an exam or optical materials but they go along with the process until the very last minute, when any little thing comes up and prevents them from keeping the appointment.
- Preappointing may result in more appointments, but many of them result in no Rx change in glasses or contact lenses because a larger percentage of patients with no complaints are seen. The average gross revenue per patient is often lower with preappointing.

- Preappointing may be used for all visits that are needed within less than one year (three month or six month checks), but a different system is used for yearly recalls.
- A good technique is to offer either preappointing or conventional mail reminders and let the patient choose.

Postcards

The simple post card is still widely used and has some advantages. There are many suppliers of cards for eye care with lots of choices for message themes, ranging from eye health to funny cartoons.

- Processing is easy since there are no envelopes to stuff or seal and no letters to print. The office management software program can print sheets of address labels for patients whose recall date is due. Staff members apply the labels to the recall cards.
- Postage cost is less with postcards than envelopes.
- High monthly card volume can be handled easily with a postage meter and automatic feeder.
- If the patient does not respond to the initial recall notice by scheduling the appointment, a second card may be sent in the following month. This second post card increases recall success significantly.
- The card is a handy tangible reminder that patients often keep (or place on the refrigerator) until the appointment is made.

Letters

Software systems allow sophisticated personalization of recall notices, which can be effective. By placing each patient in a recall category at the time of checkout, a specific recall letter may be printed that targets the reason for the next appointment. You may print different letters for patients with eye disease, children, contact lens wearers and even people with vision plans.

Some practitioners use a letter first and follow-up with a post card reminder one month later if there is no response.

Phone calls

Telephoning the patient to remind him that he is due for the next eye exam could be the main method for recall, but it's more often used in conjunction with another method. If your staff calls patients out of the blue to ask them if they want to schedule an appointment, it may be regarded as a solicitation and could be too aggressive. Much depends on the demeanor of the staff member who makes the phone call.

Friendly follow-up phone calls in conjunction with preappointing or mail recall can be a very effective method of increasing recall success. Staff members should be well-trained to not appear aggressive and to always be understanding and caring of the patient's preferences. The purpose of the call may be to determine if the recall notice was received and if the patient was intending to schedule an appointment at this time. The staffer should be well-prepared with the reason the visit is needed for this patient and may offer some basic patient education about eye health. If the patient declines making the appointment, the staff person can determine if the patient wishes to receive future reminders. If there is some dissatisfaction with eye care services, the staffer is in a great position to find out about the problem and correct it.

Email
Sending appointment reminders via email is a growing trend in eye care which brings benefits and challenges. Saving the postage cost of snail mail is a plus, but doctors who use the technique find that email is more reliable for some people than others. Anti-spam filters, changing addresses and family members who open messages but don't save them can cause issues.

When does recall end?
I've seen many practices that make a recall effort one time and if the patient does not respond, no further communication is attempted. I think that's missing a big opportunity. Many people don't see their eye doctor as frequently as they should, but will return for care if they are reminded again and again. I recommend that your practice management software settings automatically reactivate the recall date each year for five years if no appointment is scheduled.

11.2 Preappointing

Many readers were surprised to see preappointing listed in my top ten misconceptions article. After all, as I heard from many of you, it’s working great in lots of practices. And I don’t doubt that. I firmly believe there is more than one way to build a successful practice. I would not recommend dropping a preappoint system that works well. I really don’t feel all that passionately about the type of recall system used in a practice, as long as some system is in place.

Preappointing is not necessarily a bad thing at all, but it also should not be considered as the “key to building a busy practice” as I worded it in the article. My own practice and many others that I’ve seen are examples of very busy, high gross practices that use a mail recall system. That is why preappointing made my list of misconceptions.

Weigh the good with the bad

There are pros and cons with all recall systems. Preappointing enjoys a higher rate of return than other methods, but here are the negatives many proponents don't notice.

- Lower revenue per exam. When your schedule has a higher concentration of patients with no complaints, your average gross per patient drops. I like some self-selection of patients so the people in the exam chair actually want to be there or need to be there. I like to see an average gross per exam of $450 to $500.
- No shows. Even with multiple confirmations, preappointing leads to greater no shows and last minute cancellations. Some people will go along with the program each step of the way, but if they really don't want to come in (often a money issue), something will come up at the last minute that conveniently makes them miss the visit.
- Awkwardness at checkout. Setting an appointment for three to six months for needed eye health care is readily accepted by patients. We do this in my practice all the time for glaucoma patients and other follow-up visits. This is also why preappointing works so well in dentistry. But when your office tries to set an appointment for a routine eye exam one year in the future, the perception changes. Even with good education, patients want to think of routine eye care as something under their control. They generally agree that regular exams are important, but they want to decide exactly when to come in. Part of the reason is financial, although no one wants to bring that up. Most people need to plan for any purchase that runs hundreds of dollars.
- Is it an appointment or not? The more specific your staff is with the future appointment (March 30 at 2pm), the more resistance they will feel from patients. The trend is to keep it very general (we'll just reserve some space for you next year); but that technique leads to some surprised patients next year when they learn they have an actual appointment they never agreed to. The very fact that most offices use the general approach is evidence that their patients don't accept preappointing all that well.
- We need to save some space for you in our busy schedule. This is the clever line that many offices like to use as justification for why they need to set the appointment one year in advance. Otherwise they would just send a postcard and leave it up to the patient to call. The problem is that it lacks credibility. Patients know from other sources

and from experience that they could call up almost any eye care office and get an appointment within a few days. It reminds me of those often-used ads by health professionals with the line that reads "Now accepting new patients". I think almost everyone knows that very few practices don't accept new patients and it seems kind of silly.

- It smells like a business strategy. Patients really are smarter than we think and they can easily spot an effort to make them return for profit reasons. We can see it in other businesses and they can see it in ours. Be careful of overly aggressive pressure to return in the name of "patient education". That can alter the image of the practice as money-hungry rather than one with a primary concern for eye health and good vision.
- Resentment and patient loss. Realize that all practices have patients who quietly leave them for other eye care providers. It's hard to track this group, but the effect is extremely important to practice revenue. Some practices have a high dropout rate and some have a small one. Of course, when preappointing is done well, it does not actually annoy anyone, but many systems go awry over time. Many staff members simply can't implement a system with subtle nuances flawlessly. A simple, honest procedure designed to remind people when they are due for their next exam really can't be messed up.
- Staff hours. A well-managed preappoint system requires a lot of staff hours. There are multiple phone calls and mailings needed to confirm, reschedule and chase down the people who are hard to reach.

A mail/phone recall procedure

My preferred recall method is a letter or post card mailed one month prior to the recall date, with a follow up post card one month later to those who do not schedule. This approach is easily processed with every major office management software program on the market.

To improve the recall success rate, a follow-up phone call to patients who do not respond to either mailing can be added if the practice has a very friendly and caring staff member. The phone call must be very non-confrontational and not pushy. It is made to check that everything was OK with the previous service and to ask when the patient would like to be recalled in the future. Many of these will simply schedule on the spot.

The recall system should be set up to occur each year for at least five years, unless the patient instructs your office to stop.

The key to a busy practice

So what is the key to a busy practice if it's not preappointing? It's customer service. It's creating an environment where the patient knows their needs come first and where eye care is different and exciting. A successful business is one where customers want to return.

11.3 How Far Ahead Are You Booked If You Preappoint?

I recently received an email from an optometrist who asked an excellent question. It is one that I deal with fairly often, so I thought I would cover it here. The doctor started by correctly acknowledging that some important decisions, such as when to bring in an associate or whether it is smart to drop a vision plan, depend on how far out the practice is booked with appointments. Her question was how to apply that logic for a practice that preappoints, since her practice is always booked fairly solid for months in advance.

Using patient demand

First, I want to congratulate this doctor on building what is obviously a very successful practice. Preappointing can be a very effective technique in practice building, but there must be many more good things going on to achieve that kind of patient demand. I agree that some measure of patient demand is helpful in making strategic management decisions. Hiring an associate doctor, deciding if you should join a vision plan (or drop one) and raising fees are three key areas that depend greatly on how much patient demand there is. If you hire an OD and he or she simply sees patients that the senior doctor would have seen, the senior doctor will see a drop in personal income. We need the new doctor to see additional patients and it is best if a good supply is already waiting. Another example: if you do not have strong patient demand, it is smart to accept even the lowest vision plans because some profit is better than nothing.

Read on for more on how to analyze patient demand.

Recall methods

It is interesting to note that recall methods are fairly evenly divided between the preappoint enthusiasts and the more traditional recall message. Both of these methods now rely heavily on email, rather than postal mail, but postal mail is still very reliable and still has a place as a back up to electronic and telephone.

We may want to use different recall methods for routine vision exams and medical eye care. It is extremely common to preappoint when the next exam is in six months or less and when there is a medical need. Some practices ask the patient what method of recall they would like to use, and offer preappointing, email reminder, telephone or post card via regular mail. I like that customer service aspect.

Preappointing is more effective than the reminder notice methods when the system is handled extremely well by the staff, but it is fairly easy to not handle all the communication aspects and the confirmations perfectly and then it does not work so well.

Overall, preappointing is highly regarded by most ODs, but consider these drawbacks:

- Preappointing can lead to a higher no show rate.
- There is more last minute rescheduling, which can lead to some appointment slots not being filled at all.
- Preappointing can lead to lower revenue per patient because more exams are seen that result in no Rx change or no treatment.
- It can be tough to know how far ahead you are truly booked, for management purposes.
- When you bring on a new associate doctor, it can be more difficult to transfer patients to the new doctor because they already have an appointment with the senior doctor.

How to measure patient demand

If you are not preappointing, you can just scan the appointment schedule for the next couple weeks and see how many appointments are out there.

If you are preappointing and you seem to be booked solid, consider coding your appointments in some way to show which ones were scheduled a year ago as a preappoint and which ones were recently scheduled. Obviously, all new patients are not preappoints, but some established patients could have fallen out of the system and recently called to schedule an appointment. You can measure your no show and reschedule rate and apply that to the two groups – knowing the preappoint group is slightly less reliable than the active call-in group.

In addition to that, here are some more ways to gauge your patient demand.

- I would look retroactively at the recent past to judge how busy you are. Start with how many patients were actually seen per day on average. In this day and age, I think each OD should see between 20 to 25 patients per eight hour day. If you are not seeing this number, is it because you don't want to or because you don't have enough to see?
- In my analysis, the 20 to 25 number is a mixture of all kinds of exams – the majority is typically comprehensive, but it includes follow-ups and office visits also.
- If you are seeing that number on a consistent basis, I'd say you have excellent patient demand and you could easily hire an associate OD or drop a low paying vision plan or raise your fees.
- You can also use some measure of revenue production as a guide to how much demand you have. This varies based on your mode of practice and other factors, but it is quite realistic for one full time OD in private practice to produce $1 million in collected gross revenue. Many optometrists produce much more than that, but you can set your own goal.
- Get familiar with the concept of full time equivalent (FTE) and know what your OD FTE is. If you have one optometrist in your practice and she sees patients 3.5 days per week or about 28 hours, you have about a .7 FTE. If we use the $1 million benchmark, this doctor should produce about $700,000. Use 40 hours per week as the full time standard.

11.4 Is Preappointing All It's Cracked Up to Be?

Preappointing is extremely popular among optometrists in private practice. Data is a bit fuzzy because ODs often use more than one recall method, but the Management and Business Academy estimates that 44% of practices use preappointing. This method of giving the patient their next appointment at the conclusion of each exam visit is generally regarded as the most effective method of recall; meaning the recall success rate is higher than with post cards, email or telephone reminders. But even if that is true, we should acknowledge that preappointing does have its weaknesses.

In my consulting experience, doctors who use preappointing often have fairly strong opinions about how good it is. This is an aspect of practice management that I'm fairly neutral about. There are some good and bad aspects to every recall system and I think the practice owner should choose the method that best suits his or her philosophy. I'm not out to change anyone's mind on their recall method of choice, but I do think we should be very objective and aware of any shortcomings. By being objective, you may be able to initiate procedures and staff training that improve the results.

I'll acknowledge that preappointing has some strong practice benefits, but this article will only focus on some potential pitfalls that you may not have realized.

Preappointing as a recall method is great if it is designed and managed well, but it usually isn't. Success with preappointing requires a very vigilant staff that always follows all the procedures. If steps are forgotten or if shortcuts are taken, problems occur like those covered below.

- The real measure of success for any recall system is how busy the practice is; the number of patients that are actually seen. Of course, the recall system is only one of many factors at work on that point, but if preappointing is truly great, those practices should be quite busy. My concern is that the practice may look busy when the doctor looks ahead at the appointment schedule, but it may fall apart to some extent as any given day grows closer.
- To measure your success, don't look ahead at how booked you are. Instead, look back at how many patients per day you actually saw in the last six months or year. This will account for one potential problem with preappointing: a large no show and last minute reschedule rate. Generate a report for how many exams you performed in 2015 and convert that into exams per week by dividing by 52 weeks (or used 50 weeks if you took two weeks for vacation). Divide that weekly number by the number of days per week that you see patients (it is OK to have a half day). That provides a rough estimate of how many patients per day you truly see. It is often shockingly low, but you should know it.
- The reschedule rate and no show rate can really play havoc on your office efficiency because it is difficult to be staffed properly when you are not sure how many patients will be seen. It is feast or famine.
- It is interesting that reschedules and no shows are often a love-hate thing with ODs; we know they hurt revenue and profit, but on any given day when you are busy or tired, you may secretly welcome them. This may prevent you from actually wanting to recognize that they are a big problem for your business.
- When preappointing is done properly, it takes a huge amount of staff time to confirm, reconfirm, monitor responses, manage and reschedule appointments. Usually there is a combination of postal,

email and telephone communications about the appointment that begins several weeks in advance.

- Conversely, with a traditional reminder system, the patient must decide if he wants an appointment and then proactively schedule it, usually within the next few days or a week. The likelihood of a no show is minimal in this case as is the amount of staff time needed.
- Practices that use preappointing may have a lower revenue per exam metric. This occurs because preappointing results in more patients being seen with no visual complaints and often seen sooner than when the patient must call for an appointment. Seeing patients with no complaints results in more "exam-only" visits, while visits with complaints often lead to acceptance of new eyewear, contact lens fittings or additional testing.
- We intuitively know that there is the possible risk of being perceived as pushy when the office staff tells patients they are scheduling them for their appointment next year. There are some clever ways to spin that, but eventually the patient realizes he has a real appointment and some will feel they wanted more control over that.
- Many patients will simply go along with the office procedure, but if they really do not want that next eye exam in that time frame, they will cancel or no show. You could charge a no show fee, but that also creates more bad will.
- Another negative for preappointing is less known, but occurs when the practice brings in an associate OD and wants to transfer some of the loyal patients from the senior doctor to the associate. This can be challenging in general, but it is made worse when all the patients have standing appointments with the senior doc. If patients have to call to set up an appointment, the receptionist has an opportunity to offer more convenient appointment times with the new doctor and encourage patients to try him or her.
- Optometrists often look to dentists with some level of admiration and we may try to mimic their practice management techniques. It appears that dentists are quite successful with preappointing, but we should realize that teeth require regular professional cleaning and that motivates the patient into more frequent visits than routine vision care.
- By that logic, we may see a high degree of success if we preappoint patients who need medical eye care, especially because these patients are usually seen back in less than one year.
- It may well be that having multiple recall tools available is the best approach. An ideal recall system for a practice that is strongly service oriented might be to ask the patient how he would like to be

notified about his next visit. You could preappoint some, send email reminders to others, and post cards to the rest. I wonder which method most patients would choose.

11.5 Get More from Your Recall System

I'm constantly looking for ways to increase patient demand for my practice and for my clients. Everything flows from the appointment schedule. If it's booked solid and booked ahead several days, you will obviously increase gross and net revenue, but strong patient demand can also lead to other strategies you could implement:

- Have the confidence to raise fees and product pricing.
- Explore ways to see more patients per day without sacrificing quality.
- Delegate more to staff, which may require an increase in staff.
- Acquire new instrumentation to assist staff with data collection.
- Move to a larger office to handle the increased patient flow.
- Ultimately, hire an associate OD to see a larger segment of patients allowing the owner to spend more time as CEO.

Here is my list of the major factors that influence patient demand:

- Word-of-mouth referral heavily influenced by customer service
- Insurance provider lists
- Marketing projects of all kinds
- Recalling established patients for ongoing care

All of these are important and worthy of our attention, but I will focus on the last point for this article.

Recall is the core of patient demand
Established patients make up about 70% of the exams performed in an established practice. If we can find a way to increase the effectiveness of the recall system so more patients return in a timely manner, we can greatly increase the number of people in the appointment schedule.

The most popular methods for notifying patients that they are due for their eye exam are postcard reminders and preappointing. Email and texting are increasingly being used as an alternative recall method and for confirming existing appointments. These are all excellent techniques that should be a major part of your recall system, but a strong weapon that is rarely used is the human voice. The personal touch of a phone call, when done properly, can greatly increase recall success.

The telephone recall system

In my view, telephone recall occurs as a follow-up to the other methods. A telephone recall list is generated by the practice management system each month. This list consists of patients who are six months past due for their exam. These are patients who did not respond to the postcard or pre-appoint recall method.

It is extremely important that the recall phone call is performed with great care and caution. A phone call can be viewed as intrusive by some people and might feel like a solicitation for business if not handled well. I recommend an office manager or the doctor listen to a sample of these calls to ensure the patient perception is positive.

I don't use scripts very often because I prefer staff members to sound natural using their own words, but I help them with an opening statement as you'll see below. A good recall specialist can take it from there. More important than a script is getting the right staff member to make the calls. We want someone who is sweet, caring and kind by nature.

A guide for making recall phone calls

Consider modifying this list to suit your practice and print it to assist your staff with the telephone recall project.

- Before calling, check to see if the patient is eligible for eye care with a vision plan previously used. If yes, this is very important to mention early in the call.
- Check other history, such as: age, last visit date, special notes, which doctor was seen last, and type of vision problems. If patient is under 18, place the call to a parent.
- If you must leave a voice mail, just identify yourself and our office and ask the person to call back. Have a copy of the call list on hand so all our other staff members will know how to handle a call back and will not have to take a message.
- This is the basic lead-in statement when you actually speak to the patient: "Oh hello, Mrs. Smith! (warm, smiling, speak loudly, slowly and clearly). This is ______ at Gailmard Eye Center. I noticed you are past due for your eye exam and the doctor just wanted me to check to see if you are receiving our reminder notices and if everything is alright." Wait for a response.

- Respond to the patient's response with great kindness, understanding, respect and concern. If everything seems OK, ask if the patient would like to schedule an appointment. If patient declines, ask if we should continue to send reminders and if he/she prefers email or regular mail.
- If there was a problem with our service in the past, apologize and express how concerned you are. Explain to the patient that we would like to take appropriate steps to fix the problem or make up for it in some way. Invite the patient to come in if it is an eyeglass problem. Tell the patient that you will speak to the manager and she will be in contact. Thank the patient for letting you know about the issue. Report all problems to the office manager.
- Keep a call log. Write notes about each call made and indicate if an appointment was scheduled.

11.6 Reactivation of Past-due Patients

The strategy that I'm sharing this week must be done with care and caution, but with the right staff member, this technique can increase your appointment schedule faster than any other.

The concept
A staff member from your office calls patients who are due for an exam but have not responded to normal recall methods used in your practice. This technique can be especially effective for patients covered by vision plans or other insurance. Many patients intend to come in for eye care, but simply procrastinate. Speaking to a staff member from your office will be all that is needed to schedule most of these folks.

The tone of the call is one of care and concern for the patient – not a call to generate business. The staff member should simply mention that the patient was due for an eye exam in whatever month was specified and that the call is just to make sure he received the post card or email about it. After that, the staff person takes her cue from the patient. See below for tips on what to say. Since the call works with your current recall system, the exact method will vary.

- Use your office management software to search for patients who had a recall date of three months ago. A recall date in the past means that these patients are past due for their exam. If they had been in for an exam, the recall date would have been updated for the future.

- There is small chance that some of these patients are already in your appointment schedule for an exam but they have not been seen yet. Check for this before calling or modify your search factors to filter these patients out.
- You can continue to generate lists of patients by running a search for past recall dates as far back as you wish – such as four months ago, five months ago and so on.
- If you use a mail postcard recall system, consider when the last card was sent so the staff member can refer to it.
- If you use preappointing, use this concept to expand on your usual phone efforts to confirm and reschedule. Many preappointment systems also use a mail system for patients who do not wish to preappoint. Or perhaps you can generate a list of patients who did not keep their appointment.

The challenge

Telephone calls can be regarded as intrusive. Asking a patient to make an appointment can be interpreted as a solicitation for business and that can annoy people. Some may even be rude to the staff member placing the call. This perception can actually harm the image of your practice. For this reason, you must be very cautious about the technique used. You need a staff member with the right personality and with careful training to make this successful.

Another challenge is actually talking to the patient on the phone. You will connect with voice mail quite often and have to leave messages and be sure that the staff member is easily available when the patient calls back.

How to do it safely

The staff caller should take a very kind and respectful attitude. You are only looking out for the patient's best interest. It should be a very friendly call. You will do whatever the patient wishes and you will not be pushy or persistent. Review this article with the staff member you assign to the task and discuss how patients might be annoyed by phone calls they did not expect.

To be really safe, I think the doctor/practice owner should listen in on the first few calls to really understand the impression it makes. This could be done by using speaker phone or by recording the calls. If speaker phone is used, I recommend that the staff person lean in close to the phone so the voice quality is not diminished as much.

Be prepared
The staff member who is making the calls should review the patient's record before making the call. Know the following:

- How to pronounce the first and last name.
- Know the patient's age. If it is a child, call the parent.
- Find the phone number that was given as the best one to call. Don't call the work number if there is a note in the chart saying not to! Cell phones can be even more intrusive because they ring everywhere.
- Check the dates of vision plan or insurance coverage and mention this during the call.
- If there are notes indicating that a patient has been difficult, feel free to omit them from the telephone recall.
- Know the basics about the patient's visual needs. Does he wear contact lenses? Does she have an eye disease? Does he have low vision? Does he live in a nursing home?
- Is there a nice fact that you could mention about the patient's interest or personal life if the situation seems right?

What to say

- "Hello, this is Mary from Dr. Smith's office. I noticed you were due for an eye exam in November and I wanted to be sure you received the reminder card we sent by mail." Listen and take cue from the patient. Be ready to end the call if the patient is not receptive. It may even be necessary to apologize for the intrusion.
- Make a note in the record if patients do not wish to be called.
- "I see you are eligible for this exam under your vision plan."
- "Would you like to schedule your appointment at this time?"
- "I see in your record that Dr. Smith has some concern about your eye health and he noted that re-exams are important for you." Staff should clear this approach with the doctor before implementing and get guidelines. It might prove awkward if the patient did not know of an eye health problem and is hearing it for the first time.
- "How is your vision and how are your eyes feeling?"
- "Are you getting low on your contact lens supply?"
- "Do you have any questions about your eye care?"
- "Would you like me to send you another notice by mail in a few months?"

Chapter 12. Business Operations

12.1 Influence Point Analysis

One of the most important factors in practice development is the patient's opinion of service quality at your office. Evaluating his or her experience is something every patient does at every visit. The overall effect of that evaluation on practice growth is huge because word of mouth recommendation is the largest source of new patients for private practices. Word of mouth is the best form of marketing available to us.

Smart practice owners actively increase the word of mouth referral factor by analyzing and improving the typical patient experience in the office. This process is called influence point analysis. Influence points are the interactions your practice has with a patient. The Walt Disney Company and others have called them moments of truth; Ritz-Carlton hotels refer to them as key success factors and many other top organizations have studied how they interact with customers.

The best place to start this analysis is by making a list of influence points that occur in your practice. It is a very large list: there are minor influence points and major ones; we can consider direct points and indirect ones. In this tip and in the weeks ahead, I'll help you perform this powerful management project which can lead to a reengineering of your procedures and ultimately, faster practice growth.

The Analysis

Simply making the list of influence points will help you analyze them. Think about each point from the patient's point of view, not your or your staff's point of view. It may help to actually walk through your office as if you're a patient. Spend some time observing areas of patient flow that you don't usually see, such as the initial greeting at the front desk. Don't assume that the way you originally envisioned your practice operations is the way they are actually conducted at present. Office procedures have a way of changing over time.

Consider the following as you analyze each point of interaction:

- Force yourself to look at each point from the patient's point of view. How would you feel about this if you were the patient at your dentist's office?
- Who are the staff members in charge of each point?

- How much of an investment of money and resources is given to each point?
- Have patients made any comments about each point?
- Are the points coordinated with each other (are there interdepartmental gaps)?
- Are there any uncontrolled influence points? An example is negative word of mouth where a patient talks badly about your practice to others.
- Do your colleagues and competitors handle each point differently?
- How do other businesses perform each point (hotels, restaurants, big box retail stores, hospitals)?
- How well do you perform each point?
- What would be the ideal way to conduct each point?

The list of influence points

The list of influence points may vary with each practice, but here are some examples. Develop your own list by tracking each step of a typical patient visit at your office.

- The first phone call to your office to inquire about services and fees.
- The phone call to schedule an appointment.
- The appointment confirmation phone call.
- The initial greeting at the front desk.
- The forms for the patient to complete.
- The wait in the reception area, including length of wait and general comfort of surroundings.
- General cleanliness of office including the washroom.
- Condition of office furniture and décor.
- The initial greeting by a pretesting technician.
- The pretest experience including instrumentation and communication.
- The case history.
- The inner-office wait for the doctor.
- The greeting by the doctor.
- The initial conversation and demeanor of the doctor.
- The examination.
- The summary of exam findings, patient education, treatment options and recommendations.
- The explanation of the treatment plan and prescriptions.
- The ensuing contact lens fitting or eye glass selection and design. This would be a subset of influence points.

- Reappointing for additional testing if needed or discussion of recall date.
- Summary of fees and insurance coverage.
- Request for payment.
- Notification of materials ready to dispense.
- The dispensing of contact lenses or eyeglasses and instructions given.
- Final payment of balance.

The points above might be referred to as primary points because your staff actually speaks directly to the patient or the patient is in your office. A listing of secondary points is also useful and should be analyzed:

- A visit to the practice website to find out more information before calling the office.
- The recall messages sent by the practice.
- Statements sent by the practice.
- Newsletters and marketing pieces sent by the practice.
- The yellow page ad.
- Advertisements.
- Community organization sponsorships.

We'll delve into some of these influence points in the weeks ahead to discuss how to improve them.

12.2 The Initial Phone Call

An influence point analysis of your practice, as described in last week's tip, begins with making a list of all the ways your office interacts with patients. Once you have a list of these influence points you can analyze and redesign each one in order to make the total patient experience the best it can be. Using this tool will certainly reward you with practice growth based on increased word of mouth referrals.

The first influence point in most practices is the initial phone call to the office. It's important because it creates an initial perception of the practice. You never get a second chance to create a great first impression. When done well, the initial phone call is converted to an appointment, which is the core requirement for a successful practice!

Consider making the initial phone call a topic at your next staff meeting and asking your staff for their ideas about how to improve telephone interactions. What are the most challenging issues they face on the phone? Here are a few thoughts to get you started with this important moment of truth.

- Avoid automated phone menu systems. I think most consumers strongly dislike automated phone systems that require the caller to press one for this and press two for that. Some practice owners may think such systems are impressive, but truly impressive is an office that has pleasant and knowledgeable humans who answer the phone promptly.
- Voice mail can be so overused that it becomes a convenient way for employees to avoid work. It is inconvenient to have to wait for a call back. My impression of an office that puts me into voice mail is that it is inadequately staffed and does not care about my needs. Voice mail should be a rarely used back up during business hours and a helpful tool after hours.
- Start with the right people. You can train your staff to improve their phone techniques, but some individuals are just naturally friendly and outgoing. Those are the people you want to answer your phones. Realize that many people will have to answer the phone in your office; you may have your primary tier and then some backup people who take over when the primary people are busy or absent. They all should be trained and proficient.
- Let the staff members who answer phones be natural and honest. Contrived scripts have a way of sounding that way to the caller, but choosing the right words is very important.
- Be sure to have enough staff and enough roll-over phone lines to handle the vast majority of calls properly.
- Be warm, engaging and friendly and ask questions. Be interested in the caller more than your office. Are you having any eye problems now? Have you ever worn contact lenses? Even if you don't care much about the answers, asking questions shifts the discussion to the topic of most interest to the caller: himself. It demonstrates that you're interested in the caller and it's something the other eye care offices probably didn't do.
- An oldie but goodie management tip is to train staff members to smile while they are speaking on the phone. While the smile obviously can't be seen by the caller, smiling changes your tone of voice and makes you sound friendlier. Some offices place a mirror near the phone at the front desk so the employee can see herself while speaking, which is a strong reminder to smile.

- Be confident. Act like the practice is the best and the doctors and staff are very thorough. Refer to the doctor by name and praise his experience and reputation.
- Discuss the whole practice, not just the elements of an eye exam. Talk about the optical dispensary, the contact lens department, the priority you place on staying on schedule and any other positive aspects.
- Don't rush the conversation. Act like you have all the time in the world.
- Ask for the appointment. When the timing seems right, just say "would you like to schedule an appointment? I have an opening tomorrow at 10am."
- Answer questions directly without sending up a smokescreen. If the caller wants to know what the fee will be, tell her. Try to be exact, but quoting a range is acceptable.
- Tell the caller anything they should know but may not think to ask. Review insurance and vision plan information. If you plan on asking for payment at the time of the appointment, I would tell them that in advance.
- Don't act annoyed if the caller does not schedule an appointment. Refer the caller to the practice website for more information and say that you hope he will call back. Realize that some people are calling multiple offices to inquire about fees, insurance and services and they may not be willing to schedule an appointment until they've contacted every office. Your staff may not even realize that a person calling to set up an appointment now had called previously and spoke to someone at length.
- Encourage the caller to download and complete any history forms and other paperwork before the visit by logging on to your practice website.
- Review your office hours while considering phone interaction. Calling the office during standard business hours of 9 to 5 on weekdays and finding the office closed (due to lunch or half day or full day closings) is a turn-off.
- Maybe it's just me but I think the message on hold strategy is getting old. The idea was novel 15 years ago but consumers have all heard them so much that I think they are now perceived as an annoyance. I think classical or jazz music with no commercial message is a more pleasant approach to occupying the hold time. Of course, hold time should always be kept to a minimum.
- If you have more than one doctor, how are the choices offered? If there is a goal to get one doctor's schedule busier, you may want to

offer the first available appointment, rather than asking "which doctor do you want to see?"

- Find out about insurance coverage for the patient, including vision plans and medical insurance.
- Keep most insurance plan websites running in the background and the staff member can often check eligibility while still on the phone.
- Don't forget to take the insurance eligibility one step further and look at family members on the website and notify the caller if anyone else is eligible for an exam. Offer to schedule them also.
- Remind the caller about any fees that will be due at the time of the visit. This would include co-pays, but it is also best to mention the contact lens evaluation fee over the phone to patients who wear contacts. This eliminates complaints at the front desk about it after the fact.
- Let the caller know that your office confirms appointments via email or text and obtain the address and mobile phone number.

12.3 The Front Desk Greeting

Let's start with the greeting of patients at the front desk when they arrive for an appointment. This brief interaction sets the tone for the whole visit and it goes a long way to shape the patient's perception and even their behavior. It is very important, and yet most optometric practices don't handle it all that well.

Evaluate it

Take an objective look at how your office currently handles the check-in process. You may have multiple staff members who do this task and the exact process may change with each patient, but look at a typical cross section of what usually happens. You may want to sit in the waiting area yourself, although admittedly, staff may behave differently when they see the boss is observing them. But even with that, you can learn a lot by watching and listening. Also, just ask staff to tell you what happens and if there are any aspects that patients don't care for. Make some notes.

Review Your Resources

The resources for an office procedure are the people, office space and equipment that are used in providing the service. In this case, it is the staff, telephones, computers, photocopier, scanner, paperwork and the desk itself. All of these factors play a role in the efficiency of the process. More about this below, but one big resource is staff. In many offices, quite often, there is no one staffing the front desk at all! That is a very negative impression and it is not OK.

Review Your Financial Investment

Sometimes you have to spend money to make your business better. The smartest investment may not always be something tangible, like a new instrument. Have faith that investing in your process will also produce a good financial return. An improved patient experience will result in additional sales, more referrals and increased loyalty in the future.

Consider these possible ways to invest in your first impression at the front desk:

- Hire an additional employee if it seems that your current staff at the front desk is either absent or too busy to take care of people arriving for an appointment.
- Add more phones and workstations so your larger staff can take care of all tasks quickly.
- Make the front desk larger to accommodate more people. If this is not possible, consider building a call center in a back office so the front desk staff does not need to answer the phone.

Review Your Process

Much of what happens at check-in was created by you, the practice owner. That may have been years ago and many things may have changed. Many new procedures may have been added without ever taking any away. Now is the time to look at everything you do from the patient's point of view. With the goal in mind of making the check-in process easier and more pleasant, see if you can change the requirements and weed out what you can.

- Internal paperwork and file preparation. Could staff do this a couple days before the appointment (during a slow time) so everything is ready when the patient walks in?
- History forms. Do you need all those questions on every patient? Don't make every person complete all that if you don't really need it. Remember that you only need extensive review of systems, past, social and family histories if you are billing 99 codes. 92 codes can be used in many cases and do not have the onerous history requirement. Additionally, many exams are billed to vision plans and not medical and thee also do not require extremely long histories. By all means, get the history you need to do a good job clinically, but don't require more than that.
- You and a clinical tech can verbally ask what you need to know. Avoid asking for the same thing multiple times in different ways.

- Be sure your staff requests that patients go to your website before their visit to download and complete forms.
- Many offices offer a screening test of some sort for an additional fee. I think a yes/no form can work fine for this, but keep it short and have the receptionist provide a brief verbal explanation when it is presented.

Staff Training

- Staff members should smile at every person who walks up to the desk. Oddly, this simple task can be the most difficult thing to implement. Ideally, you would have hired a person for this job who smiles easily and has that kind of personality in the first place. In any case, a smile sends a huge positive message and front desk staff should understand the importance and master the technique. Talk to them about it.
- Multitask. Even if the receptionist is busy or on the phone, he or she must make eye contact with the arriving patient and gesture "I'll be right with you". We do not want the patient to feel like he is a bother or less important.
- Greet warmly. Decide what the greeting should be and train all staff to say it properly, but start with a greeting like good morning or hello, Mrs. Smith. Welcome to our office is nice. Introducing one's self is always courteous - simply "my name is Jill" works fine. Inform the patient of what to expect at the visit, such as waiting time, and describe any forms that need to be completed. "Please make yourself comfortable" sounds much better than "take a seat".
- Use the name if you know it. I am amazed at how well my staff knows the names of patients, but they don't always take advantage of that by using the name. The sound of one's own name has special power, and calling a person by name makes him feel important. Relationships are built by using a person's name. Of course, people with an appointment are pretty easy because the staff has a list of those names and they know what time it is! But don't use the wrong name and pronounce it properly. Work on details like when to use Mr., Mrs., and Miss., and when to use first names. I would not use first names for people older than you unless asked to do so.
- Let the patient know honestly about the expected wait time.
- Offer any refreshments that are available, like coffee, tea or water.
- Review the wording staff should use to explain any paperwork and forms that are required.

The patient experience

Here are a few issues that I've seen that can make or break the front desk experience.

- Is there anyone at the front desk? It is extremely common in eye care offices today for no one to be staffing the front desk at any given moment. In my view, there should always be a staff person present to greet anyone who walks in. I recognize there are legitimate reasons why a receptionist may have to leave the desk, (getting a file, using the rest room, checking on something in the lab, walking a patient to an exam room, and so on), but if we work on it, the lapses can be prevented. From the patient's point of view, walking into an empty office is not pleasant. Should you sit down? What if you sit down and someone else walks in and stands at the desk and then gets taken in sooner? You start to think no one cares about you within about 20 seconds.
- Are you understaffed? Many practices that I observe are trying to get by with too little. The goal is to hold down expenses, which is fine, but if you are trying to provide excellent service (did you really mean that when you wrote your mission statement?), cutting costs works against your goals. This is why practices that don't charge high enough fees can't provide great service. These practices become mediocre. Consider that there are many days when you don't have the staff numbers you need to due to call-offs, vacations and usual days off. The odds are good that you are understaffed.
- No sign in sheets. There are still many offices that use a sign-in sheet at the front desk. I understand that the list works well for the staff, but this is not about what's best for the staff. We're analyzing how patients feel - and they generally don't like signing in. If I'm a patient, I don't really want my name sitting there for every other person who comes in to see. I'm not concerned with HIPAA; I just want to create a great impression. Sign-in sheets are a great excuse for staff to not have to be present and to not communicate with patients.
- No glass panels. These were popular in medical offices in the 60s but they give a negative impression. Sliding doors with clear or translucent glass, or with a hole for talking through, present a closed-off feeling and a feeling that the staff should not be disturbed. It is exactly opposite of the image I want to project. If sound is a problem, see if those activities can be performed somewhere else.
- Immediate acknowledgement is key. Train your staff to acknowledge patients who approach the front desk immediately. Even if the receptionist is on the phone or with another patient, she can make eye contact with the new comer and say "I'll be right with you." If

the receptionist is speaking to another staff member when a patient walks up, the discussion should stop and the receptionist should greet the patient. If the staff person can't speak because it would be rude or an interruption, eye contact along with a smile and a nod is sufficient. A good receptionist is an expert at multitasking.
- Smile! The entire communication changes if the staff member smiles. Some people smile easily and frequently and some don't. If you have an employee who does not smile very often, talk about how important it is. It is trainable and it makes a world of difference.

Put all these elements together and you have an action plan for improving your front desk greeting and check-in process. Be sure to monitor the procedures to be sure the staff does not revert back to old habits.

12.4 Emergency Symptom List for Front Desk

I received several emails following my last tip, which was about charging more for emergency visits. Several colleagues requested my list of emergency symptoms to assist receptionists in judging the urgency of eye problems. The list is printed below.

It's a good idea to meet with your staff periodically to discuss the emergency nature of certain ocular symptoms, and how these calls should be handled. Many factors will influence this, such as the availability of a doctor in your office every day, how tightly the practice is booked, and your desire to treat various medical eye problems.

If you want to increase the emergency care aspect of your practice, consider telling each patient that you examine that he or she should call your office if they ever have an eye emergency. Many patients routinely think they should call their primary care physician or go to a hospital emergency room, when your office may be a better alternative. You may even want to print a handout or magnet card with common eye emergencies and what to do about them as a patient give-away reference.

It's tempting to simply tell receptionists to work-in any caller who says they are having an urgent eye problem, or is concerned enough to want to come in immediately. This is a good practice, but it does not solve all the responsibility of the practice. There are two scenarios where this approach alone is not ideal:

1. A caller does not request an emergency same-day appointment, but has an urgent problem and does not know it. Waiting for the patient to ask for an emergency appointment is not good enough if the patient does not know that sudden flashes of light is a concern.
2. A caller who demands an emergency same-day appointment, and is squeezed into a very full day, only to find that the chief complaint is a scratch on the eyeglass lens. Some people will push for their own convenience. While this scenario is disrupting to the office – it's better to see a false emergency than to not see a true one.

Here is a guide to emergency symptoms that will help a staff member prioritize appointments. It is not all-inclusive and you may want to add or delete some symptoms.

Post at front desk

We should ask every patient who calls for an appointment: "Are you having an eye problem?" Some appointments are for routine check-ups. If yes, ask the patient to describe it and listen to the patient's level of concern and use your judgment. Ask a doctor or technician if you're not sure. This office sees all patients who are having an urgent eye problem the same day. Try to give a specific appointment time that is soon and appears to work best with the schedule. If all appointment slots are full, just tell the caller to come right over, and we will work him or her into the schedule. Advise the patient about the exam fee and the payment requirements over the phone.

Emergency Symptoms (Work patient into today's schedule or page the doctor on call. A referral to the hospital emergency room should be considered if no doctor is reached).

- Sudden loss or blurring of vision in either eye or both eyes
- New or sudden flashes of light or floaters
- Pain in the eye
- Chemical splash in the eye (advise immediate copious flushing with water for at least a half hour, even if the event seems over)
- Injury to the eye or head
- Foreign particle in the eye
- Red eyes of recent onset
- Discharge from eyes
- Extreme swollen eyelid
- Contact lens lost or broken in the eye
- Steamy or cloudy vision of recent onset
- Sudden unequal pupil size
- Sudden double vision or sudden crossed eyes

12.5 Balancing Your Cash Drawer

I think it's important to operate the business office of your practice as if it were a bank. That means specific procedures are followed every day to ensure an accurate accounting of all monies. These steps are necessary even if you have a small practice and fully trust all employees who handle financial transactions. Monitoring the process of collecting and depositing payments lets you know if errors are being made and gives you a basis for preventing them. A daily routine to balance sales with the bank deposit prevents employee carelessness and possible embezzlement in the future.

I believe the balancing of the cash drawer and depositing the receipts into the bank should be delegated to staff, but the process should be reviewed by the practice owners. Staff members may email the production report each day to the owner or leave the printed document in a predetermined place. The deposit should be entered into a financial software program (such as QuickBooks) and the owner will review it daily. Having the ability to log onto the practice computer system remotely may facilitate the owner's supervision from home or when traveling.

Two cash drawers
Accurate accounting of deposits every day is made easier by using two cash drawer trays. These trays are used alternately every other day. Each drawer tray starts out with exactly $200 in cash in various denominations of bills and coins to make change. Cash, credit card receipts, personal checks and insurance checks are added to the drawer as the payments are entered into the practice management computer system.

When, where, how to balance
There are two distinct steps your staff will perform to balance the cash drawer. One is closing out the drawer and the other is balancing the drawer with the daily production report. Often these two activities are performed at the same time, but they don't have to be. You can decide when these activities work best into your office routine based on your staffing levels and how busy the office is at certain times of the day. But once you decide on a time of day, I recommend you stay consistent. A consistent routine improves accuracy and is less likely to be forgotten or modified.

The closing of the cash drawer is generally performed near the end of the business day. In order to help our employees leave the office promptly at quitting time, we close the drawer about a half hour early. This may mean that some of today's sales will be shown on the following day's production report, but that does not matter to me. To close the drawer, the staff runs and prints the daily production report on the practice management software system and the cash drawer is exchanged for the second drawer. At this point, the cash, checks and credit cards slips in the drawer, minus the $200 starting cash, should exactly equal the total payments shown on the daily production report.

The cash drawer and the corresponding production report can be balanced at that time or may be stored until a more convenient time the next day if you have a secure place to store the cash. You will need a place to keep the cash drawer when not in use anyway, so you may want to have a lockable cabinet or safe. Balancing the drawer consists of adding up the cash (less the $200 starting cash), checks and credit card slips and seeing if it equals the day's payments on the report. If it does, the drawer is balanced and the employee places her initials on the report. If it does not balance, the staff member must review every transaction until the error is found, and then make a correction on the daily production report.

Bank deposits

I believe in making each bank deposit exactly equal to one day's receipts. A deposit is made every day and we do not allow the receipts from one day to be added to another day or partial day. This makes it easier to track past deposits if it becomes necessary and the regimental nature discourages theft. If you do not wish to have any funds held in the office overnight you may use a night depository at the bank.

12.6 A 10-Point Checklist for Interpersonal Skills

How you act with each individual patient can have a powerful impact on your practice growth. Yet, many excellent doctors never even think about how they act or what they say in the exam room. They have a job to do and they go about getting it done.

Interpersonal skills come easily to some, and are difficult for others, but if practice growth is one of your goals, it is smart to pay attention to it. See if you consistently perform each item on this checklist when you examine patients. If not, commit the list to memory and be sure to touch every point.

- Smile – don't be so serious. Optometrists do have major responsibilities during an exam, but patients aren't impressed by serious and somewhat scary doctors. Serious behavior is usually interpreted as rude or arrogant. Keep in mind that patients may be a little nervous or worried about the exam. A smile is contagious and it makes you friendly and caring. Over time, it builds good reputations.

- Shake hands. It doesn't matter anymore if the patient is male, female or even a youngster – extend your hand in a friendly manner. It builds relationships. Not too firm, by the way, you can actually hurt some people.
- Talk non-optometry first. Don't jump right into the case history. Talk about the weather, sports, the patient's job, or a hobby that you made a note of at the last visit.
- Say the patient's name. You can't build a relationship without using a person's name. Ask how to pronounce it if your not sure, then write it phonetically in the record. Use Mr. or Mrs. for folks older than you, until they advise you otherwise. Say the patient's name occasionally in conversation – but don't overdo it so it sounds phony.
- Wash your hands in front of the patient. If your exam room does not have a sink, call a plumber right away. This speaks volumes about everything in your practice.
- Explain tests as you do them. Do this in extremely simple terms and keep it very short. This can cross over to boring very quickly.
- Summarize the exam results. Stop writing and look the patient in the eye at the end and review all the major parts of the exam. Include the pre-test data. Present normal findings as good news.
- Give treatment options; then recommend the best. As you discuss your treatment plan, list the patient's choices, even if you think they might not be interested. Then be sure to recommend what you think is the best option and state why. Always include the recall date and reason in your exam summary.
- Ask: "Do you have any questions?" This is a great way to close your visit and it gives the impression that you have all the time in the world, while implying that you are getting ready to end the exam.
- Say thank you as you leave the patient. A thank you is very polite and considerate. It is humble and anti-arrogant. You are thanking the patient for choosing your practice for eye care.

12.7 Words Make a Difference

There is no question that the way your practice is perceived by patients has a huge effect on future success. During the course of a visit, an image is formed by thousands of little things that are seen and heard in your office. We have control over most of those things to a large extent, but many doctors become so busy that there just is not enough time to train staff members on little details. I hope this list of preferred terms will help to a small degree.

The list is not exhaustive and it's not perfect because words taken out of context can have different meanings. But it's a start. I tried to balance the need to say things in a professional and pleasing manner, yet not become so obtuse that a patient does not understand what you're talking about.

Have all your staff members read this list and consider printing and posting it discreetly at your front desk (not the check-out counter). It would actually be a good idea for doctors to give the list a quick read as well; I hear many of my colleagues use some of the non-preferred terms quite frequently. Staff members tune in to the terms used by the doctor so it's important to set a good example. The list is also a must-read for all new employees.

As you hear other examples of phrases that could be expressed in a better way, just add them to the list.

- Don't say customer or client.... Say patient
- Don't say sell.... Say prescribe or dispense or provide
- Don't say buy.... Say order
- Don't say store or shop.... Say office or practice
- Don't say business or trade.... Say practice or profession
- Don't say price.... Say fee
- Don't say old patient.... Say established patient
- Don't say waiting room.... Say reception area
- Don't say back room.... Say lab or administrative office
- Don't say optical shop.... Say optical dispensary
- Don't say buy frames.... Say select frames
- Don't say girl.... Say technician or assistant or optician or staff member or use person's actual name
- Don't say employee.... Say staff member
- Don't say doctor is busy.... Say doctor is with a patient
- Don't say doctor is on vacation.... Say doctor is out of the office
- Don't say doctor is late.... Say schedule was interrupted by an emergency

- Don't say trade show.... Say conference
- Don't say trade magazine.... Say professional journal
- Don't say trade group.... Say professional association
- Don't say equipment.... Say instruments
- Don't say check eyes.... Say perform examination
- Don't say check-up.... Say follow-up exam
- Don't say trial contact lens.... Say diagnostic contact lens
- Don't say fit contacts.... Say prescribe contacts
- Don't say check contacts.... Say evaluate contacts and corneal health
- Don't say pick-up glasses.... Say dispense eyewear
- Don't say insert.... Say apply
- Don't say surgery or operation.... Say procedure
- Don't say drug.... Say medication
- Don't say steroid.... Say anti-inflammatory medication
- Don't say glasses were rejected.... Say glasses did not meet our quality standards
- Don't say pressure check or glaucoma test or air puff.... Say tonometry or measurement of intraocular pressure
- Don't say picture.... Say photograph or image
- Don't say invisible bifocals.... Say progressive lenses
- Don't say antireflective coating.... Say antireflective lenses
- Don't say no problem.... Say thank you and you're welcome

12.8 How to Handle Early and Late Arrivers

Have you ever had your schedule disrupted by a patient who arrives late? I guess we all have. And the early arriver is not much easier to deal with. Try as we might to keep a well-designed schedule, unexpected events that are not within the control of the practice can cause back-ups of patients or wasted time. Here are some tips on how to improve the situation.

The Latecomer
Assuming the usual efforts are made to tell patients the appointment time and confirm it one day in advance, I just accept that some people generally run late. Tough measures to change people's habits can have a way of being perceived as too controlling for a high-service practice. Patients can perceive it as a turn-off. When a patient does arrive late, I think it's very important to handle it well at the initial greeting by a staff member. My staff is trained to say something like "Hello Mr. Smith! It's so nice to see you again! I see you have a 1:30 appointment and it's now 1:50. We should be able to work you

into our schedule with only a minimal delay. I'll let you know right away if there will be any problem."

If the staff member feels too shy and passes the first chance to acknowledge the time situation, the opportunity is lost. The same is true if there is no staff member available to greet Mr. Smith because he or she had to leave the front desk (another pet peeve of mine that happens all too often). Mr. Smith then conveniently forgets that he was late and he can begin to resent any delay, even though he caused it! It seems fair to me that the latecomer should be the main person inconvenienced by the action – not the other patients who were on time for appointments.

The Early Bird

The patient who arrives early can also cause problems with the schedule, because a well-meaning assistant will frequently start the exam for this patient ahead of another one who should have gone first. This is fine for the early arriver – but the next patient (who was on time) may be delayed.

I recommend similar staff training for an immediate acknowledgment, just as above for the late patient. "Good morning, Mrs. Jones! I see you have a 10:30 appointment and it is now about 10:05. We will try to take you in a little early if our schedule permits, but I'm not sure about that just yet. In the meantime, please help yourself to a cup of coffee or tea at the beverage counter, and feel free to browse for frames while you wait."

An office manager or senior staff member should evaluate the schedule and make a decision about when the best time will be to begin the early or late arriver.

A Cut-off Policy?

My staff occasionally asks me if we have an official number of minutes, after which we turn away a late-arriving patient. They would like it to be a little more cut and dry than I think it should be, so I decline to have a specific number of minutes. While it would make things easy on the staff to just say "if a patient arrives more than 20 minutes late for an appointment, they will be turned away and rescheduled for another day." I won't do that. It's a good way to lose a patient and his family and to build a bad reputation. One could argue that those late arrivers are not desirable anyway and they deserve to be taught a lesson, but I don't agree. Patients are too valuable, and the patient very likely will teach the practice a lesson by going elsewhere. Most of these latecomers are good people who had something unexpected happen in their day.

I prefer to be flexible enough to handle things that throw off my office schedule. We should be good enough to manage those inconveniences well. I will generally see any patient who arrives late, unless it is right at closing time and would require staff members to stay extremely late.

What about the wrong day?

Here is another great example of challenges that can upset the schedule. By now, you probably can infer that my office is going to handle the patient who shows up at the front desk saying he has a 2:00 appointment, only for the receptionist to finally find him in the schedule one week in the future. My staff is trained to accept the blame for this mishap, and apologize for apparently recording it wrong. We then do our best to work this patient into the schedule today, which is usually no big deal. What we avoid is the confrontation of trying to prove that the patient made the mistake and should just go home and come back next week. The patient, realizing that the situation could have been his error, is always very understanding. And let's not forget that it really could have been our fault!

Flexibility and Efficiency

This customer-friendly appointment policy works if your practice is flexible and efficient with clinical procedures. Here are some factors that make that possible.

- A larger staff
- More delegation
- Automated instrumentation
- Shorter appointment slots for exams
- Doctors and staff who are aware of the schedule and can change the sequence of testing
- A supervisor to direct patient flow

12.9 More on Late Patients

I received some nice comments on last week's tip about staff members who frequently show up late for work, but several readers asked me to expand on the side point I made about patients who arrive late. I'm happy to tackle that topic here, but be forewarned: many readers of this column will not like my answer! Read on anyway. I might change your mind on this and there is one gem in here that almost every practice will like and use.

My philosophy

My method for handling late patients is based on an assumption that you want to grow your practice into a huge success and you want to make huge financial profits. I realize that financial gain is not important to everyone, so if you are not that interested in profit, I can understand that you might respond differently.

If you are interested in maximizing revenue and profit as fast as possible, then understand that my approach to late patients is one part of a larger philosophy of excellent customer service. Most ODs only get that to a point and most are not willing to go far enough to make customer service a marketing strategy. The late arriving patient is just one excellent example of how you could drive huge numbers of patients to your practice.

My strategy

My staff makes a strong attempt to confirm every appointment two days in advance, but in spite of that, we know that some patients will arrive late. Here is the part that many ODs and staff won't like: When a patient shows up late in our office; we are extremely understanding. If the patient offers a reason for why they're late, we're very sympathetic. We generally see the patient even if they are quite late, unless we are about to close the office for the day.

I realize that arriving late is disrespectful and disrupts our schedule. But I don't look at this event from our point of view. I look at it from the patient's point of view. From the patient's point of view, he could not help being late and it was not his fault. I don't get caught up in trying to judge whether that is actually true or not. That seems like a waste of time and I can't really be sure, so I just accept it at face value. I prefer to resist trying to teach the patient a lesson in life. I prefer to take advantage of the situation and show the patient how easy we are to do business with.

Moments like this can actually shock a patient, but it causes them to love our practice. As staff members provide this high level of service, it builds our office culture and they can feel that we are different and special. A situation that could easily have caused some anger ends up becoming a moment of kindness.

My tactical approach

We handle late patients one case at a time, but in general we try to see the patient as fast as we can while minimizing the impact on other patients. If we can't do a good job with both, the late patient has to wait. But we take pride in being able to provide an eye exam quickly and with flexibility. We simply make it work and we don't waste more time worrying about it.

Here are some tips that will make dealing with the late patient easier:

- We train our front desk staff to be aware of the current time and if a patient checks in more than a few minutes late, we politely get it on record by mentioning it. The greeting is really the only time we have to let the patient know that we know he is late. It is to our advantage to work from that fact because if we have to make the patient wait longer than our usual high standard, it is because he was late. We just say: "Hi Mr. Smith. So glad you're here. Your appointment was at 3:00 and I see it is now 3:25. We will get your exam started just as soon as possible..."
- A manager or an experienced staff member should look at the schedule and make a decision about when to start the visit and what procedures to do. The doctor may want to be consulted as well. If everyone works together, a solution can usually be found. I love it when the optometrist can be flexible and may take a patient without the usual pretesting. Or can see the patient briefly and then start him dilating. Whatever it takes.
- My staff would like me to set a specific number of minutes, beyond which we can tell the patient that we won't see him. I won't do it. I want to handle these on a case by case basis as we look at the situation.
- If we are near quitting time or lunch time or if there is some unusual circumstance, we just talk to the patient. We are simply honest, but very kind and understanding. We may let the patient know that because of other appointments in progress, there may be a significant wait and he may prefer to just reschedule. Or we will say that our office closes soon and we won't have time to do the exam, but our optician will be happy to help you look at a few frames today.

12.10 No Show Fees – A Costly Policy

A surprising number of practices have a fee that is charged to patients who fail to show up for appointments. There are many variations on the exact policy – such as not really charging it (but only threatening to do so) or giving a discount on the no show fee if a future appointment is kept.

We may have to agree to disagree on this, but I think these policies are damaging to the practices. Further, it might serve as a sign of a customer-tough philosophy in general for any given practice. I assume doctors who have these policies like the impression it gives the public – sort of a "we don't really need you" attitude. My way or the highway. Maybe these practices are so large and successful and booked so far in advance that they truly don't need patients. If that is the case, then I have no problem with the tough-love policy. But I've seen a lot of practices, and I hardly ever see one that could not use more patients. Lots more patients. In fact, I can't envision any practice that has enough patients. If demand is high enough, I'd hire more staff, hire associate doctors and build new offices.

Understandable logic – but flawed
I think I understand why no show fee policies are developed. It seems unfair and inconsiderate when a patient reserves the doctor's time and does not use it. Income is lost. Time is wasted. Expenses, like staff salaries, are still incurred. Another patient could have used that appointment time.

Further, the irritated doctor reasons that he is better off without these people. If they pay the fee, then fine, but if they don't recognize the value of the doctor's time, they can go elsewhere. This is where we differ. If the primary goal is making a profit, I believe we are better off letting the patient win. This is an example of customer service, which yields patient satisfaction and loyalty. That is the single most important aspect of practice building.

Fairness
When a patient misses an appointment, he invariably believes it is not his fault. And many times it isn't, but in any case, there is always an excuse. It's human nature. Smart businesses don't worry about fairness; they look at everything they do from the patient's point of view. Marketing is defined as identifying and satisfying customers' wants and needs. The patient's perception is all that matters and they never put the practice's needs ahead of their own.

One final drawback to the no show fee is that to be effective, it must be stated in advance to every patient, even though only a small percentage of people are guilty of the offense. This causes every patient to perceive the practice as tough. I think it makes them easy pickings for another practice which projects the high-service image.

12.11 Are you making follow-up phone calls?

I'm sure you've heard of the practice of calling patients one or two weeks after they receive new glasses or contacts to see how they're doing. Most eye care professionals have heard of this and even tried it for a while, but I have found that the procedure is often dropped. I'm here to recommend that you revive it.

Do you really want to stir up complaints?

The answer to this question is yes... you really do want to hear the complaints. It's far less costly to learn about problems and correct them than it is to let the problems drift. The cost of uncorrected problems is fairly invisible, so many practitioners prefer to not know, but realize that the true cost exists in terms of loss of repeat business, lack of referrals of others, and general ill will and damage to one's reputation. The cost of not knowing is great.

The follow-up phone call does not cause patients to have complaints; it only makes your office aware of complaints and problems that already exist. Every office that dispenses eyewear has some complaints. If you don't ask how people are doing, a large percentage may let the problems go unreported. Certainly some patients will return to your office to let you know about a problem, but for every one of those there may be dozens who don't bother to come back. This group procrastinates about the problem; they try to deal with it; they want to avoid a confrontation; and eventually so much time passes that they don't feel they can complain any longer. In the end, they resent having paid hundreds of dollars for glasses that "were never right." While these patients don't bother to tell you about it, they generally tell many other people in their social circle.

These glasses were never right

You may have seen a few of these patients in your exam chair. After obtaining new glasses from your office a year or two ago, they are now back for an exam again and they report that the glasses "were never right." These patients don't necessarily expect you to do anything about the problem; they seem to just want to report it. I know this is aggravating to hear and you want to say, "Why didn't you let me know?" The patient does have some responsibility to bring a complaint to your attention in a timely manner, but my point is that these patients exist in every practice and most of them do not reappear in your exam chair at all; most just go somewhere else for eye care.

It may seem that calling every patient who receives glasses is going above and beyond the call of duty, but that is exactly what I want to achieve in my practice. I want patients to know that we care and we want everything to be right. I'd rather initiate the call, find out if there are any problems, and proactively do whatever it takes to remedy the situation.

Follow-up call procedure

Placing the telephone call is a great secondary job for staff members. There are times when any office slows down and I like each employee to have a side job assignment to perform when time permits. I assign the follow-up phone calls to one of our most friendly assistants. You can track the patients who should be called in a variety of ways, depending on your practice management software or record keeping system.

This technique is also advised for a change in contact lenses, but unlike eyeglasses, contact lens patients are often scheduled for a follow-up visit in the office and that may make the phone call unnecessary.

The assistant says something like this: "Good morning, Mrs. Smith. This is Denise from Gailmard Eye Center. The doctor asked me to call to see how you are enjoying your new eyewear." If all is well, great, but if there is any problem, the assistant advises the patient to return to the office so it can be corrected. In either case, you have made a positive impression on every patient by showing how much you care.

I like the assistant to make a few brief notes after each call, such as: doing great, left message on machine, thanked us for calling, or having a problem with ____. You could compile a list of names and phone numbers in a notebook for this purpose, or you could write on the back of the optical order forms before they are returned to the files, or use a notes section in your electronic records program. A rewarding side benefit is that you quickly realize that the vast majority of patients are very pleased with the services and products they received, which makes working with the occasional unhappy person a little easier!

Was the technique dropped?

I find the follow-up phone call is frequently dropped and forgotten about because the procedure is delegated to staff and whenever the office becomes busy, it can easily be postponed. Once it's postponed it's often lost for good. The phone call is not vital to practice operations, so it's the first thing to go. The technique is important enough that management should make sure it happens.

12.12 Patient Waiting Time

As we continue our analysis of the major influence points in your practice, let's look at the typical wait time for a patient. A long wait has become the norm in health care offices today, but just because it's common doesn't mean we should accept it.

There are some medical specialties that are inherently extremely busy and have all the patient demand they could ever need but, unfortunately, eye care is usually not one of them. Most eye care practices need many more patients to reach high success levels. Rather than worry and wonder how things got this way, I'm far more interested in changing it. The way to build patient demand for private practice eye care is excellent customer service. Making people wait beyond a reasonable period of time is a huge step in the wrong direction.

An opportunity
Most practices need more competitive advantages: reasons why a patient should choose your office over others in the area. Developing those advantages can be difficult and expensive. Earning a reputation for generally being on time for appointments is a very strong advantage that doesn't cost anything and can be implemented immediately. Smart practice owners embrace the opportunity to be different than most doctors' offices by being on time and they generate patient loyalty and word of mouth buzz in the process.

Remedies for chronic problems
If your practice often runs more than ten minutes past appointment times, consider these strategies for changing your operations.

- Observe and analyze why your office runs late. Ask your staff for input as well, since they may see things differently than you. Is it in the processing before the exam? Is it a bottleneck in pretesting? Does the doctor talk too long? Are there not enough exam rooms? Diagnose the problem before trying to treat it.
- I define the beginning of a visit as the time when someone calls the patient into the clinical area to begin some aspect of testing. Usually, that is a technician. Make sure you have enough staff. Trying to keep expenses down with fewer employees is penny-wise but pound-foolish. Doing so will hold back your practice growth. Proper staffing

is a wise investment that pays for itself with improved service and higher productivity.

- Be aware of the inner waiting time as well as the reception room wait time. Calling someone into the office only to make them wait in an exam room or holding area is not being on time.
- The doctor must be interested in an excellent record of being on time. Everyone knows that occasional emergencies or complex cases can cause any doctor to run late on occasion, but what is the track record like? Some doctors really don't mind if they make patients wait. If they don't see the benefits of a great reputation for being on time, then this tip won't help. Doctors who wish to improve their track record will work on being flexible with their exam procedures.
- Doctors who are interested in the schedule will leap frog an easy patient who arrives early or may change the routine for dilation or other testing to suit the flow at the time. The order you do some things can be changed to accommodate the appointment status.
- Delegate more to staff so the doctor can concentrate on the patient rather than data collection.
- Consider using scribes in the exam room. This technique brings amazing time saving efficiencies, not the least of which is saving the doctor from walking patients around the office and explaining the treatment plan to staff.
- Be upfront and honest about wait times with patients. If your staff knows the doctor is running behind schedule, it's best to tell patients this as they check in and even offer to reschedule them if the problem is severe.
- I like to see doctors apologize directly to the patient if they are significantly late. It shows a respect for the patient's time and conveys that running late is not the norm. It reverses some bad feelings.

How to handle early and late arrivers

There is no question that people who don't arrive on time play havoc with your schedule. The early bird wants to be seen right away and the late person wonders why you are not calling him in since it's past his appointment time. Both would like to ignore that you have other appointments.

Train your receptionists to politely acknowledge the current time at the moment of check-in. Just say, "Hi Mr. Jones! It's so nice to see you again! I see you have a 3:00 appointment and it's now 3:20. We'll work you into the schedule just as soon as possible. It shouldn't be too long of a wait; please make yourself comfortable." This approach let's the patient know that you know he's late and that any wait is his fault. The same is true with early folks - mention the current time and tell them you'll try to work them in sooner than the appointed time if possible.

Staff members would sometimes like to be tougher on late arrivers, but my approach is very lenient and understanding. If you work with people and genuinely try to serve them and avoid inconveniencing them, it all works out.

Wait times for patients who drop in
As you examine typical wait times in your practice, don't forget to consider patients who stop in to pick up glasses or replacement contacts or to have an adjustment or repair. Since these folks don't generally have appointments (I don't recommend appointments for these kinds of visits), a small wait is understandable, but it should be brief most of the time. If there are often long waits for picking up glasses I would be concerned that you don't have enough employees.

12.13 Get Started Faster

The record-keeping requirements in health care today are getting more complex all the time. I'm not a big fan of all that paperwork (and electronic work), but even if I can't eliminate many aspects of the process, I can control when my staff does it. Reducing the time before starting the eye exam provides your practice with many significant benefits.

Speeding up the process at check-in greatly improves the patient experience, which is a huge goal for earning good reviews and generating more word-of-mouth referrals. No one likes to wait or fill out forms. The patient only has a limited amount of time to spend in your office; do you want to short-change the optical dispensing aspect?

Review the following points that often occur when the patient checks in and consider how your office handles each one. I'll provide some comments that may help you to reduce the time required for each point.

- Start by reviewing all the forms you ask a patient to complete in your office and try to eliminate as many as possible or at least make them simpler.
- A lengthy health history questionnaire is very time consuming. Many doctors and many EHR templates require a very long case history, including review of systems, past family and social history,

and history of present illness. Don't ask for all that detail from every patient if you don't need it. Routine vision exams that are billed to vision plans do not require it. Even Medicare and medical insurance plans don't require it if you use a 92 CPT code. Only the 99 codes require the most extensive histories and it is your choice if you use 99 or 92 codes. Of course, we always need some medical history for even a routine exam, but decide what you really need and ask only that.

- My office uses a simple one page intake form that covers basic demographics and basic medical history and we only ask for that from new patients. My technicians review and update the demographics and history verbally for established patients.
- Our intake form is on our practice website and the staff encourages new patients to complete it before arriving for their visit when they speak by phone for the appointment. Many patients don't do it, but we try.
- Don't have staff take the verbal history in the pretest room, it ties up the room too long. Our techs take the case history later in an exam lane.
- The HIPAA notice of privacy practice signature form is only required of new patients and you could add a sentence about it to another form you are asking the patient to sign, getting more than one purpose from a form. A statement like this will work: I acknowledge that I have received a copy of the Gailmard Eye Center Notice of Privacy Practices.
- Some forms are important enough that you don't want to drop them. We use a form to ask if the patient wants special screening tests like Optomap and macular pigment density testing. Some offices like patients to write out their own recall card addresses. Keep these items simple and brief.
- Try to drop patient education handouts and disclaimers at check-in. Long explanations about insurance plans, pupil dilation and other disclaimers don't really work and most patients don't even read them. It would be better to give a patient education handout to specific patients about conditions they actually have.
- I don't use questionnaires aimed at lifestyle optical dispensing or a dry eye center. I prefer my staff to engage the patient verbally

which leads them into a discussion about the products. It is quite obvious to everyone that these questionnaires are designed to increase business and they can be annoying. But when a person asks you about your outdoor activities or about your job or if you have eye discomfort, you feel like they are interested in you.

- Don't delay the start of the exam by having the front desk staff enter all the data while the patient waits. Just enter enough to open the chart and do the rest while the technician is with the patient.
- The day of the visit is way too late for staff to check insurance benefits, get authorization and print the benefit form. Do all that the same day the appointment is scheduled.
- Be observant of frequent reasons for delaying the start of the exam. If you often don't have a tech available you may need more employees. If you have a tech, but no pretest room or exam room is open, you may need a larger office.
- Train your technicians to be flexible about where they start the exam. If the pretest room is busy, start in an exam lane or photo room and come back to pretesting.
- Many technicians spend an inordinate amount of time reviewing past exam data before calling the patient in. Train them to take a quick look at past best visual acuity and diagnoses and then get going. The tech can read more details if needed as the exam progresses.
- Keep an eye on your appointment schedule all day and make an effort to stay on time. Be flexible with your exam routine: what you do and when you do it.

12.14 Taking Too Long with Optical Orders and Fee Calculations

As we all move our office procedures to electronic records and online ordering, I refuse to let software programs ruin the patient experience and staff efficiency in my practice. As a follow-up to last week's tip about staff being too busy to sell a second pair of glasses, I urge you to look at how long it takes staff to write up an eyeglass order and calculate the fees due from the patient when using a vision plan.

I recently consulted with a doctor and optical manager who felt their optical checkout process was inefficient. Patients had to wait too long, staff were stressed and the patient experience was poor. We implemented some changes in job duties which resulted in a dramatic decrease in time needed with the patient in optical.

There are several good ways to overcome a problem with slow checkout and not every practice has the same issues. Here are some ideas to consider as you customize the solution for your office.

Don't wait for the handoff

This is really not part of the checkout process, but I see so many practices that make the patient wait at the start of frame selection that it is worth bringing it up. It is possible if we improve efficiency for opticians, they will be able to handle more patients and will be more available to accept a handoff and get started. If no one is often available when the doctor pages an optician or walks the patient into optical, you need to fix that. Having patients wait or begin to try on frames by themselves is inviting them to become impatient and think about taking their Rx elsewhere. Get them engaged in the selection process with an eye care professional right away.

Move the billing aspect to the front desk

Many offices now have the optician enter the charges for frames, lenses and lens options into the electronic health record (EHR) and practice management (PM) system. This task may also include charges for the exam and other services, possibly screening retinal photos, contact lens services and contact lens products.

It can work quite well to begin a patient's fee slip in the exam room or optical dispensary and enter fees as services are provided or products are sold. But some PM systems are rather cumbersome when it comes to closing out the fee slip. There may be diagnosis codes to enter, insurance plans to transfer to, discounts to be applied, payments to be posted and that all could be on a line by line basis. Watch the time element of this and if it takes opticians a long time to complete, consider having some or all of the billing process handled by the front desk staff.

Of course, that creates more work for the front desk staff and it could be shifting the work from one place to another, but I'm very protective about the patient experience. In some cases, the data entry can be saved until a time after the patient leaves and the office is not so busy. There must be a good system for this, however, such as a walkout receipt for the patient and a method to be sure the charges are not overlooked.

You could design a specialized superbill for each vision plan you accept that has the names of optical products and places for other fees like exams, contact lenses, and retinal screenings. The optician can write the usual and customary fees in one column and what the patient owes for each item (if any) in a second column. The difference is simply billed to the vision plan. Your staff also needs the printed benefit authorization from the vision plan for complete pricing information. We use a different superbill for medical eye care which has CPT and ICD-10 codes preprinted.

Don't place the optical order at point of sale

Some ODs have the opticians place the eyeglass order to the lab directly through the vision plan claims website while the patient waits. My staff is pretty fast at filing eyeglass orders electronically, but I would not want that happening in front of the patient. We have a specialized staff for our in-office optical lab and their job is to manage all aspects of the eyeglass orders, whether it goes through a vision plan or if we make the glasses in our lab. We have an administrative assistant in the lab who enters all online vision plan orders.

Our opticians quickly write up eyeglass orders on an order form that is prepopulated with the patients name and new Rx. The paper form is half-page size (5.5 by 8.5 inches), which fits into an optical job tray.

12.15 Next: Let's Speed Up Your Check-Out Process

I got a nice response to my last article on speeding up the check-in process, but a very sharp OD (whom I happen to know) emailed me and said she needed more help with her check-out process; not check-in. I understand and agree; that part of the patient experience is also very important and it is extremely slow in many practices.

Checking-out may not get the attention it deserves from doctors because it does not slow down their patient flow and they have generally moved on to the next patient, but there are two big reasons why you should still care.

Why worry about it?

The two big reasons to make your check-out process quicker are:

1. Customer service. Look at your check-out procedure from the patient's point of view. Patients are most likely tired by the time they get back to your front desk at the end of the visit. They have typically spent over an hour in your office. They may have just spent a great deal of money. It is important that the last interaction with your practice is a good one. It will color how the patient feels about you and it may impact what they tell others. Patients don't care or understand about coding procedures or office computer software, but you have a chance to let them leave feeling very good about your practice... or not.
2. Reduce financial errors and potential embezzlement. The truth is that the data entry required by many office software systems is quite complex and the process is slow. So much so, that many staff members don't even try to enter the information with the patient standing in front of them. Many offices have evolved into a procedure where the staff member gives the patient a handwritten paper receipt and sets the paperwork aside to enter later. While efficient and in line with the patient's need to get back to his busy life, it is a bad practice. It is extremely easy for those charges to be forgotten and accidentally never entered. This delayed entry process can also be a temptation to steal. No one likes to think that their employees would be dishonest, but we all know it happens. If cash is collected but the patient's account does not reflect the charges and payment, there is no record of the money. Printing an accurate receipt from the accounting system (whether it's a software program or a cash register) is a key component of business security.

How to speed up the check-out

Start by observing the process in your office. Ask your staff to walk you through what they have to do as they check out a patient. What can you do to speed the whole thing up?

- Change the setup. Can you reduce the size of drop down lists of products and codes so staff can find what they need faster?
- Staff training. Can the staff be faster at data entry? Do they fully understand insurance processing and billing and coding?
- Do you have enough staff? Are your staff too busy and no one is available at the check-out point? Should you begin to have your staff specialize so some employees are very good at the process?
- Organization. Do you have an in-office fee slip that has all the procedures, products diagnosis codes, recall dates and out of pocket fees clearly detailed?

- Who does what? Can the technician or optician prepare most of the fee slip before going to the front desk so the receptionist only has to retrieve it? Can the technician be sure the fees and payments are correct and review them with the patient before going to the front desk?
- Prepare in advance. Do you have all the insurance benefits confirmed? Can you have most of the office work done and most printed materials ready when the patient checks out?

The check-out process is one of several influence points within the patient experience in your practice. Be sure it lives up to perception you want to create.

12.16 Your Patient Walkout Receipt

In my management consulting work with optometrists, I notice that it is quite common to furnish the patient with a receipt for services and products rendered that is not very impressive. Most optometric practices use office management software that provides a full accounting of fees, payments and amounts billed to insurance plans. These software programs can print a very nice financial summary for the patient, but in many cases, the entering of the fees, diagnosis and procedure codes, co-pays, and transferring of some fees to insurance plans is so time consuming that the office staff gives the patient a hand-written receipt at the end of a visit and returns for the actual accounting work later. My own practice has struggled with this process as well.

As challenging and time-consuming as the process may be, I think practice owners and managers must work toward entering all the fees, payments and credits at the time of service with the patient still in the office. It is important for the staff to hand the patient a printed financial walkout statement from the office software system. Let's explore the factors involved.

The patient experience
The financial walkout statement and receipt is an important document for the patient and it should reflect the high quality your office stands for. This document represents the services provided and the products that were purchased. It shows the amounts the patient paid out-of-pocket and the amounts billed to insurance that are still pending. The document shows the name of the doctor, diagnosis information, tests performed, next exam date and other important information about the practice, such as the website

address. The walkout statement may be the only document the patient keeps after an eye exam and it can serve as a public relations piece.

The entire transaction at an office visit can be fairly expensive and patients will study the receipt, show it to others and keep it in their personal records. A copy of the walkout statement may be used by the patient for many purposes, such as submitting out-of-network insurance claims, filing for flex-spending plans, and submitting to optical vendors for rebates.

I recommend you review the financial walkout documents that are currently being issued by your staff. In many cases, you may find they are handwritten copies of fee slips or superbills that have amounts scratched out, are rewritten multiple times and it may be the second or third copy of no-carbon required paper, which has very poor quality. This is not the image you want your patients to have of your practice.

Reliable systems

It is simply good business practice to enter all sales into the office software system with the patient still present in the office. Here is why:

- Recording the information on a paper form and then entering it into a workstation is double-entry and inefficient.
- It is very likely that staff will forget to come back and enter some fees properly, which results in not getting paid for services and products.
- The office software system typically has default fees and checks math, so entering and transferring fees to insurance reduces errors. It is best to find and correct any errors with the patient still present.
- Entering fees and payments into the software system and printing the receipt for the patients reduces the chance of employee theft and embezzlement.

Watch the wait time

I find that there is usually a good reason why staff members perform tasks a certain way. If you want to change the procedure, it is important to find out why they did things the old way. In the case of printing walkout statements, it may be quite time consuming for staff to enter all the information the software requires. And the staff may also be answering phones and greeting other patients.

Be aware that patients who are checking out may have already been in your office for over an hour. They may be tired and blurry. They may be running late for another appointment or work. At this point in their visit, they may really want to leave your office! An employee who is methodically entering a huge amount of data can be very annoying! Your staff may have sensed that, which led them to handing the patient a handwritten receipt. Don't make the situation worse by requiring staff to perform a very inefficient task that creates a poor image for the whole practice.

Simplify
Every office software system is different, but spend some time observing your staff in action as they enter patient data. See what you can do to speed up their process. Ask other ODs who use the same system how they handle the walkout receipt. Ask customer service at the software vendor what they recommend and ask if they can improve the process in a future update.

Here are some things to look at:

- Try to make the drop-down lists of products and services shorter. Or change the list so frequently used items are at the top.
- See if there is some data that could be entered later, but still allow the critical fees and payments to be entered now in order to print the receipt.
- Have the scribe start the fee slip in the exam room, enter some services and fees, and put the fee slip on hold so the front desk staff can retrieve it and add to it.
- Have opticians enter the optical products directly into the fee slip as the items are sold in optical. Add workstations if needed.
- You may need to hire more staff at the front desk so a person doing checkout is not pulled away to handle other tasks.

12.17 Collecting Patient Accounts Receivable

Even though your office policy probably requires patients to pay for any charges that are not billed to insurance, odds are good you have some significant balances due on the non-insurance side of your ledgers. Here is a look at the best techniques to collect amounts due long after the patient has left your office.

The new goal

Once you classify a patient's debt as past due, the immediate goal is for a staff member in your practice to speak to him or her over the phone. Speaking to the patient in person is the key to better collections, but there are two big factors working against this goal.

- Many of the people who are late with their payments do not answer the phone. They use voice mail to screen calls and they don't return messages.
- Placing calls to patients with past due accounts is one of the least pleasant jobs in your office. It is quite likely that the staff person assigned to the task will find many other duties that take precedence. It is very easy to put the job off.

In spite of those obstacles, real money is at stake and the services have already been provided, so the time spent on collection is well worth the effort. And the chances of successful collection are best if you make a personal connection with the debtor and appeal to his sense of fairness. You want to call upon your past strong relationship and use the fact that the patient will need you again in the future. The best way to do that is for the patient to speak directly to a staff member over the phone.

Overcome the two factors above by choosing a very good employee and meeting with her frequently to monitor the status of accounts receivable. An office manager should play an important role in this effort. The reluctance of the debtor to take phone calls can be worn down by repetition. If your staff member continues to leave messages day after day, it may become embarrassing (and annoying) and the patient may eventually answer or return the call. Once the patient realizes that you are not going to let the matter drift, he will be more likely to respond. But let a week or two pass between communications and the debtor realizes that he can easily ignore the bill.

What to say

When your collections manager finally speaks to the debtor over the phone, it is best to take a friendly exploratory approach at first. Many past due debts are because the patient was not satisfied with the service or product. Additionally, it is quite possible that your office made an accounting or billing error. These issues must be resolved first and then you have a good chance of collecting.

The first step in the phone call is for your staff member to review the services and charges and see if the patient agrees that the amount is due. Once you have that confirmation, you simply remind the person that the balance is long past due and must be paid immediately. Try to take a credit card number over the phone or at least get a firm date when the amount can be paid. Try to collect the full amount of the balance, but if you have to make payment arrangements, try to get authorization to process a credit card at specific dates for three installments or accept three post-dated checks to hold and deposit.

Train your staff to be discreet about leaving messages with other household members or co-workers of the patient that reveal a past due debt. These are private matters and you should only speak to the debtor or guarantor.

Send statements and letters

Of course, since you can't always speak to the debtor by phone, have form letters ready to be customized and mailed which detail the past due amount and also continue to send regular statements with interest accruing every month. Letters may start out friendly and may get tougher if the debt is ignored. At some point you may threaten legal action, damage to the credit rating and the end of eye care services at your office.

Keep records

It is extremely important to write down all the details and promises. Follow-up with another phone call and letter on the specific day something was due but did not happen. You must create the impression that your office does not forget.

Tempting to farm it out

Many doctors, managers and staffers hope to find another way to resolve the collections challenge and it's easy to understand why. My experience and that of many colleagues I've spoken with tell me that collection agencies don't usually work very well. I've also tried using a local attorney to send letters on law firm stationery with limited success. It is much easier for the patient to ignore a strange company he has no relationship with than to ignore your office staff. The best way to collect is to keep the task within your office.

The law

Always comply with any state laws that may exist protecting the consumer in the collection process and which specify how you may apply interest. Check your state government website under consumer credit.

It is far better to prevent balances from getting to the accounts receivable ledger than it is to try to collect after the fact. Next week's tip will cover ideas for collecting in the office at the time of service and preventing unpaid insurance balances from going back to the patient.

12.18 Preventing Patient Accounts Receivable

Last week's tip focused on collecting past due balances from patients, but it would be far better to prevent the debts from occurring in the first place. So let's examine the most common reasons why unpaid amounts end up on the patient's ledger in the first place and what steps you can take to collect more fees at the time of service.

Office policy

I assume you have a policy that requires all fees (not billed to insurance plans) to be paid at the time of service or, in the case of optical products, that balances are paid at the time of dispensing.

If you don't have a policy like that, implement it today. There is simply no reason to offer credit directly through your office when national credit card firms are so plentiful and easy to do business with. It doesn't matter if your practice is in a small town or if the local population has lower incomes, there is no need to offer any payment plans. Any slight improvement in sales will be offset by bad debt that you end up working to collect and then writing off.

How does bad debt happen?

Even with a pay as you go policy, there will still be plenty of dollars owed to your practice by individual patients. Here's why:

- Services that are billed to an insurance plan are not paid as expected (or as hoped) and the amount is transferred back to the patient. Of course, there may be contractual agreements that prevent this transfer back, but in many cases it is allowed, especially if an advanced beneficiary notice is signed.
- Special circumstances cause staff or doctor to make an exception to the payment policy. This might be a patient with financial problems or it might be a patient who wants to purchase several very expensive items at once and asks for credit.
- The patient does not know that the fees are due. One example might be a patient who thought his exam would be covered by insurance but is told at checkout that it will not. Or the teenager who stops in to pick up his new glasses with no parent and does not bring a check.

How to prevent bad debt

Here are my suggestions for how to minimize patient accounts receivable, especially due to the reasons noted above.

- You can't always prevent insurance from not paying, but it can be minimized if you only participate with plans that you know are easy to work with. Drop plans that are unpredictable.
- Get tougher on what you agree to bill to insurance. When you have a choice, just tell the patient that a special service is not covered and that the fee is due at the time the work is done. Doctors often assume that the patient will opt out of care if it is not covered, but I find that to be very rare. Let the patient file his own claim to be reimbursed. For example, I don't bill medical insurance for contact lens fitting for keratoconus.
- Use an advance beneficiary notice whenever you want the patient to know that insurance will not cover a service. Medicare and some plans may have specific forms and wording, so check the carrier website.
- Be firm on your policies. You can still provide excellent customer service and not offend patients; in fact patients will respect your integrity when they test you and find you can't (or won't) bend the rules. You'll be surprised to find the vast majority of people who ask for special payment options still get out the credit card or checkbook when they are told no.
- If you sell very expensive products or services, look into national consumer credit firms. Your office gives the patient a simple application form and faxes it in for financing approval within minutes. Your practice pays a fee for the financing but you are paid in full right away. Several of these companies specialize in health care.
- Tell patients in advance if fees will be due. I've written about this many times; just tell people the fee in advance and most problems are eliminated.
- Know how to handle awkward situations. That teenager who comes in to pick up the glasses was probably sent by a parent who knows your policy of requiring payment. The kid may not know or may know and act dumb, but when we are faced with that, we do not dispense the glasses or contact lenses without payment. We simply apologize profusely for not having told the patient about the policy (even though we know we did) and we suggest calling Mom for a credit card number. If that doesn't work, we offer to hold the item until he can return with the payment. And we apologize again.

12.19 Who is Managing Your Accounts Receivable?

Accounts receivable (AR) is one aspect of the practice that no one really likes. Practice owners generally agree that far too much money is owed to the practice by insurance companies, the federal government and patients. Staff members given the job of reviewing accounts receivable aging reports are not always sure what to do when people or insurance plans don't pay. Given this unpleasant scenario, it is common for doctors and staff to procrastinate about managing AR. A few months could easily pass before anyone looks at the AR reports. If that describes your office, let's turn over a new leaf and develop better habits with AR; it will save you thousands of dollars.

Accounts receivable is one aspect of the practice that no one really likes. Practice owners generally agree that far too much money is owed to the practice by insurance companies, the federal government and patients. Staff members given the job of reviewing accounts receivable aging reports are not always sure what to do when people or insurance plans don't pay. Given this unpleasant scenario, it is common for doctors and staff to procrastinate about managing AR. A few months could easily pass before anyone looks at the AR reports. If that describes your office, let's turn over a new leaf and develop better habits with AR; it will save you thousands of dollars.

Diligence and a calendar

Many of the problems with accounts receivable can be overcome with basic organization. The task of managing the AR aging reports must be assigned to a competent staff person who understands the importance of the job, and that person should be supervised by the practice owner or a manager to be sure the job is done on an ongoing basis. The best way to accomplish this is to have meetings scheduled on the calendar to meet and review AR aging reports. I suggest twice per month as the optimum interval, but one of those meetings could be very brief if procedures are followed.

As a review, accounts receivable is the term used for all fees that are owed to your practice. If your office management system is used properly to enter all charges and accept payments, then the system will produce a current AR aging report at any time. The AR aging report shows who owes money and how long it has been due. There is typically one AR report for patients and another report for insurance plans. I think it is best to print both of these reports so they can be reviewed at the meetings and notes can be written.

Insurance AR research

Before the meetings, it is the staff person's job to research every account that has a balance of over 30 days old. This research asks the question: why was this balance not paid yet? If the money is owed by an insurance plan, here are some steps to take:

- Was the claim submitted and did the practice receive any payment and an explanation of benefits (EOB) statement? If so, read the EOB and see if any amounts were rejected and if so, why? Take the time to read the comment codes on each line item that refers to a reason.
- For purposes of the meeting with the manager or doctor, make notes on each account about the reason why the balance was not paid.
- The reasons may be administrative, such as the provider is not known or a form was not completed properly.
- The reasons could be that the diagnosis code does not match with the procedure performed.
- There might be an insurance deductible that was applied and the insurance will not pay.
- The insurance AR is where you can really learn a lot about medical billing and coding. Find out what you did wrong in each case that did not pay and don't make the mistake again.
- Resubmit claims with corrections whenever possible.
- Transfer balances that are now payable by the patient (like deductible amounts) to the patient's personal account.
- Keep a log book about insurance plan rules and what they pay and don't pay.
- Implement office policies as needed to prevent payment problems in the future. Discuss these policies at staff meetings.

Patient AR research

A different research effort should be made on the patient AR report for balances over 30 days.

- Did the patient pick up their glasses or contacts? The balance may by quite normal and will be paid at dispensing, but why is it taking so long? Are the optical materials on back order? Was the order placed? Was the patient notified?

- Were invoices or statements mailed so the patient is aware of the balance due? When? It is usual practice to allow the patient 30 days to pay a bill from the time they receive it.
- Was the balance transferred back to the patient from insurance that did not pay as expected?
- Why did the patient not pay for services and products at the time of service?
- If you find that the patient owes the money and has not paid, a staff member should call and speak to the person directly. But go easy on this call; your office could have made a mistake. Look at the first call as fact finding. Is the patient aware of the balance? Is there some reason why the office has not received payment? If the patient has no complaint and acknowledges he owes the balance, find out when it will be paid.
- If there is a complaint, the staff members can handle it according to office policy or note it for discussion at the meetings.
- Make notes in a log book about all phone calls and letters sent and promises made. Follow-up as needed.

Collections and write-offs
Once you get accounts receivable under control, you will see that managing it is not so bad after all. I've never had good luck with collection agencies, so I usually manage the collection effort with my staff in house. In some cases, either by decision or because it just not-collectable, you can choose to simply write off a balance. When we write-off a balance in my practice, we place a notation in the patient's record about the amount and if the patient ever wants to be seen again, we require payment of the past due amount. It happens more often than you might think.

12.20 Who should present optional screening tests?

This week's article asks a question that I don't really have the answer to, but I've been studying the matter closely and I can present some pros and cons for your consideration. And of course, I always like to hear from readers about their experience. I'll report back with a summary of your input in a future article.

Many eye care providers (ECPs) offer optional special screening tests to patients, not covered by medical insurance or vision plans, for an additional fee. Typically the fee is nominal and designed to encourage a large number of patients to opt in and agree to the test. This allows patients who have basic routine vision coverage to obtain the most advanced technology in eye care. Patients with medical insurance have access to screening tests that are never covered without a medical diagnosis. Many ECPs report patient acceptance rates of 75% or higher, which validates the concept of special screening tests. But acceptance rates can vary widely and I believe the manner in which the test is offered can have a huge effect. What's your experience?

Typical screening tests

Here are a few of the more commonly performed exam upgrade tests:

- Digital Retinal photography
- Optos
- Macular pigment optical density test
- GDX or OCT screening
- Automated visual field screening
- Corneal topography
- Others – what optional test do you offer?

When, where and by whom the test option is offered to the patient is an important consideration. Here are some pros and cons for three possibilities.

Receptionist presents the option to the patient at check-in

- Typically, the receptionist will present a printed handout form that describes the test and the fee and asks the patient to check yes or no and initial or sign the form.
- The form prevents misunderstandings and provides proof that the patient authorized the test.
- The form presents a practice-approved message about the test and can also provide sample images.
- The patient has a chance to read about the test and think it over.
- The patient has a chance to confer with a spouse or other party.
- It offers the patient a graceful way to decline. While the goal of the practice may be to have more patients accept screening tests, think carefully about the patient experience and crossing the line to being pushy.
- Patients may tend to stand at the front desk to read the educational handout form, blocking access by other patients and creating an awkward situation.

- Patients may ask questions about the screening test to receptionists who are not as well trained in clinical eye care as technicians.

Technician presents the option during pretesting

- The technician has a better understanding about the nature of the test and what it does.
- The technician may have an incentive to discourage acceptance of the test because it is just more work for her. This may be especially true if the office is running behind schedule.
- Explaining the screening test in the pretest room takes more time and could cause a bottleneck to patient flow and block access to the room by others.
- The patient may feel put on the spot. There is little time to understand the test and the patient may feel forced to give a verbal answer quickly.

Doctor presents the option in the exam room

- May result in the highest patient acceptance rate because recommendations from the doctor carry more weight.
- The doctor can provide case-specific reasons why the test is advisable.
- Associate doctors may not have an interest in recommending some screening tests.
- The test results are not available before the doctor's portion of the exam. It is helpful to see most data before the exam and the doctor may have to see the patient twice if the test is to be reviewed and discussed.
- If the patient is dilated, some tests may have a better outcome after dilation, rather than in pretesting.

Regardless of how you offer screening tests now, it may be smart to experiment in your practice with the various options. It could reveal a method with better patient acceptance, improved efficiency or a less confrontational approach. Simply try different procedures and track the acceptance rate and revenue production for each over a period of a couple weeks. Advise staff members that you are testing different methods and ask for their feedback on each. Listen and observe patient reactions.

12.21 Employee Theft

I'll bet this title got your attention and rightfully so. I think all practice owners and managers are aware that theft by employees most likely occurs in every practice, including their own. But how do you know how prevalent it is? And what can you do to prevent it?

What can be stolen?

Employee theft can occur in many ways; some not so obvious. The first step in preventing theft is to assume it is probably occurring in your practice to some degree already. To some extent, it is a cost of doing business, but I believe employers should make a strong effort to prevent theft before it becomes a major problem.

Consider if your practice is vulnerable in the following areas:

- Cash. With most payments now in the form of credit cards, checks and insurance drafts, your exposure to losing cash is decreasing, but it is still by far the most attractive thing to steal. Cash can be stolen from your cash drawer or from a bank account when one employee has too much authority to transfer funds and write checks.
- Fraud. One example might be an employee who sells optical products to friends under the table, so to speak. Eyeglasses are ordered through your lab supplier but no charges are ever entered for a patient. The employee (who always receives deliveries) retrieves the glasses when they arrive and delivers them to the buyer away from your office. The employee is paid privately for the glasses at a greatly discounted price. You would have to really scrutinize the lab invoices to notice this is going on.
- Products. Employees can easily take products for their own personal use or their loved ones. This may include sunglasses, contact lenses, prescription drugs, low vision aids or anything else that's sold in your office.
- Supplies. A common theft category is in the form of office supplies. From copy paper to toilet paper and from alcohol swabs to coffee, supplies are easy to take home.
- Premiums, discounts and gifts. We often hear of employees making special deals with frame distributors and optical labs so they can personally receive free gifts in exchange for placing orders. I view these premiums as rightfully belonging to the practice. Even complimentary products or extreme discounts could be viewed as a form of theft if the benefit is not provided to all employees equally.
- Time. Perhaps the most invisible form of theft is embezzlement of time. This could range from falsifying a time sheet or punching in for an absent friend to just wasting time while at work. The personal use

of cell phones or office computers for texting, email, checking Facebook, internet surfing, and playing games are all forms of time theft.

Prevention

In many cases, the techniques that are used for detection of theft are also a deterrent to theft. People don't want to be caught. If employees realize that management is aware and monitoring operations, theft is too risky.

- Culture. Having a positive organizational culture that is built on fairness and respect won't guarantee a theft-free workplace, but it will go a long way in keeping basically honest people from taking advantage. Many people will steal as a form of evening the score if they believe they are being mistreated.
- Policy. Develop strong office policies that must always be followed, which in turn reduces the temptation for theft. For example, be sure that staff members always print receipts for patients as they check out. Charges and payments that are held to be posted later make it too easy to overlook the posting and keep the money. Or turn a check in and take cash out.
- Checks and balances. Have a routine that requires financial accuracy. The daily production report must always balance exactly with the cash drawer at the end of the day. Have two working cash trays with a predetermined amount of cash to start the day so the other cash drawer always stays with that day's production report until it is balanced. Any over or under cash amounts must be explained. Bank deposits should always match the day's receipts exactly in the form of cash, checks and credit card payments. Bank deposit receipts are returned to the owner and monitored.
- Spot checks. Make a habit of routinely checking patient's account ledgers with the orders that are in the patient record. You can also check office computers to see what websites have been visited recently by your staff; just press CTRL H on any computer when the internet browser program is open and see what pops up.
- Control authority. Be careful with who has the authority to write off account balances. Adjusting account balances is very common with insurance plans, but anyone who can write off balances has a great deal of power.
- Good records. Keep an eye on frame inventory and track sales and total number of frames.
- Multiple people. It is best to not have just one person always performing a job if possible. Theft occurs when no one else will notice.

- Limited people. On the other hand, allowing everyone to work with cash or inventory opens you up for poor accountability. Theft occurs when there are many people who could have done it.
- Supervision. A manager who supervises operations can greatly reduce opportunities for embezzlement.
- The practice owner should always monitor accounts payable and sign or approve all checks.
- Locks. It seems obvious, but locked drawers, cabinets and closets work well to prevent theft.
- Video camera security systems. Video camera systems are actually quite affordable today and they are a strong deterrent to theft. There are do-it-yourself systems that can be easily installed or you can work with a local security company. Camera feeds run 24 hours per day and are viewable on a monitor and recorded on digital video recorders with large capacity hard drives. The videos from each camera can be stored for several days on the DVR and segments can be located by date and time and reviewed in fast forward mode. Many offices will have four to sixteen cameras positioned in key locations to monitor cash and inventory. Of course, these systems are also strong deterrents to shoplifting by the general public and can help assist in the event a theft or burglary occurs. Some cameras can also pick up audio and are useful in staff training. These systems can be accessed via the internet and the practice owner can view operations from any computer anywhere in the world. They can even be viewed on your cell phone!

Once you know
If you are certain that embezzlement has occurred, I would discuss the matter with an attorney familiar with employment law before taking any action. Accusing someone of theft and firing him or her over it can lead to more legal problems, especially if you can't prove it.

12.22 The Appointment Manager Concept

Here is an idea that may help your practice to be more productive and increase gross and net revenue. Assign a staff member to actively monitor and manage the patient appointment schedule. Many practice owners may think they already have this in the form of receptionists or front desk personnel, but I often find that many appointment slots still go unfilled due to late cancellations or slightly low demand. The value of filling the patient schedule every day is huge! If you filled one last minute cancellation or open appointment slot per day, your practice could generate an additional $91,000 of gross practice revenue per year (based on mean exam revenue of $350).

Job description

The primary goal of the appointment manager is to keep all doctors in the practice fully booked, with special attention given to today and tomorrow. This staff member actively manages a call list and also contacts any patient who is currently on the schedule in the future and offers the sooner appointment time. Additionally, the appointment manager would handle all recall efforts and other promotions that result in appointments. This staff member would call patients who do not respond to standard recall messages or who cancel pre-appointments. These calls must be made with a great deal of tact and sensitivity to avoid creating a negative image for the practice.

The call list is an important resource for proactively filling empty appointment slots. This is a list of patients who would like to be called if an appointment opens up that is sooner than the one they currently have reserved. All staff members who schedule appointments should contribute to the list by asking every patient who schedules an appointment, but indicates that he would have preferred a different date and time or a sooner date in general, if he would like to be placed on the call list. The concept could even be expanded by asking all patients if they would like to be contacted if an earlier appointment is available, not just those who are unhappy with their time slot. The call list should contain cell phone numbers or text and email preferences so your office can get in touch with the patient as fast as possible with the fewest voice mail messages.

In an aggressive situation to fill empty time slots that are coming due soon, the appointment manager may call any patients who are booked ahead in the schedule, possibly even with a different doctor, and ask if they are interested in an appointment time that opened up.

Some practice owners may choose to provide some kind of incentive or bonus to the appointment manager (or to all employees) if the goal of a completely full schedule is achieved for a day. That will work but I'm not convinced it is necessary. I have a problem with paying staff more to do their basic job. I believe in monitoring performance on the job and providing lots of feedback and, of course, raises are in order when a job is well done. But we won't quibble on this point; bonus payments or not, an appointment manager can help your practice.

Depending on the size of your practice and your current staffing needs, you may just assign the appointment manager job as an additional duty to one employee. It could just be a part time side job that has a special focus. Or you could create a new position and give the appointment manager a dedicated workspace away from the front desk. This gives the job the importance it deserves, and it creates an environment that is conducive to making many phone calls without interruption. The appointment manager could be part of a "call center" in your office, which is an approach that is growing in popularity and offers other advantages. I'll cover call centers next week. If you create a new position for appointment manager, consider moving a veteran staff member who knows your procedures and patients into that job and bringing in a new person as a receptionist.

Why can't all staff do it?

To take the concept a step further, consider these points that illustrate why you may be better off dedicating one specialist to managing appointments.

- Offices get very busy. With current staff busy answering phones and taking care of patients, time passes and a late cancellation can easily be neglected. Staff must prioritize their actions and if they are busy with patients, trying to fill tomorrow's vacant slot will go unheeded. The appointment manager would have the time to do the job well.
- It is human nature for employees to not really want the appointment schedule full. A full schedule means more work and more stress. Of course, staff members understand that it is part of their job and if there is plenty of supervision, they will fill the empty slot, but recognize the tendency to not get around to it, especially as the time grows near.
- One person is accountable. In practices with many staff members, it is easy to assume someone else will take care of tasks like calling patients.
- Special skills and training. The appointment manager should be very good on the telephone. We want someone who is friendly, likeable and has good communication skills.
- Experience is the best teacher. When one person works repeatedly and frequently on the task of calling people and filling appointment slots, she gets very good at it.
- A dedicated process. When the job description is formalized, you will develop a specific protocol for how to handle last minute vacant slots. Most practices take a simple approach like... if we have any cancellations, we try to fill them. That could mean wait until someone calls and asks for an appointment and see if he can take the empty slot. That seems like not enough effort to me.

12.23 Appointment Confirmations: A Good Job Will Increase Your Income

Most optometric offices confirm appointments; at least that was the plan originally. It's a good idea to be a stickler on this task because it is very common for the confirmation effort to decline as staff members get busy. If confirmations are done effectively, they can result in producing $30,000 additional revenue per year for the average practice (5% of $600,000). An appointment slot that passes with no patient is production that is lost forever.

Let's review an effective plan for appointment confirmation.

Phone, text or email

I think it is smart to use all three methods of communication. Email is the primary method for confirming appointments in my practice, but a smaller group of patients love text messages and don't use email as much. Electronic messages have a few strong advantages over telephone:

- We have a better chance of reaching the patient because email and text usually goes to the individual and not the household like the telephone. Also, the message remains as a visible reminder in the inbox, unlike voice mail which is usually gone after it is listened to.
- The email or text asks the recipient to click on a button within the message to confirm the appointment. This action shows up on your office software dashboard as confirmed and no further effort is needed by your staff. We know these patients received our message and they are planning to show up.
- Links are provided within the message to the practice website and a button takes patients to history forms to complete before the appointment. Additional information about the upcoming visit can be customized and provided, including a map.
- Email and text messages from a doctor's office are impressive and can get patients talking to others about your practice.

The easiest way to use email and text to confirm appointments is to subscribe to one of the software programs that specialize in electronic communication. Some of the best known companies are Websystem3, Solutionreach, Demandforce and 4PatientCare. You need a large number of email addresses for your patients to make this work, but your staff should be gathering that information on nearly every patient seen.

Of course, email and text is still not perfectly reliable for everyone, so our staff uses the telephone to contact any patient who is not confirmed by email. Using the appointment scheduling module in our practice management software, we click next to each appointment to indicate contacted, no answer or left message.

Automated voice phone calls are also quite effective in the confirmation process and they can be surprisingly pleasant. My staff has plenty of downtime during the day when we are not seeing patients and I like to have side jobs for them, so we have no problem making these calls personally.

No shows

An excellent confirmation system will drastically reduce no shows. If you have more than 5% of appointments ending up as a very last minute cancellation or no show, you should carefully review your confirmation procedure and consider modifying it. Confirmation efforts are extremely important for practices that use pre-appointing for routine exams.

If no shows are excessive, consider asking for patients to confirm your confirmation. This happens automatically with email, but most phone confirmations are simply left as voice mail with no response. You could ask the patient to call your office back and confirm the appointment, but many people just ignore this request. On some days with very high demand, like Saturdays, you may want to require that the patient call you back to confirm, or the appointment will be cancelled.

I don't care for threats to charge a fee for no shows in most cases, but every practice is different and some with unusually high patient demand may have to go to extreme measures. In the vast majority of cases, practices need more patients and they need very patient-friendly policies to increase demand through referrals. In addition to a stronger confirmation effort, another way to decrease the impact of no shows is to speed up the doctor's portion of the exam and schedule more patients per day. Double-booking appointments that are not actively confirmed or are suspect for some other reason is also a good strategy.

Start early enough

Many offices make their confirmation calls the day before the appointment, but that does not really allow enough time to fill any appointments that are vacated. It is best to send the email or text message about 3 days in advance. If the appointment is not confirmed by the patient, I would make the phone calls two days before the appointment.

Supervise and personalize the effort
It's important that an office manager or the doctor spot check that confirmations are really getting done. Staff members may drop the procedure or simply forget to do it. In some cases, employees may actually like to see more no shows because it makes their work day easier.

If more than one staff member works on confirmation phone calls, be sure to have them initial the schedule or call list so there is no confusion where each one thinks the other is doing the job.

12.24 The Call Center Concept

Last week's tip covered the idea of using a dedicated appointment manager in your practice to keep appointment slots filled. That strategy dovetails very well with another concept that some practices are starting to adopt: the call center. A call center can improve customer service and improve efficiency at the front desk.

What is it?
A call center is an office workspace that is separate from the front desk area, dedicated to receiving incoming telephone calls and placing outgoing calls. Staff members are assigned to work the call center and take the majority of the telephone burden off the front desk staff, allowing them to concentrate on patients in the office and other business office tasks. The main employee in the call center could be an appointment manager as described in Tip # 438.

The call center staff should be well trained as telephone specialists. Customer service orientation, strong communication skills and a pleasant attitude are very important. They manage the appointment schedule, answer questions about services and fees, check to see if optical products are ready to pick up, take messages and route calls to other staff members as needed. Scripts may be supplied to this staff as needed to improve patient communications.

Call center personnel can also place outgoing calls for appointment confirmations, recall follow-ups, product satisfaction checks, and many other functions. Additional administrative tasks can be assigned to fill in downtime as needed, such as insurance billing, accounts receivable follow-up, and data entry.

When does it make sense?

A call center makes sense for a practice that is growing faster than its office space and staff size allows. If you feel like you need more front desk staff but have no place to put them, consider this concept. It could work well for you if customer service seems to suffer because the front desk staff is always too busy and patients line up to check in and checkout.

Many offices have some adjacent unused space that is not practical for patient care, but could be well utilized for administrative functions. This space may be on a second floor, a basement, or a back office area that is not finished as nicely as your public spaces. I would invest in some sprucing up of the area to make it suitable for staff to work. Make sure it is neat, clean and comfortable and well lit. You'll need desks or work counters and bookshelves

Satellite offices

Practices with multiple locations can put the call center concept to very good work by having a centralized staff to handle all incoming calls and to manage appointments for all the offices. Be sure to monitor customer service closely in these situations, since a remote call center staff may not be as knowledgeable about another office location and checking on the status of eyewear and contact lenses may be more challenging. But generally, the concept works very well.

Incoming call backup plan

Of course, a single staff call center member (or even several) can all be on calls when another phone line rings. The staff can manage this by asking if a caller can hold briefly. There should be a policy for handling multiple calls at once, such as the front desk will pick up if a call reaches four rings.

Beware of automated systems

Automated phone answering and menu routing systems are becoming quite common in businesses today, but I don't know any caller who likes them. I prefer to have adequate human staff who provide a warm and welcoming response. Having said that, a call center may be able to use some automation if it is well-managed and hold times are kept brief. There are some excellent automated voice systems for appointment confirmations and text and email systems work well for this also. Just look at the process from the patient's point of view and be sure to provide the personal touch whenever possible.

12.25 The Patient's Point of View

Regular readers of this column know that I believe customer service is the single biggest factor for increasing practice revenue production. Excellent customer service is the basis for all things that are good in a practice: patient loyalty, higher fee structure, more word-of-mouth referrals and reduced reliance on vision plans. Yet, as important as customer service is, most practices are just mediocre in this regard. I know my practice could be much better at customer service and I'm obsessed with it. I know how easy it is for great service to erode when your staff is faced with a busy day or they've brought some personal problems to work with them.

Here is a technique that I use to stay on track with customer service. I teach my staff to think this way all the time. It really just follows the Golden Rule that we all learned as children, but it turns out that rule fits quite well in business.

My practice motto

I have a motto that I use internally in my practice: "We look at everything we do from the patient's point of view." As much as possible, I set policies and handle live situations with an effort to do things the way the patient would like. It's really pretty easy to determine what the patient would like when you think about it, but most practice owners and managers don't think about it. Most office policies and procedures are based on the wants and needs of the staff or the doctor; not the patient. In business, your wants and needs are secondary.

As an exercise in reviewing your customer service level, consider your office procedures from the patient's point of view. A great way to do this is to follow every step in a typical patient experience; from the first phone call to the actual office visit to financial transactions to picking up optical products. Be objective and be tough on yourself. Review this with your staff and ask their opinions. Focus especially on areas where patients have been known to complain occasionally.

Review the following policies and ask yourself what the patient would like in each instance.

- What are your office hours ... especially evenings, Saturdays and those odd half days off? (Remember ... the patient's point of view).
- What happens during lunch breaks?
- How do you decide on billing a vision plan or medical insurance?

- How often do you begin a patient's visit within five minutes of the appointment time?
- How long is the history questionnaire and must it be completed at every comprehensive exam visit?
- When are patients told about the contact lens evaluation fee... over the phone or when they are checking out?
- If patients arrive at the office ten minutes before posted office hours, is the door locked?

I'm sure as you read the list above you have very good reasons for doing things the way you do them. Experience has shown me that there are always alternative methods that work just fine as well. Don't be stuck in your ways. Times change and we must be innovative and ask: how can we do it better? How would patients like us to handle it?

Patients are smarter than you think

As you review your policies, be wary of clever business strategies that you have implemented that may be more obvious than you think. Patients are very smart. Many own businesses themselves or work for companies in management positions. They can spot a business move a mile away. They will be too polite to embarrass you or your staff at the time, but they form impressions about your integrity and your motives.

I'll use an example to illustrate my point. An optometrist trains her staff to preappoint all patients at checkout and has provided scripts to assist with the process. A 35 year old male with excellent eye health is told that he should return in one year for re-examination. The receptionist says she has reserved a date and time for next year and she will contact the patient to confirm the appointment a couple weeks in advance. She prints an appointment card and gives it the man. The patient says he would rather not have an actual appointment and he will just call when he is ready to return. The staff member says the office uses this procedure in order to ensure there is space in the appointment calendar for our established patients (that's what the script says). The problem is that when the patient called for this appointment he was given a few choices within the next three days. And his wife called a few months ago and got an appointment the next day. The man decides to not argue the point, but he feels the office staff is dishonest and pushed him into an appointment for next year that he didn't want and probably didn't need. It's not likely that he will keep it.

What if you don't have time?

You simply have to make time for management if you want a successful, fast growth practice. I think it requires the practice owner in addition to a good office manager. The eye care professional/owner has a huge effect on the practice culture, so management and marketing cannot be completely delegated.

Most practices actually see accelerated growth when the ECP schedules more time for management. And that is the best way to correct the hundreds of little flaws that exist in every practice. Schedule time for it. Of course, no practice is ever perfect, but we must keep trying to reach perfection. You may naturally be concerned about reduced productivity if you take a day or two for management. In my experience, most practices are extremely inefficient and if you began a new plan to delegate more and speed up the exam process (without sacrificing quality or stressing out the staff) you could compress all the patients you currently see in five days into three or four days.

If you have unmet patient demand of more than a week or two, hire an associate optometrist to see some of the patients so you can work on management!

One of my favorite quotes is by Zig Ziglar and it sums up this philosophy very well: “You can get anything you want in life if you just help enough other people get what they want.”

12.26 Your Office Procedure Manual

Chances are you don't have a procedure manual for your practice. Most practices are fortunate to just have what I call a policy manual, and that is much easier to write and much shorter. A policy manual is really about the rules of employment; a staff guide about vacations, sick days, dress code and personal phone calls. A procedure manual describes how to perform all the jobs in the practice from filing insurance claims to pretesting to optical dispensing.

Why have a procedure manual?
Writing a procedure manual sounds like a formidable task, but with lots of help from your staff and some organization, you'll see it is not that bad at all. And there are many benefits from having a procedure manual – such as easier staff training and clarity on how the office is supposed to run. Over time, office procedures and policies tend to change and not always for the

better. Memories of what we are supposed to do fall short and each time a task is explained to someone new, it changes a bit. Employees put their own spin on things and eventually, the vision has changed.

We also know that staff members go on vacation, take extended absences and resign or retire. If the one employee who knows how to do a task in your office leaves, the practice can suffer and the remaining staff and doctors will feel the stress. If even the basics of how to do the job are recorded, work can proceed smoothly.

Start simple and share the work

Here are some tips on how to manage the project of writing a procedure manual:

- All offices have periods of time when they are not busy with patients. The manual can be written during these times and especially when a doctor is on vacation and production is lower than usual.
- The staff members currently doing the work know exactly what they do. They simply jot it down so someone else can do it.
- The doctor or manager can determine the topics and organize the assignments.
- Don't worry about grammar and writing style; just list the basic facts.
- A topic section can simply be a list of key points. It does not even have to be written in complete sentences.
- Include sources for help and other instructions, such as websites, phone numbers, names of people, etc.
- Have all staff members write their sections in a word processing program and save the files. The sections can be reviewed, edited and combined into one document.

What you can exclude

It is not necessary to write about tasks that are an expected part of a job skill. For example, it would not be necessary to write how to measure a seg height or perform lensometry. An optician is expected to know those things. But you could write about how to enter or write up the eyeglass order, how frames should be shown, how vision plans should be calculated and how patient fees should be collected. Other forms and patient handouts could be covered.

A very detailed procedure manual could include technical aspects like pretesting and optical dispensing, but there are text books written on those subjects. To develop a functional manual from scratch, I would start with a simple goal. It will always be a work in progress and it will evolve over time.

What you might include

You should have sections that cover the various departments in your practice. There could be topics, for the front desk, general administration, clinic, optical dispensing, optical lab, and so on.

Start by thinking of the jobs in your office that would be difficult if a key person was no longer available.

These are your first priority. Add to that list all the basic things your staff does every day. Here are a few possibilities:

- Filing insurance claims. The basic steps can be written down and it should not be a secret that only one person knows.
- What to do if the server goes down or internet access is lost.
- Converting time clock records into payroll.
- Sending recall notices or confirming pre-appointments.
- What to do when a patient shows up late or calls and wants to come in later than planned.
- Checking in eyeglass jobs and calling patients.
- What to do if a job is rejected.
- What to say over the phone to callers who want an appointment.
- Returning frames and lenses covered under warranty.
- How and when to reorder trial contact lenses for stock.
- How to do pretesting and notify the doctor that a patient is ready.
- How to open and close exam rooms at the start and end of day.
- How to offer an option for routine retinal photos.
- Key shortcuts you've learned in the operation of clinical equipment, such as the acuity chart or the settings on the retinal camera in case someone changes things.
- There are many more topics. Just break them up into bite-size pieces and let your staff work on them.

The idea of buying a template for a manual or borrowing one from a colleague is appealing to ECPs, but every office is so different that I strongly recommend that you write your own from scratch. You aren't reinventing the wheel; you are describing your unique system. The value of a procedure manual is in how well it describes your methods.

12.27 Telephone Menus Can Equal Poor Service

Optometrists often try to emulate large companies to make their practices more impressive to the public. I understand this perfectly and stretching oneself to provide a higher level of service makes perfect sense. But be sure a new technique is actually better before you implement it; many systems in use by large companies fall far short of excellence and telephone menus and some aspects of voice automation is one of them. Have you ever tried to call AT&T, Comcast or even the highly regarded Apple? My experience has usually been disappointing.

Telephone menu systems

Telephone menus in optometric practice can certainly seem like a good idea. It feels like your practice is cutting edge and it provides a way to educate callers about your services. But let's look deeper into the actual caller experience. I will present some typical menu options in a phone system for an optometric practice, followed by what might be the thoughts of a typical caller.

- Your call may be monitored or recorded for quality assurance and staff training purposes. This line has been heard so many times it is becoming old. I really would rather not have to think about your staff training.
- Please listen carefully as our menu options have changed. How condescending. As if I can't decide how closely to listen.
- Many questions can be answered by visiting our website at www.notarealsite.com. I guess they don't really want to talk to me. But I don't think the website will know if my glasses are ready, so I will stick with the telephone.
- If you know your party's extension you may enter it at any time. Wow, I thought this was my local eye doctor's office. There must be dozens of employees sitting in their cubicles waiting for phone calls. Unfortunately, I do not know any extensions.
- Please press one for eye emergencies, press two to schedule an appointment, press three to speak to our optical lab staff or to check on the status of eyewear, press five for the contact lens department, press six to speak to an operator. It feels like I've been on the phone for quite a while and have yet to speak to anyone. OK, I want option three.
- The call is routed to a specific phone in your office based on the selection, but since the size of your staff is limited, the employee in that department is busy or on a break and the call goes to voice mail. Great, I guess there is no one there who can tell me if my glasses are ready.
- The caller leaves a message and hangs up feeling like his needs were not met very well.

Patient satisfaction

One can make the argument that the public will understand that your practice is busy at times and these automated systems are necessary. Many people will understand, but these small service points add up and make a big difference in the overall impression. A caring person quickly taking care of a customer's wants and needs is always more impressive than an automated system.

If the call had gone to the front desk or to a call center, someone would have answered it. It would be part of the job description and there would be a back-up system in place if the first responder is busy. When the call goes to a department, the chances of going to voice mail increases greatly. Answering the phone should be a priority, but menus and voice mail allow staff to conveniently avoid the task. This route is definitely not convenient for the patient.

People are often in a hurry today. They may be on a cell phone and grabbing a few minutes to call you while at work. The seconds used up by listening to the phone menu can seem like minutes. I can see some callers acting a bit rude to your staff when they finally speak to someone (but the staff member wonders why).

The whole experience is made worse if the patient has to call back a few times in a short time period. Having to listen repeatedly to the menu tree and having trouble connecting with a human is extremely aggravating. The caller's conclusion will likely be that this office is hard to do business with. Many people will think they may have to shop around next time they need eye care.

Patients see beyond the show

While the menu system might seem impressive, patients can easily see beyond the thin veneer. The phone menu might be necessary if your practice was a major hospital, but it isn't. Your patients quickly realize the size and scope of your practice. They see that the fancy menu system should not really be needed in an operation of your size.

I realize I'm generalizing a bit and not all people will have a negative impression of a phone menu system, but filter it through your own experience. Look how deeply I analyzed the caller's point of view and use it as an example on how to dig into other aspects of your practice.

The alternate experience

The patient calls the optometrist's office and a cheerful staff member answers on the first ring and says "Good morning, Main Street Eye Center, Jenny speaking. How may I help you?" The patient presents the reason for the call and Jenny handles it or routes the call to the proper person.

It might seem like old school, but I'm quite sure which system the public likes best.

12.28 How Clean is Your Office?

An office that is scrupulously clean creates a very positive patient experience. Patients really do notice and will comment about it on surveys. They also notice the opposite condition: an office that is not very clean. It is easy to let an office drift from clean to dirty without noticing; here are some factors working against you.

Who does the cleaning?
When I first opened my practice, cold, right out of school, I couldn't afford many extras. It was a very lean operation in a very small office! I did some of the cleaning myself and I had one employee who also understood that we were just a small start-up and she did some housekeeping as well. As the practice and the staff grew, I assigned the cleaning duties to all my employees. I reasoned that the staff was not always busy and they were getting paid anyway, so why not? I don't recall exactly when it dawned on me that my staff hated cleaning toilets and running the vacuum cleaner, but it wasn't too long. They thought of themselves as eye care professionals and the heavy cleaning should not be in their job description. Looking back on it, they were right. I noticed that the staff would often forget their cleaning duties and they didn't do a very thorough job. I also knew that a happy staff meant better attitudes. I hired a professional cleaning service; the office has been cleaner and the staff happier ever since.

There are a few aspects of cleaning that are still in the domain of my staff, but it is best to differentiate between heavy cleaning and touch-up cleaning. Except for small practices and start-ups, I recommend that a commercial service take care of the heavy cleaning. How often the service comes to your office depends on how busy and how large it is. Keep a close watch on the cleanliness and increase the service as needed.

I assign side jobs to all staff members and day-to-day cleaning can be included in those tasks. Here are some cleaning jobs that are better for staff to do:

- Straighten up the reception room a few times each day. This includes returning magazines to the rack and picking up trash.
- Clean up the coffee area.
- Check patient washroom and tidy up as needed.
- Empty wastebaskets at the end of the day and take out trash and boxes.
- Inspect instruments, tables and exam areas; clean and dust as needed. Some instruments and mirrors require very specific cleaning methods; these items should be excluded from the cleaning service and managed by the optometric staff.
- Clean mirrors and all surfaces in the optical dispensing area.

Staff members will accept their role in cleaning better if the heavy lifting is done by a janitorial crew.

What kind of job do they do?

In my experience, commercial janitorial services often decline in quality until the customer notices and complains. That means that you or your manager must inspect the work on a regular basis and let the cleaning crew know that you notice if quality drops. This takes a bit of effort because you may not always go in some areas of your office, like the waiting room or patient bathroom. If you were to go into your waiting room right now and wipe your hand along the baseboard in one of the far corners, would you come up with dust, dirt or maybe even cobwebs? Go try it; I'll wait.

Make a decision to earn a reputation for your practice as the cleanest professional office in town.

Special areas

It is very important that bathrooms are extremely clean. Be sure the cleaning staff does a very thorough job by checking it the morning after they work. Bathrooms should also be attractive, well-lit and fully stocked with supplies. Have staff members wipe up the sink a couple of times per day.

I generally think that cleaning the floors is the job of the janitorial service, but the entrance to the office and the front desk area can need attention more frequently, especially in inclement weather. Using the wet Swiffer mop is very easy and convenient and only takes a couple of minutes. Changing floor mats as they become soiled or wet is also part of the daily job in the winter. A well-charged Dustbuster vacuum is another must-have tool.

12.29 Patient Has Insurance, But Fails to Tell You

We've all been there. Your staff asks about insurance when an appointment is scheduled by phone, but the patient says he doesn't have a vision plan and insists the exam is just routine. Your office asks again at the appointment confirmation and again at check-in, but the answer is still no insurance. The exam is done and new glasses are ordered and the patient acts like all is well. But sometime later, maybe several weeks later, the patient (or the spouse) calls to say "Oh, darn! It turns out we did have vision insurance after all! Please file for my benefits and refund what we paid."

For the practice owner, that is quite aggravating to say the least! It is not just the staff time that would be required, but this transaction already occurred as private pay and to reverse that and accept the discounted vision plan benefits would mean a loss of revenue.

I want to acknowledge that this topic was sent to me as a question via email by a colleague and I appreciate the idea for this article!

How should you handle this?
Here are your options as I see them:

- You could politely tell the patient that it is his responsibility to let your office know ahead of time what insurance/vision benefits he has and there is nothing you can do.
- You could tell the patient to file his own claim for out of network reimbursement. But that reimbursement is much lower than in-network benefits and most patients know that.
- You could honor the patients request; call the insurance company; find out what they allow in these cases; bill the insurance company and refund the patient.

I would choose the last option, but I realize that will not be a very popular decision with most eye care providers and staff members. It is, however, a very popular decision among patients. Read on for my reasoning on why I let the customer win on this issue even though my profit will be reduced.

To some extent, your options may depend on which vision plan is being used. Some plans allow you to correct an oversight in special cases and file a claim for glasses even if they were made by an out-of-network lab. Some plans do not allow a claim to be filed if the glasses were not made in its lab.

Who is to blame?

When problems occur in my practice, I look at how my staff and I can better control the situation and prevent it in the future. I don't expect much from patients and I rarely blame them for the problem. Even in this situation, where it seems so obvious that the patient caused the problem by not knowing about his own vision plan coverage and by not telling us about it up front, I look at what my practice did not do well enough. I can't control how the public thinks and I accept their shortcomings. It is just human nature. But I can control what we do in our internal process of scheduling appointments and getting insurance authorizations.

It will seem odd to many readers, but when this happens in my practice, I view most of it as our fault. We should have prevented it. So, I'm willing to learn from this mistake and help the patient on this isolated incident. Staff members will struggle with this because they hate to admit they make mistakes, but I'll help get past that by not blaming the individual, but instead blaming our office process.

It is OK if we disagree on how to handle cases like this, but I will remind you (in my defense) that customer service is the biggest factor in building a large, successful, profitable practice.

How to prevent this

By working with my employees on this issue at staff meetings, we came up with a system that makes it extremely rare for us to have a patient tell us later that they have a vision plan.

- Our staff member who makes the appointment is responsible for getting the insurance authorization that same day. We know who that was because her initials are on the appointment notes. We never wait until the day of or the day before the appointment.
- We assume all patients have a vision plan even if they say they do not. We check all our plans online until we find the patient. Quite often the patient's employer gives us a clue about the plan. This requires that we get the last four digits of the social security number, but most patients give us that over the phone when we tell them we want to make sure they do not have some coverage.
- We call patients back if they do not have insurance and we discuss our exam fee and medical insurance.

In addition to just checking the plan directories yourself, there are various software programs that can assist your staff with finding out if the patient has insurance coverage and in some cases these programs can tell you about co-pays and deductibles.

12.30 Back to Fundamentals: Five Factors to Review

Like other ODs who own their practice, I get really busy sometimes. Even though I pride myself on delegating many tasks to an excellent staff, I still like to know what is going on in all aspects of the practice. Time gets away from me and some things are overlooked for a while, but eventually I like to circle back and review key elements of our operations. Here is a good overview for you to check on five fundamental factors in your practice.

Accounts receivable
You should be running monthly reports on money that is owed to your practice from two major entities: patients and insurance companies. It is helpful to actually print these reports so you can review them with key staff members and write directly on the pages as you outline your plan. If you do not have an accurate list of accounts receivable that shows the age of the balances due, you should work with your office management software provider to learn how to obtain it (or speak to your accountant).

The key sections to look at are the accounts that are more than 30 days old. Investigate the claims with insurance companies that are older and also the balances owed by patients. If you have not kept up to date with these past due balances, your staff will need to make phone calls and send letters to find out why the balance was not paid and when you can expect to receive payment. This is not an easy job, but there is a lot of money at stake.

As account balances get older, it is less likely that you will ever collect them. It is necessary to write-off some unpaid balances once they are very old, say more than 120 days past due. If your staff reviews the AR reports monthly in the future, many write-offs can be prevented.

Insurance billing
Insurance billing is a department in the office that the OD/owner does not often pay attention to. It is a vital area that you should review. It is very smart for the practice owner to understand the basic process of how claims are generated and filed. Ask yourself if your insurance coordinator were to

resign tomorrow, would you know how to train another employee on what to do (or at least get them started)?

Be sure to review both parts of the eye care insurance world: vision plans and medical insurance. They are quite different. Find out if your staff is up to date with claims or if they are way behind from the date of service. For vision plans, who submits claims that include an eyeglass order? Who submits exams only and contact lens orders? For medical plans, what happens when claims are rejected? Are amounts that go toward a deductible transferred back to the patient and billed? Are those balances eventually paid in most cases? For all insurance, who on your staff enters the payments and adjusts off the balances? Review those write-offs and see if there is a way to overcome some of it.

Fee and price lists
Your practice functions with many price lists. Revisit them with your staff and ask how long it has been since they were updated? Here is a list of prices:

- Exam fees
- Medical procedure fees
- Contact lens fitting and evaluation fees
- Specialty services
- Contact lens products (per box and per years supply)
- Frame mark-up formula
- Base ophthalmic lenses
- Lens enhancement features (add-ons)
- Miscellaneous products

Write down your actual wholesale cost for products and see if the profit margin is what you think it is. Is it time to raise some professional fees?

Customer service
Patient satisfaction is vitally important for continued practice success. We depend on happy patients referring others based on the wonderful experience they had in our offices.

- Telephone. Make sure phones are answered promptly and there should be very little use of voice mail. I dislike menus that delay the call and end up going to voice mail. The phone is so important; just answer it!
- Office hours. Many ODs don't really separate the practice from themselves personally. Convenience is part of excellent customer

service, so try to expand your hours and be open when it is convenient for the patient.
- Check-in and check-out process. Take a close look at the forms you are asking patients to fill out and try to minimize them. Make check-in and check-out fast and easy.
- Waiting times. Develop an office culture that tries hard to be on time. Have your tech call the patients in quicker. Have the doctor be more flexible and be more aware, to minimize internal wait times.

Frame inventory
Run a simple frame inventory count so you can see how many frames you have in various retail price points as follows:
- Under $150
- $150 to $200
- $200 to $250
- $250 to $300
- $300 to $400
- $400 to $600
- Over $600

Add up the total number of frames in all categories and calculate the number in each price point as a percentage of the total. Are there some price points that have very few units? Do you have the proper distribution of prices based on your practice demographics and your market philosophy? Are there good style choices in each price point? Is there some understock and is the total number of frames on hand the correct number?

12.31 Do you want to put something down on that?

Have you ever heard the sentence above uttered by a staff member in your office? That, and the much more common "how much did you want to put down on that today?" are a reality in eye care practices every day. I cringe when I hear it. When I do hear a question like that in my office, I know it's time for retraining on the topic of collections at the next staff meeting.

You may not like the answer

The questions above actually seem fairly innocent and even logical to the untrained. After all, it is what your staff member needs to know to print a receipt – so she asks it. The problem with either question is that you may not like the answer. The answer might be: "No, I don't want to put anything down." Or, "Let's see, I think I'll put $10 down (on this $600 order)." Like attorneys in court, our staff members shouldn't ask questions if they won't like the answer.

Of course, the error can be corrected so it seems like no big deal. The receptionist simply explains the office policy of requiring 50% down at the time of order. But having to invoke "the policy" is not a good thing because it's always used to say NO. I want our staff to say YES whenever possible. The patient is made to feel badly – like he's trying to be cheap and get away with something. But the office corrected him and won the issue at hand.

Get comfortable with money

I believe these undesirable collection phrases occur in our offices because people (staff in this case) are naturally somewhat intimidated and uncomfortable about asking for money. We need to be certain they get over that. There is nothing unnatural about asking to be paid for services rendered, and the patient is actually expecting to pay something. We just need to tell them how much and when. There is often a tendency to say too much when a person is nervous or hoping to avoid a confrontation.

What should they say?

The best way to handle the payment at checkout is for the staff member to simply state the total charges incurred at that visit. For example, if a patient in my office had an eye exam and then ordered new contacts and glasses, and the total fees were $730, the technician assisting on the case would have explained the fee breakdown for all services and materials as they were selected and written on the superbill. The patient is escorted to the business office counter, and introduced to a receptionist, who would say, "Mrs. Smith, your charges today are $730." Period. It takes some practice to just be silent after that, but it can be done.

The patient often takes out the checkbook or produces a credit card and pays the whole amount. We are happy to accept it. Cash flow is important, so the sooner we're paid, the better. In other cases the patient asks if they have to pay the whole total now, and we reply that only a 50% deposit is required (with the balance due upon dispensing). It sounds so much nicer than the mean office policy scenario mentioned earlier.

By the way, if there was some amount that our office would accept directly from an insurance plan (our list of accepted plans is pre-determined), that amount would have been deducted from the total and the patient's balance would have been stated.

Talking business with staff

We recently had a staff meeting about all this in my office. I explained the importance of cash flow to my staff by telling them that our practice is actually a business and we have many suppliers to pay and the sooner the patient pays us, the better. I find staff members like to be included in business aspects, and when they're told about them, they want to help. Instead of just caring about the patient's needs, which still should come first, they are also aware of our business needs. It's now not just printing the receipt, but it's collecting revenue, which pays her salary.

A fairly new receptionist came to me about one week after this staff meeting and said she was amazed at how well it worked when she just stated the total balance. Patients were paying their full fees up front and had no problem with it. I noticed a jump in the deposited receipts also.

Free enterprise

Sadly, I think optometric practices have always been poor at collecting fees, and many have become worse over the past twenty years as our profession has concentrated on "billing and coding" everything we do. We are seeing the free enterprise system fade away in optometry as it has in health care in general, and it's too bad because it was so good for us. I'm doing my part to keep it going as long as possible.

12.32 Office Policies for Remakes and Refunds

Continuing with our series on patient satisfaction, following last week's tip on warranties and the previous tip on service recovery, let's talk about a fun topic: remakes and refunds!

Remakes and Rechecks

Most optometrists understand the need for remakes and do so willingly. The nature of our work and the conventions that exist in our society make it best to offer complete satisfaction. This would include a no-charge recheck by the optometrist, if needed, to resolve a problem.

In argument, one can offer the analogy of a physician who prescribes a drug that doesn't work; noting that the doctor does not pay for the ineffective medication, or waive the office visit fee for continuing to work on the problem. But it's different with optical than it is with medicine, because optical is close enough to retail goods that those rules apply. Optometrists get to follow the medical tradition when prescribing a drug that does not resolve a keratitis, or reduce IOP enough in glaucoma. We do make a profit on the sale of optical products, but not on the sale of a drug. If the complaint is about eyeglasses, and if we look at what is best for the practice and its reputation, the no-charge trouble-shooting visit is essential to good will. I view these visits as an opportunity to create a powerful bond by sincerely helping a patient who has a problem. How you approach these can set your practice apart from others and relieve considerable stress for the patient, who is likely to be worried over the confrontation.

As for the remake, my advice is to just do whatever it takes to make the patient happy. The tough part is often figuring out what that is... but if you know, or if the patient tells you, it's easy. Another tough part involves the time line. How long do you offer the free remakes and rechecks? Here are a few rules and tips I've found to be helpful for me and my staff.

- I will often provide some kind of remake, even if I'm not sure what is causing the complaint. I demonstrate my desire to help, and it often does solve a vague problem, or a problem that is in disguise when the patient really wants to choose a different frame.
- While I empower my staff to fix problems themselves without my input, I discourage them from guessing at the cause of a problem. A 2mm change in the PD is not going to resolve a visual complaint in most cases, and the patient ends up having to come back again. Multiple attempts at remakes is very inconvenient, costly and undermines the patient's confidence in our practice. I'd rather see that patient myself and re-refract.
- One of the clues I listen for, which can change how I resolve a problem, is when the patient states: "these glasses were never right". That is quite different than glasses that were once just fine, and something happened to change the fit or the vision. If they were never "right", and if the time frame is not too unreasonable (like years after dispensing) I'm likely to remake them at no charge.
- It's frustrating when people wait what seems to be an unreasonable time period before bringing up a complaint. My response to this helps me deal with the problem appropriately. I ask the patient, in a nice way, "what took you so long to bring this to my attention?" Then I listen. The answer will vary, but it does two things: first, it

gives me some insight into why it took so long, which can be legitimate ("I was in the hospital") or lame. Secondly, it lets the patient know that they took too long and whatever we do for them is really nice.

- After listening carefully (and empathetically) to a complaint, if the resolution is not obvious, a very effective question to ask the patient is "what would you like us to do?"
- I apologize. I'm not sure why so many eye care professionals have learned to remove the words "I'm sorry" from their vocabulary, but it is often all any of us really want to hear when a business lets us down (patient perception is all that counts here). I have no problem apologizing for the patient's inconvenience for having to return, or for making a mistake in the lens design or prescription. I don't worry about who I can blame - I'll take the blame. I also thank the patient for bringing the problem to my attention.
- I think it's smart to print all office polices about rechecks, remakes, refunds etc. on the back of your superbill or walk-out statement. Patients will read this and most will follow the rules.
- Don't forget that you can put returned frames that have not been worn back on display. I have my in-office lab make new plano demo lenses for them and put the frame back in standard adjustment.

Refunds

The topic of refunds can trigger emotions in practice owners that run very deep. Opinions vary widely on how to handle them, and all I can do here is share my views.

I will try to resolve complaints and fix problems through remakes first, but if the patient wants a refund, I'll give it with no hard feelings. It does not ruin my day. We try our best and we learn from our mistakes, but no one is perfect and we know we can't please everyone. I don't take it personally. I've learned that we often retain the patient, keep a good relationship, and provide services and products for many years to come.

Our policy, which is printed on the back of my superbill, states that refunds must be requested within 30 days of dispensing. This is reasonable, but rules can be bent when circumstances warrant it.

I would typically offer a refund only on materials, keeping examination fees totally separate - which indeed they are. If a patient requested a refund on an eye examination, I'd politely make the point that exam fees are for work that was performed in good faith, and that no one works for free. But if the patient continued to request the exam fee, I'd realize that I was dealing with an irrational person and I'd refund that fee also. This happens so rarely that it's not worth worrying about. I don't stew over the incident - just move on.

Why do it?
One very valid reason to have patient-friendly policies is to make life more pleasant in the office for you and your staff. It reduces stress when you can make patients happy, and the pleasant working environment breeds many important intangibles in the practice culture! Providing the remake or refund without a fuss even allows you to save face in the patient's eyes, because if you don't make an ordeal out of it, it's not perceived as an ordeal. But the biggest reason to have lenient policies is that you will make more money. Your practice will grow and become one of the most successful in the community. It will take a few years, but time passes. You wouldn't think giving refunds or doing more remakes would make you more money, but it's a paradox.

12.33 When You Have to Fire a Patient

Even though my last few tips have focused on the value of achieving high levels of patient satisfaction, there are situations when it is necessary to dismiss a patient from further care. In my experience, this should be very rare, perhaps in the area of one dismissal every few years, or longer.

The reasons for ending the doctor-patient relationship will vary, but you'll know it when you see it. It may be repeated complaints that are unreasonable and unsolvable, or it may be a poor payment history. You certainly don't have to provide eye care to someone you don't want to, except for our duty to provide emergency care when needed and no one else is available, and to not discriminate against protected classes of individuals.

Sending a letter to the individual you no longer wish to see is probably the best way to end the relationship. The following example is ethical, professional and puts you in good legal standing. The letter can be adapted to your needs. I prefer to have such letters signed by an office manager on behalf of the practice, because it makes it less personal. In small offices, however, the doctor could certainly sign it.

By certified mail, return receipt requested

Date

Patient name
Address

Dear Mr./ Mrs. :

Main Street Eye Center will no longer be able to provide eye care services or products for you. We are terminating the optometrist / patient relationship because it has become clear that the trust and confidence required is no longer present and it would be in your best interest to obtain eye care from another provider.

Our doctors will be available for the next thirty days to provide treatment for you in the event of an eye emergency. You may find another optometrist by visiting AOA.org. I will forward copies of your eye care records to the provider of your choice if you notify me in writing that I can release them.

Very truly yours,

Jane Doe
Practice Administrator

*Substitute in second sentence if applicable: .... because you have not met your financial obligations to this office for past services rendered.

Chapter 13. Managed Care

13.1 Do you know what your profit is with vision plans?

I find very few optometrists actually know how much profit they make with the vision plans they accept. Oh, there is a vague feeling that it is not very much or that one plan is better than another, but when it comes to actual numbers, no one really has the facts. I understand this to some extent; after all, the payment systems are rather complex. Each vision plan has different fee maximums and there are product charge backs for some items while other parts of the lab bill are paid in full, invisibly.

In spite of the complexity, however, you really should know approximately how much profit you make with each plan. After all, you made it through a very high level geometrical optics class, I'm pretty sure you can figure out the gross revenue minus the cost of goods equals your profit. Read on and I'll show you a very easy way to get a good read on this elusive but vital data.

Why you need to know
As business owners, it is extremely important that we understand the profitability of all aspects of our practices. When we know the profit margins, we can make smart choices about the resources we can devote to a specific business channel and we can also decide if we even want to continue with specific services, products or third party payers. Changes are occurring in our industry faster than ever so we should reevaluate the profit margins in the major categories of the practice on a regular basis. Vision plans are a major category of most practices!

With most businesses, different products and services have different profit margins and that is quite normal. We may enjoy a great margin on one thing and a smaller profit on another. That does not mean we should dump the service with the small profit. Some profit may be better than nothing at all. For example, my practice earns a higher profit on prescription glasses than it does on plano sunglasses. The plano sunglass market is more competitive and the same product is sold in other places, so our mark-ups are lower. That does not mean that I'm unhappy carrying non-Rx sunglasses in my optical.

It is very difficult to make a judgment about profitability by looking at the vision plan fee schedules alone. There are too many variables to evaluate and we end up looking mostly at the exam fee. That scares most doctors off, but it is more accurate to consider the complete mix of patients. This is also true if you are contemplating accepting a new vision plan. To determine profit margin, you really have to accept a plan, use it for about three months, and then run a retrospective study like I describe below.

We need facts, not emotion

It seems to me that our perception of vision plans is based on a very emotional response. If you read the OD internet chat forums and social media, there is no shortage of strong opinions and heated discussions. Of course, those forums are set up for that very purpose and they can be very helpful, but be warned that there are many myths and inaccurate statements about vision plans. There are many misunderstandings.

One good example is the emotional aspect of seeing the charge backs on the vision plan explanation of benefits (EOB). In many cases, it appears as if you are actually losing money seeing a patient. Some vision plans require the practice to write them a check if charge backs exceed payments. But realize that the more your charge backs are, the more the patient paid you for extra items. The greater your charge backs, the greater your profit.

I'm not defending vision plans; they are what they are. But let's work with facts and data, not hearsay and rumors. Do a little homework in your practice as described in the next section and find out your profit margin with each vision plan. Also, it is a good idea to actually read the provider manuals.

The analysis

I recommend you perform a retrospective study on 20 actual cases that you have recently examined or dispensed eyewear to within a specific vision plan. You will determine the gross profit you received on each case and then take the average for all 20 cases. You should repeat this process for each vision plan you work with. Once you know the mean profit level for each vision plan, you can make intelligent decisions about working with vision plans, accepting new ones and comparing them. When I conducted this study in my practice, I found my profitability with vision plans was actually greater than I expected.

- You will need to pull the clinical and optical records for each of the 20 patients and also have the vision plan statement (or EOB) that details the payment and chargebacks you received. You should also have access to the patient's personal account ledger with your practice in order to include the items the patient paid for.
- I would like you to select the 20 patients randomly without knowing what they purchased, but you should prorate the types of cases selected based on your real world experience. By that I mean select the correct mix of: exam only, exam and glasses, exam and two pairs of glasses, exam and contacts, and glasses only. The correct mix will

reflect the percentage of each of those types of cases you see in a large sample in your practice.

- When I did this analysis in my practice, I used the following mix:
    - Exam only: 10% or 2 cases
    - Exam and glasses: 60% or 12 cases
    - Exam and two pairs of glasses: 10% or 2 cases
    - Exam and contacts: 15% or 3 cases
    - Glasses only: 5% or 1 case
- I would leave medical billing out of this analysis, but know that if you bill some services for patients with vision plans to medical insurance, your profit will be even better than shown on this analysis.
- The goal of the analysis is simple: add up all the payments you received from all sources (the patient and the vision plan), deduct all costs of goods (including items you paid for and charge backs from the vision plan) and the result is your gross profit for that patient. Add up the gross profit figures for all 20 patients and divide by 20 for the average profit per patient for this vision plan.
- We call it gross profit because we are not considering your office expenses like staff or rent. We are just considering cost of goods.
- You should include all items that you sold on the first exam or the annual exam no matter who paid for the items. This includes everything, even if the vision plan did not cover the item. For example, you should include screening retinal photos or other optional tests, multiple pairs of glasses, contact lenses, nutritional supplements, etc. If you were paid to do in-office edging, factor in your lab costs and add any net payment. Too often we only look at the vision plan payments and we forget the patient paid for many items as well.
- Deduct all cost of goods that are billed through your lab or suppliers, but use the actual amount you pay so the profit is accurate. Don't use the Frames Data price, use the price you paid after any discounts. If you paid for contact lens products, deduct that cost. Also, deduct the charge backs shown on the vision plan EOB.
- Get the average gross profit per patient for this vision plan.
- You can also total up your usual and customary fees for these 20 patients if you wish and average those totals. That data is not helpful in the profit analysis of vision plans, but it is an interesting comparison to private pay.

A word about marginal costs

As you reflect on your profit margins, be sure to consider how busy you are. If your appointment schedule is not full, you are better off accepting additional patients even if they have lower profitability than your private pay patients.

If you add up all your fixed expenses (rent, staff, utilities, equipment, marketing, etc.) and divide by the number of patients you saw in that time period, you get your cost per patient (also called chair cost). That can be a big number and you might think that if the gross profit is not greater than that chair cost, you should reject the vision plan. But you must ask yourself what the cost would be for you to see an additional patient if you have empty appointment slots. That cost is called the marginal cost and that cost is actually zero. You have already met all your practice costs and seeing an additional patient costs nothing. So any gross profit you produce on those patients is pure profit. Some profit is better than no profit.

13.2 Should You Accept That Vision Plan? Three Big Questions for You.

I realize that vision plans can be a hot topic among optometrists, so it is fairly bold of me to decide to tackle the topic. Many optometrists advise their colleagues to not accept vision plans, and yet the leading plans have provider networks with over 30,000 doctors, so clearly some of these doctors do not follow their own advice.

We simply can't make blanket statements about what is right for all practices. Each doctor, each practice and each market area is unique and we must analyze them one at a time. There are many factors to consider when making the decision to become a provider for a vision plan, and I'll cover more of them in future articles, but for now I want you to consider three key questions:

1. Do you want a large practice?
This question is not as easy as it first seems. Not every optometrist wants to have a large practice with a large staff, large office facility and high gross revenues. A smaller practice could provide a very good personal income. A smaller practice could offer more specialized care and could be more private pay based. This type of practice could have a higher net income as a percentage of gross. It is by design, however, a practice that revolves around and depends heavily on the practice owner.

But don't overlook the benefits of a large practice either. It can be a joy to practice with a large staff, an office manager, multiple doctors, plenty of office space, all the advanced instruments and enough cash flow so you can ignore the small stuff that might otherwise stress you out. The large practice usually generates more net income in dollars.

If you want a large practice, I think you should accept most vision plans. There are definitely strategies to increase your profitability with vision plans and you should work on that. There are always exceptions and special circumstances, but most large optometric practices accept most vision plans. Large practices need high patient volume and that is very hard to achieve, without accepting vision plans. You need access to large numbers of patients and many of them will need medical eye care, premium eyeglasses, multiple pairs of eyeglasses, contact lenses and many more eye care services and products.

2. Do you have an associate or do you plan to hire one?

If you have an associate doctor (let's say he/she is full time and is paid a typical salary plus a benefit package), you may find that you feel differently about accepting vision plans. This is actually a great way to force yourself to look at vision plans in a purely business-like way, without the emotion of judging if your personal time is worth a lower profit margin. When you have an employed doctor drawing a salary and if her schedule is not full, you may decide that having him see a vision plan patient is better than seeing no patient at all.

Hiring an associate OD is one of the best practice management strategies there is, but it takes a lot of patient demand to make it work. Usually, vision plans are necessary to create that patient demand. The best way to ensure that the new associate generates enough revenue to cover his/her compensation and produces additional profit for the owner is to have a strong backlog of patients. Of course, before hiring a doctor, it is smart to hire more technicians and other staff to allow the first doctor to practice efficiently. This is a great formula for success, but it requires a lot of patients.

I believe that practices need to work on all the traditional methods of building patient demand including all aspects of marketing, cultivating word-of-mouth referrals and strong recall methods. But even with all those efforts, I see many practices that are not busy enough. Vision plans can bring a large number of patients to the practice; I view them as another form of marketing.

3. How full is your appointment schedule?

This question is extremely important as you assess if a specific vision plan would be good for your practice. Before you can answer the question, we must define how full the schedule should be. A doctor who sees 10 exams per day may conclude that his schedule is full because all the slots are filled. I would argue that he needs way more slots. At least twice as many slots and if he had that, his schedule would be far from full.

Preappointing can be an excellent recall system, but it can delude the practice owner into thinking his schedule is full when it really isn't. What really matters is how many patients were actually seen if we look backwards. The schedule may look full in the weeks ahead, but if a high no show rate and frequent rescheduling at the last minute makes production low, then the schedule is not really that full. A very full schedule is one where the staff has problems finding room for new patients who call or for patients who need to return for follow-up.

If your schedule is truly full I would say congratulations and let's hire an associate and get his schedule truly full too. If you already have a busy associate, then I'd say you may want to drop some of the lower profit vision plans because you have so much patient volume that you can be selective.

The truth is that all vision plans are profitable if you have open appointment slots. If you have openings, there is no cost to seeing the additional patients that the vision plan would bring. You already have an office, equipment, staff and a frame inventory. You're already paying for those things even if your exam chair sits empty. Every vision plan pays something, even after considering the cost of goods. You could argue that you would rather play golf or be with your family and that is very valid, but that is making it personal. That argument applies well to the smaller practice, but not to one that is going to hire an associate.

13.3 Determining Fees with Vision Plans

Knowing what you will be paid for eye care services and products is one of the most important factors about a vision plan, yet it is incredibly difficult to get a straight answer to this question! Most vision plans will send you a sample fee schedule in advance that will list most fees for exams and optical products, but I've seen some plans that will not even tell you the fees until you sign a contract! Also, there are often many different sub-plans and most of them have chargebacks, so it gets pretty complicated.

Usually, ODs just look at the exam fees because that seems straight forward, but those fees are often so low that the plan is rejected right away. I think it is a mistake to base the decision on only one small part of the fee structure. I've seen many doctors assume that vision plan A pays much better than vision plan B based on the exam fees, but when you factor in the profit that is earned on optical products, the plans come out about the same in total profit. That is important to know.

The best way (and maybe the only accurate way) to evaluate the fees from a vision plan is to sign up as a provider for the plan and see patients for about three months. That will allow you to take an aggregate look at all the patients seen with the plan and to accurately determine the profitability. This method takes into consideration that some patients will be exam only, some will buy glasses, some will get contact lenses and some will buy services or products out-of-pocket. We can also assess the true profit we retain after chargebacks with this method.

If it turns out that the fees and profits are not acceptable, the provider can drop out of the plan. That may seem like a lot to go through just to find out the fees, but in most cases I've seen, the total profit and average profit is better than anticipated. Clearly, the profit will seem low compared to private pay patients, but we know that going in. I think there is really nothing to lose to try out a vision plan.

After you start seeing patients, follow the procedure I described in Section 13.1 to determine your average profit per patient with the new vision plan.

13.4 Evaluating and Signing Up for Managed Care Plans, Part 1

Managed health care, including new plans under the Affordable Care Act (ACA), traditional medical insurance and even vision care plans, requires practice owners to educate themselves and make important decisions. Put this topic on your growing list of things to do as CEO of your practice. In this article, I'll give you some guidance on how to evaluate and participate in the plans that are good for your practice.

It is tempting for some ODs to try to outsource some of the tougher aspects of running a practice. Maybe you can hire a firm to take care of it for you or maybe you can delegate it to a staff member. But in most cases, other people are not going to be able to make important decisions about your practice for you. You might be able to outsource some peripheral functions of your practice, but not the core management. You might be able to delegate routine tasks to your staff, but not strategic decision-making.

More often, ODs just don't work on it
When some aspects of running the business are too time-consuming or too demanding, most ODs simply don't do it. In the case of our topic of evaluating managed care, many ODs go for years without looking into a new insurance plan. They may eventually be prompted to consider a plan if they receive an invitation to join from the insurance company or if several patients ask if the practice accepts a plan. That method will work, but I recommend you take a much more proactive approach. No one can do it for you.

There are many other business aspects that don't get enough time from the OD/CEO, like human resource management, marketing the practice, regulatory and insurance compliance, office technology updates and many more tasks. When is an OD supposed to find the time to do all this and see patients too?

The answer is simply not to avoid these business tasks. The answer is to improve time management and work smarter, not harder. It is really not difficult to do these tasks if you just had the time. It is actually gratifying once you jump in because you know your practice is getting the attention it needs. Time management is a topic for a future article, but for many ODs, a big step in the right direction is to make eye exams more efficient. Compress the same number of exams into fewer days per week and delegate more data collection to staff. Make the eye exam a shorter event in most cases.

Make some time in your schedule to research and work on managed care.

What plans are out there?
Do some basic research about the medical insurance and vision plans that are present in your area. Assign some of these tasks to your staff and you should appoint someone to be the insurance coordinator if you don't currently have an employee with that title. Keep written records of your phone calls and Google searches.

- Start by making a detailed list of all the plans you already accept in your practice. Separate the vision plans from medical.
- Make a second list of managed care plans that exist in your area and keep notes under each one, such as how popular the plan is, what

local employers offer it, and physicians and ODs who accept the plan. At first, you may not know some of this, but you'll learn.

- Ask your staff about the names of insurance plans that patients ask about when they call your office.
- Look up the websites of local optometrists and ophthalmologists and read which insurance plans are listed as those they accept.
- Research your state Medicaid plan. You may have looked into Medicaid in the past, but it has changed drastically in many states and you need to look again. Many new Obamacare plans are administered through the Medicaid program. There are often several different plans under Medicaid and some pay very well and are administered by third party plans you already work with. Some Medicaid plans are no longer just for the unemployed, but for people who have jobs that do not provide benefits.
- Do a Google search for Medicaid in your state and other medical plans. These sites are not always very user friendly, but spend time reading them anyway.
- Medicare is generally a must-have plan for your practice, but write down the names of popular Medicare Advantage plans that your patients bring in. Call the provider support line and ask about how to become a provider.
- Talk to local colleagues, ODs and MDs, about the managed care plans they accept and ask for their advice. More on this in the next issue.

I'll continue this topic next week, and we'll cover questions such as: Do you really want to join a plan? Will you be locked out of a plan? If you join a plan, will you see any referrals or patients? How do you submit an application and get credentialed?

Begin to think about how to become more informed about managed care. Read information about insurance plans and health care reform from the AOA and your state association. If you are not a member, this is reason enough to join. Read more in professional journals and newsletters. Read the news and current events sections of these publications, in addition to management articles.

13.5 Evaluating and Signing Up for Managed Care Plans, Part 2

Last week, I introduced the idea of making time to investigate and evaluate managed care plans and become credentialed with plans that make sense. The tough part is that all plans do not make sense. In this article, I'll share some thoughts on how to evaluate managed care plans. We'll start with medical plans and the touch on vision plans.

Do you want to join a medical insurance plan or ACO?
Don't make the mistake of assuming that all medical plans pay well because they are medical. Some of the newer plans pay so poorly and have so many compliance measures, they make the worst of the vision plans look good. Medical insurance today is moving away from fee for service and entering a world of value-based reimbursement. To measure "value" and "quality", providers must comply with a host of reporting requirements that can be extremely burdensome, similar to meaningful use and PQRS measures. Compliance can be very time consuming and distracting for staff. There could be financial penalties if accountability is not met. Couple this with low fees for office visits and some plans may not be worth taking.

Will we have to move to this model eventually?
Maybe, but we have seen the health insurance industry and the federal government change their policies fairly often in the past few years. In many cases, we are better off waiting and monitoring a program and not rushing in.

Will you be locked out of a plan?
It seems to me we have been down this road a few times and we should learn a lesson to not act from a place of fear. Many ODs joined low-paying vision plans for fear of being left out and that allowed the vision plan to grow stronger. I would not worry about being locked out. I would join plans quickly if you can find out the details of what they pay and what the value-based requirements are, and if it looks good to you. Otherwise, wait and monitor. If a colleague pressures you to join a certain plan, I would question the true agenda.

If you join a plan, will you get referrals?
Being included on a long list of providers for a health plan does not ensure that you will get referrals of patients from primary care physicians (PCP). Referral patterns from one physician to another develop just as they always have: locally based on relationships. Meeting local physicians is still the best way to cultivate referrals. Doing so will help you to identify which insurance plans you want to become a provider for. Drop in on PCPs in their office to introduce yourself. Joining local community service clubs is another way to

meet doctors. Start the referral relationship by sending your patients to certain PCPs along with sending short, concise report letters.

What about vision plans?
There is not one blanket right answer about joining vision plans. It is very market driven and it also depends on the practice model you want to pursue. Not all ODs want to build a large practice. Your acceptance of vision plans may change if you want to bring in an associate OD or open multiple office locations. Some ODs have plenty of patient demand without vision plans (although this is pretty rare).

Most optometrists are misinformed about the profitability of vision plans. If we only look at the exam fee that is offered, most ODs would reject the plan. But if you look at the total revenue and profit produced by the average patient in a vision plan, it is better than you think. Vision plan patients often buy non-covered services like retinal screening tests, multiple pairs of glasses, contact lenses plus glasses, nutritional supplements, optical upgrades and medical eye care. We need to look at the big picture of everything that is collected and the fact that the basic optical lab bill is covered for you. Vision plans can be smart for some practices.

13.6 Increasing Your Profitability with Vision Plans, Part 1

Rather than complaining about vision plans and the discounts they require, let's develop a strategy to maximize gross and net revenue with vision plans. Rather than wishing we could change vision plan policies, let's figure out a way to change your practice to adapt to the mandates in a positive way.

Should you join in the first place?
I'm well aware that there are some practices that do not accept vision plans. There are also some practices that accepted vision plans in the past and dropped them. The decision to become a provider for vision plans is important and complex and every practice owner should perform a careful analysis, but I'm going to save that discussion for a future article. Many ECPs have already analyzed the question of participation and have made the decision that belonging to some vision plans is in their best interest. Many ECPs realize that if they were to drop out of a vision plan, they may not be able to sustain their practices.

Read on and consider how your practice handles each of the following strategic points. The more prevalent vision plans are in your practice, the more action you should take.

Delegation

I think maximum delegation to technicians is an important step to increased profitability in all practices, but it's even more important if a high percentage of your patients are members of vision plans. The goal is to make the most out of the situation you're in. Let's play the hand you're dealt. You might prefer the practice model where the doctor does most of the testing and appointments are scheduled every half hour, but if exam fees are determined by vision plans, that model just won't work. You might like to examine patients the way you were taught in optometry school, but the real world may dictate that you find a more automated way to evaluate the eye and visual system.

It is true that a delegation model requires an investment in staff and instrumentation, but doing so puts first things first. If you don't have enough patient demand then perhaps you can see your entire patient load in two or three days per week. That is still a victory. You have created three days per week when you can do something else. Those three free days could be spent working in another practice, opening your own branch office in another community, or working on the management and marketing of your current office to increase the demand. But at least you are spending the correct amount of time on each patient based on the fees you're being paid.

Product selection

If you review the payments and charge-backs for all optical products under each vision plan, you'll see that some items yield greater profit than others. Typically, the more advanced lens designs allow a higher fee and greater profit. This should guide your decisions about what products to offer your patients. You do not have to carry all products and you should always recommend the best products. Typically, the vision plan member gets a great deal on the most advanced lenses and best frames and your practice receives a higher profit.

Selling up

This really goes hand in hand with product selection above, but you must spend time training your staff to recommend the best and to practice some basic sales techniques. I often hear staff members start a frame selection by asking the patient if they would like to see frames that are covered in full by the vision plan. We certainly know they do not have to start there. I often observe staff assist a patient with an eyeglass order and never mention the option of high index plastic, even though it provides a thinner lens with UV protection and excellent scratch resistance all in one. The assumption is that the patient does not want to spend any extra money, but that is so untrue! Sadly, when an optician fails to review and sell all the lens options, the quality of the eye care is diminished.

Fee structure

Many ECPs who have a high concentration of vision plans feel that there is no point to raising fees. The thinking is that the plan caps all the fees anyway so there would be no increase in collected revenue. I disagree with that philosophy on several levels. If a practice is dominated by vision plans I'd counter by asking why not charge high fees? The patients are not going to be upset in the least because they don't have to pay those fees. In fact the patient's perception of your practice is enhanced because many people judge the quality of the goods and services based on the usual price.

But the most important reason to charge higher fees is because there are many services and products that are not covered by vision plans. In those instances we must be able to generate a strong profit. Also, there are many services and products where a discount is mandated and you obviously will generate more revenue in those cases if your usual fee is higher. Consider the patient who needs an interim eye exam that is not covered. Consider the effect of the retail price mark-up when a frame overage is calculated. Consider the effect of price when a patient buys a second pair of glasses or must replace a lost pair of glasses in between eye exams. These are all examples of items that are not fully covered by vision plans and they happen every day in your office. Pricing makes a difference.

13.7 Increasing Your Profitability with Vision Plans, Part 2

Let's continue with our analysis of vision plans and develop a plan to make changes to your practice operations that will maximize profitability. In this issue, I'll focus on determining which third party to bill: vision plans or medical insurance.

Routine vision or medical eye care?

Many ECPs strictly define the scope of vision plans to only pertain to routine vision care or what is sometimes called a well-vision exam. If an examination reveals any abnormalities of a medical nature, then it is deemed to be outside the services covered by vision plans and the fees would then be billed to the patient's medical insurance. This approach seems smart and indeed some ODs report good success with it, but it can present problems. I advise extreme caution because patients have a bigger stake in this process than you may realize and it is possible to lose the patient and his family over it.

The difficulty is where to draw the line. An ECP can find a medical diagnosis on the vast majority of patients, which could effectively mean that nearly all exams could be billed to medical insurance, which may pay higher fees. It is easy to see that glaucoma patients are receiving medical eye care and require additional exams and special diagnostic tests that are not covered by vision plans. And the healthy 20 year old, two diopter myope would easily qualify for vision plan coverage. But what about the people in between the extremes? Consider an asymptomatic patient who mostly just needs an update on his glasses Rx to return to 20/20 vision, but has very mild signs of allergies or very slight nuclear sclerosis. Deciding when to call a case medical vs. vision can be difficult.

Why medical is not always better

Here are some factors that make aggressive conversion to medical insurance not in your best interest.

- Patients may be unhappy with the decision. In many cases, billing the exam fees to medical insurance will come back to costing the patient much more than using their vision plan. Patients will notice this and they won't like it. Many patients won't argue with their doctor over the billing but they will just go elsewhere next year so they can use their vision plan. Don't collect a few more dollars for the exam fee but lose the patient forever.
- Many patients have very high medical deductibles, so the eye exam applies to that and the patient must still pay the fee out of pocket. The medical exam fee in some offices is quite a bit higher than routine exam fees. This also requires you to transfer the balance to the patient and send a statement 30 to 60 days after the service. Some patients simply won't pay it, thinking it should have been covered.
- The refraction is typically not covered by medical plans so that must be billed to the vision plan (which does not pay well for refraction alone) or to the patient.
- Patients typically pay some part of the premium for vision plan coverage through their place of work and they feel they did not get to fully use the benefit they are entitled to.

- A disturbing trend is that some medical insurance plans are cutting their reimbursements so much that those fees are lower than the vision plan fees!
- It may be difficult for optometrists to get on some medical insurance networks due to state laws, ERISA plans, or staff HMO plans.
- Medical insurance plans may reject claims more often than vision plans, requiring more follow-up work and more write-offs.

The patient has a stake
My advice is to consider the patient's preference when it comes to billing. If you asked the patient if he would rather have today's visit billed to his vision plan or medical insurance, what would he say? Obviously, if additional office visits and diagnostic testing is needed, that is always billed to medical insurance.

13.8 Increasing Your Profitability with Vision Plans, Part 3

Thanks to the many readers who sent comments to me about parts one and two in this series on vision plans. There is no question that there are many diverse opinions about how to manage these programs in practice. Your comments will provide great topics for future *Management Tip of the Week* articles.
In this issue, I'd like to cover four more aspects of maximizing your profitability with vision plans.

Non-covered services
If a large percentage of your patient base is made up of vision plan members, then non-covered services (and products) are extremely important and you should develop a plan to maximize usage of them. Review this list and see if you can add or improve these services in your practice.

- Exam upgrades. The classic option to offer is routine retinal photos, but there are others such as macular pigment testing or other high tech screenings. The concept is that the vision plan covers basic routine eye exams, but some people will opt for more advanced technology and be willing to pay a nominal fee out of pocket. Have your staff present a simple handout at the front desk explaining the procedure and that the fee is not covered by vision plans. The patient can initial yes or no and you take it from there.

- Medical eye care. Expand your services to include diagnosis and treatment of eye disease to the maximum scope of your license. Invest in advanced diagnostic instruments. Bill these services to Medicare or private medical insurance.
- Optometric specialties. Many specialty areas like low vision, vision therapy, sports vision, industrial vision, computer vision, and corneal refractive therapy are not covered by vision plans. Build a practice in one of these fields.
- Premium optical products. Advanced lenses such as digital freeform progressives and premium antireflective coatings are either not covered or allow a higher reimbursement.
- Non-Rx sunglasses. You can sell them if you have a great selection. Great for contact lens patients.
- Second pairs of glasses. My practice offers a 50% discount on multiple pairs purchased at the same time and we sell a lot of them. The first pair can be covered by the vision plan. Do the math and see what your profit margin is after giving 50% off of your usual prices. Some profit is better than no profit.

Maximizing patient demand

This is one factor that vision plans generally do very well and it is the main reason most ECPs join the networks. Vision plans can quickly bring patients to your office just by being on the provider list, but you can attract even more patients with the following tips.

- Send special recall cards. If you notify patients who are due for their next eye exam and you remind them that the visit is covered by their vision plan, you will get a huge response. Do you run a separate search for recall by vision plan every month? Do you use a special post card with the vision plan logo? If you are confirming preappoints, does your staff mention that the exam is authorized?
- Promote vision plans on your website and in other forms of communication. Check with your vision plan companies to get permission to use the plan logo and display them in your marketing materials.
- Announce your participation in a new plan. If you join a vision plan, call the major employers who use it in your area and ask if they have an employee newsletter or bulletin board. Try to have a small article or announcement placed about your practice and that you are now a provider. You might even consider running a small ad in the local newspaper.

Contact lens services

Some ECPs tend to take contact lenses for granted. We fit contacts if the patient asks for them and we provide ongoing care for current wearers, but we are fairly passive about it. I think that approach is missing out on a huge opportunity, especially if your practice is a strong user of vision plans. Contact lens fees for both services and products are generally almost fully collectable under vision plan rules. You may want to re-read that previous sentence because you can't say that about many eye care services and products. Most vision plans require a minor discount of 10 to 15% off usual fees, but after that the plan pays an allowance and the patient pays the balance. That makes contact lenses extremely attractive in my book.

I think most ECPs should raise their contact lens professional fees and leave their product prices fairly low and competitive. After that, realize that enthusiasm sells and if you simply recommend contact lenses to more people, even if they don't ask about them, you'll fit more. Start by having lots of your patients try on a free trial pair in your office at no fee. Just try them on and have your technician check with the patient and see if a fitting exam is desired.

In-office optical lab

Reducing your cost of goods is a great way to increase profits when the prices are fixed by vision plans. One of the best ways to reduce cost of goods is to operate your own in-office lens finishing lab. Of course this is only effective with plans that allow you to use your own lab, but many do and even VSP, which historically required the use of a contract network lab, now has a program that pays you to do the lab work. With the advanced technology of lens edgers today, it's very easy to train anyone who knows how to use a lensometer to cut and edge perfect lenses. Arrange for a demo of a new edger in your office or compare several brands at the next major eye care conference. And check out the prices of lens uncuts to see how much you can save on your lab bill.

13.9 Vision Plans: Resist or Embrace?

I mentioned in my last article on marketing projects that I like to look at patient acquisition within three potential opportunities: marketing, word-of-mouth referral, and vision plan participation. In this article, I'll focus on strategies about vision plans.

Practice owners face a tough decision about joining vision plan networks and there is no blanket right choice for all. Much depends on your marketplace and your goals for your practice. The options range from saying no to all vision plans to accepting all of them to settling in between and participating in some plans. To me, the biggest factor is how busy your practice is right now and how busy do you want it to be?

The decision really revolves around patient demand. Say what you will about vision plans, but they can dramatically and quickly change the number of patients you see. Remember, even though a vision plan may be less profitable than private pay patients, if you have empty chair time in your practice, some profit is better than no profit. And contrary to popular opinion, all vision plans are profitable. But if you can fill your schedule with patients that provide higher collected revenue per visit, there is no question that is the smarter move.

A smaller or larger practice?

To determine the right patient schedule for your practice, start by thinking if you want the characteristics of a larger practice or a smaller one. This is an oversimplification, of course, but it can be a useful tool to help you determine your goals. A larger practice is not necessarily better and we all have different values for what is important in life.

Here are a few practice traits to consider along with some thoughts about each:

- Personal income. This is not as clear as one might think because smaller practices can have a very large net revenue due to lower overhead costs. But if the practice can be built into the multi-million dollar gross revenue range (with one large office or via multiple locations), personal income for the OD/owner will be higher. The practice net income as a percentage of gross revenue may actually be lower in a large practice, but a lower percentage of a much higher number can still be more in dollars.
- Work factors. There are many aspects to this: How hard does the OD/owner work? How many hours per week? What types of tasks? This all depends on what you like to do, but to me, a larger practice has the advantage here. A small practice with smaller gross revenue and a smaller staff means that more work falls directly on the OD/owner. Most of the patient care will be delivered by the OD/owner. This may be a good thing for some ODs, but the desire to see patients can also change throughout one's career. Practice income and cash flow virtually stops if the owner takes extended time off. The owner must personally handle a variety of business related tasks.

- Associate ODs. This is much easier to achieve in a larger practice and it dovetails with the point above. It is hard for a single OD in a smaller practice to afford an associate doctor. With lower patient demand, the owner would basically be paying another doctor to see the patients he/she could have seen. There is not enough net income to compensate two doctors. Smaller office facilities don't have enough room for two doctors to work at the same time. If there is a large amount of patient demand, enough to create a backlog of patients for the owner, an associate OD can come in and generate more than enough additional revenue to pay his/her salary.
- Staff. Managing a staff is considered the biggest challenge for practice owners, so many ODs want to keep the number of employees small. I actually find it easier to manage a larger staff because if someone calls off work, takes a vacation or quits, the doctors and remaining staff don't feel the pinch as much. With a larger staff, I can delegate more of the work of seeing patients and of running the business. An office manager is a must with a larger staff, so much of the staff management, hiring and training can be delegated to him or her.
- Equipment. Many smaller practices have the very best diagnostic technology available, so this factor does not have a clear winner. But advanced instrumentation can be very expensive and it is often justified and financed easier with a large patient base.
- Asset value. Business valuations are based on revenue, so practices with higher gross and net incomes will appraise higher.

Can you have a larger practice without vision plans?
This would be ideal. This may be what drives many ODs to avoid vision plans: the hope of becoming fairly large without having to accept the lower profit per patient and living within the rules of vision plans.

There are a few areas of the country where vision plans are not very strong, but this is rare, especially in urban settings. In my experience, patients who do not have vision plans and therefore, pay out-of-pocket, are more likely to seek eye care from low-priced providers and online vendors. This makes it harder for the independent OD to attract this group.

There are always exceptions and I am certainly generalizing, but the vast majority of large practices that I know accept vision plans. Many even accept the plans that are deemed less desirable. In many ways, vision plans simply provide access to large populations of patients, which often end up needing medical eye care or other non-covered services.

Some ODs try to work around the issue by accepting payment out-of-network or by providing discounts, but the vast majority of patients with vision plans won't find these doctors because they only look to the network provider list.

The largest population for eye care is for routine exams, eyeglasses and simple contact lens fittings, so it is difficult to have a large practice without catering to this group. The following specialties can be very successful within a large practice or as a core component in a small practice, but they have limitations.

- Ortho-K. A great specialty, but the population of good candidates who can afford it may be small.
- Vision therapy. Great again, but the candidate population is still small compared to primary eye care. Some parents can't (or won't) afford it and if you accept medical insurance for these services, it does not pay that well.
- Medical eye care. Great again, but is mostly office visits and diagnostic tests. The fees are good and we should work to build this part of the practice for diversification, but it is not as lucrative as optical.

One good way to find out how much patient demand is available without vision plans is to not accept them for a few years. If you see strong growth in revenue year-over-year, then keep going. But if growth is slow, don't keep waiting it out for very long. If that occurs, change strategies, embrace vision plans and learn how to be profitable with them.

13.10 Dropping Managed Care Plans, Part 1: The Philosophy of the High Fee Practice

Discontinuing managed care plans is a concept that many optometrists long to pursue, but it's a very complex issue. To cover the subject in this tip format, I'll write a four-part series, with each article focusing on a different aspect as follows:

Part 1: The philosophy of the high fee practice
Part 2: Evaluating chair costs, marginal costs and time management
Part 3: Evaluating vision plans and medical plans
Part 4: Communicating financial policies to patients

Free enterprise

As we develop our marketing plans for our practices, we run into an obstacle that most small businesses don't have to face: we are not part of the free enterprise system. When managed health care became prevalent in our society, we lost the ability to set our fees where we wanted.

That's a disadvantage, because business owners usually have the freedom to select the quality and value they wish to offer, and to set prices they deem appropriate. Ultimately, the marketplace decides if prices are appropriate, but there is a growing segment of the population that wants the best, and is willing to pay for it. When prices are fixed by a third party at a low level, business owners must make cuts in services in order to maximize profits. Maximizing profits is what business owners do; that's what business is all about. Discounted managed care plans force ODs into a low-fee / basic-service philosophy.

A better business model for optometry, in my opinion, is a high-fee / advanced-service practice, but to succeed, a large percentage of the patient base must be private pay or covered by a full-fee medical plan. For many practices today, that would mean dropping participation in some managed care plans. A common response to that notion is that it can't be done in "my practice", or in "my community", but let's not be too quick to write that off. It is possible to attract people out of their plan into a non-participating practice, if the benefits are compelling enough. It is possible to develop the private pay sector of a practice, while still keeping the best of the managed care plans available. A practice can do both, but control the mix.

Note that when I write about managed care, it could refer to either vision plans or medical plans.

Private pay and managed care coexist

The blending of the private pay and managed care components of a practice can be further enhanced in two ways:

1. Not participating in a plan, but still seeing patients that are members of the plan. These patients file for out-of-network reimbursement themselves. Granted, the benefits are often much lower this way, but it can still occur if the practice offers compelling advantages to the patient. These patients become private pay, even though they have some managed care coverage.
2. Accepting a managed care plan, and providing additional, non-covered services to its members. Even those patients who have managed care coverage can elect to purchase multiple pairs of

eyeglasses, high-end frame and lens options, sunglasses, contact lenses, low vision aids, and advanced medical testing. The mentality that says "I only want what my plan covers" can be changed in the right practice environment.

Learning from other businesses

We only need to look at dentistry to see how high-fee practices can flourish. Sure, there are dental insurance plans, but most of them allow the dentist to balance bill the patient, and dentistry has enough elective and cosmetic procedures to allow plenty of free enterprise in their practices. Professional dental fees are high, marketing efforts are advanced and patient loyalty is excellent. There are opportunities in optometry too, if we simply pursue them.

Ritz-Carlton hotels do very well, even though there are plenty of Holiday Inns out there. Exclusive restaurants in major cities are booked for months in advance and require a credit card just to make a reservation, even though there are alternatives like Applebee's and McDonald's.

How is a patient attracted out of his plan?

By offering something compelling. Let's look at a real-world scenario that happens all the time as an illustration. A patient is so impressed with the services at Main Street Eye Care that he raves about it to a close friend who needs eye care (let's call the friend Seymour). The referral is very strong, and Seymour trusts his friend. Seymour has had mediocre experiences from his previous eye doctors. Seymour decides to see the new doctor and calls the office to schedule an appointment, and the friendly, caring receptionist on the phone asks if Seymour has any insurance plans. Seymour mentions the vision plan he has through his employer, but he is politely informed that the office does not participate in that plan. The receptionist mentions that he can file his own claim with his plan, but the exam fee of $XXX is due at the time of service. Seymour decides to schedule the appointment, based on the strong referral from his friend, and because he figures his eyes are worth it.

Situations like this actually happen quite frequently when the patient chooses a practice based on reputation and referral, rather than looking up someone on a list of providers. People find optometrists in a variety of ways. If your practice routinely turns patients into goodwill ambassadors, you'll get plenty of new patients who select their eye care practitioner first – not their vision plan.

If you want to pursue the high-end market, start by making your practice high-end. It takes time to build that reputation, but in the meantime you can analyze your practice profitability and develop a plan to control managed care. More on that next week.

13.11 Dropping Managed Care Plans, Part 2: Evaluating Chair Costs, Marginal Costs and Time Management

Before we evaluate specific vision or medical plans for acceptance (or continuation) in your practice, we should first evaluate your practice costs. Knowing how much it costs you to see a patient is the first step in determining if a plan is profitable, and how profitable. This evaluation is often referred to as chair cost, as in what is the cost incurred each time a patient sits in the exam chair? You can calculate chair cost per patient or per hour; both are useful.

Chair cost calculation; the easy way

The basic premise is to divide your fixed costs by the number of patients you see in a given time period, like one year. Similarly, you could divide the total fixed costs by the number of hours your office was open during that time period. Fixed costs are considered to be everything in your list of expenses, except your cost of goods sold. One easy way to figure this is to take your true gross (collected revenue; not billed charges), and subtract all cost of goods (frames, contacts and lab bills) and subtract the practice net (or all doctors' income). If your practice has typical expense ratios, you would subtract about 30% for the COGS and 30% for the net, leaving 40% of your gross as fixed costs. If your practice grosses $1 million, your fixed costs would be $400,000.

Counting the number of patients or the number of hours can be trickier than it seems. Patient numbers are really the number of exams performed, but should that be full exams only or all office visits? It could be either way, or you could use a formula that counts an OV as a half point and comprehensive exams as a full point. The important thing is to be consistent when you make comparisons. You might want to use a value that relates to the plan you're evaluating, such as, counting full exams only if you're looking at a vision plan that will be used primarily for full exams. The hourly calculation begs the question of using all office hours or just hours when doctors are scheduled for patients.

If the million dollar gross practice above saw 4,000 patients, the chair cost would be $100 per patient ($400,000/4000). If it were open 2,000 hours, the hourly chair cost would be $200 per hour.

Marginal costs

Knowing the per patient cost in our example, we might deduce that if you accept a vision plan that pays less than $100 for an exam, you're losing money on each patient. The old joke is that you can't make up a per unit loss with volume! But it's really not that simple. In reality, when you consider participating with a managed care plan, you're fixed costs are already being met. The rent is already being paid and staff salaries are already covered. A fair question might be, what would be the *additional* expenses involved in seeing the patients that come from that plan? Those expenses may be zero, unless you have to hire one more staff person. The rent would not increase and the electric bill will remain the same with or without this vision plan. The analysis of a special group of expenses like this is often called the marginal cost.

How full is the appointment book?

A key factor in your evaluation is how well booked you are with patients. This factor goes hand-in-hand with your cost analysis. There is some truth in the common sense approach that says a low-paying exam is better than no exam. A good analogy is in the airline industry. If a commercial jet takes of with empty seats, those revenue opportunities are lost forever. The airline would be better off discounting the tickets for those remaining seats to $49 each, than having the seat be empty. In fact, that is exactly what airlines do, through the use of sophisticated pricing models. Likewise, an appointment slot with an empty exam chair is revenue that can never be recovered in your practice.

Beware of the inertia of managed care

There is danger in accepting too many managed care plans, however, just because the practice is not fully busy. Your practice develops a momentum that can be hard to change. The practice philosophy can be formed by the patients you see and by the fee levels that are generated. Policies are built around managed care plans and frame inventory is based upon plan coverage amounts. Staff training and staff attitude can shift. The practice reputation begins to reflect a managed care approach, and before you know it, you are not the high fee / advanced service practice you once dreamt about.

Remember, building time into your schedule purely for administration, and not patient care, is a good thing. Use that time for practice development and marketing that will build the private-pay sector of your practice.

13.12 Dropping Managed Care Plans, Part 3: Evaluating Vision Plans and Medical Plans

In parts one and two of this series on managed care, I wrote about the philosophy of the high fee practice and how to evaluate your practice costs. This week, let's focus on how to decide if you should participate with any given managed vision care or health care plan. This exercise does not just apply to new plans that become available to you, but also to all the plans you currently accept. Periodically, it's smart to review the plans you work with and decide if they are still meeting the goals of your practice.

Your practice goals
Your practice business and marketing plan should have considerable impact on your managed care decisions. Some practices are designed to fill a low price niche, or they are located in economic areas that dictate low fees. On the other hand, most ODs have the freedom to decide on the market niche they wish to serve, and it's possible to even change that niche if so desired. So, decide on your practice philosophy first, and then look at which plans to accept.

We also discussed the empty exam chair syndrome as it relates to accepting managed care plans. It's best to achieve a balance of private pay and managed care. If your appointment book is very full, you may be able to drop some plans. If you have many openings, you may want to look for additional plans to work with. Some appointment availability is a good thing if you use the time to grow the private side of the practice.

The first step I would take in this analysis is to gather data about the percentage of your practice that is made up of each plan that you currently accept. This should be done in two ways: the percentage of total gross revenue and the percentage of all patients seen in the past year. Armed with this list of plans and percentages, evaluate the factors listed below with a number scale with 1 being the worst and 10 being the best. Some factors are not applicable to all plans, like optical fees on a medical plan.

Managed care checklist

- Fees allowed under the plan. This encompasses exam fees and optical fees and the freedom to balance bill the patient. A rating of 10 would be a plan that pays your usual and customary fees or allows you to balance bill.
- Any caps placed on non-covered options, like ophthalmic lens add-ons.
- Ease of fee calculation and plan coverage amounts.
- Ability to do optical lab work in-office or to use the lab of your choice.
- Ease of verification of benefits in advance.
- Ease of claim filing and time required.
- Ease of claim troubleshooting if rejected and availability of human claim support.
- Accuracy and timeless of payments.
- Intrusiveness of requirements, policies and programs.
- Benefit frequency.
- Volume of patients actually seen under the plan or likelihood of high volume for new plans. What employers in the area use the plan?
- Ask your staff for their opinions about working with each plan.

Applying the analysis to your practice

The next step is to consider your practice goals and make a decision. If you are starting a new practice and need patients very badly, you can benefit from joining some managed care panels. Consider joining the largest and best vision plan in your area and Medicare right away. By the way, I really don't see any reason any OD would not participate with Medicare, unless the practice is limited to pediatrics. Medicare pays well, does not discriminate against optometrists in the medical arena, and does not require advance verification of benefits.

If you have a medically oriented practice, or want to build this aspect, join the major health care plans in your area and study billing and coding. But be cautious not to allow your medical focus to weaken your optical dispensary. Fees for office visits and diagnostic procedures alone are not enough to grow your practice into the top income levels. Optical fees are significant and this revenue stream exists without the doctor.

If you already work with many managed care plans and would like to reduce your dependence on them, perform the analysis above and drop the worst of the plans. It should be easy to figure out which one that is. Study the affect this change has on your practice gross, net and hours worked. This can be a valuable lesson on what will happen if you drop another plan, without being much risk to the financial health of your practice.

13.13 Dropping Managed Care Plans, Part 4: Communicating with Patients

Let's suppose you decide to bite the bullet and drop a managed vision care plan that your practice has been participating with for some time. You realize that you may see a decrease in patient visits because some of these patients will choose to go elsewhere, but you also know that this group of patients is the least profitable group you have. It may be possible to reduce your staff costs, since there will be less work filing claims. You may actually be able to see fewer patients and not see much change in your net income at all. You may even be able to fill those empty appointment slots with a more profitable group of patients, or use the free time to focus on practice development and staff training. In this way, your net income may actually grow, even though you dropped an insurance plan.

Patient form letters

I often hear doctors who have dropped managed care plans discussing the form letter they sent to all patients to notify them that the plan is no longer accepted by their office and provide all the reasons why this change was necessary. Why ODs do this remains a mystery to me. It seems to me that this is the fastest way to ensure these patients will look elsewhere for a provider. It is almost like telling them they need to find a new doctor. And patients don't care about the injustices you have to deal with in managed care; it's boring stuff to them.

I believe we have an ethical responsibility to inform patients if we no longer accept an insurance plan, but I opt for telling them one by one, verbally. It happens automatically when the patient calls to schedule his next appointment, because my staff always obtains all insurance information over the phone and reviews our office policy about fees and payment. This is an office policy that I think is extremely important for efficient practice management, but many practices just don't do it.

Get it over the phone!

Our standard practice is to ask every patient who calls for an appointment if they intend to use a vision or health insurance plan with their visit. If the answer is yes, we ask the name of the plan, and we then inform the patient if that plan is accepted by our practice, or not. If not, we always quote the exam fee (even if the caller doesn't ask), and we let them know that the fee is due at the time of the visit. We also let the patient know that they may file their own claim with the insurance company and that we'll provide the paperwork they need for that.

If the caller has an insurance plan that we accept, we always verify benefits before the day of the exam. If we find that benefits are not available, we call the patient back and let him know that he can still keep the appointment, but the fee is due at the time of the exam.

It may seem like a little work to train staff to do this, and to require that the information be obtained over the phone for every appointment – but it's all worth it because of the increased cash flow, reduced accounts receivable, and reduced stress in the office since we no longer have confrontations at the front desk. Trust me, this in one policy your staff will embrace once they try it. Patients actually appreciate the information; most know there will be a cost for their services and materials and they want to know how and when payment is expected. We never have a situation when we ask for payment without having told the patient about it in advance. We also never transfer fees to an insurance company without having the benefits pre-approved. Imagine, never having a situation where you are battling with an insurance company for payment after services have been rendered! It can be done; just ask the patient to pay it.

Given the above procedure, informing patients about plan participation is automatic. We may add or drop plans from time to time, just as we raise fees on occasion, and no formal notification is required.

Chapter 14. Clinical Efficiency and Delegation

14.1 Increasing Your Patient Flow

There are many good ways to design your appointment schedule. Part of that decision depends on the optometrist's clinical philosophy about eye care and how much time they need to perform an eye exam that meets their standards. However, with the increasing dominance of managed care, many ODs are trying to find ways to be more efficient. This is a very smart strategy and it can definitely increase your profitability.

Contrary to popular belief, seeing more patients per day does not have to be stressful for doctors or staff members. It does not have to reduce quality of care. It does not have to take away from the patient experience. And it does not mean that anyone must work harder.

An important question in your effort to increase patient flow is if you have any more patients to see. If you have lots of patients wanting to be seen, the change in your routine is fairly easy and very rewarding. If you don't have tons of patients, increase your flow and efficiency anyway. If your average number of exams per week is 50, see them in three days instead of four or five days. Use the newly created free time to market your practice.

Here are some key factors to work on.

Delegation

Many optometrists are stuck in an old exam process. Step out of the box and think about what you could delegate if you had the staff and the exam room set up that would make it work. There are a few high level procedures in the eye exam that only a doctor can perform, but not many. How about visual acuity measurement or routine tonometry? Pick some things and make it happen.

To achieve higher delegation in your clinical setting, you may need more instrumentation or a change in your pretesting room layout. That's fine; go ahead and decide on what you need. It is a smart investment.

Always observe the laws of practice in your state or jurisdiction.

Staffing

Many times, the toughest part of implementing change is what to do first. I find one of the best first steps is to hire another employee. Don't worry about increasing your payroll cost; it is almost a certainty that your productivity will increase and you'll bring in more new revenue than the employee costs.

Multiple exam rooms per doctor
The baseline for efficiency, unless the practice is a new start-up or very small, is two exam rooms per working doctor. More than two per doctor is even better. If you are adding a second OD and you will both see patients on the same days, you need four exam rooms. If you can't find the space to convert, you will have to look for larger office space, but be creative. Meet with a contractor and ask if he can move a wall or two, add a doorway, take out a closet, or repurpose that outdated contact lens training room.
A technician can use one of the exam rooms to complete the pretesting before the doctor comes in. That can free up the pretesting room quicker so another technician can bring the next patient in.
If you have a room that is too small for an exam room, consider making it a dilated exam room with an exam chair and slit lamp. But if you can put those items in there, why not add a phoroptor and a mirror for the acuity chart and make it a full-function room. Automated refracting systems are designed to work in very small spaces, but you need to add a slit lamp to most of the designs I see.

Dilation
The need to dilate is a professional judgment only you can make, but consider if adding an Optomap could reduce your dilation percentage. Or consider dilating in advance of seeing the patient or when you first meet the patient.

Scribing
Another form of delegation, but having a technician record your exam findings is a huge time saver. How much time would you save if you did not have to record any data in your EHR system?

Talking time
OK, I'll come right out and say it. It is possible that you talk too much. I know your patients love you and they enjoy the chit-chat and it is important they understand their eye conditions. But it might not be as interesting as you think. Slightly less talk could be a good thing. Most people want to get on with their day.

Wasted time
Be on the lookout for ways you and your staff waste time. A doctor who must walk patients in from the reception area or out to the optical is a big waste of time. Those few minutes add up!

Appointment schedule

As you implement your new efficient approach, design a new appointment template that will keep you busy, but not running behind. Three exams (a mix of all types, but most are comprehensive) per hour is a good goal. Consider having some technicians start their work day 15 to 30 minutes before the doctor officially starts his/her schedule. The same could happen with your lunch breaks. Have staff get started with pretesting so the patient is ready when you start work. But don't be late.

These changes do not have to make you rush or act crazy. In fact, the time you save with delegation or by eliminating waste can be used for the important things that only you can do.

14.2 How many patients per day?

One of the fastest ways to increase your income is to increase the number of patients examined per day. With your fixed office expenses already met, any increase in sales volume per day will fall to the bottom line and into your pocket. If your average sale per exam is $350 (that is realistic) and if we allow 30% for cost of goods, you will net $245 for each additional exam seen per day. If you see two more patients per day for five days a week and you work 48 weeks per year, you would net an additional $117,600 per year. Let me be clear that we are talking about net income. Pretty amazing, really.

Can you see more per day?

I often meet some resistance from doctors and staff when I propose the idea of changing their office procedures to see more exams per day, but when you consider the incredible financial potential, the interest level always goes up. Now that I have your attention, let's consider the changes you would have to make to see two more full exams per day.

- Change the appointment schedule. Unless you want to work longer hours or skip lunch, you will need to shorten the standard appointment slot that you currently use for an exam. If you are adding two exams and if an exam takes about 20 minutes of doctor time, you need to find 40 minutes. If your schedule currently allows 30 minutes for an exam slot, and if you have 10 of those per day and if you shave 10 minutes off each one and make it a 20 minute slot, you will have created 100 minutes. That is much more than you need, but you could insert a few block out periods into the schedule to be sure you run on time. I find that every practice is different and it is best to fine tune and customize the schedule based on actual operational experience.

- Hire an additional technician. You can certainly test the new schedule first with your present staff, but be prepared to hire an extra employee quickly if you want to maintain staff morale and if you want to continue to deliver high quality eye care. You have the potential to increase your net income by over $100,000; you can certainly handle the additional payroll cost.
- Increase your delegation. The amount of delegation that exists in eye care varies tremendously, so I can't be very specific here, but be sure you are delegating effectively. Increasing daily production is the ideal time to take a major step up in delegation so you can save more doctor time per exam. The goal is for doctors to spend more time on high level physical exam procedures and on patient communication and less time on data collection. Be sure you're delegating tasks that do not require new instruments, such as case history, visual acuity, lensometry, stereopsis, color vision, and blood pressure.
- Invest in automated instrumentation. An autorefractor and a tech-friendly tonometer are great places to start. Add a visual field screener and a digital retinal camera for screening photos and you are well on your way to an efficient practice.

Additional thoughts:

- Review your exam routine. Every way that you can save a few minutes in your exam matters. A five minute savings per patient adds up to an hour and 40 minutes if you see 20 patients per day! Retinoscopy and Goldmann tonometry on every patient requires more much more time than that.
- You need not limit your goal to an increase of only two extra patients per day. How many patients per day can an eye care professional see with excellent staff support, and still provide excellent patient care?
- Don't worry that you will have to work harder with the new schedule. Seeing 25 patients per day is no more work than seeing 10 if you have enough help. In fact, the shorter visit with each patient is actually easier because you can eliminate having to perform boring and repetitious tests and concentrate on diagnosis and treatment.

The biggest challenge to higher production

There is a fly in the ointment, though, when it comes to this ambitious plan. Many practices simply do not have enough patients to increase the number examined per day. You could consolidate the existing appointments into fewer days as I've described, but most practices will quickly run out of patients and would simply see holes in the schedule. I strongly encourage you to do it anyway, even if you don't have much patient backlog! Compress the appointments you do have into fewer days and practice more efficiently on those days. The benefits are still huge even if you have some unfilled slots.

- You and your staff learn how to work efficiently so you can quickly absorb more business as it develops in the future. You will be ready.
- Your practice looks more impressive. Patients see a busy, high-functioning practice instead of a slow, sad one. Patients who are impressed refer others much more often.
- Your time is managed better, allowing you some free days without interruption so you can concentrate on building your practice.
- You have appointments available sooner for people who call and want to be seen quickly.

14.3 A New Concept: Reduce the Time Patients Spend in Your Office

Here's an idea that many eye care professionals (ECPs) have never thought to work on: find ways to reduce the total time patients spend in the office. Achieving that goal is really a win-win situation because (a) patients actually love a shorter visit. Their satisfaction with your practice greatly increases if you get them in and out quickly. And (b) practice profitability increases when you spend fewer resources, like staff time, on each patient visit. If all visits are quicker, the practice can see more patients per day.

Total patient time
While I'm sure most ECPs try to be economical with their own time (although, amazingly many don't think about it at all), I'm recommending that you reduce the total time spent in the office by patients. Total patient time is different than doctor time because the former includes things like completing forms, waiting, pretesting, patient education, eyeglass selection, and so on. Ironically, many ECPs think they will impress patients if they make the typical visit fuller. They reason that if more things are happening, perhaps the patient will perceive greater value. This kind of thinking is even more prevalent in practices that are not extremely busy. It's false thinking. Who ever said patients want an eye exam to take a long time?! They don't. It's really not that much fun. Patients have busy lives and the eye exam is just a necessary task that most people would really rather not have to endure.

Of course, we should make the visit as enjoyable as possible and we can give patients a pleasant surprise by making the visit more interesting, but making the visit short is an important way to make it enjoyable. Don't wear out your welcome!

The new value of personal time

The practice that works to reduce wasted time, while still being thorough and delivering high quality, wins. Patients who think back about their eye care visit and realize they were able to get in and out with amazing efficiency will love your practice! They will refer more friends and relatives. Convenience and personal time is valued so highly today that people will actually pay higher fees if they can spend less time with you!

What can be done?

Here are some time consuming factors that can often be made more efficient.

- Reduce the wait in the reception area. It's easy to become complacent about the initial wait time. After all, it has become quite common in all health care, right? It behooves you to be the exception. Review your appointment scheduling system and your operations to eliminate reasons why you run late.
- Reduce the time at check in. Having a staff member at the front desk at all times can make the welcoming greeting more efficient and it gets the process started immediately. Have staff members complete most of the records and paperwork the day before the visit so there is less to do when the patient arrives.
- Reduce the number of forms for the patient to fill out. Don't overdo the history form, lifestyle questionnaire, various disclaimers, insurance forms, retinal photo approval, pupil dilation form, etc. I don't think established patients need to complete another history form; we just update the original one in person.
- Reduce delays waiting for technicians to review the record and call the patient into the clinical area. Some employees simply procrastinate. Maybe the tech likes to chit-chat with the receptionist before calling the patient. I realize the tech needs to review the history form or the last exam results a bit, but train staff to move things along.
- Reduce unnecessary pretesting. There is a balance between being thorough and being wasteful. It is efficient to delegate data collection, but don't run tests that don't yield valuable information and don't duplicate tests. For example, it makes no sense for the technician to spend time on a subjective refraction with a digital

refraction system if the doctor is going to repeat the refraction anyway.

- Reduce the inner wait. Patients don't just wait in the reception area; they wait again in the exam room. Develop a system so the doctor knows when there is another patient waiting.
- Be flexible with your exam routine. Can you change your process on the fly and shift when some procedures are done in order to stay on schedule?
- Reduce unnecessary tests by the doctor. It is never impressive for the patient to sit behind the phoroptor; the novelty wears of in about 60 seconds. Are there any tests that you do routinely, but don't really need?
- Reduce the wait for dilation. Beyond the actual time needed for the drug to work, dilation is a huge drain on time in many ways. It's easy to put the drops in and say "we'll call you back in when you're ready", but do staff members let the time run over by several minutes? Are the exam rooms tied up and there is no place to go? Is the doctor too busy to see the dilated patient? Review your process with your staff and make this more efficient. Consider when the drops are instilled and what kinds of drops are used. Try to avoid having patients return on a different day for dilation (a huge time drain) or frame selection (a potential loss of business).
- Be economical with your patient education time. Choose your words carefully and get to the point. Don't over-explain and don't be too technical. Ask the patient if he wants to hear more on a topic. Computerized education video clips can be great, but don't hold people captive watching commercials that they are not interested in. It can backfire on you.
- Use a scribe in your exam room. Having a technician record data and make notes as you talk to the patient is the ultimate time saver.
- Don't waste time walking patients around the office and waiting for a staff member. Scribes eliminate this.
- Reduce the time spent at checkout. At this point, the patient usually really wants to leave. Streamline the process and don't make patients stand around very long.

There is a fine line between providing advanced services, new technology and personal care, and going on too long to point of being boring. Choose your procedures carefully and spend your patient's precious time on things that deliver maximum punch. Remember that the time spent in the optical dispensary or trying on contact lenses is a very profitable part of the visit. The less time spent in the waiting area, pretesting and exam rooms; the more time available for optical and contact lenses. Patients will only spend so much time in your office; use it wisely.

14.4 Advice for Success: Work Faster

As a consultant, I talk with a lot of optometrists. My goal is to help them to be more productive and profitable. I love to find the low hanging fruit first, which are the easy things to change that will produce a dramatic increase in revenue. In many cases (certainly not all), optometrists simply take too long to perform an eye exam.

There are many factors in your practice that are difficult to change, but the time you spend on each exam is directly within your control. You may be surprised to read that spending less time could be good for your practice, but read on.

I know the eye exam length is a sensitive subject. Your exam is part of your professional philosophy and it is completely in your domain. I respect that, and I realize that in the end, the decision is completely yours to make. But I have found there are many misconceptions about what patients really want and what constitutes high quality eye care.

Times have changed drastically since many of us graduated from optometry school. Diagnostic technology has greatly advanced and collected revenue has not advanced due to the increase in managed care. These are two very good reasons for us to look at the time we spend on an eye exam. Why should our eye exam procedures be the same as they were ten years ago?

Factors to consider

- Eye care economics. Let's consider the fee you are actually paid for an eye exam. Most ODs define routine vision exams differently than medical eye exams and the fees reflect that. Vision plans typically pay between $40 and $70 for an exam. When you consider the expenses of running your practice, this fee does not support a high amount of doctor time.
- Patient perception. What makes us think patients want an eye exam to take a long time? They don't. It may seem like your patients love spending lots of time in your exam room, but patients are naturally polite to their doctor. You're the expert and they are paying you for your service. They are not going to tell you they wish you would

speed it up. But their experience may actually be somewhat unpleasant.

- How do you measure quality? Patient surveys? Percentage of eyeglass remakes? In my experience, in my own practice and in working with many other high volume practices, the quality measures are as good or better as in slow-paced practices. Patients love their doctor and staff members in the high volume practice. Patients tell these doctors that their exam was the most thorough they ever had.
- Allow more time for contact lenses and glasses. When you take a long time for pretesting and the eye exam, the patient will want to rush the dispensing aspect of the visit because they have other plans for their day. Many ODs tell me they do not bring up contact lenses to many patients because they just don't have the time. What a shame! Contact lenses can be very financially rewarding even with vision plans because many provide an allowance and you can collect the balance from the patient.
- Create more dedicated time for practice management. Working faster allows you to create large blocks of time for non-clinical tasks. If you can see the same number of patients you see now in fewer days, you can use the time saved to work on your practice. Use it for marketing projects, staff training and for improving the patient experience.
- If you work five days per week and produce $600,000 of gross revenue, it would be possible to produce that same amount in half the time. Why not compress the patients and be very busy when you are in your clinic?
- Change something! Take control! For many ODs, the procedures that have been in use for many years have not proven effective. The result is not likely to change unless you change something. If you want big results, change something big.
- Always follow local laws and contractual obligations. Your exam should meet the medical standard of care, insurance plan mandates and regulations by the state board of optometry.

What if the practice is not that busy?

One of the major reasons that ODs provide long eye exams is because they are not that busy anyway. You may reason that the patient will be impressed with the extra time provided and the thoroughness. I actually think they will be more impressed if the exam was efficient and they were allowed to be on their way. I also think that the slow approach leads the doctor to develop bad habits. The doctors and staff become accustomed to the slow pace and eventually can't see any other way. My advice is to be quick and delegate as much as you can based on the size of your staff. A small practice can't afford a huge staff, so the doctor must do more, but work toward growing the practice and becoming more efficient over time.

How can you do a faster exam?
It is best if you figure out how you can do a high quality exam in less time, but I'll provide some general guidance.

- Delegate more. What can you do to save doctor time? Even highly delegated practices can usually delegate more. How about scribing or technician refraction?
- Some small talk is good for the patient relationship, but let the staff handle some of it.
- Learn how to politely stop a patient who talks too much. Take control.
- Don't do tests you don't need. They do not impress anyone.
- Make the subjective refraction fast and easy.
- Limit the patient education and treatment options. Patients generally want just the simple highlights. Recommend the best option; don't provide the whole list of options.
- Reduce the patient's waiting time, such as waiting in the reception area, too much paperwork, waiting for the doctor and waiting for the optician.

14.5 The Super-Tech Concept

More and more optometrists are trying the “super-tech” concept that I have been using in my practice for many years. I have written and lectured about this strategy many times, but I receive a lot of questions on this topic, so I'll review the highlights in this article.

The concept of a scribing technician/optician works extremely well in my practice, but like most practice management strategies, it is not a good fit for every practice.

What is a super-tech?
A super-tech is a clinical technician who is also a scribe and is also an optician. This person assists the optometrist with all aspects of direct patient care. The doctor delegates a great deal of the clinical and optical management of each patient to a super-tech.

The super-tech approach to scribing differs from the idea of hiring one assistant to follow the doctor and record exam data. The super-tech is a well-trained ophthalmic technician who performs the case history and extensive pretesting before the doctor sees the patient. That technician becomes the scribe for the doctor's exam and can enter exam data at a higher level than an administrative scribe. The super-tech assists the doctor as needed during the exam, listens to the case summary by the doctor and can carry out whatever final care is needed.

The super-tech is also a trained optician and walks patients who need glasses to the optical area and conducts the frame selection, takes all measurements and writes up the fees. No hand-off is needed because the optician was in the exam room to hear the recommendations first-hand. The super-tech also carries out the treatment plan if it does not involve eyeglasses, such as additional medical testing, contact lens fitting, referral to a specialist, or patient education.

The super-tech concept assigns one technician to stay with each patient at all times throughout the entire visit. Multiple super-techs are needed in a busy practice; the doctor will work with several technicians as they rotate and go to wherever they are needed most. Super-techs are also paged to the optical dispensary as needed to handle walk-in patients who are picking up glasses or need an adjustment or repair.

Why implement this?

There are many benefits of the super-tech concept, but here are a few key points:

- Extremely high level of customer service; the patient is never left alone.
- A high degree of bonding occurs between the technician and the patient. The patient experience is improved.
- The full benefits of scribing: a huge amount of doctor time is saved and the doctor's attention is always on the patient with no distractions.
- Patients are impressed with the clinical exam process; hearing the exam findings spoken out loud is interesting to them.
- Better clinical records in the EHR system because the scribe has the time to make them complete.
- A more accurate billing and coding process because the data is entered properly at the time of service. Fee questions are handled by staff, not the doctor.
- The doctor never has to search for a technician or optician.

- The doctor never has to waste time walking patients to another part of the office.
- A higher eyeglass retention rate occurs because the transfer from clinic to optical is seamless.

How many super-techs does a practice need?
It is best to arrive at the proper staffing number through some experimentation, because there are many factors at play. In my practice, we schedule three super-techs per working doctor. On a three doctor day, we would have nine super-techs. That may seem like a lot, but these technicians are often pulled to optical for dispensing tasks and they also have some side administrative duties. And we see a high number of patients; each doctor does an exam every 15 to 20 minutes. We also have three master opticians who do not do any clinical work. They are always on the optical floor and they could take a handoff from a super-tech if we needed the tech on the clinic side.

A good way to test the super-tech concept is to introduce a pilot program. Train one of your best technicians to scribe and to do basic optical dispensing and try it on a few patients. Decide from there if you want to implement the strategy on a practice-wide basis.

Staff resistance
It is fairly common to meet some resistance from staff members when you present the idea of super-techs. Staff members who are mostly clinical are not always interested in retail sales and traditional opticians may not want to learn clinical skills. When I introduce change in my practice, I try to see the situation from the employees' point of view and I try to identify their fears. Once I do that, I can usually reassure the staff and overcome their objections. I approach change with great patience and understanding and I promise to provide the resources the staff needs, such as training and additional staff if the pilot program is successful and if it makes economic sense.

As I work through change with my staff, I also position the new program as an opportunity for career advancement. That is not always an easy thing to find in optometric practice and I expect employees to be interested in expanding their horizons. If an employee has a very poor attitude about trying new strategies, I may realize that he or she was not as valuable as I previously thought.

14.6 A Novel System for Patient Flow

I never really thought the patient flow and staffing model I use in my practice was all that novel, but after analyzing many other practices, it seems so. I have used this model for over 20 years and it's worked well, so I'll describe it here. The unique aspect of the system is that one technician begins to work with a patient and stays with that patient throughout the entire visit. The patient is never left alone or handed off to another person. A strong relationship develops between the technician and patient and we are able to deliver outstanding service, while maximizing office efficiency.

The exam sequence

Typically, after a patient checks in at the front desk, a receptionist will page for an optometric technician over the office intercom. This page is only heard in areas of the office that are not open to patients, but available technicians will hear it and respond. The tech calls the patient in and introduces herself (or himself) and explains that she will perform some tests before seeing Dr. _________. If the appointment is for a comprehensive eye exam, the tech begins an extensive pretest work-up, which includes retinal photography and corneal topography for contact lens wearers. The technician and patient move into one of the exam rooms for additional pretesting. Technicians act as scribes with every patient encounter, so the pretester becomes the scribe when the doctor arrives.

Doctors don't page technicians; technicians page doctors

As the technician nears the end of pretesting, she uses any office telephone to page the doctor who is scheduled to do the eye exam. All doctors wear small numeric pagers, set to vibrate mode, and each pager phone number is programmed into speed dial on the telephone system. So the tech pushes one speed dial key, waits for the pager service to answer and just hangs up. No message is needed since we just use the pager as a signal device.

Because the doctor is silently notified that the next patient is ready, he or she can decide how to best respond in order minimize patient wait times. There are really many ways the doctor can be flexible and by doing so, stay on schedule. If the previous exam is nearly over, then just complete it and move on to the waiting patient. Otherwise, since a scribe is assisting on this exam also, it may be a good time to have the tech instill mydriatic drops, or apply diagnostic contact lenses, or do some special testing, or whatever may be helpful. The doctor can come back to this patient if needed.

The examination

The doctor joins the technician and greets the patient. With all the pretest data and images on display, the exam moves along fairly easily. During the exam and refraction, the doctor states the findings and lens values aloud and the technician records the data. She also makes notes of any additional information elicited from the patient and records any advice the doctor gives. The doctor focuses on the patient's history and complaints and on recommendations for treatment. The technician listens to the doctor/patient consultation at the end of the exam because she is going to carry out whatever steps are needed. As time permits during the visit, the technician completes the record with the diagnosis and plan, enters all fees, checks off the proper codes, and applies any insurance plans. Written copies of lens prescriptions for the patient are completed by the technician and recall dates are indicated. The doctor says goodbye and leaves the technician and patient.

The technician continues to work with the patient with whatever care is needed. If the visit is over, the tech walks the patient to the front desk. If contact lenses are to be fitted, the tech retrieves the lenses ordered by the doctor and inserts them. If more testing is needed, the tech either does it or reappoints for it. Any questions that remain about insurance or other matters are answered by the technician.

The best handoff is no handoff

In many cases, the next step after the exam is that the patient wishes to order eyeglasses. In that case, the same technician that did the pretesting walks the patient to the optical area and does the frame selection. The tech becomes an optician at this point, educating the patient about lens design options, checking the frame fit, and taking all measurements. The eyeglass order is written, fees are written up and vision plans are applied, if any. Because the technician heard the doctor's recommendations for lenses at chairside, no further communication is needed and we have maximum continuity. At the completion of the eyeglass order, the technician escorts the patient to the front desk and says goodbye. A receptionist enters all fees for the visit into the office management system, makes payment arrangements and prints the final receipt statement.

Appointment scheduling

We have a very simple appointment system. Every exam is given a 15 minute slot no matter what kind of visit it is and I don't try to control what kind of visits are accepted on various days or times. In this way, we can fill any slot easily. We schedule doctors, not technicians, and I don't worry about the lag time required to do a pretest. All staff members and doctors work hard to be on time for appointments and to start the day on time and quit on time.

Cross-training

All clinical technicians are trained in optical dispensing, but we have two full time opticians who only work in optical and do not do any pretesting work. We have additional staff for the business office and for the optical laboratory. This patient flow system may seem sophisticated, but it's really quite doable.

How many technicians?

When comparing numbers of employees from one practice to another, it's important to be aware that every office is different and how the office functions effects staffing numbers. Having said that, I've found that I'm optimally staffed with three technicians per working doctor. If we have two doctors working, six techs would be ideal. There are times when I don't have the luxury of the three to one ratio (due to call-offs, vacations, etc.), but that is my goal.

14.7 An Introduction to Utilizing and Training Scribes

Long-time readers of this Tip of the Week series know that I've been an advocate of using scribes since way before the advent of EHR systems. But EHR is certainly creating a huge increase in the number of doctors interested in the concept of scribes and I'm very pleased to see that. In this share some of the benefits you'll realize if you adopt the scribing concept and I'll help you create a plan for training and implementation.

Long-time readers of this Tip of the Week series know that I've been an advocate of using scribes since way before the advent of EHR systems. But EHR is certainly creating a huge increase in the number of doctors interested in the concept of scribes and I'm very pleased to see that. In this article, I'll share some of the benefits you'll realize if you adopt the scribing concept and I'll help you create a plan for training and implementation.

Benefits of scribes

The biggest reason for using scribes in your exam room is the same benefit we derive from most aspects of delegation: we save doctor time. And record-keeping requires a very large segment of time. Many doctors would say that record-keeping takes longer with EHR systems than it did with paper. My experience bears that out as well. With most optometrists trying to keep their exam time with each patient at 15 to 20 minutes, we don't want to spend 10 of those minutes typing on a keyboard and searching drop-down lists to click on. We care about the patient experience and we need to get rid of the burden of the computer or tablet.

Fortunately, there are several other benefits of using scribes, such as:

- Always having a technician available to assist the doctor
- Saving time walking patients in and out of the exam room
- Contact lens fitting is amazingly fast
- Optical dispensing and sales are improved because there is no handoff to an optician (the scribe is the optician)
- Records are often more complete and accurate
- Patients are impressed with the efficiency and with learning more about the exam data
- Having a third person in the exam room can protect the doctor

Presenting the concept

There are two main ways to use scribes: the first is what I call the super-tech concept where the scribe is also an optometric technician, pretester and optician all rolled into one. This technique requires an advanced level of cross-training, but it brings many advantages. With this concept, one technician stays with the patient throughout the entire visit. This system requires several super-techs and any available technician can work with any patient. I find the ideal number of super-techs is three per working doctor, but realize that these employees are also opticians and they do much more than just assist the doctor.

The other method of scribing is to have a staff member trained on the EHR system and the only job is to record the exam data. In this scenario, one scribe could stay with one doctor for the whole day. There is some benefit in that this dedicated scribe learns the doctor's recording preferences quite well. But it is easier to train a fully qualified technician to scribe than a lay person.

After deciding which approach you want to take, I would hold a staff meeting and explain that you would like to test the concept of scribes with your staff and ask for their feedback. I view this as an opportunity for some of your staff to grow within their careers and I hope they see it that way also. Explain the benefits of the process and reassure the staff about any worries or concerns they may have. The idea is to try it on a small scale and see how it works.

Training staff

I would begin by training one or two of your best technicians on how to record the exam data in your EHR system. Review some previous patient charts and have them watch you while you record data on a fictitious practice patient. Tell them what tests you will be doing and some of the things you may say out loud. They can just assist you with one or two patients per day to start.

As you work with staff, realize that you do not have to speak all findings out loud if you are not ready to share them with the patient yet. You can wait until you speak to the patient. The tech will learn that if you don't dictate anything, to simply wait. Also realize that you can still record some things yourself if it is too complex for a technician. If the office is very busy and staff are needed, let the manager or someone else know they can just knock on the exam room door and ask the technician to come out. You can carry on alone if needed.

I always recommend that doctors review all their records fairly soon after the exam and make any changes or additions, before signing the record. This can usually be done between patients and you can work out a routine for listing the patients who are ready to review and finalize.

The logistics

Depending on the EHR system you have, think about the best way to input data. My current system does not work well with a tablet, but more are going that way and there advantages in portability. But realize that typing and clicking can be faster with a real keyboard instead of the virtual one taking up a third of the screen on a tablet. Be careful to not allow patient flow to slow down because the scribe is inputting data in the pretest room. You may want to hold off on some aspects, like the case history, until the assistant and patient are in an exam room.

In my office, we use a laptop for the scribe and we have a second desktop PC and monitor for the doctor. The scribe works off of the end of the refraction desk. It is generally not possible for two people to make changes to the same data base at the same time on different computers, but one workstation (the doctor's) can have a read-only version of the exam data for viewing only.

The best approach is to just jump in and try scribing. You will quickly learn as you go along.

14.8 A Guide to Adding Scribes to Your Practice

I wrote about the concept of using scribes last week and how one technician can be cross-trained to serve as scribe, pretester and optician. In this article I'll present some tips for actually making it happen in your practice.

A pilot program

There are many details to work out as you change your clinical routine and the role of staff members. I'll provide some help with that, but every practice is different and if you try to predict and plan for every consideration, you may never actually start. So, as they say in the Nike ads: "Just do it." I would tell your staff that you are trying a pilot program to test a new procedure with the use of scribes in the exam room

Hold a staff meeting and explain that the practice is a business and based on the challenges of managed care, new forms of competition and a weak economy, you must re-invent the way your practice provides eye care. Discuss the business challenges with staff and ask for their input on how the practice can increase revenue and efficiency. Discuss that having the doctor work at his or her highest level is a key factor. Explain that seeing more patients per day does not have to be more work or stressful. Remind staff members that taking on new responsibilities are the best way for them to advance their own careers.

Pledge your support

As you describe how the exam process will work with a scribe, try to see the new role from your employees' point of view. If you think about it, you can understand that they may worry that they will have to work harder or that they may not be able to handle the task. Reassure them so they can get beyond those fears. Admit that you don't have all the answers yet and that the system will evolve as you go along, but that you want to try the concept of scribes and cross training. Let the staff know that if it works like you hope it will, you will hire more employees and provide all the support and training they need.

Go on to tell them that you will not embarrass them in front of a patient by using terms they are not familiar with. You can still record the more complex findings yourself – and you may not want to say everything out loud anyway until you've had a chance to counsel the patient first. Tell staff members they can always ask questions during the exam if they didn't hear something. Just go over all the "what-ifs." You can also tell your office manager or front desk person that if the office is ever running way behind schedule or has a rush of patients; she can just knock on the exam room door and ask the technician to step out for a minute. You can still record the data like you always have.

Think about where the scribe can sit and create a small area with a stool at the end of the refraction desk. I added a small extension of the countertop so there is space for the knees.

Start with paper forms

One of the biggest advantages with scribes is that they can take over all the data entry in the electronic medical record (EHR), but if you are just starting with scribing and if your staff is not familiar with the EHR system, you might be smart to start by using paper exam forms. Paper forms are easier and they can guide the scribe through the process with a specific place to enter data. After the staff is used to scribing for a few weeks, you can then train them to use the EHR.

I found an exam form with two pages worked best. The first page is for the case history and all the pretesting. The second page is for all the tests performed by the doctor. When the doctor begins to work with the patient, he or she will have the pretest form with all the data, which is very helpful to refer to throughout the exam. The scribe keeps the blank form for the doctor tests, which she will fill in. The scribe should just take notes and write down all the findings the doctor says out loud.

Can you afford all those staff members?

In my practice, I try to schedule three scribes/pretesters/opticians for each working doctor. That may seem like a lot, but these staff members also provide optical dispensing services. They do repairs, adjustments and dispensings. Our business office staff uses the telephone paging system to call technicians to the clinic or to the optical as needed. All staff members have secondary jobs to work on if they are not working with patients.

You may need to add some employees to your practice if you introduce scribing, but I see that as a good thing. Additional staff provides more resources and three good things happen:

- Customer service improves because you have more staff to take care of people.
- You will delegate more because you have more people to delegate to.
- Productivity increases because you can see more patients per day and doctors and technicians can spend more time with patients, which causes them to buy more goods and services.

Because of these factors, I doubt that you will notice any increase in payroll cost. Revenue will increase much more than the increase in payroll. To maximize the profitability with scribes, change the appointment schedule to shorter time slots and see a few more patients per day. It should be no problem because scribes save the doctor a great deal of time.

14.9 Solve Your EHR Problems with Scribes

Many eye care professionals (ECPs) are switching to electronic medical records (EHRs), and for good reason... the advantages far outweigh the drawbacks. But most of us who have made the switch still find that EHRs can be time consuming and inefficient. In this article, I'll share my experience with having scribes record the exam data into the EHR and why I think that is the way to go.

Readers familiar with my practice model know that the doctors in my practice have a scribe assist them with all patient visits. We did this long before we went to electronic records because there are many advantages, but I now see that scribes offer tremendous additional value in a busy practice with an EHR system.

As a side note, we use scribes in a unique way in my practice: the scribe is also pretester, clinical technician and optician all rolled into one. Scribes don't work with specific doctors but rather go wherever they are needed most. We try to schedule three scribe/tech/opticians per working doctor.

How do scribes help with EHRs?

I find scribes to be nearly indispensable with EHRs because I don't want to use my time entering data and I don't want to be distracted by the software. I want the patient to have all my attention during their visit.

The good news is that scribes can make your EHR system a breeze to use. The bad news is that there are a few rough spots that must be worked out as you integrate scribes and EHRs.

How can doctor and scribe both be in the record at the same time?

The short answer is they can't. Databases don't typically allow two users to work in the same file at the same time and that can be difficult for optometrists because of the way we work. When I do an eye exam, I like to have the pretest data in front of me. As I talk with the patient, I'm reviewing the history, current medications and chief complaint. As I refract, I like to see the entrance acuity, habitual eyeglass or contact lens prescription, autorefraction data, patient's age and other information. As I progress through the exam, I look back at today's results for tonometry, field screening, blood pressure, and other findings.

I resolved this issue in my practice by using a paper worksheet for the scribe to record all pretest data. This data is transferred by the scribe into the EHR later (see below). I keep the worksheet with me as I examine the patient and I refer to it as needed (just like I always did in the past). We then discard the worksheet after the patient visit. Yes, a worksheet is a bit of a crutch and it makes us not really paperless, but it really helps us through a rough spot and I see no need to change.

A side benefit of the pretest worksheet is that it helps speed up our pretest process because the technician does not have to enter data at that time. We also don't have to make room for a desktop, laptop or tablet PC. Our pretest rooms have several automated instruments and they can easily become a bottleneck to patient flow. I want our techs to get in and out as quickly as possible so the next patient can enter.

When and where to enter data

When the technician completes all the pretesting, she pages the doctor on a silent numeric pager by pressing the speed dial phone number on our office phone system. She simply hangs up when the call goes through as no message is needed. When the pager vibrates, the doctor knows the next patient is ready. Our doctors are prompt and flexible in their routine, so we keep the internal wait time to a minimum, but typically the technician and patient may wait up to five minutes for the doctor to enter. The tech used to wait outside the exam room, but now we use the time for the technician to enter the pretest data from the worksheet. The patient watches educational videos about eye care during this short waiting period.

The technician could enter the pretest data in the exam room (with the patient) or could do it on a laptop or tablet PC (on our office wireless network) in a work area in the center of the clinic. If the doctor shows up very quickly, the data can be entered anytime while the doctor is refracting or working with the patient.

How do you view the record if you leave the exam room?

We had a challenge when the doctor or tech needed to see the exam record outside of the exam room. One example is when the doctor wants to review the record so she is familiar with the case before entering the room. Another example is when the technician or doctor goes into the contact lens lab to select trial lenses to put on the patient and needs to refer back to today's refraction to select the correct powers. This is where we find that tablet or laptop PCs are a big advantage over desktop PCs that are tied to the exam room.

Training issues

Training multiple technicians to record exam findings in an EHR was a major task. We had a professional trainer visit our office for three days and that was a key boost in our progress. From then on, we just kept practicing. Fortunately, my staff had a very positive attitude about the concept of EHRs and they wanted to master the skills. In spite of the work involved, I love our EHR system and having scribes to record the data.

14.10 Scribes Dramatically Increase Contact Lens Profitability

It's obvious that I'm bullish on scribes, but the benefits of using them in contact lens practice are so profound that you really must consider adding the technique to your office routine.

Efficiency is as good as raising fees

There are two very important factors in your contact lens profitability: your fees and your time. I assume you have already set your fees as high as you can, given market conditions, but most practices I see are still very inefficient when it comes to contact lens fitting. If you can reduce the chair time and doctor time needed to fit a patient, you will have more appointment slots available for other patients and your revenue will increase.

Most optometrists are still fitting contact lenses the same way they were taught in school and have not made a significant change in office procedures for many years. Yet, contact lens technology has changed markedly along with managed care trends and competition for contact lens product sales. We must adapt our practices to the new market conditions to remain viable.

Analyze your fitting philosophy

We really should think of contact lenses differently than we did in the old days. Consider these traditional ideas.

- Most ECPs only discuss contact lenses if the patient asks about them or is already wearing them. This causes your practice to miss many good candidates. This approach can often be traced to the fact that the appointment given to the patient only allows enough time for an eye exam and to begin a discussion of contact lenses would throw the office off schedule. What a shame! Is your scheduling process holding back your revenue production?

- Patients today are more impressed with services and products that are easy and quick than they are with those that are complex. If you think you are impressing patients by making the contact lens fitting process appear to be so advanced and complex that it requires much more time and effort, I would think again. That's old school. Today's consumer is more impressed with a practice that fits the new contacts that are super-easy! Of course, it's how you fit them that makes the difference.

Scribes can change your fitting process

Let's take a look at typical contact lens procedures in use today. Let's assume a patient is in for a comprehensive eye exam and has an interest in contact lenses – either a new fit or a significant refit. The doctor usually performs the following steps and the amount of time really adds up.

- After the eye exam, the doctor talks about contact lenses with an overview about the types of lenses, the risks and complications, the fitting and follow-up process and the fees.
- After deciding on the lens design and brand, the doctor goes into the CL inventory room and searches for trial lenses with the correct parameters.
- Upon returning to the exam room, the doctor opens the lens package, removes the lens, rinses it with saline and inserts it for the patient. After waiting for the lens to settle, it may need to be removed and reinserted if there is any discomfort. This is repeated for the other eye. More waiting is needed.
- The fitting procedure may vary, but usually the doctor takes monocular visual acuity with the contacts and may take near acuity as well. An over-refraction is performed. A slit lamp exam is performed and the fit is evaluated. One or both trial lenses may be changed based on test results.
- The steps described above can easily take more than 15 minutes – possibly 30 minutes. That is enough doctor time to conduct another comprehensive eye exam! If we consider that the average gross revenue produced per exam is about $350, it is very expensive to fit contacts this way! The cost of a missed opportunity is very real.

Let's look at the process in my model using a scribing technician:

- After the eye exam, the doctor enthusiastically recommends contact lenses and encourages the patient to simply try on a pair.
- The doctor tells the technician/scribe what brand of lenses to insert and the doctor leaves the room to see another patient.
- The technician gets the trial lenses and follows the steps outlined above to insert the contacts.
- Depending on your state law, the technician takes visual acuity and may perform a spherical over-refraction with the phoroptor. An over-refraction without cylinder testing is quite easy, but if you would rather not have the tech use the phoroptor, she can also take the patient into the pretest room and do an auto-refraction with the lenses in place.
- The technician discusses lens types, lens handling and hygiene, follow-up visits and fees.
- The doctor pops back in and checks the fit of the contacts with the slit lamp. The lenses are dispensed if possible.
- Total doctor time: about three minutes.

14.11 Questions and Objections about Scribes

My latest series of tip articles about scribes has produced a lot of interest from readers so I'll conclude the topic this week by answering some questions I've received.

Three scribes per doctor
I mentioned that I schedule three scribes per working doctor, but I phrased it as
"scribes/technicians/opticians" and that was a bit confusing. I meant that to be read as one job title that is cross-trained for all those duties, not three separate people. To sum it up better, we have three technicians per working doctor and each tech also acts as a scribe and frame stylist as well. On a three-doctor day, we try to have nine technicians.

The technicians do not stay with a specific doctor but they go wherever they are needed most. They may be paged to the optical area to do an eyeglass dispensing or they may take the next patient into the clinic for pretesting. In addition to the three technicians per doctor rule, we have receptionists, an office manager, insurance coordinator and lab technicians to make glasses. We also have two full time opticians who always remain in optical and do not perform pretesting or scribing. These opticians take care of walk-ins and are available to take a handoff from technicians if the clinic side is very busy and we need the techs back for patient care.

Every practice is different and those exact staff requirements may not work in every practice. Having the technicians cross-trained in optical gives us many resources that we can move to any part of the practice that gets busy. It allows a high-level of customer service in optical because that side of the practice is not by appointment and we can get a rush of people at times.

Should smaller practices also use scribes?

No, probably not, but I would recommend the practice owner set a goal to use scribes in the future. I also believe ECPs can use scribes sooner than they might think. Let's consider the extreme of a new startup practice. This practice may have only one employee and that person is primarily at the front desk, but may also be cross-trained for some optical dispensing. The doctor in this situation must perform many tasks that I would eventually recommend delegating. But in the beginning, with limited cash flow and a small number of patients, it is best for the doctor and staff member to handle multiple tasks.

Over time as the practice grows, the doctor should delegate more and more duties and scribing would be one of the more advanced tasks. The point is for the ECP to continue to push for more delegation. This should be accomplished even before there is an obvious need to delegate. Don't wait for the practice to be extremely busy before delegating at a high level; put delegation into effect first and the practice will become busier. How? If you compress patients into fewer days of the week, you create free days or half-days when the practice owner can be scheduled to work solely on practice management.

Cross-trained scribes may not be good at optical sales

I've heard the concern before that clinical technicians may not be stellar at optical sales. The thought is that the cross-trained super-technician might not be as good at selling as a dedicated optician. In over 25 years of using scribes, I have not found it to be a problem and in many cases, the clinical techs surprise me at how well they sell. Consider these points:

- The power of the doctor recommending optical products at chairside and having the technician in the room to seamlessly make it happen goes a long way to boost sales. This advantage elevates the average technician to a level on par with a very good salesperson.
- I still employ opticians who are great at selling, but I really can't find enough of them. I need more staff to keep our patient flow at a high

level. We ask our best sales staff to train our clinical technicians in the art of selling and they learn by observing.

- A great optical dispensary is a huge aid to sales. After investing in beautiful frame displays and extensive inventory, our approach is to educate each patient about optical products and to ask them verbal questions about their lifestyle. When we do all that, we sell a lot of products.
- I don't really want a slick, high-pressure sales approach. We sell more by keeping optical under our healthcare umbrella and not making it feel too retail-oriented.

Dilation and contact lenses

A question was asked about how I handle pupil dilation with the contact lens fitting process that occurs on the same day as the comprehensive eye exam. We use full dilation in about 90% of comprehensive exams, but it really does not present a problem with contact lens fittings or frame selections. We are simply a little creative about when we instill the drops with the goal of managing all aspects of eye care.

In the case of all new contact lens fittings and many refittings, we are scheduling a follow-up visit in one week. This visit is included in the fitting fee. Unless the patient had signs or symptoms of a serious eye health problem during the initial exam, we just perform the dilated fundus exam after the contact lens follow-up one week later.

Another approach would be to just delay the drops until the technician or doctor has performed most of the contact lens procedures. I can still evaluate the fit of a basic soft lens with a slit lamp even if the pupil is dilated. Vision can be evaluated before the drops are instilled. A big advantage of having the visit managed by a technician instead of the doctor is that more time can be devoted to a patient without disrupting the appointment schedule.

14.12 How to Get Staff Onboard with Scribing

I presented a webinar last night on the topic of scribes and super-techs. There was a lot of interest and some excellent questions, so I'll continue to write and lecture on this topic. Many of the questions revolved around how to motivate staff members to want to take on this task and how to train them.

Three ways to implement scribing

There are three different ways you can approach the staff assignment to scribing:

- A dedicated scribe. This staff member should be proficient with keyboarding and also have some knowledge of medical and optical terminology, but she does not need to be a clinical technician. Each working doctor would have one scribe.
- A pre-tester who is also a scribe. This is a natural extension for the clinical technician who already knows a lot about eye care. The practice would need at least two of these per working doctor because one needs to be working up the next patient while the first one is recording for the doctor.
- A supertech, which I define as a pre-tester who is also a scribe and also an optician. This highly cross-trained individual can stay with the patient from the beginning to the end of the visit and the patient is never left alone. There is a seamless transition from the exam room to optical with no searching or waiting for an optician.

The first two job descriptions would still require a handoff to an optician for frame selection and lens design, while the third one does not.

Any of these three methods will work well and you should consider which one will work best for your practice and with your staff. You may want to start with one system and transition to a different one as more staff are hired.

Staff needs leadership

Leadership is an intangible skill that is hard to describe, but we all know it when we see it. Staff members frequently resist change and the best way I've found to overcome this is by respecting them and being honest with them. If you would like your staff to embrace the concept of scribing, have a staff meeting and explain to them why you believe it would benefit your practice. Don't be afraid to discuss the business aspect of the practice, such as the need to generate a greater profit which may involve seeing more patients per day.

Also, be sure to discuss how EHR software is not actually faster than paper, and it requires a large amount of time to enter the data. Explain how the patient experience suffers when the doctor spends most of the time typing, clicking and searching drop-down lists. Discuss how efficient it would be to have a scribe in the exam room.

It is important to look at the new task of scribing from the employee's point of view. Some staff may be concerned that they will have to work harder with this new task, or that they may not be able to master it. Once you understand the fears that staff may have, you can overcome them by pledging resources (such as hiring more staff) or by promising plenty of time for training and that you can do a trial run first.

Opportunity for career advancement

As you encourage your staff about the idea of scribing, get them to see the project as an opportunity for career advancement. I don't think it is necessary to be specific about raises at the outset of this process, but it is understood that as new skills are learned, raises will occur. In some cases, careers in optometric assisting have not had enough opportunities for career growth, but new responsibilities are just that.

Also realize that you may learn something about an employee that you did not know. You may find that an employee who you thought was excellent is really not much of a team player and does not support your vision for the practice. That does not mean the employee does not have other good traits, but this is new information that enters into your ongoing review process.

Training

When you are first starting out with scribing, it is best for the doctor to train the first few scribes. Start with a pilot program. Work with your best technician and show her your EHR software or your paper exam forms. She most likely already knows quite a bit about these documents, but review some previous records with her and show her when you free-form type and when you use drop down lists. Tell her the most common things you will say out loud when you scribe. Then have her sit in on a few exams and record the results as you speak.

Keep in mind that it is perfectly fine for the doctor to still make some notes (on paper or in the software) and the patient will not think anything of it. The doctor does not have to say everything out loud if it is sensitive information or if it would upset the patient. After the exam, review the record with the scribe and consider how the process could be improved. Implement changes that will make the experience better.

14.13 Benefits of Scribing Are Much More Than EHR

Last week, I wrote about how to get your staff on board with the concept of scribing. I will expand on that topic in this article and will focus on the benefits doctors derive from using a scribe in the exam room. Most doctors are interested in scribes to help them with entering data into the electronic health record (EHR), and that is a great benefit, but there are many more. For those of you who miss David Letterman on late night TV, here is my top 10 list for why you should use scribes.

Benefits of using scribes

1. The EHR record is no longer the doctor's responsibility. Spend more time with the patient instead of typing, clicking and searching drop-down lists. Make eye contact with the patient.
2. Patient records are more complete. Doctors are usually rushed, but the scribe is able to sit quietly at the end of the desk and enter all the test results as dictated by the doctor and also summarize what the doctor tells the patient.
3. The scribe is a witness to what happens in the exam room; this can prevent poor patient behavior and can protect against an untrue legal claim.
4. The scribe can go get things as needed. This could be a special instrument that is stored in another room or it could be to take a pair of glasses to the lab for a repair while the exam is underway. The scribe can even go fetch a parent or loved one near the end of the visit.
5. The doctor leaves the exam room first, leaving the scribe to finish with the patient. This can put an end to small talk if desired and the doctor does not have to walk patients in or out of the exam room. This saves time.
6. Patients are impressed with the presence of the scribe and hearing the terminology that the doctor uses for the record. Patients love having the full attention of the doctor. The patient experience is enhanced.
7. If the scribe is trained as a frame stylist/optician (supertech), there is no optical handoff needed. The doctor does not have to repeat his or her recommendations. The scribe hears the doctor's recommendation first hand and carries it out.
8. Increase the eyeglass retention rate because the flow from exam room to optical is seamless. The scribe has already bonded with the patient.
9. The doctor does not have to search or page for a technician or optician (who are often too busy to respond). The scribe can take care of additional testing, contact lens insertion or frame selection as needed.

10. The scribe takes care of all coding, fees, insurance discussions with the patient, and the recall date. The doctor can assist if there are questions and should review the charts as time permits.

Try scribing on a small scale as a pilot program. Just have one of your techs sit in with you and record the data. Once you see all the benefits, you'll wonder how you ever did without it.

14.14 How to Train a Scribe

I have written many articles on scribes (just do a key word search for "scribe" in the tip archive), but I continue to receive many questions about the topic, so I know there is a lot of interest. Today I want to focus on the training aspect.

For purposes of this article, I'll assume you are training an employee who is already a pretester / optometric technician. This means the staff member has at least a basic understanding of the eye, common ocular diseases, refraction, special diagnostic tests, eye care terminology, contact lenses, eyeglasses, and medications. If not, you should train him or her for those job skills first.

If you are just starting to use scribes, it is best for the optometrist to train the first one or two scribes. You may want to start with your best technician and consider it as a pilot program at first. Have the technician assist you with a couple of patients and then learn as you go. Eventually, if scribing becomes the norm in your practice, your existing scribes can help train new ones.

Here are some things to consider:

- Review the hardware and workspace. Consider your technology options for how to enter the data. Does your EHR software work well with a tablet or would it be easier on a laptop? Will you use a network cable for better speed and reliability or does wi-fi work well for you? Will the device have enough power to last all day? Where will the scribe sit in the exam room? You may need to modify your countertop or refraction desk to accommodate scribing, but you can test the scribing concept before going into that.
- Make an outline of what, when and where the scribe should record exam data. Break down your typical eye exam into sections and keep it in the usual chronological order. List the items you will want the scribe to record and note if the procedure will be performed by

the scribe or the doctor. Will the scribe enter items in the pretest room or wait until she gets to the exam room? When and where should the history be taken? There are usually a few minutes between the end of pretesting but before the doctor arrives. The scribe can use this time to enter data collected in pretesting.

- You may want to design a cheat sheet form for the tech to quickly jot down a few items in pretesting or to use if he/she can't find the exact right spot in the EHR record. This worksheet can be shredded after the data is transferred to the EHR. There may be some paper forms used in the exam process that can be scanned before shredding.
- Develop your list of abbreviations. This is smart to have in case you are audited by an insurance carrier, but it also helps the scribe know how to abbreviate properly and save time. You may also have macros stored in your exam templates for commonly entered statements.
- Meet with the technician for a couple hours to show her the EHR software. Some techs are already using these records, but this training session will go into detail about where everything is recorded and the essential elements of the record. The tech should have a notebook and pen and take her own notes.
- Have a technician shadow the doctor in the exam room. In the early going, the scribe-trainee can simply watch the exam and watch closely as the doctor enters the data.
- Talk about what the scribe should do. I think it is best for the scribe to remain mostly quiet during the doctor's part of the exam. Of course, questions are allowed. The scribe should assist the doctor and record everything that is said to the patient.
- Discuss what the scribe should do at the end of the exam, including printing or sending prescriptions, doing a handoff to optical, rescheduling for more testing, coding for procedures and diagnoses, setting recall dates, totaling up fees and walking the patient out. The doctor can assist with all of this until the tech is up to speed.
- Begin scribing on a few patients. The doctor should remember to take it easy on the new scribe and dictate exam results clearly and slowly. Avoid dictating complex medical descriptions in the beginning and realize that the doctor can still reach over to the scribe's computer and enter some findings. The doctor should also use caution about speaking some results out loud that might worry the patient prematurely. It is OK to do a test and not say anything at the time and come back to it later after you have talked to the patient about it.

- How many scribes do you need? It depends on how many patients you see per day and what else the scribe does. If the scribe is always by the doctor's side, you only need one. If the scribe also does pretesting, you need at least two, so one can stay with the doctor and another one can start the next patient. If you use supertechs, like I do, you'll need about three per working doctor because they also go to optical to do dispensing tasks.
- The doctor reviews the record, makes changes if needed and teaches the scribe. This can happen between patients. Work toward not making this too burdensome or time consuming.

Using scribes in your practice will create many benefits and efficiencies. Payroll cost may go up slightly with more staff, but the time saved for the doctor more than makes up for it with increased productivity. Once you try it, you won't want to go back.

14.15 Pagers as In-office Signal System

There are several systems available to assist with in-office communication of doctors and staff, from colored lights and audible tones to colored flags mounted outside exam room doors. These can work, but the simple, standard beeper offers some great benefits when used inside the office to notify the doctor that the next patient is ready to be seen. We have used this for many years in our multi-doctor office - but it would work equally well in any practice where technicians perform pre-testing and the doctor works between two or more exam rooms.

The doctor uses a standard numeric paging device, which works with a local phone number. The cost is nominal - about $10 per month. The pager can be used for typical business and personal use. They work great for after-hours doctor on-call duties, and if our office needs to speak to a doctor when he or she is out of the office. But these are side benefits.

The main use of pagers in our practice is to signal a doctor that his next patient is ready. It reaches the doctor in any location in the office, and it does so silently when placed on vibrator mode. The optometric technician who has just completed the pre-test data collection initiates the page. All office phones are programmed on speed-dial with the pager number of each doctor, so placing the call is a snap. When the tech hears the message tone, she enters the exam room number where the patient is waiting and hangs up. The doctor receives the page in about two minutes.

We hate to make patients wait in our office, so just knowing the next patient is waiting is very helpful. Quite often, the page is received when I am in the other exam room, seeing another patient. I simply hit the pager button to stop the silent signal. I don't even need to look at the display - I know what it means. I can now make on the spot decisions to improve patient flow. I may decide I am at a good point to instill mydriatic drops and finish this patient later, or I may ask my tech to apply diagnostic contact lenses, or I may be nearly done and I will just finish up. On the other hand, if I'm working with a patient and haven't been paged, I know I have plenty of time.

Try it - you will find your office is more efficient and your patient satisfaction ratings will improve.

14.16 Pre-Exam Dilation Protocols

Long-time readers of this tip series know that I've been a proponent of having a clinical technician instill mydriatic drops during the pretesting phase of an eye exam. I've tried many different protocols for this in my practice over the years. In this article, I'll review our past procedure and give an update of where we are now.

Phenylephrine

For many years, my staff instilled phenylephrine drops during pretesting (10% for several years, then 2.5% due to safety). I first wrote about this in 1989 in the print version of *Optometric Management*. This technique provided a better view of the fundus than no dilation, but we often added tropicamide later in the exam process when we needed a better view of the retinal periphery. It is still very popular among many doctors because it opens up the pupil without any cycloplegic effect.

As the standard of care evolved and as I added associate doctors to my practice, we found that we were fully dilating nearly all patients during comprehensive eye exams. We still do this today even though we have an Optomap instrument with high utilization rates. This dilation practice made the instillation of phenylephrine unnecessary since the doctor was almost always adding additional drops anyway. So, we dropped the practice of using phenylephrine as a pre-dilating agent several years ago. I use the term "pre-dilate" to refer to having a technician instill the mydriatic drop before the doctor sees the patient.

Pre-dilation with tropicamide

My practice has experimented with many different protocols for pre-dilating patients in an effort to overcome the obvious inefficiency of the doctor having to see each patient twice (before and after dilation). We have had some success, but we still face a number of challenges and I still search for the perfect method.

As we discuss and compare these clinical procedures as colleagues, we should remember that there are a variety of professional opinions about the need to dilate under various situations and the process to be followed prior to dilation.

As a quick review of the commonly available ophthalmic drugs used for pupil dilation, tropicamide is available in .5% and 1% concentrations. Tropicamide is popular because it is relatively short-acting, so it offers minimal inconvenience for the patient in the form of blurred vision and glare. Tropicamide produces mild cycloplegia. A very popular drug with the brand name Paremyd has tropicamide in only a .25% concentration and it is combined with hydroxyamphetamine, which is a sympathomimetic that increases the dilation effect. Even with the combination, however, many practitioners find they need stronger concentrations of tropicamide to obtain adequate dilation in some patients, such as those with dark irises. The other sympathomimetic eye drop that is often used with tropicamide is phenylephrine.

Here is a list of factors to consider as you develop a protocol for pre-dilation in your practice.

- You may wish to only pre-dilate established patients, so the doctor has the chance to evaluate important factors like pupil response, chamber angles and systemic conditions in new patients. In many practices, the vast majority of patients seen are established, so this technique still provides a big increase in efficiency. Some practices have technicians evaluate those factors in new patients and pre-dilate everyone who meets certain criteria.
- Which drug to use? Paremyd may be used as the pre-dilation drop since it is fairly mild, but it may not provide full dilation in every case.
- The technician should be trained to take a special case history and to perform a pupil test before instilling mydriatic drops.
- Technicians may be trained to not pre-dilate under the following situations:
    - New patients.

    - Patients with chamber angles of grade 1 on the last exam.
    - Patients who are pregnant or nursing.
    - Children under age 8. The only concern here is if the child becomes overly upset about eye drops, the doctor may have trouble obtaining any clinical findings.
    - Patients over 40 years old wearing multifocal contact lenses.
    - Patients wanting a new contact lens fitting today.
    - Patients with an abnormal pupil exam.
    - Patients with extremely red eyes.
    - A good policy: if you are unsure, ask the doctor.
- Script about dilation: "I'm going to put a drop in your eyes that will dilate your pupils so the doctor can do a thorough eye health exam. This is the same drop that you had at your last eye exam with us. The drop will make your vision a little blurry for a few hours."

Challenges

Here are some of the difficulties we have faced with pre-dilation:

- Frame selection can be difficult with dilated pupils because the patient can't see well enough. This one is a big concern for me, but we also faced this problem with the traditional dilation process when the doctor instilled the drops.
- Due to all the exceptions we impose, we end up with some patients being dilated in advance and some dilated by the doctor and seen twice. This makes it difficult to predict our patient flow and it is harder to stay on schedule.
- If pretesting proceeds too quickly, the drops have not had a long enough time to take effect when the doctor wants to perform the fundus exam.
- Some tests, like macular pigment density, are better performed with normal pupils.

14.17 The Pretesting Bottleneck

Scheduling more patients per day brings up a common dilemma that most practices face as they try to increase efficiency: a bottleneck of patient flow at the point of pretesting.

The cause

As patient demand grows and as the practice attempts to process more patients per day, there is an evolution of office procedures. This includes delegating more clinical data collection, hiring more staff members, purchasing automated instrumentation, changing the appointment schedule and time allotted per exam, and adapting office space to serve new functions. These changes often occur incrementally so the financial investment and staff training can occur over time.

Since there is typically only one set of automated pretest instruments and one pretest room in the practice and since every patient receiving a full eye exam goes through pretesting, it's understandable that a bottleneck can occur. In many cases, the amount of time the doctor is spending with the patient is much less than the time spent with a technician. If the doctor is working out of two or more exam rooms (which is highly recommended for efficiency) there will be many occasions where the doctor is standing around waiting for the next patient.

Some remedies

Here are some thoughts on ways to improve patient flow through pretesting so the doctor stays busy. Remember that the potential increase in revenue that occurs when you see more patients per day is very great, so it behooves us to think big.

- Work with your staff to minimize the time spent in the pretest room in order to turn it over quicker and allow the next patient to come through. Just make them aware of the problem. We train staff to not take case histories in the pretest area and to not reinsert contact lenses and try to avoid chit-chat. They just wait until they move into an exam room for those things.
- Don't have the technician perform stereopsis, color vision testing or blood pressure measurement in the pretest area. Duplicate those inexpensive tools and have one set in each exam room so those procedures can be performed away from the bottleneck.
- The visual field screener is almost a self-testing device, so our techs read the habitual Rx on the lensmeter during that time.
- You may need two or more pretest areas with duplicate equipment. This is a big investment because autorefractors and retinal cameras are expensive, but if you have enough patient demand it is the right thing to do. Many doctors have multiple exam rooms, so why not multiple pretest rooms?
- You may need a larger office. I know many offices were designed when the patient demand was much less, but moving to larger quarters is one price of success. Embrace that and start looking for more space rather than let your facility hold you back.

- You may be able to remodel your present office to allow rooms to function in new ways. Making a large room into two smaller rooms can increase productivity in some cases. Perhaps you can use off-site storage units to free up space for purposes that increase production.
- There is always a dilemma about how many instruments to place in one room. If you have only one instrument in a room the room turns over quicker, but if you have to move the patient from room to room you can waste a lot of time. If the test takes a longer time, like threshold visual fields, a small separate room works well. Other considerations, such as the need for darkness or privacy, enter into this decision. I like to have most pretest instruments in one room on an arc shaped table so tests can be completed quickly at one sitting, but special pretests, like retinal photos can be done in a separate private room.
- As diagnostic technology increases, more special testing rooms are needed.

14.18 Communicating in Subjective Refraction

I'm sure we all discover phrases that work well in day-to-day patient communication. These special words may make our interaction with the patient more efficient, may put the patient at ease, or may build your image as a caring doctor. In this article, I'll share a few phrases that work well for me along with some thoughts on overall communication during the subjective refraction process.

Communication

It occurred to me that optometry relies on communication more than most health care disciplines, because of the importance of the subjective refraction. Granted, all doctors who work directly with patients find verbal interaction important, starting with the case history, but ODs use verbal skills for that and much more. Primary care physicians rely on patients to describe symptoms. Dentists rely on that also, but because they work in the mouth, the patient does very little talking. Perhaps only psychologists and psychiatrists rely on communication more than optometrists.

Subjective Refraction

Isn't it ironic that you almost never see an article in our professional publications on the topic of refraction, even though that test encompasses a major part of what we do? Of course, I know we do much more than that, but even as we assess ocular disease conditions, best-corrected visual acuity is of major importance. Refraction takes a large chunk of the time we spend with all patients, including contact lens care, low vision, pediatrics, and geriatrics.

I suppose the lack of articles on refraction is due in part to the fact that ODs mastered the mechanics of the procedure long ago, but the communication aspects can challenge even the most seasoned practitioner. Often comical, the responses we get from patients as we interrogate them about their quality of vision (under adverse circumstances) can be highly variable. Some people get it immediately, and some never will. Examples of refractive miscommunication include these classics:

- Doctor: Which is better, number three or number four? Patient: Number two was better.
- Doctor: Which is better, number three or number four? Patient: T Z V E C L
- Doctor: Which is better, number three or number four? Patient: Actually, neither one is very good.
- You can fill in more of your own favorites.

In fairness to patients, we do ask what must seem like some very odd questions. We want to know which lens is clearer, even though they are both somewhat blurry. Our ultimate goal is to make both images look the same, but we keep asking which one is better – and the decision gets harder as we get closer to that elusive goal of equality. We also have a big advantage over patients since we do the procedure 20 times per day and they do it once every 2.3 years.

Digital Refraction

One of the many benefits of computerized refractors is that they can offer two images side by side, which greatly aids communication. The patient does not have to remember the quality of the previous image and the doctor does not have to repeat the options several times when the patient can't decide. It's just easier to tell the clearer image when they are side by side. Of course, computerization is not required to achieve that practical approach... I remember using the Zeiss Simultan test in optometry school, which simply attached to the lens well of any phoroptor and used a split prism to present two images at once. But that's just a museum piece now, although I'm not sure why some inventor hasn't pursued the principle. It was brilliant.

Cardinal Rules of Refraction

- Simplicity. Avoid long, scientific speeches about refraction and complex descriptions of what you are going to ask. Just ask it. There is a cute story about a man who is asked what time it is, and he responds by telling you how to build a watch.

- Patience. You will get better results and the procedure will be easier if you don't reveal any frustration you may feel. Always be kind, polite and friendly to the patient even though, at times, you may become a little annoyed. Once the patient senses some dissatisfaction on your part, he or she will become more defensive and distracted from the task, and you end up looking like the jerk. Go slowly when needed and make the choices easier.
- Encouragement. The more difficulty the patient has, the more encouragement they need. Words like "you're doing fine" or "we're almost done" can be helpful.
- Speed. Boredom and fatigue can lead to poor subjective responses. Work on your technique so you don't offer more choices than necessary. Don't fog and unfog more than necessary and don't seek reversals you don't really need. A quick refraction is a pleasant refraction.

Favorite Phrases

You may want to reserve some of these statements just for the group of patients who have difficulty grasping the concept of subjective refraction. It doesn't take long to identify people in this group.

- This statement is my favorite: "I'll have you look through two different lenses. Even though neither choice will be perfect, I want you to say which one looks clearer".
- If the patient is indecisive, remember to add: "... or do they look about the same? It's always OK if you think the choices look about the same."
- For the nervous patient: "Many people dislike this test (as you gesture toward the phoroptor), but I'll make it very easy for you, so don't worry.
- For those who struggle: "Some of these lens choices are very easy, and some are difficult, but that's OK; you're doing fine".
- For the difficult refractive case: "I'm going to have to ask you lots of questions during this test, but it's important so I can make your vision as clear as possible. Just relax and bear with me".
- For the impatient patient: "Even with all the examination technology we have in this office, I still like to know your personal preferences, and that's why I do this test. We obtained this information by a computer analysis earlier, but now I want your input".

14.19 Do You Dread Seeing Rx Trouble on Your Schedule?

We may call it by different names, but all optometrists deal with eyeglass rechecks, Rx problems, refractive troubleshooting or just the simple redo. I'm pretty sure most of us hate seeing these on our schedules, but let's take a closer look at them and why you should learn to love them.

Why is the visit no charge?
It just is. That has become the norm in our industry for decades and we have to just accept it. ODs love to use the analogy that when a physician prescribes a medication that does not work and the patient returns, another exam fee is usually charged. It makes sense in theory that we should be compensated for our work, but the market prevails and very few optometrists charge for a recheck due to a complaint about new glasses. It is not uncommon for a mistake to be made at some point in the process of making new glasses and we owe it to our patient (customer) to troubleshoot the problem.

If we fix the problem at no charge, it is usually not necessary to determine and reveal exactly who was at fault. If we charge the patient additional fees, it would be necessary to explain why.

Why not just tell staff to handle it?
Opticians can and do play a major role in troubleshooting eyeglass complaints. The level of involvement depends on the skill and knowledge of the optician. I encourage you to train your staff on how to listen to the complaint and ask the right follow-up questions. A protocol should be followed to carefully verify that the lens prescription and all the optical measurements are within tolerance compared to what was ordered. Once all the measurements are confirmed to be as ordered, the optician can double check that some measurements like the PD and seg height were taken properly and visual acuity at far and near point can be measured. Additional factors like lens material, base curve, and progressive lens design should be noted. When all this data is considered along with the patient's complaint, the problem may be discovered; or maybe not.

If the problem has been correctly diagnosed, the glasses should just be remade to fix the error. Most eyeglass problems do not ever need to reach the optometrist. But big trouble can occur if there is an attempt to fix a problem and that attempt fails. The problem remains. The cost of the remake is going up. If that happens, the patient will lose confidence very quickly and the time spent waiting for the correct glasses can become intolerable. A refund may be requested. The patient may write a negative review on social media.

This is why the optometrist may want to become involved earlier, rather than later. The optometrist may be able to help with the troubleshooting. If there is a possibility that the lens prescription is wrong, it may be easier and more certain to just recheck the refraction. That usually requires the optometrist. ODs are also very good at listening to visual complaints and understanding what the cause is, that can help your office to pinpoint the problem.

Better to see them than not see them

As you see patients back for eyeglass issues, don't take it personally. Eyeglass problems will occur and your practice will be judged on how well you handle them. Fix it right the first time and patients will actually be glad they came to you. They may be glad they did not go to some cheap place or order online, where it may be harder to find a resolution.

This is why we should love Rx rechecks, if you did not see them, I would be worried that the patients were not getting the best care and may not be completely satisfied with their services and products.

Don't send a bad message to staff

I think it is best to encourage staff members who do the initial troubleshooting on glasses to let the patient see you if they have any doubt about the cause of the problem. This goes beyond just telling staff that is OK to put these patients in your schedule. If you act annoyed or complain behind the scenes about seeing these patients, staff get the message. Welcoming Rx trouble might get you a few false positives in your exam chair (patients who did not actually need to see you), but that is better than false negatives (patients who should have seen you but the staff tried remaking the job due to some imagined reason).

Remember that these patients spent a lot of money in your office and they are having a bad experience. Your office most likely had something to do with that. It may have been an error by your lab or your staff or maybe even you. Get these patients in to see you quickly. Make room in your schedule. Remember also that Rx problems are almost never as bad as you think they will be. Just greet the patient with a positive attitude and a smile and reassure him that you will resolve the problem.

I think I am a true expert at Rx problems. It must be all the practice I've had with it.

14.20 Clues that you're not delegating enough

A sensitive subject

In speaking with optometrists about practice management over the years, I've found that the topic of delegation is a sensitive one for many. I've heard many objections to the concept – although I never really understand the resistance. I'll be the first to say that optometrists should practice any way they wish, so it's really an individual philosophy and decision, but my objective is to help my colleagues build more successful and more profitable practices, so if you're in the group that wants that, you owe it to yourself to analyze your delegation practices.

Even if you're comfortable with the concept of delegation of clinical and optical procedures to well-qualified technicians and opticians, you may say that there is no need to do so in your situation, and there is no one to delegate to. That's where we would disagree. All successful businesses need to have the owner move away from the task of doing the technical work and into the task of managing the business – it doesn't matter if you repair cars, cut hair, bake donuts, or examine eyeballs.

The early stages of practice

Granted, you can't practice maximum delegation if you're in the early stages of practice development – but you should be thinking about how it should be. I started my practice cold, so I'm quite familiar with all the phases. A fatal mistake occurs when the doctor/owner is performing tasks that could be delegated and becomes complacent about it and rationalizes that it's the best way. I want you to feel just a little bit badly when you do routine duties (like the ones listed below and many others) so you'll act on devising a plan to change it. You may have to do certain procedures at times for practical reasons, but don't lose sight of the master plan for your practice.

One common objection

A typical objection by an OD to the delegation concept might be: "Why should I hire someone and pay him or her to do something that I can do, and have time to do, in my current schedule?" That certainly sounds logical, and it's why optometrists don't delegate very much. This objection is built around the fact that many optometric practices have appointment schedules that are not completely full – and if the spotty schedule in question is structured to allow about 12 exams per day, the doctor will have plenty of extra time.

The fallacy of the objection above is that you don't have as much free time as you think. Not if you were doing the right things – and it's not all about patient care. Many ODs don't realize how and where they are needed in their practice. If you're practice is not booked solid, you need to spend even more time on practice marketing, self-training in business, staff training and customer service. So the non-busy practitioner should delegate some routine tasks because he or she will be using all non-clinical time on management activities. Ideally, you should reorganize and consolidate the schedule as you make the shift toward delegation. This would involve seeing a few more patients per day, so those days are really busy, while freeing up some half days or full days for management.

Clues about delegating

This list is just an example of a few tasks that are often performed by optometrists, which I think can and should be done by staff members. Are you doing any of these procedures? Do you plan on doing them forever?

- Ordering contact lenses by phone, fax or on-line
- Measuring a seg height
- Taking visual acuity on every exam
- Edging spectacle lenses in your lab
- Calculating payroll hours
- Teaching contact lens insertion, removal and care
- Performing automated pre-tests, like auto-refraction or non-contact tonometry
- Performing threshold visual fields
- Performing corneal topography
- Making bank deposits
- Adjusting a frame
- Doing routine lensometry on a patient's habitual Rx or on finished glasses as they arrive from the lab

14.21 Delegation: The Usual Excuses

I'd like to focus the next two tip articles on clinical delegation; or the lack thereof. Delegation is a major key to success in practice, yet most optometrists think it does not apply to them. They often think that delegation is something they will do when they become more successful. They don't get that delegation must occur first in order to become successful.

Let's look at the usual excuses optometrists cite for why they don't delegate more. Are you guilty of believing any of these myths?

I'm not busy enough to justify the extra staff member I would need.
This is the number one reason I hear for not delegating very much and I don't agree with it at all. Look at the big picture. If you think of the practice as a separate entity that must pay a salary to the doctor/owner, then doctor time is the biggest expense there is. If you can save doctor time or maximize its purpose, you are saving money. Even if you do not have enough patient demand to fill the appointment schedule, you would be better off seeing all the patients in fewer days with the help of a technician. Why? Because you would then create open days during the week that you can use to work on the practice. And if your schedule is not full enough, that is exactly what you need the most. Call on other physicians and introduce yourself. Join a community organization. Develop marketing programs. Improve your practice website. Read a book on business development. Start a Facebook page for your practice. There are countless things you can do to promote your practice, so don't just sit in your office and slowly see a few patients.

My patients would not like having an assistant do tasks that I typically do.
Sorry, but I don't buy it. If this is true it is because the doctor creates the perception that his staff members are inferior. And that perception can be reversed quickly if the doctor simply displays confidence and praise for the staff. Patients are very accustomed to technicians and paraprofessionals delivering health care. In fact, a practice that operates that way is more impressive than one where the doctor does everything.

I can perform the tasks better than any technician.
The clinical tasks that I recommend delegating are simply forms of data collection. Anyone can be trained to do it perfectly and in many cases an automated instrument is involved which simplifies the procedure and confirms the accuracy of the result. If patient flow is limited to just one person, it is impossible to see the number of patients necessary to generate a strong profit. In this age of managed care and discount vision plans, it is imperative that practices become more efficient. Train your technicians to perform tests and record the outcome the same way you would do it. Don't condemn a new approach until you have tried it.

I do not have the office space needed.

There are generally ways to delegate more even with limited space, but if that is truly an obstacle to delegation, then you should begin to look for new office space. A small office will definitely restrict the growth of your practice and limit your income. You must have multiple exam rooms per working doctor and pretest rooms for technicians. As you explore the possibility of moving to a new location, see if there is a way to take on vacant space adjacent to your present office or use your existing rooms differently. Maybe the contact lens dispensing room can become a pretest room or perhaps you can use a storage room for patient care and move all the stuff to a remote storage facility.

I can't find enough good employees.
With unemployment at an all-time high, it has never been easier to find good employees. You must advertise the position in the local paper as well as online resources. Help-wanted ads can be expensive, but you should run the ad until the position is filled. Being understaffed is even more expensive. If you are not seeing high enough quality in the applicants, you may have to pay more and be willing to accept people without eye care experience. It is time consuming to train someone with no experience, but it is far more important to find the right person. Look for an outgoing personality, plenty of smiles, good eye contact, a passion for customer service, intelligence, a knack for computers, and strong communication skills.

Chapter 15. The Medical Model

15.1 Practical Tips on the Medical Model

The term "medical model" is used quite often among optometrists, but it can have different meanings to different people. To me, it means more than just providing medical eye care, which most optometrists do quite often. I use medical model to refer to billing medical insurance plans for a medical eye condition, even if the patient has vision plan benefits available. Most ODs are network providers for Medicare and medical insurance plans and we are increasingly billing these plans for services when appropriate. But patients are often confused about the difference between medical insurance and vision plans. Here are some tips on how and when to bill various insurance plans that cover eye health and vision care.

The term “medical model” is used quite often among optometrists, but it can have different meanings to different people. To me, it means more than just providing medical eye care, which most optometrists do quite often. I use medical model to refer to billing medical insurance plans for a medical eye condition, even if the patient has vision plan benefits available. Most ODs are network providers for Medicare and medical insurance plans and we are increasingly billing these plans for services when appropriate. But patients are often confused about the difference between medical insurance and vision plans. Here are some tips on how and when to bill various insurance plans that cover eye health and vision care.

- **Is it legal to bill medical insurance if the patient has a vision plan?** Certainly, as long as the patient had a chief complaint that was medical in nature and a medical diagnosis code. Vision plans clearly state that they provide coverage for routine vision care services and optical products.
- **Is it legal to bill a vision plan if the patient has a medical diagnosis?** Vision plans will pay for a vision exam as long as the patient is eligible for benefits, which occurs based on a timetable, such as once per year. The vision plan would not reject a claim for patients who have medical eye problems; after all, they could also need a refraction and glasses at some point. But a vision plan is not the correct insurance for medical eye care and it is not a good practice to use it for that purpose. However, there is a gray area where the exam could technically result in a medical diagnosis, but the patient's intent was to receive routine vision care. That is when the situation can get tricky. It is in the best interest of your practice to

work on this gray area so you communicate well, educate patients and keep patient satisfaction high.

- **Should you bother with the medical model?** Yes! Medical eye care is a more advanced level of service and you deserve to be paid at higher fees, which medical insurance typically pays. Many optometrists just bill the vision plan first in every case and if they need any additional testing, they would bill that to medical insurance. That is OK in those gray areas, but if the case is truly medical in nature, the exam should be billed to medical insurance. In my experience, the vast majority of patients with medical eye problems understand that their services should be billed to medical insurance and they are fine with it. There are some patients who don't like it, but it is a minority and we can work with them to keep them happy.
- **How to present it to the patient.** The best way to start is to give the patient a brief educational handout at check-in that explains the difference between vision plans and medical insurance. Beyond that, the doctor or a clinical technician can just say to the patient at the end of the visit: "Mrs. Smith, your exam today will be billed to your medical insurance plan because you have a medical eye problem as the doctor discussed with you. We will save your vision plan and use it on a future visit and we can always use it for new eyeglasses. Judy at the front desk will go over all your charges with you."
- **Use the vision plan at some point.** The one factor in all this that vision plans feel strongly about is that the member (patient) should be allowed to use their vision plan at some point. That seems perfectly reasonable to me. The patient and his employer pay for that benefit and they have a right to use it. Whether you perform the routine exam and refraction first or later can depend on the case and the nature of the chief complaint.
- **Coordination of benefits (COB).** This is an underutilized benefit that is available with some vision plans and with some limitations. If a vision plan allows COB, there will be section about it in the provider manual. COB is a great way to begin using the medical model because it limits the patient's out-of-pocket expense. Basically, you bill the medical plan first with a medical diagnosis and you also bill the refraction. Some medical plans will cover the refraction, but most do not. The patient may also have a medical co-pay, which can be collected at the time of the visit or can be held on the patient's personal account. If the medical insurance rejects the refraction, you may then use the COB procedure to bill the vision plan for the

refraction and in some cases the plan will also cover the medical co-pay or part of the deductible.

- **Back to billing patients?** There is no doubt that this trend to work with managed care causes us to have to send invoices and statements to patients. This seems counter-productive to optometrists who worked hard in the 1980s to eliminate the practice of billing patients. We got good at collecting the fees in the office. As we bill medical plans, we have to let go of this to some degree because we often find out later that a deductible was not met or some service is not covered. I'm happy to report that my practice has had very little bad debt as we transfer fees back to the patient and bill them. They generally pay quite well. Perhaps it is because they also receive the explanation of benefits from their insurance company and it shows clearly any amount that is owed to the physician. Perhaps the patients don't want to have credit problems and they know they will need care in the future. At any rate, billing medical insurance has more pros than cons and we should embrace it.
- **Let the patient win**. The most important lesson in the medical model is to keep the patient happy. The last thing I want to do is lose a patient and his family over which insurance plan we bill. Most patients are perfectly happy letting us bill the appropriate insurance for the care they receive, but if we have a patient who feels strongly about it, we let him have his way. Talk about the medical model and the gray areas at your next staff meeting.

15.2 Routine Vision vs. Medical Eye Exams: Fees and Insurance

Optometrists are doing a much better job with the medical model of eye care, but this is still a sensitive area in practice management because patients naturally want some input into whether we bill their vision plan or medical insurance. Two major factors to consider are the exam fee structure and how to decide which insurance to bill. I'll present an analysis of both these factors here, along with some tips on how to bill for the maximum fees without upsetting the patient.

Fees

A good place to begin your fee strategy is to decide if your practice should have a lower fee structure for routine vision exams compared to medical eye exams. If the patient has a vision plan that the practice accepts, it may not make any difference because the practice ultimately accepts the vision plan payment, but in some cases, routine vision exams are private pay. It is not an easy decision but we should start there.

Let's begin by looking at medical eye exam fees because they are a bit easier to determine. Many doctors use the published fee levels for Medicare as the minimum to charge for a service. You could use any medical insurance plan fee schedule as your basis, but Medicare is often considered the standard. This makes sense because doctors want to be paid the maximum for a service and the popular expression is that we don't want to "leave money on the table" by billing less than insurance will pay. Of course, you could charge more than the approved amount and many doctors do, but that fee will be adjusted down to the approved fee level and you can't balance bill the patient for covered services.

S-codes and TOS discounts

For a 92014 the Medicare approved fee is about $126. That does not include refraction and let's say that averages about $35. So the eye exam with medical insurance is at least $161. So, will a routine private pay patient pay $161 for an eye exam? In many cases, they will. I know many ophthalmological and some optometric practices that charge more than that to private pay. My practice charges more than that and we only have one comprehensive exam fee for all types of patients, regardless if it is routine or medical, regardless of no insurance, vision plan or medical insurance. If you can charge the same fee to all, then you don't need S-codes or a time of service (TOS) discount.

But many practice owners feel they would lose a lot of patients if they charged that high of a fee for a routine exam. There are always optical places in every community that charge very low exam fees. If you feel you need a lower fee for routine and private pay, then S-codes or TOS discount are both good ways to go. To my knowledge, there is not a published maximum for TOS discounts but it must be reasonable and represent the true administrative cost that would be incurred for billing and collection. If we use 20% as the TOS discount, that would bring the fee down to $128 for the private pay patient. If you feel that is still too high for a routine exam fee, then you can use an S-code like S0621. An S-code exam is a different service than a medical eye exam and it can legally have a different fee. S-codes include the refraction. You can make an S-code exam fee any amount you want. S-codes are never billed to medical insurance; they don't recognize them.

Billing medical or vision?
We give each patient in my practice at check-in a short handout explaining that vision plans only cover routine vision wellness exams, eyeglasses and contact lenses. Medical eye exams (the diagnosis and treatment of eye health problems) are billed to medical insurance. From there, the doctor determines how the case is billed. Much depends on the chief complaint and the medical diagnosis.

- In some cases, we will bill the vision plan first for a routine exam and reappoint for follow-up medical care which is billed to medical insurance.
- In some cases, such as emergencies, we perform a medical eye exam and treatment first and then reappoint for a routine exam and refraction.
- In some cases, we simply do not need to see the patient for two visits within a close time frame and we do not routinely manufacture a second visit. In the first place it would be unethical and in the second place, patients are smart and many will sense the unnecessary visit and quietly change doctors. In those cases, we may bill the vision plan or we may bill the medical plan depending on the primary diagnosis and complaint.
- We use coordination of benefits with both types of insurance when allowed, which means the vision plan may cover some of the fees that medical insurance does not cover, such as co-pays and refraction fees.

Questions from patients
If patients ask why you have two different exam fees or why you bill medical insurance instead of the vision plan, your staff must explain that a routine eye exam is different than a medical eye exam. A routine exam is faster and easier to perform and there is no medical decision-making or disease treatment in a routine exam. That is fair, but there is a gray area in between routine and medical that the patient may not understand or accept, and ODs need to be careful with that. You might find a very minor medical issue, let's say a very mild dry eye condition that does not require treatment or follow-up. You could insist that it is a medical exam because of that finding, but the patient may feel that he did not really have a medical problem and he just wanted an exam for new glasses.

I let the patient win on borderline medical cases like that and also if I know there is a high medical deductible in play (if there is an exam co-pay, the

deductible is usually not a factor). I just consider those exams as routine and bill them to the vision plan. My practice treats and bills a high number of medical cases, but the patient relationship is more important than a higher exam fee. If a case is clearly medical and the patient still objects - let's say diabetes for example - I might let the patient have his way on this initial visit, but I'll explain that he has a chronic medical eye problem that requires a higher level of care and in the future, we will have to charge a medical exam fee and bill medical insurance. We mark the record accordingly so my staff knows how to handle it next year and we know what we said. I might lose a few of those patients next time, but that is OK with me because I'm doing the right thing. I will keep most of them and I let the patient get out of the issue gracefully the first time. I also avoid a negative online review and bad word of mouth and I keep the stress level low for my staff.
There is usually a way to achieve your business goals and keep patients happy if you work on it.

15.3 A Patient Education Form for Medical vs. Vision

I received a lot of reader email following an article that was published a few weeks ago: "Routine Vision vs. Medical Eye Exams: Fees and Insurance". I appreciate the comments and support on this important topic. I mentioned a patient education form that we provide to patients at check-in in my practice that explains the difference between vision plans and medical insurance. Many readers requested a copy of this form, so I'll provide it below.

I think it is important to keep signature forms and disclaimers short. Realize that many patients simply don't read them and they don't want them long and complicated. You may be able to combine this vision vs. medical form with other educational documents you offer to the patient at check in, such as HIPAA acknowledgment and retinal image screening forms. You may be able keep the combined form to one page and have one patient signature cover several topics.

Your Practice Name and Logo
About Your Insurance

There are two types of health insurance that will help pay for your eye care services and optical products. You may have both types and Main Street Eye Center accepts most insurance plans in both categories: 1) Vision plans (such as VSP, EyeMed and others) and 2) Medical insurance (such as Blue Cross/Blue Shield, Medicare and others).

- Vision plans only cover routine vision wellness exams, along with eyeglasses and contact lenses. Vision plans do not cover medical eye care (the diagnosis, management or treatment of eye health problems).
- Medical insurance must be used for medical eye care.
- If you have both types of insurance plans it may be necessary for us to bill some services to one plan and some services to the other. We will follow a procedure called coordination of benefits to do this properly and to minimize your out-of-pocket expense.
- If some fees are not paid by your insurance, we will bill you for them, such as deductibles, co-pays or non-covered services as allowed by the insurance contract.

Please provide your insurance cards to our staff member so we can make a copy. We need to have your medical insurance card or Medicare card on file in case we should need it in the future for billing your insurance.

I have read and accept these policies.

Patient signature (parent if child) Date

15.4 Billing Medical Insurance or Vision Plans?

Optometrists are both blessed and cursed to be paid by two forms of third-party managed care plans: medical insurance and vision plans. Usually I feel more cursed than blessed, but I firmly believe in playing the cards we're dealt, so let's look at ways to determine when to bill which plan, given the system we have in place in the United States. I will say at the outset that I don't have all the answers to the complex issue of how to bill insurance companies for the legally maximum amounts while keeping the patient perfectly happy. I think it's important to balance those two factors and recognize that there is a gray area between routine vision care and medical eye care that must be handled well.

Bill the plan that pays the best

There are many circumstances where an eye care provider (ECP) could bill either a vision plan or a medical plan for the same visit. It is, of course, illegal to bill both plans for the same work, but it can be perfectly legitimate for the doctor to choose one plan or the other. Vision plans approve claims based on the calendar. As long as the patient is eligible, the diagnosis does not really matter. Medical insurance approves claims based on an appropriate medical diagnosis and medical necessity. If a patient has both types of insurance and if there is an appropriate medical diagnosis, either plan could be billed and will be paid.

In the absence of any other factors, it makes perfect sense to bill the plan (and the specific code) that pays the best (usually the medical plan). But there are many other factors. Vision plans generally pay much lower fees than medical plans and they clearly indicate that the covered service is a routine vision exam. So when does a routine vision exam become a medical exam? Many ECPs have office policies and definitions to try to differentiate the two types of exams, but it is still quite common (and understandable) for patients to be confused.

The gray area

Many case examples are extremely easy to determine if they are routine or medical. A patient who has no complaints or only wants to check if his prescription for glasses is correct should use a vision plan. A patient who is a glaucoma suspect or has a foreign body in his cornea should use medical insurance. But there are a large number of cases that may not be so clear. Some medical diagnoses are rather minor in nature and do not need additional treatment or follow-up. There is wide variation among ECPs on how to handle the cases in the gray area and even on what is the gray area.

The patient is a stakeholder

It's important to consider the patient's point of view as the decision is made about billing vision plans or medical insurance. The terms of all these plans vary, but it is quite possible that the medical plan can carry a higher co-payment amount or the vision plan may have zero co-pay. There may also be a high annual deductible with medical insurance that has not been met. The medical plan may not cover the refraction test (but some do).

If the practice makes the unilateral decision to bill the medical plan without educating the patient, it's quite easy for patients to be unhappy with their part of the bill. The patient may complain to the front desk staff in some cases, or may not say anything and just decide to not return for future care. It is clearly not a good strategy to be paid a higher exam fee, only to lose the patient and his family forever.

Some insurance management tips

- Have a patient handout that explains the two types of insurance and defines routine vision exams and medical eye exams. A one-page handout is actually your office policy written in simple language. It can be used for patient education and it also reminds staff members of the key points and works like a script. I'll give an example in a future tip article.

- Tell patients in advance. This goes a long way to keeping patients happy. Many successful practices train the front desk staff to take a mini-history over the phone as the appointment is being made. If the nature of the complaint or history is medical, the staff member can indicate right then that a medical eye exam is needed and that your office will be billing the medical insurance. It is always better to discuss these matters before the services are performed.
- Always obtain both the vision plan and medical plan information over the phone. This task alone will educate patients as many will ask why you want it. This is a clue that this patient does not understand that eye doctors can provide medical care and there is a high likelihood of confusion about insurance. Your staff should see this as an opportunity to provide patient education. Some patients, however, will not want to hear the education.
- Learn about the insurance plans that are common in your area by keeping a log book about what they cover and how much they pay. This should be specific for the employer or group since each insurance company has many different plans.
- Help the patient as much as possible with keeping his out-of-pocket costs low. After all, that is the main concern the patient has with regard to which insurance is used. Patients don't know the specifics about their vision or medical plans, so help them with it. In many cases, the difference in the out-of-pocket dollars is not that great. If you can show that, then all the fuss goes away.
- Find out which services go toward the deductible for all the medical plans you see. Many medical plans do not apply office visits to an annual deductible at all, but rather only the co-pay applies. If that is the case, high deductibles do not cause any problem at all. This could be different for 92 codes vs. 99 codes.
- Consider coordination of benefits. In many cases, you can bill the medical plan for services, including non-covered items like the refraction. When the payment and explanation of benefits (EOB) is received by your office, you may be able to send the claim on to the vision plan with a copy of the EOB. The vision plan may pay up to the plan limits for the non-covered amounts. The vision plan may even pay the medical co-pay. You may need to file a paper claim for these cases.
- Don't reappoint unless you really need to. This is another sensitive area, but many ECPs routinely make the first exam visit go to the vision plan and if there is a medical diagnosis, they bring the patient

back for additional tests and those are billed to medical. This is a perfectly fine way to go and it is very clean, if additional testing is needed like an OCT or visual field. But if the second visit is simply to examine the same thing that was seen at the first visit, patients and insurance plans will rightfully have an issue with it.

15.5 Retinal Image Screenings: What Are Your Options?

Offering patients the option of having digital retinal photos or ultra-widefield laser retinal images as an optional screening test is a great way to enhance a routine eye exam. This procedure has been used for decades, but has grown in popularity and acceptance. Patients understand that their vision plan only covers a very basic vision exam, but many want the benefits of more advanced technology and are willing to pay out-of-pocket for it.

Chances are very good that you already offer some kind of retinal screening test, but you may wonder if you are doing it the best way. Or, perhaps you are new to retinal imaging and you are wondering how to position it in your practice. I have provided retinal screenings in my practice for a long time and I've tried many different methods. Here is a quick rundown of your options.

Always read the provider manual of any vision plan you work with and stay within the contractual guidelines you agreed to.

Which instrument and multiple tests?

The first step is to determine what type of screening to offer. Most optometrists offer retinal photos of some kind and for good reason; they provide useful clinical documentation for comparison with future exams and they offer a very high degree of the wow factor. Patients never get tired of having their doctor show them an image of the inside of their own eye and explain what the structures are and if it is healthy. Which retinal image device to buy depends on your budget and your preferences, so all I can say is shop around.

Many ODs are also offering other screening services in addition to or instead of retinal photos. There are wellness screenings available in OCT instruments and macular pigment optical density (MPOD) testing is also quite popular. These choices are up to you, but keep in mind as you bundle more tests, the cost is generally higher to the patient and the time it takes the technician to run the tests will increase. Keep an eye on the total patient experience and don't let a very good wow factor turn into a drain on the patient's energy and time.

I was always concerned that offering two optional screening tests would be too much, but we have had a very positive reaction from patients when we offer the Optomap and MPOD test as a bundled package.

Include in exam fee or charge additional?

Many doctors adding advanced technology to their exam tell me they just want to include it in the exam fee and have the test on all patients. I get that, but we have to look at the economics of the situation as well. The decision may come down to how prevalent vision plans are in your practice. You can't raise your exam fee within vision plans and since the technology is quite expensive, collecting an out-of-pocket fee is an excellent way to generate a lot of revenue.

High fee or low fee?

Consider the tipping point of fees: at what price will many more people say yes? As an example, you could charge a fee of $40 and you might find 50% of patients opt in, but if you charge $20, you could find almost 100% say yes. The revenue you collect would be the same in both cases, but the time needed by your staff would increase greatly with the lower fee. You would also gain the exam efficiency and more people would have the wow factor with the lower fee. Your call.

Leverage dilation?

Another big factor for your opt-in success rate is if you can make the claim that patients who have the screening test will not need to be dilated as often. Optometrists vary widely with their opinions on this matter. It really only applies to ultra-widefield laser imaging, because standard retinal photos do not provide a very wide view of the posterior pole. All I would say is represent your clinical philosophy honestly. We dilate almost every patient in my practice, so we don't make any claims about reducing the frequency of dilation.

Written handout or verbal?

Some doctors like the technician to discuss the screening option during pretesting, some doctors prefer to recommend it personally, and others have a staff member at the front desk hand the patient an educational paper form at check-in (and the patient checks a yes or no box and initials it). You can try all those methods and choose which way works best in your practice.

Surprisingly, I found a higher opt-in rate when our receptionists gave the patient a handout at check-in compared to having our techs explain the test and offer it during pretesting. I'm not sure why that was, but I suspect the technicians often feel rushed and they did not want to take the time to do the extra test. We went back to having the receptionist hand out the form. Some offices pay a bonus to staff members if they reach a certain goal on the opt-in percentage or for each screening test performed.

I prefer a low-key approach to offering the screening test. I don't want the patient to feel pressured into having the test and I want to let them opt-out gracefully if they so choose. The patient experience is more important than the extra fee in the long run.

Maximize the wow factor
If you are going to offer retinal screening tests, I think it is important to obtain the full wow factor. The instrument should be in a pretest or special diagnostic room and it should be on the office computer network system. The screening test is performed by a technician and the images are brought up on a monitor in the exam room for the doctor to review and discuss with the patient. You may want the images from the previous exam also brought up for comparison.

15.6 Medical Optometry: Is There a Downside?

Talk with a group of optometrists today about the latest trends in the profession and you'll hear about the increased emphasis on medical eye care. New grads and seasoned practitioners alike; everyone is embracing diagnosis and treatment of eye disease; in some cases as if it is the savior for all of what ails optometry.

My personal position on medical eye care in my own practice is very positive. I became certified to treat eye disease in my state when the legislation was passed many years ago. I'm in group practice with three other doctors and we all actively diagnose and treat everything from infections to glaucoma. We all obtain a considerable amount of continuing education in this field. No doubt about it, prescribing pharmaceuticals for the eye is an important part of optometric practice.

From a business standpoint, medical eye care can be a financially rewarding addition to our other services, but there is also a potential drawback.

Driving the medical trend

There are many good reasons why optometrists are increasingly pursuing management of ocular disease.

- Training. Professional training drives what happens in practice and it has now been many years since optometry schools, internships, externships and residencies started teaching medical eye care at the practitioner level. The concentration in this area keeps improving, but there are now enough graduates who experienced these programs that it shapes what they do. This specialized training extends into continuing education courses, journals, text books and simple sharing within group practices.
- Medical insurance vs. vision plans. Fed up with the extremely low fees allowed by vision plans, doctors realize that medical insurance also covers eye care services if there is a medical diagnosis. Medical insurance usually pays at a much higher fee level.
- Technology. Optometrists aspiring to provide the highest level of care invest in advanced instrumentation for their practices. Most of this new technology is focused on diagnosis and management of eye disease. As ODs are armed with more information, disease is detected earlier and managed more aggressively.
- Ego and status. ODs have always been sensitive about being misunderstood by the public and the medical community. Because one aspect of our care involves a product with a retail and fashion orientation, optometry is sometimes viewed as non-medical. Some optometrists emphasize the medical model in order to overcome the retail perception and to educate others about what we can do.

So what?

So, is there a downside to medical optometry? Not directly maybe, but concentrating on eye disease can pull your focus away from optical dispensing and that can lead to a loss of significant potential revenue. Revenue is not everything, of course, and each practitioner must do what makes him or her happy, but our premise for this article is the business standpoint and the primary goal in business is revenue. If we're honest, personal income is a very strong goal for most of us.

Many ODs think they can practice both medical and optical care, and some actually do it. That would be ideal. Unfortunately, as is the case in any business, it is difficult to pursue two diverse services and do both well. There is only so much time and the CEO can only work on so much.

Optical suffers

In many cases, the optical department in a medically oriented eye practice is mediocre. There is often a lack of attention from the top and the staff develops a complacent attitude about customer service. Optical is not fun and exciting, but it is a medical adjunct to functional vision. A necessity. The doctor who loves treating eye disease usually could care less about the latest designer frame style or about policies to create sales of second pairs. In some cases, the doctor proudly states that he has no interest or knowledge of optical dispensing, preferring to delegate all aspects of that to the staff. I'm big on delegation, but that approach severely limits practice growth and revenue.

Big revenue

Optometric practices that earn top revenue have great optical departments and generate an amazing amount of revenue from eyeglasses. Without surgical fees, a primary care practice is limited to what it can bill for diagnostic procedures alone. That may seem like good revenue, but it pales when compared to what a practice can produce when it offers excellent clinical and optical service. Consider what you get paid for procedures like office visits and visual fields. It's satisfactory, but it's not big money and it all depends on you to do the work.

Vision plans may be so dominant that it can affect the philosophy of the doctor and staff. You may feel like medical procedures produce excellent revenue because you compare it to the exam fees paid by vision plans. You may feel like optical is not that profitable because you have not broken away from providing what the plan covers. What many ODs don't seem to know is that patients will still pay for services and products that they really want, even if it's not covered by a plan. We have to make those services and products available and attractive.

Don't place all your energy into eye disease and billing and coding. Embrace optical as well.

15.7 Top Ten Misconceptions in Practice Management

Conventional wisdom is often wrong. In this week's tip, I will present ten commonly accepted management strategies that I generally disagree with. I admit that there is more than one way to be successful in practice, so some of these concepts may seem to be working for you. But that's really the point of this article; read over this list and see if you are surprised to find something you believe strongly in may not be as effective as you thought. Granted, these are simply my opinions and nothing more, but I assure you that I have strong evidence to lead my thinking.

Taking the contrarian approach to some management theories can sometimes yield excellent results. With all due respect, many optometric practices are not doing all that well, so following the usual procedures that are prevalent in our profession may not lead to outstanding results.

I won't go into details here as to the reason I think these ideas are misguided, but see if you can infer why I take the opposite point of view. If there is enough interest, future tip articles may focus on the theory behind each point.

My top ten misconceptions in practice management

10. I don't need a larger frame inventory.
9. Pre-appointing is the best recall strategy and is the key to building a busy practice.
8. Delivering glasses in one hour or one day is no longer important in practice building.
7. Annual employee evaluations are an important part of staff management.
6. Saturday hours are not that important to practice growth and they are inefficient due to no-shows.
5. A good bonus or incentive program for staff is a smart way to increase optical sales and improve performance.
4. For a fee increase to be well accepted, it should not be greater than 10%.
3. Using scribes in the exam room would drive payroll costs too high and it is simply not practical.
2. Medical billing and coding are the keys to financial success in optometry today and it's smart to have a higher fee for medically-based examinations.
1. It is smart to bring in an associate to buy into my practice earlier in my career so I have a secure exit strategy.

15.8 Response to the Ten Misconceptions Expanding on Medical Billing

I received an outstanding response from readers on my article two weeks ago on the top ten misconceptions in practice management. One reader said I really opened a can of worms and another said she hoped I was ready for the storm I probably created. Many of you simply said you wanted me to expand on all ten items while others listed a few by number that piqued your interest. At any rate, your interest is truly gratifying to me professionally and I will definitely be expanding on all ten concepts in future tips. Many readers noted (correctly) that I was probably happy to have ten weeks of future topic ideas.

I listed the ten items in an order loosely based on my view of the impact each one has on revenue production. Of the items that were identified by readers, however, here is how the interest ranked from most to least:

- Medical billing and preappointing (tied)
- Staff bonus system and employee evaluations (tied)
- Associate OD
- Frame inventory
- Scribes
- Saturday hours
- One hour glasses
- Fee increases

Medical billing

So, let's tackle them in the order you want. This week, we'll cover medical billing. The statement in my article was: #2. Medical billing and coding are the keys to financial success in optometry today and it's smart to have a higher fee for medically-based examinations.

This misconception, like a few of the others on the list, is not based so much on the premise that I don't believe in the concept, but more that the concept is often taken too far in a practice at the loss of something else that is more important.

Here are my thoughts on the trend of billing medical insurance and having a higher fee for medically based examinations.

- Patient satisfaction is still the most important factor in practice success. I think it's easy to lose sight of that when the doctor thinks he is dealing with a corporate third party like an insurance company. The patient still has a strong interest even if it appears that a third party is paying. The whole area of fees and payments has a huge potential to upset patients.
- Many practices work too hard to find a medical diagnosis or to justify a higher fee. Patients are very smart people and they know a

business strategy when they see one. Strategies that may call integrity into question can cause more harm than good.

- Most optometric practices (not all) provide a high percentage of routine exams and refractive care. To base fee decisions on a small percentage of cases does not make sense. I know many practitioners who proudly say their exam fee is $250, but they only charge that in less than 10% of the cases. Eventually the patient gets to the "real" fee, but it shouldn't feel so convoluted.
- There is no harm in billing medical plans for legitimately covered services, but if the patient is put out because he has a high deductible and just wanted an eye exam, or he wanted to use his vision plan but the doctor insisted that it was a medical problem, or any other annoyance that may arise when a patient does not get what he expects, harm could result. The invisible harm that doctors aren't even aware of is the number of people who decide to go somewhere else for eye care next time. That is a significant loss that occurs in some practices much more than others and it is very hard to track.
- Assuming that private pay routine patients will not pay $150 for an eye exam, therefore the fee must be altered for that group in some way, is an expensive mistake. People will pay that fee or more for eye exams and I think the nature of the service is worth fees in that level. Why don't most optometrists think they are worth it?
- Many practices would be better off improving their level of care and service and increasing their routine fees to the level paid by Medicare or other major medical insurers. Having a higher fee for medically-based eye exams is the same thing as having lower fees for non-medical exams. I don't like offering low fee eye exams.
- Patients really like to know what the fee will be for a service they are buying (an eye exam) and they want to know what their insurance will pay. It may influence their decision on where they go for eye care. If an office can't tell a caller exactly what the fee will be for an eye exam and if an insurance plan (vision or medical) is accepted, then I think there is a good chance of upsetting some patients. I have trouble with the concept that the fee varies based on the diagnosis. I do all the same tests in a comprehensive eye exam and I have medical decision making even if the eye is healthy. Of course, additional procedures and follow-up visits will vary based on the diagnosis, but those are extra services that only need to be explained to people who need them. I have some patients with binocular disorders that require prism in their glasses who take an inordinate amount of my time in an examination, but it is not

> medical. And I have senior patients, who have 1+ nuclear sclerosis, but they take very little time or medical decision making and they could be called medical. Some exams will always be easier than others, but for practical reasons, a system with one fee for a specific service works very well.

Medical billing and coding are not the keys to financial success in optometry. High fees in general for excellent service and a high percentage of revenue from optical dispensing are the keys.

15.9 Routine Vision Exams vs. Medical Eye Care

Topic ideas for tip articles continue to be sparked by reader emails and I greatly appreciate the interaction. In Tip #311, I cited several scenarios that frequently occur in eye care offices that can upset patients. The area of greatest interest is in the differentiation between routine and medical eye care. I think this topic deserves a great deal of attention because it is one of the strongest trends in practice management, but it has the potential to damage patient relationships through misunderstandings.

Vision or medical?
Here is one scenario I described from a patient's point of view:

They told me my vision insurance would cover my exam, but when I got there they said they had to bill my medical plan. I think it's just a way for them to make more money.

That statement prompted this question from a reader that accurately describes the dilemma that many eye care practitioners (ECPs) face every day:

What is an OD to do when he or she discovers a non-threatening sight/ocular condition that does require evaluation, education and management (limited management at the very least) of the patient? They came in expecting the lower vision exam fee yet now they should be "upgraded" to the medical level. Of course, a variety of insurance scenarios can occur: the patient has both vision and medical insurance, no vision or medical insurance, vision plan but no medical insurance, medical insurance but no vision plan, or the worst of all: super high deductible with an MSA/HSA?

My reply:

My opinion may differ from many ECPs on this issue, but I think every exam should include some evaluation, education and management. If the only diagnosis is astigmatism, you had to detect it, measure it and decide how much of it to prescribe. You should tell the patient what astigmatism is and what to expect in the future. You may have to explain further, such as telling him that reading in the dark or watching TV won't cause astigmatism to increase. You may discuss when to wear eyeglasses and if contact lenses are an option. I don't find that kind of work any easier than diagnosing dry eye or mild allergic conjunctivitis and managing those conditions. Patients don't see any difference either.

I don't need to look hard to find a medical diagnosis because my fees are the same whether the case is visual or medical (see next section below). I just do an eye exam and I cover and treat everything I find. I see some medical cases that are extremely easy and fast and I see some refractive cases that are very complex. One comprehensive exam fee still applies in either case and it all averages out in the end. Of course, if I truly need an additional visit for more testing, or a special diagnostic procedure, or a follow-up visit to monitor a condition, I'll order it and charge for it. Those fees may be billed directly to the patient or to any third party plan the patient wishes as long as my office accepts it.

I don't change the exam fee based on whether it's routine or medical. An important point here is that I didn't lower my medical exam fee to the routine level, but rather I raised the routine fee to the going rate for medical exams. I believe ECPs are incorrect with the usual assumption that they will lose patients if they charge a high fee for routine exams. Of course, if the patient has a vision plan, my usual and customary fee will not be covered in full, but that's a business problem that I accepted when I signed up for the vision plan. Finding a medical diagnosis and increasing the fee looks too much like bait and switch to the average patient, and that's very bad for business.

If I'm ever unsure whether to bill a vision plan or a medical plan (assuming the service is covered by both with no clear coordination of benefits), I'll ask the patient which one he wants me to bill. I'm also never shy about charging the patient privately and letting him file his own claim. We tell patients over the phone in advance what the fee will be and we discuss their insurance and advise accordingly if they will be expected to pay at the time of the visit. They don't mind; quite the contrary... patients appreciate knowing what the fees will be.

No surprises

In Tip # 311, I wrote: *Patients hate surprises about fees. Tell people in advance what to expect.*

A reader responded: This would be interesting to expand on. What is a surprise anyway?

My Reply:
Of course, only the unpleasant surprises bother people. Examples would include situations when the patient didn't know that a fee would be charged (a contact lens evaluation, perhaps) or when the fee is higher than expected. Another unpleasant surprise would include not being able to use the insurance plan the patient intended to use. Patients view insurance as an extension of their own personal resources and they want to maintain control over it. They generally pay something for the insurance or earn it as part of their employment. Patients may prefer to use one plan over another for many reasons, but co-payments, deductibles and paying for refraction fees are frequently a consideration.

It's easy to quote exact fees over the phone and inform callers if an insurance plan is accepted or not. We do this in my practice even if the patient doesn't ask. All you need to do is keep the fee constant for each type of exam offered. Staff members actually like the procedure of disclosing the fee in advance because it eliminates misunderstandings and confrontations in the office.

15.10 Medical Eye Care and Optical Dispensing

I consult with many optometrists who have built very successful practices with a strong emphasis on medical eye care. In many cases, they lament that their optical sales are lower than what is found in most traditional optometric practices. One might infer that it's normal to find a lower percentage of eyeglass prescriptions in a practice like this and therefore, a lower amount of revenue generated by optical products. When I really dig into the details of these practices, however, I find that some of the ODs have made a mental shift away from refractive care. Many of these medical optometry practices could produce much more revenue and profit in the optical if the doctor approached the patients differently.

Traditional optometric practices typically produce about 50% of gross revenue from eyeglass sales, although there is a wide range for this metric. Some ODs are so happy about their strong performance in medical eye care that they proudly tell me that 80% of their practice revenue comes from medical. I'm never really sure if that stat means that the practice does a lot of medical eye care or if it means the optical is just poorly managed and should be producing more. We really need more information.

Consider the following factors if your practice provides medical eye care to a large degree.

Don't make the refraction optional

This came as a surprise to me the first time I ran across it, but it is actually becoming fairly common for ODs to ask their medical patients if they want a refraction. To me, a refraction is just part of an eye exam and if it has been over a year since the patient had one, they need one. Some ODs are so busy with medical eye care, they have adopted procedures that deemphasize refractive care, such as:

- If entrance acuity with the habitual glasses is near 20/20, they don't perform a refraction.
- Since the refraction test is not covered by Medicare, the doctor or a technician asks the patients if they want the test performed and lets them know what the out of pocket fee will be.
- Clinical technicians do not ask patients if they have complaints related to eyeglasses or if the patient is interested in getting new glasses.

In my opinion, an objective and subjective refraction should be performed at every comprehensive eye exam on an annual basis. It is a requirement for patients who receive care in my practice. Patients can't opt out of it. If insurance does not cover the refraction fee, then the patient will have to pay it. We have operated this way for many years and we have no resistance from patients.

Patients are not in a good position to make a decision if they need a refraction any more than they should decide if they need tonometry or visual fields. Even medically oriented optometrists know that visual acuity alone is not a good indicator of optimum visual performance. We have all seen patients who think they see just fine only to find a large shift in refractive error, sometimes in just one eye.

If your practice is fortunate to be so busy that you tend to drop refractive care to save time, I recommend you look for other ways to gain efficiency, such as hiring more techs or an associate doctor. Regular refractive care greatly benefits the patient and it increases practice profitability at the same time. If you do fewer refractions, you will definitely prescribe fewer glasses.

Recommend an update in the spectacle Rx

Since you are now doing refractions on a large number of patients, the next step is to use your professional judgment and decide if the patient needs a change in his spectacle Rx. This is based on the change in refraction as well as the patient's visual needs and complaints. Just be the doctor in the same way you would if you were to prescribe a medication. You can say "I'm going to prescribe new glasses for you today because…".

Train scribes to begin frame selection

If you have scribes in your clinical setting, consider training them to walk the patient into your optical and begin frame selection. How far they go with this will be based on your practice model. An optician could take over at some point and the scribe will return to the clinic or the scribe could be a super-tech and handle the whole optical process. In any case, starting optical dispensing quickly increases the Rx retention rate.

Have a great optical

A medical optometric practice can mix very nicely with an optical dispensary; they do not have to be mutually exclusive. Invest in the design of your optical, carry great frame lines, offer a wide range of price points, and employee excellent opticians and you'll see your optical revenue climb.

Chapter 16. Contact Lens Practice

16.1 Contact Lens Practice: Your Key to Profitability

Later this month, Vision Service Plan will begin to introduce its new enhanced contact lens benefit. The Contact Lens Care Program is being phased out. This is good news for many optometrists and it is a great time to review all aspects of your contact lens practice.

For many eye care practices, a change in attitude about contact lens wear along with some changes in marketing and clinical operations can provide a nice increase in practice profitability. Many vision plans provide an allowance that is used toward contact lens services or products, and the eye care provider can charge the difference to the patient, less a small discount. This gives contact lens practice excellent potential for higher profitability.

Consider the following factors and make changes in your contact lens fitting process.

- **Recommend contact lenses enthusiastically.** Stop being so neutral! Instead of starting a discussion with your patient about the potential problems of contact lenses, try presenting them in a very positive way. Tell the patient that new contact lens technology is fantastic and the vast majority of patients can wear contacts with ease, even if they have had difficulty in the past. Tell patients that presbyopia and astigmatism are now easily corrected and new lens modalities and materials have helped many people with dry eyes and allergies. Here is a real bold idea: bring up the idea of contact lens wear to patients rather than wait for them to ask about it.
- **Put free trial lenses on more people.** I believe the free trial lens inventory already sitting in your office is a huge underutilized resource. Coupled with the enthusiasm in the previous point, if the OD personally asked most patients to just try on the newest and greatest lens in the office, the vast majority would agree. Make this trial process free of charge and consider it as part of your marketing program. Delegate the insertion of the trial lens to staff members so the doctor is not involved unless the patient decides to proceed with a fitting. At that point, the doctor would evaluate the lenses, consult with the patient and a fitting fee would apply. If the patient does not want to proceed with contact lenses, the technician removes and discards them. The point is that if you put trial contact lenses on many people, a high percentage will decide they want to wear them. Let the free trial take place in your optical while frames are tried on

and many patients will purchase contact lenses, eyeglasses and sunglasses!

- **Set your fees appropriately.** Many eye care professionals (ECPs) charge too little for their services. It is not necessary to try to match fees or product prices with optical chains, discount stores or Internet providers. Your patients are generally quite loyal to your practice and they want to buy from you. They value your expertise and it is convenient to get everything in one place. Test higher fee levels and judge the response, including monitoring your contact lens Rx retention rate (see more below). Generally, most patients won't go anywhere if you raise your fees to an appropriate profit margin.
- **Use advanced instrumentation and build the fee into the evaluation or fitting.** Position your practice as the best, not the cheapest. People will seek you out for your service and reputation rather than low prices. Establish this position by providing a higher level of service with technology such as corneal topography or specular microscopy performed on an annual basis.
- **Don't make contact lens fitting more complex.** Some ECPs have developed their contact lens procedures to appear more complex as a strategy to impress patients. I disagree with that approach. I think patients are more impressed when contact lenses are easy and convenient. If you delegate more of the fitting process and reduce the chair time and number of office visits, your profit margin improves. Don't reappoint for a fitting, just dispense the lenses today!
- **Train your staff to sell full year supplies.** Most patients will buy a full year's supply if given an incentive to do so. Here are the main points: 1) Train staff to not ask "how many boxes do you want?" Just assume the patient wants a full year. 2) Have staff members discuss the manufacturer rebate amount and assist with the process. 3) Give an additional 5% or 10% discount off your usual lens prices when patients purchase a full year's supply.
- **Track your CL Rx walk-out ratio.** This is very important data and it is worth the trouble to track. One way to measure it is to count the number of patients each month who receive a contact lens exam but do not buy any new lenses. Divide this number by the total number of contact lens exams performed that month. The walk-out ratio should be less than 10%. If greater than that, find out why by asking patients.

16.2 Contact Lens Fees Are Not Always Simple

Eye care practitioners frequently ask how to handle the sticky situations that can arise with contact lens fees. Is it always smart to charge a refitting fee if you want patients to try new lenses? When should a refitting fee apply and how do you explain it to the patient? Should follow-up visits be included in a refitting or itemized separately? If you didn't charge a fitting fee, how do you handle patient complaints and ensuing office visits that arise right after prescribing a new lens? What should you charge if you evaluate diagnostic lenses in the office on a new fitting, but you or the patient decides to not go through with the order? Is it a good practice to charge a fee only to adjust it out if anyone complains? How do we respond to patients who don't understand the need for contact lens professional fees?

Clearly, there are many scenarios that can occur and the fee issues can be challenging. I think the best way to analyze this topic is by presenting individual case reports and I'll do that over the next few weeks. It behooves us to have a clear understanding of contact lens services and fees so we can train staff members and communicate well with our patients.

Definitions

Before we jump into managing some of the real world situations stated above, we should review some of the terms that are often used in contact lens services. If I've learned anything about eye care practice it's that there are many, many different office policies and procedures in use for contact lenses. Accordingly, communication can be confusing and it's easy to misunderstand another practitioner's fees.

For example, a contact lens exam may include a general eye exam plus any additional testing needed to fit contact lenses, all for one fee. It may include patient education and training and follow-up visits or those could be an additional cost. Or, it may include all office visits for a year. On the other hand, a contact lens exam may be structured as an additional service from a comprehensive eye exam with a separate fee charged and itemized on the bill.

There are many definitions for the terms contact lens fitting and refitting, although some doctors don't like the term "fitting" and may call it contact lens prescription and management or various other descriptions. And what is a contact lens evaluation? Are exams, fittings and evaluations all the same thing? Should there be different levels of complexity in CL fittings with different fees? How do contact lens service agreements fit into this?

A system to consider

There is no right or wrong to how contact lens services are packaged or organized and the terms really don't matter as long as people understand what we are talking about, but I'll share with you my preferred system for contact lenses. Here are some definitions that I use for CL services.

- Contact Lens Evaluation. The evaluation of the fit and Rx of an existing pair of contact lenses on an established wearer, usually performed at the time of an annual eye exam. This evaluation includes additional tests that are not always done in a routine eye exam, such as slit lamp evaluation of the lens on the eye, over-refraction, keratometry and corneal topography. This service carries a separate fee from the eye exam fee and it's itemized on the patient's statement. I do not have different levels of complexity for a CL evaluation because by definition it is only performed on successful cases that do not need a fitting change. If a fitting change is needed, then the CL evaluation is replaced by a different service: a contact lens fitting. CL fittings have various levels of complexity and fees that increase accordingly. A CL evaluation leads to the renewal of the contact lens prescription and I include power changes as part of that process, not as a refitting. It's important for practitioners who accept vision plans to charge a separate CL evaluation fee because vision plans generally consider this a non- covered service and will allow the practitioner to charge the patient privately for it. It has become a widely accepted standard procedure in eye care in the United States.
- Contact Lens Fitting. I have four levels of contact lens fittings based on the complexity of lens design and each level has a different fee. I don't differentiate among patients new to contact lens wear and those who have worn them in the past but discontinued. A CL fitting includes dispensing, training and follow-up visits for two months.
    - Basic fit - Spherical soft or gas permeable lenses on a daily wear basis. While the fitting period is defined as two months, I usually will only need one follow-up visit. The two month period just gives us some reference for the follow-up care, but if we are actively pursuing a successful fit, we will continue to work beyond that period.
    - Advanced fit - Includes extended wear, toric and presbyopic lenses, including monovision.
    - Keratoconus or post-surgical fit - This service includes six months of follow-up care.
    - Orthokeratology or Corneal Refractive Therapy

- Refitting. I use the term refitting whenever I make significant changes in lens design or lens brand for a current contact lens wearer. I will typically reduce the usual fitting fee because the patient does not need training and I can use the past and current experience to help me with the fit. These cases are handled on a case by case basis but the refitting fee will often be 50% to 75% of the full fitting fee for that type of lens, but if the case is very challenging there may be no reduction in the fitting fee. Follow-up visits are included.

A comprehensive eye exam by a doctor in my practice is always required before a contact lens fitting (within six months). The eye exam has a separate fee. Contact lens materials are always charged separately.

16.3 Contact Lens Services, Part 2

We covered the common terminology used in contact lens services last week, along with some basic definitions, but since definitions and office policies vary widely, we must try to compare apples to apples when we discuss services or quote fees. It's the little details and special situations that make contact lens fees challenging for doctors and staff members, so let's look at some hypothetical case examples in the coming weeks. How would you handle the following case?

Case example

An established, successful, daily wear contact lens patient is in for her annual exam. You routinely charge a comprehensive eye exam fee plus an additional contact lens evaluation fee. The patient presents no eye or vision complaints. No change in the Rx is found and the eyes are healthy. You discuss the benefits of silicone hydrogel lenses with the patient and offer to let her try the lenses at no extra charge. You put on a pair of diagnostic lenses; the fit looks fine and visual acuity is 20/20; the patient is intrigued; you dispense the lenses and tell her to call and let you know whether she wants her next supply of lenses to be the new ones or stay with the lenses she was previously using. You can order a new supply without seeing the patient back again. She calls back in a week, likes the lenses very much, but thinks the prescription may need to be adjusted a bit. She wants to come in for a recheck before ordering the full year supply. Do you charge her a progress exam fee for this next visit?

Points to consider

- Should you have allowed a change in lens brand or material without a fitting fee? Many eye care professionals (ECP) would say that charging a higher refitting fee at the time of the exam would have prevented the problem in the case above because follow-up visits could be incorporated into the fee, and I agree. On the other hand, charging a higher fee when you encourage a perfectly happy patient to try a new type of lens can place your motives into question.
- It's certainly a refreshing and easy approach to tell a contact lens patient who is in your chair that even though he's doing fine with his current lenses, you always want to let him know about the latest and best technology in contact lenses. Offering a free sample pair of trial lenses, with no hidden agenda for an increased fee, is a great way to show patients that you care about their best interest and that your practice is on the cutting edge of technology.
- It's easy to say that we should charge a higher fitting fee when a new lens is tried on or dispensed, but what often happens with such a policy is that doctors often avoid trying new lens designs with perfectly happy patients because of the very real possibility that the lens won't be received as well as the old brand. That would put the ECP in an awkward position.
- If you charge high enough fees for the comprehensive exam and for the CL evaluation, you can afford to be magnanimous with patients. You can give away a few things and not worry about it. You can be very generous with your services. If you cut the profit to the bone, as do many ECPs, you have to nickel and dime the patient at every turn. The high fee practice has a competitive advantage because it can offer nice perks to patients, which results in higher loyalty and referrals than that seen in average practices.
- When deciding if a higher refitting fee should be charged, it's smart to consider how often a follow-up visit or a complaint will occur and that may vary by the type of case. If that only happens rarely, a higher fee and required follow-ups may not be necessary. You might consider any additional time spent as a form of practice marketing.
- Some ECPs would disagree clinically with the approach that no follow up visits are needed in the case above. I consider that professional judgment and I would not make a sweeping conclusion either way. It could even be handled on a case by case basis, but I would not say that a follow-up visit is always needed just because we change the brand of lens, especially if we are assuming daily wear lenses.

Back to the original case

I would not charge a fee for a follow-up exam to recheck the contact lens power, based on the way this case was presented in the first place. I would handle this visit the same way I handle any patient complaint about a new prescription, whether it be for eyeglasses or contact lenses. We call these visits "Rx Trouble" or "CL Trouble" visits and there is no charge. If I elected to proceed without a fitting fee and without requiring follow-up visits at the initial exam, then the risk is on me if a problem arises. I would do well to monitor the frequency of such complaint events and if they seldom occur, there is no need to change my practice.

I've heard all the complaints that eye care seems to be the only health care field that's burdened with not always being paid for our time and the analogies with primary care physicians, who would still charge for a second visit even if the first antibiotic didn't work. But the reality is that the two professions are different and the public's perception and expectation is different. It's in our best interest to see complaint cases at no charge (within a reasonable time after a new Rx); I just roll that cost of doing business into my exam fees. Every eye care practice has patient complaints that warrant a recheck and I let my staff know that I want to see those patients. It's far more costly (to your reputation) to not see them!

16.4 Contact Lens Services, Part 3

This series on contact lens services and fees seems to have struck a chord with our readers, judging from the number of emails I've received in the past two weeks. I appreciate that interaction very much because it often makes me look at things in a new way. I generally believe that if one person takes the time to write in a question, there are probably many more people who wonder the same thing, so I will reprint some of the questions here in a Q and A format. All of the following are actual questions from readers.

Q. An established CL patient is in for his annual exam and I need to make a change in the lens type... this might be a spherical case which now needs a toric or a daily wear patient who wants to switch to extended wear. I typically charge an exam fee and a contact lens evaluation fee, but in these cases I would like a follow-up visit. Should I charge an additional fee for the contact lens progress exam (CLPE)?

A. Yes, but I would charge the fee in advance and call it a refitting fee rather than charge for the progress exam when it occurs. I agree that you need a follow-up visit in these cases and it could turn out to be more than one visit.

In my practice, the evaluation fee is simply replaced by a higher refitting fee. Follow-up visits would be included in this fee. I would tell the patient that I need to see him back in one week (or possibly even sooner than one week for the new EW case) and the appointment would be scheduled before he left the office.

Q. Do you specify the number of follow-up visits that are included in a CL fitting or refitting?

A. I prefer that contact lens fitting and refitting fees include a period of time for follow-ups rather than a specific number of visits. I like that because it may be hard to predict exactly how many follow-up visits are needed. A toric fit may look easy enough at the outset, but it may not remain that way! Furthermore, I like to avoid the situation where a patient does not return for the second progress visit, but a year later starts having a problem and declares that he is now ready for that second visit he was supposed to receive. I typically set the time period for covered follow-up visits at 60 days. In many cases, that will only be one visit if all goes well, the patient is seeing great and corneal health looks great. My protocol for required visits has decreased over the years as lens technology has improved.

I prefer to include follow-up visits as part of a global fitting fee rather than charge them on a per visit basis because the patient may not return for a visit if an additional fee will be incurred. I view the follow-up care as a necessary part of a fitting, so charging a global fee encourages good follow-up care and eliminates the cost factor in the patient's mind.

Q. How does one determine an appropriate contact lens fitting fee?

A. I have four levels of contact lens fitting fees, based on the complexity of the case, the evaluation of diagnostic lenses, additional tests like corneal topography, time for patient training and the typical number of follow-up visits anticipated. I believe we should set fitting fees fairly high. Contact lens practice must be profitable and I believe we should be well compensated for our skill and expertise. Since lens materials prices are somewhat market sensitive (although not as sensitive as many ODs think), I prefer to see most of the profit in the services.

As you determine your fitting fees, consider your usual fee for an intermediate office visit as the appropriate charge for a contact lens progress exam. I see many doctors with global fitting fees that would barely cover one office visit, but that's much too low when you consider that the progress exam is only one small part of the total fitting service. If the usual fee for an office visit is $80, the entire fitting fee can't be only $90.

Q. One aspect of CL fees that I would appreciate your opinion about concerns patients who are new to your practice, but are successful contact lens wearers. Do you charge these patients for a fitting on their first visit to you? Would it matter if they came in for their exam with their old CL Rx, and/or if they were wearing their contact lenses?

A. If a patient is new to us but is a successful wearer and knows their CL Rx (has the boxes or the written Rx) then we just charge a CL evaluation fee (in addition to the exam fee of course), assuming we do not need to change the fit for some reason. If I have to put on trial lenses because I don't know what the CLs are, then it would be considered a fitting and a higher fee would apply. We tell the patient this in advance and we'll help the patient obtain the old CL Rx if necessary to avoid the extra work and fee. It's helpful if they just bring in their boxes or foil wrappers.

16.5 Contact Lens Services: Expired Rx Issues

Our series on contact lens fees continues to generate a lot of reader interest, so I'll continue to publish some interesting questions.

Q. Part A. What do you do when a patient comes in for his yearly exam and states "I do not want to be fit for contact lenses today because I'm using my insurance benefits for new glasses only"? (As is often the case, the plan covers glasses or CLs BUT NOT BOTH!!!). Then the patient usually comments..."besides I still have two more boxes of contacts at home and I feel like I'm seeing fine with them".

Part B. Then the patient calls two months later and either wants to order more contact lenses from my office or worse, wants me to give him a prescription he can fill at a mail order company. How do I handle this without angering the patient??? Remember I did not do a contact lens evaluation or fitting and did not charge for that because he specifically requested me not to do so at the annual exam. These are always sticky situations that I am sure docs everywhere run into.

A. My answer to part A is to only provide the services the patient wants, but educate him about the consequences of his choice. It appears we are talking about an established patient, so during the pretest work-up my technician would inquire about the contact lenses. If the patient said he did not want to have the contact lens evaluation, the tech would comply with that request, but would also say that the contact lens Rx is expired (or will expire on...), and that we can't renew the prescription without doing additional tests. If the patient wants to come in on another day for the CL evaluation that would be fine (cost could be an issue right now for the patient), or perhaps he is considering not wearing contacts any more. At that point in the discussion with the technician, some patients will elect to have the CL evaluation performed now after all, and some may still want the exam only. It's the patient's choice, but at least he's informed. The record should be documented.

The issue created in part B of your question should have been prevented by handling part A as indicated. The patient might act like he did not know a CL evaluation was required, but of course, we would know better. And if he did act like he didn't know, my office would not make an issue of that, but would simply inform the patient that his contact Rx is expired and that the doctor needs to do a few tests before it can be renewed. We will stand firm on needing the CL evaluation to renew an Rx, but we'll assist the situation by helping the patient obtain an appointment quickly and in other ways. See the question below for more on how to handle a request for more contacts after the Rx has expired.

Q. My dilemma with contact lens fits involves two areas - patients showing up after running out of contacts and expecting their prescription and expecting not to be charged for their trials and how to handle a red eye during the fitting process. I have had two red eye cases and both patients expected the fitting fee to cover it and threatened to leave the practice if it didn't.

A. Responding to patients who need more contact lenses after the Rx is expired is a frequently encountered issue in most practices. We've all learned from experience that patients feel passionately about this issue, and my business sense tells me to listen carefully when patients display passion. My professional fees and lens prices are far from the lowest, so I really want to go above and beyond in other areas of service because that's how I intend to attract patients and build loyalty.

I have a practice philosophy that is based on an obsession for excellent customer service (I use customer here rather than patient to emphasize the non-clinical aspect of service). Most eye care professionals think they are good in the area of customer service, but it can quickly break down if there is a cost involved or if staff members play a large role. In my view, ECPs tend to focus too much on small costs often creating a much larger loss. Staff members don't have the judgment and authority of the doctor, so they stand firmly on the rules they were taught; sometimes too firmly.

The last thing I want is an angry patient because he ran out of lenses and my staff wouldn't let him have any more. Of course, that would be the patient's perception and patients often don't understand the eye health aspects of contact lens wear, but it's important to realize that the patient's perception is all that really matters when it comes to success in practice.

That was a long warm up to my answer to the question, but here it is. My receptionist would tell the patient that the CL Rx has expired and that a new exam is needed for the doctor to renew it. Patients may not like hearing this answer, but I know they understand the concept because it is analogous to any other medical prescription. Once we've shared that news, my staff's job is to help the patient in any way possible to get them more contacts with maximum convenience. We should find out how many more lenses the patient has, or how much more wearing time we have to work with. We should offer an appointment within the next day or two so he can get the needed exam. Once the patient agrees to schedule the exam, we should offer to provide replacement lenses in some convenient manner if needed to get the patient to the exam time. This could be in the form of a free trial lens or perhaps selling him a box of lenses with an open box exchange offer if the CL Rx is found to have changed at the exam.

Are you shocked at the idea of offering to exchange an open box of lenses that might only have five lenses inside? Don't be. Think bigger. That is the kind of gesture that wins great patient loyalty! What a fantastic practice to do business with! The patient would feel like his needs were all you cared about, and that's a great feeling. OK, let's think about the cost... first, how many patients would you really have to make such an offer for... second, what percentage would not need an Rx change anyway? Of the remaining group, how much is your cost on a box of lenses? If that amount is a big concern it tells me that your professional fee basis is set too low. You could raise your CL evaluation fee for everyone by the average cost of two boxes of lenses and no one would likely notice at all.

Let's go further - what could you do for the toric or bifocal patient? That cost may be too much to absorb, but most of us have trial lenses that would be close to the needed Rx. But what if you did not have the exact Rx? Your staff could probably not do much in that situation alone, but the doctor could. A close Rx is better than no Rx in many cases. A -7.00 sphere in one eye could help a patient who needs -6.00 -2.00 X 180 get by for a few days. Be creative. How could you help if you really wanted to? What would you do if the patient was your spouse or sibling?

Some ECPs might wonder why they should jump through hoops when the patient should have noticed he was getting low on his supply of lenses or should have responded when he received a recall notice from the office. I think that's an example of a doctor not thinking like a business person. We need to be business-savvy if we want to build successful practices, and business-savvy CEOs understand human nature and don't try to teach lessons. They find a need and fill it.

Let's also get a grip on the reality of eye health risks in contact lens wear. Most of the cases which we stand firm against releasing more contact lenses are patients we examined and prescribed for less than two years ago. Because these patients want more lenses, chances are quite good they are seeing pretty well and have eyes that are healthy. Granted, I don't know that for sure on any given case, but helping patients for a short period of time until I can perform the needed exam does not carry much risk. Let's compare it to a patient you are treating for glaucoma who does not show for a scheduled exam and calls up needing a refill on his medication. He tells your staff that he is all out of drops, and can't get in to see you for at least a week. I'm likely to stress the importance of the exam, but I'll call the pharmacy with one more refill to give this patient the care he needs until he can get in to see me. I wouldn't keep prescribing the drug forever without an exam, but one grace period is better than no treatment. And that's how I handle a drug Rx for a pair of eyes that I know is sick! I can't see a tougher policy on CL Rxs than glaucoma.

As for the red eye cases, I would design my fitting service to cover a set period of time, like two months from the lens dispensing, and I'd take care of anything that occurred during that period. Why not consider red eyes a part of that global care? I think you'd be hard pressed to assume that the contact lenses did not play some role in the etiology and it would be even harder to convince the patient. Of course, if you were concurrently treating other conditions while fitting contact lenses, additional tests would not be included in the fitting fee (like visual fields or nerve fiber analysis for example), but that would be explained at the time of the eye exam and it would be pretty rare. I would just take care of anything else. If you don't feel you would be compensated enough to care for red eyes during the fitting period, raise your fitting fee.

16.6 The Contact Lens Evaluation Fee

Show me ten eye care practitioners (ECPs) and I'll show you ten different ways to structure contact lens fees. The names and definitions of services along with the prices can vary greatly. Some ECPs charge separately for every service while others prefer to bundle services and products into a package. Those differences are fine; we certainly don't have to all follow the same fee system and many different approaches can be successful. But many fee systems that I see are priced too low and the practice is missing out on much needed profitability.

The actual fees and prices that are selected will depend on the mode of practice and the price sensitivity of the patient base. If your practice marketing strategy is based on low price, you may have to keep fitting fees and product pricing very low and in line with large corporate retailers. ECPs in private practice have much more flexibility in pricing if they build a reputation for great customer service, advanced technology and a high level of clinical expertise. In that situation, I think ECPs can take control of fees and contact lens practice can return to one of the most lucrative specialties we can offer.

Contact Lens Evaluation Fee
Charging a professional fee, in addition to a basic eye exam fee to cover the additional procedures needed to evaluate an existing contact lens fit, has become extremely common. This fee applies when no change is needed to the contact lens prescription, but the prescription is renewed for one year (typically). Here are a few considerations:

- The CL evaluation fee is sometimes replaced by what some ECPs call a contact lens exam, which is an annual eye exam for a contact lens wearer that includes a CL evaluation. It's really just a matter of either charging one higher exam fee or charging the usual exam fee plus a CL evaluation fee. I don't really like the term eyeglass exam, which often becomes the lower priced alternative to a contact lens exam. It feels like we are measuring someone for a pair of shoes. I prefer to itemize the exam fee and the CL evaluation as two separate services.
- The CL evaluation service typically covers the slit lamp evaluation of the lens fit on the cornea, corneal health assessment, some measurement of corneal curvature, an over-refraction with the lens in place and any other tests deemed necessary. Many ECPs include corneal topography in the CL evaluation fee and the procedure is performed as a pretest on all contact lens patients by a technician. I use this approach and the corneal images are displayed on the

computer monitor in the exam room. Including corneal topography in the CL evaluation justifies a higher fee for the service.

- Some ECPs have a few different fee levels for the CL evaluation, depending on the complexity of the case. I prefer to have just one CL evaluation fee since it's only used when all is well with the patient and with the existing fit. One fee is simpler for staff to quote in advance and to explain. If there is a problem with the CL evaluation and a change in lens fit is required, then we no longer have an evaluation but the case changes to a refitting and there are now different fee levels based on complexity. Evaluating a perfectly fitting toric lens is no more difficult than evaluating a perfectly fitting spherical lens.
- I do not consider minor adjustments in contact lens prescriptions as a refit. A power change, for example, would still be charged as a simple evaluation. No follow-up is needed. One of the best things about charging high professional fees to begin with is that you can be generous with your policies and build patient good will. ECPs who operate with low profit margins may feel they are forced to nickel and dime their patients.
- The CL evaluation fee should be incorporated into the fee system for most ECPs because it's allowed by vision plans and it's a non-covered service. Since most vision plans require significant discounts of the usual fees, ECPs need to take full advantage of legitimate ways to charge the patient for some services.

Contact lens evaluation fees can be a source of patient misunderstanding and dissatisfaction if not handled well. I strongly recommend that the fee be quoted in advance over the phone. My staff quickly brings up the patient's file on the office computer system while speaking to the patient by phone. If the caller is a new patient, the receptionist asks if he currently wears contacts. Once it's known that the patient wears contacts, the fee for the CL evaluation is quoted in addition to the exam fee. If there are any questions about what is included in a CL evaluation or why it's needed, the staff handles it then. The fee is hardly ever questioned in my practice when presented in advance. This is strongly preferred to a confrontation at the front desk after the exam.

16.7 More on Contact Lens Fees

Last week's column was devoted to the contact lens evaluation, which I define as the additional services provided for contact lens wearers at annual eye exam visits. This week we will focus on contact lens fitting fees and pricing for contact lens products.

Fitting and refitting

It's pretty common in most practices to have a few different contact lens fitting fees based on the complexity of the case. I agree with this approach and the fees in my practice are described as a standard fitting (basic spherical daily wear), advanced fitting (toric, multifocal, extended wear) or medical fitting (keratoconus and post-surgical cases). Each of these levels has a higher fee. Corneal refractive therapy (orthokeratology) represents a fourth category with a higher fee.

In developing a fitting fee, one should consider the number of follow-up visits that are typically included in a case and the likelihood for lens fit changes and other complications that require more chair time. Patient training on lens care and handling must also be considered. While follow-up visits could be itemized separately, I prefer to charge more and include them in the global care of the patient. Including follow-up visits in the fitting fee avoids the problem of a patient not showing up for progress visits because they are not having any problems and wish to avoid an additional fee.

I think it's better to specify a time period in which all follow-up care is covered, rather than a specific number of visits. If you include a certain number of visits and if the patient doesn't utilize them all, there is the possibility of the patient returning a year or more later, with the idea that the visit should be at no charge. I include two months of follow-up care in my fitting period, but that is usually only one visit if all goes well with the fit. More visits are scheduled only if problems occur. The patient is then recalled for annual examinations from that point forward.

The contact lens fitting fee is charged in addition to a comprehensive eye exam fee. A comprehensive exam is required before beginning a CL fitting. Be sure your contact lens fitting fee is high enough to cover all the components of care that are provided. One follow-up visit alone is worth the fee usually charged for an intermediate exam.

I would never include additional follow-up visits that aren't really needed in order to justify a higher fee. Just charge the higher fee anyway and don't waste doctor time or inconvenience the patient.

Refitting an existing wearer was discussed last week to some extent. Eye care practitioners generally agree that some of these cases are simpler than a new fitting. But some aren't. Refittings may be based on professional judgment on a case by case basis. Quite often, a 20% discount off the usual fitting fee for that type of case (basic, advanced or medical) is appropriate.

What kind of follow-up visits are covered?

This issue is more controversial than I expected, but there are a large number of ECPs who differentiate between follow-up visits that are contact lens related and those that are not. The contact lens fitting fee is only meant to cover contact lens related follow-up. If a medical eye problem occurs during the contact lens fitting period, the fees for that care would be billed to the patient's medical insurance or to the patient directly. I understand the theory, but I don't like it because the situation often leads to patient misunderstanding and dissatisfaction.

I can easily see the patient's point of view if he gets a red eye within the first few weeks of being fitted with new contact lenses that he would likely conclude that the red eye was caused by the contacts. Granted, it may not technically be true, and it could be just a coincidence that an infection occurred at this time, but I don't think the average patient is going to buy that. The last thing I want at a time when a new contact lens patient is experiencing difficulty is to create a confrontation and distrust. I would be hard pressed myself to honestly be certain that the contact lenses did not play some role in most external inflammations of the eye. I prefer to set my fitting fee at a high enough level where I can handle most any kind of problem during the global contact lens fitting period (two months).

When should fees be charged?

It has come to my attention that many ECPs write up and enter contact lens fees over time as each case progresses. The advent of free diagnostic lenses played a role in this gradual evolution, because the practitioner can now wait until success is proven before charging for any materials. This approach works, but I prefer to charge all fees up front, all at once for the following reasons:

- I want the patient to know the total charges for all exam and fitting services and contact lens materials at the beginning of care. I don't want to surprise them with a second billing for lens products later. Even if explained, patients don't always hear us and they can easily misunderstand.
- I don't want to forget to enter some of the charges. By always entering all fees up front, we avoid patients having lenses dispensed that were never charged. Sometimes it appears there is no balance

on an account, not because the fees were paid, but because none were entered!

- I prefer to show the sale as soon as possible in order to speed up payment and cash flow.

I generally know what type of lens I want to prescribe at the fitting visit. My technician reviews exam, fitting and lens fees at that initial fitting and asks if the patient wishes to order contact lenses from our office and if so, how many boxes are desired. All fees are written up at that time and entered into the patient's account, even if the patient is leaving the office with only a trial pair of lenses. The boxes of lenses are ordered if we don't have them in stock. We do not require payment in full until the supply of lenses is actually delivered, but I prefer to have the total of all fees entered and acknowledged. Most patients just pay the balance in advance. Of course, in the rare event that the first lens design is changed to another type or brand at the follow-up visit, we simply exchange any lens boxes as needed. Generally, the revenue boxes have not been dispensed yet and the new lens supply is ordered. If the lens price category changes with the lens fit change, a credit or debit adjustment is made to the patient's account.

We always release a written copy of the contact lens Rx when the fitting is complete.

16.8 Need more patients? Host a multifocal contact lens event.

I really like to see practice owners take control of their destiny. Most optometric practices need more patient demand, so if you're in that category, consider this idea: host a bifocal contact lens seminar and screening event. I like this marketing strategy because it works with contact lenses and presbyopia. Contact lens business is highly desirable because you can set your fitting fees wherever you like and collect at least 85% of that even with vision plans, plus a good profit on the lens product side. Presbyopia is a great vision problem to specialize in because it affects such a large segment of the population and it is a demographic with high income levels.

Do something

The whole point of hosting an event like a contact lens open house is that you are doing something! Don't just sit back and hope more patients start calling. What have you done lately to market your practice in a big way? When you decide to host an event, a whole world of promotional opportunities opens up; you have something to talk about. You create a buzz among patients, staff and your community at large.

The basic concept I have in mind is for the doctor to present an in-office seminar on contact lenses and presbyopia and follow that with a screening to allow interested people to try on multifocal contacts in their prescription. Refreshments will be served and the doctor and staff can answer questions about contact lenses and presbyopia. The goal is to schedule appointments at the open house for a complete contact lens fitting for as many people as possible.

Plan it

I suggest you work with one of your contact lens reps and a staff member to plan the contact lens event. Here is a good list to start with:

- Choose a date and time. Set it for a couple of months out to allow time for promotion. I would choose a time like 4pm to 6pm to catch people coming home from work.
- Do a target search in your computer system for people over 40 years old who have an Rx in the range you wish to fit. You may wish to limit astigmatism and remove emmetropes.
- Invite the general public as well.
- Design a nice invitation that can be sent by email or postal mail. This should have your practice logo and describe the nature of the event.
- Always state that space is limited and must be reserved in advance. Call all people to confirm and plan to get 20% no shows. Accept enough to make it a full house.
- Decide on refreshments: Starbucks coffee and cookies from Panera Bread? Wine and cheese?
- Design your seminar. This is important: do not make it complicated! You are not teaching how to prescribe and fit contacts! Patients can be easily bored. I would limit the presentation to 15 minutes then take questions.
- Don't worry about public speaking – you can do it just fine. I would use PowerPoint slides which makes it easy to remember all the points you want to cover – but limit the number of slides to less than ten. Consider buying a small LCD projector and a screen for this and many future seminars and staff meetings. Just plug in your laptop. The projector is tax deductible and makes your events very professional.

- You might (but you don't have to) offer a discount on the contact lens fitting and full year supply package if the appointment is booked at the open house event.
- Be sure your multifocal fitting set is fully stocked in all powers.
- Have all your staff present for the open house and place each one at a work station. Call patients in who want to try on multifocal contacts and use their previous record if they are established with you, or do an autorefraction if they are new to your office. Place the trial lenses on and have the doctor meet with each person for a few minutes. The doctor and techs can take near and far acuities, and look at the lenses with the slit lamp. Questions are answered, but any further work will require an appointment for a fitting. Lenses are removed and discarded before the patient leaves the office.

Promote it

The great thing about planning a contact lens open house is that you now have something to promote! Even if people don't attend, you and your practice are now considered as experts in this field in your community! People will seek you out months later for bifocal contacts because they saw you held this event. Your patients who are not even interested in bifocal contacts will see that you are doing something big and they will call for that routine exam they are overdue for. The major benefit to your practice is in the promotion of the event.

- Put the invitation on your practice Facebook page.
- Use other social media to promote the event.
- Have regular updates and more information on Facebook.
- Post about the event afterward on Facebook.
- Add a blurb about the open house on your practice website. (If you can't make easy updates yourself on your website, you need a new website).
- Put up posters around your office about the event.
- Place an ad in the local paper, inviting the public.
- Send invitations to your patient base by mail and email.
- Print flyers and ask other businesses to cross-promote it for you.
- Mention the open house to patients in your practice who are good candidates.

I am quite confident that this process will result in several new contact lens fittings for you, but the publicity and promotional value is worth even more.

16.9 Host a Cosmetic Contact Lens Open House

We are seeing some exciting new developments in a category of contact lenses that has been rather dormant for many years: cosmetic enhancing lenses. Contact lens manufacturers are taking different approaches to this category and you'll see various terms being used, such as color, beauty, cosmetic, enhancement, tint, and more. Regardless of the terms or product differences, it is great news to see new products and new life in this category. I think it has the potential to create a lot of consumer interest in contact lenses.

We are seeing some exciting new developments in a category of contact lenses that has been rather dormant for many years: cosmetic enhancing lenses. Contact lens manufacturers are taking different approaches to this category and you'll see various terms being used, such as color, beauty, cosmetic, enhancement, tint, and more. Regardless of the terms or product differences, it is great news to see new products and new life in this category. I think it has the potential to create a lot of consumer interest in contact lenses.

The new cosmetic lenses bring a huge improvement in lens comfort and the technologies used to make the color more natural are amazing. These lenses are not like the color lenses we had years ago. Be sure to let patients know that the new lens designs are much different and be enthusiastic about it. Enthusiasm sells. Read up on these products and meet with your sales reps. Have your staff wear the lenses and talk about them.

We are already seeing some national consumer advertising campaigns on these new cosmetic lenses, which will drive patient interest and create an excellent opportunity for your practice. In this article, I'll present an idea on how to capitalize on the growing excitement and make cosmetic contact lenses a huge hit in your practice.

Host an event

Nothing creates excitement and buzz quite like an event, but coming up with an idea or theme that is new can be challenging. Cosmetic contacts are new again and it is the perfect product for an open house. Here are the broad strokes on how to plan and promote this event:

- Choose a date and invite patients and the public to your Cosmetic Contact Lens Open House.

- I would choose a weekday from 4pm to 7pm. Block your appointment schedule so you won't see any patients for exams during that time period. Your entire staff should work the event.
- Serve beverages and snacks.
- Consider offering a discount of some kind for people who attend your event and proceed with a complete fitting and a full year supply of lenses. The goal at the open house is to get attendees to schedule an appointment for an exam and fitting before they leave the event.
- Use multiple media channels to promote the event in a big way. The event is fun and educational, but the real value to your practice is that it gives you something to promote. It positions your practice as different and better than your competition. Get the word out with email blasts, a banner on your website, multiple posts on your practice Facebook page, signs throughout your office, consider local radio (and see if they can do a live broadcast from your office at the event), consider newspaper and use direct mail in the form of invitations.
- Ask people to RSVP to reserve a spot at the open house. Space is limited. Determine how many people you can handle, but make it full and busy and count on 30% no show rate.
- Work with your contact lens rep on the planning of this event and see if he or she can attend and assist.
- The open house can include a brief seminar by the doctor on contact lens care in general and the latest technology of cosmetic lenses. The rep can speak to the group as well and may be able to supply PowerPoint slides.
- Offer some kind of screening to see if patients can wear contact lenses and help them choose the color or enhancement they like best. Decide if your open house will use free trial lenses, try-on technology or both. If you use virtual try-on technology, your staff can use your computer work stations throughout the office to assist patients with the virtual try-on. You can invite them to bring a photo with them on a USB drive to upload or your staff could simply take a photo using the patient's own smartphone or tablet.
- See if you can arrange a cross marketing alliance with a local cosmetic store or salon. They can send some make-up artists to your office and provide free mini eye makeovers at the open house. They can assist as judges if you hold a contest for best eyes (see the next point). The idea is that the cosmetic store will also market the event to their customer base and bring new patients to your practice.
- Have several prizes available for raffles and contests. Raffles add excitement and they bring people out. Raffle off a year's supply of

cosmetic contacts along with a complete fitting service. Have a contest for best eye makeover. A pair of designer sunglasses makes a great prize. Promote the contests in all your marketing.

Social media
Cosmetic contacts offer a clever opportunity to use social media to market your practice. Invite and assist patients to post some pictures of themselves with the new eye appearance to their own account on Facebook, YouTube, Twitter, Instagram etc. They can ask their friends to vote or comment on which ones they like best. Be sure to ask them to mention your practice name. This social media marketing effort has more punch than most because patients would really like to show off their new look and would really like the feedback. The power of each attendee's social circle is a great marketing opportunity for your practice.

Also, ask patients if you can post before and after shots on your practice Facebook page. Document that they gave you permission by having them sign a simple statement and scan it into the record.

Trial lenses
You can decide how liberal to be with attendees trying on free trial lenses at your open house. Speak to your contact lens rep about it. You could hold off and not offer trial lenses until the actual fitting appointment that will follow or try some lenses on during the open house, after the doctor performs a screening with the slit lamp. Since you are not doing complete eye exams on these attendees, it may be best to not allow trial lenses to leave the office.

Cosmetic contact lenses have the potential for great word-of-mouth referrals to your practice and an open house can get you started with a large number of new fittings.

16.10 Quoting Contact Lens Prices

I love a simple idea that makes money and that's what I have for you today. This is under the category of why didn't I think of that sooner, but better late than never. I'm sure some of you are already doing this, but if you aren't, you're going to like it.

My practice recently implemented a small price increase for contact lens products. I monitor our profitability on the product side and we need to pass along wholesale price increases that occur every year or so. As we were printing up new price lists to distribute to staff members and various locations around the office, I realized that patients often ask us the price per box. Some of these patients compare prices with online sources or other places. Many services and products sold in our offices are not very price sensitive, but contact lens products can be.

The price quote

Our practice has a policy of discounting contact lens products by 10% if the patient buys a full year supply. I find this to be quite effective. Most patients want to buy their lenses from our office and they respond well to the discount and opt for the full year most of the time. We also help the patient to obtain the manufacturer's rebate they are entitled to with a full year supply. The light bulb went on for me that we should quote contact lens prices to patients after the full year discount and rebate, expressed as a per box price.

Our office (and I think many others) does not usually quote the price this way because every manufacturer has different rebate amounts and the rebates change from time to time. A pretty weak reason, don't you think?

To be clear, we do not typically quote the price per box unless we are asked. We prefer to not talk about boxes at all but rather a full year supply of lenses. My staff is trained to simply say "your full year supply of contact lenses after your discount and rebate is $XXX." When patents ask what the price is per box, we say "The price is $XX per box after your discount and rebate." We used to quote our price per box and then mention that there is also a full year discount of 10% and also a manufacturer rebate. But the patient only heard the first price and the discount was vague and not calculated as a dollar amount. Our new way is better.

This process of quoting the price after rebate and discount is easy to do if you simply put it on the price list in parentheses.

Price lists

Our contact lens price list is stored on a spreadsheet on all our office PCs, but we also rely on a low tech method for technicians to have prices at their fingertips. We print the price lists of contact lenses, all exam services and all optical products on paper, then we shrink the size on our photocopier, and we laminate the sheets to become pocket cards. These cards are about five by seven inches and we punch a hole in the corner and put them on a ring.

Our contact lens price list provides every factor the technician needs to know. Here are the columns that run left to right on our list:

- Lens brand name.
- Recommended replacement period (daily, two week, monthly, etc.).
- Our price per box.
- How many boxes make up a full year supply.
- The total cost for a year supply before discount (helps us write up the fees).
- The total cost for a year after our 10% annual discount and the manufacturer rebate.
- The price per box after discount and rebate.

With our price per box after discount and rebate, we are quite competitive with online sellers and big box stores. Once you show patient s you are in the product price ball park, most will buy their lenses from your practice.

16.11 Fitting More Daily Disposable Lenses

There is a very simple reason why you should prescribe more single day disposable contact lenses: they are the best. If you asked a large sample of optometrists what type of contact lens they think is best, with cost not a factor, a huge percentage would say daily disposables. That is certainly what I would say. In spite of that very positive point of view, optometrists see thousands of contact lens patients every day who are about to buy more lenses and the vast majority don't bring up daily throw-aways. It makes no sense at all. I guess we're just too timid to say what we believe.

An analogy that hits home

As I step back and look at our typical contact lens prescribing habits, I must conclude that we don't practice what we preach. We try to train our staff members to never prejudge our patients and what they think they can afford. We tell opticians to always present the best products first. Start with the high-end frames. Recommend premium lenses with the best AR, high-index and digital surfacing. If the optician were to say that the patient was doing fine with his old type of lens and there is no need to even discuss the newest lens options, most practice-owning ODs would have a problem with that.

I believe this approach that we urge our staff to follow is well placed. We shouldn't prejudge what we think a person can afford. We should offer the best eye care possible. If the patient has a budget problem, he'll let us know and we can find a more economical option, but we can't hit a home run if we don't even swing the bat.

The doctor's domain

Why should everything change just because the product is now contact lenses instead of glasses? Or just because the doctor is interacting with the patient and not an optician? Does the OD degree confer some ability to know the patient's financial condition? There was a best-selling book a few years ago called "The Millionaire Next Door". The premise was that you really can't tell a person's financial condition by appearance. In fact, the ones who try to look like they're wealthy often are not and the guy wearing the overalls might very well be.

I think many of us ODs have an inferiority complex and we fear rejection! We presume the patient won't want to pay slightly more for contacts, when in reality, many would happily pay more in order to have:

- The convenience of never having to clean lenses or bother with them at the end of the day.
- Much better comfort all day.
- Ability to leave contacts in a few hours longer each day.
- Whiter, healthier looking eyes.
- Less dryness.
- Fewer allergic symptoms.
- Ease of low cost replacement lenses and spares on hand in every situation.
- Not having to purchase lens care products.

Our professionalism hurts us

I think we are often so professional and so afraid of being perceived as selling a product that we become too conservative. We let the patient down by not being forthright with what we think. Daily disposable lenses are actually better than other modalities in many respects, but ODs often don't even touch on the subject.

I think we miss the biggest opportunity when we tend to not change a patient's lens type if they have no complaints. We all see many of these patients every day. Rather than giving the patient something new and better, we tend to leave them in their old brand and design. It is certainly safe and it may help you get finished faster, but is that the goal? If you step up and recommend the best, you will make patients happier, create more reasons for referrals and increase revenue and profitability.

We've all had that case where we tried really hard to give the patient a great improvement in their vision with some change (in prescription, ophthalmic lens type, contact lens material, or whatever) only to have the patient prefer what they had before. Maybe we are so sensitive to that possibility that we shut down and just play it safe. I hope not. I'd like to think we can snap out of it and take a stand.

How to present daily disposables

I love the Mark Twain quote: "If you tell the truth, you don't have to remember anything!" That is exactly the case with daily lenses; just tell the truth with confidence and enthusiasm. Act excited about them; don't act bored and serious.

- Tell the patient that the best contact lens on the market is a daily disposable. Talk about comfort and clear, healthy eyes.
- Have enthusiasm when you say... "Many of my patients tell me they can't even tell they have lenses on!"
- Connect with the patient. What do you know about the person in your chair? Does he play sports? Does she like to swim? Does he have allergies? Does she have dry eyes? Does he travel frequently?
- Make it easy to try them. Offer a free trial without a lot of testing and bother.
- If the patent mentions the cost, just agree with him. But also mention the savings on lens care products, which is more money than one thinks.
- I would not prescribe the lowest priced daily disposable; I'd prescribe the best one. The most comfortable one.

16.12 Dispensing Annual Supplies of Contact Lenses

We all know that selling an annual supply of contact lenses is a good thing when we see patients for their annual exam, but most practices still do a rather poor job of this. I'm trying a new approach that is causing more patients to opt for the full year purchase.

Benefits of annual supplies

Just to review, there are several great reasons why we should make an effort to encourage patients to purchase a full year supply of contacts.

- We take the patient out of the market for a year.
- We get the use of the cash sooner.

- Patients tend to use their vision plan at the time of their eye exam to help them with the cost of their initial lens order, but many go online to buy the second six month supply at a lower price.
- Staff time is greatly reduced by not having to handle the second six-month order.
- Most contact lens companies offer free shipping to the patient's home or office with a yearly supply.
- Most contact lens companies offer larger rebates with an annual supply.

After studying these issues in my practice, I'm convinced that I need to do more to greatly encourage the annual supply purchase at the time of the exam.

A new larger incentive

Doctors have a strong advantage over online vendors and big box stores and when it comes to retaining the contact lens sale because the patient has an abundance of trust for the practice. The patient would actually like to buy his contacts from your office. But price does become a major factor when the decision is ultimately made about how many boxes to buy.

I have always offered a 10% discount off our usual contact lens prices when the patient buys a full annual supply, but I decided I wanted to increase that incentive to convert more patients. To facilitate that without losing profit, I raised my contact lens prices about 15%. I typically kept our prices very close to the major online contact lens vendors. We are still close enough to retain the vast majority of the CL prescriptions, but this price allows us to now offer 20% off on an annual supply.

We also are well equipped to present the manufacturer rebates in addition to our own discount. The dollar amounts of these rebates are quite significant. We total up the dollars saved for the patient if they go with the full year supply and it is too much to resist!

Staff training

It is important to get staff members on board with the importance of selling yearly supplies. Talk about it at staff meetings and have staff members practice how to present the lens order. Here are some ideas we have had success with:

- Don't ask the patient "how many boxes do you want?" Just assume he wants a full year supply.

- The technician can say "The doctor has approved you for a full year supply of lenses."
- "Ordering a full year supply is by far your best buy. You will save $170 off the regular price!"

Consider spiffs

Paying the staff a small monetary bonus for each full year supply really elevates this project and will increase the percentage of annual sales. I like each technician to keep her own scorecard in her pocket and she simply records the date and patient's last name. This self-scoring keeps motivation high as the reward keeps growing. We can spot check a few names to confirm the annual sale, but basically we just count them up and pay the bonus.

16.13 Reinvent Your Contact Lens Practice

Contact lenses have been at the core of advanced optometry since they first became popular in the 1950s and 60s. Optometrists pioneered the development and created the success that is enjoyed by so many people today. In spite of that leadership position, it seems to me that contact lens procedures have not changed much in the past 30 years. Contact lenses offer an excellent opportunity for profitability, but I think many ODs have lost their enthusiasm for this form of vision correction. It is time to rediscover the rewards of prescribing contact lenses. Embrace them and you will grow your practice.

There is a strong resurgence in fitting specialty contact lenses, including scleral lenses, reverse geometry designs and other exotic lenses. These are useful in a variety of hard to fit cases, including keratoconus and also orthokeratology. I think it is smart to embrace this specialized work, but let's also realize that the population that is interested in these specialty lenses is limited. We should also build an excellent system for prescribing disposable soft lenses that appeal to a huge population. Specialty rigid lenses require significant time and expertise, while many soft contact lenses can be prescribed quite easily and quickly.

Here are the key factors I would change to maximize contact lens profitability:

Bring up the idea

This has been a problem for decades: very few optometrists bring up the idea of wearing contact lenses to patients, unless they brought it up first. I don't know if most ODs don't have time during an eye exam or if they would just rather not fit contacts. It is crazy to me. Let's make contact lens fitting so easy and so well delegated that you break this habit. If doctors simply act enthusiastic about contact lenses and ask patients to try on a free trial pair, they could fit twice as many patients as they do now.

Contact lenses can be extremely profitable with vision plan patients because you can still set your fees and collect most of it in many cases.

Understand vision plan benefits

Some vision plans provide an allowance to be used toward the fitting and lens materials and you are allowed to bill the patient for the amount not covered (less a small discount). These plans are excellent and if you see many of these patients, you should proactively recommend contact lenses. Other vision plans place a cap on your fitting fees and allow very little profit on the sale of contact lens products. In these cases, it may not be in your best interest to be so proactive.

Raise fitting fees but keep product prices competitive

We've been hearing this strategy for years, but most ODs I work with still charge too little for fitting or evaluation fees. We must remain fairly competitive on lens products (although we simply can't match the lowest of the discount retailers), but you can and should charge a healthy evaluation or fitting fee. Cover your additional time and expertise and include one or two follow-up visits plus some time for your technician to review lens handling and care. I also require corneal topography on all new fittings and at every annual exam. The professional fee is expensive, but we provide excellent care and people want that level of service. If our fitting fee is too high for some patients, we happily let them go elsewhere. We know contact lenses are available at lower prices and we understand. We manage to stay extremely busy with contact lens patients in spite of low priced alternatives.

Delegate more of the fitting and follow-up

To truly maximize profitability in contact lens practice, we must delegate more of the process and reduce chair time! Technicians can gather most of the data, review the lens types and place an initial trial pair on the eye. The technician, working under the doctor's supervision, can also over-refract and record acuity. The doctor will check the fit with the slit lamp and the fit is done.

Technicians can also perform the entire follow-up visit if the patient has no complaints, good acuity, and a normal slit lamp exam.

Don't make it complicated

Years ago, contact lens fitting was fairly complicated, but most of it really isn't today. Some ODs still favor complex office policies and procedures with the hope of impressing patients with the big ordeal. In my experience, patients are more impressed if the fitting process is fast and easy.

16.14 Take Contact Lens Follow-ups Off Your Schedule

I'm constantly looking for ways to increase clinical efficiency which can save doctor time and allow more revenue-producing exams. In an era where physicians must accept fees that are discounted and capped by insurance plans, efficiency is a key way for us to increase profitability.

One way to save a lot of doctor time is to not see very many contact lens follow-up visits. Let me be quick to add that I'm not advocating that you stop doing contact lens follow-ups, only that you delegate most of them to a qualified optometric technician. To be clear, I'm referring to the short exams following a new fitting or a refitting, not the annual contact lens evaluation which also includes a comprehensive eye health examination.

If you have some advance patient demand, this strategy would effectively replace a non-revenue patient visit with a revenue-producing visit. Many optometrists see two or three contact lens checks per day or more. This technique could conceivably produce a significant increase in practice revenue and profit.

The concept

Begin by creating a separate provider in your appointment scheduler where most contact lens follow-ups will be scheduled. You could use a generic provider name like technician or contact lenses; that way, if you have more than one technician who is trained to do contact lens checks, the patient can be seen by whoever is available. These appointments should be on the same day that the doctor is also seeing patients under his or her own schedule. You should always follow state law and most states allow technicians to work under a doctor's direct supervision.

It works well to set a policy that the technician should consult with the doctor if the patient has any of the following:

- A complaint about the contact lenses.
- Visual acuity that is worse than expected, based on the fitting exam.
- A questionable over-refraction.

- Any sign of redness, edema, corneal distortion, discharge or any insult to normal physiology.
- A lens that does not fit well.

Most contact lens patients are doing quite well at the one week follow-up, so it should not be very often that the tech needs to consult with the doctor or have the doctor examine the patient. It is best if the OD is flexible and fast enough to be able to handle an occasional additional patient without usually running behind schedule. Quite often, the doctor can decide on the treatment plan and the technician can carry out additional diagnostic lens work or patient education.

Of course, there will be some types of cases where the doctor will still want perform to follow-up visits and those will just be appointed as usual.

The exam procedures
Basically, your tech will perform the same tests you would do. You will train your technician on any examination techniques that she is not familiar with, such as possibly the slit lamp exam and over-refraction.
Here are the typical test procedures the tech will conduct:

- Case history
- Visual acuity with contact lenses
- Over-refraction (in most cases, this will be with spheres only so this is an easy test for a technician).
- Slit lamp examination and evaluation of lens fit.
- Corneal topography or keratometry
- Review of lens wear and care

Contact lenses have evolved to a point where most fittings are extremely successful and the follow-ups are routine. Those are ideal for your technician to handle. In my experience, patients are perfectly happy with this arrangement as long as the doctor acts confidently about it.

16.15 Your New Attitude about Contact Lenses

I think many of us take contact lens practice for granted. As optometrists, we prescribe contacts and manage patients who wear them every day, but we do very little to promote the category. That is our loss because contact lens practice can be extremely profitable and it results in very loyal patients who often refer others. Let's take a new look at this specialized service and reinvent how you position it in your practice.

Stop being old school

Have you noticed that everything is changing quickly in the retail world? The younger generations want products faster and simpler. Technology and e-commerce is leading to new expectations even when consumers visit retail stores and offices. I realize that the products we prescribe are health care devices and we have responsibilities and liabilities that the public may not understand, but I also realize that optometrists tend to be very professional and have a hard time with change.

Now is a good time to evaluate your contact lens fitting process. With the improvements we have seen in lens technology, the majority of contact lens patients can be fit easily and successfully. Try to reflect that by making your fitting procedure convenient and simple for the patient.

- Let patients try a pair of contacts on in your office at no charge. Charge a fitting fee if the patient wants to go further than a try-on with your technician.
- Let the free try-on occur at the same appointment as an eye exam – no reappoint necessary.
- Suggest the free try-on to patients who are good candidates – even if they don't ask.
- Broaden your definition of good candidates – let it include presbyopes and astigmats. Even dry eye and allergy patients can often succeed with the right lenses.
- Ask some patients if they would like to enhance their eye color.
- Ask some patients if they would like to wear contacts for special activities only, like sports (including swimming) or social events. Most patients don't know that daily disposables work great for part time use.
- Don't make the fitting process a long process. Make it simple and quick. If you did an eye exam, you have what you need.
- Don't have follow-up visits you don't really need and let your technician perform them if there are no complications.

What would it take to get your interest?

Most ODs only fit contact lenses if the patient asks for them. We generally do not bring the subject up even to excellent candidates. We rarely recommend contacts with statements about how great they are; we are more likely to talk about the problems that could occur. It is almost as if we don't have any time for it and we hardly make any profit. But that should not be the case. Most ODs are not that busy and you can usually control the profit margin by setting the fees where you need them to be.

Begin your new attitude about contact lenses by raising your fitting fees and ongoing evaluation fees. You may get a few patients who don't proceed because of fees, but most will and at least you will feel good about working with them. Let the ones who are looking for the lowest price go elsewhere. Charge higher fees because you are the best and be enthusiastic about the specialty.

Vision plans

When we think of raising fees, we must also consider how any change will be impacted by vision plans. Contact lens fees and profits vary widely depending on the vision plan, but many still operate with a dollar allowance and the OD can collect usual and customary fees, less some discount like 15%. That makes contact lenses one of the most profitable services covered by vision plans.

Host an open house

Talk to your contact lens account rep about helping to host a promotional event in your office.

- Give a brief (15 minutes) PowerPoint presentation to patients in your waiting area or optical. Present a seminar on a topic like multifocal contacts or colored contacts. Your rep may help with slides and content.
- Invite good contact lens candidates to your open hours and seminar from your patient base and also invite the general public. Send email flyers or post cards and promote on social media.
- Serve refreshments: coffee, soft drinks, cookies and snacks.
- Offer free try-ons in your office, have all your staff work the event with you. The contact lens rep can help also.
- Provide a discount off the fitting fee for any attendee who proceeds with a fitting within 30 days. Have your staff ready to schedule appointments at the event.
- Schedule it in the late afternoon on a weekday and run into early evening to get the after-work crowd.
- Take photos at the event and post those on your practice website and Facebook page.
- Take photos of patients with contacts on using their own smartphone so they can post on their own social media sites.

16.16 How to Make Contact Lenses More Profitable

I don't mind admitting that I'm old enough to remember the glory days of contact lenses when professional fees were high and we made a high margin on the materials. A very high margin. I started my professional career in the late seventies when we were still fitting some PMMA lenses and single use soft contact lenses did not mean daily use, it meant a year or two or when they started to turn brown! Contact lens fitting and follow-up care was more complicated back then, so fitting fees were relatively high.

Many changes occurred over the past few decades, such as the proliferation of vision plans, the advent of disposable lenses and the launch of e-commerce. But it's really not my style to reminisce. The advancements in contact lens technology have led to easier fittings and healthier patients and we can still be very profitable in this modality. We just have to change the way we prescribe and manage contact lenses.

Speed it up

Many optometrists still rely on some of the old procedures we were taught in school and some of those might have been outdated then. In addition, many ODs actually try to make the fitting process longer and more complicated because they believe it will impress the patient and might justify higher fees. I think we should reinvent the fitting process. For most types of lenses, we could make the fitting process so fast and easy, the patient is not even aware of it. That would impress patients much more than an old, outdated process. Professional fees for elective contact lenses need not be based on time; they are based on skill and patients will happily pay for speed and convenience.

To start with, we should stop reappointing for a trial lens fitting. Reducing chair time is the same as increasing profitability. You really can do the contact lens fitting at the same visit as the initial exam. If you are using a scribe, simply tell him/her what trial lenses to apply and go see another patient. A huge amount of doctor time is saved by having the chairside assistant find the diagnostic lenses and put them on the patient. After that, the assistant can take visual acuity and do an over-refraction with spheres only in the phoroptor. What's left? The doctor pops back in the exam room and does a slit lamp evaluation. Many scribes could do that too, but I'm assuming the OD still wants to be involved.

Do you really need a follow-up visit? If you feel like the answer is yes on new fittings, fine, but can a technician do most of them? And certainly one follow-up visit is enough if the patient is doing well.

Charge all the fees up front

We have developed a bad habit since we started having free trial lenses readily available. It's OK; we can overcome it. Many optometrists routinely do not charge for the contact lenses at the initial fitting visit because they are not sure what brand or lens type they are going to use. These doctors may charge a professional fee, but since they are working only with free trial lenses at this point, they reappoint for a follow-up visit and do not charge for lenses yet. They may have some concern that they will want to change the lens type. This is a mistake in my view, because:

- It is possible that the patient will not return.
- It is possible that your staff will order and dispense boxes of lenses, but forget to enter the additional charges.
- Patients may think they already paid their contact lens fees and when you finally get around to charging them for the product, they are shocked and very unhappy.

The remedy is simple. Make a decision about what type of contacts you are prescribing and enter all the fees on day one; this includes services and products. If the patient is not actually taking any product with them, you do not have to demand full payment that day, but at least let the product be shown on their account.

Raise fees and add technology

You are entitled to make a decent profit when fitting contact lenses. Revaluate your fees for a new fitting, a refitting and for a contact lens evaluation (as part of the yearly eye exam even if there is no change in lens parameters). Charge more for specialty lenses like torics and multifocal. Add technology like corneal topography or specular microscopy and increase the professional fee.

Many vision plans provide an allowance for contact lens fitting fees and the patient pays the balance after a discount. These plans still provide a fair profit picture for the practitioner. Some vision plans are putting a very low cap on contact lens professional fees and that is unfortunate, but even in those cases, it pays to be more efficient.

16.17 Do You Really Need That Contact Lens Training Room?

Most practices I consult with need more space and if they had it, they could increase productivity and profitability. Of course, moving to a larger office or buying a building are good ways to go, but in many cases, that is not practical. At least not right away.

Utilizing the space you have now for the highest purpose is a smart strategy. There may be several ways to rework your present floor plan with minor expense, but I find the contact lens room is often a very functional space with a low priority purpose. Let's dig deeper.

The contact lens room

- There can be various purposes for a contact lens room in an optometric office, such as:
- Storage of diagnostic lenses
- A place to instruct patients on insertion, removal and hygiene of contact lenses

A place for staff to work, possibly for ordering contacts and tracking them for patient pick-up or delivery.
While all those tasks are needed, they do not necessarily need a dedicated room. Consider how you use your contact lens room and if there might be another area you could use for each function. All you really need for diagnostic lens sets is open shelves to set them on. If you have an open space or a wide hallway, a carpenter could build a custom design of shelves with the depth and height needed to display most of the sets from the manufacturers. Ideally, this would be near the exam rooms. I don't think the lens sets need to be hidden; I think they are impressive to patients. Diagnostic lenses could also go into a closet or laboratory.

I actually believe that contact lens training rooms are kind of outdated. They make me hark back to the old hard contact lens days when ODs would hold classes and training sessions took a long time. Today, soft lenses are quite easy to insert and the vast majority of fittings are on patents who have already worn lenses. Sure, we still train patients but I don't think it is a big deal and I don't want to make it seem as if it is. I also don't think it requires much privacy. I could easily see a technician and a patient sitting across from each other at a dispensing table in a corner of the optical and the patient practicing in front of a mirror. If other people see that, maybe they will be interested in contacts also. CL training can also occur in an exam room with a hospital table rolled up to the exam chair.

Staff members certainly need a place to work and if that occurs in the contact lens room, perhaps you can find another place for them with a computer and a phone, such as in a lab or other office space. I realize that staff may dislike changes that disrupt their work space, but you must consider the potential for a higher purpose in that space: a revenue-producing purpose.

What to do with the space

The first thing that comes to mind when I think about how to use the space is an additional exam room. The size of most contact lens rooms is usually perfect for this purpose and they usually have a sink. The extra exam room can be used by technicians and the doctor. The goal is for the staff to get the next patient ready while the doctor is in the other exam room. Ideally, the doctor just moves from one exam room to the other.

Another great purpose is for special diagnostic testing. That could be an OCT, dedicated visual fields, retinal imaging or macular pigment density screening.

All of these purposes produce revenue. What can you do with your contact lens room?

16.18 Contact Lenses: Why Don't You Bring Up the Topic?

I'd like to share a pet peeve of mine about ODs: most of us only prescribe contact lenses if the patient asks for them. Many of those patients are current contact lens wearers who want to renew their Rx and some are people who want to try them for the first time. How did we ever get to this situation where the optometrist does not bring up the contact lens treatment modality for good candidates in the rest of the population?

If you change your approach on how your recommend contacts and if you change the way you fit them, you can build a huge contact lens practice. Those patients will buy contacts, eyeglasses and plano sunwear and they return for regular eye care much often than non-contact lens wearers.

You can have a huge impact

The power of the doctor is really amazing and if you simply act enthusiastic about contact lenses and recommend them to a large number of patients whom you already see, you can double the number of contact lens wearers in your practice.

I'll cover the obstacles you face and I'll show how to be more profitable with contact lenses, but begin by recognizing that you can greatly increase the number of contact lenses you fit if you stop waiting for patients to ask for them. Instead, tell a high percentage of your patients, that they can wear contacts and educate them on the benefits. Good candidates are from kids to senior citizens and the group includes presbyopes and astigmats.

Clinical obstacles

The obstacles that we face in fitting far more patients with contact lenses are really of our own making, but our habits are quite ingrained and change can be difficult. Here are three factors that I think causes ODs to not fully embrace contact lenses:

- Too much time needed. On any given day, when you are with a patient, you are probably short on time. There may be other patients waiting to see you or you may have a number of other responsibilities waiting for you. To bring up the topic of contact lenses seems impossible in many cases due to lack of time. Theoretically, you could reappoint for the contact lens fitting, but you would still have to discuss the concept now and patients seem to resist the idea of coming back for more eye care. We need to fix this time problem. I'll tackle it in the next section, but you can't be too busy to make more money. Hire more staff, delegate more and make your fitting process more efficient.
- Feels like selling. Optometrists are sensitive to being viewed as a salesperson and if you bring up the idea of contact lenses, the patient might see it as selling. Please get over this antiquated idea! Contact lenses and eyeglasses are the tools we work with to correct vision defects and no one thinks poorly of you if you bring it up. You can even be excited about it.
- You think the patient must be motivated. Some ODs feel like the patient must have a desire to wear contacts if they are to be successful. They think it should be the patient's idea. This may have been true back in the day of PMMA lenses, but today, the average person can hardly even feel a contact lens on the eye. We need to move past our old outdated ideas about contact lenses.

Reinvent how you fit contacts

The best advice I can give you on how to increase your CL practice is to SIMPLIFY! Technology today has brought us products that are easy to fit and healthy to wear. The best way to improve profitability with soft contact lenses is to reduce the chair time.

- Fit the patient the same day as the eye exam using technicians to assist you with all aspects of the service.
- After the eye exam, tell patients they are good candidates and that you have a new contact lens that is amazing. Tell patients you'd like them to try on a free sample, just for fun and it will only take a couple of minutes. Let the patient wear the diagnostic contact lenses while they try on frames and sunglasses with the technician.
- The technician will insert the trial lenses, check acuity and over-refract if needed. You can see another patient in the meantime and then circle back to approve the fit with a slit lamp.
- Do not charge a fee to try on lenses in your office.
- Use daily disposable lenses for the free trial without talking about any other modality. Don't bring up wearing periods, but if asked, act like daily disposable is the best way to go.
- If the patient seems uncertain, mention the benefits of part time contact lens wear for sports and social occasions. Talk about how easy contacts are today.
- Do not discuss all kinds of bad things that might happen when wearing contact lenses.
- If the patient opts for contacts, make insertion and removal training easy and fast. Ideally, this is also on the same day as the exam. The technician can review proper lens care and give the patient an educational handout.

Chapter 17. Optical Dispensing

17.1 Dispensing Eyeglasses: The Tangible Details

The delivery of a pair of eyeglasses to a patient is a very important aspect of practice building, yet it is a part of our service that can easily under-perform because the optometrist is not often directly involved. The Rx delivery process should be reviewed frequently from an objective point of view. I'll offer some tips on dispensing in two parts: the tangible and the intangible.

The tangible details of dispensing finished glasses are extremely important because optometry is a service "business" in which patients don't really understand the service or the product. They have no way of judging spectacle lens quality, or eye exam quality. With no basis for evaluating what was purchased, people use other clues to help them decide if a service or product was a good value. The physical surroundings play a huge role in this perception of quality – which influences future referral patterns.

The act of dispensing is what the Disney Institute would call a "moment of truth", and marketing experts may call an "influence point". It is one important way the firm interacts with the customer.

Here are a few physical things to consider as you analyze your dispensing interaction:

- Is it set up efficiently? It should look like this is a place that does glasses well. Are adjustment tools, salt pan and sink easily accessed? Can more than one patient be dispensed at one time if needed? Does it seem convenient to the patient?
- How does the dispensing furniture look? The table or counter; the patient's chair; the tech's stool; the area where the patient looks straight ahead with the new glasses. Remodel this area and replace furniture before it is obviously needed.
- Where are glasses stored? Where the glasses are retrieved from makes an impression as the patient watches. Invest in the storage cabinet and make it look efficient and properly sized.
- How are the glasses packaged when they are brought to the patient? This is often not even looked at from the patient's point of view – but I believe it makes a huge difference. Avoid the "lab look" that is so common – such as glasses in job trays, lab ticket wrapped around them with a rubber band, lens markings still present, etc. We even remove the progressive lens markings when the glasses are verified in our lab, and we've had no problems fitting them. The glasses

should look like fine jewelry. Consider presenting them in a beautiful tray, or bringing them in their case.

- How is the case? The case speaks volumes – don't skimp and don't advertise on it. Make it something that the patient would be proud of. Obviously, match designer cases with designer frames.
- Other give-aways? We like to dispense a complimentary bottle of lens cleaner and a microfiber cloth. In my opinion, these are good places to put your practice name and logo.
- Is the frame already in standard adjustment? You want it to fit well and feel good upon the first wearing.
- What does the reading material look like? Avoid dog-eared, worn acuity charts. Replace them often with high quality materials. Printed text is better than a Snellen chart.
- Is there an attractive, large mirror present?
- How is the lighting? As an expert in vision, we must have plenty of light to read comfortably, and pleasing illumination on the patient's face to make the first viewing in the mirror a success.
- The dispensing visit may be the last interaction with the patient for some time and last impressions are just as important as first ones because they stick. Be sure to make this service special. More next week on what to say when delivering glasses!

17.2 Dispensing Eyeglasses: The Intangible Details

Last week's tip covered the tangible aspects of dispensing eyewear, so I'll focus on the intangible details this week. Don't underestimate the importance of these details - over time, they can make the difference between a thriving practice and an average one. Be sure to monitor these operations frequently, they have a way of drifting away from what was once standard procedure. Continual re-training of staff members on these points is time well spent.

Here is a good question for a staff meeting, along with some points that I think are important. Compile your own list and print copies for all dispensing staff members.

What should a technician say and do when dispensing a new pair of glasses?

- Greet the patient with a cheerful and warm statement. Use the patient's name and ask to be corrected on pronunciation if you're not sure (it should be spelled phonetically in the chart).

- Present and handle the glasses gracefully (see last week's tip also).
- Verbally review the features of the lenses and frame. For example, say: "Mr. Smith, I see you've ordered progressive lenses in a high index polymer. These are no-line multifocals, in the lightest and thinnest material available. You also have anti-reflective lenses to reduce glare and look better on your face. WHY do this? Two reasons: (1) Patients forget everything we tell them and they pay a lot for glasses; reminding of the special options builds value. (2) You want patients to talk to others about their new glasses and arming them with knowledge gives them something to say.
- Make some adjustment, even if they fit perfect. This enhances the perception of professional, custom fitting.
- Perform a final quality check of frame fit and that materials are free from defects. Acknowledge any problems you discover and propose a solution. You may wish to dispense the glasses so the patient can wear them while you re-order or re-make the correct part. Offer an apology without blaming co-workers and without becoming angry or upset. It should be very rare that a problem is found at dispensing.
- Complement the patient or the new glasses in some way. Be sincere and natural.
- Instruct the patient on use of the glasses, especially if this is the first time wearing this type of lens. Verify the quality of vision at appropriate viewing distances.
- Instruct the patient on the care and use of the glasses. Try to keep this simple and easy.
- State the balance due and ask how the patient wishes to pay. This requires a system to make this reliable and smooth.
- Close with something positive, like "I'm sure you're going to get many complements on your new glasses! Don't hesitate to let us know if they should need any adjustment."

17.3 Frame Board Management, Part One

Optometrists often ask me about frame board management (FBM). I get the feeling they would like a very short answer that would completely solve all aspects of this task. I think they might really love an app on their iPhone that would take care of it for them. While I don't have a super-short answer or an app, I will make FBM fairly easy for you in this article. I urge doctors and their key optical staff members to give this task more personal attention. I believe your frame inventory is important enough to warrant your best personal judgment on an ongoing basis.

I think the best approach to frame board management is for the OD/owner to meet with the optician, frame buyer or optical manager on a quarterly basis and review and rebalance the inventory. I like having a frame board committee because I want input from several people on what frame styles, brands and price points the practice needs. It might be tempting to delegate all of this to the staff, but I highly recommend the OD owner become involved. Optical dispensing may not be high on your priority list as an optometrist, but as CEO of the practice, it should be. The frame selection you have on display is extremely important to the success of your optical and there is a great deal of profit riding on that.

Before you meet with your frame committee, I would like someone to prepare what I call an FBM worksheet. The only way to make smart decisions and design a good plan going forward is to have data about your current frame inventory: Make up a document template with places to insert the following items:

- List all parent frame companies that you carry.
- Below each parent company, list all frame brands sold by that company that you carry.
- Put the sales rep's name after each brand.
- Show the current number of frames you have on display after each brand. This is easier than a true inventory. Just count the frames in each brand and show the total.
- After each frame brand, show the range of prices for that brand. I'd like to see a range for the Frames Data wholesale prices and your current retail prices. Also, make a note of the discount you receive on this brand.
- Add up all the frames-on-hand quantities to give a grand total of frames on display.
- If you have frame understock, count them and show that total.

You may have an inventory module in your practice management software that will provide some or all of this data, which would be great, but doing it manually once per quarter is not very difficult. We want accurate numbers. Be sure to date and save all these FBM worksheets so you can review the changes you make over time.

Committee meetings

Once the frame inventory data has been collected, set up a meeting to review the worksheet with your key staff members and have an open discussion of frame buying. I recommend setting aside at least one hour. The first meeting may take longer than subsequent meetings because you should review all aspects or frame buying and pricing. Many good side topics may branch off from this discussion, including how to display frames, what mark-up formula is used, how to reorder fast-selling frames and how much understock is needed.

The goal is to make decisions about the frame inventory and to develop a plan for buying frames in the future. As you review the list of frame brands, consider these points:

- How is this line selling? Is the brand perceived well by the public?
- Does this brand look similar to other brands? Is it repetitious?
- Does this brand fill an important niche demographic?
- How does this brand fit into the desired mix of retail price points?
- Do we like working with this company, the rep, the discounts and the service?
- Do we have the correct number of frames within each brand? Should we increase or decrease?
- Are there some brands we should drop completely?
- Are there any new brands we should consider adding?

Active frame board management requires judgment that only the practice owner and staff possess. You know your market and patient base better than anyone. It is perfectly normal for some frame lines to sell down quickly while others take longer. It is quite possible to overbuy in some brands. The quarterly FBM meeting is designed to adjust the numbers of frames in each brand in the coming months to reflect the current goal.

Price points

As you review the FBM worksheet, do some calculations to determine the percentage of the total frame inventory in various price ranges. You want a nice representation at the low end and the high end. What is the lowest price point you should offer? What percentage of frames are currently in the following retail price points:

- Under $150
- $150 to $250
- $250 to $350
- $350 to $450
- $450 to $600
- Over $600

Once you have your current mix, talk to your staff about what it should be. Consider your local market and income levels. Consider your eyeglass Rx retention rate.

A popular idea is to assign a specific number of spaces on the frame boards for each brand and let the sales rep manage those spaces as he/she sees fit. The theory being that the rep is incentivized to provide the best frame models at all times to maximize sales. I think it is smart to work closely with frame reps and rely on their advice, but it is important for the practice to monitor and coordinate the big picture of diversity of frame styles and price points. I want to retain the ability to change the number of frame board spaces allotted to a brand at any time.

17.4 Frame Board Management, Part 2: What Price Points to Carry

Last week, I started a series on frame board management (FBM) and I'll continue with that for the next few issues. In this article, I'll give you some ideas about frame price ranges to select for your inventory and how vision plans might influence your decisions.

I believe most independent optometrists should have a good representation of all frame prices from the budget-conscious low-end through the mid-range and including the high-end. Of course, how we define low-end and high-end will differ based on your market demographics, such as median household income, but we really do want something for everyone. You want to make the strong profit that comes with exclusive luxury frames. You also want to prevent some folks from walking out with their Rx if they feel you don't have a good selection of affordable glasses or glasses that are fully covered by a vision plan.

Understand vision plan pricing
To maintain strong profitability in your optical, it is important for everyone on your FBM committee (see last week's article), including the doctor/owner, to understand how vision plans work. Vision Service Plan is one of the largest plans in the U.S. and the system they use is a bit different, so let's review VSP frame pricing. Opticians generally understand the procedure very well, but if I ask ODs if they know how it works, the answer is usually no. It is not that difficult and it may affect the frame prices you decide to carry.

VSP lists two allowances in dollar amounts on each patient's benefit authorization. We find it helpful to print this benefit sheet in advance of the patient's visit and we refer to it during the frame selection and lens design process. You will see a wholesale frame allowance (WFA) and a retail frame allowance (RFA) on the VSP benefit form. If a patient selects a frame with a wholesale cost (as shown in the Frames Data book) of less than the WFA, the frame is fully covered by the plan and the patient owes nothing on the frame. Obviously, that means your practice makes a lower profit.

If the patient selects a frame with a wholesale Frames Data price of higher than the WFA, the patient will pay some frame overage and we look to the RFA to calculate that. The RFA is subtracted from the retail price you set for the frame and the patient pays 80% of that difference in price. If you priced the frame at $400 and the RFA is $170, the difference is $230. The patient pays 80% of that or $184. It is important to note that you have the freedom to set the retail price at whatever you wish. The market will drive that decision.

Lessons to learn

Of course, if VSP is not very big in your practice, then you don't need to consider its pricing system in your frame buying. But if VSP is a large managed care plan for you, you can buy smarter and make more profit if you keep the following points in mind.

If you could buy fewer frames with wholesale prices less than the typical WFA value in your practice, you would have more patients paying something toward their frame cost. Of course, the vision plan contract requires providers to maintain a specific minimum number of frames that are fully covered, and you want to do that anyway to satisfy patients' budgetary needs. But you could opt to buy frames with a wholesale cost that is well below the typical WFA and make a better profit. This would include low priced frame vendors and closeout frames. The least profitable scenario is when you buy frames that are just slightly less than your typical WFA. How do you know your typical WFA? Look at your patients' benefit forms and average them.

If you increase your frame mark-ups up a little bit, patients will pay more in frame overages. Only you can decide if your market will accept that, but if you feel the vision plan does not pay enough in fees, you may have to collect more from the patient. Many optical consultants feel the old 2.5X or 3X mark-ups are out-of-date. You may be able to mark-up some brands more than others.

17.5 Frame Board Management, Part 3: Reordering

In this installment of my series on frame board management, I'll write about the importance of reordering best-selling frames on a regular basis. While this sounds like it should be easy, it has always been a challenge because when a frame is sold, we don't really know if it is a hot seller or not. We generally have only one frame unit in each color, so when it sells, we don't know if it is the start of a trend or a one-off sale.

I believe it is very important to present a complete collection of frames within a brand. I'd rather have fewer brands and more units in each one. Patients who are interested in the brand want to see a lot choices. The brand should be well-represented. A few oddball shapes and colors are not impressive and it looks like old stock. Based on this premise, it is not good enough to sell a bunch of frames and then wait for the sales rep to return in a few months. The good styles are likely gone very quickly.

A new reordering system

We have been using a new method of reordering frames on a weekly basis that is working well for us and our frame reps like it as well. Here is how it works:

- We use bar-coded inventory tags on our frames that slip onto the temple. In addition to the bar code, the tag shows the frame name, size, color, our date of acquisition, our wholesale cost (in code so it can't be read by patients) and the retail price.
- We prefer to use the frame off our board with each Rx order because it gives us more control on the job and prevents backorder issues. We will special order frames as well, but we have a large inventory of frames to choose from and a small amount of understock to replace sold frames.
- When a frame is sold and sent to our lab, we remove the tag and place it in a tray.
- Once per week, our office manager reviews the tags in the tray and removes any frames that we do not want to reorder. This may be a brand that we decided to drop, or a frame with a very old acquisition date, or a model that is highlighted with a yellow marker. We highlight tags in yellow while they are still on the frame board if we decide we do not want to reorder it.
- After removing the frames we do not want, a staff member reorders all the other frames in the tray.

- We reuse the inventory tags when the new frames come in.

Seeing reps for new styles
Seeing frame reps has proven to be very easy and quick with this new system and the reps like it because we buy frames sooner and always have a good representation on the boards. We see reps quarterly, which is less often than we used to see them. When a rep comes in, we generally have most of the spaces allotted to that line full. All that is needed is to look at the new styles since the last visit and exchange some frames that have been slow movers.

Here are some benefits we see with this system:

- Even though we must exchange frames at times, our exchange rate is lower with this new method than it used to be. This is because we do not overbuy like we used to and then we would have to freeze our ordering to let us sell through. This would cause us to go too long between rep visits and we would have a lot of old inventory to get rid of.
- Frame buying is more evenly distributed throughout the year so we see fewer big spikes in bills to pay.
- The rep's visit in our office goes much faster; generally less than 30 minutes.
- Less understock is needed because we reorder so often.
- We always have a nice selection within each frame line and we always have the hot sellers on the boards.

This reordering method is low tech and very accurate. It does not require that you use a frame inventory software system, although that can be a helpful adjunct. Talk to your frame reps and consider trying this system in your practice.

17.6 Frame Board Management, Part 4: Frame Lines

This final installment of my series on frame board management will focus on which frame brands and models to choose for your inventory. If you use a frame board management work sheet as described in part one of this series, you can divide your current inventory into four divisions as shown below. It is important to have some representation in each of these categories.

The high end
You want to have some beautiful luxury frames for patients who want the best and have the financial ability to buy it. These frames may not sell as

quickly as the others, but they are very profitable on a per unit basis. It can be hard to know what retail price point is the high end in your practice. You might assume it is $X dollars, but you could be underestimating your market. The only way to be sure you hit it correctly is to stretch a bit and test a price point higher than what you previously thought was the maximum. When I did this in my practice, I found the high end was much higher than I realized.

You may have to accept some sales policies that are different than the ones you are used to with the major frame companies in our industry. Exclusive upscale brands may specify a minimum order, minimum stock on hand, no discounts and no exchanges. For many ODs, those tough policies are enough to make them give up, but I urge you to be flexible and make an investment in a truly high end line. If it does not sell well, you can mark it down and get rid of it, but if you never try, you will never know what your high end is.

The low end

Possibly even more important than high end frame lines is the low end. If possible, we do not want patients to take their eyeglass Rx to go, and having a great selection of cool styles that are affordable will often do the trick. You should train your staff to not start with this value line when showing frames, but it should be there if you need it. You can segment the low priced frames from the rest of your inventory somewhat, but I would not give the impression that these frames are inferior or low status by making them hard to find. They are good frames because your practice would not carry junk.

Here are some sources for value priced frames:

- Value priced frame companies. There are several good ones in our industry that sell good quality products, with a warranty, in stock for immediate shipment. These companies have frames that are extremely low price or moderately low. The styles in the moderately low price range are very up to date. These may have a brand name or no name, but they do not have the expensive licensed brands. An important feature with most of these companies is that they list the frames at fairly high wholesale price in the Frames Data book, but offer very strong discounts to your practice.
- Closeouts. There are many frames from the major companies, including designer lines, that are soon to be discontinued (or already are) and they are marked down to sell fast. These closeout frames offer very good prices for current styles and name brand recognition, but you must be willing to buy deep in each model, size and color. You and your staff must also accept the fact that you may not be

able to reorder replacement frames or parts for repairs. Some offices make it clear at the time of sale that the frame has no warranty and others will select a new replacement frame and make new lenses in the few cases that have a problem. I recommend you let your frame reps know that you are interested in closeouts.

The unique lines

There are many high quality, beautiful frame lines that have a brand name that is not well-known to the consumer, which can be a good thing. These lines may not be available online, in big-box stores or from national optical retail stores. These frame companies often offer unique styles and colors that are not the run of the pack. You can differentiate your practice by offering a nice selection of unique brands that are tailored to the segments of your market from funky to conservative.

The name brands

Some optometric practices simply refuse to carry the major frame brands in our industry, including some of the best known designers in the fashion world. The reasoning is usually that the frame buyer does not want to carry frames that are sold in local shopping malls. Some are also trying to make a statement against vertical integration in the optical industry. To each his own, but based on how well these brands sell in my practice (and at very strong margins), that could be a mistake. The truth is that most of our patients do not shop for frames at the mall or online. Most fully intend to buy their glasses at my office when they make the appointment. We help them do that by giving them what they want and a large segment of our market loves those brands.

17.7 Four Steps to Higher Frame Profits

Most optometrists don't pay much attention to the pricing of frames that are carried in their practice's optical department. This is an area that is usually on autopilot. A frame mark-up formula was created many years ago, and that is how frames are priced. If that describes your practice, you are missing out on some profits.

Here are four tips on how to improve your profitability of ophthalmic frames:

A modern frame mark-up formula

Let's review your mark-up formula and be sure it is up to date. Chances are your pricing system has not been revised in many years. While some consumers will shop around for frame prices, the vast majority of patients who visit independent private practices want to obtain their eyeglasses there. And many of these patients have vision plans covering the majority of the frame cost. Given these trends, the frame price is not that price sensitive. The old method of something like 2.5X plus $30 is outdated. Many successful practices today use a sliding scale that starts at a 3X mark-up for frames with a higher wholesale cost and shifts to a 4X markup on frames with a lower wholesale cost.

Mark-up formulas work well for most frames in your office because it lets staff know how to price most frames without special decisions or input from the owner.

Go off the mark-up formula

While the general pricing formula works for most frames, there are times when it is smart to go off your system. For example, I believe in offering a budget line of frames (although we don't promote it and we keep it separate from the main frame lines). These frames are purchased at a very low price, possibly as low as $5 to $10. Obviously, these frames can't be sold at $15 or $20. There are too many services and overhead costs that go with the sale of a pair of glasses to support that low of a price. These frames could easily retail at $90 or more.

Another opportunity exists to simply set a price based on the quality and the public's perception of the frame, without a direct relation to the wholesale cost. You could buy a frame at a very low price, often much lower than the price published in the Frames Data list, which is used to determine the price covered by vision plans. There are several frame lines that offer such pricing. This frame line could be priced any way you wish. There is nothing wrong with having some frame lines that provide a much higher profit margin. Having a higher retail price on these lines creates a higher frame overage after the vision plan allowance is calculated.

You may be able to buy some close-out frames in very popular designer brands at a very low price and mark them up based on the usual wholesale price. You may need to change your buying habits with this type of frame, such as buying ten pairs of the exact same model, size and color. You may not be able to get other colors or sizes for patients to view and you may not be able to order replacement parts for repairs, but you can increase profits very nicely with close-outs.

Move price points up

Here is a smart way to analyze your frame inventory: count the numbers of frames you have on display in price ranges similar to this: Below $150; $150 to $250; $250 to $350; $350 to $450; $450 to $550; over $550. This creates six price points. Convert the number of frames into percentages of the entire inventory. Examine these percentages and try to decrease the number in the lower price points and increase the higher price points. You will still have all prices available, but more choices in the higher range will result in a higher average sale.

Explore your true high-end

Test your market by bringing in a frame line that is much higher price than anything you carry now. Many practice owners have a preconceived notion of what is the high end of what local consumers will spend for frames. For many ODs, that upper end might be $600. What if you brought in an exclusive high end frame brand that retailed at $1200 and what if it sold very well? We would have proven that the initial assumption was wrong. I experienced this scenario in my practice about 15 years ago. We have been selling high end frames ever since.

Be aware that some exclusive frame lines may operate with different rules than we are used to. There may be an expensive buy in. You may not be able to return frames that don't sell well. There may not be a discount. Don't let these different policies scare you off and prevent you from investing in a brand that would be good for your practice. There is always some risk in business strategies and this one is relatively small.

17.8 Optical Remakes

I recently returned to my office after a vacation and among all the mail and messages left for me by our office manager was a file labeled optical remakes. My office uses a special optical order form when we remake or replace eyeglasses at no charge. The form is on pink paper and has three copies so we can track the frequency and cost of remakes. Some of these optical jobs are covered under a warranty program, some are due to our own errors in prescribing, measuring or fitting, and some are due to breakage or damage of materials by our staff. Remakes are always approved by a doctor or a manager before they are ordered.

The optical remake file is nothing unusual; reviewing it from time to time is part of my normal duties. In this instance, based on the stack of pink slips, I assumed at first glance the file was for the year 2007. It turned out it was just for January! Houston, we have a problem. OK, I'm exaggerating a little bit, but the number of no charge remakes was higher than I would like, so I investigated the reason for each job.

Basic overview

In assessing the remake problem, I realize that my practice dispenses a high number of eyeglasses, so even with a low remake percentage; I will have a high absolute number. It's tempting for me to try to quote some percentage that might be considered normal, but it would be a disservice because the definition of the remake policy varies so much from one practice to another. It's hard to compare apples to apples in an expense category like remakes.

I also realize that my practice has a culture that places a high value on total patient satisfaction. While I strongly believe in that philosophy and it's the main reason my practice does well, that philosophy also promotes more frequent remakes. As a business person, I want to reduce remakes but not reduce the excellent customer service that often requires a remake. I want to stop what I consider unnecessary and preventable remakes.

Reasons for remakes

Let's examine some of the factors that cause an eyeglass prescription to have to be remade or reordered at no charge.

- Doctor error. This happens to all of us. I don't get hung up on why a spectacle Rx is not working the way it should, I just find the problem and fix it. I don't try to shift blame to the patient or the lab or my instruments. I strongly believe in excellent customer service; it's the most important factor in practice success.
- Optician error. There are lots of possibilities... incorrect measurements of PDs or seg heights are high on the list. Also, poor frame choice for a given lens Rx or poor frame fit to the patient. The error could be in the form of an omission, such as not specifying a vertical optical center measurement.
- Optician damage. If we break or harm a patient's product, we replace it. We use a disclaimer form when we work on older frames, which relieves us of some extreme risk, but I know a temple can snap on a new frame also. I'll cite another example and admit that I didn't know this until recently... antireflective lenses should not be heated! We are now dispensing more plastic frames and some of my opticians place the frame front (with lenses) into the salt pan or under the hot air blower to adjust it. My lab manager advised against that because crazing or clouding can occur to the lens surface. The lenses should be removed from the frame before it's

heated. One optician asked, "How can I get the lenses out without heating the frame?" It turns out the lenses should be snapped out cold, but the frame can be heated to allow easy reinsertion.

- Lab error. This would not be considered a remake in my office because the job is rejected upon inspection and is returned with the original order. My definition for a no charge remake is when a new order is written, but no one paid for it.
- Product defect or poor performance. This may not be anyone's fault but if a lens tint or coating does not work to the patient's satisfaction the blame often goes back to the optician or doctor with the assumption that he should have known better. A truly defective product is easy to spot and may be covered under a warranty (see that point below).
- Buyer's remorse. Often disguised by the patient looking for a way out of the purchase, you may hear that some aspect of the glasses is not right when it's really the cost or the style that is the problem. It doesn't really matter. I'd let the patient save face and fix the problem. Patient satisfaction is king.
- Warranty. Show me ten practices and I'll show you ten variations of eyeglass warranties. Many warranties are in place from the manufacturer or laboratory, but those are typically provided to the practice and the practice is free to decide what warranty is provided to the patient, if any. There are often different warranties for frames, lenses, antireflective materials and non-Rx sunglasses. Some practices are very lenient on warranties, some are very strict, some are given free, some are sold for a price, some are for one year, some are for life, some are no charge when used and some require a co-payment.

Of all the reasons cited above, there are two that I feel are the easiest to attack: optician error and optician damage. I would like to reduce the remakes from the other categories as well, but I feel these two are the most amenable to change.

Remakes from the warranty category result in the largest number by far in my practice and those should really be viewed separately from all the others. Warranty remakes generally have the cost covered by the supplier of the product, so while there was no charge to the patient for the order, there is no lab cost either. We should not overlook the labor cost, however. An established practice that does a great deal of warranty work will incur a significant expense in the time needed by employees to process the orders and re-deliver the products. If a warranty remake is not covered by a supplier and must be covered by the practice (such as with in-office labs), that's based on a business policy decision that the practice owner decided was in his best interest.

How to reduce remakes
It's very important to reduce the number of no charge optical orders for two major reasons: 1) the lab expense is significant and cuts into the practice net income and 2) many of the remakes are caused by errors which even if corrected create an inconvenience for the patient.

I think the best way to reduce remakes due to optician error or damage is through staff training. This should be an ongoing effort in every practice, but in reality it usually gets dropped by the wayside. I'm going to rededicate my efforts in this area and design a program of weekly staff in-service meetings. I'll write more next week on how to plan and produce staff training sessions that will improve your services and reduce your remake cost.

17.9 A Guide to Troubleshooting Eyeglass Complaints

It's not lost on me that if I consider myself an expert with vast experience at handling patients with eyeglass complaints, then it follows that perhaps I'm not a very good optometrist. But the fact is that I am a very good optometrist, if I do say so myself, but all ODs who see many patients over the course of their career will have quite a few who are unhappy with some aspect of their new glasses. It happens to all of us.

Here is a guide to efficiently correcting the problem, keeping the patient happy and loyal, and not losing any sleep over it.

An attitude adjustment
To be completely successful in managing an Rx problem, you may want to examine your own attitude about it first. It is easy to become a bit apprehensive when you first learn that a patient you recently examined is unhappy with the product you prescribed. You really must get over that feeling... that is for complete rookies with no self-confidence! Realize that the vast majority of these patients are as nice as can be and as soon as you show that you are concerned and want to help, they are like putty in your hands! So eliminate any stress or dread and know that these office visits are usually not bad at all.

This change in attitude should carry through so that you let your staff know that you do not mind seeing these patients at all. It is actually best if you see them as soon as possible with little inconvenience. It is OK to see these patients by appointment if you must, but if a patient with a problem is in your office and you can find the time, it is best to just see them right now. After all, you have no apprehension, right? And if you save the patient a return trip and get it over with, you will have a big advantage.

Train your staff to handle these cases properly before you even see the patient:

- When the patient states a complaint, immediately show great concern and agreement that the problem must be corrected. Ensure the patient that you will find the cause of the problem and fix it.
- It is usually appropriate to apologize. At the very least, apologize for the patient's inconvenience and if you find that your office made a mistake, admit it and apologize for that as well. An apology immediately makes most people more tolerant and understanding. It is what we all want to hear when we are inconvenienced or wronged in some way.
- Forget about trying to blame others. Go ahead and accept the blame if it will help get to the issue.
- Staff should know when they can fix a problem on their own and also know when to ask the doctor or senior optician to get involved. Taking a weak stab at the problem and not really fixing it only makes the issue worse. It is far better to solve the problem right the first time.

A scientific approach

Okay, let's get on with identifying and fixing the eyeglass problem. That is not always as easy as you might think. There can be many factors for an eyeglass complaint, including buyer's remorse. Remove the emotion and follow a specific scientific protocol like this:

- Do it yourself. As much as I believe in delegation, I prefer to handle complaint cases myself once my staff feels they need my input. These cases are very important and can go very wrong if not handled perfectly. I have many excellent staff, but I'm in the best position to put together all the variables of eye health, refraction and optical correction.
- Meet and greet the patient is a compassionate way. "I'm so sorry to hear there is a problem with your new glasses, Mr. Jones. I'll do whatever I can to take care of it. Tell me about it."

- I begin by listening very carefully to the patient. Look him in the eye and understand what he is saying. Nod in a supportive way. Don't interrupt. Ask questions to be sure you understand and enter this history data into the patient record.
- Recheck everything. Don't assume you know things; take a very scientific approach. Review the previous case history and any visual complaints that led you to prescribing the new glasses. Confirm these original factors with the patient. Verify all the prescription lens parameters, retest the subjective refraction and recheck visual acuity. Compare the new Rx with the old glasses subjectively, if appropriate.
- I like to do lensometry on the problem glasses myself, not give them to a staff member to check. I need to know exactly what the readings are. Don't use an auto-lensmeter unless you paid over $10,000 for it. These $3,000 auto-lensmeters are not accurate enough. A manual lensmeter is actually better for troubleshooting. Spot the PDs. Spot the PAL markings on the lenses and draw the seg location. Put the glasses back on the patient's face and check the alignment.
- Consider lens materials and base curves and review the previous lenses. Polycarbonate has some advantages over CR-39, but optics can still be a problem.
- Be sure that visual acuity is as good as previously recorded and if not, suspect a change in ocular health status. Examine the eye as needed. I've seen Rx complaints turn out to be a fresh retinal hemorrhage.

Explain and fix the problem

In most cases, the process above will lead you to an obvious cause for the complaint. It should make sense; there should be a cause and effect relationship. In that case, just explain what happened in simple terms to the patient and proceed to fix the problem by remaking the lenses or whatever you have to do. Do not spare any expense at this point. The lab may make new lenses at no charge, but worry about that later. The cost is very minor in all this. It is part of the cost of doing business.

Unfortunately, there are plenty of times you won't know for sure what is causing the problem. The Rx and the optical measurements all seem perfect. In those cases, you might try just starting over. Ask the patient if she loves the frame or if she would be willing to choose a new one. The response can tell you quite a lot. I'm extremely easy on patients. If the new glasses are within

30 days from dispensing, I am happy to select a new frame and make new lenses.

Service recovery
Complaints cases can bruise your ego and they can become emotional, but resist the urge to blame others. If you handle the customer service aspect well, you can come off as a hero. Once you show a patient that you truly care and you go the extra mile for them, they become extremely loyal. Many of these complaint cases can turn into your very best patients.

If I feel like we dropped the ball in some way, or the patient thinks we did, I like to give a small gift as a goodwill gesture. It might be a coffee mug with the practice logo, a $10 Starbucks gift card or a $50 gift card to our eye center. We have all of them on hand.

17.10 Is it Time to Start Charging for Frame Adjustments?

As most readers know, I favor a very patient-friendly approach to practice management; I've always been in the camp that does not charge patients for eyeglass adjustments or even for minor repairs. But as I monitor the still very small number of patients who buy their glasses online or from other local providers, I realize I should treat those patients differently. I now propose that we still perform the usual optical adjustments and repairs at no charge for patients who bought their glasses from my office, but that we charge a fee to those who need services and bought the glasses elsewhere. I'm sure many of you arrived at this point before I did, but better late than never!

Online optical
In the past, so few of the glasses we worked on came from other sources that there was no reason to bother checking on that point. In the rare case that the glasses did not come from our office, we chalked it up as a goodwill gesture and hoped the patent would buy from us next time.

The gradual increase of eyeglass sales on the internet is causing more people to call on us for adjustments and repairs to eyeglasses than we had before. We've always had some patients opt to take their spectacle Rx out and buy glasses elsewhere, but until recently, they could always return to that office or store for repairs and adjustments. Obviously, there is no place to go when you buy glasses online and you need service later. These folks will naturally go to their optometrist. This need is cumulative over the years that online optical has existed and is becoming significant, even though sales of prescription glasses online is still around 3% and have not increased over the past four years.

Is it worth the identification step?

To begin charging an adjustment fee for non-purchased eyewear, your staff will need to require the patient's name before they do any work on his glasses. In addition to the patient's name, we should also know the name of the frame and color in order for the optician to identify if some pairs of glasses were purchased from the practice by this patient and other pairs were not. While this checking process is time consuming, there are some big benefits.

One of the benefits is that many of the patients we see in optical every day are past due for eye exams. If your receptionist obtains each person's name before calling an optician, she can check the last exam date and write it down. The optician can then mention the need for an exam to patients who are past due and ask if they would like to schedule the appointment right now. This definitely works and you can read more about this technique in Tip #539.

The policy helps Rx retention

Another great reason to adopt the policy of charging for optical service on eyewear bought elsewhere is that you can tell that to patients when they are considering going elsewhere. Generally, these patients are in your optical with your staff and they have not decided if they will walk or not. Some of them are "showrooming" you, as it is called. It does not happen often, but some people try on frames and speak to your optician, and then Google the frame name and model on their smartphone. They can instantly see many online vendors selling the exact same frame for much less than you. But just because a product can be purchased for less does not make it a good value. There are many optical services that come with buying a frame from my office and it is only fair that none of those services should be available if the frame is purchased elsewhere. The price on the internet is just for the product – our price reflects our service, our facility, our expertise and much more.

When my optician is working with a patient who is considering his options, I want to let him know that we offer lifetime service on eyeglasses that are purchased from us, but we charge a fee to work on glasses that are purchased elsewhere. We even have a handout that describes our optical services in more detail.

Frames on the internet; not lenses

Be aware that a growing number of patients will buy a new frame on the internet and bring it to your office to have lenses made for it. This is a trend we should keep an eye on. Patients realize that a specific frame model is exactly the same no matter where they buy it, but lenses are not as easily compared. Lenses are more complex and many people want our expertise and custom measurements on that aspect of the glasses.

This could become a reason to carry more independent frame lines that are only sold to eye care professionals. I am not making a big shift just yet because many people love the designer name brands and they sell well, but the mix is always up for evaluation and could change over time.

Monitor your Spectacle Rx retention rate!

A key metric to monitor as you navigate these new factors in the competitive optical landscape is your actual eyeglass Rx retention rate (capture rate). This should be more accurate than just dividing the number of glasses sold by the number of refractions. I get this data every month in my practice and my retention rate for July was 92%!

17.11 Eyeglass Problems, But Purchased Elsewhere

Last week's tip article explored the idea of charging patients a fee for eyeglass adjustments when they are purchased elsewhere. I received quite a few email comments from readers, many agreed with me and some did not. That's what makes optometry so great; there are many ways to be successful in practice. One colleague liked the article, but asked what he should do when a patient returns with a problem with new eyeglasses he prescribed, but they were purchased from another eye care professional or even online.

Still your patient

I view the complaining patient as a person who needs our help, even if he bought the glasses elsewhere. After all, I'm still his eye doctor and plan to be for many years to come. I accept what the patient tells me with understanding and empathy and I believe them completely (until they prove untrustworthy, which is not usually the case). I believe patients have a right to fill their eyeglass or contact lens Rx anywhere they wish. I work hard at trying to make my practice their best choice, but it is their choice.

Generally, all patients with eyeglass complaints are received by one of our opticians or technicians. This obviously depends on the size of the practice and available staff; the optometrist can certainly follow the same steps. I genuinely want to assist the patient with identifying the cause of the problem and advising them about what to do about it. I also want to do this efficiently and not provide services that were not paid for. Building some goodwill with the patient that converts to loyalty and referrals is worth some time and effort.

Here are the steps I would follow:

- Listen to the complaint and think about what could cause those problems. This is important because it can lead you down the right path to identifying the problem. If the patient is angry or upset, show them that you want to help and that you are also unhappy with the issue.
- Most visual complaints will require you to check the spectacle Rx and some basic lens parameters. Use extra care in handling the glasses because they are the patient's property and they were purchased from another source. Inspect the glasses in front of the patient before taking them away for lensometry or other tests. If you see any defect in the frame or lens, show it to the patient. You could say, "Were you aware that..." Using care not to scratch the lenses on your lensometer, read the lens Rx and note the optical centers. You may need to mark the optical centers and measure the PD, but not in all cases and maybe not yet.
- Compare the Rx with your record. It is best to not compare the Rx as read with a written copy of the Rx or a lab invoice because those could have been written incorrectly. Let's see if the Rx is what your record indicates. Here is where you need some optical experience. The Rx may not be exactly perfect. There is a tolerance, which is often considered to be the published ANSI standards, but use your common sense. If the cylinder axis is 5 degrees off, that would be significant if the cylinder power is 2.00 D. But if the cylinder power is .25 D., I'm not so sure 5 degrees would even be noticeable. Maybe, but I'm still looking for more than that.
- Depending on the complaint, you may want to evaluate the seg height of a bifocal or the major reference point of a progressive. Bifocals are easy; progressives will require you to find the invisible markings and draw the segment with a washable pen. Put the glasses on the patient and look at the seg in relation to their eye and determine if it is set properly.

- This may seem like a lot of effort for glasses that were not purchased from you, but I believe this is a courtesy we should show our patients. It is not very many that need this extra time. I'm willing to check the Rx, the PD if needed and the seg height.
- Complaints about frame discomfort are easy. That is really not your problem, because you did not sell this frame.
- If you have found the likely cause of the problem, I write the patient's name and date on an Rx blank and write a short note with what I found. You might write the Rx you found and rewrite what was prescribed or write that the seg height is too low, etc. I give the note to the patient and advise him to return to where he got the glasses and have them remade. There is usually no problem with this because the glasses were not made correctly.
- If lensometry shows the Rx to be substantially what you prescribed, the problem may lie with you. It happens and I don't get defensive or try to shift blame. Just take the next step which is to recheck the refraction. I happily do this at no charge because it is expected by the public. I know the often quoted analogy that a physician would not see a patient for a second exam at no charge just because the first drug Rx didn't work. It's different.
- Be very exact about your recheck refraction. Also review the visual complaints at the time of the last exam and review the habitual Rx. You will know what to do at this point. If you find a different Rx, just explain how that can happen and confirm with hand-held trial lenses how you can fix the problem. Read on for how to proceed if you need to change the Rx.

How to be a hero

Quite often, you or your optician can be a hero in the process of working with this problem patient. At first, just listening and caring gets you some points. You come off as the true expert in visual science. You are the one that can unravel this mess of variables and help the patient get some glasses he can see with. If the Rx needs to be changed, I would write it out for the patient and add a note like "Rx change needed". I would advise the patient that most reputable optical stores will remake glasses at no charge within 30 days of purchase when there is a change needed. If there is any chance that my staff or I made an error in our exam or our records, I advise further that if the optical store will not remake the lenses at no charge, I want the patient to bring the glasses back to my office and we will remake them at no charge.

17.12 Showrooming: What Should You Do About It?

So here's a good topic to get you going today... showrooming. It's one of those new verbs that has sprung up to describe a fairly new phenomenon in the retail sales world. Showrooming refers to customers (or patients) who shop in brick and mortar stores with the express intent of making a decision about products so they can go home and buy the item online at a lower cost. If you happen to own one of those brick and mortar places, such as your office, it definitely strikes you as unfair and just not right.

Most of us have seen this in our own offices by now: the patient with a notebook and pen who writes down frame model numbers and sizes and prices (often asking your staff for help with the process). Or worse, takes photos of the frames with a cell phone and then uses the phone to browse the internet for online vendors selling the same product. It's enough to give you one of those gloom and doom moments, but take heart... rumors of the demise of brick and mortar opticals have been greatly exaggerated.

Look at major retail

If you think the occasional (rare) patient who showrooms your office is concerning, how would you feel if you were the CEO of Best Buy and you had to face this same trend on a huge national scale, with Wall Street watching very closely. According to Drew Fitzgerald of the *Wall Street Journal*, analysts warned last year that the company's 1,400 stores were becoming little more than a testing ground for Amazon.com customers. Fast forward to the current holiday season and Best Buy is running TV commercials proclaiming its stores as the "ultimate holiday showroom"! I've been in Best Buy recently and it is true. The place is amazing and I bought a tablet PC!

Best Buy CEO, Hubert Joly, has been quoted as saying he loves showrooming! "A year ago, people said that showrooming would kill Best Buy. I think that Best Buy has killed showrooming," Mr. Joly said in an interview, as he referenced price matching strategies and improved customer service.

The WSJ article goes on to describe how some big box stores are benefitting from "reverse showrooming", as shoppers search online for products before buying them in a traditional store! I love to think that it works both ways in our offices, too. Target stores have gone so far as to install free Wi-Fi to encourage customers to browse the internet with cell phones.

A reversal in optical

Another sign that brick and mortar offices have a bright future in optical is that two major online optical vendors have recently opened brick and mortar stores. Warby-Parker has a number of stores in major U.S. cities and Coastal Contacts, a Canadian retailer of eyeglasses and contact lenses, just opened its third store. What's that about?

What can you do about it?
As interesting as those trends are, let's get back to what you and your staff should do when a patient says he does not want any assistance, but he blatantly writes down data or takes photos. I must acknowledge my friend and colleague, Mark Hinton, who is an excellent speaker and optical consultant, for getting me to see this the right way.

I found I was way too worried about staying removed from the patient's right to buy glasses wherever he chooses. Of course, he has that right, but why should we stand by silently? Why should we never say anything against the idea of buying glasses online, as if it were sacred? I happen to believe it is a bad idea in the patient's best interest. And most patients in my office have a lot of respect for my opinion and that of my staff. So, the best way to handle showrooming is to engage the shopper. Ask him questions, like "Are you thinking of buying glasses on the internet?" Ask some more questions and you'll know where to go from there.

Be sure to share some stories of other patients who have bought glasses on the internet and how it did not work out well. Talk about how important precise measurements are in order to obtain the clearest vision and how those measurements and fittings are not possible over the internet. Quote the research study from Pacific University and reported by the AOA that found over half of all glasses ordered on the internet failed tests for prescription accuracy or safety specifications. Advise patients that they are better off buying glasses in person from an optometrist.

17.13 Lens Packages Revisited

I have designed and used lens packages in my practice several times over the years, but I've never been completely happy with them until now. In some cases, I felt we were giving a discounted price for lens features that the patients would have happily bought at full price. In other cases, my optical staff would review all the lens features that are included in the package, only to have the patient say he wanted it, but would like to remove one item. Well, then it is not a package! We would end up going al a carte. Finally, I found that our packages revolved around presenting good, better, best options and I don't really like that approach. I like my staff to just present the best products.

For my practice, I'm happy to say that we have found a great solution by offering only one lens package, which includes the best of everything.

Just one package

This concept really makes the design of eyewear very easy and a high percentage of patients just say yes and go with the lens package.

We tell patients that our doctors have carefully selected the most important lens features and the very best brands available and we designed our premium lens package. We guarantee this package to be the lightest, thinnest, safest, best-looking and best-performing lenses available. We list the brand names of all the products in our package and they are well-respected and often nationally advertised. Our patients really trust our doctors and opticians and they know they are not in a good position to make all the choices themselves.

My optical staff goes on to explain that while the prices for the premium lens products in our package are higher, we are able to discount the package significantly saving the patient $65. We even offer the package to vision plan patients and offer them a small savings over the usual approved co-pays for all the features. I analyzed the profitability of this package program and we are definitely dispensing enough premium products that we are generating more profit even after the discount.

Some of the lens features included in our package are:

- Digital free-form design
- Premium progressive lenses if an add is prescribed
- Premium antireflective with hard coat
- High index plastic
- Transitions
- Aspheric lens surface
- Ultra-violet protection
- Scratch resistant finish
- Polished edges
- Lens warranty

We only have one lens package, but we have pricing alternatives without Transitions and in single vision or progressive.

Saves time
While I love dispensing premium lens products, I also love saving time for me and my staff. The single lens package does that because the patient does not need to make many decisions. Most patients just choose a frame and then go with the lens package and we are done.

For vision plans, we quote the total of all the co-pays instead of each co-pay. The package also prevents the sticker shock of so many add-ons. There is a psychological advantage to just giving one price instead of six or eight items all added together.

I find that making things simple for patients is a big advantage and patients love it.

Consider spiffs
I know that paying an individual bonus to an employee for selling a specific item is not very popular, but I'm not sure why. It is actually quite effective and extremely simple to pay an optician a small bonus for selling a specific item, like the lens package. The reward has a high correlation with the desired behavior instead of being filtered by what all the co-workers do or don't do. We don't have the disappointment if we come close to a goal but don't quite make it. I track the sales of special items and I see a big jump in sales when we attach a spiff. Bonus systems work best when there is a high degree of correlation.

17.14 The Profitability of Multiple Pairs of Glasses

It's a neglected area in most optometric practices: the sale of multiple pairs of glasses to the same patient. At a time when most practices are looking very hard to find new profit centers, especially with the dominance of discount vision plans, most ODs sell very few multiple pairs. It is an opportunity for improvement and it can mean an increase of $100,000 or more to your annual net profit.

Read on for my three-prong approach to selling more second pairs of glasses... and third and fourth pairs.

An incentive for the patient
I've been doing this part for many years in my practice, but most ODs have not adopted the strategy of applying a deep discount to the second complete pair of glasses purchased at the same time as the first pair. I like the nice

round figure of 50% off on all additional pairs. My only rules are that the discounts must be on the less expensive pairs of glasses, they all must be complete pairs and the multiple pair discount may not be combined with other discounts. They may be combined with vision plans however.

The most important thing to do before offering the multiple pair discount is to make sure your optical prices are high enough. You need to still make a profit after the discount. Higher mark-ups in optical can help with general profitability as well.

This 50% off tactic alone helps us sell many multiple pairs of glasses. In no small way, we sell them because the discount makes our staff feel comfortable about bringing up the idea! I find many opticians do not feel comfortable talking about multiple pairs, but once the concept is presented, many patients go for it.

There are many efficiencies in selling two or more pair of glasses at the same time, which makes the discount more bearable. We take the measurements all at once, place the orders together, check the jobs in together, call the patient once, and dispense all pairs at the same pick-up visit. It is very quick.

Be sure to check with your wholesale lab about its policy on multiple prescriptions for the same patient. Many labs extend a 50% discount to your practice when ordering multiple pairs for the same person.

An incentive for your staff

I'm not usually very big on bonus or incentive programs for staff. I don't think they work as well as most people think and they can become a morale problem and create an entitlement mentality. But paying a bonus or spiff directly to the people who sell additional pairs of glasses does make a big difference. It does work. Of course, with a 50% discount already given to the patient, the bonus can't be extremely large, but it doesn't need to be. Five or ten dollars per pair works very well.

I don't really care that all employees don't share equally in this bonus opportunity. I think bonus programs that divide a pool of money equally are fairly weak. They don't usually do any harm, but they do not really change people's behavior because the reward is too abstract and the goal is not within anyone's direct control. But selling a second pair of glasses is directly within the optician's control, and the more they do it, the more money they earn.

If you want all staff members to have a goal, design a different program for the various departments. For example, front desk staff could be rewarded each day that is completely filled with patients.

Sales training for doctors and staff

Don't be offended by my use of the word sales. It is the most straightforward word and there is nothing wrong with it. We all sell our services and ourselves every day in a professional way. As a doctor, all I really mean is for you to prescribe the best eye care without regard for the cost. Don't prejudge patients and their ability to pay for what they want and need. The best eye care often requires more than one pair of glasses. You know this like the back of your hand. Simply prescribe for the patient's needs: computer glasses, sunglasses, TV glasses, golfing glasses; whatever the need is. Use the power of the doctor and recommend the best. Plant the seed.

For staff, you may want to provide more sales training. After all, your optical dispensary is a retail environment and you compete with some the best retailers in the world.

- Read books on sales techniques and share them with your staff. Present the core elements at a staff meeting.
- Bring a professional speaker into your office to present to your staff. Close the office for a half-day seminar.
- Send staff to some of the best optical sales programs in existence at Vision Expo or at meetings held by practice management groups.

Be sure to help your staff understand how important their contributions are to the profitability of the practice. As the practice grows, so does their career.

Train your staff to ask the patient questions when they start a frame selection. It is the best way to sell. Even if the optician already knows some of these factors, it is best to ask anyway and act like the answers are fascinating! After all, this is the patient's favorite topic: himself!

- Tell me how you use your eyes at work. What do you do?
- Do you participate in outdoor activities?
- Do you drive long distances?
- Do you use a computer or tablet very much?
- Do you have any hobbies?

Track multiple pair sales

We know that whatever you measure will improve, so track your multiple pair sales every month. Consider a contest or a goal with a reward that all the staff can have fun with.

17.15 Is Your Staff Too Busy to Sell a Second Pair?

We all know that prescribing and ordering multiple pairs of glasses for a patient is not only good for profitability, it is the best eye care. If glasses were completely free, how many would you recommend on average for each patient you see? I'm sure at least two pairs and very likely three or four! So why do most optometric practices wallow away in mediocrity when it comes to multiple pair sales? There are many reasons, but I think the biggest one is that the idea is often not brought up to the patient. Optometrists and opticians don't think about two pairs of glasses often enough. Let's look at the reasons for that and devise a plan to overcome it.

The huge impact of multiple pairs

First, let me motivate you to design a plan of attack on this topic. Vision plans have made it more important than ever to sell two or more pairs of glasses to each patient. With profitability reduced and capped on the first pair of glasses, we need to increase sales of second and third pairs. Even if you give the patient an aggressive discount on the second pair, you can easily produce a gross profit of $200 per pair of glasses. If you sell two more per day than you do now, you would generate over $100,000 per year in gross profit (after cost of goods).

The right number of staff

I have often found that hiring another employee boosts practice revenues and one reason for that is that sales go up. Observe your staff in action at several different points per day over the course of a couple of weeks. If the opticians are often busy and there is another patient waiting for them or there is lab work waiting for them, it is very likely they will not take the time to offer the second pair option. It takes a lot of time to select another frame, review the lens options and write up the order.

You may think you are keeping your expenses down by not hiring another staff member, but it may be false economy if you are losing sales because no one has time to sell.

Second pair discount

A strong incentive to the patient makes a huge difference in multiple pair sales. My practice offers 50% off the second complete pair of glasses and we have been doing it for 20 years. If you have fairly strong mark-ups to begin with on optical products, you can still make a very good profit on the second pair. And many wholesale labs will give you 50% off on the lenses of additional pairs for the same patient. It does not matter if the first pair is through a vision plan; we still want to sell the second and third pair.

The discount is an obvious incentive for buying the additional pairs, but it also gives my staff a reason and a duty to bring up the concept of a second pair. If they just bring it up, many patients will order two pairs.

Try a spiff
If you want to gauge the potential of multiple pair sales in your practice, offer your staff a spiff of $5 or $10 for each additional pair of glasses sold. I make these special bonus programs for a limited time and then it ends, like for one quarter. I found a big increase in multiple pair sales when I offered the spiff. I like to change the goal of the bonus program each quarter so the staff does not take it for granted and it stays fresh.

It can be difficult to track second pair sales because our practice management software does not differentiate first pairs or multiple pairs. But your in-office lab orders should be able to gather this data fairly easily. You should track it as a baseline before starting a new program so you can evaluate the success of a spiff, discount or additional staff members. To track the spiff program, I just have opticians and super-techs record their own multiple pair sales on an index card with the date and patient name. We just count them up and multiply by the spiff rate. Keeping one's own record continues to remind staff about how much they are earning.

17.16 Achieving a High Dispensing Capture Rate

Your capture rate (or retention rate, which may have a nicer ring to it) is one of the most important factors we can look at for practice profitability. There are plenty of optical retailers (both online and brick and mortar), that are working hard to attract your patients for their eyewear purchases. But you have the patient in your office first and you should be able to retain the vast majority of them when it comes to buying glasses.

Here are my top eight factors that lead to higher eyeglass retention rates:

- Start by measuring your capture rate on an ongoing basis. Design a routine that will automatically report this metric to you on a monthly basis. You can assign it to a staff member or use a business analytic software system. There are many ways to measure eyeglass retention rate, but the simplest and most widely used is to divide the number of eyeglasses sold by the number of refractive exams performed in a given time period. Details like the number of outside Rxs filled, the number of multiple pairs sold and counting pairs of lenses or complete pairs of glasses will have an effect on this measurement, but as long as you are consistent with your method, it won't matter much. The national norm for independent ODs is about 65%, but I would set a goal to reach closer to 75%. Of note with this metric is that it uses all refractive exams as the divisor and we all know that many refractions do not result in a change in Rx or a recommendation to buy new glasses. But refractions are a convenient and readily available data point, which makes it good to use.

- The doctor prescribes specific products and talks about them at chairside. Optometrists are historically very conservative when it comes to recommending products, but we really should get over that. Patients want our professional opinions and they want to know about the latest and greatest technology in eye care. Present the best eye care possible to your patient at the end of the exam. The more specific you are about lens features and the best types of frames, the more likely the patient is to buy them in your optical.
- Design a better handoff or no handoff. The transition from the exam room to the optical dispensary is the most vulnerable time in the patient relationship and this is when most patients decide to go elsewhere for glasses. Don't give them a reason to. If your optician is often not available when you are ready to do a handoff, you have a problem. You may need more staff or more cross-training of existing staff. You may need better support from staff to drop other tasks and take care of live patients. I avoid the handoff and the search for opticians completely in my practice by using super-techs, which are scribing technicians who are also opticians.
- Faster start and more efficiency. A major reason patients leave your office prematurely is that they have other things to do. They often say they will return for the frame selection, but once they leave, you will lose many optical sales. If you are taking an hour or more on the clinic side, some patients will have to leave without ordering glasses because they did not allot enough time. Speed up the check in time, reduce the waiting periods and increase exam efficiency.
- Tie in frame selection with dilation. Don't let the need to dilate pupils prevent the patient from ordering eyewear. Review how and when the drops are instilled and train staff to coordinate dilation and frame selection. Waiting for the drops to work is an opportunity

to use that time effectively in optical, but prioritize which steps to do first.

- You may already have this going for you, but it is very important to provide a great patient experience during the entire exam process. If that part goes extremely well, the patient will become loyal and want to buy glasses from your office. If something goes wrong, the patient may decide he can do better elsewhere for the optical products. It is a comprehensive, team effort to impress patients with the exam experience.
- It is easy to forget the obvious, but one big way to influence where your patients choose to buy glasses is the state of your optical. If you invest in it and make it more beautiful, larger, and better, people will decide early on that they want to get glasses from your office.
- Great looking value frames. When I ask ODs why patients take their Rx to go, by far the most frequent response is "price". I believe that is true. Most independent ODs will admit they are not the cheapest place to buy eyewear, but that business model serves us well. In addition to offering high end designer frames and premium quality lenses, you should also have a nice selection of value priced frames. Many ODs carry budget frames (and they are required by most vision plans), but some practices strategically make these styles outdated. I think that is a mistake. There are some very current and fashionable shapes and colors available at low price points and it is smart to carry those. If your staff can show the value line with pride, you can change a patient's mind about leaving.

17.17 How is your Dispensing Process?

Sometimes doctors and staff members are so close to the day-to-day operations of their practice that they can't see the forest for the trees. As the needs of the practice set in over time, it's easy to gradually stop working the vision of greatness you once had. I'm guilty too.

That's why we must step back and review key elements of the patient's experience. This week, let's tackle the delivery of new eyeglasses.

Is it special or mundane?

From the patient's point of view, new glasses are a very special event. As eye care providers, you and I wish it was not quite such a landmark event and that the public would buy them more often... but the fact is, they do not.

Patients don't think about the fact that you dispense and adjust hundreds of glasses per month; they just think about their new pair that will soon be on their face for the world to see. They hope it will make them look cool. They hope they will see really clearly. They view glasses as very expensive with a lot of technology they don't understand very well.

To maximize the patient experience and to garner as much positive word-of-mouth chat as possible, the act of picking up the new glasses should be made very special. Review the process as it is now in your office. Has it turned into a quick in-and-out visit with a busy optician? Does it seem routine and boring? Are the glasses treated like a commodity?

Tips for maximum dispensing

Consider these simple steps to make the most of the dispensing visit and make it memorable. You will elevate the importance of the eyewear and increase the perceived value.

- Trays to hold the eyeglasses. This is a great place to start and I think it is a must-have. The act of retrieving the glasses and carrying them to the dispensing table greatly affects the patient's perception. We place the eyewear on a black tray that is lined with black velvet. We train the receptionist and optician to handle the glasses as if they were expensive jewelry. We've all heard of this idea but most ODs don't bother.
- There are many sources for trays; just Google "jewelry trays".
- Get rid of the paperwork and plastic bags. Consider everything the patient sees and make it better. Most offices just put the glasses in a case and wrap the job ticket around it with a rubber band. They may be in a reused plastic bag. Then the case is placed in a drawer heaped with other glasses. The receptionist rummages around searching for the correct glasses and pulls out a pair.
- A better approach is to direct the patient to the dispensing table and then locate the glasses. Take the glasses completely out of the case and place them open on the tray. The glasses should already be clean of lab markings. Yes, I know those can be helpful in confirming the fit of a progressive, but the patient's impression trumps that in my view. It is rare that there is a fitting problem and you can always re-mark the lenses if needed. The dispenser carries the glasses to the table on the tray. Keep the paperwork separate – don't place it on the tray.
- Train dispensing staff to compliment the patient's new eyewear and be excited about the process!

Other niceties

Here are some ideas for additional items you can place on the dispensing tray.

- Place the eyeglass case on the tray, along with a cleaning cloth and a bottle of lens cleaner.
- A single chocolate truffle is a nice touch.
- A high quality business card with the optician's or doctor's name. You want referrals don't you? Be sure the card has the practice logo, web address and an email address.
- An office brochure is a possibility.
- A list of eyeglass features included on this pair of glasses. If patients know what type of lenses they have, they are more likely to talk about their new glasses to others. Their perception of quality and value is also increased. You could use a checklist that is preprinted with the practice logo on heavy paper stock. You could also generate a word processed document that is more customized, but the checklist has the advantage of showing and describing the lens features the patient didn't choose this time, but might next time. I like the form to specify which pair of glasses it pertains to and again, you could preprint the common options like: general purpose, sunglasses, computer/office use, driving glasses, etc. This promotes patients thinking of multiple pairs.
- These documents could be in a nice folder and presented separate from the tray. You could add the patient's receipt and eyeglass warranty form.

Make dispensing of new eyewear a fun and important event in your practice. Celebrate it and start the patient off with enthusiasm!

17.18 The Lost Art of Adjusting Eyeglasses

I'm very fortunate to have a really great staff in my practice. My office manager and I work hard to create a positive organizational culture and to provide excellent training programs. So, I was a bit surprised when my manager recently told me that we have a problem that is affecting our quality. She said many of our opticians and optometric technicians who dispense eyeglasses are not doing a great job with frame adjustments. This manager is an excellent optician herself and she noticed patients who returned for adjustments often did not have an ideal fit.

I understand how this can happen and I think the same issue may exist in many optometric practices. We try to hire highly skilled opticians, but we often can't find anyone. We try to hire people with extensive optical experience, but we also need to find the right personality and someone who is successful at selling. We have to watch the payroll budget as well and when an employee quits, we need a replacement relatively fast.

Along with these human resource challenges, we have seen a gradual decline in formal training in optical dispensing. There are still some excellent college programs in dispensing, but much of the training actually occurs on-the-job all over the country. Optometrists no longer have training in optical dispensing in school, so we have dwindling resources available for training staff members. Since we have lost some aspects of the art of dispensing, especially the frame adjustment part, we end up with new staff members learning from others who are not well-trained in the first place.

Start your own training program

I decided that my managers and I will make training on frame adjustments a high priority for our practice. We designed a program that will be presented over several weeks at special staff meetings and then we will continue to provide refresher courses a few times per year.

Hopefully you have one or more employees, who are still very good at frame adjustments, who can present a similar course in your practice. The doctor may have learned some dispensing skills and can assist in the design of the course and help with content. If not, you may have to invest in hiring a really great optician who can bring these skills to your office.

I should note that there are some excellent training programs for optical dispensing online and also at major eye care conferences. I use these resources in my practice and I recommend other ODs use them for new employees and to enhance the skills of veterans. But even with these large-scale educational programs, you should also have your own in-house training, because frame adjusting requires lots of hands-on practice with actual frames. You can't get good at it by reading about it or listening to a speaker.

Course format

Here are some ideas for how to develop your own training program on the art of adjusting eyewear.

- Write a course outline with the help of a skilled optician from your staff. This is easy! Just make a list of the common frame adjustment problems you see every day. Add bullet points on how to look for these problems and how to fix them.
- Use PowerPoint or other slide production software. PowerPoint gives your seminar a professional look while keeping your content organized. You can save the course and present it again to new staff in the future. Use your laptop or iPad and plug it into a computer monitor, large screen TV or a projector with a white wall.
- Add photos to your slides showing frames with problems and more photos of how to use tools to adjust them. Take some photos of poorly fitting frames on a person's face.
- Add slides with just text to make your points.
- Print handouts and give them out. Staff members need to have a reference to refer back to. You can print your PowerPoint as a handout.
- Have lots of frames in metal, zyl and rimless along with dispensing tools and a salt pan or hot air blower to use for demonstration. You'll also need nose pads and screws.
- Have even more frames that you don't mind if they break to allow lots of opportunities to practice. We collect used frames for mission trips on a continuous basis and some of these could be used for your training project.

Topics

You will come up with plenty of ideas on how to properly adjust frames, but here are a few thoughts to get you started.

- Start with what a properly adjusted frame looks like on a face. What is proper alignment and size?
- Once your staff can recognize a good fit, stress that they must achieve this at the time the glasses are ordered. Fit the frame at the time of the order so the patient gets the right size and shape to start with.
- Teach staff to inspect a frame in front of the patient before working on it and point out any scratches or defects. This prevents the patient from thinking the optician damaged the glasses.
- Know when to decline doing anything to the glasses, or get the patient's approval to try and if it breaks, the patient will bear responsibility.
- Many eyeglasses fit too tightly at the temples, which actually pushes the frame off the face. Pressure on the sides of the head is

uncomfortable. Teach your staff how to widen the frame temples when needed.

17.19 How Is Your Low-end Frame Selection?

I have written and lectured about the importance of carrying upscale frame lines and offering brand names that your patients want. Nationally known brand names are the best-selling frames in my practice and we also do well with high-end frame lines that are not as well known, but offer leading edge fashion. I think this is still a good strategy and these upscale lines provide the best profitability, but it is also important to have a great selection of lower priced frames.

You need a large range of frames prices to satisfy the diverse needs of patients. Most offices have a selection of budget frames, but in many cases, this group is designed to be undesirable in an effort to move people to buy more expensive products. I think it is smart to make your budget section larger and include styles that look current and cute. We want to prevent patients from going elsewhere to buy glasses, whether it be online or at big box optical stores. We want the entire patient experience to be great and we give them what they want! We expect patients to come back next year and to refer their friends and relatives to us.

Just what my insurance covers

Eye care professionals hate to hear those words, but be careful to not alienate patients by being too forceful or pushy in an effort to move them up to higher level products. Rule #1 in sales is to listen to the customer's wants and needs! We care about the entire patient experience and we try to say yes as much as possible.

My opticians usually start the frame selection process by showing some of the newest and best frames on display, but if a patient says he wants to see frames covered by insurance, we say "sure!" We have a large selection of frames in very current shapes, sizes and colors with a retail price of less than $200. Some are less than $100. The majority of frames in this section are covered in full by vision plans, but there are a few styles that would have a slight overage and we find most patients do not mind paying $20 or $30 more if they really love a frame style.

In some cases, since the patient is feeling happy about all this, he or she wants to see frames with higher price points and find out what their cost would be. The important thing is that we make the patient happy.

Closeouts and value lines

I find I can still make a good profit if we buy smart on our lower priced frame lines. We look for closeouts as much as possible by telling our frame reps that we are interested in them. Closeouts typically offer excellent style and quality from major frame manufacturers, but the models are being phased out. When a rep brings you an opportunity to buy closeouts, you must be ready to act quickly and think differently than you do with your usual frame lines. Think no returns and maybe no replacement parts, because these frames are being discontinued. That is OK though; the low cost makes it worth it. You will buy these frames in bulk. Maybe 100 or more pieces at a time. You may not even get to see the frames in advance. You may buy five or more frames in the exact same size and color.

Educate your staff to understand the value in these closeouts and be aware that opticians may avoid showing them at first because they are afraid that can't get replacement parts. You may raid the other frames on your board for parts as needed for repairs. You may have to let a patient select a new frame and make new lenses at no charge. This happens infrequently and does not bother me in the least.

We also do business with some frame vendors that specialize in low wholesale prices. They offer very low wholesale prices and go up to a moderate price point. As prices go up, the quality and styling improves, but we watch the price carefully and strike a balance.

Not the usual mark-up

We price our value line frames at various retail price points that are attractive to the consumer. We do not use our usual frame mark-up formula for the value lines because we buy them very cheaply, but we must remember that there are many optical services built into the retail prices. Eyeglasses are not like a sweater or other retail item where there is virtually no service at all. With eyewear, we need a trained professional to advise the patient on the products, measure and fit the frame, order the glasses and verify the accuracy of the Rx, dispense and adjust the fit, instruct the patient on use, repair and adjust the frame for life. We must have a strong mark-up on a low priced frame.

17.20 Measure Twice; Cut Once

I've always liked the old carpenter's adage mentioned in the title above. With great simplicity, this statement describes the essence of economy and efficiency when doing a job right the first time. I've recently applied this axiom to the optical department in my practice.

Appalled by the number of remakes of glasses my practice does every month, I analyzed the reasons for the do-overs:

- Seg height or PD measurement error by my staff
- Rx error by our doctors or transposition error
- Non-adapt by patient
- Lab error or quality problem in fabrication
- Warranty replacement of frame or lens (breakage or scratches)
- Optician damage
- Buyer's remorse

The first reason noted above caused a large percentage of remakes and it is the easiest for us to control. I'm targeting PD and fitting height measurement accuracy with a staff training program and a new "measure twice; cut once" policy.

Let's realize that not only are optical remakes expensive in staff time and material costs, but they also come at a high price in the loss of patient satisfaction and confidence. In many cases, we see multiple remakes occur with the same patient for the same pair of glasses, because the problem was not properly diagnosed the first time. This is extremely inconvenient for the patient and causes real harm to the practice reputation. The first remake due to a measurement error may be covered at no charge under a lab remake policy (with some limitations), but additional remakes are a significant cost to the practice.

Review of measurement methods

Basically, we have two methods for measuring glasses: digital and manual. The most critical measurements are PD and seg height, but digital devices add additional factors like vertex distance, pantoscopic tilt, wrap and other proprietary features.

From big, free-standing towers to desk-top units to iPad devices to cameras built into mirrors, I own and have tried many different digital measuring devices. Most of these work with a photograph of the patients face and eyes. I'll conclude that some systems work better than others, but all of them are just tools and when used properly by a well-trained optician, they all can produce accurate measurements. These devices have undergone many improvements over the past five years to speed up and simplify the process.

Our old measurement standard, which has come under much ridicule in recent years, is a pupilometer and a Sharpie felt-tipped pen. While these techniques are definitely old school, years of experience tell us they are accurate. Perhaps the simplicity of this method is more important than we first realized.

A good test of your own opinion about optical measurement methods is revealed by how you answer this question: Assume your optician measured a patient for progressive eyewear using a digital photographic device and measured again with a pupilometer and dotting the center of the patient's pupils on the demo lenses. Assume the measurements for the PD and seg height were different by at least 4 mm with the two methods. The patient already left your office. Which measurement method would you have more faith in?

I love the wow factor we get from the use of digital measuring devices and I'm well aware of the need to be perceived as up-to-date as we face competition from online vendors and new uses of technology. I also think the measurements we take for eyeglasses are important enough that we can do them twice. If they differ by more than 2 mm, we can redo them or get another opinion from another staff member.

Measure twice

I implemented a new procedure for ordering glasses in my office that requires my staff to measure the PD and fitting height by both a digital method and the old school method. Our optical order form now has a place for two measurements of the PD and seg height labeled digital and manual. The data produced by this is interesting to gather: how often are the measurements different and by how much? Interestingly, many of our technicians and opticians told me they were already doing the double measurements, but not recording them.

I believe this extra measuring step will significantly reduce our remakes.

17.21 Eyeglass Complaints: Let Them See the OD!

As optometrists, we are rightfully proud of our lens prescriptions that help people to see better and improve their lives. The vast majority of these prescriptions work out very well and patients are extremely happy. But, what about the glasses that are not working so well? As a percentage, this number may seem small, but many ODs are not even aware of the actual number per week. We may think we don't want to know about those unhappy outcomes and just let the staff handle them, but mistakes do happen and these patients deserve special attention to correct any deficiencies in their care. I'm convinced that many practices are damaged by weak efforts to work with unhappy patients.

How does your office handle eyeglass problems?
Many practices are set up with policies that make it a slightly difficult for patients with eyeglass complaints to see the doctor. With good intentions, most ODs empower opticians and other staff members to "do whatever it takes" to make patients happy! It sounds good, but what if the opticians don't know what to do? What if after all their best troubleshooting, the staff takes their best shot at fixing a problem and it turns out to not fix it?

Multiple attempts at remaking eyeglasses (without success) quickly cause the patient to lose confidence. It becomes clear that the practice does not know what they are doing. Unfortunately, this happens fairly often. Some of these patients will just ask for a refund and others will quietly find a different optometrist next time they need an eye exam. Virtually all of these patients will tell other people about their horrible experience. Optical labs may absorb the cost of one remake, but additional ones carry a product cost to the practice. Those outcomes cause real damage to the practice.

Let them see the OD!
In my opinion, we should make it much easier to see the prescribing doctor for a no charge recheck when the patient has a visual complaint with new glasses purchased from your office. If we really cared about the success of this patient, from both a clinical and business perspective, we would recheck all the major factors in the prescription. If we can fix the problem the first time and get it done quickly, we can save the patient relationship, help the practice reputation and keep cost of goods lower.

I think we should pull out all the stops in troubleshooting a pair of glasses that are not working well. I think we should let the optical staff work on the problem and also let the OD recheck the refraction and review the plan for the remake (seg heights, PD, base curves, lens material, brand, etc.). What is the worst that can happen? The OD might see a patient who could have been handled by the staff. To me, having better outcomes on these at-risk patients makes the office visit well worthwhile. The goodwill and confidence perceived by the patient is extremely valuable.

What are your roadblocks?
Optometrists today are increasingly delegating all things optical to staff. Some of these staff members have excellent training and skills in optical and some don't. Regardless of the skill level, a better outcome is achieved when two or more experts review the case and decide on the plan. ODs today do not receive as much training in optical dispensing as they once did, but that really does not matter. We still receive excellent training in the human visual system and the scientific process. That is what we need. Don't cop out and say you don't know anything about glasses. You know plenty.

Here is a quick checklist of factors that can impede a positive outcome:

- Is the doctor willing to see the patient?
- Can the patient be seen quickly? It may be necessary to hold back a few appointments per week or per day so urgent needs can be met. This includes any patients we want to see quickly, such as medical eye emergencies and new eyeglass complaints.
- Does the doctor or staff have an attitude? Does the doctor take the complaint personally, like a criticism of professional skill?
- Is the doctor defensive (assumes a position that he/she was right and the patient is imagining the problem)?

If the staff and doctor act as if they want to see the patient and they give no hint of annoyance, then no one will focus on whose fault it was. Move past that and don't be sensitive.

What kind of problems
Obviously, there are many optical problems that the staff can handle without the doctor. The main factor might be if vision is part of the complaint. If the complaint is frame fit, quality, product selection or frame comfort, the optician can handle it. If the complaint is about vision, I'd get the OD involved.

17.22 The Optician Who Is Not Great at Sales

I received a question recently from an OD about how to manage an optician employee who is not doing very well with optical sales. This optician does an excellent job in other respects: she is reliable, hard-working, loyal, and has strong technical knowledge about optical products. The employee is very well paid and the OD/owner has provided her with numerous courses and books on sales in an effort to improve her sales ability, to no avail. The office manager has met with the optician numerus times on this topic.

The first reaction by many ODs when faced with an employee who is not very good at selling is to structure an incentive or bonus program. The reasoning makes sense on the surface: if you reward a person with enough money, surely they will sell more. But relying on bonus programs to take the place of good staff management and training won't yield the best results. A bonus program could be helpful, but my first response is to ask about the one-on-one discussions the OD has had with the employee.

Employee chats

I'm amazed at how many times I speak with ODs who are unhappy about some aspect of an employee's job performance, only to find out that they have really not talked to the staff member about it. Maybe some practice owners are not comfortable with confrontation or maybe they don't know what to say, but communication with employees is the key to building a better staff. Here are a few points on how to meet with staff members with the goal of getting them to improve.

- Have the meeting in private. Job performance reviews are personal and could be embarrassing, so ask the employee to step into a private room and close the door. It is fine to have a manager in the meeting also, but that is not mandatory and you also want to avoid the perception of ganging up on the staff member.
- Telling the whole staff that some aspect of the practice needs improvement is not as effective as telling the main person who has an issue with it. It is fine to talk with all staff at some meetings, but when an issue is really with one person, set up a private chat.
- Start the first chat very carefully. Ask questions at first: how is the employee doing? Be prepared to hear another side of the situation and give the employee a chance to speak early. There are always two sides to every story and it is best to listen first.
- Staff members are quite sensitive to criticism. Mention some of the positive traits of the employee first. Project an attitude of caring and patience as you explain the factor that needs some work
- Try to have some general data to back up your criticism. If this optician's sales are not good, how do you know? Do you track sales for all employees? Is it based on sales from the prior year?

- Keep some notes of your discussion in a file with dates. The employee does not need to sign your notes or even be aware of them, but you can't rely on your memory and you need a record.
- At some point, you have to tell the employee what the problem is. This may seem basic, but you can't dance around the issue and never get it out in the open. Also, be sure to let the employee know that this is an important part of his/her job.
- Read on about how much of this to delegate to a manager.

Office Managers
I view office managers as a boss and one of their key duties is to train staff, so it is fine for office managers to hold the chat with the employee. It may even be preferable to the OD doing it. This is especially true when the talks are working and progress is being made. But if an issue with an employee becomes serious, I think the OD/owner should dig deeper and get involved.

In some ways, when an employee underperforms, the manager is implicated too. It may be partly the manager's fault, or maybe not, but I would be wondering and looking into it. It may be appropriate to retrain the manager at the same time you are working with the problem employee. In this way, the manager may be able to handle it next time.

Be an expert yourself
Providing outside resources like courses and books are fine, but I also believe it is my responsibility to simplify things and just tell the employee how to improve. It is up to me to be an expert first. It is up to me (and the manager I delegate to) to train the staff.

In this case about anemic sales, I would reflect on the key elements of selling. I would read a book myself if I needed help on a topic and then I would boil it down to become our system. I would not tell an employee they need to improve their selling techniques; I would tell them how I want them to improve their selling techniques. Then we can supervise the employee's efforts and provide feedback.

As part of my preparation for an important meeting and to train the optician the best way possible, I would listen (covertly) to him or her doing a frame selection with a patient. What does he say and do? What would I do differently?

For example: How to improve sales

So, how do we sell glasses? We sell by asking questions. That would be a key factor I would look for when I observe the employee.

If we ask questions about the patient's life, we will sell more glasses and more premium products. Many opticians do not ask questions at all, but they simply start telling the patient what their options are and why some products are good. Telling is not selling. Here are some examples of questions to ask:

- How do you use your eyes at work?
- Do you participate in any outdoor activities? Tell me about them.
- Do you have any hobbies or a secondary career?
- Do you use a computer, iPad or smartphone?
- (For multifocal patients) Do you watch TV? How do you sit?

Another factor to observe: Is the employee rushed (often needs to get to other patients/walk-ins) and does not have time to bring up the idea of a second or third pair of glasses? Does she always bring up the idea and recommend a second pair when you listen to her? Once you know the reason why sales are poor, you can find the remedy. If an optician is too busy to sell multiple pairs, you need another optician.

17.23 Form Your Own Frame Advisory Committee

In an effort to maximize sales and revenue in your optical in the coming year, let's do a comprehensive review of your frame inventory. The brands you carry, the size of the inventory and the price ranges offered are all key factors for optical success. The goal is to retain a high percentage of the prescriptions written in your office and to dispense multiple pairs to the same patient. Taken further, a great frame selection can become a competitive advantage for your practice and may serve to increase word of mouth referrals of new patients. Optical is far too important and generates for too much revenue to take a passive approach to the frame inventory.

Committee members
My idea is for every practice to form an advisory panel which will meet from time to time to analyze the frame lines and ordering policies and to make recommendations to the frame buyer. Every practice is different, but see if you can adapt the idea to fit your needs.

I think the following individuals would make great members on your frame advisory committee. I would look for about four people to serve, but the size of the practice will influence this.

- The optometrist / practice owner. Many ODs have delegated all aspects of optical and have little or no input anymore. I think that is a big mistake. The practice CEO should have an interest in the products the company sells and the optometrist has much to offer in the overall plan for the inventory – from styles to sizes to finances.
- The frame buyer. Most practices have a designated person to buy frames and this person naturally must sit on the committee. If you have a few people who handle this duty, select one for the committee simply to keep the number of voices reasonable.
- An optician or technician. The frame buyer is often an optician, but you may want to bring another one into the mix. We're looking for people who can tell us what frame styles we are missing and why patients decide to take their Rx out. The frame buyer can be slightly defensive about this and, even if that is not a factor, we want different points of view.
- A person with a strong fashion sense. This could be any of the three people above, but find someone who likes fashion, knows clothing fashion trends and the ins and outs of designers and brand names. It could be a spouse, a patient or a friend.
- Any other person who can give valuable input is welcome. Possibly a lab technician or the office manager.

The meetings

Start by holding an initial meeting for about an hour and then hold additional meetings as needed, but at least quarterly. The goal of the meeting is to develop a plan for your frame inventory that will increase eyeglass sales and profits. That comes from having the right frame for more people and from generating excitement among staff and patients.

If you use an inventory management system, have a current report printed for the meeting. Have a list of all the frame companies your work with including sub listings showing the frame rep's name and the brands that person carries. Indicate the retail price range of each brand and the approximate number on display. Include plano sunglasses, budget lines, safety frames and any other lines that do not have a rep. Also have a count of any understock on hand and bring any other data and forms that are used in optical, including pricing formulas.

If you have any data from patient surveys that pertains to frame selection, have that available. If you don't have any idea about patient satisfaction with your frames, you should develop a program to record some data for that. You must know the customer's wants and needs for your products and it is best to not simply guess. Of course, the people on your frame advisory committee work with patients every day, so they know the wants and needs including what is selling well and what you are missing.

Be sure to assign someone the job of taking minutes of the meetings and file the notes for later review.

Ideas to consider

Here are a few topics to consider for your first meeting. This will lead to more brainstorming which should result in more innovations for your optical.

- What patient categories are well represented and under-represented? Start by defining the style categories such as: elegant, conservative, funky, sporty, and business. Do you have an appropriate number in each category based on demand? What categories are you light in?
- Are there unmet needs for special sizes? Do you have an insufficient selection for the big man or the petite lady? What would appeal to teenagers? Seniors? What would you show if you needed a small bridge or a very long temple?
- You may have to work hard to seek out frames in some size or style categories because the industry is not serving that segment very well. For example, it is hard to find many styles with a deeper B measurement for full use of progressive lenses because current fashion favors the wider, shallower shapes. You may have to search catalogs and ask your reps, but when you find a few that meet this need, order heavier in those models.
- What is your current offering for economy frames covered by insurance? Consider your strategy to encourage patients to upgrade to better styles while still offering enough choices for those who want to stay within their allowance.
- What percentage of frames do you carry in various price levels? List your retail prices in $50 increments and calculate the percentage of frames that are in each one. Can you shift the percentages upward? What is the new high end for your market? Most offices underestimate the high end which limits sales potential. The best way to find out is to experiment with higher priced lines.
- What are some new hot brands that you hear about but do not carry? Shop upscale optical boutiques, read the ads in the optical magazines, attend Vision Expo East and visit the frame fashion booths. Do you carry anything that is exclusive in your territory?
- How do you currently know when to reorder hot sellers? How often do you need to meet with reps?

- What can you do to improve your displays and merchandising? Be creative. Is there a better way to group frames other than men, women and children? Possibly group by designer, color, or by patient type (executive, sporty, fun, high fashion, conservative, etc.)

A great frame inventory is more than just having a large number on display; it's about having the right frame for each person.

17.24 How Many Progressive Categories Do You Need?

Like most optometric practices, my office once offered three different levels of progressive lenses to our patients. Our opticians would review the features and benefits of the most advanced progressive and how it differed from premium and standard progressives. We always tried to start with the best, but many patients would still buy the lower level products to save money. Some of our staff members struggled with explaining why one level of progressive is better than another. Heck, even I struggle with that a bit!

Now, I'm simplifying our product offerings in our optical and I believe we are improving the patient experience, saving staff time and making a better profit margin on optical products. I asked myself why we give the patient so many choices about lens design and material when they are really not in a position to make the best decision. I don't think most patients really want to make those decisions and they do not enjoy the process. It is too technical for most patients. What if we just offered one progressive, one antireflective lens and let's consider something innovative for the lens material? Life would be better.

Progressives
Your lens design and brand of choice and even the optical laboratory may change from time to time, but you can simplify all that for the patient and just offer one progressive at one price point. You as the optometrist and practice owner can decide what that lens design should be and set the price wherever you see fit. We must remember that the prices for optical products also include a lot of professional dispensing services at the time of the sale and for years to follow. Our markups are higher than many retail products because of this built-in service.

Your decision on what lens to use can be based on a combination of factors such as visual performance, availability of various materials, professional experience and wholesale cost. You may use a different lens brand for private pay and for each vision plan. You may have a long corridor and a short corridor. But all of that can be behind the scenes with zero patient involvement. You could offer patients one progressive at one price and have a lens usage guide for your staff to use behind the scenes when the order is placed.

Antireflective

The same principle applies to antireflective levels of quality. Why offer the inferior product at all? We could just have one AR coating at one price. Of course, we strongly recommend AR on all eyeglasses. There may be some choices for the patient now with blue-blocking technology, but I would keep the choices to a minimum and not add inferior categories.

Vision plan options

What about participation with vision plans that offer many different levels of quality with each at a different co-pay and profit margin? We need to honor our provider agreements and make products available to patients who want them, but that does not mean we must review every product and every category. As eye care professionals (ECPs), we are permitted to give our recommendation to the patient on the best lens design for their prescription and visual needs. In my office, we start with the best and most advanced product in each category. In most cases, the patient is perfectly agreeable to that. If a patient asks for a lower priced option, we have those available also. We want patients to be happy and we work with them.

Lens materials

As ophthalmic lens technology has evolved, we are now presented with many options for lens materials, such as CR-39, poly, Trivex, high index 1.60, 1.67 and 1.74. Optometrists and opticians have their preferences and we don't always agree, but it can be very confusing when patients are asked to make a choice. This is another lens product decision that really is handled better by the ECPs in the practice and it can easily be made based on lens power. We can specify ranges of lens prescriptions and what lens material is advised. You could indicate if the sphere power is from plano to -1 we use this and -1 to -2 we use that and so on. You may feel that plus lenses should be made with different material.

Of course, some lens materials cost more than others, so simply build that into the base lens price. There is no need to burden the patient with all that; some prescriptions are more expensive than others because they require a different type of plastic. We always design lenses for the best combination of features, such as clearest vision with few distortions, thin and light weight, UV protection, etc.

Imagine how much easier the eyeglass ordering process could be if your optician said: "Mrs. Smith, the doctor has prescribed a progressive lens for you with AR. Let's select a frame." The time saved from all the lens discussions can be used to design a second or third pair of glasses. There will still be a few lens options that need to be offered in some cases, such as Transitions, the type of sun lens, task-specific glasses, and once in a while other special features, but I think simpler is better.

17.25 Dispensing Records: Practice Building Power

Leading companies recognize the value of data and they find innovative ways to collect it, but optometrists often don't keep any record of one of the major services they provide. Eyeglass adjustments, repairs and replacements are often treated as goodwill freebies in optometric offices, but they have some major hidden benefits. People visit your office every day for eyeglass services; read on for ways to use it to your advantage.

Optical record-keeping
Many ODs do not keep very good records of routine adjustments and repairs because it seems like it is not worth the time and effort. My practice used to be in that camp. After all, efficiency and speed is important to me and if we are not charging a fee for a basic frame adjustment or repair, then why bother pulling up the record? The issue of charging a fee for adjustments or limiting them to eyeglasses purchased at your office is a worthy discussion, but let's table that for now. By far, most ODs do not charge a fee for a basic frame adjustment at this time.

It turns out that even if you are not charging a fee, there are some big benefits to collecting some data about optical dispensing visits.

Why collect dispensing data?
Here are some practice building benefits of collecting data about routine dispensing visits:

- Use the face-to-face visit as an opportunity to check the date of the last exam and reactivate patients who are past due for eye care. This strategy alone will help fill your appointment schedule and it makes pulling up the record well worth the effort.

- Track the number of non-selling dispensing visits handled by your staff per month. The amount of staff time devoted to adjustments and repairs will stagger you.
- Track the number of no charge optical remakes performed by your practice; some covered by a manufacturer warranty and some not.
- See the number of optical remakes that occur with a fee charged and the amount of revenue generated though that service.

An idea for optical record-keeping
You can certainly keep dispensing records in your EHR system by having your staff use a laptop or other workstation, but I find paper forms to be far more flexible and efficient. Using an iPad or other tablet sounds great, but most software I've seen for dispensing visits requires the user to enter text in a freeform manner and tablets are not that easy to type on.

I designed a paper form that in a half sheet size (4.25 X 5.5 inch) and I had our printer make them in pads of 100 sheets. We use these at optical check-in to ask the visitor (patient) to print his or her name in the blank at the top. The form has check boxes that list the most common reasons for a dispensing visit, such as: eyeglass adjustment, repair, lenses are scratched, not seeing well, eyeglasses not comfortable and select new glasses or sunglasses.

The bottom half of the form indicates that it is for staff use only. It has blanks to handwrite the last exam date, recall date, and type of insurance. Check boxes keep a record if we advised the patient that they are past due for an exam and if an appointment was scheduled. We also have check boxes and blank lines to indicate if these specific glasses have a warranty, what type of work we did, and if any frame parts or lenses were ordered along with the pricing, if any.

We collect these forms and I review them at the end of the month and then they are scanned into the patient's EHR file. The paper is discarded after scanning.

17.26 Optical Dispensing: Quick Record Form

I had quite a few requests for the dispensing visit form I mentioned in last week's tip article, so I will provide it here.

The key point in using this paper record form is to make it easy for your staff to obtain patients' names when they drop in for a repair or adjustment.

These forms are in pads of 100 with a cardboard back and each patient can print his own name at the top. The size of the paper is 4.25 X 5.5 inches.

The staff can then look up the last exam date and the optician can let the patient know that he is past due for eye care and recommend scheduling an appointment right now. Other useful data can be collected and the form can be scanned into the EHR system.

Name of Practice and Logo
Eyeglass Adjustment or Repair

Patient Name, Date

Reason for visit:

- Eyeglasses don't feel comfortable / frame does not fit right / frame slips.
- Frame or lens is broken. Repair needed.
- Lenses are scratched.
- Not seeing well with eyeglasses.
- I want to select new glasses or sunglasses.
- Other

-- For Staff Use Only --

- Last exam date Recall date Type of insurance
- Patient notified Appt. scheduled
- Warranty status
- Frame adjusted: Successful Success uncertain
- Repair or replace: Nosepads Temples Front Lens R L both

Notes
Charges today
Shipping and handling
Total

17.27 Reusing Patients' Own Frames

In keeping with last week's tip on waivers, disclaimers and informed consents, I'll share another office form with you this week. As I stated, too many of these are a big turn-off to patients, so pick your battles carefully and adopt these only if they present a significant problem in your practice. I try to balance the need to keep things simple and positive with my desire to inform patients in advance of things they need to know. I have found that telling people in advance about our policies on such things as payment of fees, insurance plans, and warranty coverage works very well. It's always fair if it's known in advance.

Smaller offices can rely on a verbal statement, but with multiple technicians it can sometimes be hard to know if patients were really informed of a policy, or not.

We are always happy to re-use a patient's own frame, as long as it's in good condition and fits well. But there are a few technical issues about frame re-use that the average consumer is not aware of, and we must educate them. Our concern is the responsibility of breaking or damaging the patient's frame while in the process of placing new lenses into it. See the handout below for how we handle this.

We always inspect the frame first for defects or cracks, and we may decide that the frame is not in acceptable condition to accept new prescription lenses. In those rare cases, we show the patient the problem and decline to re-use it.

One final problem that exists when using the existing frame is that the patient may have to go without his or her primary eyeglasses while the frame is sent to the lab for new lenses. Since my office has an in-house surfacing and finishing lab, this is only a problem when a patient has a vision plan that requires the use of a vision plan lab.

As we point out defects in the old frame, the importance of a spare pair of glasses, and the sharing of responsibility of frame breakage, some patients change their mind and decide to select a new frame, which may be a smarter decision in some cases anyway.

Here is the handout we use whenever we place new lenses into a patient's own frame. A signed copy is kept in the patient record.

Policy for Placing New Lenses in Patient's Old Frame
We are happy to make new prescription lenses for your own frame if it's in good condition and fits your face properly. If we accept your frame for re-use, we pledge to use the utmost care in handling it. But in a small percentage of

cases, the frame material will be worn or brittle to the point that it will not support a new pair of lenses.

Please be aware that older frame styles are often discontinued by the manufacturer and replacement parts are usually not available. This presents a problem if the frame breaks and can't be repaired.

If your frame breaks during our lens insertion process, the lenses initially made for that frame cannot be re-used for a different frame style. We will make new lenses at no additional charge for any new frame you choose, but the cost of the replacement frame will be at your expense.

I understand and accept this policy.

Patient's signature, Date

17.28 Dilation and Frame Selection

My goal is to never hear the words: "My vision is blurry from those drops so I think I'll just come back on another day to look at frames." I'm sure most eye care practitioners have faced this issue due to the cycloplegic effects of mydriatic eye drops, but what are you doing about it? After all, if the patient needs a change in the spectacle Rx and wants to buy glasses, it's logical and efficient to instill the drops and proceed with frame selection while the drops are working. If activities occur quickly this can work out fine, but there are certainly cases where the drops interfere with the process.

Why care?
I'll come right out and say the main reason I work on this issue is to increase optical sales. Sure, the patient may come back and place the eyeglass order on another day, but a basic rule of salesmanship is to strike while the iron is hot. If a patient decides to buy glasses in my office, we'll see that it happens. It's really not difficult to achieve both pupil dilation and a frame selection at the same visit if, as long as the doctor cares.

If frame selection does not occur on the day of the exam, patients may...

- Change their minds and decide they don't want glasses.
- Decide to shop around.
- Forget much of what my staff and I recommended as frame and lens options for the new eyewear.

Additionally, new glasses may be a primary reason in the patient's mind for visiting our offices. My practice achieves high satisfaction ratings and referrals by caring about patient's wants and needs.

One technique

A simple solution that I often use is to instruct my assistant about which drops I'd like to instill. She places that bottle in her pocket and escorts the patient to the optical area. This works especially well with the use of scribes who also perform the frame selection, but that's certainly not mandatory. My technician proceeds with the frame selection process until the patient has narrowed down the choices and is close to a decision. Some people decide quickly while others take a long time, but we don't want to rush anyone. At that point the technician instills the drops with the patient still seated in the dispensing area. We have a tissue available and the patient simply leans his head back and it's done. The tech can then continue to finalize the frame choice, check the fit, take measurements, discuss lens options, enter all data needed for the order, write up all charges and complete insurance paper work. There are plenty of duties to use up most of the necessary dilation time. The patient is then worked back into an available exam room for the doctor to complete the examination.

Optical dispensing is simply too important to patient satisfaction as well as practice revenue to make frame selection a difficult process. It should be a fun experience for the patient!

Additional thoughts

- The blur from mydriatic drops causes problems mostly for hyperopes, although high myopes and astigmats can have problems seeing frames on their faces with or without drops.
- A virtual dispensing video system that allows patients to see themselves wearing various frame styles while wearing their habitual Rx glasses is a big help.
- A magnification mirror and good lighting is beneficial.
- The use of lens flippers with trial lenses of the right Rx (or pre-made with plus lenses) may assist when held in front of the new frames, although they do get in the way.
- I've heard of doctors inserting trial contact lenses to assist with frame selection in cases with a high prescription, and also as a way to introduce contacts to patients who might not have considered it.
- If the case is routine, the dilated fundus exam can be done when the patient returns to pick up the new glasses.

17.29 Don't Rush the Frame Selection

I recently asked readers for some suggestions on tip topics they would like to see covered and I received some very good ones. More are always welcome, but read on for this tip from a colleague who has had the opportunity to work in many practices. He makes an excellent point.

Reader email

I am a private practice owner of two years and an avid reader of your tips. Before purchasing my practice, I used to do a lot of fill-in work and I think this tip would be helpful for many ODs. Basically, I am amazed at how many ODs really short-change the eyewear selection experience for the patient. The patient is often dilated and given 15 minutes to select frames and make lens choices before being hustled back to the exam room, or it is rushed because the schedule doesn't allow adequate time before office staff leaves for lunch, or people are running vacuums, and covering equipment, etc. at the end of the day. Or, the doctor tries to squeeze in a comprehensive exam and visual fields, review findings and adjust therapy, then have the patient (dilated, blurry, and tired) try to select eyewear...the result being "just give me what I had last year"!

At my office, we schedule plenty of time while the patient is fresh to do the eyewear selection, offer complementary CLs for the high Rx patients, and for new patients (if we get good VA and feel OK with health screening) we schedule a separate visit for the DFE so the patient doesn't feel rushed. At the very least, we dilate AFTER the frame selection. We also always make VFs a separate visit from refraction/eyewear selection, and make every effort to run on time at the end of the day. We also have a policy that the radio stays on and there are no visible "end of day" procedures going on that could subtly make patients feel rushed as the end of the day approaches. I feel this has made a significant difference in our average optical sale.

My thoughts

This reader basically wrote this tip article for me, which is much appreciated! I have seen many practices that follow the examples provided and I have had to work on the procedures in my practice to avoid these mistakes.

It's easy for ODs to let other tasks supersede frame selection because we delegate the frame selection process, so it is easy to not give it much thought. Another reason is that we consider the eye exam to be the most important factor in the patient's visit. I think we can all agree that ocular health is most important, but that does not mean we need to neglect optical dispensing. For most patients, we can provide a thorough eye health exam and give the patient plenty of attention.

- Don't waste time in the exam process. If you take too long on the clinical side, the patient will need to leave and will rush through the optical. He may say the dreaded "I'll just come back some other day when I have more time."
- The patient only has a limited amount of time for the entire visit. Some personal chit-chat is good, but too much can hurt your bottom line.
- Don't dilate too quickly. In my practice model, which uses scribes who also do the frame selection, the technician often takes a bottle of mydriatic eye drops with her in her pocket to optical. When the frame selection is nearly over, the tech instills the drops right there in optical.
- Consider having the patient select frames before the exam when there is more time and the patient is fresh. Especially if there will be a slight wait before starting the exam.
- Have plenty of staff and train them to not rush. Selecting second pairs of glasses takes more time. We want them to do that, right?
- Reappoint for special testing, like visual fields, OCT, medical photos, etc.

17.30 Pick One Thing: Frame Selection

As we continue with my "Pick One Thing" (and get really good at it) series, this week's topic is a really big one. So big, we will devote two articles to it. Frame selection (and I will include lens design here) is really the essence of optical dispensing. This includes the sales aspect of optical and that drives a huge part of practice revenue; usually about 50% of gross revenue.

The other reason that frame selection is such an important part of the patient experience is that patients care so much about it. Many patients still see their family optometrist to obtain routine refractive eye care and new glasses. They want to see clearly, but they also want a new look that freshens up their self-image.

Most ODs today are increasingly embracing medical eye care, which is a great move for many reasons, but I caution these doctors to not lose sight of the importance of optical dispensing and to remain actively involved in it.

Evaluate it

While I firmly believe in investing a portion of profits back into the practice to make it great, I'm also a strong proponent to starting small and modest in order to generate profits quickly. That is the way it is with optical: the practical budget aspect may limit what you can do in the early stages, but don't become complacent and drift along in mediocrity for a long time. Think big and think great.

Frame displays

The frame displays and general office décor have a huge impact on the perception of your optical by the patient. Many offices start out with a do it yourself approach in optical, but it is smart to obtain the professional skills of an interior designer, either as a free-lance advisor or by using one of the optical display companies who employ these experts.

Frame inventory

I believe optometrists need a larger frame inventory than most of them have. I know it is expensive, but people want choices and it is not very difficult to find more choices at the local mall or online if their family OD seems small and out of date. Investing in your optical pays off with increases sales.

To do a good job in frame buying, start by considering your target market. What does your patient base usually buy from you? What are the demographics of your community and what are the opportunities? It is smart to carry some high end frame lines to stretch the price points that you think are in the normal spending range of your patients, but you also need a good selection of value-priced frames to prevent price-conscious buyers from waking out with their Rx.

Most practices need several choices of well-known fashion designer name brands, but they also do well with the lesser known, independent labels that have shapes and colors that do not look like every other frame on the boards. Of course, you need styles that are designed for men, women and children and a nice selection of sunwear.

To accomplish all this really well, you need about 800 frames as a minimum and maybe 1,200 or more when your practice is in a growth mode from medium to large. Part of the challenge of larger frame inventories is often the lack of office space. After all, we don't want the frame boards or shelf systems to be packed with frames! We want to break up the rows of frames with product displays, branding materials, merchandising, mirrors, posters, and all the tools you see in nice retail stores. See if you can add more space to your existing optical and make it a priority in your floor plan the next time you move to a new office.

Review Your Resources

Much of the success of your optical lies with the people on your staff. Designing and fitting the right pair of glasses takes knowledge and skill. Optometrists are busy professionals and many believe in fully delegating all aspects of optical, which I think can lead to problems. In my view, the independent OD who owns his/her practice must be competent enough (and interested enough) in optical dispensing to be able evaluate the opticians who work there. If you are one of the ODs who has not paid attention to optical, now is the time to dive in. Set up some meetings with your opticians and start asking questions. Gather some data about your optical product sales. And find time to take a seat in your optical way off to the side and act like you are working on your laptop, but really observe and listen.

The handoff

The transfer of the patient from the clinical side of the practice to the retail side is crucial. Patients are observing this closely as they decide what to do about buying glasses. They often missed what the doctor said at the end of the exam, so this is a chance to hear it again and decide what to do. The patient also obtains clues about how well the office operates.

Time is a big enemy in the handoff. If patients are frequently left to wait for an optician and browse on their own, many will think about it and decide to wait. Many patients will say they will come back when they have more time, but never do.

Optician skill levels

In start-up practices, it may make sense for the optometrist to serve as the optician. Don't be shocked; owners must do all kinds of tasks in a start-up. But hopefully it will not take long for that approach to stop being economical and then it makes sense to hire a well-trained, experienced optician. Eventually, with more growth, the practice needs several opticians to handle the flow of patients.

Not every employee who works in optical needs to be a master optician. Some optometric technicians also serve as opticians. Some staff members are trained as frame stylists and they understand optical products and can take basic measurements, but they do not have the skills to handle complex prescriptions or troubleshoot optical complaints. Always follow your state law if opticians are required to be licensed.

Evaluate the skill levels of your current optical staff and provide training and support if there are areas of weakness. Some opticians are very skilled on the technical aspects of optics, but may not be good at selling or may have poor people skills. Identify the needs of your practice and get the right people.

17.31 Pick One Thing: Frame Selection, Part Two

In my last article, I covered the basics of frame selection, but focused more on how to set up your optical. In this issue, we'll cover the sales aspect and the patient experience.

Is it OK to "sell"?
"Selling" has long been a very sensitive word in optometry. After all, doctors do not sell. I understand that point of view, but the act of selling can take on many different forms and times are changing. In the world of eye care today, when a patient moves from the clinic area to the optical area, the patient moves from health care to retail. Selling does not have to be in conflict with the patient's best interest or with the doctor's professional philosophy. You and your staff can take a very low-key approach to selling and be very successful. Selling in optical is really more about patient education, which is actually part of our duty and if we educate well, the products sell themselves.

In many ways, we don't sell anything. Rather, we help the patient buy.

Go back to your mission statement
The highest level of optical sales occurs when the doctor and optician work together. Great success occurs when the doctor recommends specific optical products to the patient in the exam room during the summary of the visit. This summary should include eye health issues as well as eyeglass, sunglass and contact lens recommendations. The optician should be quite capable of supporting and fulfilling these recommendations. Or, if there are no recommendations from the doctor, the optician can and should make them.

When I work with doctors and opticians on selling, I remind them of the mission statement of their practice. Just follow that. For most independent practices, most mission statements have some element about providing the best eye care in the region. It would be very unusual for the mission statement to be that the practice is designed to provide the cheapest eye care (although, if that is the mission, then follow that). If your goal is to provide the best eye care, then all I ask is to recommend that and design glasses based on that. If you are providing the best for the patient, then you want to update the lens Rx to be the best. And you would prescribe premium progressive lenses in high index with a premium AR. And the glasses would include a new frame of high quality and good looks. And the best eye care would probably include a second pair of glasses for sun wear or other purpose. That would be the best glasses, so always start with that.

It is up to the patient to let us know if there is a financial issue and if they do, we have alternative options that we can go to. But let's presume the patient wants the best. It is not our job to save the patient money. Remove money from the equation unless the patient brings it up. We all know, but need to be reminded, that to prejudge a patient is rude and somewhat discriminatory. And you will often be wrong in your assumption about a person's wealth or spending habits.

Sales techniques
There are many books and courses on selling and I recommend them, but I can boil selling down to extreme simplicity, which makes it easy to remember in a busy office. If your opticians will do the following two things, they will be very successful in selling:

- Ask questions first – then show product.
- Put on a big smile.

Asking questions gets the patient talking about himself and it creates a relationship. The answers to the questions provides the needs that you can fill. Try these questions:

- How do you use your eyes at work?
- Do you use a computer, laptop or tablet?
- Do you participate in outdoor activities?
- Tell me about your hobbies; what do you do in your free time?

The big smile may be the harder task, but enthusiasm sells more than anything else. It is not that hard to smile. Just make yourself do it and you'll see what I mean about how it impacts sales. Get excited about what you are showing. If you are not smiling, you are moping.

The "yes… but" technique
We all have tough patients at times, who seem very resistant to following our recommendation for optical products. An example is the patient who says: "I just want what my plan covers." Or, "I just want my eyeglass Rx."

My favorite response is to agree with the patient first and say "yes... but."

Using this technique, a possible answer might be: "Sure, Mrs. Smith, we can select a frame that is fully covered by your vision plan, but I also want you to know that if you are willing to pay a few dollars over your benefit, it opens up many more style choices that you might like and you'll get better quality. Can I show you few options that are less than $20 over your allowance? We just got this new frame line that is so cute." If Mrs. Smith sticks to her preference of a fully covered frame, then we help her with that. We can try once, but we are not pushy. We care about the patient's wants and needs.

We always agree first, like this: "Yes, Bob, we will give you a copy of your prescription and you can buy your glasses anywhere you wish." This disarms the patient and gives you a chance to offer one more statement that might change his mind:

- "But, remember that not all optical vendors are providers for your vision insurance like we are. And you have an excellent plan that provides an eyeglass benefit worth hundreds of dollars."
- "But, we have a great selection of very affordable frames in the most current styles. They start at $95; would you like to see them before you go?"
- "But, we would love the chance to earn your business. If you don't mind my asking, is the reason you want to buy glasses elsewhere due to price, selection, or the quality of our service?"

Chapter 18. Associate Optometrists

18.1 Exit Strategy and Associate ODs

Deciding on the correct management strategy is difficult in any business and ideas that seem good on the surface often have an unexpected down side. I acknowledge that any of my top ten misconceptions can work in certain practice settings and with the right leadership, but I also want to point out that taking the opposite approach can also work well; often better in my experience. I like to challenge the popular wisdom and make us all think about the strategies we adopt.

Based on the number of requests I received for further explanation, I'll cover what I listed as the number one misconception: It is smart to bring in an associate to buy into my practice earlier in my career so I have a secure exit strategy. I think this one is important because there is a lot of money and professional happiness at stake.

A popular scenario
Understandably, there is quite a bit of concern over exit strategy among eye care practitioners who are nearing the midpoint of their careers or beyond. Here is a typical scenario: a solo OD realizes that his successful practice is an asset that has considerable value. While he or she is not quite ready to retire yet, the equity that has accumulated in the practice is somewhat intoxicating. Many practices sell for 50% to 75% of annual gross revenues, which looks pretty good! Around this time, the practitioner is also getting tired...

- Tired of seeing so many patients
- Tired of staff management hassles
- Tired of taking a vacation and realizing that it is doubly expensive because practice income basically stops during the absence
- Tired of working evenings and Saturdays
- Tired of everything in the practice depending on the owner

The thought occurs that if you brought in a junior partner, you could sell a portion of the practice now (who couldn't use the cash?) and have a buyer in place for the rest of the practice in the future. Pretty neat! My advice: don't do it.

Here is the flaw: by cashing out a portion of the practice, you also lose a large part of the income stream. After all, your new partner just put up big bucks to buy in and he or she has a right to a prorated share of the profits. One must question which is more valuable, the one-time sale of part of the practice, or the future years of maximum cash flow. One more negative factor in the popular scenario of selling part of the practice well before retirement: you end up with a partner who will not always want to run the practice the way you do. All business decisions from now on must be agreed upon.

Dividing income among partners

There are all kinds of reasons that partners become unhappy, but let's look into one of the big reasons for dispute: money. Partnership net income is typically divided based on a formula that attempts to be fair to all. When we think about being fair, it seems logical to say that some of the income should be divided based on productivity. If one doctor works more hours or is simply more gifted in generating revenue, he or she should be rewarded. Good business in theory, but it also creates some potential problems.

- The doctors end up in an unspoken competition for patients, which are probably in short supply since a one-doctor practice became a two-doctor practice. Competition between partners is a recipe for disaster.
- The senior doc usually has a large and loyal patient base, but he finds himself reluctant to facilitate the transfer of some of them to the new doctor. To do so would jeopardize some of his personal income. And the reasoning follows that the senior doc had to build his following, why shouldn't the junior doc do the same? Some resentment about the new generation of ODs not being what it used to be follows.
- The office staff has more loyalty to the senior doctor and they soon get the message that the senior doc should be kept busy with appointments. The junior doctor can feel alienated by the staff.
- The senior doctor can't reduce his patient schedule without reducing his income, which causes him to continue on the road to burnout. He still can't take a long vacation or reduce his number of days in the clinic.
- The junior doc is not seeing enough patients and is not making enough personal income and he's unhappy with his role in the practice.

An alternate plan

In my opinion, a better route for the senior doc is to hire an associate optometrist on an employment basis. Contrary to old school opinion, there are many excellent doctors out there who don't want to own a practice or worry about the business aspects. One doesn't have to offer ownership to attract a good doctor to the practice. There are many clinicians who just want to take care of patients and they would like to do so in a professional private practice environment.

Here are some tips for success with employed associates:

- Pay the doctor well. Associates brought in on a partnership track are often paid fairly low salaries at first because they will soon be gaining ownership. But if the plan is for the new doc to be an employee, it's not fair to offer that low compensation and you won't be able to retain a good doctor if you do. There should be plenty of new revenue to pay the associate well and still allow the owner to make a nice profit from that work. If there isn't, you aren't busy enough to hire an associate or your fees are too low.
- Offer excellent employment benefits. High level employees, like doctors, expect it and deserve it.
- Make the new doctor busy. There is no competition felt with a doctor who is paid a salary. It behooves the practice owner to keep the associate's schedule full and to foster efficiency through staff delegation. One of the best ways to achieve this is for the senior doctor to take himself out of the clinic schedule one or two days per week. The increased backlog of appointments for the senior doc encourages more patients to move to the new one. Some will move. These days off can then be devoted to practice management, which results in more practice growth!
- Don't expect practice building efforts from the associate. Unlike the days of old where the associate had to build his or her own following, the practice should bear most of that responsibility. That's one of the perks of being an employee. Of course, just providing good patient care will result in some practice growth, and that is the associate's responsibility.
- Give the associate professional freedom. It's OK to expect continuity of services, fees and office policies, but allow associate doctors to exercise their own clinical judgment with patients, listen to their input and be responsive to their needs.

Selling the practice

The best time to sell most optometric practices is when the owner is truly ready to retire completely. Ironically, that might be at an older age if employed doctors are brought in to see patients. The owner avoids clinical burnout and may be happy pursuing the management responsibilities of the practice longer than anticipated. We may not know who will eventually buy a practice, but if it's profitable and well-managed, it will have value and some entity will want it. In the meantime, selling a portion of a practice early in one's career is like killing the goose that laid the golden eggs. The years of the greater income stream are often more valuable and the practice equity is still there upon retirement.

18.2 Your Goal: Adding an Associate OD, Part 1

For many optometrists who own practices, hiring an associate OD should be one of the ultimate goals. This is the first step in achieving the CEO of your practice model. Adding an associate allows you to quickly increase practice revenue and net income while allowing you to spend less time on patient care and more time on practice management.

When to do it

It takes a lot of work to prepare a practice to successfully add an associate doctor, but it is so worth the effort. The main requirement is lots of patient demand, so you may need to reassess your goals and your marketing plan. In my view, it is the responsibility of the practice (and the owner) to provide a strong supply of patients for the associate right from the beginning. With this approach, the associate OD is fairly busy right away and generates a large increase in gross revenue without taking away any personal income from the practice owner. The factors to look for are: how far ahead is the senior doctor booked and how many patients does he/she currently see?

To consider bringing in a full time optometrist, I like to see a practice that already uses a system of high delegation to clinical technicians, sees at least 20 patients per day (all types of exams) and is booked ahead at least seven days solid. Greater patient demand than that is even better. Less demand than that may be sufficient for a part time associate. If the practice owner wants to reduce his/her clinical work days per week, that will increase patient demand for the associate, but it also reduces personal income for the owner somewhat because the owner will be paying the associate to see those patients. Regardless of that, if there is excess patient demand there will be plenty of new revenue to cover the new doctor's compensation and create additional profit for the owner.

I don't believe the old model where the new associate is expected to build his or her own patient following is a good approach. This method usually does not produce enough income for the new doctor to make a living. Increasing the patient demand can take longer than expected. If the established OD is not seeing enough patient demand, it is hard to imagine that the new OD will be able to attract a significant number of new patients.

How to increase patient demand

For most practices, patient demand is the limiting factor to being able to hire an associate. If that is true in your practice, it may be time to step back and reevaluate your marketing plan. What would it take to attract more patients in your community? If your goal is to attract far more patients than needed to just keep your schedule full, what can you do? What big changes can you make? Consider these points:

- Vision plans. While many ODs believe the smartest way to build a practice is to avoid participation in vision plans; that philosophy may change if the goal is to bring in an associate. Vision plans can provide a fast increase in patient flow.
- The medical model. Be sure you are actively providing medical eye care and billing Medicare and medical insurance plans.
- Customer service. Making your practice convenient and easy to do business with can have a profound effect on patient demand through word of mouth referrals. Ask yourself the tough questions like how many evenings and Saturdays are you open?
- A larger, nicer office. This requires a financial investment and some time, but moving to a better office is one of the most powerful marketing strategies I've seen. Make your optical better also.
- Referral sources. Can you build a network of physicians or educators or business leaders who will recommend your practice to others?

Financial aspects

I prefer to pay associate ODs a straight salary, which is contrary to how many practice owners want to do it. Many owners I speak with want to pay some kind of percentage of production. The biggest problem with paying a percentage is that no one really knows how much money that will be. In the early days after joining the practice, the production will be low and the income may be insufficient. A few years later, I would expect patient flow to be quite good and production will be very high, which means the compensation could be much higher than the going rate for an employed OD.

I believe a fair salary and benefit package is the best way to go. Raises are provided on a yearly basis, commensurate with performance. Employment benefits for full time doctors should be quite generous including health insurance, paid time off, paid holidays, continuing education expenses, AOA dues, retirement programs, malpractice insurance, etc. Part time doctors are typically paid on a per-day or per-hour basis and typically no benefits are provided.

What about incentives?
I don't think associate optometrists need a financial incentive; they just need to practice excellent eye care. I control the production of the associate OD by controlling his or her patient schedule. If I can fill the doctors schedule (or nearly fill it), the financial production will be there. Tracking the gross revenue per exam is a good way to monitor production and if that metric is significantly below the owner's performance, the reasons should be determined followed by discussions and mentoring. Ultimately, if a doctor's production is sub-par, he or she may not be the right person for the job.

I'll present Part 2 on this topic next week and I'll cover topics such as finding the right doctor for the job, preparing your practice for the change and more.

18.3 Adding an Associate OD, Part 2: Recruitment and Preparation

Last week, I wrote about the wonderful opportunity that exists for your practice when you can bring on an associate optometrist. In this article, I'll cover additional details that will help you make your group practice a big success.

How to find associate doctor candidates
As with any employment position, when you want to recruit a doctor for your practice you need to get the word out. Start by writing a position available ad that can be posted in several media outlets. I would describe the job available including the name and location of the practice, the type of practice and specialties, full time or part time and who to contact and how to send the curriculum vitae (resume). Try to sell the position by describing some of the desirable things about the city or region and the practice. If you are located in an area that has difficulty attracting a doctor, plan to pay a higher salary and indicate that in your ad.

There are many resources available to list your position available. I would use them all:

- All the schools of optometry have a placement service and they have graduates from all over the country. I would send your employment ad to all the schools.
- The AOA placement service is Optometry's Career Center, which is now part of the ExcelOD.com website.

- All the state optometric associations have a newsletter or magazine to communicate with members and they accept job position available ads. State associations are especially good because the readers are fairly local to your practice.
- There are many online job search websites, such as Craig's List and even optical-specific services like LocalEyeSite.com.
- Consider attending any "meet the students" events that may be hosted by professional organizations and schools of optometry.
- Use your network of colleagues and business associates. Let other ODs know you are looking and ask them to refer anyone who may be interested. Perhaps you know a doctor who is doing fill-in work and might like a steady position; if so, call him or her. Ask your sales reps if they know any ODs looking for a new job opportunity.

Is there a buy-in opportunity?
Decide well in advance if you are looking for a future partner or an employed doctor. It is important that you not mislead a candidate by agreeing to consider partner of the practice in the near future if you are not truly ready for that step. Even an offhand comment that you are open to the idea of someone buying in can be construed as a promise. Don't let the excitement of a good prospect make you say things that are not true. A good response to the question might be: "At this time, I'm only offering an employment position." There are plenty of excellent doctors out there who do not want to own a practice. Many optometry graduates just want to be good clinicians and do not want the risk and headaches of ownership. A good, private practice of optometry is very appealing as a career option.

How to prepare for another doctor
When your practice is ready for an associate OD, you have an opportunity to change some aspects of your practice for the future. It is far better to state the things you want during the interview process and when you make an offer than to come to your associate some time later and try to make a change. Your negotiating strength is when you are making the offer. The policies and procedures in place when the new doctor starts becomes the agreed upon norm, even if they are not written down. So set your policies the way you want them to be before you start the relationship.

Even though you will have great respect for your associate and treat him or her very well, don't be a pushover and give in on everything. Stand firm on the factors that are important to your practice.

- Office hours. Bringing in an associate is often the best time to expand your office hours and offer some evenings until at least 7pm and every Saturday. Yes, you will have to arrange staff coverage for the expanded hours, but that is not so hard. Offering convenient hours is a huge practice builder.

- Lunch breaks. Set the rules in advance. The new doctor is an employee not a partner.
- The appointment template. Even though you won't be able to completely fill the associate's schedule right away, the new doc should know what the appointment schedule will be and should agree that she can handle the very busy flow. Some doctors can't or won't see three patients per hour and you should know that and decide if it is a deal-breaker.
- Emergencies during office hours. I think the new doctor should see all emergencies. Is he ready and willing to do that?
- After hours on call. How will you handle phone calls after hours and emergencies? Will you share that responsibility? I don't think any doctor should meet a patient at the office alone after hours; we don't get paid enough for that for one thing. But we should take the phone call and give advice over the phone.

18.4 Adding an Associate OD, Part 3: Transferring Patients

In this third part of my series on adding an associate optometrist, I will cover how to transfer patients who have traditionally seen the senior doctor over to the new doctor.

As I mentioned in the first part of this series, having a backlog of patients of at least one week of solid appointments is an important prerequisite for bringing on a full time associate doctor. If you are fortunate enough to have that and if you hire an OD, how do you get those loyal patients to see the new doctor instead of you? Read on and I'll provide some tips for that.

I believe it is the responsibility of the practice (the owner and office manager) to fill the new doctor's schedule. Sure, some patients will like the new doctor and will refer their friends and family, but I don't think it is a good approach to assume the new doctor will build his or her following from scratch. They need to be fairly busy fairly fast for the employment relationship to work financially. The senior doctor should want to move as many of his patients to the new doctor as possible. If you are not sure on that point, you may want to reassess the plan for an associate. There should be a non-compete restrictive covenant in place (if allowed by law) to prevent the associate from leaving the practice and soliciting the patients.

Get staff on board

Once the senior doctor is on board with the goal of trying to move patients to the associate, the next job is getting the staff on board. Many staff members are not sure what they are supposed to do when patients call to schedule an appointment for an eye exam. You need to tell them clearly and repeat it often that the goal is to fill the new doctor's schedule. The staff should work hard on that goal. Keep in mind that staff members naturally think the senior doctor is the best doctor in the world. They know that the patients love the senior doctor and since the staff want to do their best for each patient, they tend to offer those appointments first. Tell the staff that for business reasons, you want to move patients to the new doctor and discuss the factors below as tools for that.

Tactics

We always want to honor the patient's choice of doctors, but we need to be creative in finding ways to help the patient accept the new one. Here are a few ideas:

Make the new doctor the only doctor who is available for highly desired appointment times. Schedule the new doctor to work a couple of evenings per week until 7pm or later and every Saturday. Early morning appointments are also in demand. The senior doctor should no longer work these hours at all. These are the easiest appointment slots to fill and the new doctor will quickly be very busy during these times. Don't be too worried that the new doctor (and many staff members) will have a work schedule they don't like, it is really not that bad. When employees work a couple of long days and 8am to 1pm on Saturdays, they get a day off during the week and still reach their 40 hours. If you want to build your practice, you need to be convenient for the public; especially those patients who have jobs!

- Reduce the senior doctor's patient care schedule. If the senior doctor usually sees patients four days per week, cut it to three days when the new doctor comes on board. This increases the senior doctor's backlog and makes it more convenient for some patients to switch. Some patients will want to stay with the senior doc and that's fine; he is still available if they don't mind waiting.
- Sell the new doctor. Teach your staff to say something good about the new doctor when patients call to schedule appointments. Start by offering an appointment with the new doctor first by saying: "Dr. Smith has an opening at 4pm on Thursday." If the patient has

questions about Dr. Smith, reply with: "Dr. Smith is a wonderful doctor. Our patients just love her! She is so nice and she has excellent training. She is my eye doctor now as well!" Avoid positioning the associate as second best.

- If patients act unsure because they always have seen the senior doctor, your staff can reassure them that they can see the associate doctor this time and return to the senior doctor next time. There is no problem with seeing either doctor and they share all the records.
- You could have the associate doctor see all urgent squeeze-in visits. These patients need to be examined today and they really don't have much choice if the only doctor available is the associate.
- The senior doctor could refer some of his patients directly to the associate and reappoint them for her. Let the new doctor be an expert in some areas. Consider dry eye, ortho-K, vision therapy, and glaucoma as some possible specialties to refer in office.
- Preappointing is very popular, but there are some drawbacks and one is that it is harder to move patients over to a new doctor if they have an actual appointment with the senior doctor. It is just bit awkward for the staff member to suggest changing doctors. If the patient is calling for an appointment, it is easy to offer the new doctor first. If you have a long time to plan ahead, you could switch routine vision plan patients to traditional recall via email or post card.
- Introduce the new doctor when there is time and have him introduce himself. If the patient flow is a bit slow, ask the associate to drop into the exam room so you can introduce him to your patients. Some practices have the new doctor perform part of the exam along with the senior doctor, but I have some concern that the associate will come off as the junior assistant, which would be very bad for the reputation. I think it is great for the associate to hang out in optical and say hello to patients who drop in. An optician can still do the work, but a little chit chat about eye care is a good practice builder.

18.5 Adding an Associate OD, Part 4: Increasing Production

In this final installment in my series on adding an associate, I will cover how to get the associate doctor to produce at a high level. We can measure production in various ways, but collected gross revenue and number of exams performed are the key indicators. I'll also describe a few miscellaneous factors to consider when you bring on another doctor.

Revenue production

The main reason I would bring an associate doctor into a practice is for the potential to increase gross and net revenue. A secondary benefit is that the senior doctor may be able to reduce the amount of time spent on patient care, possibly allowing the owning OD to devote more time to practice management, but increasing profit is a highly desirable factor. If the practice has built up enough patient demand and if the senior doctor is seeing a strong number of patients per day with good delegation to staff, adding an associate doctor will cause a dramatic increase in gross and net income.

It does take time for a new associate to become busy enough with patients to first cover his or her own salary and benefits, and then to make a profit for the practice. That time table will depend on how actively the staff moves patients from the senior doctor to the associate (I covered this last week) and how busy the practice is in general. I would expect a new doctor to have roughly half of his appointment slots full after the first six months. At that level of activity, the practice should easily pay the doctor's salary and benefits and make a small profit from the doctor's work. As the appointment schedule is filled further, the profit level increases.

Absolute revenue metrics

It is important that the practice management software system can produce accurate reports that indicate the financial production for the practice as a whole and for each provider. Production reports can be produced on demand for any time period, such as daily, monthly, quarterly or yearly. Typically, all services and optical products sold to a patient are credited to the doctor who did the exam. If patients bring an outside prescription for glasses into the office, those sales are not assigned to a provider, but rather to the practice as a group.

When we look at gross revenue for a provider, we always should look at gross collected revenue after insurance adjustments. The usual and customary fees that were entered are really of very little consequence. All that matters is amount of payments that are collected and deposited. The practice management software should be able to show those adjusted revenue figures and that is what we use.

The median collected gross revenue for a full time OD who sees patients about 40 hours per week is around $680,000 according to the Management and Business Academy (MBA). That is a perfectly good guide to use as a comparison for your associate, but be aware that a very busy practice often has each full time equivalent OD producing about $1 million or more. I would look at the senior doctor's production as a guide as well, after considering the amount of time the associate has been with the practice and the number of hours worked per week. In most cases, there is no reason the associate OD should not produce the same revenue as the senior doctor.

Variable revenue metrics

While the total dollar amount produced by the associate is of interest, we can tell much more if we calculate the total revenue produced per exam. This removes the factor that the senior doctor may be naturally busier than the associate. Calculate this metric by taking the total revenue produced by each provider from all sources and dividing by the number of comprehensive exams performed during that time period.

The national average according to the MBA is about $308 total collected gross revenue per comprehensive exam, but a more relevant guide would be the senior doctor's production per exam figure. If the senior doc produced $498 per exam on average over the past 6 months and the associate produced $308 per exam for the same time period, I would want to know why there was such a big difference.

Consider the types of patients

A large difference can sometimes be explained if you look at the types of patients each doctor sees, so think about that. If one doctor sees a lot of Medicaid and the other does not, that makes a difference. Also, if one doctor sees a different age group or different types of insurance plans or practices a lucrative specialty; that can explain a lot. If those factors seem strong enough, you might conclude that the associate is producing at an acceptable rate. If not, you should meet with the associate and discuss the likely reasons for the difference.

You can also uncover more if you analyze other sources of revenue on a per exam basis. For example, are the optical sales lower for the associate doctor on a per patient basis?

What to do about low production

The most important thing to do if your associate has much lower production than other doctors in the practice is to have a meeting in private and discuss it. I would share the revenue per exam data and ask the doctor if he/she has any thoughts about why such a difference exists. I would conduct the talk in a

very respectful way and I would look at it as an opportunity to train or mentor the associate doctor.
You may want to discuss if the doctor is rather conservative in prescribing eyeglasses or contact lenses. This may lead to a discussion about not prejudging patients and their ability to pay and how that is really not our concern. You may want to revisit the mission of the practice, which could revolve around providing the best care; not the cheapest. I often tell my associate doctors that all I ask of them is that they prescribe and recommend the best eye care for every patient and not worry about the cost. The patient will let us know about his budget. I'm also happy to discuss the business aspects of operating a practice and how we face many challenges, such as managed care, competition and increasing operational costs. We must find a way to increase practice revenue every year.

It may be helpful to have the associate doctor observe the senior doctor in clinical practice to gain insight into how to communicate and recommend products at chairside. Often, just letting the associate know that you track the production numbers and discussing this aspect is enough to increase the revenue per exam number. Continue to monitor that data point and consider it when it is time for an employment review and possible raise.

Miscellaneous factors
Here are few important details to consider when you employ an optometrist:

- A new associate is not much good to the practice if he is not a provider for most medical insurance and vision plans. I would not try to bill for services by the associate under the senior doctor's provider number; it is best to follow all regulations. You may want to make the start date for a new doctor after all licensing and credentialing is in effect.
- I would have the associate sign a simple written employment agreement which includes a non-compete clause.
- You will need more staff members as the practice sees more patients. That is not a concern because much more revenue will be generated.
- Consider hiring a consultant who is experienced in recruiting and managing associate doctors. Many expensive mistakes can be avoided.

18.6 Ten Tips on Adding an Associate OD

I view adding an associate optometrist as one of the best management strategies a practice owner can implement. If done properly, it can greatly increase the practice gross and net income and pave the way for the senior OD to spend less time seeing patients and more time as the practice CEO.

My experience in my own practice and in working with other practice owners shows me that the conventional wisdom prevalent in our profession about hiring associates is not always the best approach. Here are ten points to consider as you plan to add a doctor to your practice.

1. The new doctor does not have to be a partner. The old school model in optometry was that if a doctor wanted to move from solo practice to group practice, a new doctor would buy in as partner or work on a track to earn partnership over time. The new doctor was expected to build his or her patient following and not take patients from the senior doctor, except for some overflow. The model I advocate is completely different: the senior doctor seeks an OD who will be an employee and does not want to be a practice owner. Owning and operating a business is not for everyone and many excellent ODs today just want to see patients, be well compensated for their work, and not worry about a business. I think private practice optometry should be a major source of employment for these ODs and they should not have to go to commercial chains or ophthalmology practices. Decide early in the planning process if you want a partner or an employed associate. It makes a big difference in the doctor you choose and how you structure the compensation. Of course, you can always decide later to sell all or part of your practice and the associate could end up being a buyer. It is much more difficult to become an employee.
2. When to proceed. To make my model work, the associate OD must have a minimum base of patients to see. The practice needs some backlog of patients in the form of appointments booked in advance. The goal will be to convert as many patients as possible to see the new doctor, while always honoring the patient's preference of doctors. Ideally, I like to see two weeks of advance appointments if a practice wants to add a full time doctor. You may be able to get by with less than that if the senior doctor wants to decrease his or her clinical hours. You will also need a plan for the practice to be able to see more patients, such as multiple exam rooms so to doctors can work at the same time, or extended office hours so the total number of doctor hours per week is greatly increased.
3. Set compensation fairly but don't overpay. Most practice owners want to pay associate ODs on a percentage of their production, but I have not found that system to be necessary to obtain high production and it has

some drawbacks. There really is no standard on what a fair percentage is and what metric to use in the calculation. It is certainly possible to set the percentage too high or too low and if that occurs, one of the two parties will be unhappy. Most percentages are figured out by trying to set what a reasonable salary will be and then working backwards by trying to guess what production will be and what percentage will work. Seems rather imprecise to me. A straight salary can actually work quite well and most ODs do not need a commission to practice good eye care and to prescribe appropriately. To find out what the going rate for an employed OD (not an owner), just ask some new optometry graduates what they expect to earn in their first year out of school. A good benefit package should also be included for full time doctors; this would include health insurance, paid vacations, holidays, etc.

4. Set expectations clearly. Avoid discontent later by talking about everything in advance. Don't be too shy to bring up sensitive topics; talking about them early lets you get to know the candidate better and that is a good thing. It's important to set some standards for your practice that all doctors will follow. This will include fees, insurance plans, number of patients seen per day, some exam elements and more. There is also a need to let each doctor have his or her own professional judgment, so not everything should be dictated. The expectation of how many patients will be seen per day and who sets the doctor's schedule is very important. I make it clear those issues are determined by the senior doctor. It works out well that the associate will not be instantly fully booked with patients. This allows time for the doctor to adapt to the office process and to gain efficiency. But it should be clear that eventually the new doctor will see patients at a given pace. He can't decide that he needs longer exam slots or that he wants to see fewer patients.
5. Decide on the schedule that is best for the practice. When you reach the point of bringing on an employed OD, it is a perfect time to reconsider your office hours. Many practice owners build their practice around hours that cater to the owner and perhaps to the staff, but are not extremely convenient for patients. Adding an associate doctor is a perfect opportunity to expand the hours. Evenings and Saturdays are the easiest appointments to fill and they offer a great way to move patients to the new doctor.
6. Have an employment agreement including a restrictive covenant. Assuming you are just hiring an OD as an employee, as described in last week's tip, you should have a basic written understanding. You can decide if you need an attorney to draft this agreement or if you want to keep it simple and just write your own letter of understanding. Of course,

if the new doctor will be a partner, I strongly recommend both parties have legal counsel.

7. Provide for observation and training. The associate doctor will have outstanding professional training and can begin to care for patients right away, but your practice has hundreds of policies and procedures that will take time to learn, and most of these are not written down. A good face to face discussion with the senior doctor and with the office manager can cover many important points. I also find that much can be gained by having the associate OD observe the staff in pretesting and the senior doctor examining patients. Additionally, I like the new doctor to observe and even participate in optical dispensing when possible.
8. Don't micromanage cases. I think it is important to separate practice activities, which are best if handled the same for all doctors, and patient care activities, which can be managed differently by different doctors. Part of being a good employer of a doctor is to respect his or her professional judgment and not expect every case to be treated exactly the way you would.
9. Meet often and talk freely. I think it is very important for the doctors to communicate. This could be to review cases and clinical management or it could be to discuss the business aspects of the practice. Even though the associate is an employee and may not have as much interest in practice management as the owner, he or she should understand that business is still part of the job. I stress that all I expect is that the associate OD practice the best eye care. That is the goal. The doctor should not focus on what is the cheapest for the patient. We should not prejudge a patient's ability to opt for quality services and products.
10. Review production data and surveys. One of the best metrics for evaluating a new doctor's performance is gross revenue per exam. This benchmark is good because it removes the lower patient volume we expect to see for the new doctor and expresses revenue per patient. Simply take the collected gross revenue for the month and divide by the number of comprehensive exams. I measure this data for the practice as a whole, for me individually and for each associate OD. Comparing the performance of each doctor speaks volumes. If the associate has a much lower figure than the practice owner, they should examine individual cases to see where the difference lies. It is also important to gauge patient satisfaction with the new doctor. Use one of the electronic marketing firms that offer patient surveys via email after each exam.

18.7 When Is the Right Time to Hire an Associate OD?

Adding an associate optometrist to your practice is one of the best management decisions you can make. It can increase practice revenue and profit dramatically while allowing the practice owner to reduce time spent on patient care. The additional free time can be used to concentrate on practice administration or to just enjoy life. In this article, I'll cover ideas that will help you know when the time is right to hire an OD.

Do you mind if your personal income drops?

It might seem obvious that most practice owners do not want to see a drop in their personal income, but it is a good question to start with. This question gets to the heart of the timing for bringing in an associate OD and what the goals and expectations are. In some cases, a senior OD might place so much value on gaining some free time that it does not really matter if personal income drops a little.

If you want to maintain or even increase your personal income from the practice, you need to avoid the situation where you are paying a new doctor to see patients that you could have seen. If you do that, your personal net income will decrease by that portion of the new doctor's salary. Read on to learn how to predict and avoid that.

Will you see more patients per week?

This is the most important point that relates to paying the new doctor's salary and benefits, and possibly making some additional profit. Project how many exams per week you will be able to see with the new doctor on board. This will require you to answer some questions:

- Will you be decreasing your patient care days per week? If you hire an OD to work two days a week and you drop two days, you did not increase the number of patients.
- It will help if the new doctor works a couple of evenings per week and every Saturday. Those are highly desirable days to patients and those days may be booked far in advance.
- It might seem difficult at first to get patients to accept seeing the new doctor, but there are ways to improve that. One good way is to decrease the senior doctor's patient care days per week so his or her backlog gets much further out. Some patients will see the new doctor because appointments are available sooner.

How far ahead are you booked?

This is the key element to look at, even though it is not perfect. In general, how far ahead in your schedule is the next appointment opening? Of course, you may have a cancellation tomorrow, but if you look at your patient schedule, how many days ahead are you booked fairly solid? Be very cautious in evaluating this if you preappoint because your schedule could appear fairly full, but in reality, you may get a fair amount of last minute cancellations, reschedules and no shows. In that case, look backward and see how many patients you actually see per day and make a judgment if you consider that to be a full day or not.

If your schedule and that of all associate ODs in your practice is booked ahead at least a week, and you have a well-delegated practice and see at least 20 patients per day, I think you are ready for a full time associate. If you are booked a few days in advance, you may be ready for a part time doctor. If you are not booked ahead much at all, you should not hire an associate, unless you don't mind having your personal income drop.

Why not just expect the associate to build his or her own following?
Some doctors who are not booked ahead very much will reason that they had to build their patient following, why shouldn't the new doctor do the same? In my experience, that approach does not work well. Usually, the new doctor will not be able to do this fast enough and will not produce enough revenue to pay himself a fair salary. When that happens, the new doctor will be unhappy and will eventually quit.

The validity of the earn-your-own way approach also comes down to the question: is the new doctor an employee or an owner? This point sometimes gets blurred because the senior doctor wants to respect the new doctor, but it is best to keep this clear. An employee does not typically agree to take on the business risk of an owner. In my view, if you hire an associate doctor, he or she is an employee and it is up to the owner to supply the patients.

18.8 Finding the Right Associate for Your Practice

A reader asked me to write about how to find the right doctor for the practice with an eye on reducing turnover and setting realistic expectations. I'll cover that in this piece.

Plan for your needs
As you interview and evaluate candidates for the associate optometrist job position, a big factor to consider is how many choices you have. Some markets have many ODs who are looking for work and others have very few. You can be more selective if you have several candidates or if you are not in a

hurry. Of course, you can attract more candidates if you are willing to pay more in salary.

There are many advantages to hiring a doctor on a full time basis, including less turnover, but some practices do not have enough patient demand to keep a doctor busy full time. Part time optometrists generally do not receive employment benefits, like paid vacation, continuing education payments or health insurance.

While we want to reduce doctor turnover, realize that you can't force an employee to work for you. Either party can end employment at any time. It helps to retain doctors if you pay well and treat them well, but some factors that make employees quit are beyond your control.

Don't think of this employee as a partner. I think it is your job to fill the new doctor's schedule. Don't hire an associate optometrist if you don't have a backlog of patients. Reducing the senior doctor's patient care load, however, will encourage some patients to move to the new doctor if handled properly by the staff.

Decide what is good for the practice and don't make too many concessions in your enthusiasm to attract someone. Hiring an associate is a perfect time to expand into evening and Saturday hours. The practice owner should decide on the appointment schedule and it should be fast-paced.

Personality match

For a new doctor to fit well into the practice, the personalities of the senior doctor, the new doctor and the staff must interact well together. At the most simple level, you determine this by getting to know the candidate through general conversation. Do you hit it off well? Do you have some things in common? Do you see eye-to-eye on most issues?

To carry this effort further, read up on personality types and consider giving the job candidate a personality test.

One factor that I'm especially wary of is the possibility of an over-sized ego. If some jobs in the office seem beneath the new doctor, or if the new doctor thinks he is more important than the staff, problems are likely to develop. I want an associate who is friendly, down-to-earth and respectful of others. This personality not only fits in with the office culture, but it builds a good relationship with patients, which results in more word-of-mouth referrals.

Professional match

After a general discussion about optometric practice and trends in our industry, be sure to focus on some practical real world issues like the following:

- Dilation preferences and frequency, with and without retinal imaging.
- Discuss interest in specialties like orthokeratology, scleral lens fitting, vision therapy, low vision, dry eye, nutrition and ocular disease.
- How does the new doctor feel about seeing urgent medical cases that are worked into the schedule?
- Electronic health record-keeping can be time consuming and managed care requires records to reflect the level of care provided. Ask the new doctor about his or her skills in that area and also in billing and coding.
- Discuss how the practice will handle after-hours emergency phone calls and eye care.
- Discuss evening and Saturday hours. I prefer the practice owner to decide on the hours and make it non-negotiable.
- Given some time to adapt and learn new techniques, will the new doctor be able to perform about 25 eye exams (a mix of comprehensive exams and office visits) in an eight hour day? Set the expectations early for the schedule the practice needs and give doctors who prefer a slower pace a chance to bow out before they start.

Career goals

There are plenty of optometrists who do not want to own a practice and operate a business. Those of us who own practices can understand that; it is no bed of roses. Many new graduates want to practice clinical eye care and would love to do that in a traditional optometric private practice. The professional image, the great staff, the excellent instrumentation and the full service optical are all positive factors.

The ideal OD candidate for this CEO model of practice is one who does not want to be a partner or owner. If the candidate asks about opportunities to buy in, I think we owe it to him or her to be honest and reply that the position available is for employment only and at this time, there are no other opportunities. Of course, some years down the road, anything can happen and an associate may become a natural buyer of the practice, but don't mislead or make promises.

A restrictive covenant is an important consideration and should be presented and discussed openly and early in the discussion.

Resources
Here are a few good resources for advertising your available job position:

- The AOA national placement service is an excellent resource: Optometry's Career Center.
- Your state optometric association may list practice opportunities in its publications.
- Most optometry schools provide placement services for their graduates. I'd post a position available announcement in all of them.
- There are many online career placement services available.
- Use your own network of friends and colleagues to spread the word about the position and to recommend someone.

18.9 Recruiting an Associate OD

A colleague emailed me about hiring an associate OD and she suggested that I use the questions for a tip article. Great idea!

Here are the questions that led to this article: I am having trouble recruiting a new doctor. What are your suggestions for recruitment? What questions do you ask an optometrist during an interview? How do you gauge if a doctor will commit to long term or move around?

Determine your job position
The first question is: do you want a partner (now or in the near future) or do you want an employee. The terms are not fully standardized, but "associate" usually is a synonym for "employee". Partner implies someone who has ownership in the practice. You should think this point through before you begin to recruit so you can advertise the position in a way that attracts the right candidates. If you are not sure, you may want to start with an employment-based arrangement since those are much easier to control and to terminate. I will keep my comments to the employed doctor arrangement for this article.

Another consideration is if the position will be full time or part time. This one is mostly based on how much patient demand your practice currently has. You should be able to find some interested doctors for either full or part time, but the former is more likely looking for a career and the latter may be working in another practice besides yours. There is more turnover with a part time associate, but they can fill a void in patient care and it is less expensive and less risk

Consider your office hours carefully before you bring in an associate because this may be a great time to change them. Will you be able to have two doctors working at the same time? This works well if you have at least four exam rooms (two per doctor) and a large optical. Do you currently offer two or more evenings per week until at least 7pm and every Saturday? If not, consider speaking to your staff or hiring more staff members who are willing to work on those less popular hours. Patients love those convenient hours and expanding your schedule increases production and revenue.

What you start with - you may have to stay with
Realize that the policies and rules you begin with may be very difficult to change later. Here are a few sticky points where you want to start off on the right foot:

- Hours. As mentioned above, start with the evening and Saturday coverage you want.
- How many patients per day? It is best if the practice owner sets the schedule. Even though the new doctor may not be fully booked in the beginning, make it clear what the normal schedule will be and that the associate can't change it.
- Lunch breaks. Are they included in the base pay or is the time deducted. How long is a normal lunch break?
- Other assignments. Discuss what non-clinical duties you may ask of the employed doctor. This might be staff training, marketing, community outreach, office technology, etc.
- Can the doctor decide to leave the office early if there are no more appointments that day? Will time off affect pay?
- Emergencies. Will the new doctor see urgent cases the same day and how will you handle after hours calls from patients?

Where to look for a candidate
There are several well-known channels for posting a job position available for an OD. It is the same resources that doctors who are seeking employment will use to find a position.

- Optometry schools placement services. Certainly the ones closest to you are of main interest, but many practice owners post positions available at all the schools.
- State optometric associations.
- The AOA placement service: Optometry's Career Center.
- Commercial placement services and head-hunter firms.

- Craig's list.
- Optometric consultants and alliance groups.
- Industry sales reps from frames, contact lens, drug, and equipment companies.

The interview

This process is not so different than an interview you would do for a staff member. You want to get to know the applicant and see if he or she is a good fit. Try to ask open-ended questions and let the candidate speak most of the time.

Ask about the doctor's training, special interests, experience, and career goals. Delve into the aspect of prescribing and recommending products. Discuss pupil dilation preferences, comfort working with staff, expertise with computers and EHR software.

I'm on the lookout for people who seem to have large egos, even though they usually hide that during an interview. If a doctor thinks he is extremely important, he may not fit in well with the staff and with patients.

Review the sticky areas listed above to see how flexible and open the candidate is. The best fit occurs when the new doctor is willing to adapt to the systems in place in the practice.

Long term relationship

There is no perfect way to be sure an employed doctor will stay with you for a long time. Your odds improve if the candidate as roots in the community such as he grew up there or has a family or spouse there. You can also just ask the candidate and you'll be surprised how candid some will be.

18.10 Interviewing Associate OD Candidates

With a new crop of doctors of optometry graduating soon, many practice owners are looking to hire an associate. If your practice is fortunate enough to have ample patient demand, adding an associate OD is one of the best ways to dramatically increase profitability. This can also be an opportunity for the senior doctor to reduce his or her patient care days per week. This will allow the senior doc to dedicate more time to practice management duties and possibly take some personal time off as well.

Just as in the hiring process with any employee, finding the right person can be challenging. While there is no way to be absolutely certain in advance about an OD job candidate, the interview process is extremely important. Here are a few tips and topics that I have found helpful:

- As you evaluate the candidates, keep in mind the overall job market for ODs in your area of the country. Some regions have many ODs to choose from while others may have trouble finding anyone to even apply for the job. Your ability to be selective should reflect the size of the applicant pool.
- Start the interview process by making it a casual conversation. Help the candidate to relax so you can find out more about his or her personality. Just let the OD talk about himself, his education or his interests. Ask open ended questions. Resist the urge to talk about yourself and your practice in the early going.
- Watch for signs that the candidate has an oversized ego. It usually won't work out if the young doctor thinks he is better than the staff or the patients. Of course, there is a natural tendency for the candidate to want to impress the senior doctor, but move the conversation away from that. Is he friendly and outgoing?
- Try to judge how open the candidate will be to adapting to the procedures that you already use in the practice. There will certainly be some differences among how doctors provide eye care, but there are many factors that improve efficiency and profitability if they are common for the whole practice. Is the new doctor open to preferred brands of contact lenses and ophthalmic lenses? Can she adapt to the office software programs?
- Discuss dilation protocol, which can be quite time consuming and could be a source of disagreement.
- What optometric specialties is the candidate interested in? Do you have hopes that the new doctor can provide low vision or vision therapy services?
- What is the comfort level for treating eye disease? Don't assume that the candidate will be an aggressive star in this area just because he is a recent grad. What specific types of cases will he treat or refer out?
- Can the new doctor help market the practice? Will she be willing to present a seminar to patients or call on physicians in their offices? Will she join a service organization in your community? Will she be willing to work on marketing projects and social media during slow times in the office?
- Discuss willingness and ability to see up to 25 patients per day someday. It will usually take some time to transfer existing patients

who may have a preference for the senior doc, but you want to be sure the new doc can handle that flow when the time comes. If your practice does not typically see patients at a fast clip, you may want to achieve that before seeking an associate.

- Will the new doctor be willing to hang out in the optical when not busy with patients? This can be a great practice builder if the doctor introduces herself to patients who drop in for optical service. I would love it if the new doctor could actually pitch in and help sometimes! I did plenty of dispensing in my early days of practice; why not the new doctor?
- Ask the candidate about his aptitude with computer technology and judge his willingness to help the practice in this vital area.
- The work hours are extremely important and should be discussed openly without sugar coating your expectations. A key benefit of hiring an associate is the opportunity to expand the office hours. I want the new doctor to work at least two evenings per week until 7pm and every Saturday. Doing that will also allow the doctor to have a day off during the week and still reach full time hours. If these hours are a change for your office, then there will also be some staff challenges to deal with, but convenient hours are a huge practice building strategy. For me, the hours can be a deal breaker.
- Ask what the salary expectation is. He may try to deflect that question, but it's best if the candidate is the first one to mention a number. I prefer to pay straight salary with no incentives or percentages to start because it allows you to determine what level of production is possible. Be careful about paying a percentage; when gross revenue goes way up in future years, you could pay much more than the going rate for ODs.
- Discuss the possibility for partnership vs. straight employment. Neither party may be sure at the outset, but it is best to avoid a complete mismatch of goals in this area.
- Let the candidate ask questions. Explain your practice procedures and strategies.
- Once you have a strong candidate in mind, consider having the new OD observe the practice over a few days. This becomes more than en extended interview; it lets you see if the new doc fits into the culture.

A valuable orientation technique I've used with new associate doctors is to let them begin to work as an optometric technician right out of school before the board issues the license. The salary level is obviously reduced until the license comes through, but it can be very educational for the doctor and helpful to the practice. Letting the associate observe (or scribe for) the senior doctor performing eye exams is extremely beneficial.

18.11 What If Your Associate OD Has Low Production?

I've consulted with many optometrists about bringing on an associate OD and I've had much experience in my own practice as well. The term associate can have various meanings, but in this context it is another word for an OD who is an employee of the practice; not a partner or on a partnership track. There are many factors involved in the successful recruitment, training, and ongoing management of an associate doctor, but it is a valuable strategy that can greatly increase practice profitability. Building an independent optometric practice to the point that an associate OD can be added is a very worthwhile goal.

Once a doctor is in place, seeing patients and drawing a salary, the practice owner should monitor production. The whole point of hiring a doctor is to increase practice profitability. For that to happen, the associate must produce enough additional net revenue in the practice, after deducting cost of goods and all other practice expenses, to more than cover his or her compensation. Read on for how to evaluate this and how to increase it.

What kind of low production?
When I hear from a practice owner who tells me the associate OD does not produce enough, I need to understand which of the following two problems is occurring:

- The associate OD does not generate enough gross revenue.
- The associate OD does not generate enough gross revenue per exam.

There is a big difference between these two issues and the remedies are different as well. It is possible that both problems are occurring at the same time.

Low revenue
This problem is most likely due to insufficient patient demand for the new doctor. In my view, the practice bears most of the responsibility to fill the new doctor's appointment schedule. Of course, it is normal for this to take some time. It is not often easy to transfer patients who are used to seeing the senior doctor over to the new one, but there are many strategies that can be implemented to help the process.

The bigger challenge may be that the practice does not have enough patient demand to keep both doctors busy. This should have been considered before the new doctor was hired. It is advisable for the existing doctors in the practice to be booked solid well in advance before seeking an associate. Two weeks advance booking for a full time OD is a good rule of thumb. While hard to achieve, once that advance booking exists, the practice will almost always see an immediate increase in net income when the new doctor joins.

If the associate's low production is due to insufficient patient demand for the whole practice, the practice owner should work harder on marketing projects and also consider joining more vision plans, Medicaid or other vehicles for patient access.

Low revenue per exam

In some cases, the associate's patient schedule is fairly busy, but the gross revenue per exam is low. It is very important to measure this benchmark on a monthly basis and compare it to the revenue per exam of the senior doctor. Obviously, the popularity of one doctor over the other is no longer a factor in this metric. The senior doctor may be much busier and therefore would have much higher gross revenue, but on a per-exam basis, the two doctors' revenue production should be about the same. We might allow up to a 5% difference to be acceptable due to experience and differences in personality, but in my experience multiple doctors in the same practice are usually extremely close in this metric. The median gross revenue per exam in the United States is about $306.

If the associate is under-performing in this metric, we need to find out why.

- Start by reviewing the type of patients each doctor sees. A high concentration of vision plans or Medicaid could explain some differences. There may be fewer eyewear sales in an older Medicare group or in a pediatric group, compared to the 30 to 50 year olds.
- Review some of the associate's charts. This is very important and I don't know why more practice owners don't do it. If you read the chief complaint and look at the habitual spectacle Rx or type of contact lens, and then review the exam data, you will be able to tell if you would have prescribed new lenses or not. Then look and see if the associate prescribed and if the patient actually ordered glasses or contacts. If not; why not?
- Can you monitor the eyeglass and contact lens Rx retention rate for each doctor? They should be about the same and if they are

different, we need to find out what one doctor does to drive patients away.

- Were there additional tests that you would have ordered that were omitted? Any other treatment options that might have been offered?
- If there is a pattern of under-prescribing and under-recommending, it is best to have a meeting with the associate in a private setting to discuss the differences of philosophy.
- Proceed with caution as you question another doctor's professional judgment. You must always remain respectful and realize that you will not agree on exactly how to manage every case. Pick your battles carefully, because you want your associate to like working in your practice. But a senior doctor may be able to serve as a mentor for a new doctor if the discussion is positive rather than a complaint.
- It is perfectly fine to educate the associate doctor about the business side of optometry and that he or she plays an important role in that. All I really ask is that all our doctors practice and recommend the very best eye care. I ask that they not focus on what they think the patient can afford; it is up to the patient to tell us that. It is our job to recommend and prescribe the best first, whether that is in medical eye care, eyeglasses, contact lenses or any other service or product.

What about incentive bonuses?
Incentive payments based on a production goal might work or they might not. It is just not as simple as most people think. It's quite possible that an incentive bonus could cause the practice to pay the associate OD too much. It also might not be effective at helping to achieve the desired goal (low correlation). I've even seen bonus programs help create an undesirable office culture. It is a big topic and I'll cover it in a future tip article.

18.12 Keeping the New Doctor Busy

Bringing a new associate optometrist into your practice is an excellent way to boost revenue, if you have enough patient demand.

Here are some thoughts about how to get a new doctor busy once they join you.

When to bring in a new doctor

Before I present tips on how to promote the new doctor, consider that nothing makes for a successful association like being busy in the first place. Insufficient patient demand is often at the core of all kinds of disagreements and disappointments. Consider these points before seeking another doctor.

- Delegate first. Add more technicians before adding a doctor so you are working at a high level of production. Acquire automated instrumentation and design your procedures so technicians do most of the data collection in pretesting.
- Get busy. A reasonable goal might be for a single OD to see about 25 patients in an eight hour day (a mixture of all types of visits, but mostly comprehensive exams). If you are booked with that volume for about two weeks in advance, you will benefit from an associate.
- Change internal operations before the associate joins you. The system a doctor starts with is what he or she will consider normal. (For the rest of this article I will alternate between male and female pronouns for the sake of simplicity.) It is not likely that the doctor will want to increase production or patient flow unless there is a big incentive to do so. It is best to make most changes that you want to make before bringing in an associate.

Do you want the new doctor to see your patients?

We don't see this issue addressed much, but I think it is a major stumbling block for associateships. In many cases, the senior doc does not really know the answer to the question above. There are all kinds of possible dynamics and emotions at play, but if the practice owner is not sure of where the new doc's patients will come from, trouble will ensue. In my opinion, the right answer is yes, the senior doc should want many of his patients to move to the new OD.

Consider these points:

- Many senior ODs don't really want to share the patient base. The subliminal reasoning may be that they worked hard for their following and it feels pretty good to be wanted by so many people.
- If the new doctor's pay is heavily based on production or a percentage of revenue, then the senior doc can be in a quandary. If he actively moves patients to the associate, he'll have to pay more to the new doctor and subsequently will reduce his own net income.
- Patient loyalty is job security for the independent OD and it can feel scary to let it go. Of course, you aren't really letting it go; it's staying with your practice.
- Many patients feel more like personal friends and it can be uncomfortable to think about not seeing them again.

- A restrictive covenant is very important to facilitate the transfer of patients without a business risk.
- There is a tendency to just drift along with no plan if the practice owner is not sure.
- It is very difficult for a new OD to build a following all by herself in the shadow of a well-established and successful practitioner. It is likely that there will not be enough cash flow increase to support the new doctor.
- The senior doctor is smart to try to build a system that does not depend on her. Develop loyalty to the practice - not to the person.

Internal strategies

Here are some smart policies you can implement that will get the new doctor busier:

- The senior OD should reduce his patient care schedule by one or two days per week. This creates a bigger backlog in patient demand which will create an incentive for some (not all) patients to accept a more convenient and sooner appointment with the associate.
- A side benefit of reducing the senior doc's clinical schedule is that she can spend more time on practice management, which is critical at this time of growth.
- Train the front desk staff to try to move patients to the new doctor. They should at least offer an appointment with the new doctor and not assume the patient wants to stay with the previous OD. This effort should be made gently as a suggestion, but a skilled staff person can make a huge difference. Often times, the receptionists are never even told what the plan is! Who should new patients go to first? What about established patients?
- Of course, patients who have a preference for a certain doctor should have that wish honored. And the receptionist should always be clear over the phone about which doctor the patient is scheduled to see.
- Train receptionists to "sell" the new doctor. Simply telling a caller that the new doctor is very nice and everyone really likes her is often enough. It is effective to add that the patient can see the new doctor this time and can always revert back to the other doctor the next time. We have our new ODs examine our staff right away; then the staffer can say: "Dr. Jones is great; she is my eye doctor!"
- All patients calling for emergency same day exams can be appointed with the new doctor. No choice is available in these cases.
- Consider positioning the associate as a specialist in certain areas, and having the senior doc "refer" his patients. The specialty area

could be dry eyes, glaucoma, bifocal contact lenses, binocular vision or any other.

- The senior doctor could introduce the associate to many of his patients, just as a friendly gesture.
- The associate could participate in some aspect of each patient's care, even though the senior doc is still the primary provider. The new doctor could perform pretesting or just the refraction, and the other doctor then takes over. This allows the patient to work with the new doctor and sets up a possible future transition.
- While I would normally not advocate an optometrist handle optical dispensing duties, I see nothing wrong with a new associate "hanging out" in optical to introduce himself to patients who drop in and performing some basic optical services, perhaps with an optician as backup.

Marketing

The addition of an associate is a strong marketing opportunity for the practice since it signals growth and positive change to the community. Here are some ideas for promoting the new associate:

- Newspaper announcement with the new doctor's photo and short bio.
- Direct mail announcements.
- The associate can visit other professionals to promote referrals
- Involvement in community organizations
- Consider having the new OD start a specialty that has not been offered before. Low vision, sports vision or vision therapy are possibilities. Then, promote the new specialty.

18.13 Should Your Associate Be an Independent Contractor or an Employee?

Many associate optometrists are treated as independent contractors, but in most of these cases, the IRS would disagree. I generally recommend that practice owners who hire an associate treat the doctor as an employee because if you read the IRS regulation on this topic that is the definition we meet. I'll give you a quick summary below on the key elements that lead me to making the associate an employee.

There may be some resistance by practice owners to using the employee classification because that requires the practice to withhold employment taxes such as Social Security and Medicare (FICA) and pay 50% of that FICA tax. The employee pays the other 50%. If the associate OD is an independent contractor, no taxes are withheld by the practice, which might sound good to the associate at first, but the same taxes are still due in any case. The independent contractor must file quarterly estimated income taxes and must also pay all of the FICA tax which is currently at 15.3% of the salary. Clearly, the associate would be better off with the employee status.

The practice owner is ultimately better off as well by choosing to treat the associate as an employee because the IRS has often ruled that way on audit and the employer must pay back all the taxes that should have been collected. In fairness, this issue is subject to some interpretation and I'm sure some ODs have had the IC status upheld by the IRS. It is always smart to get the input of a CPA or financial advisor, but read on and form your own opinion based on your situation.

The IRS website (IRS.gov) lists three common law rules to help guide employers into the correct decision. The IRS makes a judgment about the degree of control and the amount of independence a worker has.

1. **Behavioral**: Does the company control or have the right to control what the worker does and how the worker does his or her job?

In my experience, the practice owner usually controls these aspects and should want to control them to maintain high standards for the practice. The practice owner typically sets the work schedule, determines the fees, decides about the record keeping system and controls the length of appointment slots.

2. **Financial**: Are the business aspects of the worker's job controlled by the company? This includes things like how the worker is paid, whether expenses are reimbursed, who provides tools/supplies, etc.

Associate optometrists do not typically collect fees directly from patients or insurance companies. Those entities pay the practice and the practice pays the associate on a regular basis. Also, the practice generally provides most of the equipment, supplies and product inventory.

3. **Type of Relationship**: Are there written contracts or employee type benefits (i.e. pension plan, insurance, vacation pay, etc.)? Will the relationship continue and is the work performed a key aspect of the business?

The use of a contract or employment benefits often falls more to the associate doctor being full time or part time, but "employee" is usually the right classification in either case. The big factor here is that you expect the associate to continue working indefinitely and the work is certainly a key aspect of the business.

All three of the above factors generally lead to the conclusion that associate ODs are employees and not independent contractors.

If you currently have an associate who you would like to convert to employment status, it should be pretty easy: just say it is mandated by the IRS and the rules will provide for the practice to cover half of the FICA taxes.

18.14 Preparing Your Practice for an Associate Doctor

Adding an associate optometrist to your practice brings great potential for growth, but it is best to analyze and prepare the practice well in advance for this change. Once a new doctor begins work in your office, your standard operating procedure becomes the norm. It becomes the office policy, even if it is not written down. Associate doctors tend to accept the procedures that are in place when they start employment, but it can be difficult to change office procedures afterward. Here is a list of important factors to consider well in advance of hiring a new doctor.

Patient Demand
It is very important to have strong patient demand in the practice before a new OD is hired, especially if the goal is to be able to fund the compensation of the associate without decreasing personal income to the current practice owner. I generally recommend that doctors begin to seek a full time associate OD when the practice is well delegated and seeing a high volume of patients per day. A rule of thumb is to be booked ahead with appointments at least one week solid. Of course, a part time doctor may work well if patient demand is less than that.

In my experience, bringing on an associate with the hope that the new doctor will grow the practice does not work out very well. Certainly some growth will occur if the new doctor does a good job, but it is generally not fast enough to cover the increased payroll cost. Most practice owners will want to avoid a situation where they are paying an associate to see patients that the senior doctor could have seen.

Delegation and patient flow

The single biggest factor affecting profitability for the associate is how many patients they see per day. If the senior doctor normally sees patients at a slower pace and does not utilize high level delegation with clinical technicians, then that pace becomes the policy for the new doctor as well. That is the normal routine and it will be very hard to change after the associate works for a few months. Associate doctors, especially those who are paid on salary or per diem, do not typically want to see more patients per day. It is viewed as more work and who wants that? You could provide a financial incentive of some kind, for the associate to see more patients, but that could lead to paying more than the going rate.

The best advice is to hire enough staff and delegate actively before adding an associate doctor. The existing doctor(s) should work at their highest level of efficiency first because hiring technicians is more economical than hiring a doctor. And it sets the policy for patient flow at the right level so when a doctor does join, he or she will have proper expectations.

Office hours

In the earlier phases of practice development, it is often not possible to have the office open for extended hours. The doctor/owner may not want to work excessively long hours and may prefer to not work evenings or Saturdays. That is very well, but one of the benefits of adding another doctor is to be able to offer more convenience for patients. Expanding the hours not only provides more production in terms of number of patients seen and eyewear dispensed, but the convenience factor results in a better patient experience and more word of mouth referrals.

I recommend that the work schedule for the new doctor be designed by the practice owner and based on the needs of the practice. If the work schedule is presented during the interview process and it includes two evenings (until 7pm) and Saturdays (9am to 1pm for example), the candidate will most likely agree. After all, she wants the job offer. If the salary is based on a 40 hour work week, a schedule like that will provide the needed hours but also allow a full day off during the week. The doctor may not like working evenings and Saturdays, but it is nice to have a day off in the middle of the week in addition to Sundays off.

Office design and space

A nice jump in revenue is realized if the new doctor allows the practice to see more patients per week, but one must also consider if there is enough physical space to handle more patients at the same time.

- Additional staff members will be needed and they need a place to work, when they are with patients and for behind the scenes work as well.
- If two doctors are working at the same time, four exam rooms are needed for maximum efficiency.
- Additional pretest rooms may be needed if patient volume is greatly increased.
- Consider how you will handle frame selections for more people at the same time. You may need additional dispensing tables and more room in the optical.

You will have some time to create this additional work space, because a new doctor is not usually busy immediately, but it is best to have a plan in mind for where the space will come from.

18.15 Ten Quick Things on Hiring an Associate Optometrist

I view hiring an associate OD as one of the best practice management goals a practice owner can set. When you reach the point that your practice is ready for that, many good things happen: revenue and profitability should increase and patient care hours for the senior doctor can decrease. Read on for my quick list of ten things to consider when you want to bring on an associate.

1. Patient demand. This is the ingredient for success when adding a new doctor. Your practice should be booked solid for several days (or weeks) in advance. A full schedule also presumes that you are already actively delegating to technicians and seeing a strong number of patients per day; if not, do that first and see if you stay booked in advance. Adding a doctor when there is strong demand for services allows the practice to see more patients per day, which results in more revenue and profit. Adding a doctor when there is weak demand only moves the existing patients from one doctor to another, causing no increase in revenue while adding the new doctor's salary as a big expense.

2. Consider office hours. Adding an associate is the ideal time to expand office hours by adding evenings and Saturdays. Doing so allows the office to be more productive and patients love the convenience, which creates a higher level of satisfaction and more

word-of-mouth referrals. Most job candidates agree to work evenings and Saturdays when asked about it in the interview process, but it can be very difficult to change their schedules later. Hire more staff if needed, but expand the hours with the new OD.

3. Consider the appointment schedule. Be sure the new associate understands the fast pace that your office works at and feels comfortable with that. Of course, it will take some time to move patients and attract enough new patients to fill the new doctor's schedule, but that is the goal. The practice will supply plenty of staff support, instrumentation and multiple exam rooms, so the new doctor should realize that fast-paced care is not stressful. It is up to the practice to fill the associate's schedule with patients; the new doctor plays a role in that as well by providing good care, but most of the burden is on the practice owner (assuming the new doctor is an employee and not a partner).

4. Insurance credentialing. I would not start paying a new associate at full salary until he or she is credentialed with the major insurance plans the practice works with. The practice can assist with the application process, but it often takes months to be approved and the new doc can't produce much until that occurs. Do not bill insurance under the senior doctor's provider number if he or she did not see the patient; it is generally against the contract terms. Don't take chances.

5. Full time or part time. Decide how many hours per week you can keep the new doctor fairly busy. I strongly prefer hiring doctors on a full time basis, but part time is fine if patient demand is not enough. I recommend paying a straight salary plus benefits for full time doctors and paying by an hourly or daily rate with no benefits for part time. The cut-off for full time status is often around 32 hours per week. IRS rules are such that associate doctors should generally be paid as employees and not independent contractors.

6. Need to incentivize? I don't think paying percentages, incentives or bonuses works as well as you might think. I don't find that it actually changes the behavior of most ODs and I'm not sure I would want it to. It is possible to pay too much or too little if you don't really know what the dollars will be. I find that if the practice can fill the associate's appointment schedule, revenue production will be quite high. That is the factor to work on and the rest takes care of itself.

7. Reconsider vision plans. It is very difficult to maintain enough patient demand for an additional doctor. Adding a vision plan that did not make sense before could be a big benefit now. Any profit is better than an empty appointment slot.

8. Restrictive covenant. A non-compete agreement with the new doctor is quite standard and it protects the practice against the associate quitting, setting up a practice nearby and taking patients. The terms are generally softer for part time doctors because, by definition, they need to work in another practice in the local area.

9. How to move patients to the new doctor. The most important step, which is often overlooked, is to tell the staff that you want to move as many patients as possible to the new doctor. They need to work on it; be creative and charming about it. They must overcome their loyalty and bias for the senior doctor. Additionally, reduce the patient care hours of the senior doctor and do not have the senior doc work any evenings or Saturdays. We need some tough love for patients.

10. Review gross revenue per comprehensive exam. This is an important metric for associate doctors and it should be calculated for the senior doctor as well which can serve as the norm for the practice. If the associate doctor has much lower average gross revenue per comprehensive exam, sit down and talk about the cause. Review some patient records with the new doctor and discuss how you might handle things differently. Serve as a mentor and consider having the associate observe the senior doctor while performing some exams.

18.16 A Real World Indoctrination for a New Grad

I've had excellent success hiring associate optometrists directly out of school, and in doing so I have come up with a tip that has eased the transition from optometry school clinics to private practice. We all know that there is much to learn, but this concept accelerates the learning curve and makes the new grad a good value to hire.

The no-license syndrome

This idea was born from the inconvenient lag time that exists between optometry school graduation day and the official issue of the state license to practice. Depending on the state where you practice, that can easily be 3 months of down time for the new doctor. If you have been interviewing candidates for an associate position in their senior year, you may easily have made a selection by the middle of May. Many new grads are very anxious to begin work right way – at least the best ones are, in my opinion. Sure, they could take the summer off, but it says a lot about ambition and drive if they are eager to get to work. The new grad is not only at the height of professional enthusiasm, but also has a real financial need for a good paycheck.

The idea is to simply have the new doc work as a technician in the practice, on a temporary basis, until his or her license comes through. This may not seem like rocket science, yet the benefits are much greater than you might think and the situation is quite different from the part-time employment many students experience before graduation.

This concept works extremely well in my practice, because I already delegate a great number of tasks to technicians, and I use scribes in the exam room with me. Our clinical techs also perform frame selection and dispensing tasks, so the learning continues for the new grad. But even if you typically delegate fewer procedures, this new technician with an OD after his or her name will be the most skilled one you've ever employed. This experience may even help the senior doctor move toward a higher level of delegation in general.

Work as a tech

Let's take a look at the work the new graduate would perform and how it helps assimilate him or her into the practice.

- **Pre-test instruments**. It's very valuable for a doctor to be able to operate all the instruments in a practice, even the pre-test equipment that will usually be performed by a technician. Instruments differ, and the brand or model that was used in school could be very different. The doctor should be able to do the test herself without hesitation if a tech is not available, and should be able to supervise and train staff as needed. Topographers, field units, retinal cameras, nerve fiber analyzers, contact lens radiuscopes, and pachymeters are just a few examples of instruments the new doc must develop skill with. Nothing does that faster than repetition.
- **Problem focused exam procedures**. Taking this a step further, letting the new doctor scribe for the senior doctor provides

tremendous learning opportunities. As great as optometric education is today, very few students actually spend much time observing experienced optometrists performing actual eye exams. It's mostly the other way around, with clinical faculty ODs observing students. And in this case, the observation is with the optometrist who has built the practice the new doctor is joining! The real world education that occurs is obvious, from the selection of what tests to run for different cases to how to do a refraction quickly.

- **Interpersonal relations**. Just as important as observing the testing is how to communicate during case history, chairside consultation and patient education.
- **Timing and flow**. Performing the pre-testing, observing the senior doc and conducting frame selections helps the new doctor get a sense of timing that is needed in the world of private practice.
- **Record keeping and abbreviations**. Each practice is unique with regard to record keeping conventions, and scribing the whole record and the optical order is the fastest way to learn.
- **Office policies**. Technicians are the people in the office that actually apply the myriad of policies that exist and answer patient's questions. The new doctor learns from the ground up.
- **Contact lens practice**. What types of lenses does this office fit and what are the standard clinical and administrative procedures? The new doc gets experience with the brands of choice.
- **Dispensing and optical lab processing**. What can be promised when? How to troubleshoot a complaint? What options and materials don't go together? How to communicate lens features and benefits, and drawbacks? Optometry schools may be a little light in this area (admittedly, they have a lot to cover); so new ODs must learn it in the real world.
- **Fees and insurance coding**. Our techs write up all procedures and fees on the superbill and indicate the diagnosis codes. They also calculate vision plan benefits and complete forms amid an increasingly complicated set of rules. Is it good for doctors to know this also? Absolutely.

An ego problem?

So how does a young doctor – filled with professional pride – react to the concept of being in the trenches with staff members who are paid by the hour? In my opinion, that reaction could actually prove to be a big indicator as to whether or not the new doc gets a job offer. If he views that kind of work as beneath him, especially in this short non-licensed period, then his ego could end up causing lots of other problems in the future.

I'll admit that it could seem a bit awkward at first and it may take some getting used to, but it actually works very well in practice.

Salary level

This can be any amount deemed fair by all, but I've found that paying a salary of 50% of the agreed upon future salary when this graduate becomes licensed, works well. Even at 50%, that pay level is usually generous for technician duties. I would schedule the new doctor-tech for a full 40-hour week, with evenings and Saturdays.

After the license is issued

The new OD makes an immediate shift to become a real doctor as soon as the license arrives. The receptionists begin to schedule actual appointments, but for the first couple of months, I would space those appointments out so the new doc has about twice the time allotment as usual. This lets the doc get acclimated to the new role, and it won't matter much anyway, since she will not be fully booked for a while.

It's helpful during the first couple months to schedule some private one-on-one meetings with the associate, and to pull several of his patient records at random to review and discuss. This should be done diplomatically and with great respect for the associate's own professional judgment – even if a case was handled differently than the senior doc would have. There can be a good exchange and discussion of patient management if both parties approach this with a constructive attitude. After a short period of time, I would stop reviewing cases and let the doctor practice. At that point, both senior and junior can learn from each other.

With all there is to cover, it may seem like a three month period is not long enough, but these new optometrists are quick studies. They get it.

In addition to learning valuable skills, the new doctor will bond with the staff and will be introduced to a sample of the patient base. It's a winning situation on many levels.

18.17 An Observation about Optometric Education

As a practice owner who hires associate optometrists, I've noticed a way to improve the basic clinical skills of new ODs, especially in the area of refraction. Students are typically first taught clinical procedures and refraction techniques in a laboratory setting where they practice the test procedures on fellow students. Instructors observe the activity, provide hands-on training and correct errors made by the students. After proving proficiency in clinical procedures, the student is permitted to examine real patients in an eye clinic setting associated with the school. These eye exams are monitored closely by clinical faculty who teach the finer points of the art and science of vision care. As students reach their final year of training, they are assigned to clinical externship sites all over the country, ranging from major eye hospitals to private optometric practices. Once again, an experienced optometrist observes the student, reviews the data and teaches how to exercise professional judgment.

What's missing?

I believe the quality of optometric education is at an all-time high and the process described above results in top caliber graduating clinicians, but here is what would make it better. I think the students should spend more time observing experienced optometrists at work. As basic as that might seem, it rarely happens in our present system. Highly skilled ODs observe students all the time, but rarely is it the other way around. Students often observe fellow students, including those a year or two ahead in the curriculum, but so much more could be learned by watching a veteran OD. Students who have mastered the mechanics of refractive testing with the phoroptor stand to gain more from the observations than the uninitiated. If you don't know how to refract it does little good to watch an OD fog and unfog, select various lines of acuity, use the JCC, obtain reversals and perform a binocular balance.

Much of the value of observing a veteran OD in action comes from the communicative and interpersonal skills that are so closely tied to the testing procedures. This is how one becomes an excellent doctor. Expanding on the case history, relating the exam findings to the complaints, explaining the tests and treatment recommendations without overdoing it, and confirming tests with the use of hand-held trial lenses are all examples of how patient communication is critical to a good outcome.

If you are an experienced optometrist who works with students, consider inviting (requiring?) them to observe you in the examination of patients.

Associate ODs

Here is a technique that I've used in my practice to help new associate optometrists improve their clinical skills while training them on the policies and procedures that are unique to our office. If you hire a new graduate right out of school, he or she generally graduates in May but will not receive a state license until July or August. Consider hiring the new doc to work as a technician in your practice until the license is official. I would pay the doctor-tech a generous wage at the high end of the tech scale and I would expect the same work as any tech, but include scribing even if that is not typically done in your practice. Recording for the senior OD should be easy and the observational training occurs automatically. Additionally, the new grad will learn real-world skills in optical dispensing, automated instrumentation and insurance calculations.

This "learn-from-the-ground-up" approach will make the new associate a better doctor. With the right attitude, he or she will form a strong bond with the other staff members while working as one of them. If the new doc acts like he is too important to do technician work or dispense eyewear, I would question if this is the right associate for your practice.

Why don't we ever talk about refraction?

At the risk of sounding like Andy Rooney on 60 Minutes, did you ever notice how optometrists never seem to talk about refractive testing? Why is that? When was the last time you saw a continuing education lecture or journal article on the topic of refraction, or the art of prescribing glasses? ODs seem quite comfortable sharing knowledge about diagnostic procedures for ocular disease, why not refraction and lens prescriptions? It seems to me that we all spend considerable time doing refractions and interpreting the data, one would think we would have some ideas to share.

Chapter 19. Practice Finance and Metrics

19.1 The Nuts and Bolts of Your P&L Statement

The profit and loss statement (P&L, also called an income statement) is a summary of the income and expenses that occur in your practice. I'm sure most readers are very familiar with P&Ls and use them all the time, but I get asked about them quite often so a quick review is a good idea. I'll follow that with a list of nuances and tips about how to use the data in a practical way.

The basic review

The P&L statement is a report that can be generated by most financial software programs (like QuickBooks) and it is also produced by accountants. I recommend that practice owners use both of these methods; it is smart to manage your finances yourself, but an accountant will include more advanced information in the P&L and will help you understand it.

P&Ls are quite simple: there is a top line, the middle stuff and the bottom line. The top line is the total of all the income generated by the practice; also referred to as sales in the business world. It is shown in total dollars collected for some specified period of time (often six months or one year). This dollar amount is also known as gross revenue.

The middle stuff is a list of expenses. This list can be very long and detailed or it can be quite short. You get to design that aspect of the P&L by selecting the expense categories you want to see. When you enter a payment in your accounting software, you generally give it an account code, which becomes the expense categories in the P&L. Most QuickBooks P&L statements show many expense categories, but it may be more meaningful for you to categorize them into fewer categories. My business partner, Jerry Hayes, O.D., selected seven expense categories that have become well-accepted in optometry and are currently used by the AOA and the Management and Business Academy (MBA) program. I'll list the seven expense categories below.

The bottom line is the profit of the practice over the period of time that the P&L covers. Also referred to as net income, it is simply the gross income minus all the expenses. There are often some subtotals inserted at various places in the P&L statement.

It is important to remember that the P&L is a summary over time and that time period is always listed at the top of the page. The P&L is more accurate if it is for a longer period of time, like one year, because some expenses do not occur monthly and purchases like frame inventory can be higher in some months than others. But it evens out over a year. Income and expenses are always shown in dollars, but it is also helpful to express the dollars as a percentage. Some expenses go up as sales increase, such as eyeglass lab bills, so it is helpful to look at those as a percentage of sales.

P&L statements are useful as a way to measure the growth of your practice and to be sure that expenses are in line. If optometrists can define the expense categories and use them the same way, we can develop national norms for those expenses. Actually, the AOA and other groups have been doing that for years and I'll provide that data below.

Special notes on P&L statements

You may want to take your last P&L and reallocate some items that are currently not in the right category for practice use. Just take some of the costs out of one category and put it into another. Once you have your P&L the way you want it, show it to your accountant and have him/her format it that way in the future.

Realize that the expense percentages that I provide are only median figures, adjusted in some cases based on my philosophy. They can vary widely and for good reason. Every practice is different.

- Gross revenue. This should be the amount you actually collect and deposit into the bank after insurance adjustments. Usual and customary fees can still be tracked if you wish, but it does not mean much anymore. You can get this number from your practice management software production reports, but it really comes down to your bank deposits.
- Cost of Goods Sold (COGS). All the payments for frames, lenses, contact lenses, low vision aids and any other items you resell. By convention, optometrists do not typically include the charge-backs from vision plans, but we really should. It would be complicated, however and some of the lab costs for basic products are covered but no actual value is shown on the explanation of benefits report. Thirty percent of gross revenue is considered the norm for this, but I like to see it at about 27%.
- Staff expense. This should include all costs of employees, including benefits, uniforms if paid for, taxes, etc. It does not include ODs even if they are employees. To be really accurate, the cost of staff members who make eyeglasses in an in-office finishing lab should not be included here; it should be added to COGS. The median for

this is about 19%, but I like to see it higher at around 23%. Why would I like to see any expense higher? I'd like it to be a bigger percentage of a much larger gross revenue figure.

- Occupancy cost. We think of this as rent, but it includes taxes, insurance, maintenance, utilities, and any expense related to the facility. If you own the building, you should assign a true market rent value to analyze your P&L properly. The rent is not really free even if there is no payment being made. And some doctors may charge themselves excessive rent just to get more cash flow. Adjust it to be normal for your area. This expense is usually about 8%. A new start-up practice can't maintain that percentage figure because it has to pay normal rent, but it has not generated much income in the first couple years.
- Marketing. Typically 3%
- Equipment. Should include lease payments and interest in equipment loans. Typically 3%.
- General office overhead. This is everything that is not covered in the other expense categories above. It is typically about 7%.
- Practice net. This bottom line is theoretically everything that is left over after deducting the six expense categories above, but your net is probably better than it looks. It should include all payments, bonuses, distributions and salaries to doctors, even employed associates. This is simply by convention. It should include all benefits such as health insurance and retirement funds for all doctors. You should add back depreciation if that is shown on your P&L; it is just an expense on paper. Consider if there are any quasi-personal expenses that are shown in other categories, such as car expense, travel that was actually personal, other items that you use personally. Technically, that is part of your net. If there is any retained profit in your company, that is also part of the net income.

Spend some time analyzing your P&L statements and looking for trends. It will help you manage your practice.

19.2 A New Look at Practice Expense Ratios

Even though the topic has been covered before, I continue to receive many questions about expense ratios and benchmarks. Today, I'll cover the basic expense categories, how to define the nuances of those categories, the typical percentages from national surveys, my goals for these categories and what effect vision plans have on the data.

The seven expense categories

Practice gross income can be divided into seven categories, but six of them are expense groups and the one that's left over after all expenses are deducted is practice net income. Based on surveys by the AOA, the following are typical percentages of gross income by optometrists practicing in the U.S.

• Cost of goods sold	30%
• Staff expense	17%
• Occupancy costs	7%
• General office overhead	7%
• Marketing	3%
• Equipment	3%
• Practice net income	33%

Category definitions

It is extremely important to understand and apply the correct definitions to the categories if you want to make any meaningful comparison to the national data or to other individual practices. If you don't, you will be comparing apples to oranges. It's very likely that your accounting system has many more categories than the seven listed above. That's fine, but you may want to reallocate those expenses to meet these accepted standards. Sometimes, having fewer categories allows you to analyze data in a more meaningful way.

There are some surprising nuances to the definitions. Here are the most commonly misunderstood factors.

- Gross income. It should be collected revenue from all patient services and products. It is the actual total of bank deposits. It is not what is written up before insurance adjustments and write-offs.
- Cost of goods sold. Seems simple enough, but did you know it should include the payroll costs for lab staff who make glasses if you have an in-office lab? It should also include a prorated share of the rent equal to the percentage of office space a lab uses.
- Staff expense. All costs incurred with non-doctor employment including all benefits and payroll taxes. Uniforms and staff continuing education goes here if paid by the practice. Associate OD compensation does not belong in this category. That is considered part of the net even if the doctors are employees.
- Occupancy costs. Rent, utilities, maintenance, janitorial, real estate taxes, commercial insurance and any other cost associated with the facility. If you own the building, your practice should still pay you a

fair market rent in order to account properly for the other categories.

- General office overhead. A catch all category for all general office expense that is not covered elsewhere. All office and clinical supplies go here.
- Marketing. Include postage for marketing projects and recall notices. Include yellow page cost, but not the whole phone bill. Phone expense goes under occupancy.
- Equipment. Clinical equipment only, not business office or optical lab. Those would go under office overhead and cost of goods, respectively. Include lease payments, interest on loans, service contracts and maintenance. Do not include capitalized purchases.
- Practice net income. Include all doctors' salaries and benefits plus any retained practice net income and depreciation. Include a prorated share of business expenses that are actually deemed to have personal value, i.e., auto, travel and entertainment.

My preferences

Here are the same benchmarks with percentage goals that I believe are achievable and desirable. Of course, this would vary based on the age of the practice, for example, a new practice would have higher equipment and marketing expense. The biggest differences below are a greater investment in staff expense (which is necessary for the high service practice) and a reduced cost of goods sold (which can be achieved with an in-office lab and with higher volume purchasing).

- Cost of goods sold 27%
- Staff expense 21%
- Occupancy costs 7%
- General office overhead 8%
- Marketing 2%
- Equipment 2%
- Practice net income 33%

The effect of vision plans

Vision plans have become so large in many practices that they cause some special considerations. First, some plans pay the lab bill directly. This is an invisible payment, if you will, which could be recognized as gross income and then would be allocated out to cost of goods sold. If recognized, the gross income and cost of goods would be higher.

The second effect is in the "charge-backs" that are deducted from your payment by the vision plan company to cover lab costs of non-covered items.

You are allowed to charge a fee to the patient for these items, but the costs of the items are your responsibility. They are paid for by the vision plan but then they are deducted from your check. This has the effect of reducing your gross income and lowering cost of goods sold.

These two factors offset each other to the point where it is not necessary to analyze it in most practices.

19.3 Manage Your Practice Data Better

Business executives today are increasingly looking to data to manage their enterprises, but most optometrists don't gather much data or analyze practice metrics. Looking ahead to 2016, let's change that and make data a bigger part of your management decisions.

Why look at data?

You should look at data because it tells you how you are doing and if things are changing. From a very practical standpoint, some doctors may think so what; what am I going to do about it anyway? If that describes you, your first step to a more successful practice is to stop thinking that you have no control over it. By analyzing data, you can easily see what parts of your practice are doing well and what aspects are underperforming. From there, you can try new strategies and procedures (see more below). As you implement new things, the data will tell you if they are working and should be continued, modified or dropped.

How to get data

One reason ODs don't use data in practice management all that much is because it can be hard to gather. Some office management software programs make reporting too complex or the system was not set up properly in the first place (although the programs are getting better). But it really is up to the doctor/practice owner to spend some time exploring the report module built into the software. Run some sample reports with various parameters and see what you get. Makes notes when you figure out what you want so you or a manager can generate the report with ease in the future.

What would you like to know? Ask yourself that and figure out how to find it in your reports. You may have to add up a few items manually and do some basic math. Here are some ideas:

- Number of exams performed per month

- Number of screening retinal photos performed per month
- Numbers of glasses and boxes of contacts sold
- Gross collected revenue for the whole practice year to date
- Revenue compared with same period last year
- Revenue per doctor
- Revenue per staff FTE
- Revenue per office location
- Revenue generated in optical products only
- Revenue collected from vision plans
- Number of patients with vision plans
- Eyeglass retention rate

The other source for your data is your practice bank account ledger. Essentially this is your check register, even though payments today are typically made by auto-debit or credit card. Most practices use QuickBooks, Quicken or other accounting software to keep track of all this. When managed properly, this register is the basis for your profit and loss (P&L) statement and you can run it anytime you wish. It is an accurate record of all the money your practice took in and paid out in any given time period. If you code each payment with a category, you can see what you spent on cost of goods, rent, payroll or other items. When you express the payment as a percentage of revenue, you can compare your practice with a colleague or against national norms.

Third party software solutions
Several excellent companies exist in our industry to help you collect and analyze your data. These may be obtained on a monthly subscription basis or as part of membership in a doctors' alliance group. These programs generally have access to your office management software and pull the data out in a more user friendly format. They do behind-the-scenes calculations of that data and present it to the practice owner on demand, often in a dashboard format or with charts and graphs.

Daily, monthly, quarterly, annually
You can decide how often you should run various reports. When you look at specific reports frequently, you will begin to know what is normal for your practice, and it is very exciting to see stronger than normal performance. The data will inspire you to enjoy the business side of your practice and to work on it proactively.

My staff sends me the daily production report at the end of every day. I like to see the revenue generated, insurance adjustments and the bank deposit.

But one day is not enough time to determine trends. Monthly or quarterly is better for revenue per exam or Rx retention rate because the n value is larger. P&L statements can be run quarterly, but the annual one is really important because it includes payments that are annual and it evens out inventory purchases. Compare revenue and expenses for the current year with the previous year. How much did your collected practice revenue increase as a percentage?

What to do about it

Once you have data, the strategy for improving it is a management decision. There are many things you can do and there is not just one right way. Read practice management articles, hire a consultant, talk to your CPA, talk to your staff, talk to colleagues or chat on professional forums. Try whatever feels best for your practice, then analyze your data to see if it's working.

Here are some random examples of strategies.

- Raise prices; lower prices
- Add staff; add an associate doctor
- Change the appointment schedule template
- Add office hours
- Join a new insurance plan; drop an insurance plan
- Buy a new instrument
- Provide a new service
- Add a new frame line
- Start a staff bonus program
- Change your recall method
- Implement a staff training program
- Move to a new location
- Remodel the office
- Start a marketing campaign

19.4 Understanding Key Practice Metrics

Practice data can provide crucial information in many areas of practice management. Statistics can help you make decisions that will improve your practice. Here are some of my favorite metrics to analyze. I'll include a description of each item along with ideas on how to collect it and what it means.

- Collected gross revenue. This statistic is the easiest to track and it is very clean and not subject to variables. It is the total of all sales made in the practice over some known period of time. I watch it daily, monthly and yearly. This data point is only useful if we look at the money that was actually collected by the practice after insurance adjustments (write-offs). This could also be described as that money which is deposited into the practice bank account. That is the true gross. This is important because insurance write-offs have become very large. Your practice management system software (PMS) should be able to produce this number for you in a daily, monthly or yearly production report. This number describes the ability for your practice to generate income and it is the basic yardstick for how the practice is doing. It is useful to compare the current collected gross revenue to the same period last year to show your own growth. The average optometric practice with one full time OD generates about $650,000 per year.

- Gross revenue per exam. This is a very useful metric that can be determined for the whole practice and per doctor. It is found by taking the collected gross revenue for a month (or a year) and dividing by the number of comprehensive exams performed. Both of these items are on the PMS production report Comprehensive exams are chosen because they are a convenient unit of service. This stat is useful because it removes the variable of how many patients are seen to produce revenue and instead asks how much revenue is generated by each patient. So a very busy senior doctor can compare her production with a new associate on a per patient basis. The national average for this stat is about $310, but many practices generate at or above $500 per exam.
- Gross revenue per OD FTE. It is useful to look at gross revenue per doctor in the practice. To standardize how many hours a person may work, we use full-time equivalent (FTE). This simply uses the standard definition of full time as 40 hours per week. A practice that has one doctor who works 30 hours per week and another who works 20 hours has an FTE of 1.25 optometrists. The mean production for 1 FTE optometrist was stated above at $650,000 per year, but many single ODs can produce $1 million or more per year.
- Gross revenue per staff FTE. If you calculate the number of FTE staff members you have (total number of staff hours worked per week divided by 40), you can divide your collected gross revenue by that FTE number and get this metric. Experts vary somewhat on what this number should be, but I like to use 1 FTE staff per $135,000 as the desirable rule of thumb. If your gross per staff FTE is more than that, you may be understaffed and if your gross is less than that, you could be overstaffed. Please realize this is a very rough guideline and

does not take the place of a careful evaluation of staffing in action. Also realize that the practice can suffer if it is over or understaffed. Producing a very high gross per staff can cause stress and poor customer service.

- Eyeglass Rx retention rate. This metric can help with many decisions, such as pricing of optical products.
- Practice P&L. The profit and loss (P&L) statement (or income statement) is a report that is generated from your financial management software (QuickBooks or similar) and it may often be generated as a service by an accounting firm. It covers all income to the practice and all expenses over a period of time. This set of data is large enough that I will cover it in next week's tip article.
- Special metrics. There are many other very interesting statistics you can gather for your practice if you look at the reports your PMS can generate. You may have to do a little math, but here are a few examples:
    - Retinal photo screening acceptance rate. Divide number of screening photos by the total number of exams to get a percentage.
    - Multiple pair eyeglass purchase rate. You may have to track it manually.
    - Antireflective lens purchase rate. Divide total number or AR sales by total pairs of lenses sold.
    - No show rate. Many PMS can track this if you click on each appointment that is checked in or not.
    - Appointment fill rate. The total number appointments seen divided by the total number of appointment slots available.

19.5 Three Stats You Should Be Tracking

I get it. Most ODs who own an independent practice are so busy seeing patients, managing the day-to-day operations and trying to have a personal life, there is no time left to analyze practice data. While not ideal from a practice management standpoint, I'll describe three practice metrics that will tell you a lot about your practice.

Gross revenue per OD FTE

Gross revenue has always been the key yardstick of any business, but here are the nuances to make the stat meaningful for optometric practice.

- It is typical to express revenues on an annual basis when comparing to national norms.

- We only care about collected gross revenues. The total of usual and customary fees entered into your management software system does not mean much because most insurance companies don't pay that and you must write-off the difference. Find your collected gross revenue by running a software report after insurance adjustments or add up all bank deposits generated by services and product sales.
- Gross revenue by itself is a good measure of how a business is doing, but it is hard to compare with other practices that have multiple ODs.
- Calculate your OD full time equivalence (FTE) by adding up the average number of hours per week spent by all optometrists seeing patients. Divide the total OD hours by 40 (we consider 40 hours per week to be full time) A single OD practice with the doctor seeing patient four days per week means 32 hours / 40 = .8 FTE. A five doctor practice with each doctor seeing patients two days per week would be 80 doctor hours per week / 40 = 2 FTE.
- Divide the gross revenue by the FTE.

The national average for this stat is about $680,000 per OD FTE. Many practices produce over $1 million per OD FTE. If your practice is producing below what you would like, ask yourself if it is growing from year to year. If it is under-producing and not growing much; you need to find a way to attract more patients.

Gross revenue per comprehensive exam

This data point is useful in a solo practice and also if measured for each doctor in a group practice. It removes the factor of patient demand and tells us how much money the practice generates per patient. If the stat is low, it may mean that the doctor is too conservative in prescribing or the fees are low.

- Count the number of full eye exams performed in a given time period. You may have to add up a few exam codes from your office software reports. Include routine exams and medical eye exams, but do not include follow-up visits, brief office visits and contact lens checks.
- Find the collected gross revenue for the same time period as the point above from all sources (all products and services are included).
- Divide the revenue by the total exams.

The national average is about $307 but many practices generate over $500 per exam. Obviously, each exam did not actually result in prescribing all the products that were included in the revenue total. This metric is just an average.

Eyeglass retention rate
With e-commerce and all the other forms of competition, it is very important to keep a pulse on this metric. Measure it every month so you can see small changes early and adapt your product mix and price points.

There are two ways to measure the Rx capture rate:

- The easy way
    A. Total number of Rxs sold per month. Count lens pairs; not frames. Do not include outside Rxs and multiple pairs.
    B. Total number of refractive exams per month.
    C. A/B = Rx retention rate as a percentage of all refractions.
    D. The national norm is about 60%.
- The accurate way
    A. Total number of Rxs sold per month. Count lens pairs. Do not include outside Rxs and multiple pairs
    B. Total number of Rxs walked out per month. Must be managed carefully. A good way to track it is to have staff print two copies of each Rx to go; give one to the patient and file one for counting purposes.
    C. Add A and B for total Rxs written.
    D. A/C = Rx retention rate as a percentage of Rxs actually written.
    E. The national norm is about 85%.

If your eyeglass retention rate is low, think about how to improve it. The best way to get patients to buy glasses from your office is to make your optical bigger and more beautiful. Also, survey your patients and find out what they want and need.

19.6 Two Practice Metrics based on FTE

A quick way to obtain a basic report card on your practice can be found by calculating the full-time equivalent (FTE) number of optometrists and staff members and then expressing those values in relation to financial production. I use the FTE numbers to get a rough idea if a practice is producing a high level of revenue (total sales) and also to determine if it has the correct number of employees. It's really easy, so take a minute and do some rough calculations for your practice.

FTE review
Full-time equivalence is simply a way to count the number of workers in an organization even when some are full-time and some are part-time. We use a 40 hour work week as the standard for full-time status, even though the legal definition may vary on that. Another way to look at full-time is five days of work per week at eight hours each day.

As an example, let's determine how many FTE staff members you have working in your office by adding up the typical hours per week each person works. This includes all employees who are not doctors. Let's suppose you have four full-time staff members and three part-time. The full-timers work 40 hour weeks, two part-timers work 15 hours per week and the third part-timer works 20 hours per week. The total hours for all seven employees is 170. Divide this weekly hour total by 40 hours and we get an FTE of 4.25. This means that this practice has 4.25 full-time employees.

A practice with five optometrists, with each one working 15 hours per week, has 1.87 full-time equivalent ODs. The total OD hours worked per week is 75, divided by 40, equals 1.87.

Production per OD FTE
We can look at national data to determine the median collected gross revenue for a practice with one full-time OD. The Management and Business Academy pegs that at about $686,000 per year and the AOA data is close to that as well. That is the middle range of gross revenue per OD FTE, but what is the high end? It is debatable, but I would use the round figure of $1 million. I know many practices that exceed that figure on a per-OD FTE basis, but it is a good yardstick for a highly productive practice.

Now that you have determined how many FTE optometrists you have in your practice, all you need is your collected gross revenue for last year and you can compare how you are doing. Divide your annual collected gross revenue by your optometrist FTE; if it is above $686,000, you are producing above the mid-earning practice. If it is close to the $1 million mark, you are in the very top echelon of production.

If your revenue per FTE OD is less than you would like, what can you do about it? Well, determine what the problem is. Do you need more patients because the schedule is not very full? Do you need to be more efficient in order to see some of your backlog of appointments? Do you have too many doctors and if one left the practice, the remaining docs could still see all the patients?

Production per staff FTE
You can do the same calculation for your employees. I like to see the collected gross revenue per FTE staff member at about $135,000. The normal value for this metric is sometimes cited as high as $150,000. This statistic is tricky because unlike the OD production, where the higher the revenue number the better, I don't want to see the production number per staff person too high or too low. If the revenue per staff member FTE is lower than $135,000, there is a good chance you have too many staff and if the number is above $150,000 you may be understaffed. Both are bad. A very high production per staff person many not simply mean you are doing awesome; it could mean you have a stressed-out staff with poor customer service and a low amount of delegation. In that case, you may not be able to sustain that high production.

19.7 Financial Data to Help You Manage

When I consult with optometrists, I often find that many of them do not look at financial reports very often. In this article, I will cover some financial data points that seem simple, but have some confusing details that I'm often asked about. I'll cover additional metrics and reports in future tip articles.

The key data points below should be easily available from the reports in your office management software and you can do some simple math to obtain the ratios indicated below. These metrics will show you how your practice is performing compared to national statistics and they can show you if the practice is growing.

Collected gross revenue
Years ago, optometrists simply tracked the total of their usual and customary fees generated over some period of time and called it "gross revenue". It was simple and accurate. You can still track this number for historical comparison, but it is fairly meaningless today due to our managed care environment. The only number that is used now by practice management consultants and national organizations is "collected gross revenue" or gross revenue after insurance adjustments. This is your true gross and it is also the total of your bank deposits from your practice. It is the total payments received, not the fees that were entered.

I have found that for many optometric practices, collected gross revenue is often around 60% of usual and customary fees. Of course, this percentage can vary widely based on the fee structure and if the practice accepts a large number of insurance plans. The insurance write-off amount is generally growing as managed care grows in our practices.

Here are some key points about collected gross revenue (CGR):

- This metric tells us how the practice is doing as a business, but we need more information as shown below.
- What time period is covered? It could be daily, monthly, quarterly or annually.
- Is it for a single or multiple locations?
- Does it include single or multiple doctors?
- Within a practice, I like to compare this metric to the same month of the previous year to see if it is growing. Divide the difference by the previous year amount to obtain the growth as a percentage.

Collected gross revenue per OD

This one really tells us how the practice is doing, because it takes into account a part-time doctor and multiple doctors. Let's assume it is for a single office location.

- Determine the full time equivalent (FTE) for optometrists. Add up the hours worked per week seeing patients and divide by 40.
- If you are the only doctor and you only see patients 24 hours per week, you are an FTE of .6. If your CGR is $300,000 per year, your gross revenue per OD is actually $500,000 per year.
- The national average according to the AOA and the Management and Business Academy is about $680,000 per year. The maximum production one OD can produce is hard to determine because there can be some unique factors, but $1,000,000 per full time OD is certainly achievable and is a good goal.

Collected gross revenue per exam

This metric tells us how each OD is doing if there are multiple doctors. It also tells us how much revenue your practice produces for each exam.

- We typically use comprehensive eye exams only for this data point. That number should be on your office software report, but you may have to add a few items together.
- All sources of revenue contribute to this stat; the fees do not have to literally be generated by an exam.
- Divide your CGR by the number of exams in any time period. The national average is about $308 and many practices achieve around $500 per exam.

Collected gross revenue per staff member
This stat can help indicate if the practice is overstaffed or understaffed. It is a general rule of thumb and it does not replace direct observation of the practice operations.

- Determine your FTE for non-OD staff as described above. Divide your CGR by this figure.
- On an annual basis, I like to see $135,000 CGR per staff FTE. Some experts put the number at $150,000, so that is a good range. Having a higher number does not mean your staff is just more productive, it may mean you are understaffed which can lead to stress and poor customer service. It may also mean you don't delegate enough.

What about the net?
Of course, the net income is what really matters since that is what you get to keep. But the fastest way to increase your net is to increase your gross. You can cut some expenses to increase the net, but that strategy may be short-sighted because it could lead to reduced service or quality.

- The national benchmark for net income is about 30% of CGR.
- The net includes all doctor compensation, even employed ODs. Include all employment benefits.
- Reallocate your expense categories to move personal items to your net. Depreciation is an expense on paper only, so it should be added to your net.

Develop a system to track these key metrics on a regular basis in your practice. We tend to improve what we measure!

19.8 Your Eyeglass Rx Retention Rate

Do you know your eyeglass Rx retention rate? I don't just mean a wild guess; I mean do you actually measure it? It could be one of the most important metrics you have, yet the vast majority of optometrists don't measure it. Or if they do, they base it on the total number of refractions (or exams) divided by the total number of eyeglasses sold. That method is easy because the data comes right from your office management software reports, but it is not very accurate. We all know that there are many refractions performed that do not result in a spectacle prescription in the first place. We do refractions all the time as part of comprehensive eye exams, but there may be no prescription change or we may find the patient to be emmetropic. How can you expect to sell a pair of glasses when there was no Rx?

Tracking the true eyeglass capture rate is pretty easy, but it takes a system. Read on for a very good method.

Track the walkout number

In order to track the Rx retention percentage, it is easiest to count the prescriptions that actually walk out. This is a smaller number to count than those who fill their Rx for glasses with your office (at least I hope so!). The Rx retention rate is simply the inverse of the Rx walkout rate, so if you count one, you know the other. Your staff generally knows exactly which patients are taking their eyeglass Rx with the intention of buying glasses elsewhere.

You can review your office procedures to refine this any way you wish, but if the patient buys glasses from your practice and wants a copy of the Rx for his records, I do not count that as a walkout. If he wants a prescription for safety glasses which are provided by his employer, I don't count that either. If I recommend a new prescription and the patient does not buy glasses but wants a copy of the Rx, I count that as a walkout. There is some judgment, but your staff can be pretty accurate about the patient's intent.

Train your staff to always print two copies of the Rx in these cases where the patient is walking with it; or you could write it on spectacle Rx blanks made with two-part paper. Give one copy to the patient and drop the other copy in a tray or a box. At the end of every month, count the Rx copies that went elsewhere.

Convert to a rate

The rest is easy, but there is a bit more to it than you might think. We need the number of eyeglass prescriptions written for the month. Count the total number of eyeglass orders you had for the month. I count pairs of lenses sold. But you have to also add the ones that walked out to get the total!

Technically my "pairs of lenses" sold includes outside Rxs that walked in and it includes multiple pair sales to the same patient. Those should be factored out to be truly accurate. Some practices just let the walk-ins cancel some of the walkouts; that is up to you.

Divide the total number of walkout Rxs by the total number of Rxs as determined above and you have the walkout Rx rate as a percentage. Let's say you made 220 pairs of glasses and had 28 walkout Rxs last month. Your total Rxs was 248. Divide 28 by 248 and you get 11.29% or round off to an 11% walkout rate.

The retention rate or capture rate is the more positive way to look at this statistic, which is simply the difference needed to make 100%. Your Rx retention rate was 89% for the month in our example.

A spreadsheet

The simple math involved in these calculations can easily be programmed into a spreadsheet with the following cells:

A. Total number of Rxs sold per month. Lens pairs. Not including walk-ins and multiple pairs.
B. Total number of Rxs walked out per month. Must be managed carefully. Staff must write or print two copies and file one.
C. Add A and B for total Rxs written.
D. Divide B by C X 100 for Rx walkout %.
E. 100 – D for Rx retention %.

Your staff can simply plug the numbers into cells A and B and the math is carried through. You now have a monthly record for future comparison.

How does it help?

Many management decisions can be aided by this important metric.

- You might try raising fees and seeing if it has an adverse effect on the retention rate. And how big of an effect? Did you still net more income?
- You could try a better eyeglass warranty or no warranty and see if it matters.
- You could see if your retention is better with the use of scribes who can also measure and dispense eyewear.
- You can try different scripts for your staff.
- You can test lens and frame packages or a new budget frame line and see if retention improves.
- You can look at the absolute value of the retention rate and make a management decision that it could be better. This may be determined by comparing your rate with colleagues or national data. In the end, you could decide to improve your optical by making it larger or remodeling it and then track the improvement in retention rate.

19.9 Measuring Other Practice Benchmarks

Last week's tip covered measuring the Rx capture rate for glasses and contact lenses. Today, let's look at a few of my other favorite practice metrics.

Measuring and tracking these on a monthly basis is a smart move. First, we know that the mere act of measuring something often causes it to improve because there is an increased awareness of the task by doctors and staff members. Secondly, you will find ways to influence the result in a positive way, possibly through a staff incentive program, a contest or more staff training.

Gross revenue per exam

This stat is very easy to gather and tells you so much about your practice. It is also referred to as average sale per patient. Every practice management system (PMS) provides some kind of monthly production report and I'm assuming you are reviewing this each month. To determine your average gross per exam, simply take the total collected gross revenue for the month (this is gross fees minus adjustments, discounts and returns) and divide by the number of comprehensive eye exams performed that month. We use comprehensive exams simply as a matter of convention; we need some definition in order to compare with other practices. To determine your comprehensive exams, you may have to add a few line items together from your production report, depending on how it is set up. You may need to add new patients, established patients, 99 codes, 92 codes and S-codes. The goal is to count all full exams and not count brief office visits or follow-ups.

The national median gross revenue per exam is $306 according to the Management and Business Academy, but I know many optometric practices where this figure is over $500. Realize that everything you sell affects this number, so if you often prescribe multiple pairs of glasses along with contact lenses and also order advanced diagnostic testing, your value will be higher. Charging higher fees also increases this metric.

It is helpful to calculate this data point for the whole practice and also for each doctor individually.

Multiple eyeglass rate

This metric is not easily seen on a production report, but it is very useful. If you implement a new program like 50% off on multiple complete pairs or if you hold a special sales training session, you can gauge the result.

Start by defining multiple pairs. I say they must be complete pairs of glasses and the orders must be placed at the same time, but you can make it any way you wish as long as you are consistent. You will have to design a simple method to count the additional eyeglasses. I find it easiest to have this occur at the place in the office where orders are sent to the optical labs. The staff members who process the eyeglass orders can easily see when two or more pairs are for the same patient. I have the staff make a notation in a simple notebook divided by dates. You can use hash marks or record the patient's name, but you end up with a count of all additional pairs of glasses for a month. You do not count the first pair of glasses for a patient, only the extra pairs.

Determine your additional pair percentage by getting the total number of frames sold for a month. Divide the additional pair total by the total frames to obtain a percentage. I have not seen any national data on this, but I can tell you my practice averages about 18%.

A/R percentage

This one is fairly easy. Do you know what percentage of all glasses sold in your practice have premium or standard antireflection lenses? Just use your monthly production report to determine the total number of lenses sold (be sure to know if this is in pairs or single lenses). You can also see the number of antireflective treatments sold, often broken down into premium and standard depending on your set up. Just divide the total number of AR treatments by the total number of lenses (pairs) and you have your percentage. The national mean is about 34% in the US, but it is 70% in Europe and 98% in Japan.

Annual supplies of contact lenses

You can track what percentage of patients buy full year supplies of contact lenses if you offer a small discount for the group purchase and set it up in your PMS program as a specific type of discount only to be used for that purpose. Most PMS software will count the number of these discounts on the monthly report. Divide the number of discounts given by the total number of contact lens evaluations and fittings and you can see your full year dispensing rate.

Appointment fill rate

Your PMS system can most likely provide this if you run a special report, or you can do it manually by counting the number of appointment slots available each day and counting the number of patients actually seen. For this, I would use all kinds of exam visits, but do not count eyeglass dispensings. Most offices do not use appointments for eyeglass dispensing, but some do. If you offer different exam lengths for different exam types, you will need to know the ratio of full exams to brief exams to determine your number of available slots. For example, if 75% of all exams are comprehensive and 25% are brief, then you should analyze each day of appointments with that ratio in mind, deduct the lunch period and make 75% of the time double slots and 25% of the time single slots. Divide your total number of all exams performed for the month by the total of all exam slots and you have your appointment fill rate.

19.10 Achieving a High Dispensing Capture Rate

Your capture rate (or retention rate, which may have a nicer ring to it) is one of the most important factors we can look at for practice profitability. There are plenty of optical retailers (both online and brick and mortar), that are working hard to attract your patients for their eyewear purchases. But you have the patient in your office first and you should be able to retain the vast majority of them when it comes to buying glasses.

Here are my top eight factors that lead to higher eyeglass retention rates:

- Start by measuring your capture rate on an ongoing basis. Design a routine that will automatically report this metric to you on a monthly basis. You can assign it to a staff member or use a business analytic software system. There are many ways to measure eyeglass retention rate, but the simplest and most widely used is to divide the number of eyeglasses sold by the number of refractive exams performed in a given time period. Details like the number of outside Rxs filled, the number of multiple pairs sold and counting pairs of lenses or complete pairs of glasses will have an effect on this measurement, but as long as you are consistent with your method, it won't matter much. The national norm for independent ODs is about 65%, but I would set a goal to reach closer to 75%. Of note with this metric is that it uses all refractive exams as the divisor and we all know that many refractions do not result in a change in Rx or a recommendation to buy new glasses. But refractions are a convenient and readily available data point, which makes it good to use.
- The doctor prescribes specific products and talks about them at chairside. Optometrists are historically very conservative when it comes to recommending products, but we really should get over that. Patients want our professional opinions and they want to know about the latest and greatest technology in eye care. Present the best eye care possible to your patient at the end of the exam. The more specific you are about lens features and the best types of frames, the more likely the patient is to buy them in your optical.

- Design a better handoff or no handoff. The transition from the exam room to the optical dispensary is the most vulnerable time in the patient relationship and this is when most patients decide to go elsewhere for glasses. Don't give them a reason to. If your optician is often not available when you are ready to do a handoff, you have a problem. You may need more staff or more cross-training of existing staff. You may need better support from staff to drop other tasks and take care of live patients. I avoid the handoff and the search for opticians completely in my practice by using super-techs, which are scribing technicians who are also opticians.
- Faster start and more efficiency. A major reason patients leave your office prematurely is that they have other things to do. They often say they will return for the frame selection, but once they leave, you will lose many optical sales. If you are taking an hour or more on the clinic side, some patients will have to leave without ordering glasses because they did not allot enough time. Speed up the check in time, reduce the waiting periods and increase exam efficiency.
- Tie in frame selection with dilation. Don't let the need to dilate pupils prevent the patient from ordering eyewear. Review how and when the drops are instilled and train staff to coordinate dilation and frame selection. Waiting for the drops to work is an opportunity to use that time effectively in optical, but prioritize which steps to do first.
- You may already have this going for you, but it is very important to provide a great patient experience during the entire exam process. If that part goes extremely well, the patient will become loyal and want to buy glasses from your office. If something goes wrong, the patient may decide he can do better elsewhere for the optical products. It is a comprehensive, team effort to impress patients with the exam experience.
- It is easy to forget the obvious, but one big way to influence where your patients choose to buy glasses is the state of your optical. If you invest in it and make it more beautiful, larger, and better, people will decide early on that they want to get glasses from your office.
- Great looking value frames. When I ask ODs why patients take their Rx to go, by far the most frequent response is "price". I believe that is true. Most independent ODs will admit they are not the cheapest place to buy eyewear, but that business model serves us well. In addition to offering high end designer frames and premium quality lenses, you should also have a nice selection of value priced frames. Many ODs carry budget frames (and they are required by most vision

plans), but some practices strategically make these styles outdated. I think that is a mistake. There are some very current and fashionable shapes and colors available at low price points and it is smart to carry those. If your staff can show the value line with pride, you can change a patient's mind about leaving.

19.11 Achieving a High Multiple Pair Sales Rate

Optometrists generally realize that prescribing and dispensing two or more pairs of glasses for a patient is good for vision care and for practice profitability. But, most ODs don't do anything to try to increase the multiple pair sales rate. With the prevalence of vision plans taking a big bite out of the profit on the first pair of glasses, selling a second pair at the same visit can restore a great deal of total profit.

In this article, I'll show you a multi-level strategy that is easy to implement and will result in a much higher number of multiple pair eyeglass sales.

Measure first

In order to determine if our new approach to multiple pair sales is working, you must measure your current level of those sales and re-measure after implementation. Unfortunately, second and third pairs of glasses can be difficult to track with most office practice management software systems (PMS). Work with your staff and review your record of lab orders to see if you can obtain a basic count of the total number of eyeglasses (complete pairs) ordered per month and also how many of those were a multiple pair. If you have a special multiple pair discount, your PMS may be able to track that number. If you sold 100 complete pairs of glasses last month and 10 of those were an additional pair sold at the same visit, then your multiple pair rate is 10%.

We don't have a lot of data on national norms for multiple pair sales, but 10 to 20% is the typical range that I see.

Four steps to multiple pair sales

There are four important tools that can combine to help your practice achieve a very high rate of multiple pair sales.

- Doctor prescribes additional pairs of glasses. The power of the doctor has a big impact on multiple pair dispensing. As part of the treatment plan, which should be presented to the patient at the exam chair, the doctor should recommend and design multiple eyeglass prescriptions. This takes into account the vision problems, chief complaints and patient's lifestyle. Advise your patients that one pair of glasses can't meet all of their vision care needs. Talk about sunglasses, glasses for computer screens, occupational needs and hobbies. It is helpful for the doctor to write out separate Rx forms for each pair of glasses to give to the optician.

- Opticians sell by asking questions. The optician plays a major role in selling a second pair of glasses and one strong technique is to understand the patient's lifestyle needs. Asking about the patient's occupational and avocational interests paves the way for multiple pairs of glasses. Informing the patient about any discounts on the second pair is a great way to bring up the concept.
- Give the patient a large discount on additional pairs. My practice has found big success in offering a substantial discount to patients on multiple pairs of glasses purchased at the same time. We offer 50% off the usual price for additional pairs of glasses. It is important to realize that we gain many efficiencies when we measure, order, process, communicate and deliver multiple pairs of glasses to one patient. This is how we justify the large discount.
    - All glasses must be complete pairs (frame and lenses).
    - The discount is given on the less expensive pairs.
    - The first pair may be ordered through a vision plan.
    - This discount works well if there is already a strong mark-up built into the regular pricing. There should be plenty of profit in the additional pairs even after the discount.
    - Many wholesale labs offer 50% off the lenses on multiple pairs. Be sure to use this.
- Pay staff a bonus for selling multiple pairs. Many staff bonus programs sound good logically, but fail to actually change behavior in the desired way. I find the most effective incentives for staff are when there is a high degree of correlation between the reward and the desired behavior. That occurs when a person who sells eyewear is directly spiffed each time he or she sells a second pair. Strong individual effort earns the most rewards and is not influenced by co-workers. The bonus can be a percentage or dollar amount (we have found $10 per additional pair works well). Our staff tracks their own multiple sales on index cards by listing the patient name and date, which can be spot checked for accuracy.

19.12 Reduce Your Expenses to Increase Practice Net

It's certainly logical that if you cut your operating cost, you will increase your net, at least in the short term! But I urge you to consider the big picture of your practice and be very careful where and how you reduce expenses; I often say you can't cut your way to prosperity! Cutting expenses often means cutting service and quality, and that can lead to a loss of patient loyalty and reduced referrals. This can create a downward business cycle with reduced patient demand leading to reduced cash flow requiring more cuts to services. I think it's great to buy smart and shop for good values, but in some areas of your practice spending more will lead to higher profits in the long run.

Shop around

Most optometrists and their staffs already do an excellent job of finding good deals on all the supplies, products and services needed to operate a practice. We all have a natural tendency to shop for good values, change vendors when service or quality suffers and buy in bulk when it makes sense.

Some practices provide an incentive bonus to staff members based on net income or expense percentages, and I'm sure that can be effective, but if there is a good system of management and supervision in place, I don't think it is a necessity. My staff can only order from specific suppliers that are pre-approved.

How to negotiate with suppliers

While most ODs do a good job of comparing prices, most do not try to negotiate better deals. If they tried, they could save money. The best way to negotiate a better price is to have some form of leverage. You can't go to a supplier and just say you would like a better price. A better approach is to go to a competitive vendor and say you are considering moving some business to them and you would like the best price quote they can offer. Compare this pricing with what you are paying for similar products now. If it is much better, go to your current supplier and tell them XYZ company has offered you better pricing and you wanted to give them a chance to keep your business and see if they can do better.

It is very important, however, to realize that changing suppliers can easily result in unhappiness. The cheaper company may not provide as good service or quality or speed of delivery. Your staff may be very unhappy dealing with the new company. Patients may be disappointed in the product. All of this may not be worth the lower price! Be careful not to burn bridges. I would send only a small percentage of orders to the new company first and even if you switch to a large degree, keep a good relationship with the first vendor because you may want to go back.

I think we have a responsibility to negotiate in an ethical way with suppliers. It will work in your best interest in the long run because business relationships are important. One way to do this is to not share price lists or invoices from one competitor to the other. In my example above, you obtained the pricing information and made the decision yourself without giving copies of invoices and saying can you beat this pricing? Each vendor quotes the best price they can offer and they compete in the marketplace.

Return products

Be sure your staff keeps up to date with returning products that are covered under warranty or can be returned or exchanged. Sales reps may assist with this in many cases, but there are plenty of returned products that must be packaged and addressed and shipped back. If an office is understaffed, there may not be time to get around to this and the products pile up in a drawer or a box and eventually no one knows what to do with them.

Every staff member should have a side job that he or she is responsible to manage as time permits. Be sure products are retuned for credit in a timely manner and the credits are received on your account.

Buying groups and doctor alliances

One way for independent ODs to get optimum pricing is to belong to a group purchasing organization. By way of disclosure, I am currently employed as Chief Optometric Officer at IDOC, a leading alliance group that offers vendor savings, education, networking and consulting services to independent optometrists. There are many different ways that these groups work, but the new generation of alliances is different than traditional buying groups because they additionally bring practice management services and educational programs to doctors and staff members. The member doctors maintain direct accounts with vendors and they are afforded excellent discounts and rebates that are typically not available to individual practices or small chains. The basis for the increased discount is that the alliance group will work to build loyalty and increase purchasing volume for these preferred vendors. There is often some exclusivity of vendors within business categories with alliances, while buying groups typically represent nearly all vendors. Alliance groups typically charge a membership fee in the form of monthly dues; buying groups often keep a percentage of the discount the account earns as an administrative fee.

19.13 Patients per Day: You're Seeing Fewer Than You Think

I have an interesting exercise for you and I'm sure the result will make you think about your practice in a different way. My hope is that if you measure this simple data point for your practice, you will be motivated to change some of your procedures. Try it; it might be a wake-up call for you.

Most optometrists have a general idea of how many exams they perform in a typical day and we form an opinion on the right number for our practice and our preference. If we try to gather this data in a fairly accurate way, you will have to decide if we should count all patient visits or just comprehensive exams. We also need to define a day. You probably have some long days and some half days of patient care. As long as you understand the data in your measurement, it does not really matter, but I'll suggest a standard to follow so we can compare your results with what other ODs do.

Let's agree to count comprehensive eye exams (you can define what this means, but I would take it to mean a complete eye health exam and a refraction). Let's also agree to count a day as about eight hours of patient care, but we won't get too picky about lunch breaks.

Exams per day metric
I'm going to give you some guidelines on how to collect and measure your exams per day, but before we do that, I'd like you to make a mental note of the number you think you see. Don't use data at all for this. Just based on your experience, how many comprehensive exams do you perform on an average day?

Next, I'd like you to calculate this metric in the following way:

- Use a long time period, like all of 2016.
- Calculate the number of doctor days that occurred in 2016 by adding up all the days worked per week by all doctors. For example, if you worked the whole year and you usually work 3.5 days per week, use that number. Or, if you work about 28 hours per week on patient care, divide that by 40 hours to get your full-time equivalent and multiply by five because we consider five full days per week as full time. 28/40 = .7 X 5 = 3.5 days per week.
- There are 52 weeks per year, but reduce that by whatever time you took off in 2016. For example, you have three weeks of vacation,

one week of sick days, one week of holidays and two weeks of continuing education. So you worked 45 weeks out of the year.

- You had 3.5 X 45 = 157.5 doctor days in 2016.
- Do the same for any additional doctors who worked in your practice and add them up.

Now we need an accurate count of how many comprehensive exams were performed in your practice in 2016. The best way to do this is by running a report in your practice management software, but you can use any method that you know is accurate. If you run a report of all services and products sold in 2016, you may have to add up some sub-totals like new patient and established patient. And you may have to add up several CPT codes like 92004, 92014, 99204, 99214, 99205, 99215. Just think about what codes or services are used to describe a comprehensive eye exam in your office and include all of them and be sure to get the data for all doctors.

Divide the total number of comprehensive exams by the total number of doctor days and you have the true number of exams per day. For example, if you saw 1,250 comprehensive exams in 2016 and you had 157.5 doctor days, you saw 7.9 exams per day. Call it eight.

What do you think of your number?

In my experience, the vast majority of ODs overestimate the number of exams they think they perform. I asked you above to make a mental note of the number you think you see per day. How did that compare with your real number? Feel free to challenge the calculation and make it as accurate as possible, but numbers don't lie.

Your production report may not show exams that are no charge, but I assume you don't have too many comprehensive exams that are given away. We might have some office visits like contact lens checks that are covered in a fitting fee or eyeglass trouble visits that are no charge, but we used comprehensive exams to avoid that issue.

If your presumed number and true number are vastly different, use this a-ha moment to make some changes in your practice.

What to do

Here are a few ideas on how to increase your exams per day metric:

- Change the appointment template. If you have many appointments booked ahead, consider adding more slots per day.

- Delegate more. You can see more patients per day if you hire an additional technician and delegate more of the exam procedures. Or teach the tech to scribe.
- If you are not booked far ahead, it might make sense to reduce your number of doctor days per week so you are busier when you are in the clinic. Then you will have some days off or days to work on management without interruption.
- No shows and last minute cancellations can cause a significant reduction in productivity. This is especially common if you preappoint. You should review your confirmation procedure to be sure it is still happening the right way.
- Increase patient demand. If you need to fill your schedule, there are three big ways to do it: Increase word-of-mouth referrals (improve your customer service), add vision plans and increase your marketing efforts.

Why does it matter?
Your basic productivity matters. If you think you are seeing twelve comprehensive exams per day on average, but it is really eight per day, you may begin to understand why your revenue and profit numbers are not as good as you would like. Knowing the real number of patients seen may motivate you to change your appointment template and delegate more procedures to staff in order to increase your patient volume.

19.14 Reviewing Your Past Year and Looking at the New One

Another year has gone by and this week between Christmas and New Year's Day is always a great time for reflection. It is the perfect time to analyze your business trends for the past year and to set goals for the year ahead. Here is a guide with some factors to look at.

Your business year in review
Generate and print your practice profit and loss statement (P&L) from QuickBooks or at least tally up your collected gross revenue for 2015 and 2014. Basically, this is a total of all your payments from patients and insurance plans. Did the revenue increase in 2015 as compared to 2014 and if so, by how much? Of course, you always want to see some growth, but a large practice may grow at a slower rate than a small or new practice. We

might say we want to see at least 5% growth for a very large practice, but 10% to 20% growth would be a good goal.

If you have a P&L, look at your major expense categories and see if they are in the normal range for optometry. We especially want to look at cost of goods, employee payroll, rent and other occupancy costs, equipment, marketing and miscellaneous overhead. We would like the practice net income to be 30% of the collected gross revenue, but by convention we include all doctor salaries in this net figure, even if a doctor is an employee.

Also, print your practice production report for 2015 and spend time analyzing the products and services you sold. Where did the revenue come from? What was the total revenue generated per eye exam?

Put your ideas on paper

As you analyze your practice, think about what should be better. I find writing things down on a pad of paper helps me think. Make lists of the services and products that did well and more lists about what you would like to improve. These ideas will become your business plan for 2015.

If your personal income is not as good as you would like, what number would you prefer? Work backwards from that. If you want to earn $240,000 personally, what would the gross revenue of the practice need to be? If you net 30%, your gross would need to be $800,000. That is quite doable. What do you have to do to generate that much revenue? Maybe attract more patients. Maybe raise fees. Maybe sell more goods and services to each patient. Make more lists about how you could improve on each of these big factors.

Here are a few points to consider:

- Review your office lease. Don't wait until the lease is due for renewal to think about your office space. If you do that, you'll have to make a quick decision and you'll just end up renewing the lease because it is easy. Is it time to move your office to a larger place with better visibility or other benefits? Moving to a better location is a great marketing strategy; it gets your practice noticed. More space can convert to a larger staff and more sales.
- Is it time to open a branch office? If your practice is not growing, it may be due to the local population size in relation to other eye care providers. You might do well to keep your present office, but also open a new one in a different market area that is growing faster.

- Should you appoint a marketing director? Is there someone on your staff who could take on this additional duty and work under your direction on all kinds of marketing activities? If this new job takes that employee away from other tasks, hire a new employee to do those tasks. If the plan works right, you will generate enough new revenue to more than pay for the salary of the new employee. What if the marketing doesn't work? That is a business risk and you need to take some risk to move the practice forward. It won't fail all at once. You can adapt your plan as you move forward.
- Can you increase your eyeglass retention rate? There is no clever way to stop patients from taking their Rx out or buying glasses online. The way to do it is to make your optical great. Make it more beautiful and more impressive. Make it larger. Make the service better.
- Office hours. What would happen if you kept the office open a couple of evenings until 7pm and added hours every Saturday until 1pm? What if you were open that weekday that is generally closed? Think about it. You might make more money if you would see more patients. You might make enough additional money that you could hire more staff and maybe even hire an associate OD. Your office could be open 55 hours per week; that does not mean that you or any employee would work all those hours. People can have different days off. Some people can work Saturdays while others do not. One thing I know for sure: patients love office hours that are convenient for them. Offering more convenience to patients is the first step toward great customer service and more word-of-mouth referrals.
- Raise fees. Does it make any difference to your bottom line if you raise your fees, considering vision plans are so prevalent? Yes, it absolutely makes a big difference. Even vision plan patients must buy some things from your office that are not covered and when they do, you must make a strong profit.

Long-term plans

As you plan for the year ahead, look beyond as well and consider how much longer you want to practice optometry. When could you sell your practice and retire? If you could own the practice as a business and hire an associate to see most of the patients, would you still be in a hurry to sell? Would you enjoy retirement or would you become bored? How old are you and how long might you live? How much money would you need on hand to live as you wish if you had little or no earned income?

These are all good questions and there are many more. Talk to your spouse and a trusted advisor, such as a financial planner or a practice consultant. Join a study group of ODs and ask them what they are planning to do. Share your experience and ask your colleagues to share theirs.

19.15 Is It Time to Raise Your Fees?

Many practices have not raised fees in a significant way for many years. That could be due to a tough economy or to a general fear that if we raise fees, we may lose some of our valuable private pay patients. Competition is fierce for most eye care providers (ECPs). In spite of those concerns, optometrists routinely tell me the last time they raised their fees, nobody noticed. My experience shows me that patients are quite loyal to their doctor and not that sensitive to price.

Raising fees is one of the fastest ways to increase practice net income. You can decide if you want to use that increased cash flow to invest in your practice or take it as personal income.

What about insurance plans?

Many ODs scoff at the concept of raising fees because they have so many patients with vision plans or medical insurance that they think it won't make any difference. That is not true. Raising fees actually helps you to increase your profit on patients who have vision plans, because invariably, patients buy some services and products that are not covered. Besides that, if your practice is so heavily dominated by insurance, why not raise your fees? After all, patients won't mind one bit since they all have insurance.

When you raise your fees, the perception of your practice by the public and by your patients goes up. People judge the value and quality of your services by the fee.

How to determine fees

Most ECPs set their fees and prices by calling the other practices in town and finding out what they charge. It is quite useful to know the price range in a marketplace if you are selling a commodity, like a gallon of gasoline or a pound of sugar. But eye care is not a commodity and most ECPs set their fees way too low. Should you set your fees too low just because all the other providers under-value their services?

I would prefer that you do some market research and find the true value of your products and services. You may have to experiment with various prices to see what price point causes a drop in sales or complaints. The good news is that a short experiment with higher prices can reveal quite a lot and really can't do any lasting harm to your practice.

Most ECPs would like to use a mark-up formula to help set fees, but it is really not that simple. It is often more intuitive and to some extent it is based on what the traffic will bear.

Your practice positioning

As you set your fees, be sure to consider the demographics of your local market area. Is the median household income level high, low or in between? Additionally, what is your market strategy for your practice? Consider that first. Is your practice designed to be high-end with advanced services? Are you trying to appeal to the budget conscious blue collar family? Any of these can be a good business model, but be true to your goals.

Services and products to review

When we discuss setting fees, we must consider a wide range of products and services. You may be out of date on many or all of the following:

- Exam and procedure fees. Consider using the Medicare approved fees as a good starting point. Many doctors go slightly higher than those. Many ODs feel they need to discount those fees for routine exams that are paid out of pocket. You may not charge different fees for the same service, but you can offer a time of service discount for cash payment and you can use S-codes for routine exams and charge less that your fee for medical exams.
- Contact lens service fees. Many ODs set these fees way too low in my opinion. I would have one fee for a contact lens evaluation, which is charged in addition to the comprehensive eye exam fee because you perform additional testing on contact lens patients. A contact lens evaluation fee is charged if there is no change in the lens fit. I include corneal topography and that increases the fee quite a bit. For contact lens fittings and refittings, I would have different fee levels based on the complexity of the lens design. A fitting generally includes a follow-up visit, so that means the fitting fee must be much higher than an intermediate office visit fee.
- Contact lens products. With Unilateral Pricing Policy (UPP), we are now able to compete with any vendor and no one can sell the products for less. You are allowed to charge more than the UPP price, but I find a big advantage in saying that we charge the lowest possible price for this product. For lenses that are not yet on UPP, you should set prices fairly competitively with large online retailers.

- Frames. A mark-up formula works well so that your staff can always set the price properly as new frames come in, but the old 3X mark-up is really not sufficient anymore. Be sure to have a good selection of low priced frames as well for the budget conscious patients.
- Lenses. This category of product may be the trickiest to price correctly. To a large extent, it is what the traffic will bear, especially for premium products. The mark-ups are not linear. Some items can have a 10X mark-up while some lens add-on features might only be 3X. Remember that there are many dispensing services built into the price of eyeglasses, so the pricing must be higher than most retail products.

I advise you to gather all your fee schedules and price lists and review them. Raise the prices you feel are too low and just tell your staff what the new prices are, effective immediately. Staff members can get a bit worried about fee increases, but just plow forward and it will work out better than they think. If any patient indicates he was recently quoted a lower fee, your staff can honor that without question. Most people will not notice.

19.16 Raising fees: Why It's Important Even with Vision Plans

Most of the optometric practices I analyze need to raise fees, yet practice owners are extremely reluctant to do so. Staff members echo that fear. I realize that the economy is still very shaky, but most practices have not implemented a fee increase in well over a year and even when they did, it was too little, too late.

Optometrists routinely undervalue their services. Just look at a few other fields as a guide to relative value. Have you had a plumber come to your house lately? Do you know what dentists charge for a routine cleaning and x-rays? Have you experienced lawyer fees? For female readers: what do you pay for a "cut and color" at the hair salon? I rest my case.

What is your worry?
Most eye care professionals (ECPs) worry they will lose patients if they raise fees, yet if you think back to the last time you actually implemented a fee increase; you will likely agree that the vast majority of patients do not even notice. Eye care services in independent private practice are just not very

price sensitive. Patients come to you because they trust you and want the best eye care; price is secondary.

Even if you lost a small percentage of patients, which I highly doubt, most practices would still make a greater profit with a moderate fee increase. Anything wrong with that?

Think of a fee increase as market research. Implement it and monitor the reaction. Ask your staff if patients make any comment in the first week or two. See if you can detect any dip in sales or appointments. The great thing about running a small business is that you can make changes very easily and quickly. If you detect a strongly negative response to a fee increase, you can always just move them back to the old fee levels. How much harm can you do in two weeks? Virtually none.

Why do it if vision plans dominate?

In many cases, practice owners don't bother to raise fees because they reason that vision plan payments are fixed anyway, so it will not make much difference. My response to that logic is: then why not raise them? Who will care? Most of your patients won't be affected by the increase anyway so it is extremely safe to do it. But there are two very good reasons why you should raise fees even with strong participation in vision plans.

- A higher fee increases the patient's perception of your services. Vision plan patients may have the exam fee covered, but they are still aware of the usual fee. They may hear it quoted over the phone or see it on their office receipt. And when patients see a higher fee they place a higher value on your services. People judge services based on the price, especially when they don't have the technical expertise to judge it in other ways. Why not build a reputation as the best eye care provider in the region?
- Patients with vision plans still buy many non-covered services and products from your practice and when they do, you must make a good profit. The discount provided to vision plans by panel doctors is substantial, so you must make up for that with non-covered services. Don't write off vision plan patients as low-profit margin cases; consider that the following services may be non-covered:
    - Exams. Patients may need a mid-year progress exam or may have an eye emergency. Why not make your routine eye exam fee the same as your medical eye exam?
    - Special testing. This could be for routine screenings like retinal photos or could involve medical diagnostic procedures.

- Contact lenses. Most vision plans provide an allowance to use towards contact lens fittings and products. The plan may also require a small discount, but you can still bill the balance to the patient.
- Frames. Many patients select a frame that is not fully covered by the vision plan. Raising your frame mark-up formula can increase your frame overage fees. Besides that, patients with vision plans sometimes buy a second pair of glasses or need to replace glasses when there are no benefits available.
- Lenses. Base lens prices and additional lens features may be capped by vision plans, but think about additional pairs of glasses throughout the year.
- Other non-covered services. Medical eye care, low vision, sports vision, vision therapy, non-Rx sunglasses and many other services and products are not covered by vision plans and should carry a high fee in your practice.

Customer service can improve

When you increase your exam fees, you will find that customer service can also improve. You and your staff will develop a mental attitude that allows you to be more generous and creates a feeling of letting the patient have his way. As much as some practices try, you really can't have great customer service and low fees. The high fee – great service combination will generate an upward business cycle for your practice. The new emphasis on customer service creates more patient demand through loyalty and word of mouth referral. The strong patient demand will allow you to raise fees again because there is always a market for the best. The increased revenue from higher fees will allow you to invest in your practice, creating more competitive advantages.

Chapter 20. The CEO Model

20.1 The CEO Model of Optometric Practice

The CEO model of practice is really just a mindset. It is a way of thinking about your practice as a separate business. It encourages optometrists who own their own practices to think of themselves as CEOs of a small business and not as a doctor who sees patients. Of course, in reality and to some extent, most OD owners will continue to see patients some of the time, but the CEO model implies that he or she would not have to see patients. Other optometrists could be employed to see patients. The degree to which the OD works as an OD can change throughout one's career.

I believe this CEO mindset is extremely helpful in building a successful practice. Optometrists who can embrace business principles become better leaders for their organizations. The ground-breaking publication on this concept is "The E-Myth Revisited" by Michael Gerber, which can be an epiphany of sorts for any small business owner. The "E" in the title stands for entrepreneur.

The E-Myth Revisited
My favorite part of the book is this passage:
The Fatal Assumption is: if you understand the technical work of a business, you understand a business that does technical work. And the reason it's fatal is that it just isn't true. In fact, it's the root cause of most small business failures! The technical work of a business and a business that does technical work are two totally different things!

The carpenter becomes a contractor, the hairdresser starts a beauty salon, the engineer goes into the semiconductor business and the musician opens a music store. Rather than being their greatest single asset, knowing the technical work of their business becomes their greatest single liability. For if the technician didn't know how to do the technical work of the business, he would have to learn how to get it done. He would be forced to learn how to make the business work, rather than to do the work himself.

Think like a CEO
To help you to look at your practice as a business, ask yourself this question: If you could no longer see patients yourself, but you still came into your office every day, what would you do?

Here is a list of possible answers:

- Review and observe processes and procedures
- Buy products smarter; work with suppliers and labs
- Manage and train staff
- Implement marketing projects
- Build patient loyalty
- Develop referral sources
- Monitor expenses and compare to norms
- Improve technology systems

These tasks can be converted to the following subjects that are all courses found in business school:

- Strategic planning
- Business operations
- Human resources
- Marketing
- Organizational behavior
- Accounting and finance
- Information technology

Start your new approach to the business of optometry by devoting at least one day per week to practice administration. Organize your management work into the topics listed above and become self-educated in these areas.

Work on your practice, not in your practice.

20.2 Act As You Mean to Go

If we examine why some eye care practices grow into large, highly successful firms that gross millions of dollars while others seem to stall at an average income and size level, there is a key factor that jumps out at me. It is the entrepreneurial spirit. Some people seem to have a passion for business that fuels them to become strong leaders. There seems to be a natural aptitude in some people for business, but not every ECP who opens or buys a practice has that spirit. Many doctors end up as practice owners because it is a common career path but they didn't expect all the challenges that come with building a successful business venture.

While it may take more effort for some, I believe many of the factors that make up a great entrepreneurial spirit can be learned. Evaluate your own strengths and hesitations as you read these concepts.

Tactical vs. strategic

The differences between tactics and strategies are much like the differences between a manager and a leader. As business writer Peter Drucker said, "Management is doing things right and leadership is doing the right things." Said another way, tactics are the how; strategies are the what and why. I think ECPs who are successful in business need to be good at both. I think it is well accepted that the practice owner needs to be a good leader, but it is a mistake to try to delegate all the management duties. The successful ECP is also a good manager of people. As the practice grows, the balance between being the doctor and the CEO shifts toward less clinical time and more management time.

Think big

An entrepreneur visualizes the practice well into the future. This technique goes hand in hand with goal setting, but it is more than that. There is a visual image of what the successful practice will look like someday and how it will operate. It is the essence of a business plan that comes to life. The vision is typically very special and advanced; successful business types do not envision mediocrity.

Business involves risk

The successful CEO is not risk averse. He knows you must spend money to make money and the successful practice owner will stretch to make the practice look like the vision. There are regular investments into the practice, even if it requires a bank loan or lease at times. The entrepreneur is always looking for what he or she can do next. It might be a larger office or multiple locations. It might be a larger optical, an in-office lab, a larger staff, or new clinical instrumentation.

This technique involves making your practice look like the way you hope it will become. I often advise ECPs to "act as you mean to go." Some have referred to this as "fake it until you make it." If you make your practice look large and successful, it will become that.

Positive change results in growth

As you progress through any growth phase in your practice, many good things happen. It doesn't really matter which item on your wish list you take action on first because in any case, the staff senses a feeling of excitement and success. This elevates their attitudes and patients sense it as well. This eye care practice is doing great things. Productivity is increased by the new resources and word of mouth referrals grow by leaps and bounds. Quite often the new services or environment provides the confidence that the owner needs to raise fees and patients don't care because they love what they see in the practice.

When should you take the next step?
So, when should you take the next step in your practice? When should you hire the additional employee, or move to a larger office, or bring in that expensive new instrument? My best advice it to not wait until you see a clear signal to act, such as increased patient demand. Instead, develop a safe plan to finance the venture now and you'll be amazed at how the patient demand will follow. That is how all great businesses are built.

20.3 Your Exit Strategy Could Be to Not Sell

Many optometrists who are at the midpoint in their career or later are worried about their exit strategy. Who will buy their practice? Should they get another OD in place now who might be able to buy the practice? In some cases, the practice owning OD is working too many hours and suffers from some degree of career burnout.

I think financial planning for retirement and estate planning is a smart idea. It is certainly never too early to have an attorney draw up a will or a living trust. You should have some retirement investment accounts. But selling your practice or even selling part of it just so you have a buyer lined up can be a mistake. You could give up a large portion of your income stream to a partner, you could give up some degree of control over the practice that you built and you could settle on a sale price that has not reached its maximum level.

An alternate exit strategy
Instead of selling your practice or taking in a partner to reduce your patient load and your stress level, what if you hired an associate OD to see a large percentage of your patients? You could reduce your days per week spent on patient care, gradually or quickly. Over time, you could see patients very little or not at all, but still own and operate the practice. I call this the CEO practice model.

When this model is implemented effectively, your timeline for complete retirement from the practice usually changes dramatically. If you did not have to see the patients, would you still be in a hurry to sell and retire? Many optometrists are happy to transition to more emphasis on practice management and ownership and less on clinical optometry. They still enjoy a nice income stream that is semi-passive along with a very flexible schedule. The practice really can function just fine without you and it can even produce revenue without you.

Many ODs find that the new horizon for retirement under these circumstances is 10 or more years further out than what they were thinking. And they can still sell the practice eventually, probably for more than it is worth now. The income stream you can derive from owning the practice for many more years is more valuable to you than the one-time asset sale.

Is your highest and best use seeing patients?
Most optometrists think of their practice as an extension of themselves, but it really could be managed as a separate business. Many ODs feel that their best purpose in the practice is to examine eyes, but I actually believe that a practice that has grown to a successful level needs the OD/owner to work on the business.

Some good things happen when you hire an associate and you don't have to see all the patients:

- You can spend more time on the business side of your practice, working with your office manager. Ironically, this attention to the business by someone at your high level almost always causes the practice to grow. The business operation improves and patient demand increases.
- The associate OD and some additional staff members can allow the office to be open more convenient hours, such as a couple of evenings until 7pm and Saturdays 9am to 1pm. This is convenient for patients and good for the practice.
- More revenue is produced because the new optometrist is allowing the practice to see more patients.

Why not a partner?
I know some excellent partnerships in optometry that work out very well. Partners can also apply the CEO model as described above. Just because the practice has some partners now does not mean all future ODs must be partners.

Here is why I think employed doctors work better in most cases:

- Partners get to share in the business profit, in addition to the normal compensation one would receive as an optometrist. I would rather have you keep all that business profit.

- You will have to share all your practice decisions with a partner and you won't agree on everything.
- Items charged to the practice as business expenses can be scrutinized and argued.
- Ending the business relationship can be sticky with a partner; it's easy with an employee.

Here is a good analogy about your exit strategy for your practice. Someday, you will want to sell your house. That really does not worry you right now and you really don't know who will actually buy the house. When the time comes, you will put the house on the market and there will be a buyer. I think it is the same for your practice.

20.4 Think of Your Practice as a Separate Entity

Most optometric practices are tied very closely to the practice owner. In many cases, doctors identify so closely with their practices that it feels like they are one and the same. But they aren't one and the same. It is best to think of your practice as a separate entity. Thinking of the practice as a business and thinking of yourself as an employee (the CEO, perhaps, but still as an employee of the company) helps you focus on the needs of the business and not on your personal needs. This will also help you implement change that is vital to your growth.

For medium and smaller practices, the doctor/owner typically wears many hats and many things depend upon him or her. It is easy to develop a habit that the owner must be involved in many of the smaller details of operating the practice. This is usually quite practical in the early stages because it is not financially feasible to have a large staff, but think of it as temporary. Someday, you will not want the practice to be so dependent on you. Tell yourself that you are doing things this way for now for practical reasons, but eventually, many policies and procedures will change. Visualize how you want your practice to be someday.

Here are a few aspects of your practice that are impacted by how you think:

- Practice name. If you want to have a practice that does not depend solely on you, select a practice name that is not simply your first and last name. Instead of Jane Doe, O.D., consider Doe Eye Care or Doe Vision Associates.
- Office hours. When you are the only optometrist in the office, the clinical hours become quite personal. You may want your family to

be the priority, so you design the office hours around that. But if you think of your eye center as a separate entity, you'll realize that office hours that are convenient for patients are an important part of the business plan. It may be necessary to have limited hours with no evenings or Saturdays for now, because of your personal life, but think about how you can eventually expand the hours when you are able to hire more staff and another doctor.

- Lunch policies. Similar to the thinking above, some offices close at lunch time because it is convenient for the doctor and staff. Someday you can have enough staff to take lunch in shifts, allowing patients to drop in over their own lunch hour if needed.
- Staff. If the doctor thinks of staff as his helpers, there can be a tendency to want a small staff. A large staff feels like too much work. But a large staff leads the way to less work and less dependency on the doctor. I tried to hire more staff as soon as possible. It helped my practice to grow.
- Size of the office. The office you are in now may not be your final office. You might move several times with each location getting bigger and better.
- Delegation. Push yourself to delegate more to your staff, including optical, clinical and administrative work. Teach others to do the tasks you do now. Always maintain supervisory control and know enough so that if a staff member quits, you can show a new employee what to do. Set up a process where the office is opened and closed without you being there.
- Practice image and reputation. As the leader of your practice, the reputation of the practice will always be tied to your reputation, but work toward letting the practice get the credit for doing great things rather than you personally. Let your staff be experts in their areas of the practice.

As you reflect on your present practice model and what it might become, be sure to think big. It may take time, but continue to invest in the practice in many ways. Make your practice look and act as much as possible like the center of excellence you dream of.

20.5 Managing Your Practice While Away From the Office

I realize that most eye care professionals (ECPs) do not get the chance to be away from their offices much, except for a vacation here and there. But more and more ECPs are working part time and some are increasingly dedicated to practice administration while leaving patient care to partners or associate optometrists. It is certainly possible to manage your practice from your home in town, from a second home out-of-town or while traveling.

I've long been an advocate of designing a practice that does not depend solely on the doctor/owner. Consider these benefits:

- The owner operates at a higher level as both a doctor and as a CEO.
- It is easier for patients to accept delegation of services to staff members.
- It is easier to transfer patients to associate doctors.
- It is easier to sell the practice in retirement.
- It is possible for the practice to generate income without the doctor/owner being present.

Managing the practice remotely is a great goal because it forces you to think of the practice as a business that has important people running it besides you.

A full time manager

A full time office manager is a necessity for a practice that does not have the owner always present. Someone must be in charge and have the authority to direct work and make decisions. And since everyone gets a regular day off, calls in sick sometimes and takes vacation days, it is a good idea to have an acting manager or an assistant manager as a backup for the manager. The actual duties of the manager can evolve and increase over time, but the basics begin with telling employees what jobs to do, supervising the flow of money and properly closing the office at the end of the day.

The owner can work quite closely with the manager while away from the office. Over time, the manager becomes trained to think the way the owner does. Eventually, it's up to the owner to decide how much micro-managing he or she wants to do. It is best to let the manager function at a high level and not have to check with the owner on every routine decision.

Clear office policies and a functional employee manual are tools that greatly assist with remote management. If you don't have them when you start such a venture, you will develop them quickly.

Daily communication

Even though information will always be available to the absent owner, it is best to have some items delivered as a matter of daily routine without having to ask for them. The following items can be emailed or faxed every day that the owner is away from the office.

- Daily appointment schedule. At the beginning of the day, each doctor's schedule should be sent. Review for openings and speak with staff about efforts to fill gaps.
- Employee call-offs. Send a list of people who called off for any reason.
- Daily production report. All reports of interest from the practice management software system should be sent at the end of the day. The owner should review gross revenue and receipts along with the quantities of services and products that were sold. Spot check that appropriate fees were charged.
- Manager's email summary. The manager can send a short email at the end of the day reviewing any events of interest that occurred.
- Drawer balance worksheet and deposit ticket. Send a summary of the day's receipts and the bank deposit.

Technology

Technology certainly makes it easier to keep track of your practice from any computer in the world. Consider these ideas:

- You need a secure method that allows you to log into your office computer system from another computer – at home or on the road. Microsoft has a system called Remote Desktop Protocol built into Windows PCs and there are other software programs you can purchase. With a high speed internet connection, you can see and operate your office PC from home and you can hardly tell the difference. You can even email a document from the office to yourself and receive it at home.
- If you travel a lot, invest in the nominal monthly fee for a USB wireless modem. Just plug the device into your laptop and you can be online, using the internet and email, anywhere. These devices now offer fast internet speeds.
- Faxing is very old school. Sign up for a service that gives you a toll free fax number and all faxes come to your email inbox as a PDF file. You can print the file if you want to, just like a fax, but now you have it stored electronically so you may not need to. Instead of sending faxes, you can scan a document using your multipurpose printer and save it as a PDF file. Then attach that file to an email and send it. This is better than faxes because you now have the document stored in your system.

- To create a PDF file from any document in your PC, you download free software that lets you "print to a PDF file." Instead of printing the document, you select a virtual printer and create a PDF file for it.
- A smart phone is very helpful in remote management because email and texting are important business tools and you will always have access to it. You can communicate easily with your manager via text. Plus you have your cell phone, contact list, calendar, and to do list all in one device.
- Overnight delivery service is not high tech, but it is a great tool when you need original documents or mail fast.
- Video conferencing. This sounds pretty fancy but most laptops have built in webcams and add-on models run about $35. The software is free from suppliers like Skype, Apple Facetime and Yahoo. There isn't even a long distance phone expense. Why not see the people you are talking to?
- If you really want to monitor the operation remotely set up a security camera system with webcam access. You can position cameras at key locations and just log on to any PC, or even from your smart phone, and watch what's going on. Some cameras can even have audio. You will reduce the chance of theft or embezzlement.
- Don't forget the telephone! It's not high tech but it still works great!

Practice finance

Most practices I know use business financial software like QuickBooks to manage their bank accounts and track expenses. This works perfectly for a practice owner to keep close tabs on the practice finances by using the remote log-on system described above. If you simply log on from any computer in the world via a high-speed internet connection, you can access your accounting software and see all transactions and accounts. You may even develop a system where invoices to be paid are prepared electronically by a manager or bookkeeper, but the checks are placed on hold. The practice owner reviews the entries every few days and decides which ones to pay and when by placing a check mark next to the approved items. The bookkeeper then prints those checks that are marked, uses an official signature stamp and mails the payments.

More and more suppliers can be paid by auto debit with a bank draft or on business credit cards, and this process offers many advantages. Major insurance payers are also moving toward electronic deposits of funds. This makes administration much easier and instead of making deposits and payments, the practice owner simply reconciles the accounts, which can be done from anywhere.

20.6 Work on your business; not in your business.

The title above is a brilliant statement often attributed to Michael Gerber, author of the ground-breaking book *The E-Myth Revisited.* The advice is quite applicable to eye care professionals who own their practices and I believe it speaks to one of the major factors that holds most of us back from achieving greater success. One of the best things you can do for your practice is to not spend all your time seeing patients! Your practice is a business and it requires the leadership and vision that only the owner can provide. Yet, a recent survey revealed that the median ratio of OD office hours spent on patient care is 85%! How does your work week stack up against that? With the doctor spending almost all of his or her time on patients, who is running the business?

Generating high income in optometry

Is it possible to generate high income levels in optometry, given our challenges of discount vision plans and increasing competition from internet-based vendors? Of course it is. All industries and professions have their challenges and eye care is as good as or better than other fields. Think of practice net income as belonging to two sources: the business and the optometrist. Optometrists earn very good incomes but the really great income potential comes from owning the business. There is a going rate for work as an optometrist; it is a range with a high and low end. There really isn't a limit on the income from business ownership. Over an entire career, I advise practice-owning optometrists to gradually spend less time as a practicing OD and more time as a CEO. This shift in work focus occurs as the practice is growing larger and there is a greater need for a higher level of management. The higher volume of exams, increased optical sales, a larger staff, more office space, and associate ODs all require more management effort to make the practice run well. Without increased management, the practice will stop growing and even decline.

Examples outside of eye care

Did you ever know of a carpenter who built beautiful custom homes mostly by himself, with the help of a few subcontractors? This guy worked long hours out of the back of his pick-up truck, completing one house at a time and then selling it for a profit. As demand for these custom homes grew, based on a reputation for quality, the carpenter gradually hired more employees and subcontractors. Eventually, the carpenter becomes the owner of the premier home-building company in the region. He is now a wealthy business person; the CEO of his firm. It's extremely valuable that he is a master carpenter as he works with employees and other trades and as he evaluates his company's finished products, but he no longer swings a hammer.

We can find similar examples in any field: a hairdresser who builds a high-end salon, an auto mechanic who owns a chain of service centers, or an optometrist who leads a successful multi-location practice. Many of these very successful business people stop doing their craft directly.

Hire an office manager

Conventional wisdom in optometry has long included a philosophy by the OD that his or her best use is to be a doctor. The thinking is that the OD has the training and the license to provide eye care, so as the practice grows, the best strategy is to hire an office manager to take care of the business and the OD will see more eyeballs. I certainly recognize the important role of office managers and agree with hiring them, but I also believe that the optometrist/owner is needed in day-to-day practice management as well. In many cases, the practice owner would do better financially if he would hire an associate OD to see some of the eyeballs so he could spend more time managing the practice!

A management day (or two)

I recommend dedicating one or more days per week as a management day for the practice owner. There would be no patients scheduled on those days (for the owner), but she would still come into the office and work on operations, staff issues, marketing, fee structures, the coding and billing process and any of the hundreds of issues facing optometric practice every day. In many cases, the same number of patients that were seen per week can be compressed into fewer days with more delegation to staff and shorter time slots. If the practice is already highly delegated and very busy, it makes sense to hire an associate OD.

20.7 Optometrists with Little Interest in Optical

Eye care professionals in other countries may have a hard time understanding this, but optometrists in the United States are increasingly disinterested in optical dispensing. It would be reasonable to think that optometrists' primary interest would be in all things optical, but American ODs are very focused on medical eye care and in my experience, they often delegate all aspects of optical dispensing. I think that is a big mistake. In my view, it's smart to delegate the dispensing work; but not the management.

I admit I'm painting with a broad brush here, but it seems to me that many older ODs have grown bored with refraction and optical dispensing and they spend most of their effort on ocular disease and billing and coding. Younger ODs have not received nearly as much optical training as their senior colleagues, so they feel slightly inadequate in optical dispensing. We should be concerned because there are plenty of other folks in the business world who will be happy to take optical off our hands if we are not interested.

In this article, I will encourage optometrists to embrace optical for one major reason: greater net income. You may not be drawn to optical dispensing as an optometrist, but at least be drawn to it as the CEO of your practice. If you currently delegate the management of your optical dispensary, I encourage you to review all aspects of your operations. This is nothing against your optician or optical manager, but by simply digging into it yourself, I'm sure you'll find things you would do differently and you'll find ways to make a lot more money in the process.

Areas to dig into

Here are some factors I believe the optometrist should be knowledgeable about.

- Optical labs. If you find a decent wholesale optical lab and get comfortable with it, most practices will stick with it for years. That could be good or bad. Cost of goods is the single largest expense category for most practices and if you can cut your labs bills by 15%, your net will increase substantially. Of course, trying a new cheaper lab could mean a drop in quality that is not acceptable. Evaluating and changing labs is not an easy decision, which is why the doctor/owner should be involved. Take a look at your options.
- The in-office lab. As you consider your lab and lab bills, talk to manufacturers of lens finishing equipment. You may be smart to bring the work in-house. If you already have an in-office lab, where are your buying your uncuts and what are your paying?
- Frame lines. Bringing in a new frame line creates more work and it's certainly easier to use fewer companies, but there is a very strong reason you should do it. It brings enthusiasm to your staff. Nothing sells like enthusiasm. And your patients will sense that your optical is up to date and always changing. That builds loyalty, referrals and repeat purchases. Picture this: A patient you've been seeing for years is in for her annual eye health exam and your optician

excitedly says, "Oh, hi Mary. I'm so glad you're here! We just received our new frame line by Designer Name and there is a style I think is just perfect for you – come see it and try it on for me!" See what I mean? Find out what fashion brands are cool and hip. Which ones offer an elegant look like jewelry? What is a little bit funky and retro? Bring in new lines and drop the ones that are stale.

- Lens pricing. Many ODs have no idea how much their office charges for a pair of single vision lenses in CR-39. And many have never really looked at the prices for their lens packages. How much should you charge for premium antireflective? Checking your actual cost for these options is the first step and that can take some digging. But you really should know. You're probably leaving money on the table.
- Frame pricing. The frame mark-up formula used in most practices has been in existence for years. Most optometrists figure it's fine since it is a mark-up and if the wholesale prices go up, so do the retail prices. But what if the basic formula is out of date? Two and a half times plus $30 is so old school. Frame pricing makes a big difference in profit, even with vision plans when there is a frame overage. Run some examples of what the patient would pay at different price points and see for yourself.
- Delivery time. Is your staff pretty much telling every patient that their glasses will take two weeks? Oh, excuse me, ten working days (that sounds better, but is not really better). Patients tolerate this slow service but they do not love it.
- Suppliers. Do you know your suppliers for eyeglass cases, half-eye readers, economy frames, nose pads and screws, sport goggles, hand-held magnifiers, lens cleaners and cloths, and dozens of other products? You may be able to save money and improve quality.
- Warranty jobs and remakes. Do you know how many "free" optical jobs your practice makes per month? If not, prepare to be stunned. From scratched lenses to incorrect seg heights to broken temples, it adds up to a huge number in most practices. Don't make the mistake of generalizing that it's mostly "free" because the lab covers it. It is definitely not free when you consider the staff time that goes into ordering, receiving, assembling, calling, and dispensing. And your practice is being charged for shipping and handling by the supplier. You could still provide the free remake to patients but charge them a shipping and handling fee. They generally accept it just fine when they are getting free glasses.

How to learn about optical

First, understand that as an optometrist, you already know much more about optical dispensing than you realize. With your education and experience, the basics will come back to you quickly and the new developments will be easily understood.

My best advice for understanding optical is to meet with sales reps in the field. This can occur in your office by appointment, or a crash course can be had by attending a major conference like Vision Expo, SECO, AOA or AAO and visiting the booths in the exhibit hall. Talk to reps from lens manufacturers, frame companies and wholesale optical labs. Listen to them explain their newest products and then ask questions if there is some aspect that is not clear. No question will appear dumb. These optical experts would like to attract your business and they will be happy to discuss their products.

Armed with knowledge, you'll be in a great position to work with your optical manager to revamp your policies, update your offerings, change your price strategy and work with new suppliers. Very exciting stuff!

20.8 Doctors: Observe in Optical

I met with a top executive with a leading frame company last week and he estimated that 80% of optometrists in the U.S. have little or nothing to do with their optical dispensaries. My own experience with practices agrees with that. Most ODs delegate everything optical to staff members and really don't monitor it for years. Or decades. It's almost like we have a phobia about it.

While I'm not implying that staff members don't do a good job in the management of the optical departments, I strongly recommend that the doctor/practice owner spend some time observing and listening to staff members as they care for patients in optical, especially when performing frame selections.

You will be shocked

I think optometrists naturally tend to think our staff is carrying out our vision in various aspects of the practice. After all, the OD probably trained the original staff on how to do it, or at least discussed it at a staff meeting. And if that original staff trained the others then of course things are going well. I'm kidding, of course, but there is a difference between optical and the rest of the practice. If operations get off track at the front desk or in the clinic, the OD probably becomes aware of it at some point. He or she is close enough to that part of the office. But frame selection is often more isolated. It is semi-private and doctors are too busy to hang around.

Here are some things you might observe:

- Starting with poor frame choices. There may be no rhyme or reason to how the process is started, but it is actually very important. How many times is the first frame tried on the one that is finally ordered? Consider a tour of the entire frame area first, including a look at sunglasses before starting the frame selection. Come back to them.
- No enthusiasm. Enthusiasm sells. How many designer frame upgrades would you sell if your staff member said "Mrs. Jones, we just received the newest frames from XYZ Designer and I would love for you to try them on! I think they would be perfect for you!" More likely you will hear "Did you want to look at frames today or are you staying with your old one?" Or you will see a rather serious, matter-of-fact approach that implies the office is busy and let's get this done.
- Lack of patient education. Do you think your staff members are actually discussing all the lens options and frame design choices that are available? I'll bet not in many cases. I think many staff tend to pre-judge what they think patients will want and what they can afford. I tend to think of the Julia Roberts character in the movie "Pretty Woman": Mistake. Big mistake.
- Incorrect explanations. When staff members explain lens features like premium free-form progressives, high index materials, antireflective and Transitions, how accurate are they? You might be surprised at what they say. And why not use demonstration items? Your office is not the internet.
- No recommendation of second pairs. Your staff can sell second pairs by just asking the patient questions. "Do you participate in outdoor activities? Do you have any hobbies? Do you use a computer?" Another good way to dramatically increase multiple pair sales is to make the additional complete pairs 50% off. Your staff will finally bring up the idea on a regular basis.
- Mistakes on pricing.

How to observe

I mention this because I know it is a bit awkward to try to observe and listen to staff while staying in the background. Here are some tips, but practice makes it easier.

- Watch from a distance or behind glass. The disadvantage is you can't hear this way, but you can still learn a lot and it is more discreet.
- Act busy nearby. Work on a computer or paper work.
- Walk through the area rather slowly on several occasions. You will see and hear a lot.
- Install security cameras with audio. This is the best way. Watch from your office.

What I saw
So you don't think I try to give the impression that my practice is perfect (trust me, it isn't), I'll share with you what I noticed recently in my office. Two different staff members on separate occasions did a poor job of managing frame selections. The patient was walked directly to our budget frame display to begin the process. These frames are not in the area of our nicest frame styles. These patients had not indicated any need or desire for low-priced frames. The optician simply presumed it. I was shocked. I thought we had covered this!

Retraining
I recommend you take some notes about what you observe that could be better and discuss the issue in detail at regular staff meetings. Staff will actually open up and share their best sales techniques and communication skills. I would not criticize any individuals at a group staff meeting. There may be value in working with specific staff on specific issues, but do it in private.

I understand that optical dispensing may not be your favorite activity as an optometrist, but as CEO of your practice, it should interest you very much.

20.9 Do you ever speak to your staff about sales?

Let's face it; we are pleased when our optical dispensaries do well. If we sell a high number of eyeglasses and contact lenses, we're happy about it. There is nothing wrong with that; your optical is a business and the goal of all businesses is to generate a profit. And the bigger the profit, the better. Given that, do you speak to your staff very often about selling? Do you encourage them to sell and train them in sales techniques? Probably not, but with this tip I'm going to make it easier for you to start by sharing some ideas I use to motivate my staff to sell.

Understand selling yourself

The first step is to educate yourself about sales and to get over any professional hang-ups you may have about it. If you're an optometrist, you probably have no background or training in sales and maybe no interest. But if you own a practice the business owner side of you should care. CEOs understand the core principles that drive revenue. I'll give you some quick ideas here, but buy a book or two on sales techniques at your local bookstore. There are many but Jeffrey Gitomer is one author I like very much.

Encouraging sales

Many ECPs today take an approach that the best way to motivate staff to sell is through some sort of incentive pay system. I don't believe incentives or bonuses work as well as most people think and the other approach is to position selling as part of the optician's professional responsibility. I find staff respond very well to this. They view finding out about the patient's visual and lifestyle needs as their job. Educating people about eyeglasses and contacts is their duty and they take it seriously. They understand that generating profit for their company is also their job and that is how they advance in their career and receive raises.

My staff knows this because we talk about it often. It is a regular topic at weekly staff meetings, but we occasionally close the office for an entire afternoon for a more detailed presentation on sales and other business topics. A key part of those meetings is to allow the staff to discuss and share their experiences and techniques.

Presumptive selling

Teach your staff to presume the patient wants the best in eye care, not the cheapest. Of course, if the patient tells us or implies that he wants more economical options we are responsive to that. But short of that, we presume he wants to get glasses and contacts from our office – today. We presume he wants the best glasses and contacts. We presume there is some interest in multiple pairs of glasses since one pair can't provide the best vision for all a person's various needs. Why would we presume otherwise?

Teach your staff to never prejudge what they think a person wants or can afford. To do so based on a person's age or clothing would be a big mistake and it's actually a discriminatory insult. Some of those overall-wearing 70 year-olds are millionaires.

The F-A-B technique

You may have heard this one, but it is a great place to start with staff. Every product has features, advantages and benefits and it's important for the salesperson to know all three, but he should know above all else that people only buy products for the benefits. A feature is a physical characteristic, an advantage is a performance characteristic and a benefit is the result the buyer receives. Benefits are the only things consumers care about and the smart optician will quickly concentrate on that.

Great salespeople focus on what the customer is really buying. The classic example is the hardware store salesman who is not really selling quarter inch carbide drill bits – he is selling quarter inch holes! People buy the product of the product.

Using an example from vision care: a patient does not buy the multilayer chemical, oleophobic, hard lacquer, anti-reflective coating that is applied to ophthalmic lenses (a feature), and he does not buy the increased light transmission and decrease reflectance of the lenses (an advantage), but he does buy the reduced glare when night driving (a benefit).

If we take the F-A-B sales approach one step further, we should have asked the customer about his lifestyle wants and needs before we even started. We may have found out that this person does not care much about reducing glare, but an attractive appearance is most important. In that case, the benefit the optician should play up is the cosmetic benefit of an AR coating; that it makes the lenses virtually disappear and other people will see the wearer's eyes and not lens reflections.

Axioms
To help your staff remember the thrust of great selling techniques, here are some old sayings that I like:

- Telling is not selling! (Don't just tell people about the product, ask them how they will use it and what they like about it. Selling is listening.)
- Don't tell me how good you make your goods; tell me how good your goods make me!
- People don't care how much you know until they know how much you care!

20.10 Pushing the Mid-Level Practice Upward

I like to think of optometric practice in terms of three levels for simplicity. The optimum management strategy is different at each level. Consider these:

- New startups and small practices.
- Mid-level practices; annual gross revenue from $300,000 to $800,000.
- Large practices with approximately $1 million or more in revenue.

The largest group by far is the mid-level and it is also the hardest to break out of, so I'd like to address that today. The high grossing practice can still have many challenges, but it has already proven it can generate revenue. The very small or new practice needs to do the right things to build patient referrals and loyalty, but these require nurturing over time.

Some mid-level practices are growing quickly and are already setting themselves apart. These practices are passing through average on their way to greatness. But most mid-level practices are kind of stuck. The owners may begin to accept average as good enough; they may rationalize that they don't want to see more patients per day. The owners may become accustomed to doing many things themselves. Everything depends on the doctor and that becomes the norm.

Consider the following factors within an average practice. Each factor is usually average as well and therefore it can't become a competitive advantage.

- Office size. Usually medium to small; the space can restrict the number of patients that can be seen and staff. Close quarters can become a customer service issue. The office and the optical are not impressive.
- Signage and exterior image. Nothing that stands out in the sea of businesses.
- Office hours. Usually not all that convenient for the patient. The doctor and staff like them though.
- Clinical instrumentation. Generally average, perhaps a retinal camera.
- Frame selection. Average brands; about 600 frames.
- Office décor and optical merchandising. Nice but not memorable.
- Staff skill and service. Average; not above and beyond.

How can a mid-level practice break free?

To make an average practice grow, the owner must make some things happen. Not wait for them to happen. The interesting thing is that there are a number of "things" that will work. That may actually make growth more difficult because the owner will have to choose one or maybe two things to work on and invest in. That is what CEOs do. They have a vision. They make a judgment about what would serve their company best. And they take some risk.

Here are some ideas for possible projects that can boost a practice out of the mid-level blues. These are your possible "things" to make happen. Which one do you feel would give your practice the most lift?

- New office facility with more space. A great way to push the practice upward; current patients and the community at large see the change as a signal that the practice is doing well and service is improving.
- Add a branch office location. When growth stagnates due to insufficient population, a second office in a different market can attract new patients. See patients efficiently and quickly with a more compressed schedule.
- New instrumentation. What is on your wish list? A new high-tech instrument generates buzz. Show your patients you are up to date and get them talking.
- Remodel and expand the optical display. Patients judge your entire practice based on what they understand, and they understand interior décor and retail displays very well. Making your optical look great is a smart investment.
- In-office optical lab. This not only reduces your cost of goods, but it also improves patient service.
- An additional exam room. This is a huge step up in efficiency even if you are not extremely busy yet. Patient service improves and that results in more word-of-mouth referrals.
- Electronic medical records. Some of the benefit is for internal operations, but patients will be impressed to see the practice becoming cutting edge. Add scribes and you'll gain many benefits for patient care and service.
- Reception room lift. How about adding a flat screen TV and a Keurig coffee maker?

Making it happen

Once you decide on the most important project (in your opinion), take action! Many ODs feel they can't take on a new business expense unless they see a sure way to pay for it. That may be true sometimes, but in other cases you should just arrange the financing or go to your savings. A great example is a new, larger office. On paper, the build out cost and the increased rent may seem like a challenge, but in nearly every case I've seen, a new nicer office results in a nice boost in patient demand. Production and revenue increase more than the cost.

Of course, you want to take on new debt with some caution and have a plan for paying for it, but in most cases business will improve, you will easily handle the increased expense, and you find yourself leaving your old mid-level practice in the dust. You begin to enjoy the benefits of a larger, more successful practice. Act as you mean to go.

20.11 A Plan to Reduce Stress in the Office

Many optometrists and staff members feel stress on the job. It's an uncomfortable feeling that leads to bad attitudes, negative office culture and more frequent errors. If you feel stress fairly often in your workplace, review these tips and take some action to reduce it.

Weekly staff meetings
Stressful situations can be due to many causes, but if you communicate about them with your team, things will improve. Enhance the communication by scheduling staff meetings at least once per week and allowing at least a half-hour per meeting. You can hold daily meetings as well, but you need more time to flush out issues and set policies for the future. Simply pick a day and time of the week that will be your regular staff meeting and block it off from appointments. Block it way ahead in your schedule, like six months or one year. You are always going to need the meetings.
Review the problems of the past week and discuss how to improve and prevent these situations. Don't blame anyone and keep the meeting positive. Ask staff members to tell you about one thing that makes patients unhappy.

Work on office policies
Review all your office policies with an eye on customer service. Let most policies be patient-friendly. The goal is to identify and satisfy patients' wants and needs. Convert your office culture to one that is based on excellent service and letting the patient win. It will create a happier office.

Lunch breaks are required
Work toward requiring all staff members to take a lunch break. Try to change habits if some staff have decided to work through lunch in order to finish their work, but be careful in the process because staff often use this tactic to increase their paid work hours and taking lunch could mean reducing their pay. Nevertheless, taking a legitimate break and not thinking about work is a

good way to decrease stress. Talking to co-workers about one's personal life or going out to lunch helps people relax. My staff get a 45 minute lunch period and they must take it.

Reserve some openings in the schedule

I'm a big believer in efficiency in the clinic and seeing a high number of patients per day, but if you are constantly running behind schedule, you will feel stress. Begin by finding ways to save time in the exam process by delegating more to staff and possibly talking less. But also consider inserting a couple of blocked appointment times every day to allow everyone to catch up or to create some space to add an emergency.

Have enough staff

This may be the best way to reduce stress: be sure you have enough help. More employees reduce stress for the doctors and staff. I know we must keep an eye on the payroll cost, but most of the time, an additional employee increases production and gross revenue more than the additional salary. Having enough staff means the phone can be answered and not go to voice mail. It means there will be someone at the front desk and patients will be served well. It means someone can check on insurance benefits before the day of the appointment. And it means if someone calls off sick, you will still have enough staff to not go crazy.

Hire a true manager

Optometrists feel stress when they try to handle too much at once. A busy week of patients along with managing the staff and handling administrative duties is too much. Delegate some of the staff issues and administrative duties to a manager. A manager can be trained to handle most of the problems that arise with staff and also resolve patient complaints. That feels like less stress already! But don't expect a manager to know how to do it all; the practice owner will still have to lead and will have to coach the manager on how to do a good job. That takes time, but not as much time as doing it yourself.

It is important that all staff know that the manager is now their boss. That can ruffle some feathers, but a manager can't be effective as a supervisor unless she/he has the authority that only the practice owner can give.

Hire an associate OD

Most optometrists hire a manager to run the business side of the practice so they can continue to see patients. I think that is the wrong way to look at it. I would rather you hire an associate optometrist to see patients so you can have time to run the business! Obviously, a manager is still needed, but he or she can't replace the OD/owner. The practice needs the leadership and vision of the owner. It needs a CEO mentality and no one can do that better than the owner. The transfer of patients can occur gradually, but as the practice grows larger, it needs more management time.

Acknowledgments

I'm fortunate to have many friends and mentors who have helped me achieve some level of expertise in the field of optometric practice management. I'd like to thank the following people:

- Susan Gailmard, OD, my wife and partner in practice. We have collaborated on every aspect of our practice for over 35 years and it has been wonderful to share the challenges and the victories with her. I may be the more visible OD in this partnership, but much of the success of Gailmard Eye Center is due to Susan.
- Irving Bennett, OD. Originally a mentor and later a good friend when Susan and I bought a home in Florida, Irving was the founder and first publisher of Optometric Management magazine. I wrote an article for OM during his era when I was still an optometry student in 1974. Irving also founded the OptiFair conferences (became Vision Expo) and he helped me develop a career in practice management by inviting me to lecture many times.
- Jack Runninger, OD. Jack was Editor of OM magazine in the early days; he encouraged me to submit articles and he taught me how to be a good writer.
- Jerry Hayes, OD. A long-time friend, an outstanding businessman and a true entrepreneur, Jerry proposed the idea of Prima Eye Group to me and we became business partners in that venture in 2011. I'm proud of what we accomplished together at Prima, which was acquired by IDOC in 2015.
- The folks at PentaVision, the current publisher of Optometric Management and several other eye care publications. This includes Roger Zimmer and Rob Verna, who supported me from the beginning of the Tip of the Week and are partners with me in this book venture. Kathy Shafer, who proofread and edited my tip articles for nearly the duration of the series. She is the one person who I'm sure has read all the tips! Jim Thomas, Doug Perry and others have supported me over the years. And Pat Herron, former VP at Boucher Communications who approved my request to try the tip idea and let me run with it.
- The doctors, managers and staff at Gailmard Eye Center, for their loyalty and dedication and for implementing my vision of excellence in eye care. They make me proud every day.
- Alfred Rosenbloom, OD, who was President of Illinois College of Optometry when he offered me a full-time faculty position upon my graduation. I continued to teach at ICO for 20 years.
- Dwight Akerman, OD and Tom Steiner, two industry leaders with CibaVision when they invited me to help design and lecture in the

Management and Business Academy (MBA) program. This curriculum broke new ground in practice management and I enjoyed being part of it for eight years.

- All my colleagues at IDOC and formerly at Prima Eye Group, who have been extremely supportive and great to work with. I want to thank Mark Feder, OD, IDOC Founder, Dave Brown, CEO and Oliver Spandow, CFO, for their confidence in me during the transition with Prima and as we continue to expand IDOC's services and value for the independent optometrist. Also, thanks to Nathan Hayes, Terri Abraham and Steve Vargo, OD, MBA for their dedication to Prima in the early days and now IDOC.
- My friends in the Vision Enhancement Council. We had over 25 years of sharing and learning from each other and great fun in the process.
- Whit Lord, OD, the best businessman who was also an optometrist that I ever knew. A dear friend and a wonderfully funny storyteller. I miss him greatly.

Made in the USA
Monee, IL
13 September 2026

62979552R00410